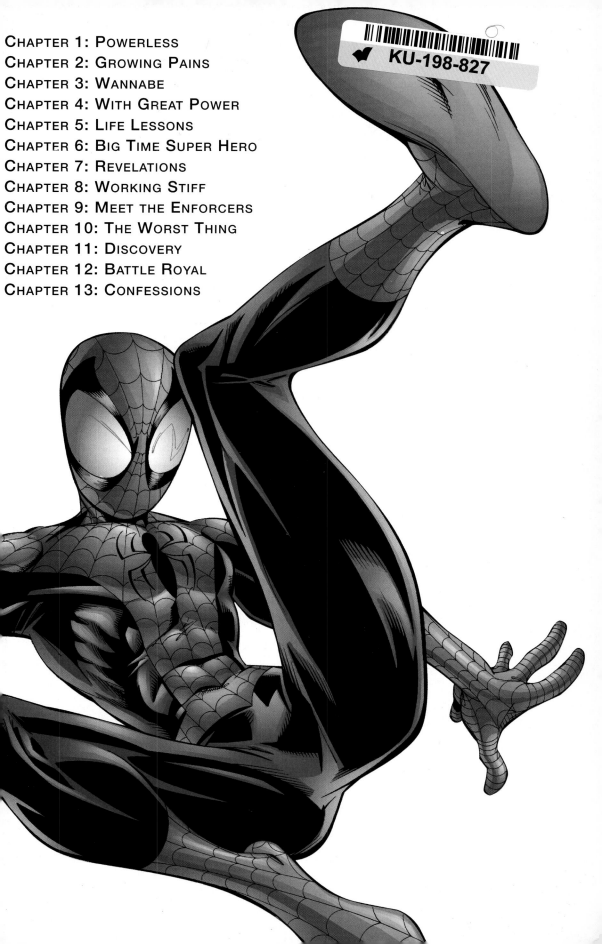

1

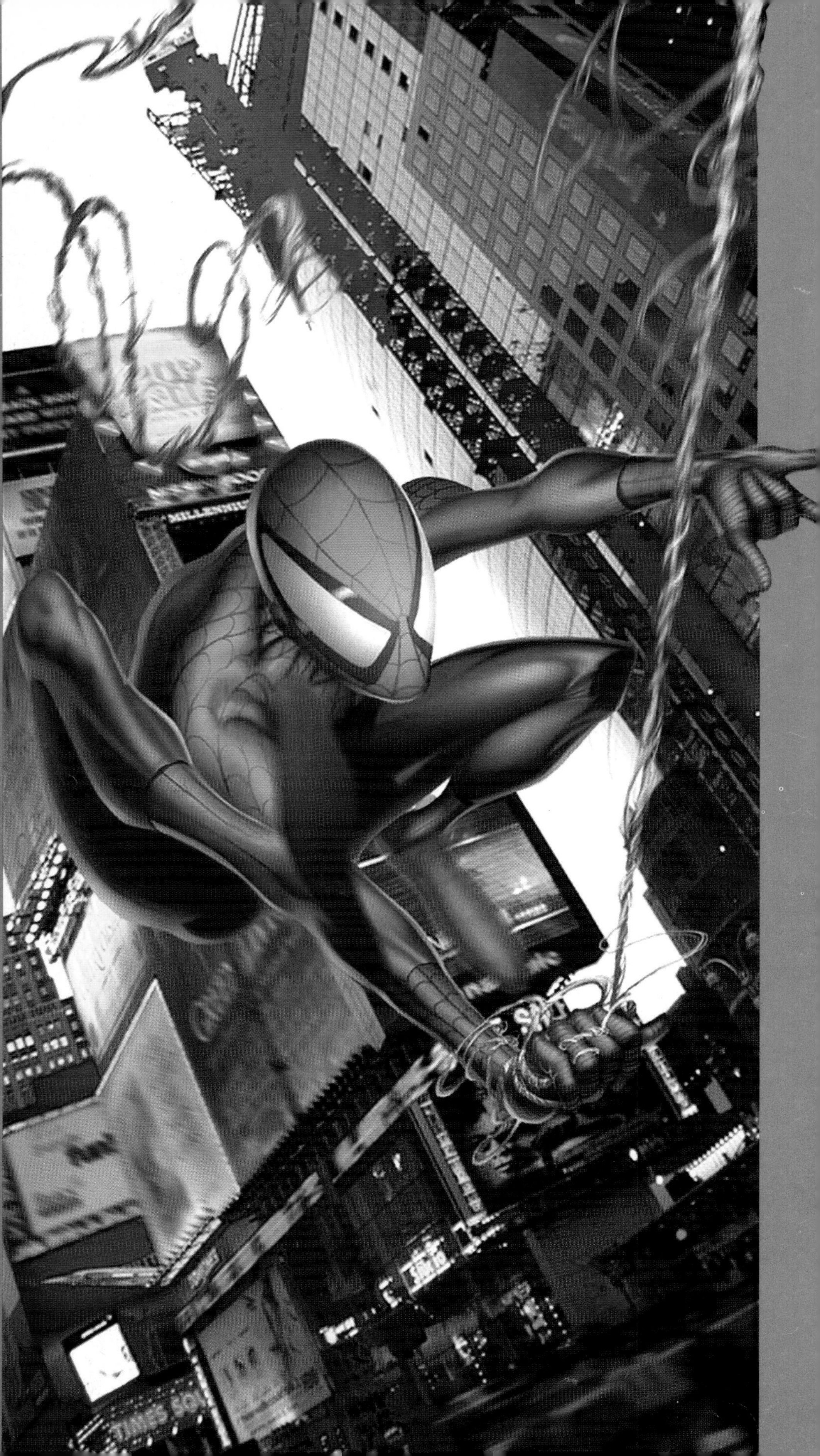

ULTIMATE SPIDER-MAN

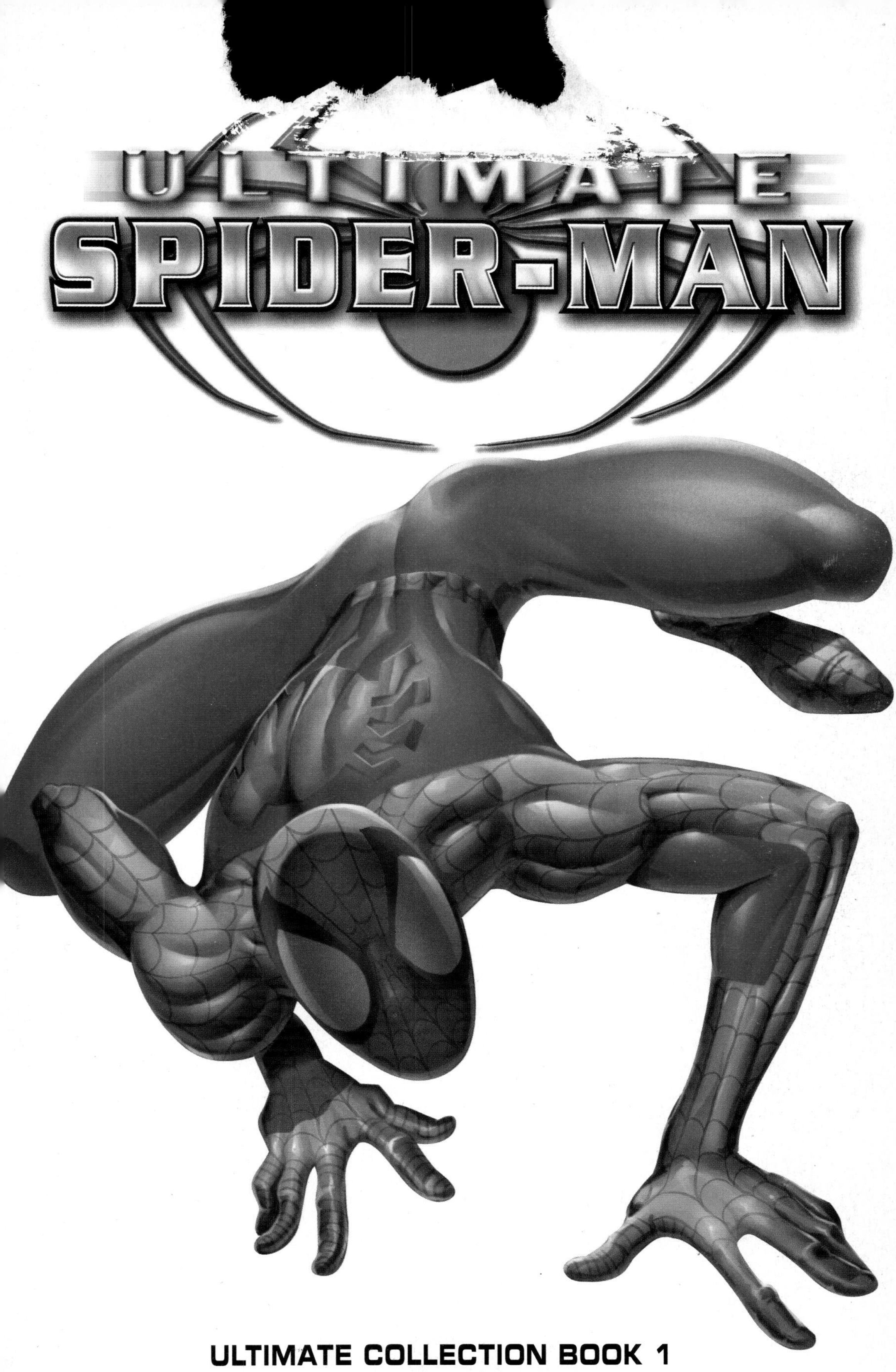

ULTIMATE COLLECTION BOOK 1

ULTIMATE SPIDER-MAN

ULTIMATE COLLECTION BOOK 1

STORY: BILL JEMAS & BRIAN MICHAEL BENDIS
WRITER: BRIAN MICHAEL BENDIS
PENCILS: MARK BAGLEY
INKS: ART THIBERT & DAN PANOSIAN
COLORS: STEVE BUCCELLATO, MARIE JAVINS,
COLORGRAPHIX & TRANSPARENCY DIGITAL
LETTERS: RICHARD STARKINGS & COMICRAFT
ASSISTANT EDITOR: BRIAN SMITH
EDITOR: RALPH MACCHIO

COLLECTION EDITOR: JENNIFER GRÜNWALD
ASSISTANT EDITOR: MICHAEL SHORT
ASSOCIATE EDITOR: MARK D. BEAZLEY
SENIOR EDITOR, SPECIAL PROJECTS: JEFF YOUNGQUIST
SENIOR VICE PRESIDENT OF SALES: DAVID GABRIEL
BOOK DESIGNER: CARRIE BEADLE
VICE PRESIDENT OF CREATIVE: TOM MARVELLI

EDITOR IN CHIEF: JOE QUESADA
PUBLISHER: DAN BUCKLEY

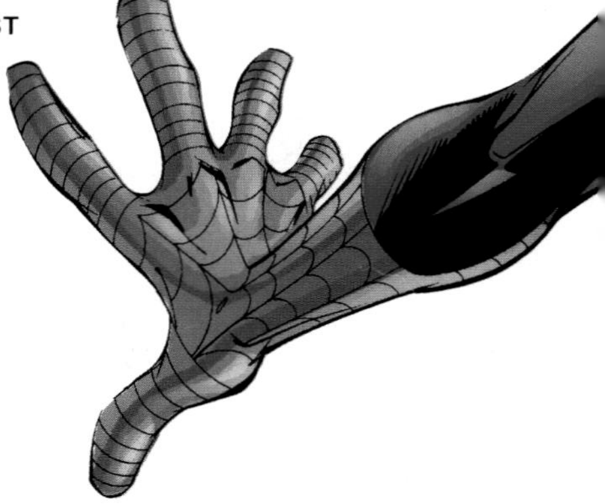

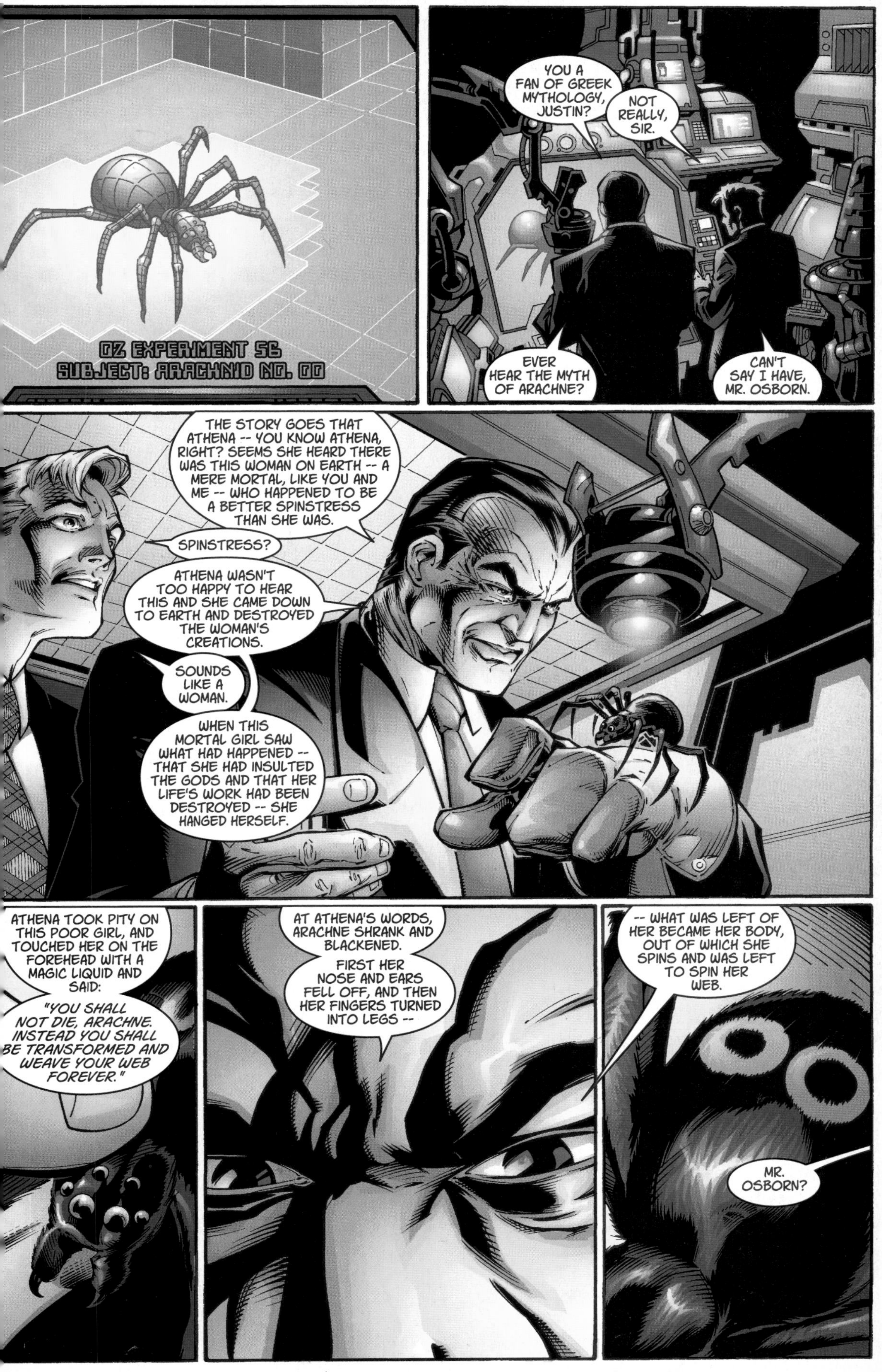
OZ EXPERIMENT 56
SUBJECT: ARACHNID NO. 00
YOU A FAN OF GREEK MYTHOLOGY, JUSTIN?
NOT REALLY, SIR.
EVER HEAR THE MYTH OF ARACHNE?
CAN'T SAY I HAVE, MR. OSBORN.
THE STORY GOES THAT ATHENA -- YOU KNOW ATHENA, RIGHT? SEEMS SHE HEARD THERE WAS THIS WOMAN ON EARTH -- A MERE MORTAL, LIKE YOU AND ME -- WHO HAPPENED TO BE A BETTER SPINSTRESS THAN SHE WAS.
SPINSTRESS?
ATHENA WASN'T TOO HAPPY TO HEAR THIS AND SHE CAME DOWN TO EARTH AND DESTROYED THE WOMAN'S CREATIONS.
SOUNDS LIKE A WOMAN.
WHEN THIS MORTAL GIRL SAW WHAT HAD HAPPENED -- THAT SHE HAD INSULTED THE GODS AND THAT HER LIFE'S WORK HAD BEEN DESTROYED -- SHE HANGED HERSELF.
ATHENA TOOK PITY ON THIS POOR GIRL, AND TOUCHED HER ON THE FOREHEAD WITH A MAGIC LIQUID AND SAID:
"YOU SHALL NOT DIE, ARACHNE. INSTEAD YOU SHALL BE TRANSFORMED AND WEAVE YOUR WEB FOREVER."
AT ATHENA'S WORDS, ARACHNE SHRANK AND BLACKENED.
FIRST HER NOSE AND EARS FELL OFF, AND THEN HER FINGERS TURNED INTO LEGS --
-- WHAT WAS LEFT OF HER BECAME HER BODY, OUT OF WHICH SHE SPINS AND WAS LEFT TO SPIN HER WEB.
MR. OSBORN?

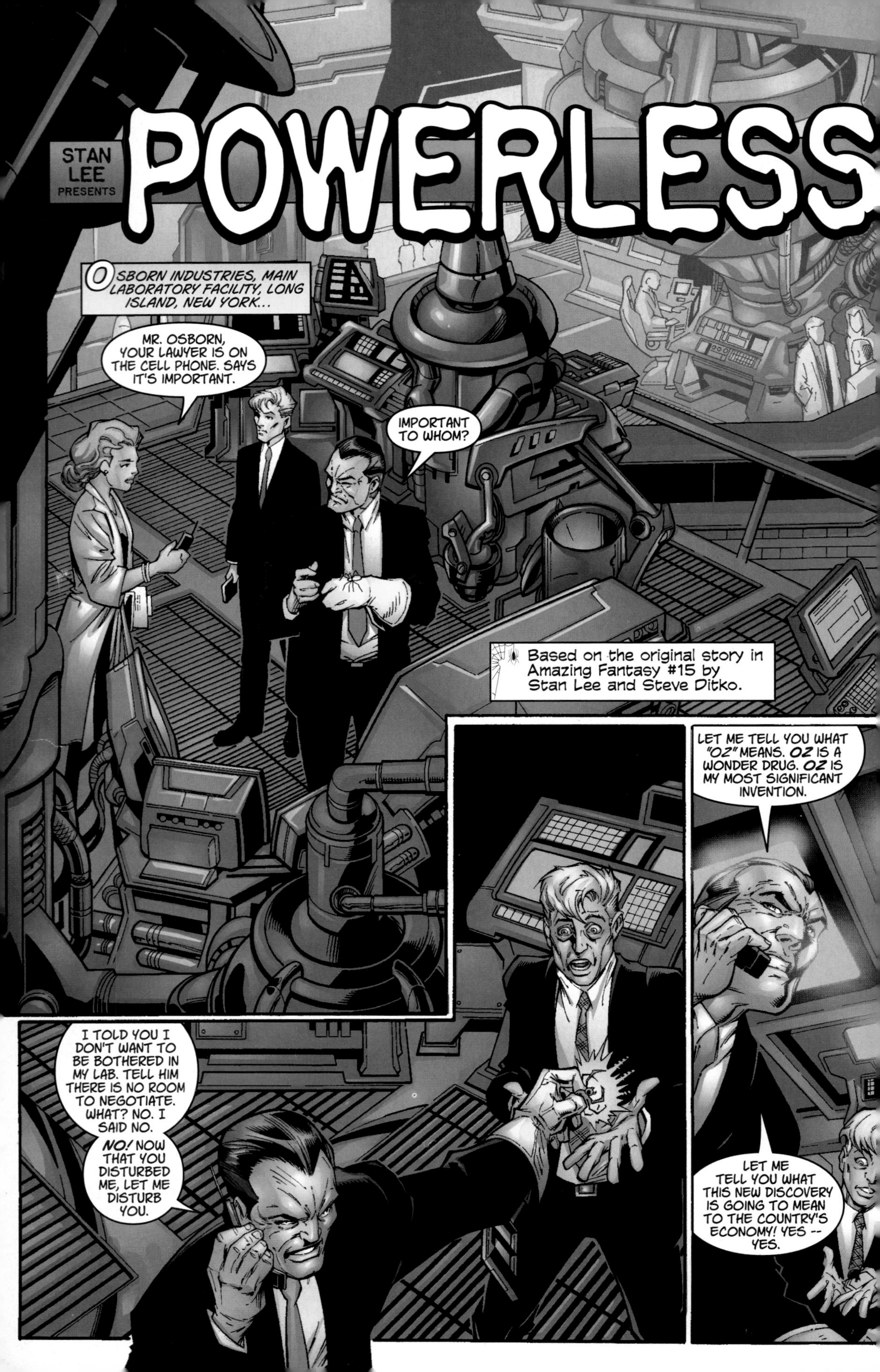
STAN LEE PRESENTS
POWERLESS
OSBORN INDUSTRIES, MAIN LABORATORY FACILITY, LONG ISLAND, NEW YORK...
MR. OSBORN, YOUR LAWYER IS ON THE CELL PHONE. SAYS IT'S IMPORTANT.
IMPORTANT TO WHOM?
Based on the original story in Amazing Fantasy #15 by Stan Lee and Steve Ditko.
I TOLD YOU I DON'T WANT TO BE BOTHERED IN MY LAB. TELL HIM THERE IS NO ROOM TO NEGOTIATE. WHAT? NO. I SAID NO.
NO! NOW THAT YOU DISTURBED ME, LET ME DISTURB YOU.
LET ME TELL YOU WHAT "OZ" MEANS. OZ IS A WONDER DRUG. OZ IS MY MOST SIGNIFICANT INVENTION.
LET ME TELL YOU WHAT THIS NEW DISCOVERY IS GOING TO MEAN TO THE COUNTRY'S ECONOMY! YES -- YES.

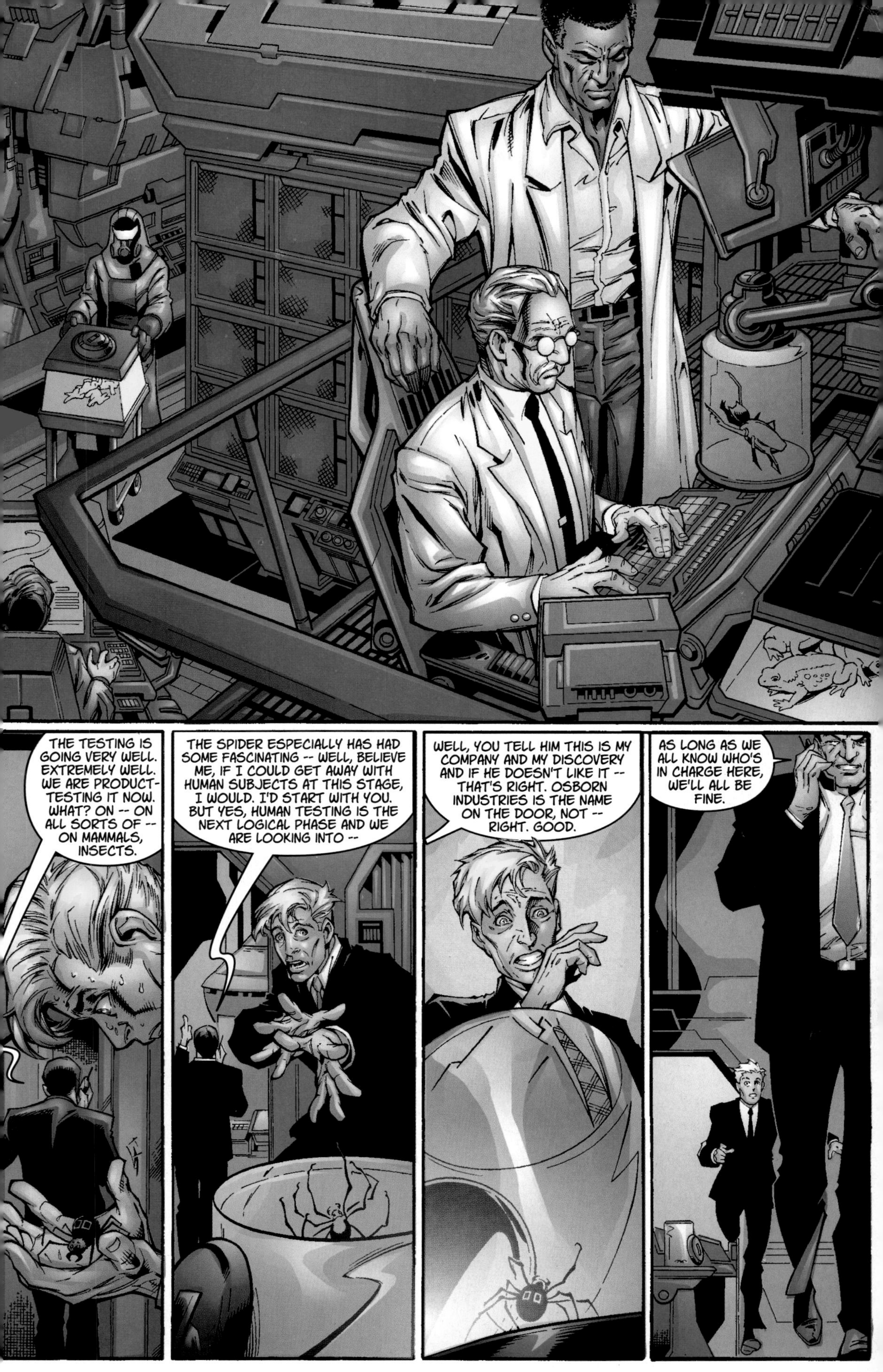
THE TESTING IS GOING VERY WELL. EXTREMELY WELL. WE ARE PRODUCT-TESTING IT NOW. WHAT? ON -- ON ALL SORTS OF -- ON MAMMALS, INSECTS.
THE SPIDER ESPECIALLY HAS HAD SOME FASCINATING -- WELL, BELIEVE ME, IF I COULD GET AWAY WITH HUMAN SUBJECTS AT THIS STAGE, I WOULD. I'D START WITH YOU. BUT YES, HUMAN TESTING IS THE NEXT LOGICAL PHASE AND WE ARE LOOKING INTO --
WELL, YOU TELL HIM THIS IS MY COMPANY AND MY DISCOVERY AND IF HE DOESN'T LIKE IT -- THAT'S RIGHT. OSBORN INDUSTRIES IS THE NAME ON THE DOOR, NOT -- RIGHT. GOOD.
AS LONG AS WE ALL KNOW WHO'S IN CHARGE HERE, WE'LL ALL BE FINE.

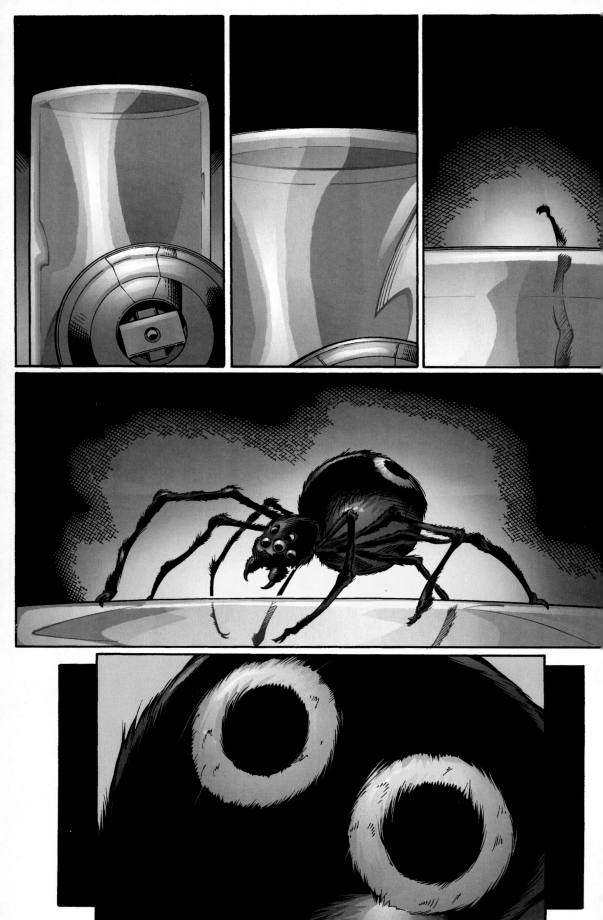

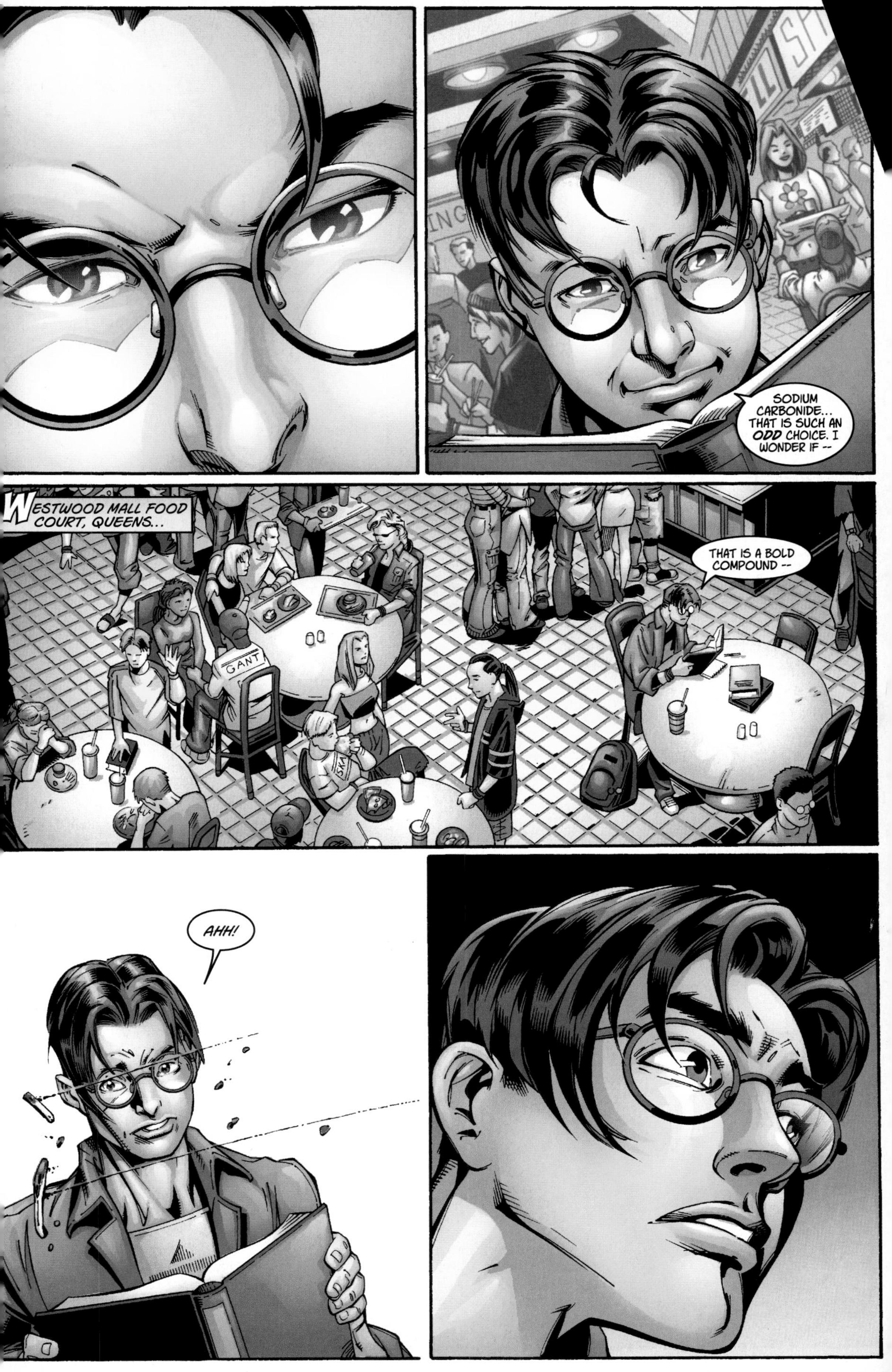

SODIUM CARBONIDE... THAT IS SUCH AN ODD CHOICE. I WONDER IF --
WESTWOOD MALL FOOD COURT, QUEENS...
THAT IS A BOLD COMPOUND --
GANT
AHH!

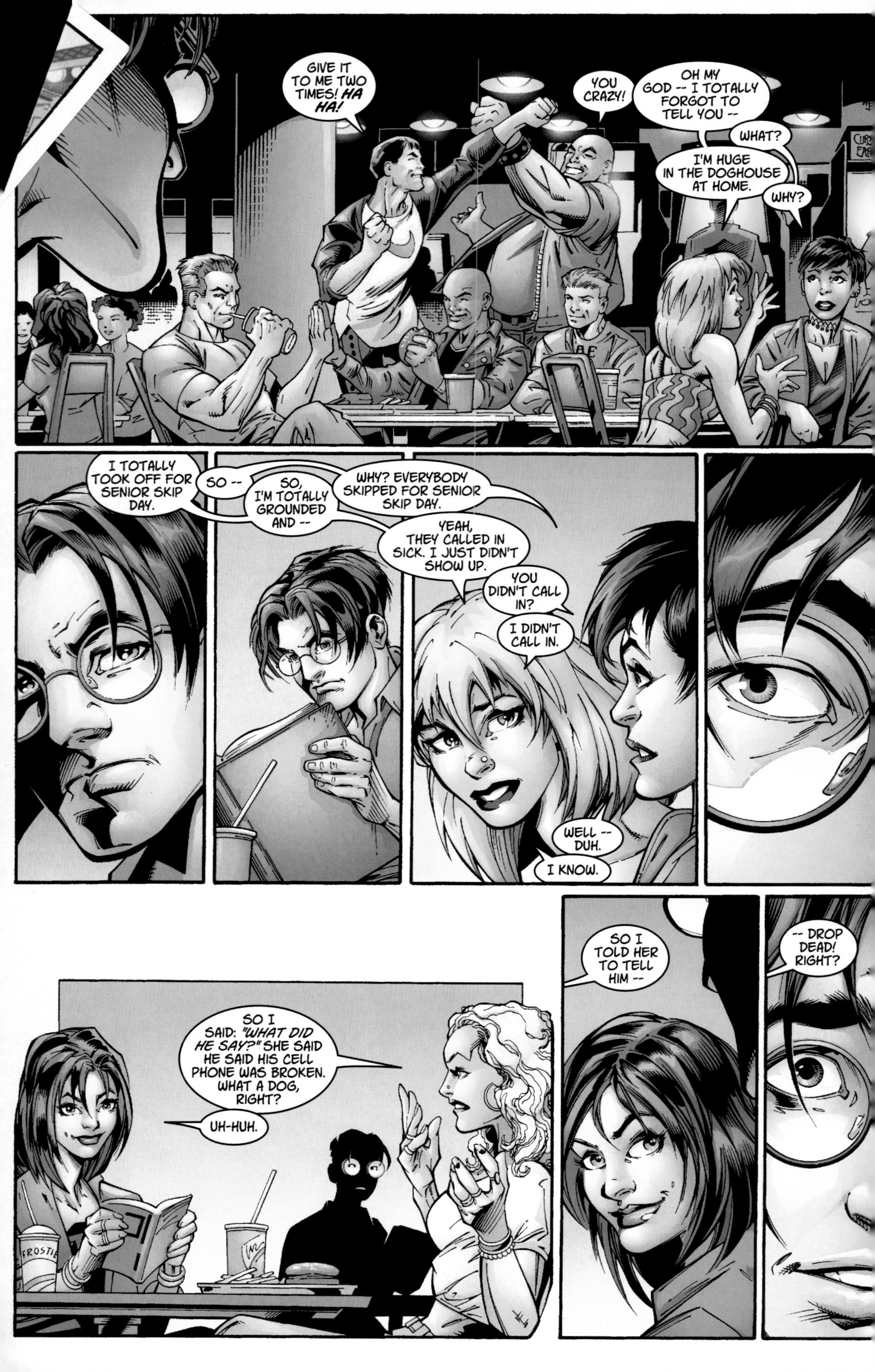
GIVE IT TO ME TWO TIMES! HA HA!
YOU CRAZY!
OH MY GOD -- I TOTALLY FORGOT TO TELL YOU --
WHAT?
I'M HUGE IN THE DOGHOUSE AT HOME.
WHY?
I TOTALLY TOOK OFF FOR SENIOR SKIP DAY.
SO --
SO, I'M TOTALLY GROUNDED AND --
WHY? EVERYBODY SKIPPED FOR SENIOR SKIP DAY.
YEAH, THEY CALLED IN SICK. I JUST DIDN'T SHOW UP.
YOU DIDN'T CALL IN?
I DIDN'T CALL IN.
WELL -- DUH.
I KNOW.
SO I SAID: "WHAT DID HE SAY?" SHE SAID HE SAID HIS CELL PHONE WAS BROKEN. WHAT A DOG, RIGHT?
UH-HUH.
SO I TOLD HER TO TELL HIM --
-- DROP DEAD! RIGHT?

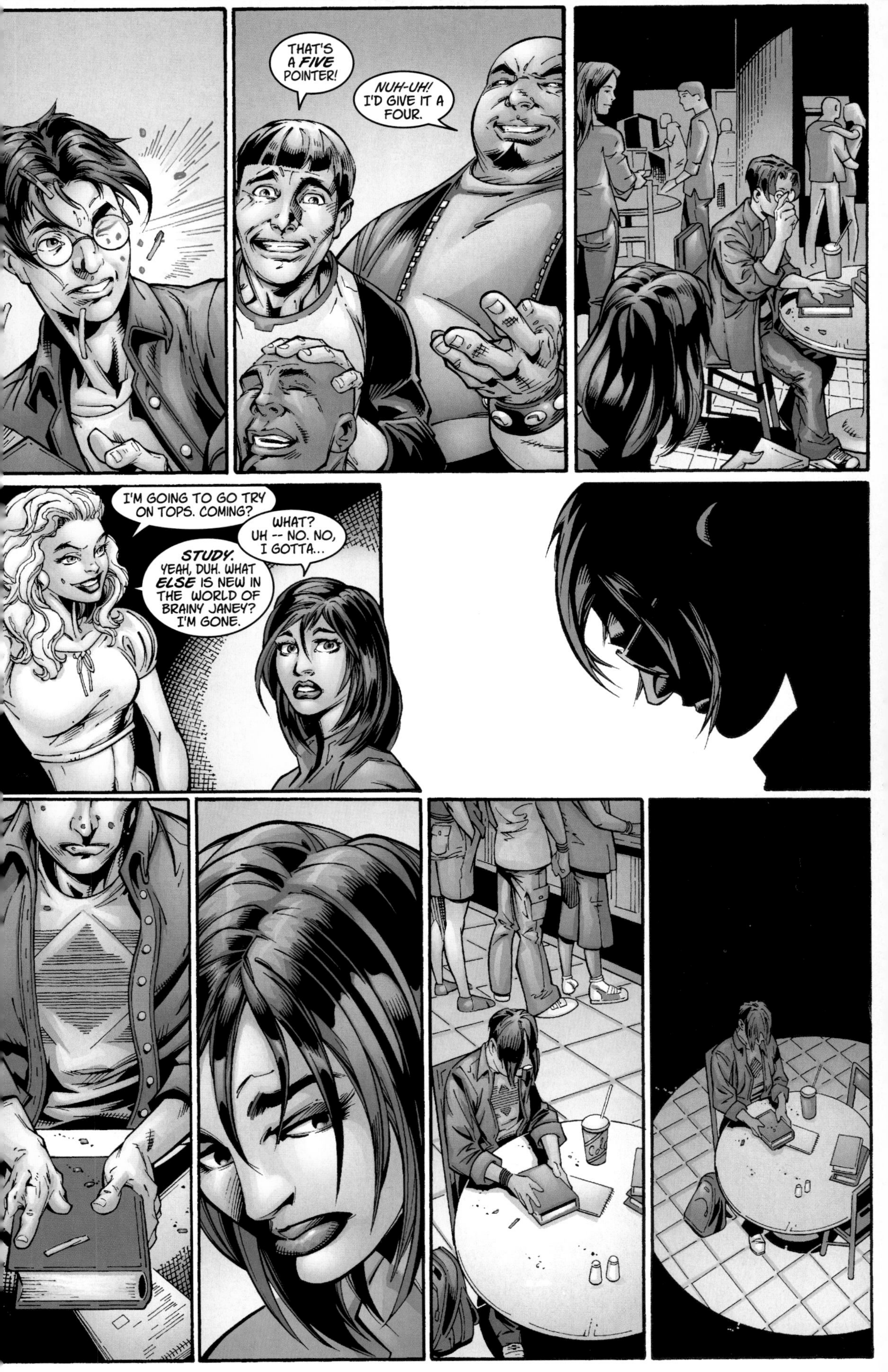
THAT'S A *FIVE* POINTER!
NUH-UH! I'D GIVE IT A FOUR.
I'M GOING TO GO TRY ON TOPS. COMING?
WHAT? UH -- NO. NO, I GOTTA...
STUDY. YEAH, DUH. WHAT *ELSE* IS NEW IN THE WORLD OF BRAINY JANEY? I'M GONE.

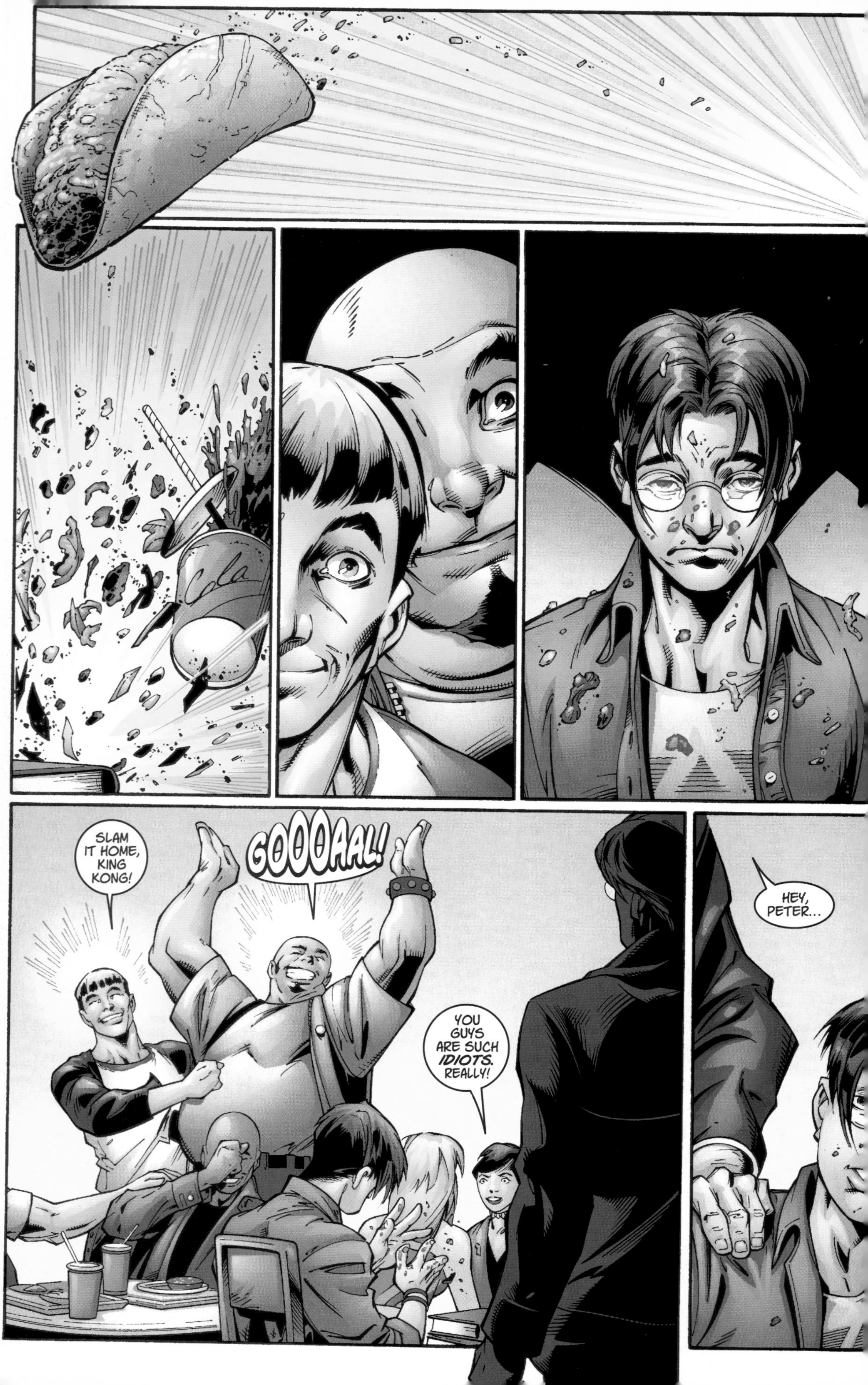
SLAM IT HOME, KING KONG!
GOOOAAL!
YOU GUYS ARE SUCH IDIOTS. REALLY!
HEY, PETER...

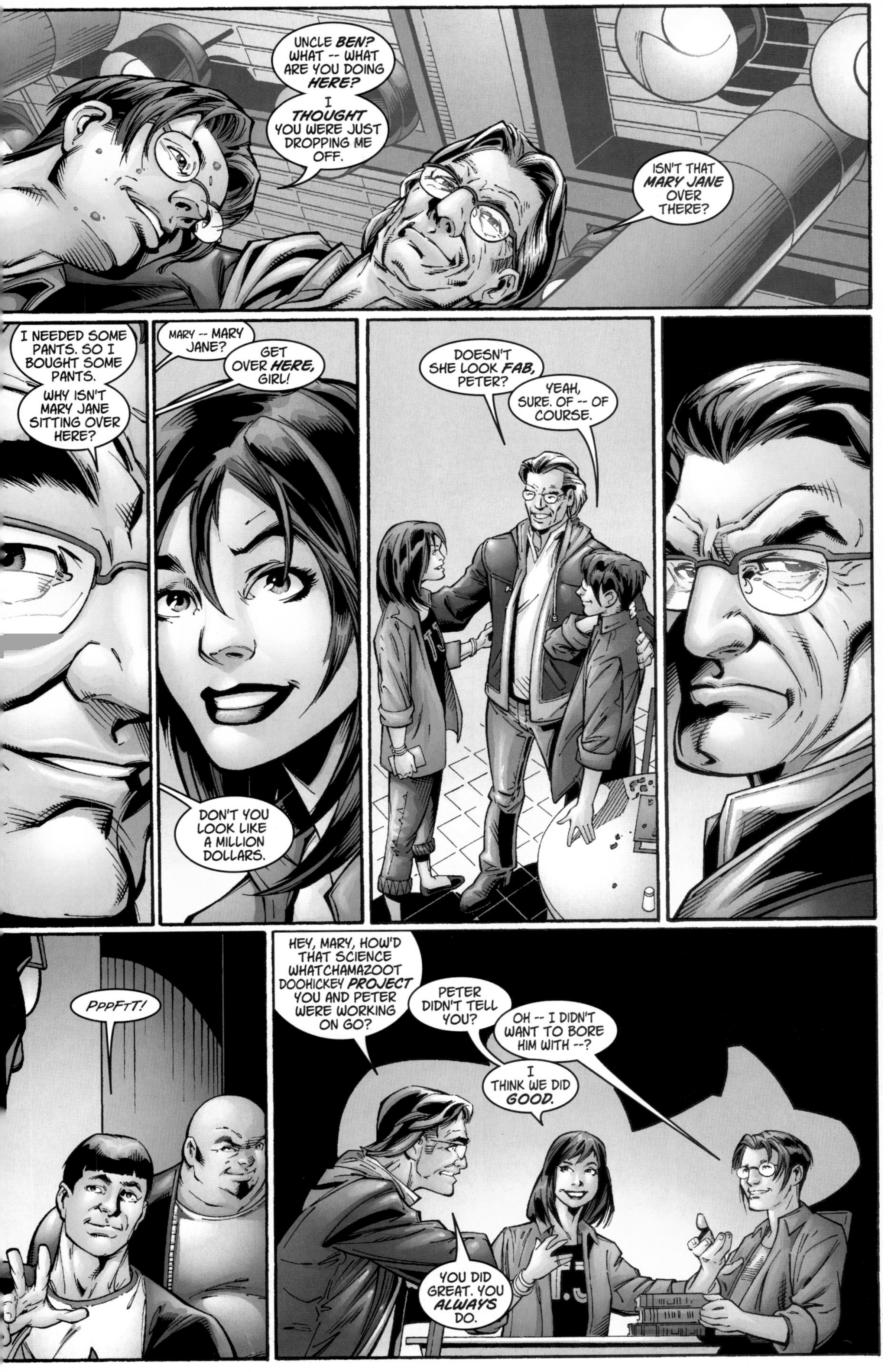
UNCLE BEN? WHAT -- WHAT ARE YOU DOING HERE?
I THOUGHT YOU WERE JUST DROPPING ME OFF.
ISN'T THAT MARY JANE OVER THERE?
I NEEDED SOME PANTS. SO I BOUGHT SOME PANTS.
WHY ISN'T MARY JANE SITTING OVER HERE?
MARY -- MARY JANE?
GET OVER HERE, GIRL!
DON'T YOU LOOK LIKE A MILLION DOLLARS.
DOESN'T SHE LOOK FAB, PETER?
YEAH, SURE. OF -- OF COURSE.
PPPFTT!
HEY, MARY, HOW'D THAT SCIENCE WHATCHAMAZOOT DOOHICKEY PROJECT YOU AND PETER WERE WORKING ON GO?
PETER DIDN'T TELL YOU?
OH -- I DIDN'T WANT TO BORE HIM WITH --?
I THINK WE DID GOOD.
YOU DID GREAT. YOU ALWAYS DO.

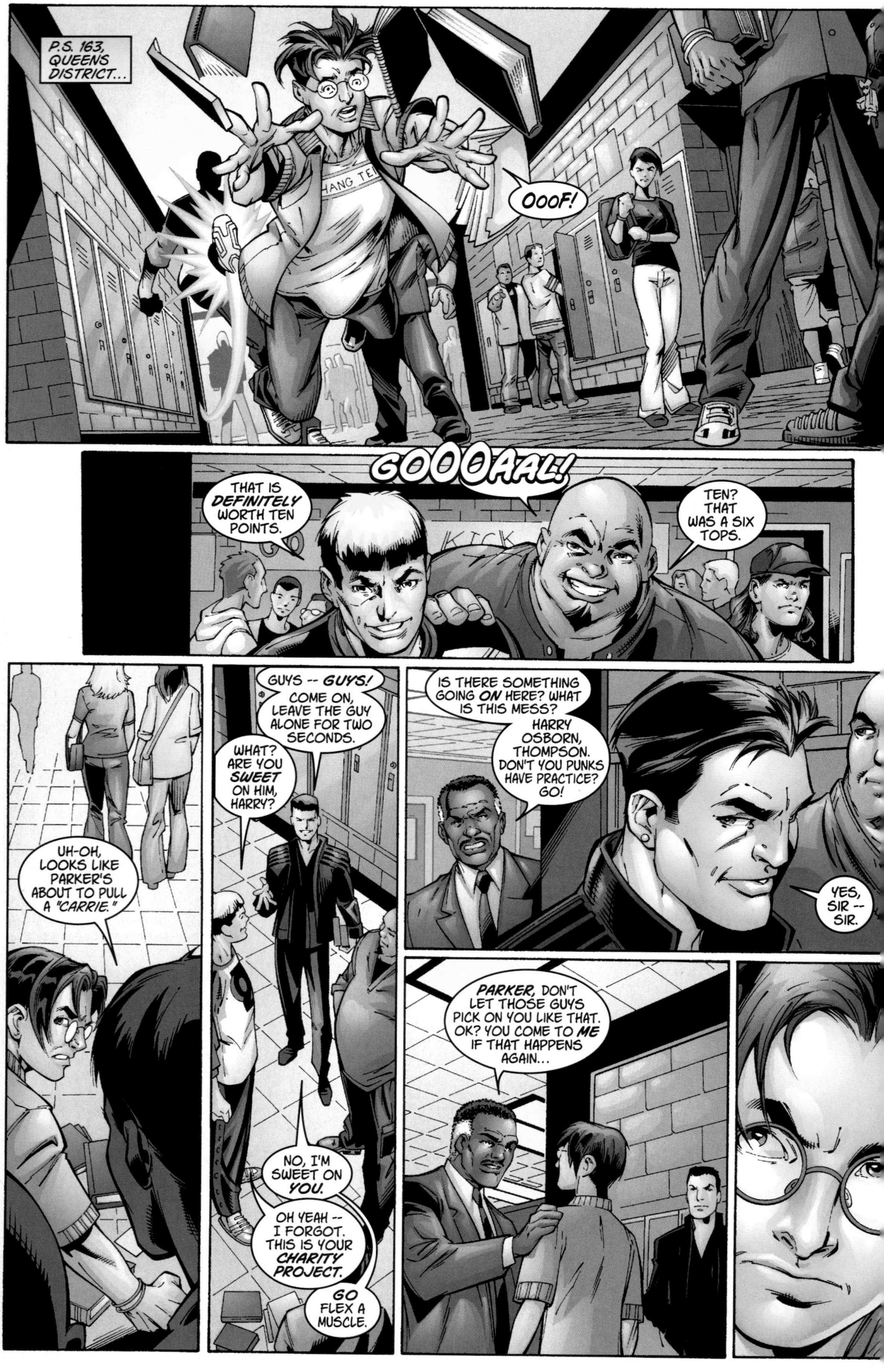
P.S. 163, QUEENS DISTRICT...
HANG TEN
OOOF!
GOOOAAL!
THAT IS DEFINITELY WORTH TEN POINTS.
TEN? THAT WAS A SIX TOPS.
KICK
UH-OH, LOOKS LIKE PARKER'S ABOUT TO PULL A "CARRIE."
GUYS -- GUYS! COME ON, LEAVE THE GUY ALONE FOR TWO SECONDS.
WHAT? ARE YOU SWEET ON HIM, HARRY?
NO, I'M SWEET ON YOU.
OH YEAH -- I FORGOT. THIS IS YOUR CHARITY PROJECT.
GO FLEX A MUSCLE.
IS THERE SOMETHING GOING ON HERE? WHAT IS THIS MESS?
HARRY OSBORN, THOMPSON. DON'T YOU PUNKS HAVE PRACTICE? GO!
YES, SIR -- SIR.
PARKER, DON'T LET THOSE GUYS PICK ON YOU LIKE THAT. OK? YOU COME TO ME IF THAT HAPPENS AGAIN...

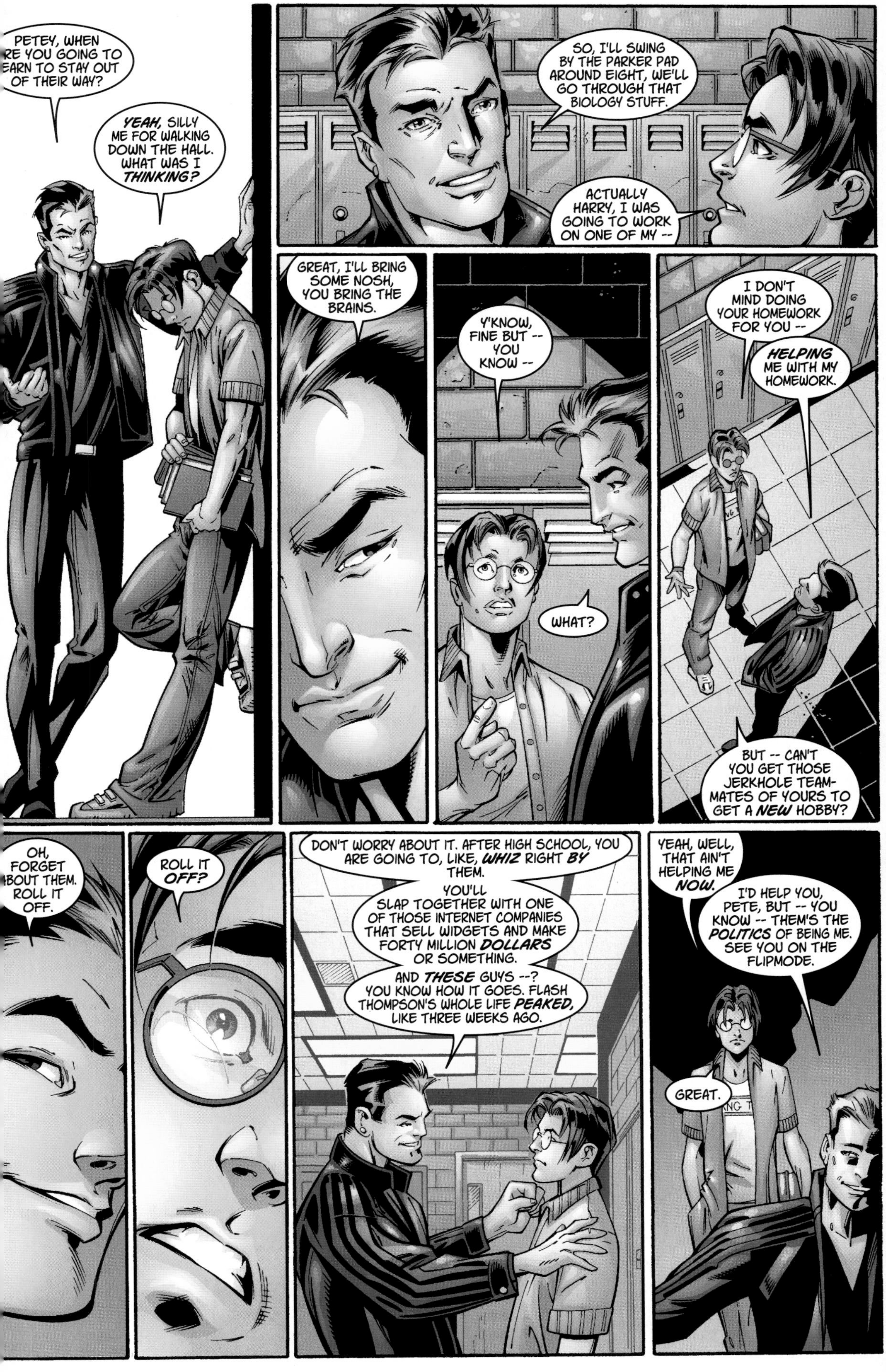
PETEY, WHEN ARE YOU GOING TO LEARN TO STAY OUT OF THEIR WAY?
YEAH, SILLY ME FOR WALKING DOWN THE HALL. WHAT WAS I THINKING?
SO, I'LL SWING BY THE PARKER PAD AROUND EIGHT, WE'LL GO THROUGH THAT BIOLOGY STUFF.
ACTUALLY HARRY, I WAS GOING TO WORK ON ONE OF MY --
GREAT, I'LL BRING SOME NOSH, YOU BRING THE BRAINS.
Y'KNOW, FINE BUT -- YOU KNOW --
WHAT?
I DON'T MIND DOING YOUR HOMEWORK FOR YOU --
HELPING ME WITH MY HOMEWORK.
BUT -- CAN'T YOU GET THOSE JERKHOLE TEAM-MATES OF YOURS TO GET A NEW HOBBY?
OH, FORGET ABOUT THEM. ROLL IT OFF.
ROLL IT OFF?
DON'T WORRY ABOUT IT. AFTER HIGH SCHOOL, YOU ARE GOING TO, LIKE, WHIZ RIGHT BY THEM.
YOU'LL SLAP TOGETHER WITH ONE OF THOSE INTERNET COMPANIES THAT SELL WIDGETS AND MAKE FORTY MILLION DOLLARS OR SOMETHING.
AND THESE GUYS --? YOU KNOW HOW IT GOES. FLASH THOMPSON'S WHOLE LIFE PEAKED, LIKE THREE WEEKS AGO.
YEAH, WELL, THAT AIN'T HELPING ME NOW.
I'D HELP YOU, PETE, BUT -- YOU KNOW -- THEM'S THE POLITICS OF BEING ME. SEE YOU ON THE FLIPMODE.
GREAT.

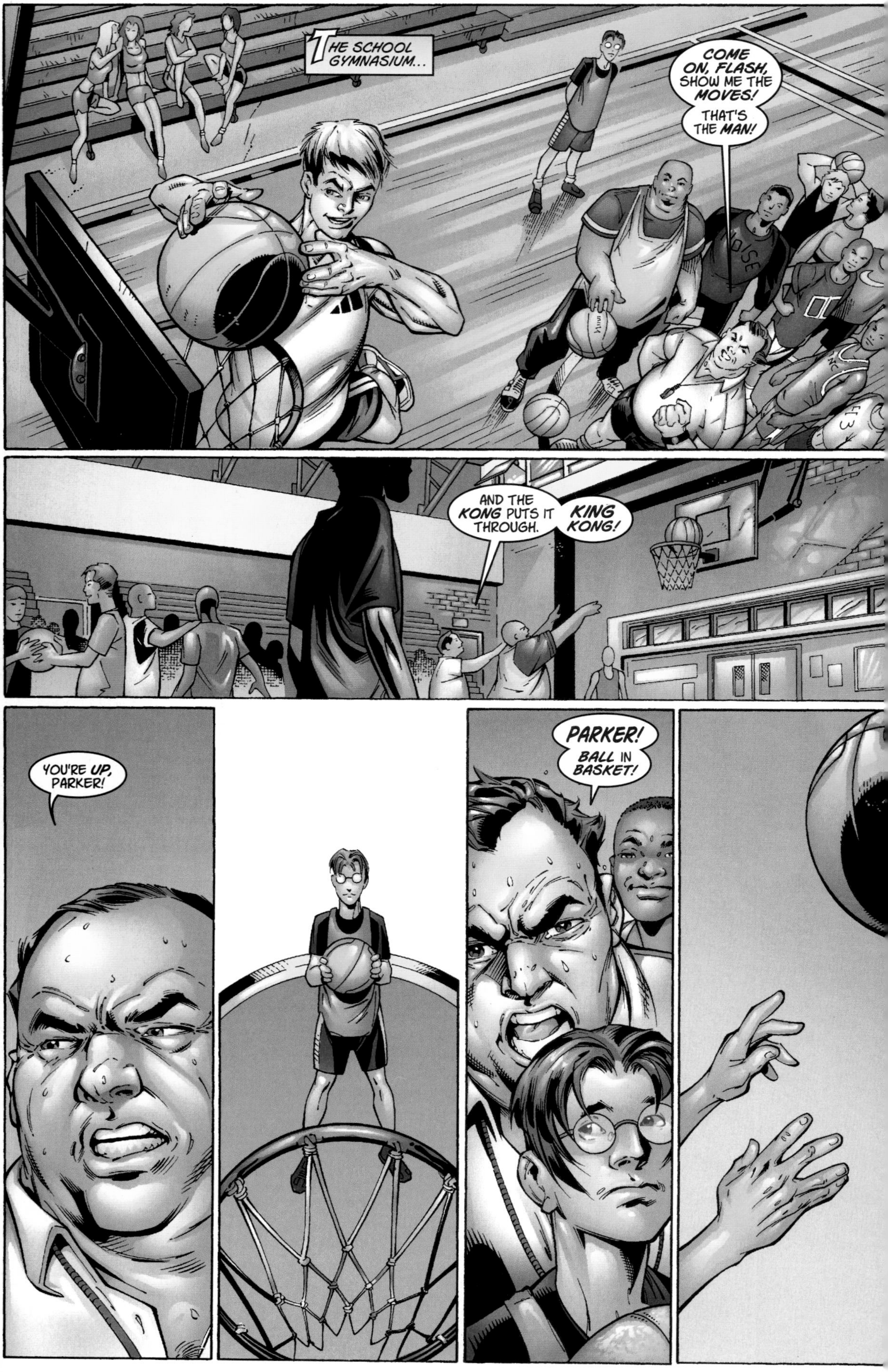
THE SCHOOL GYMNASIUM...
COME ON, FLASH, SHOW ME THE MOVES!
THAT'S THE MAN!
AND THE KONG PUTS IT THROUGH.
KING KONG!
YOU'RE UP, PARKER!
PARKER! BALL IN BASKET!

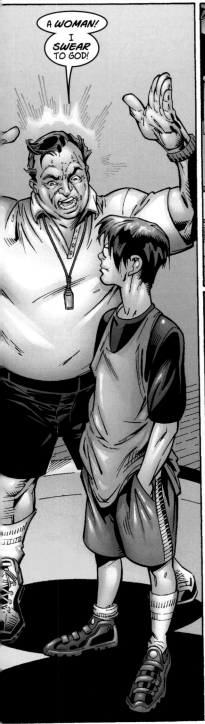

A *WOMAN!* I *SWEAR* TO GOD!

IF I HAD TO BET *CASH MONEY*, BASED ON THAT THROW, I'D SAY I WAS LOOKING AT A *WOMAN.*

TRY WEARIN' A *SUNDRESS* NEXT TIME.

MAYBE YOU CAN BORROW ONE FROM THE *PONY-TAIL-WEARIN'* UNCLE.

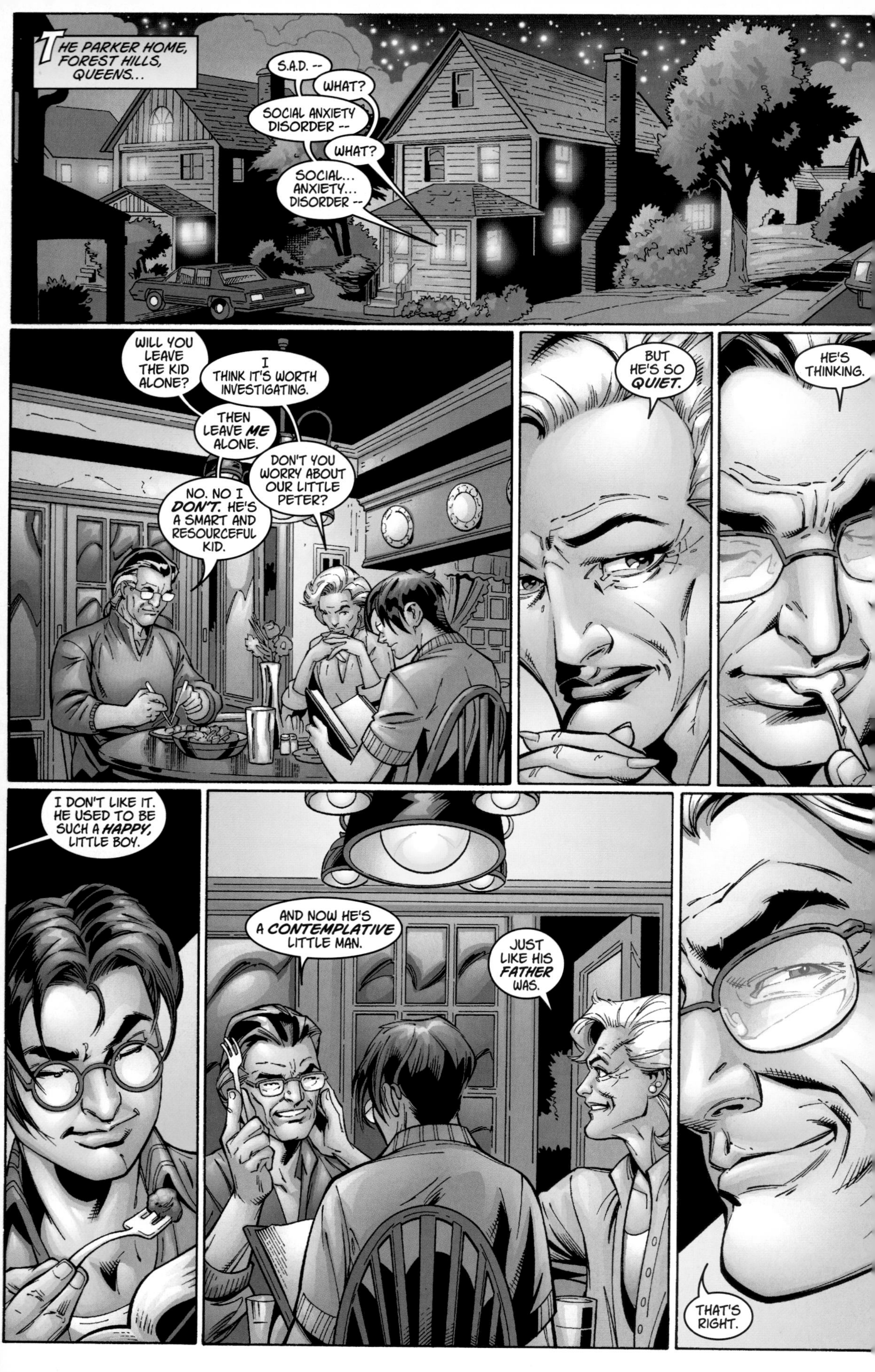
THE PARKER HOME, FOREST HILLS, QUEENS...
S.A.D. --
WHAT?
SOCIAL ANXIETY DISORDER --
WHAT?
SOCIAL... ANXIETY... DISORDER --
WILL YOU LEAVE THE KID ALONE?
I THINK IT'S WORTH INVESTIGATING.
THEN LEAVE ME ALONE.
DON'T YOU WORRY ABOUT OUR LITTLE PETER?
NO. NO I DON'T. HE'S A SMART AND RESOURCEFUL KID.
BUT HE'S SO QUIET.
HE'S THINKING.
I DON'T LIKE IT. HE USED TO BE SUCH A HAPPY, LITTLE BOY.
AND NOW HE'S A CONTEMPLATIVE LITTLE MAN.
JUST LIKE HIS FATHER WAS.
THAT'S RIGHT.

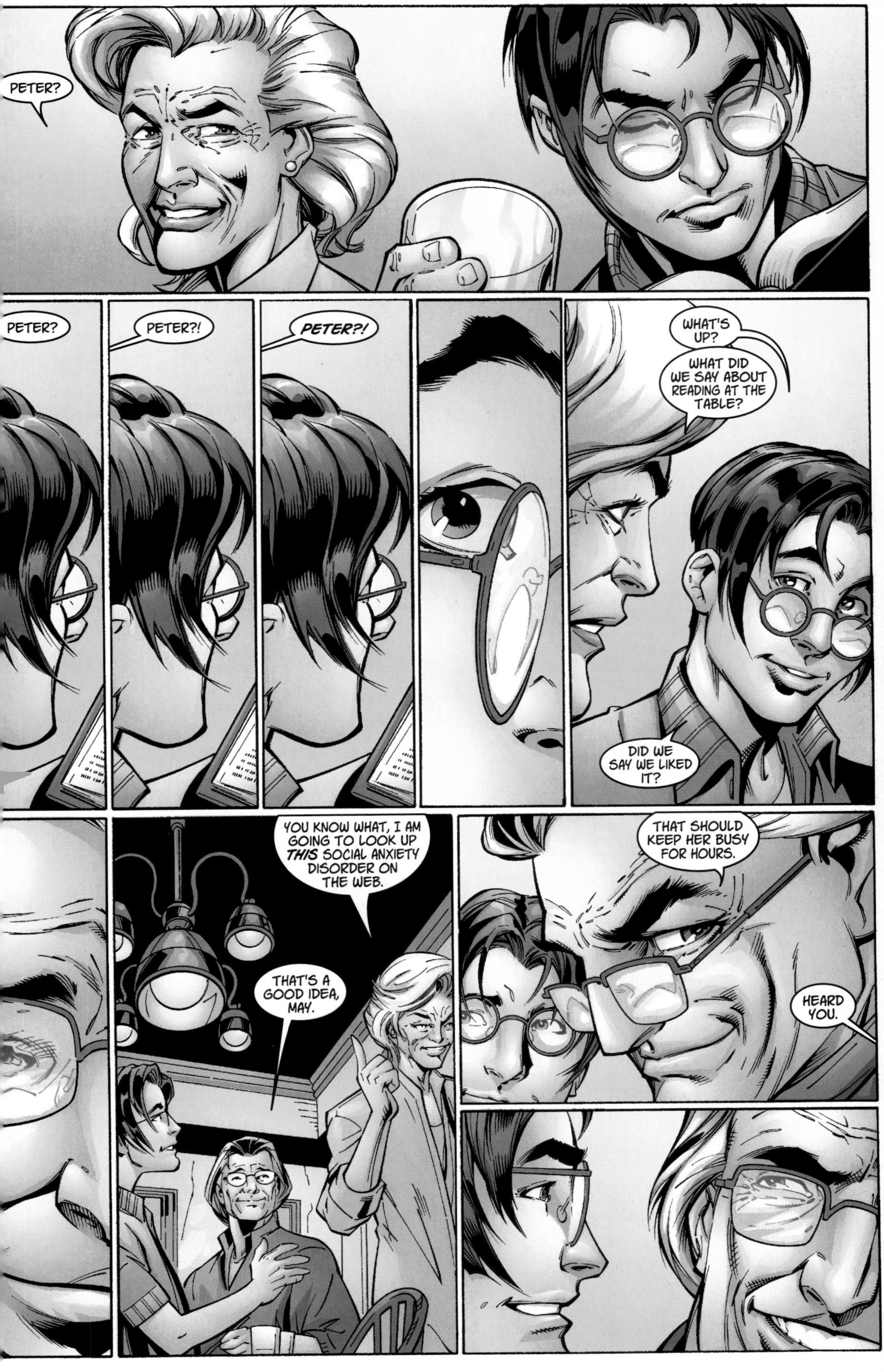
PETER?
PETER?
PETER?!
PETER?!
WHAT'S UP?
WHAT DID WE SAY ABOUT READING AT THE TABLE?
DID WE SAY WE LIKED IT?
YOU KNOW WHAT, I AM GOING TO LOOK UP THIS SOCIAL ANXIETY DISORDER ON THE WEB.
THAT'S A GOOD IDEA, MAY.
THAT SHOULD KEEP HER BUSY FOR HOURS.
HEARD YOU.

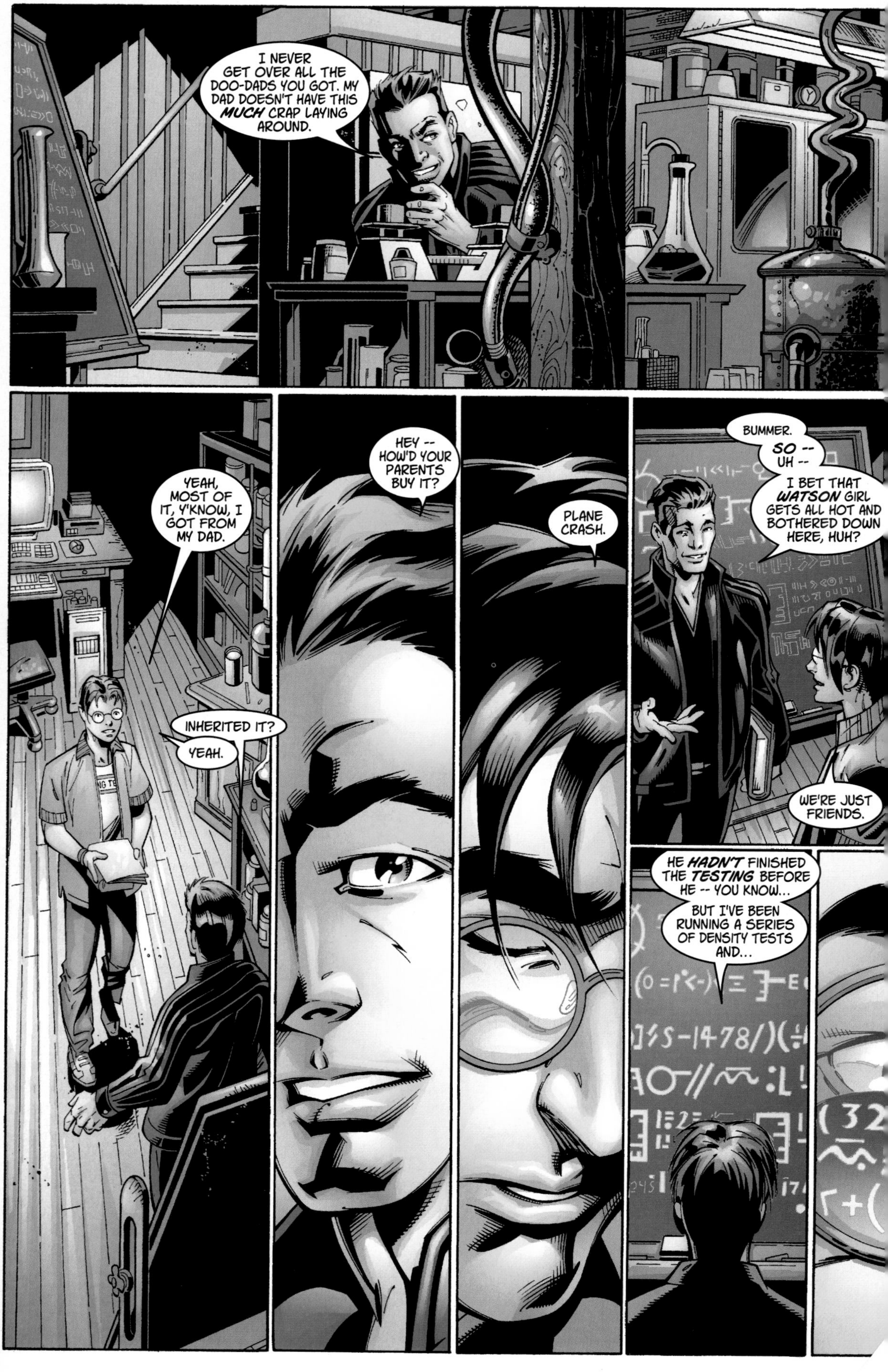
I NEVER GET OVER ALL THE DOO-DADS YOU GOT. MY DAD DOESN'T HAVE THIS MUCH CRAP LAYING AROUND.
YEAH, MOST OF IT, Y'KNOW, I GOT FROM MY DAD.
INHERITED IT?
YEAH.
HEY -- HOW'D YOUR PARENTS BUY IT?
PLANE CRASH.
BUMMER.
SO -- UH --
I BET THAT WATSON GIRL GETS ALL HOT AND BOTHERED DOWN HERE, HUH?
WE'RE JUST FRIENDS.
HE HADN'T FINISHED THE TESTING BEFORE HE -- YOU KNOW...
BUT I'VE BEEN RUNNING A SERIES OF DENSITY TESTS AND...

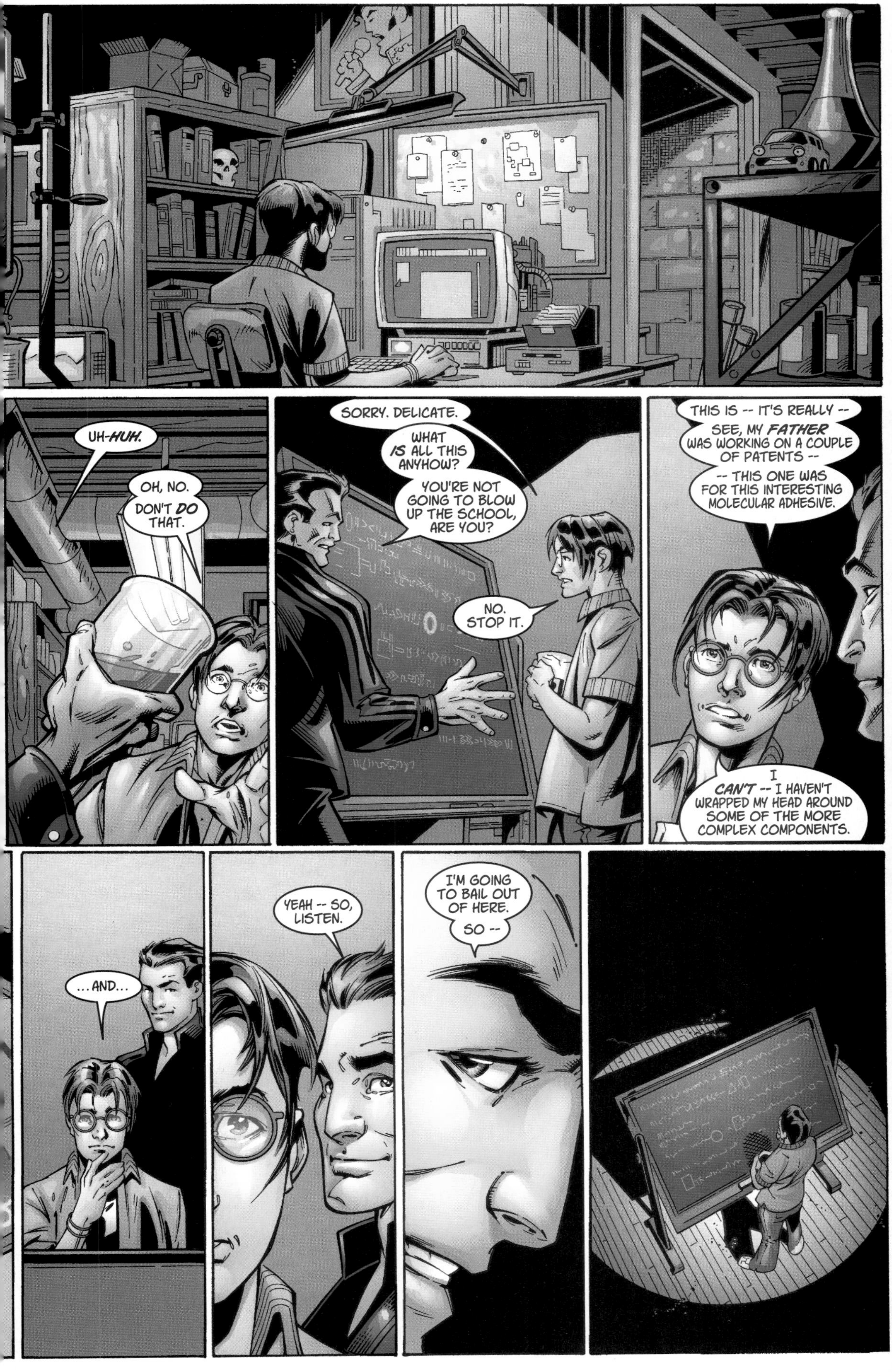
UH-HUH.
OH, NO. DON'T DO THAT.
SORRY. DELICATE.
WHAT IS ALL THIS ANYHOW?
YOU'RE NOT GOING TO BLOW UP THE SCHOOL, ARE YOU?
NO. STOP IT.
THIS IS -- IT'S REALLY --
SEE, MY FATHER WAS WORKING ON A COUPLE OF PATENTS --
-- THIS ONE WAS FOR THIS INTERESTING MOLECULAR ADHESIVE.
I CAN'T -- I HAVEN'T WRAPPED MY HEAD AROUND SOME OF THE MORE COMPLEX COMPONENTS.
...AND...
YEAH -- SO, LISTEN.
I'M GOING TO BAIL OUT OF HERE.
SO --

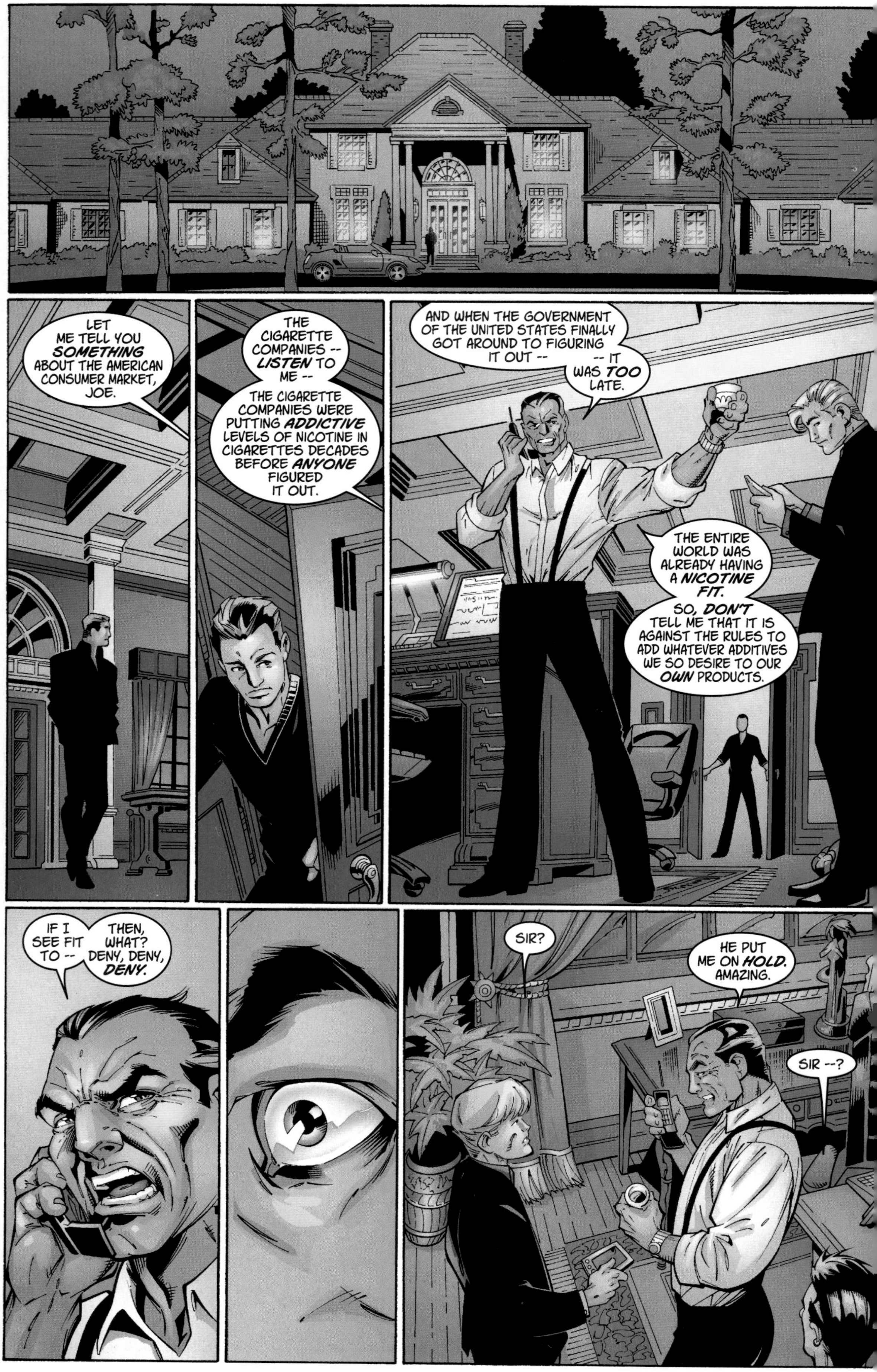
LET ME TELL YOU SOMETHING ABOUT THE AMERICAN CONSUMER MARKET, JOE.
THE CIGARETTE COMPANIES -- LISTEN TO ME --
THE CIGARETTE COMPANIES WERE PUTTING ADDICTIVE LEVELS OF NICOTINE IN CIGARETTES DECADES BEFORE ANYONE FIGURED IT OUT.
AND WHEN THE GOVERNMENT OF THE UNITED STATES FINALLY GOT AROUND TO FIGURING IT OUT --
-- IT WAS TOO LATE.
THE ENTIRE WORLD WAS ALREADY HAVING A NICOTINE FIT.
SO, DON'T TELL ME THAT IT IS AGAINST THE RULES TO ADD WHATEVER ADDITIVES WE SO DESIRE TO OUR OWN PRODUCTS.
IF I SEE FIT TO --
THEN, WHAT? DENY, DENY, DENY.
SIR?
HE PUT ME ON HOLD. AMAZING.
SIR --?

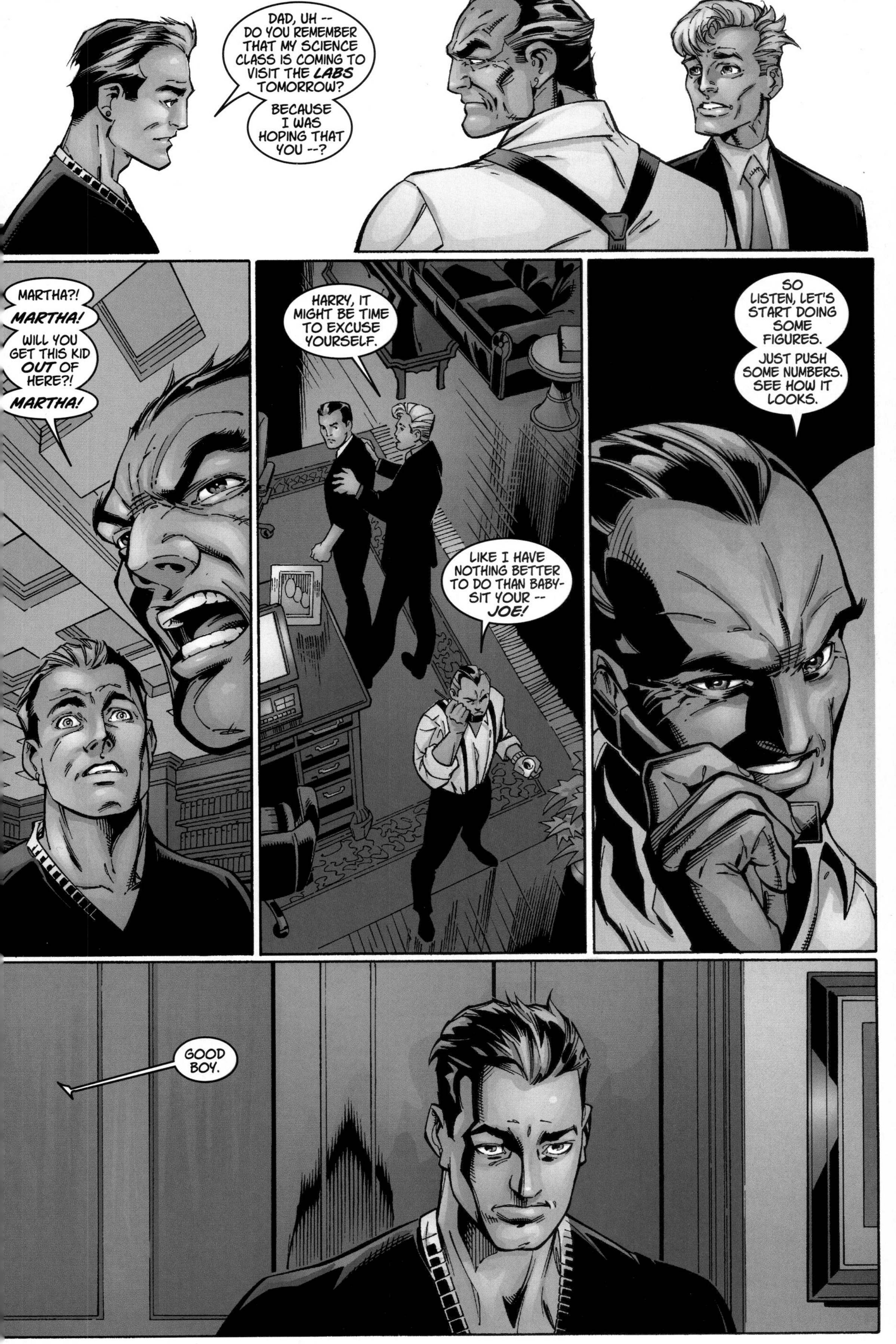
DAD, UH -- DO YOU REMEMBER THAT MY SCIENCE CLASS IS COMING TO VISIT THE *LABS* TOMORROW?
BECAUSE I WAS HOPING THAT YOU --?
MARTHA?!
MARTHA!
WILL YOU GET THIS KID *OUT* OF HERE?!
MARTHA!
HARRY, IT MIGHT BE TIME TO EXCUSE YOURSELF.
LIKE I HAVE NOTHING BETTER TO DO THAN BABY-SIT YOUR -- *JOE!*
SO LISTEN, LET'S START DOING SOME FIGURES.
JUST PUSH SOME NUMBERS. SEE HOW IT LOOKS.
GOOD BOY.

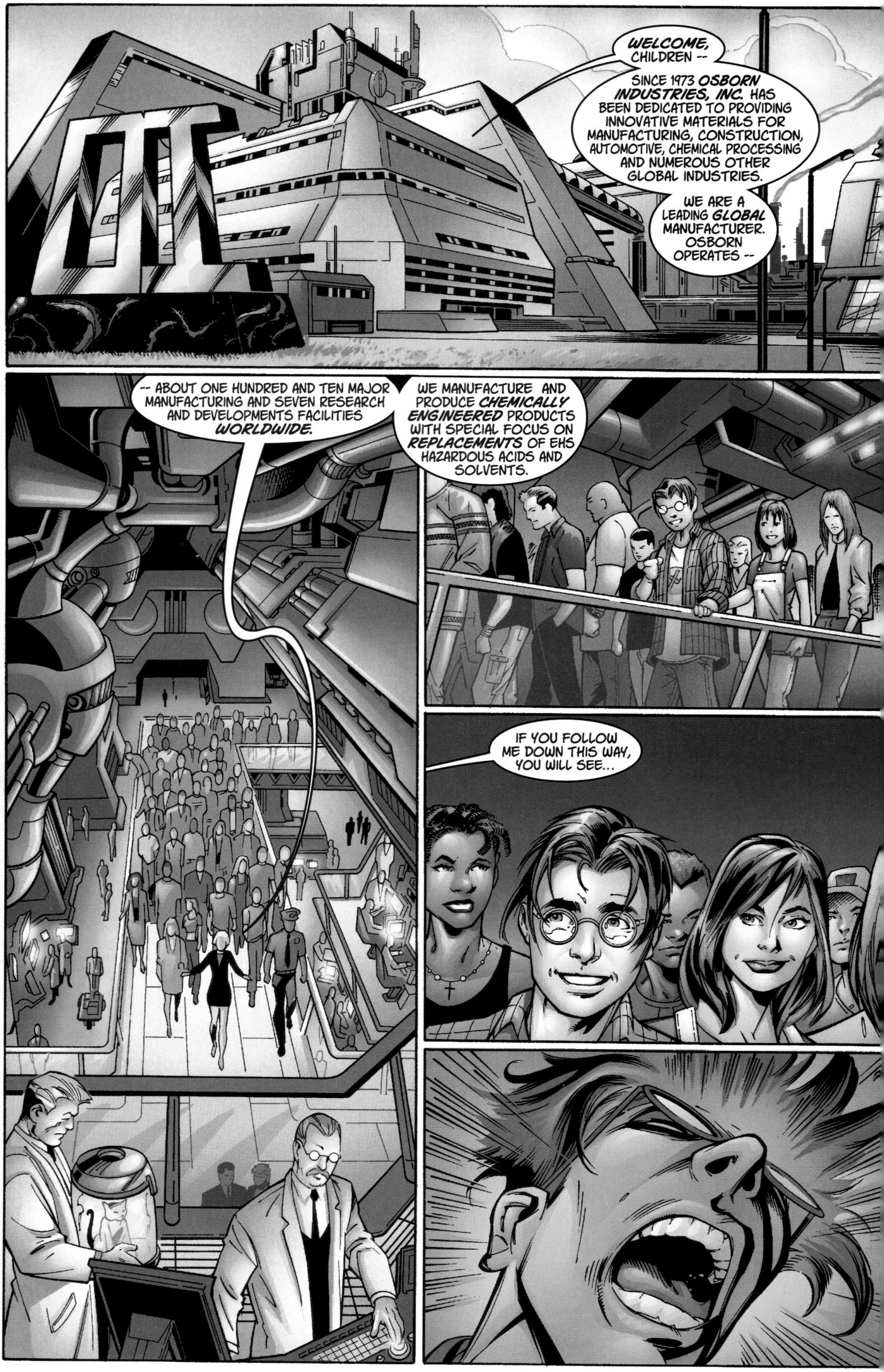
WELCOME, CHILDREN --
SINCE 1973 OSBORN INDUSTRIES, INC. HAS BEEN DEDICATED TO PROVIDING INNOVATIVE MATERIALS FOR MANUFACTURING, CONSTRUCTION, AUTOMOTIVE, CHEMICAL PROCESSING AND NUMEROUS OTHER GLOBAL INDUSTRIES.
WE ARE A LEADING GLOBAL MANUFACTURER. OSBORN OPERATES --
-- ABOUT ONE HUNDRED AND TEN MAJOR MANUFACTURING AND SEVEN RESEARCH AND DEVELOPMENTS FACILITIES WORLDWIDE.
WE MANUFACTURE AND PRODUCE CHEMICALLY ENGINEERED PRODUCTS WITH SPECIAL FOCUS ON REPLACEMENTS OF EHS HAZARDOUS ACIDS AND SOLVENTS.
IF YOU FOLLOW ME DOWN THIS WAY, YOU WILL SEE...

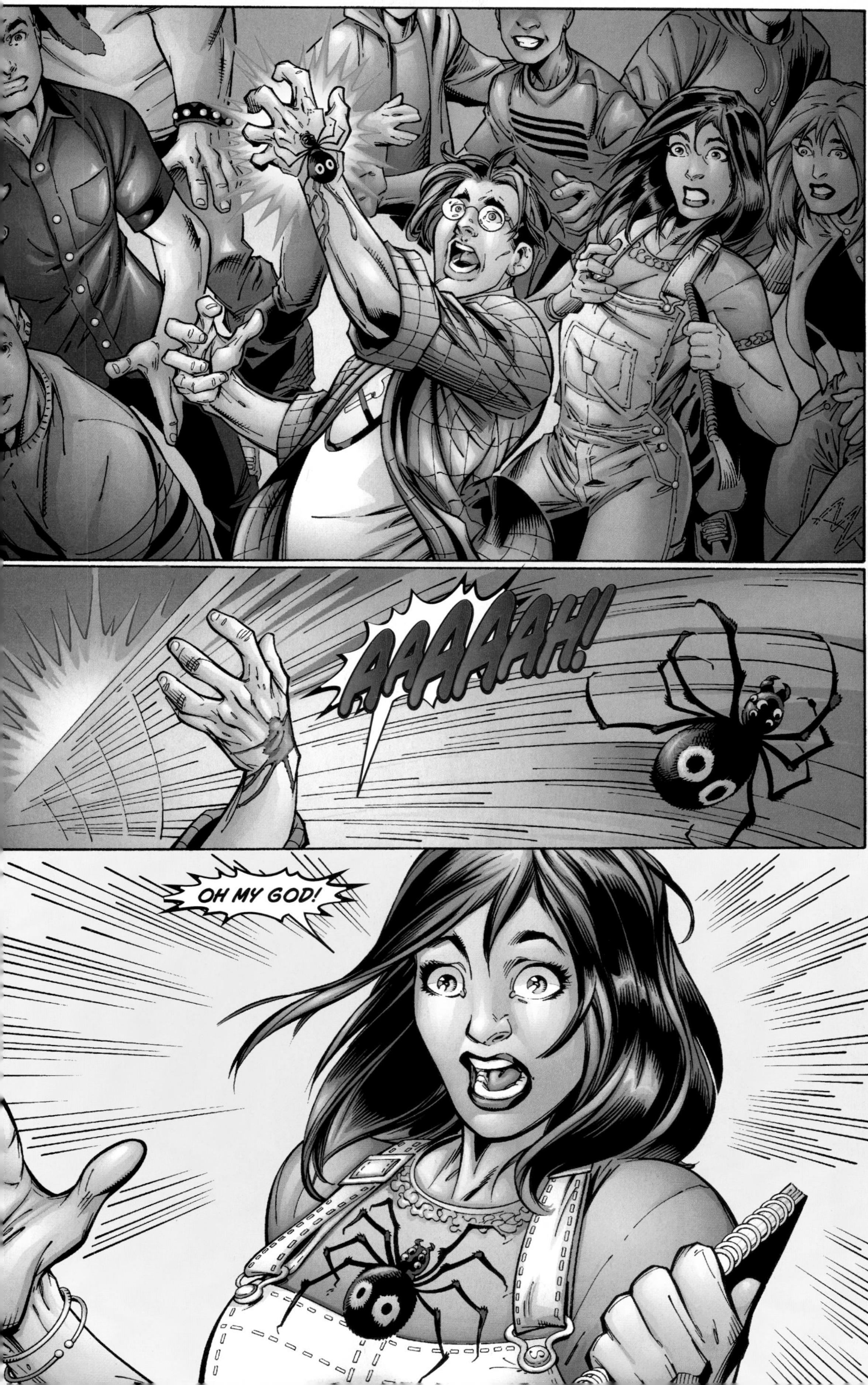
AAAAAH!
OH MY GOD!

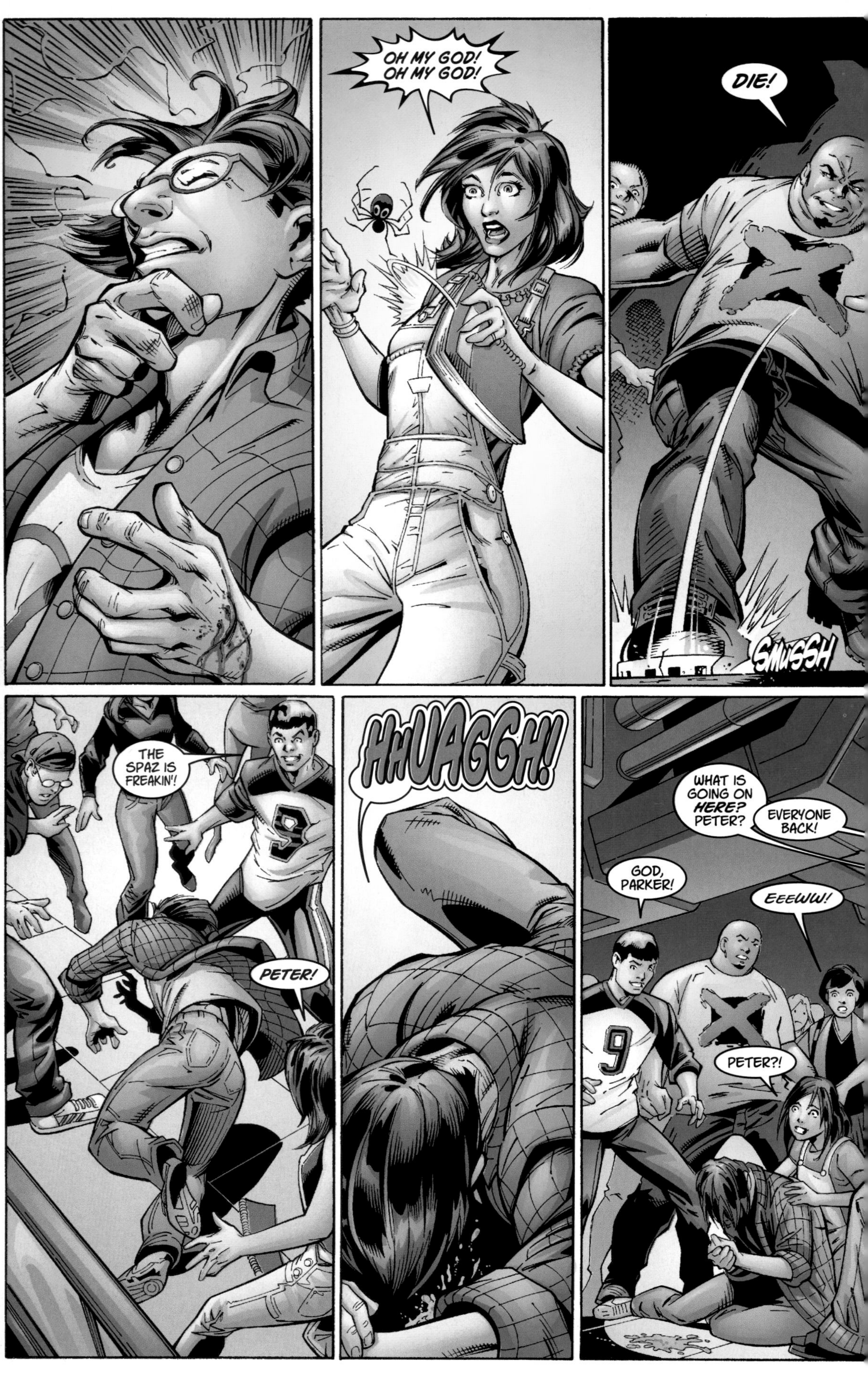
OH MY GOD!
OH MY GOD!
DIE!
SMUSSH
THE SPAZ IS FREAKIN'!
PETER!
HHUAGGH!
WHAT IS GOING ON HERE? PETER?
EVERYONE BACK!
GOD, PARKER!
EEEWW!
PETER?!

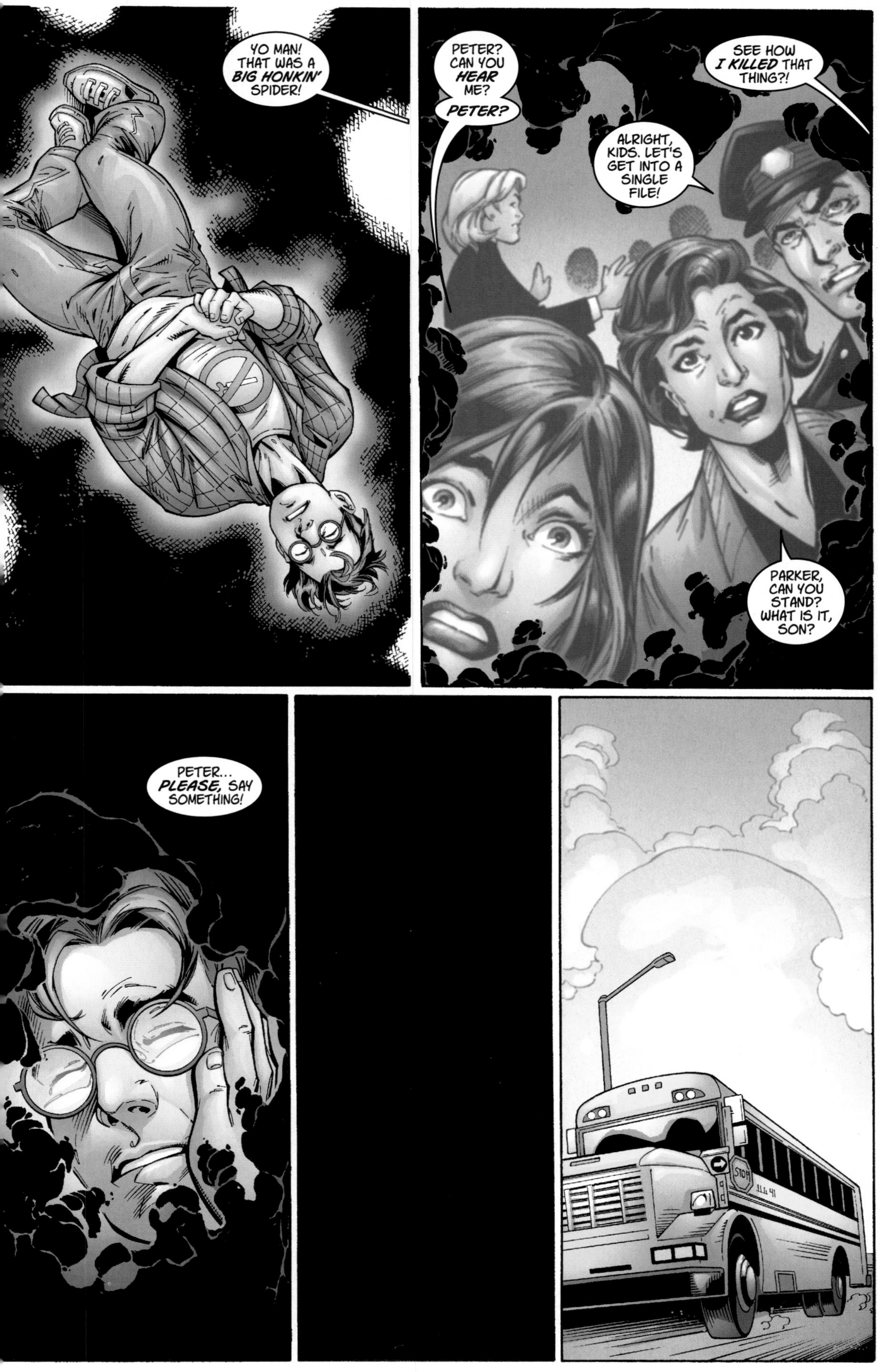
YO MAN! THAT WAS A BIG HONKIN' SPIDER!
PETER? CAN YOU HEAR ME?
PETER?
SEE HOW I KILLED THAT THING?!
ALRIGHT, KIDS. LET'S GET INTO A SINGLE FILE!
PARKER, CAN YOU STAND? WHAT IS IT, SON?
PETER... PLEASE, SAY SOMETHING!

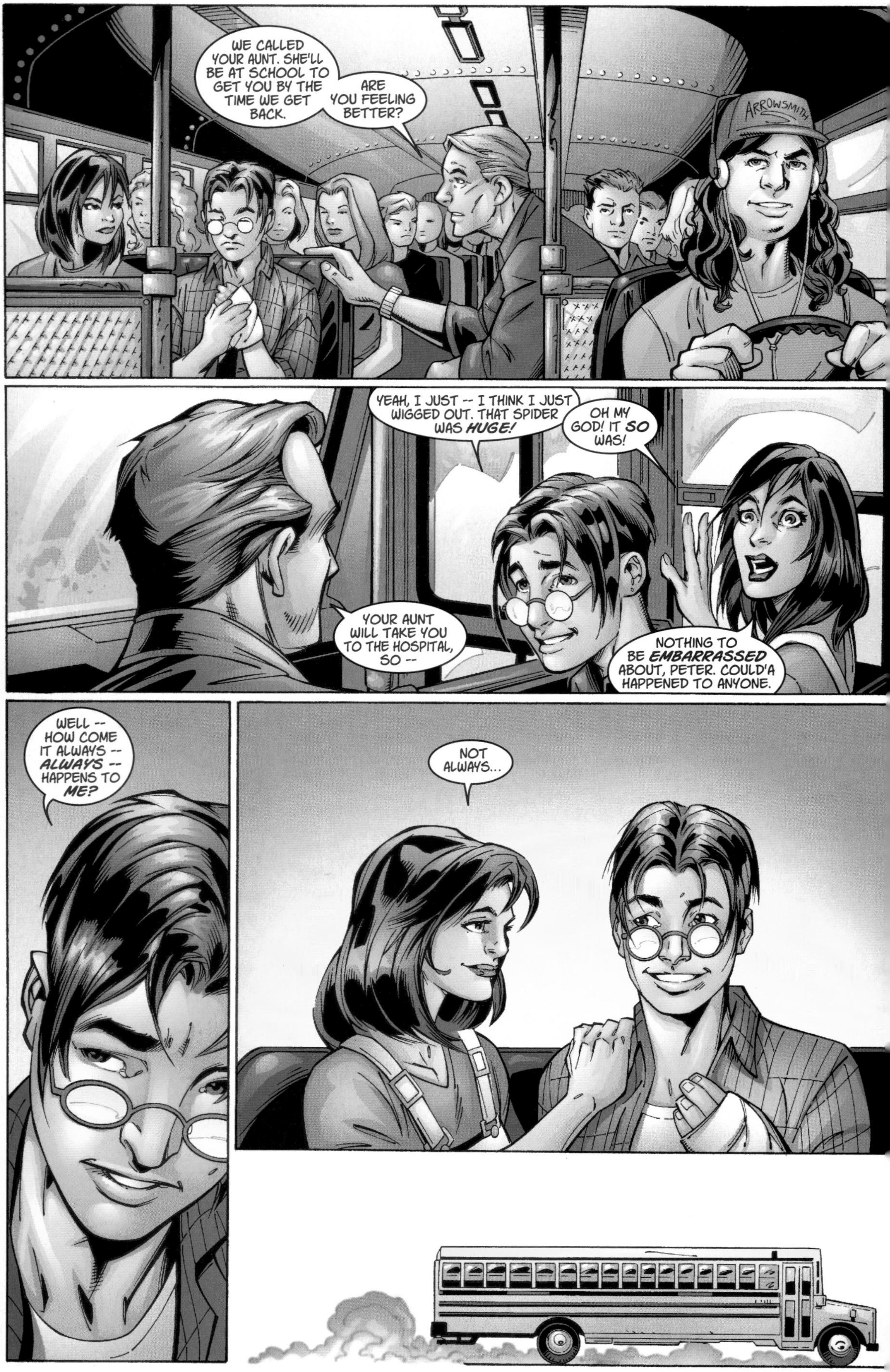

WE CALLED YOUR AUNT. SHE'LL BE AT SCHOOL TO GET YOU BY THE TIME WE GET BACK.
ARE YOU FEELING BETTER?
YEAH, I JUST -- I THINK I JUST WIGGED OUT. THAT SPIDER WAS *HUGE!*
OH MY GOD! IT *SO* WAS!
YOUR AUNT WILL TAKE YOU TO THE HOSPITAL, SO --
NOTHING TO BE *EMBARRASSED* ABOUT, PETER. COULD'A HAPPENED TO ANYONE.
WELL -- HOW COME IT ALWAYS -- *ALWAYS* -- HAPPENS TO *ME?*
NOT ALWAYS...
ARROWSMITH

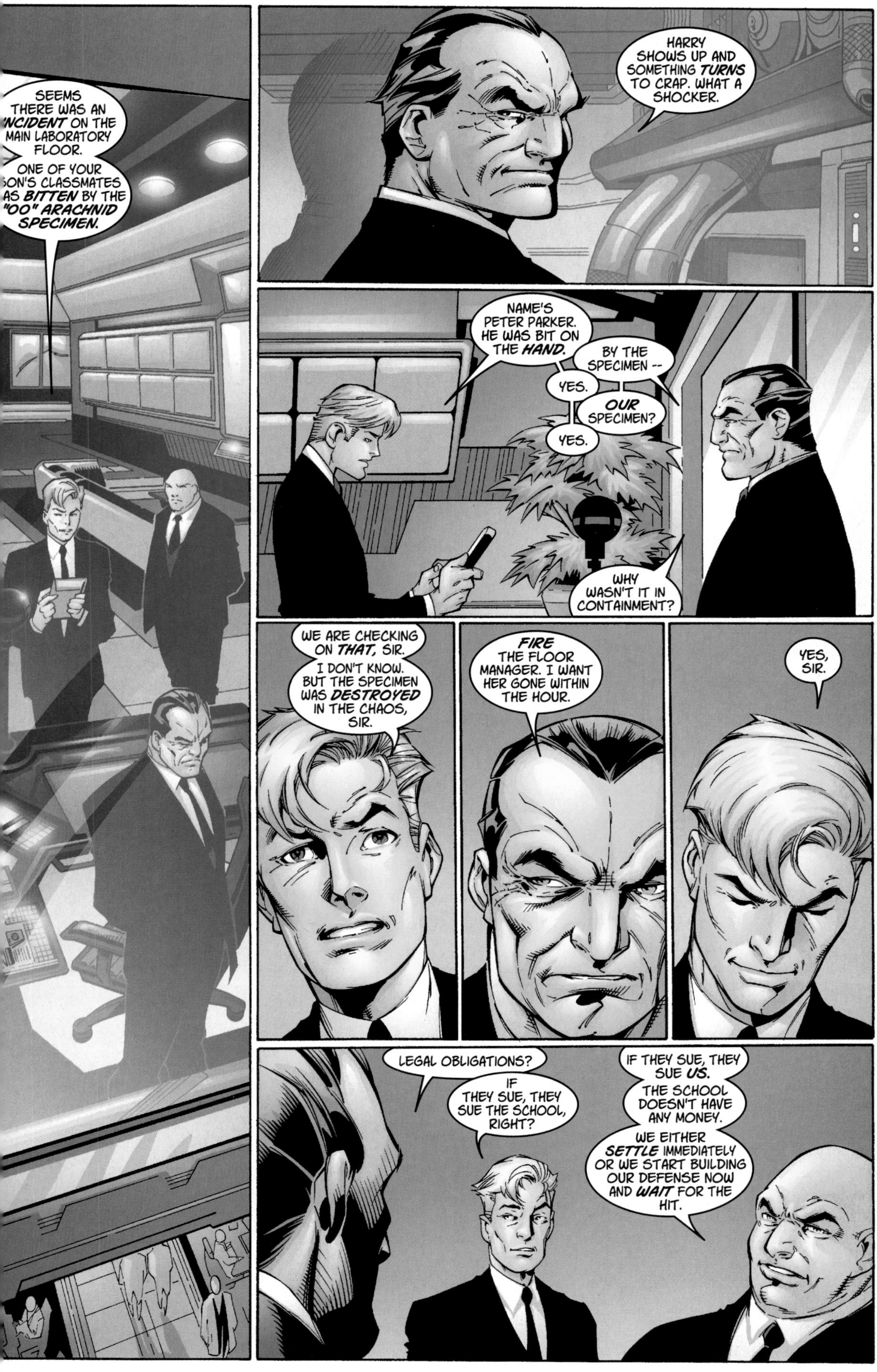
SEEMS THERE WAS AN INCIDENT ON THE MAIN LABORATORY FLOOR.
ONE OF YOUR SON'S CLASSMATES WAS BITTEN BY THE "OO" ARACHNID SPECIMEN.
HARRY SHOWS UP AND SOMETHING TURNS TO CRAP. WHAT A SHOCKER.
NAME'S PETER PARKER. HE WAS BIT ON THE HAND.
BY THE SPECIMEN --
YES.
OUR SPECIMEN?
YES.
WHY WASN'T IT IN CONTAINMENT?
WE ARE CHECKING ON THAT, SIR.
I DON'T KNOW. BUT THE SPECIMEN WAS DESTROYED IN THE CHAOS, SIR.
FIRE THE FLOOR MANAGER. I WANT HER GONE WITHIN THE HOUR.
YES, SIR.
LEGAL OBLIGATIONS?
IF THEY SUE, THEY SUE THE SCHOOL, RIGHT?
IF THEY SUE, THEY SUE US.
THE SCHOOL DOESN'T HAVE ANY MONEY.
WE EITHER SETTLE IMMEDIATELY OR WE START BUILDING OUR DEFENSE NOW AND WAIT FOR THE HIT.

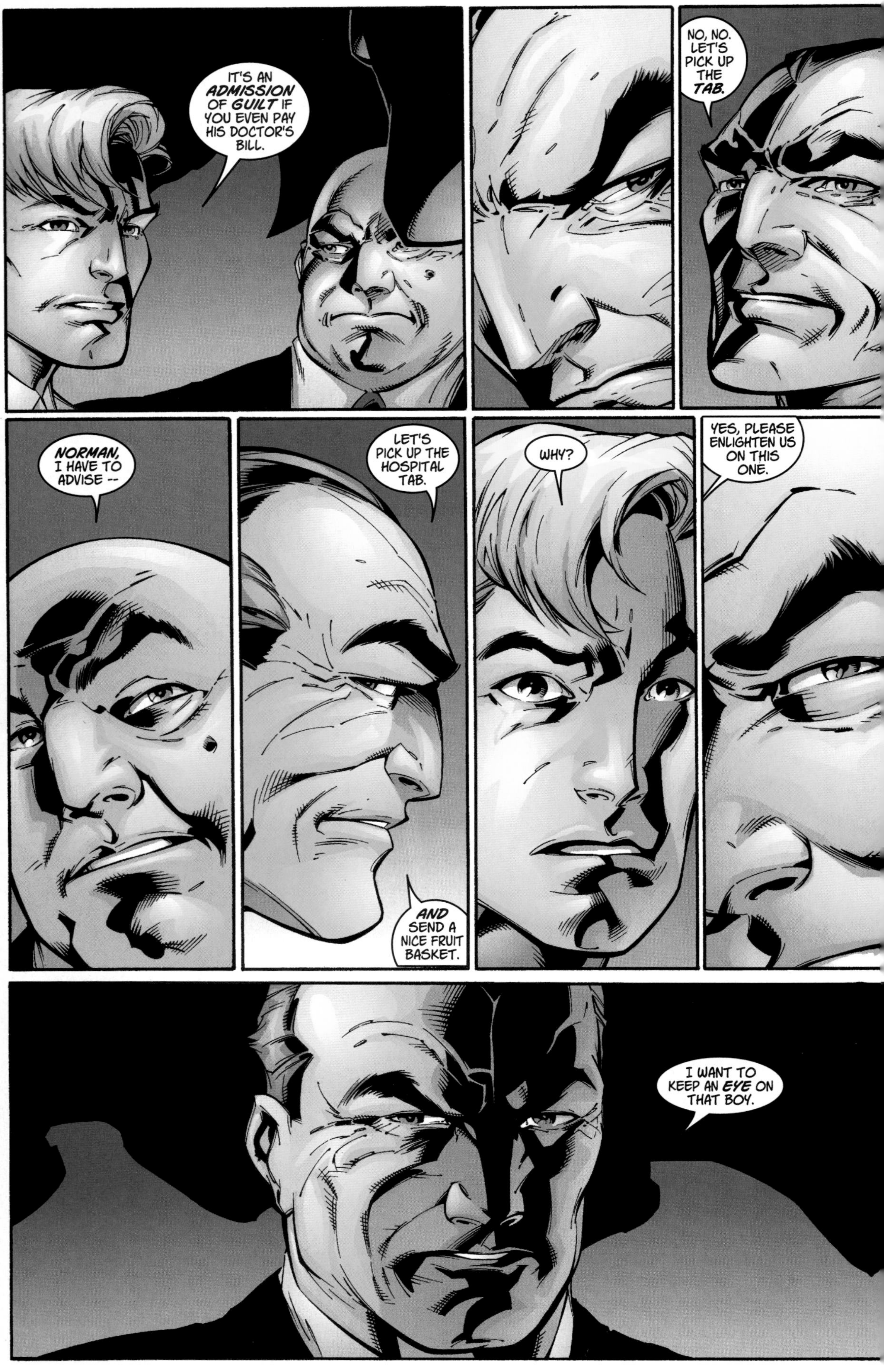
IT'S AN ADMISSION OF GUILT IF YOU EVEN PAY HIS DOCTOR'S BILL.
NO, NO. LET'S PICK UP THE TAB.
NORMAN, I HAVE TO ADVISE --
LET'S PICK UP THE HOSPITAL TAB.
AND SEND A NICE FRUIT BASKET.
WHY?
YES, PLEASE ENLIGHTEN US ON THIS ONE.
I WANT TO KEEP AN EYE ON THAT BOY.

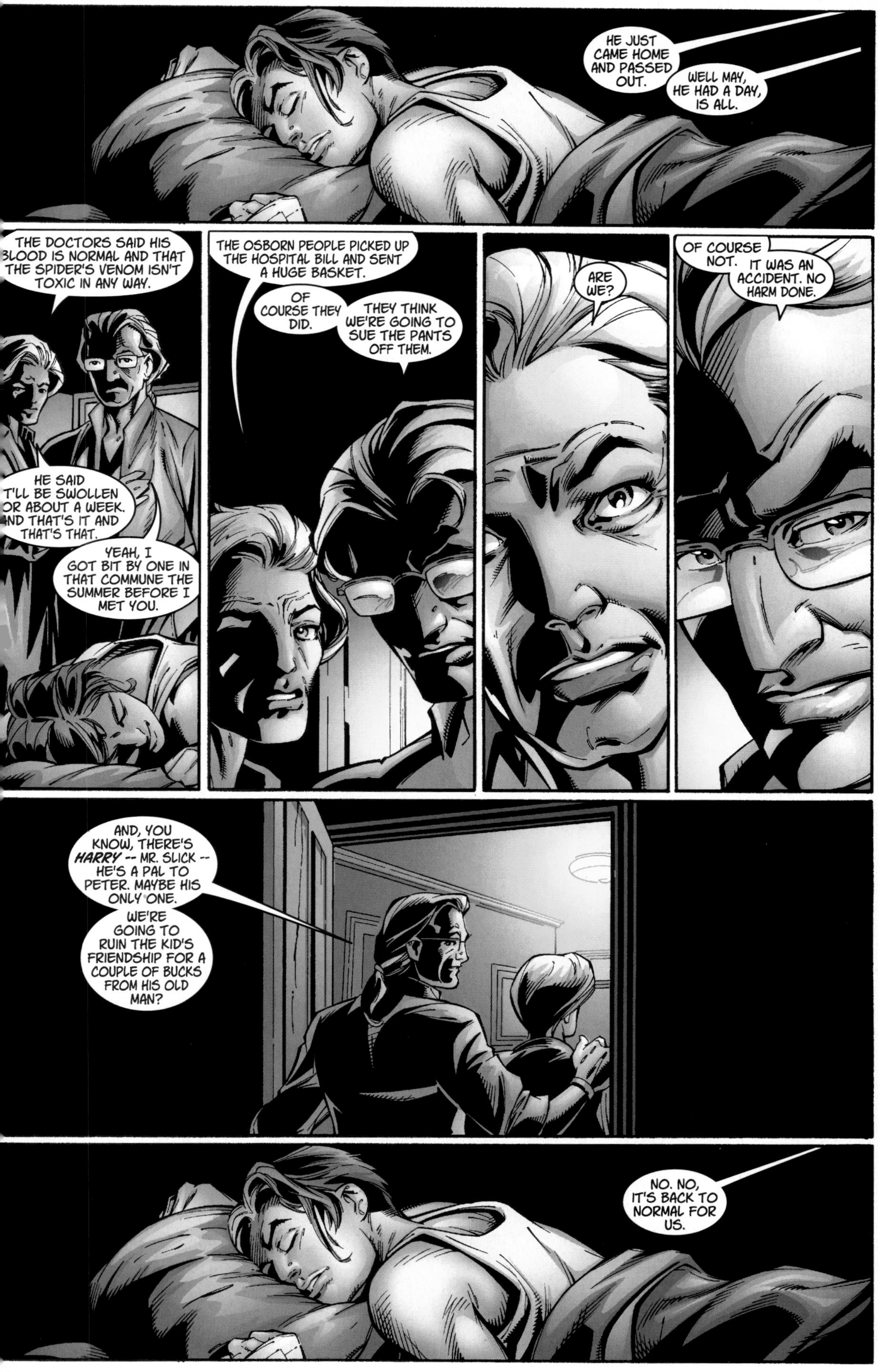
HE JUST CAME HOME AND PASSED OUT.
WELL MAY, HE HAD A DAY, IS ALL.
THE DOCTORS SAID HIS BLOOD IS NORMAL AND THAT THE SPIDER'S VENOM ISN'T TOXIC IN ANY WAY.
HE SAID IT'LL BE SWOLLEN FOR ABOUT A WEEK. AND THAT'S IT AND THAT'S THAT.
YEAH, I GOT BIT BY ONE IN THAT COMMUNE THE SUMMER BEFORE I MET YOU.
THE OSBORN PEOPLE PICKED UP THE HOSPITAL BILL AND SENT A HUGE BASKET.
OF COURSE THEY DID.
THEY THINK WE'RE GOING TO SUE THE PANTS OFF THEM.
ARE WE?
OF COURSE NOT.
IT WAS AN ACCIDENT. NO HARM DONE.
AND, YOU KNOW, THERE'S HARRY -- MR. SLICK -- HE'S A PAL TO PETER. MAYBE HIS ONLY ONE.
WE'RE GOING TO RUIN THE KID'S FRIENDSHIP FOR A COUPLE OF BUCKS FROM HIS OLD MAN?
NO. NO, IT'S BACK TO NORMAL FOR US.

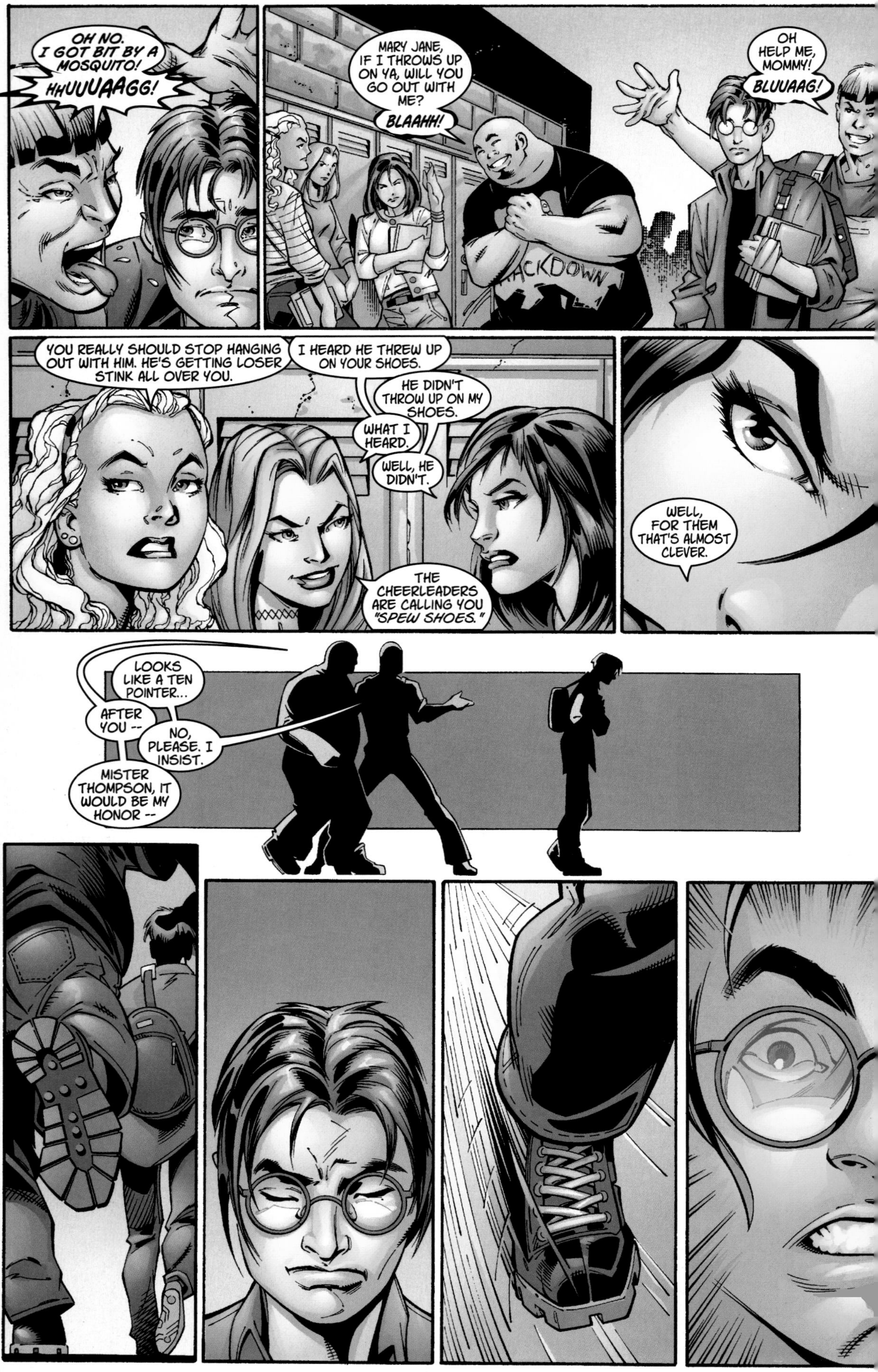

OH NO. I GOT BIT BY A MOSQUITO!
HHUUUAAGG!
MARY JANE, IF I THROWS UP ON YA, WILL YOU GO OUT WITH ME?
BLAAHH!
OH HELP ME, MOMMY!
BLUUAAG!
YOU REALLY SHOULD STOP HANGING OUT WITH HIM. HE'S GETTING LOSER STINK ALL OVER YOU.
I HEARD HE THREW UP ON YOUR SHOES.
HE DIDN'T THROW UP ON MY SHOES.
WHAT I HEARD.
WELL, HE DIDN'T.
THE CHEERLEADERS ARE CALLING YOU "SPEW SHOES."
WELL, FOR THEM THAT'S ALMOST CLEVER.
LOOKS LIKE A TEN POINTER...
AFTER YOU --
NO, PLEASE. I INSIST.
MISTER THOMPSON, IT WOULD BE MY HONOR --

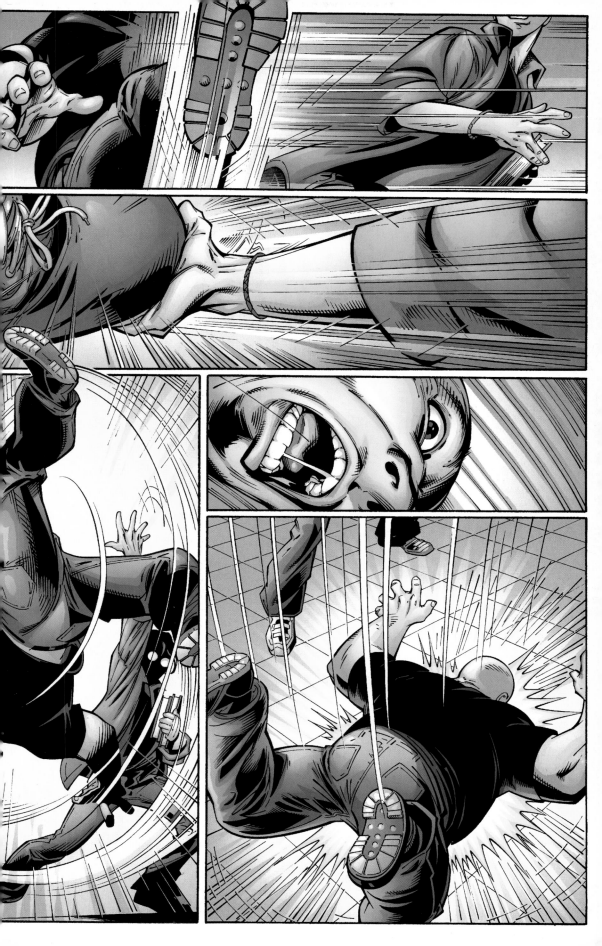

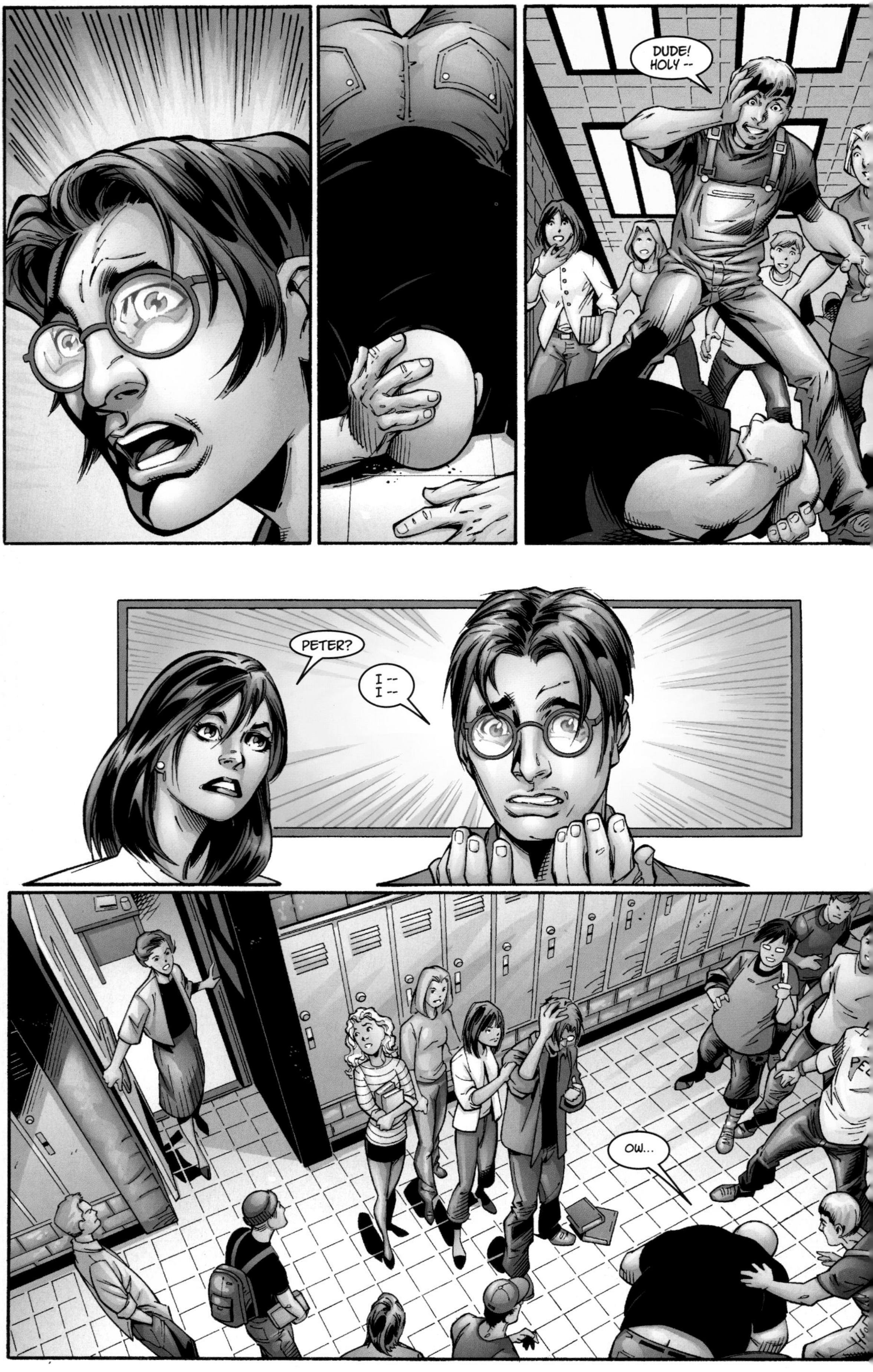
DUDE! HOLY --
PETER?
I -- I --
OW...

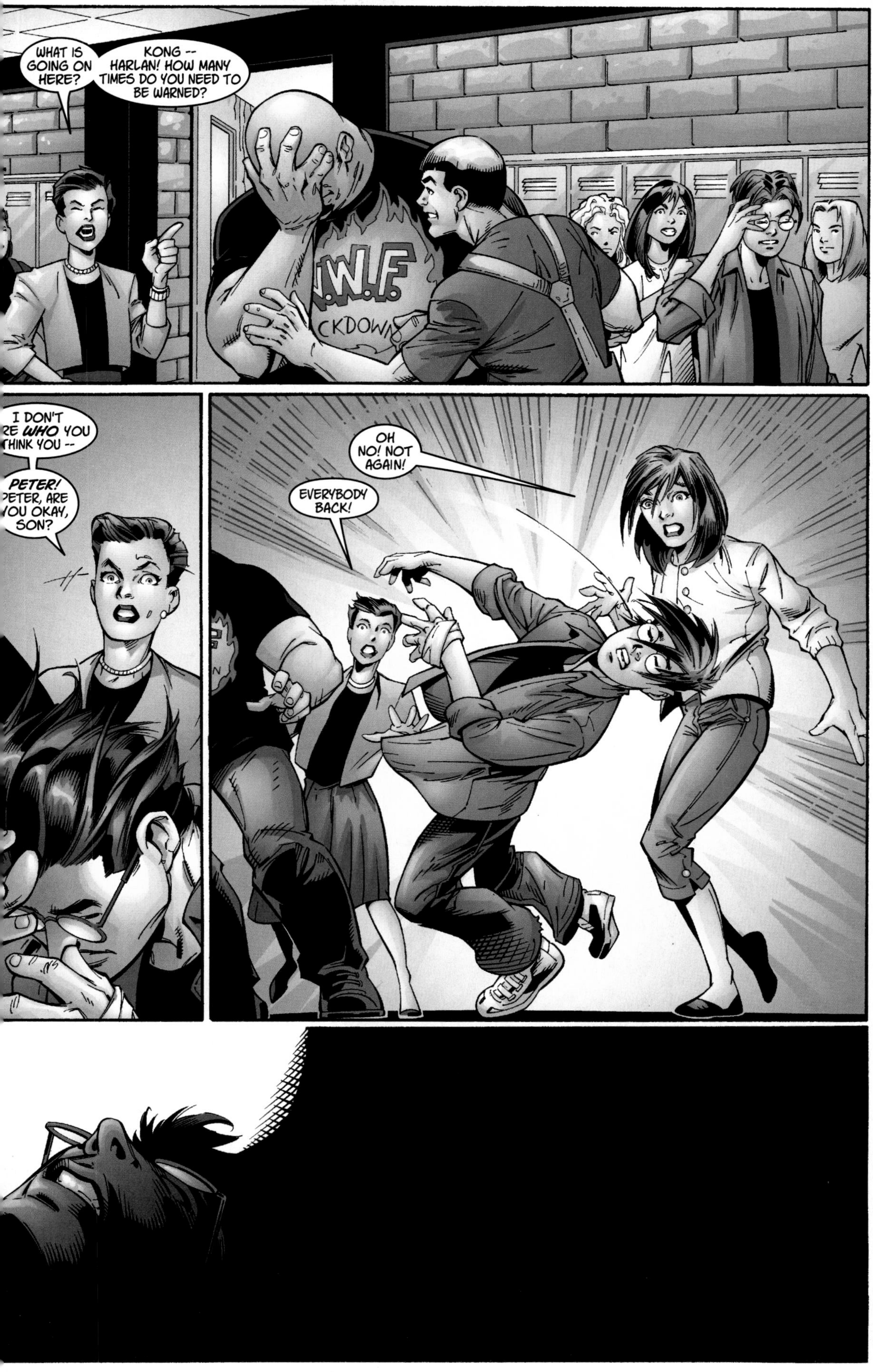
WHAT IS GOING ON HERE?
KONG -- HARLAN! HOW MANY TIMES DO YOU NEED TO BE WARNED?
I DON'T ...RE WHO YOU THINK YOU --
PETER! PETER, ARE YOU OKAY, SON?
OH NO! NOT AGAIN!
EVERYBODY BACK!

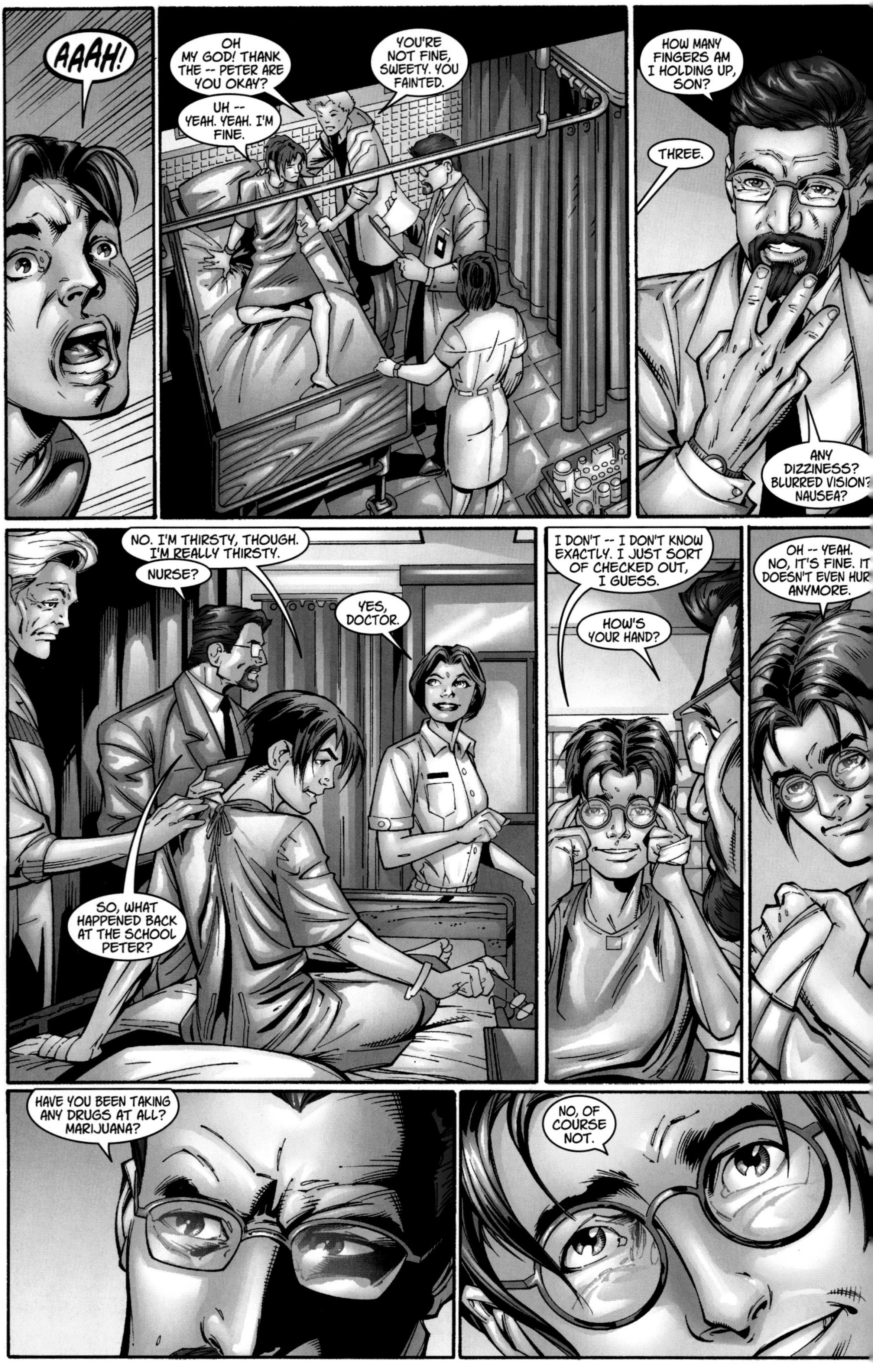
AAAH!
OH MY GOD! THANK THE -- PETER ARE YOU OKAY?
UH -- YEAH. YEAH. I'M FINE.
YOU'RE NOT FINE, SWEETY. YOU FAINTED.
HOW MANY FINGERS AM I HOLDING UP, SON?
THREE.
ANY DIZZINESS? BLURRED VISION? NAUSEA?
NO. I'M THIRSTY, THOUGH. I'M REALLY THIRSTY.
NURSE?
YES, DOCTOR.
SO, WHAT HAPPENED BACK AT THE SCHOOL PETER?
I DON'T -- I DON'T KNOW EXACTLY. I JUST SORT OF CHECKED OUT, I GUESS.
HOW'S YOUR HAND?
OH -- YEAH. NO, IT'S FINE. IT DOESN'T EVEN HUR ANYMORE.
HAVE YOU BEEN TAKING ANY DRUGS AT ALL? MARIJUANA?
NO, OF COURSE NOT.

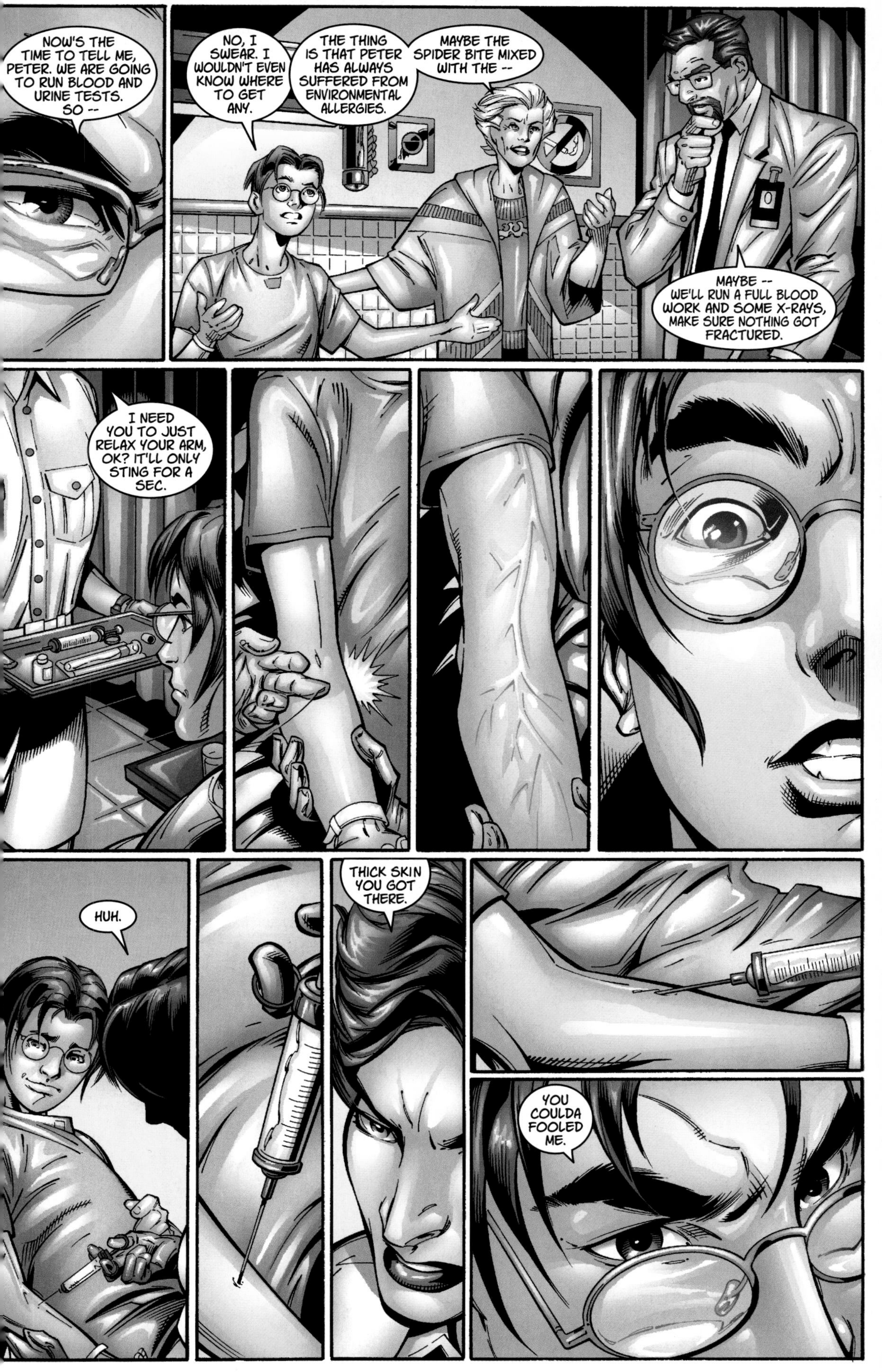

NOW'S THE TIME TO TELL ME, PETER. WE ARE GOING TO RUN BLOOD AND URINE TESTS. SO --
NO, I SWEAR. I WOULDN'T EVEN KNOW WHERE TO GET ANY.
THE THING IS THAT PETER HAS ALWAYS SUFFERED FROM ENVIRONMENTAL ALLERGIES.
MAYBE THE SPIDER BITE MIXED WITH THE --
MAYBE -- WE'LL RUN A FULL BLOOD WORK AND SOME X-RAYS, MAKE SURE NOTHING GOT FRACTURED.
I NEED YOU TO JUST RELAX YOUR ARM, OK? IT'LL ONLY STING FOR A SEC.
HUH.
THICK SKIN YOU GOT THERE.
YOU COULDA FOOLED ME.

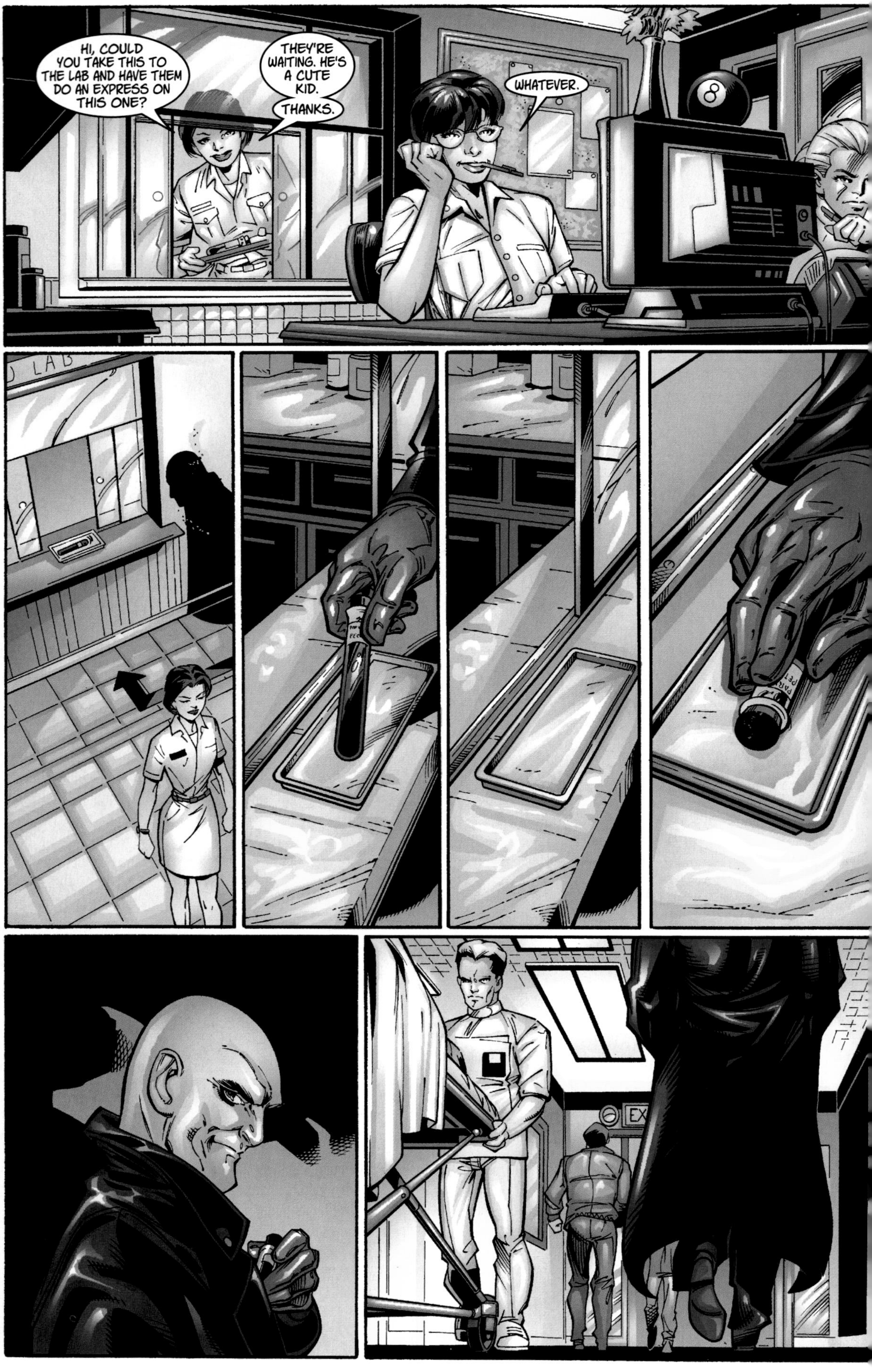
HI, COULD YOU TAKE THIS TO THE LAB AND HAVE THEM DO AN EXPRESS ON THIS ONE?
THEY'RE WAITING. HE'S A CUTE KID.
THANKS.
WHATEVER.

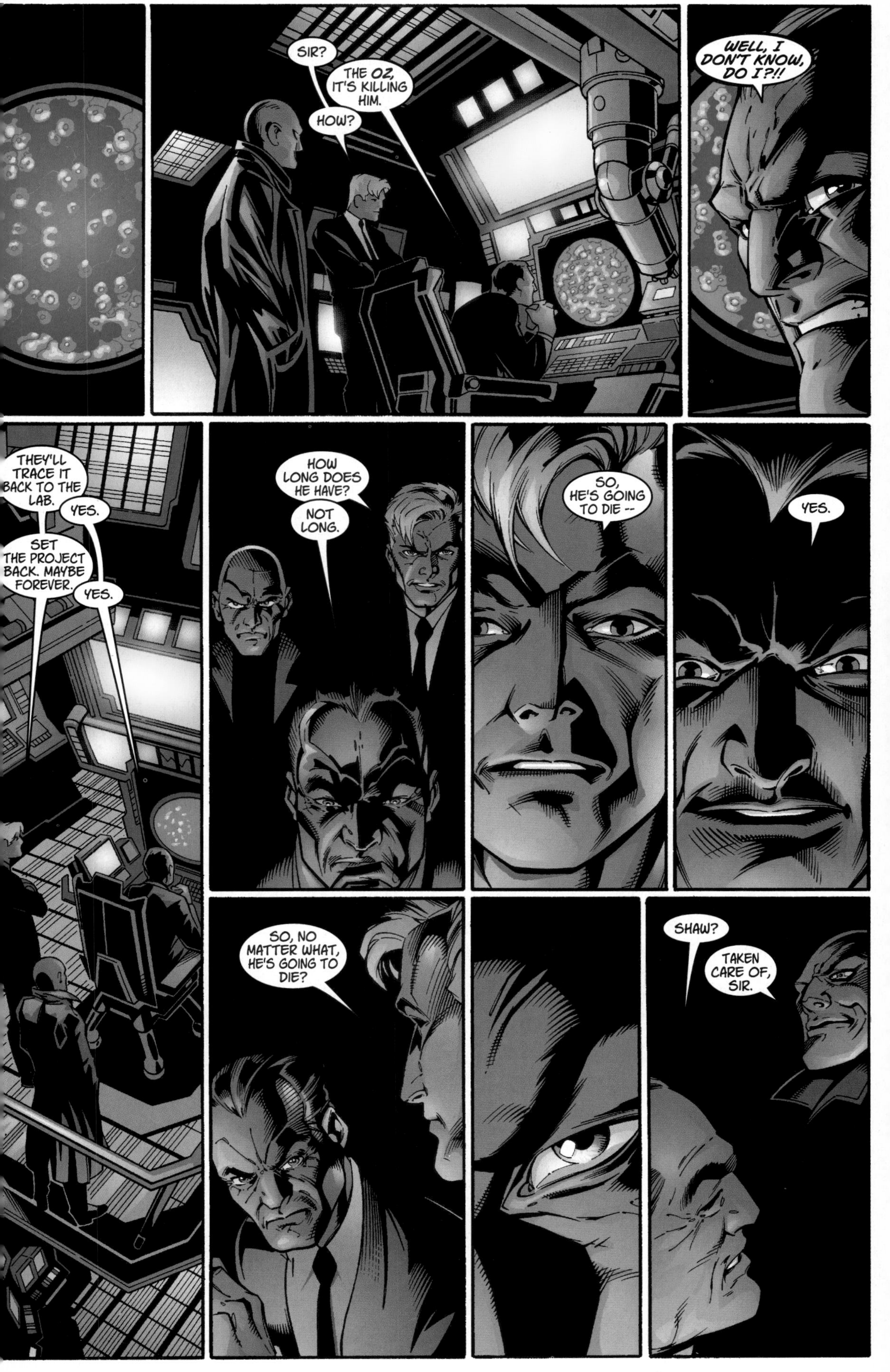
SIR?
THE OZ, IT'S KILLING HIM.
HOW?
WELL, I DON'T KNOW, DO I?!!
THEY'LL TRACE IT BACK TO THE LAB.
YES.
SET THE PROJECT BACK. MAYBE FOREVER.
YES.
HOW LONG DOES HE HAVE?
NOT LONG.
SO, HE'S GOING TO DIE --
YES.
SO, NO MATTER WHAT, HE'S GOING TO DIE?
SHAW?
TAKEN CARE OF, SIR.

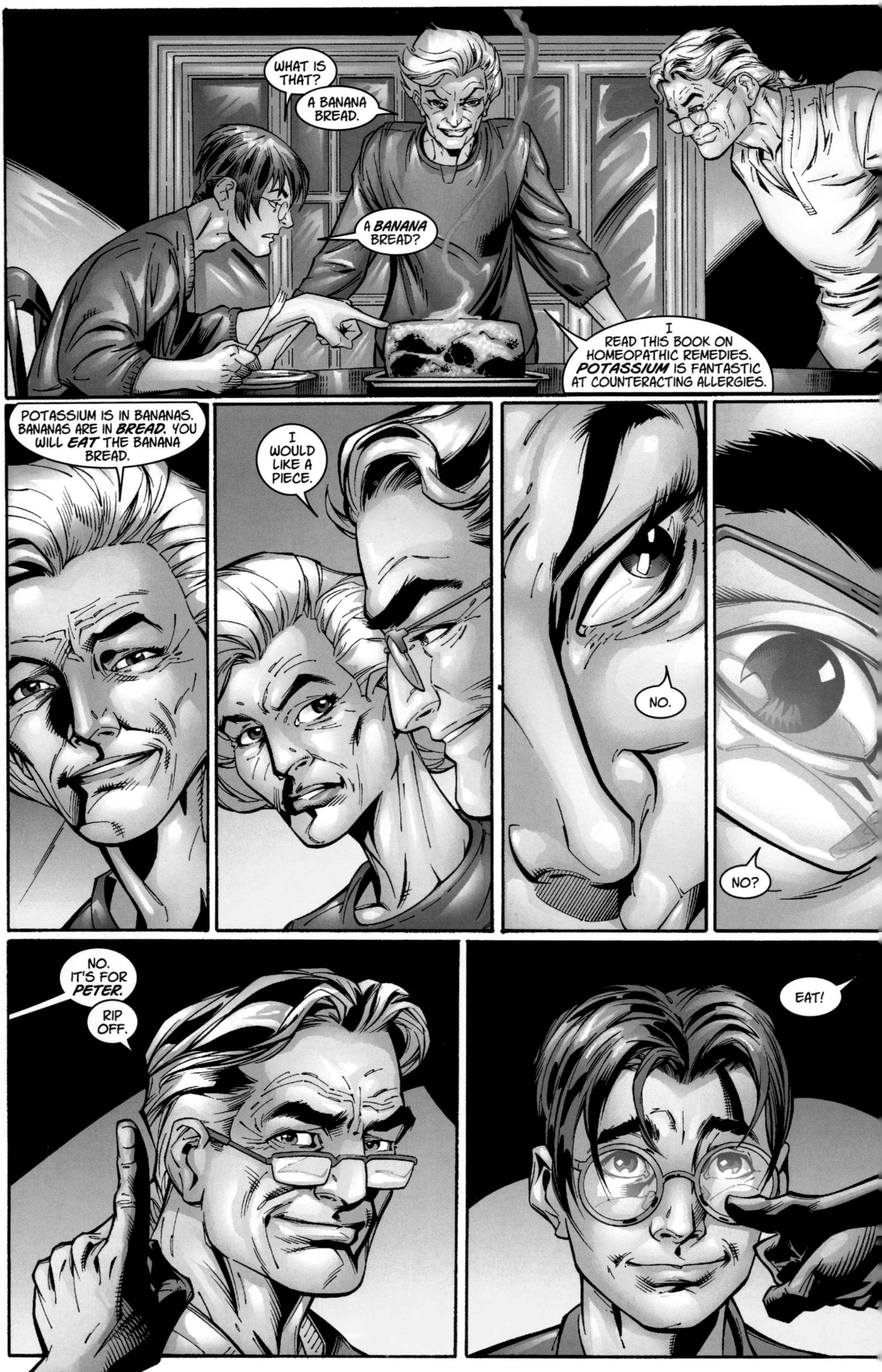
WHAT IS THAT?
A BANANA BREAD.
A BANANA BREAD?
I READ THIS BOOK ON HOMEOPATHIC REMEDIES. POTASSIUM IS FANTASTIC AT COUNTERACTING ALLERGIES.
POTASSIUM IS IN BANANAS. BANANAS ARE IN BREAD. YOU WILL EAT THE BANANA BREAD.
I WOULD LIKE A PIECE.
NO.
NO?
NO. IT'S FOR PETER.
RIP OFF.
EAT!

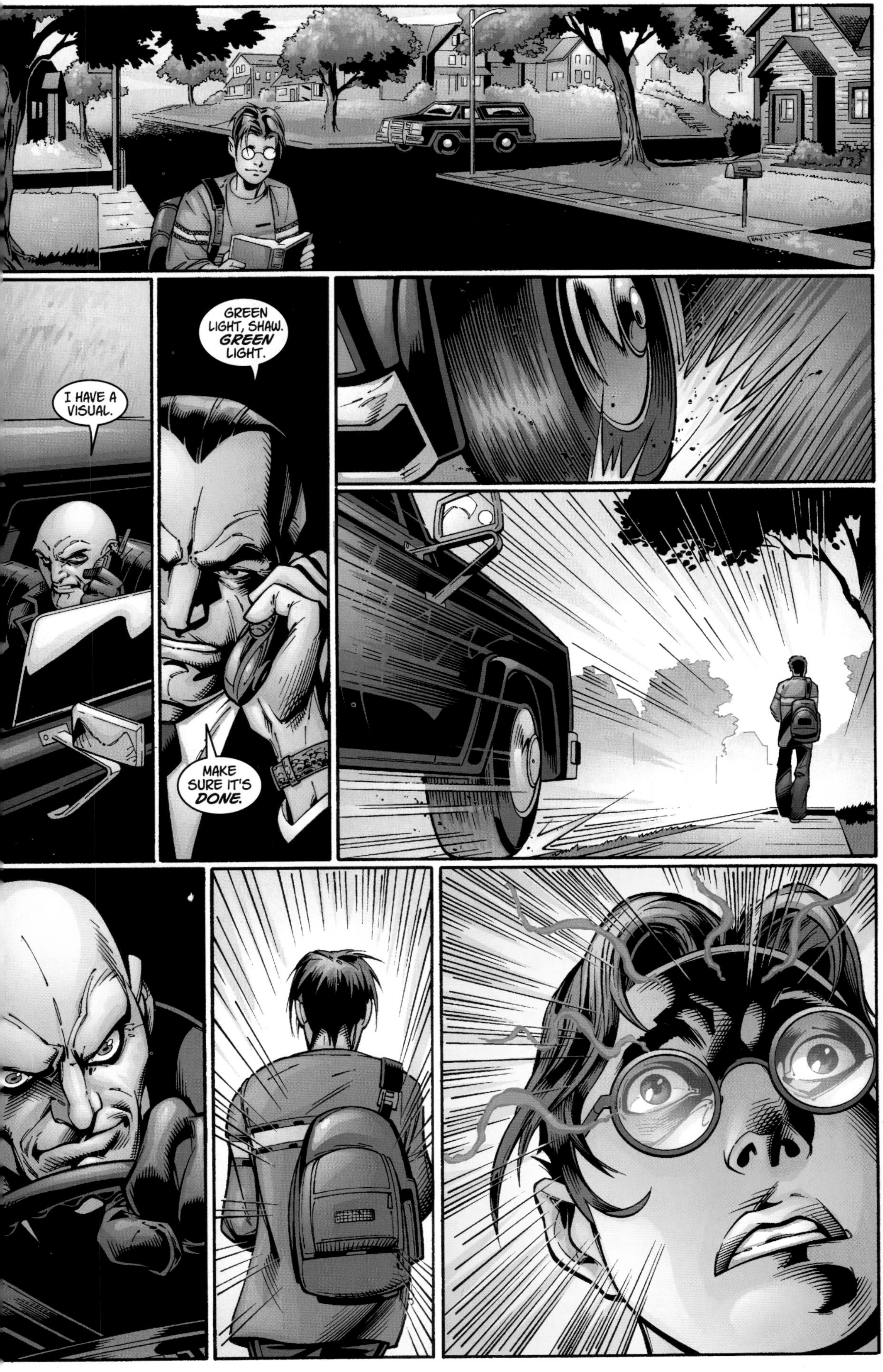
I HAVE A VISUAL.
GREEN LIGHT, SHAW. GREEN LIGHT.
MAKE SURE IT'S DONE.

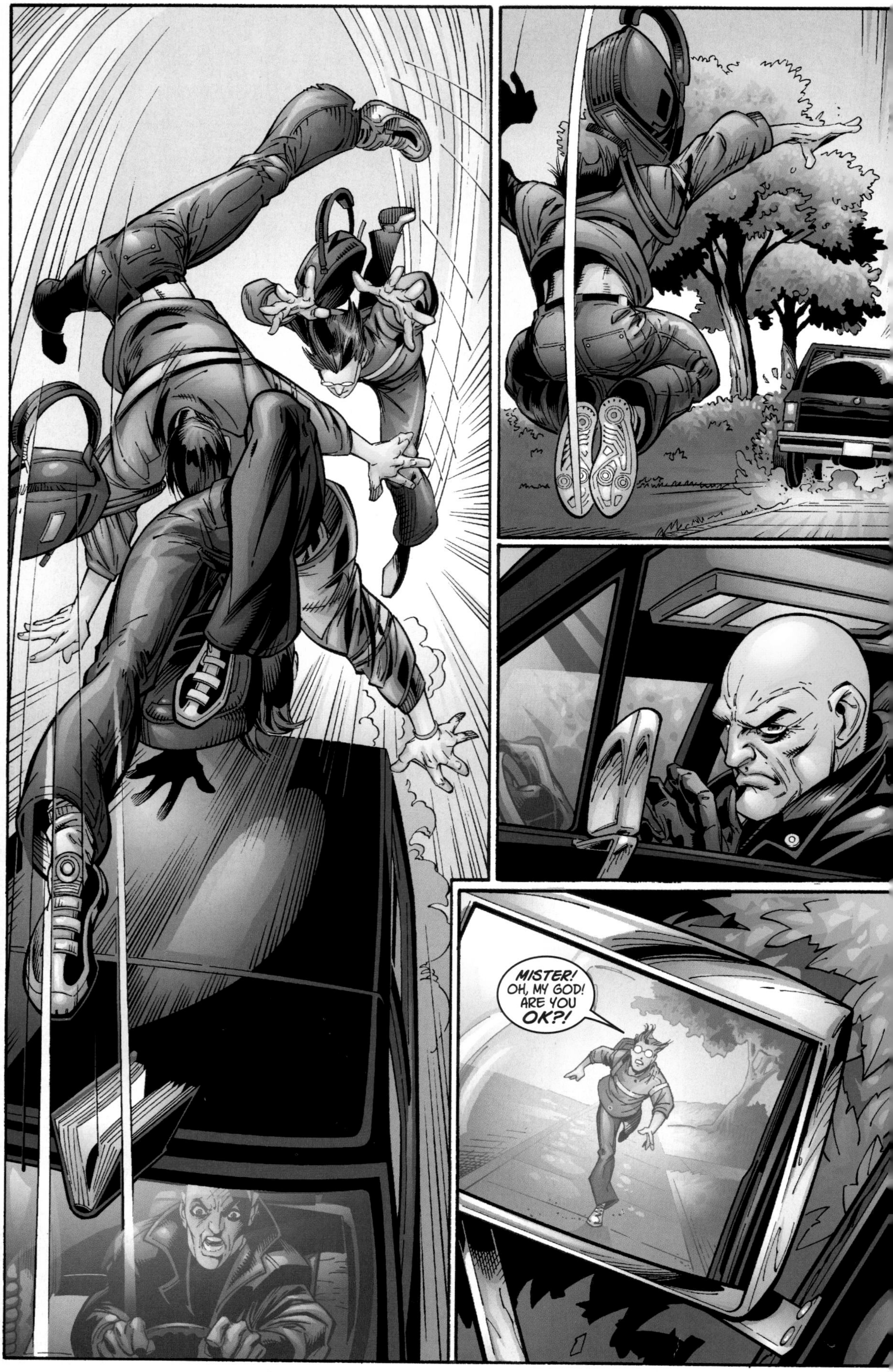
MISTER! OH, MY GOD! ARE YOU OK?!

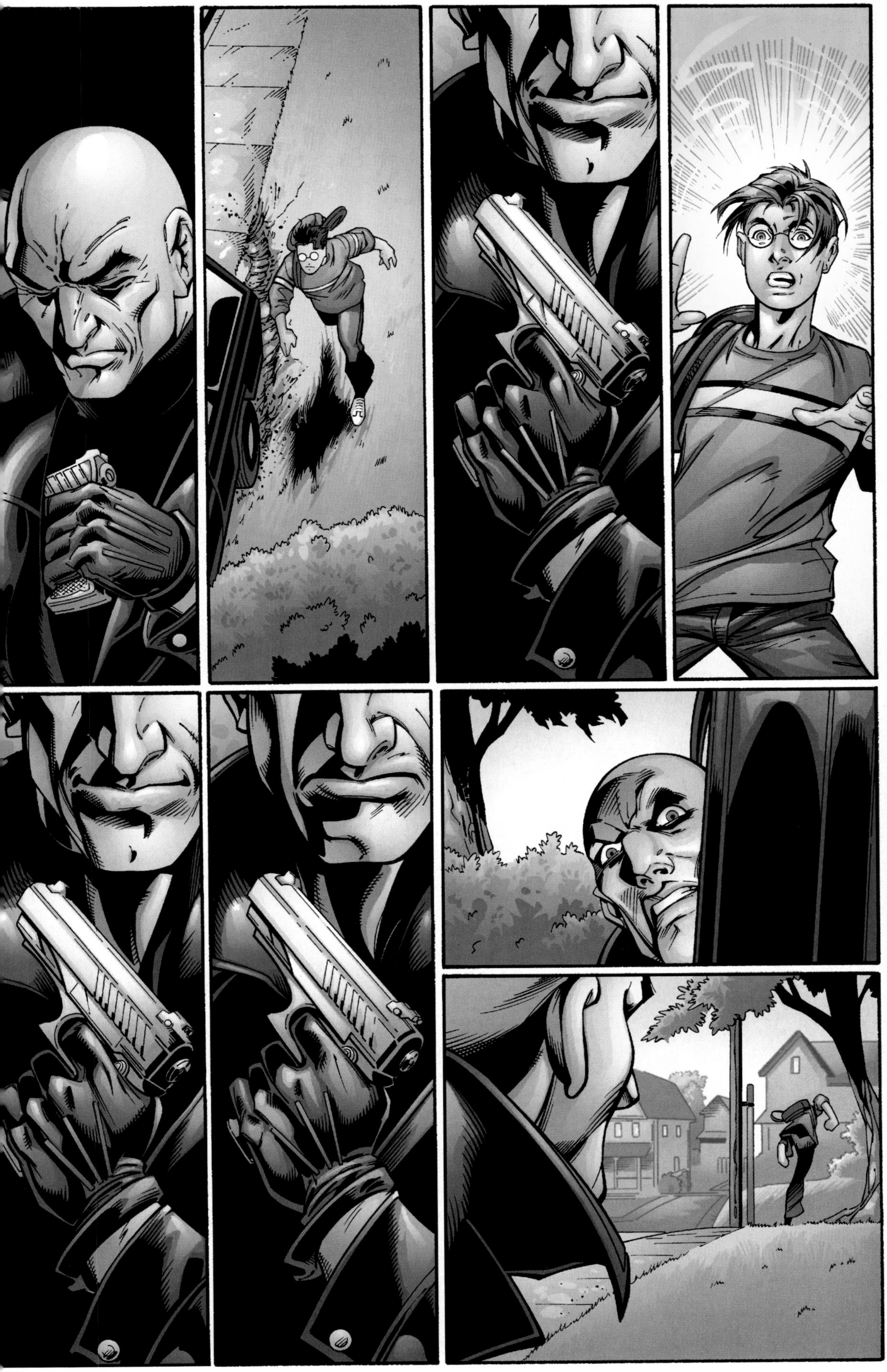

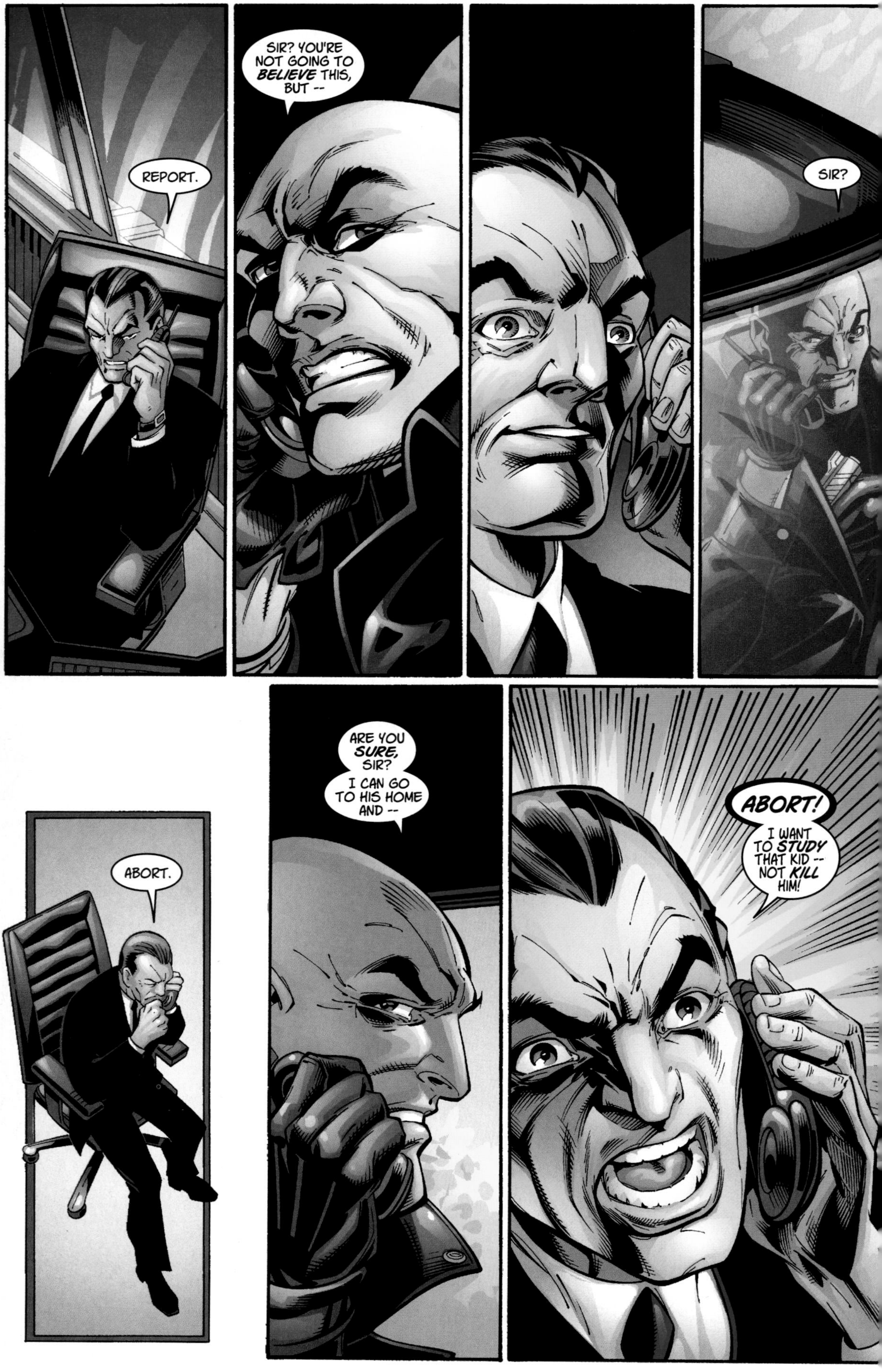
REPORT.
SIR? YOU'RE NOT GOING TO BELIEVE THIS, BUT --
SIR?
ABORT.
ARE YOU SURE, SIR? I CAN GO TO HIS HOME AND --
ABORT!
I WANT TO STUDY THAT KID -- NOT KILL HIM!

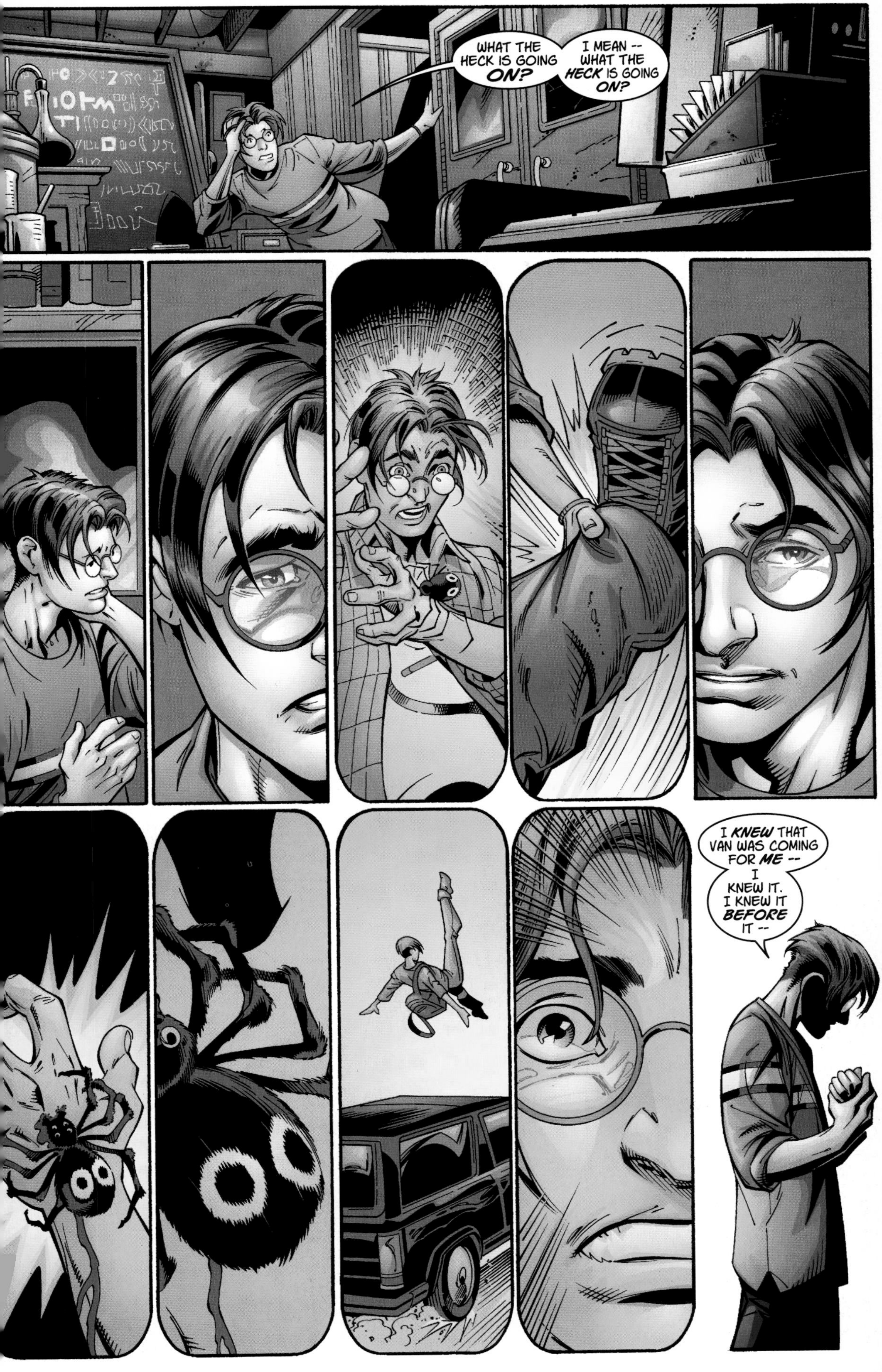
WHAT THE HECK IS GOING ON?
I MEAN -- WHAT THE HECK IS GOING ON?
I KNEW THAT VAN WAS COMING FOR ME --
I KNEW IT. I KNEW IT BEFORE IT --

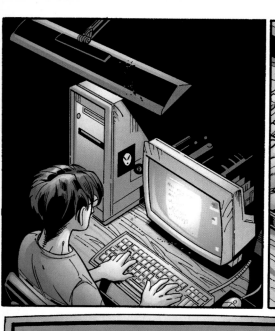

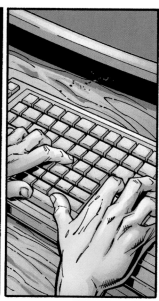

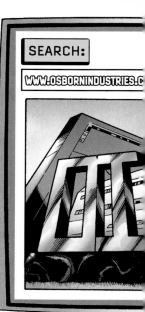

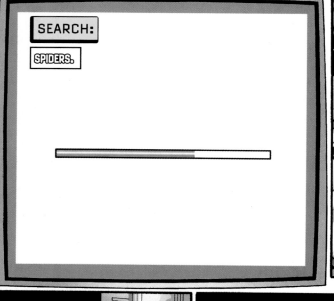

SEARCH:
WWW.OSBORNINDUSTRIES.C
SEARCH:
SPIDERS.
MANY PEOPLE CONFUSE SPIDERS WITH INSECTS. BO BELONG TO THE PHYLUM ARTHROP IN THE ANIMAL KINGDOM --
WELL, WHADDAYA THINK OF THAT.

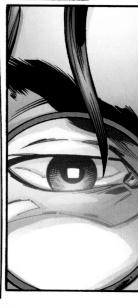

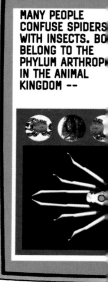

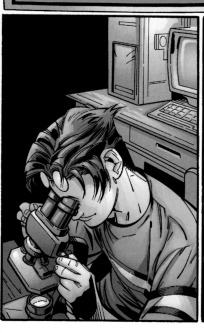

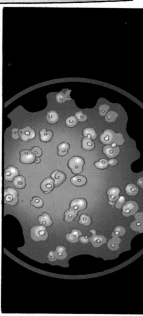

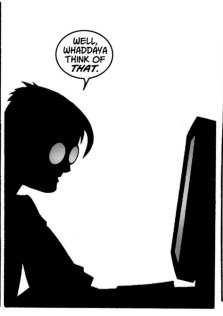

Up Close With
SPIDERS!
Prosoma

A spider's body is divided into two main
parts, the cephalothorax, or prosoma,
and the abdomen, or opisthosoma. Eight
legs attach to the prosoma, which
houses the brain, stomach, fangs and
eyes, usually eight.

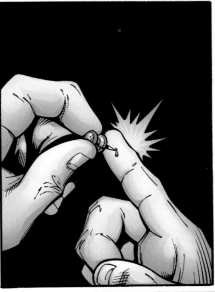

Up Close With
SPIDERS!
Prosoma

A spider's body is divided into two main
parts, the cephalothorax, or prosoma,
and the abdomen, or opisthosoma. Eight
legs attach to the prosoma, which
houses the brain, stomach, fangs and
eyes, usually eight.

-- HAVE A GOOD
DEVELOPED FEELING
MECHANISM THAT
MAKES THEM CAPABLE
OF DETECTING
MOVEMENTS OF --

NO WAY!

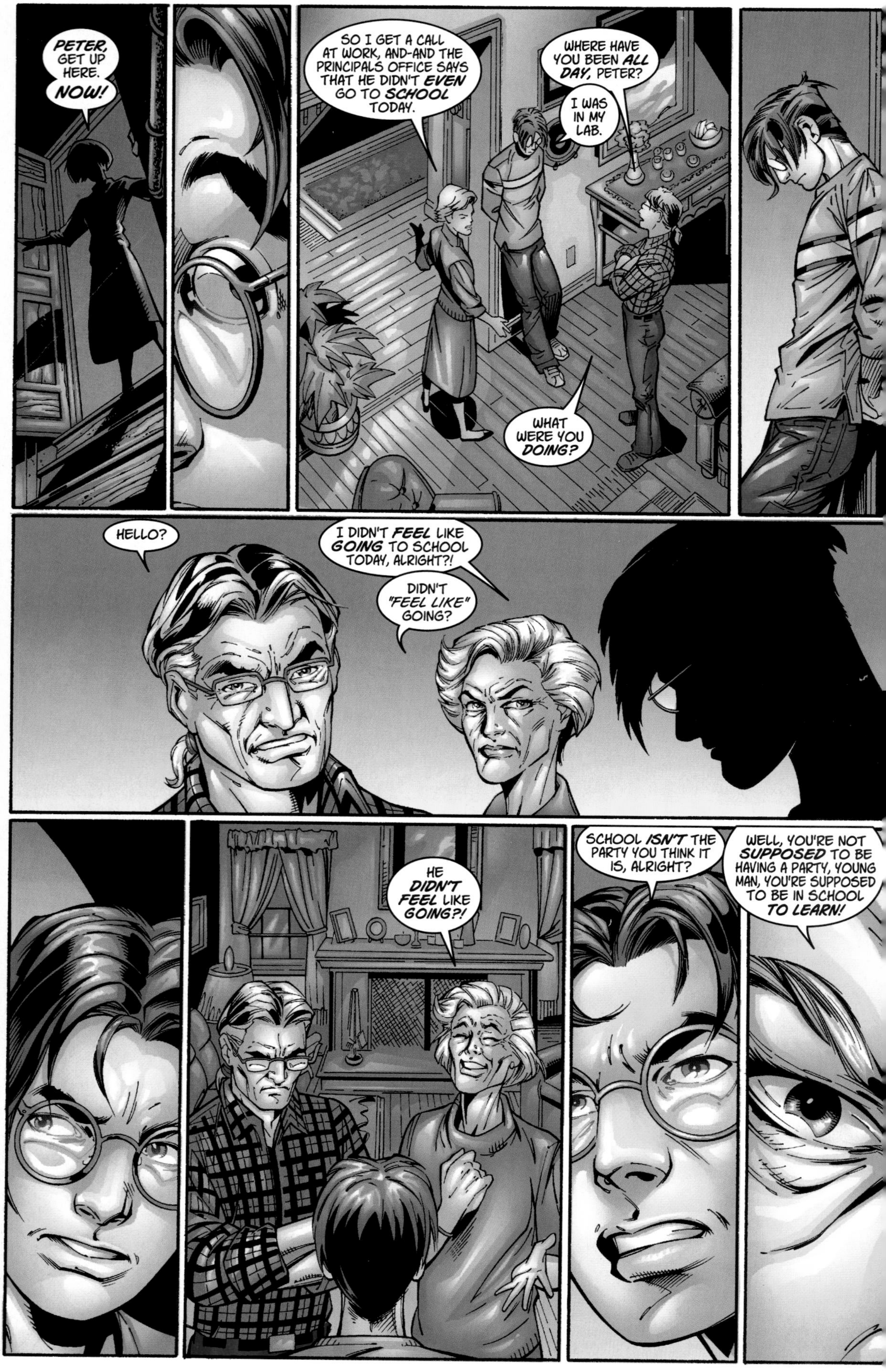
PETER, GET UP HERE. NOW!
SO I GET A CALL AT WORK, AND-AND THE PRINCIPALS OFFICE SAYS THAT HE DIDN'T EVEN GO TO SCHOOL TODAY.
WHERE HAVE YOU BEEN ALL DAY, PETER?
I WAS IN MY LAB.
WHAT WERE YOU DOING?
HELLO?
I DIDN'T FEEL LIKE GOING TO SCHOOL TODAY, ALRIGHT?!
DIDN'T "FEEL LIKE" GOING?
HE DIDN'T FEEL LIKE GOING?!
SCHOOL ISN'T THE PARTY YOU THINK IT IS, ALRIGHT?
WELL, YOU'RE NOT SUPPOSED TO BE HAVING A PARTY, YOUNG MAN, YOU'RE SUPPOSED TO BE IN SCHOOL TO LEARN!

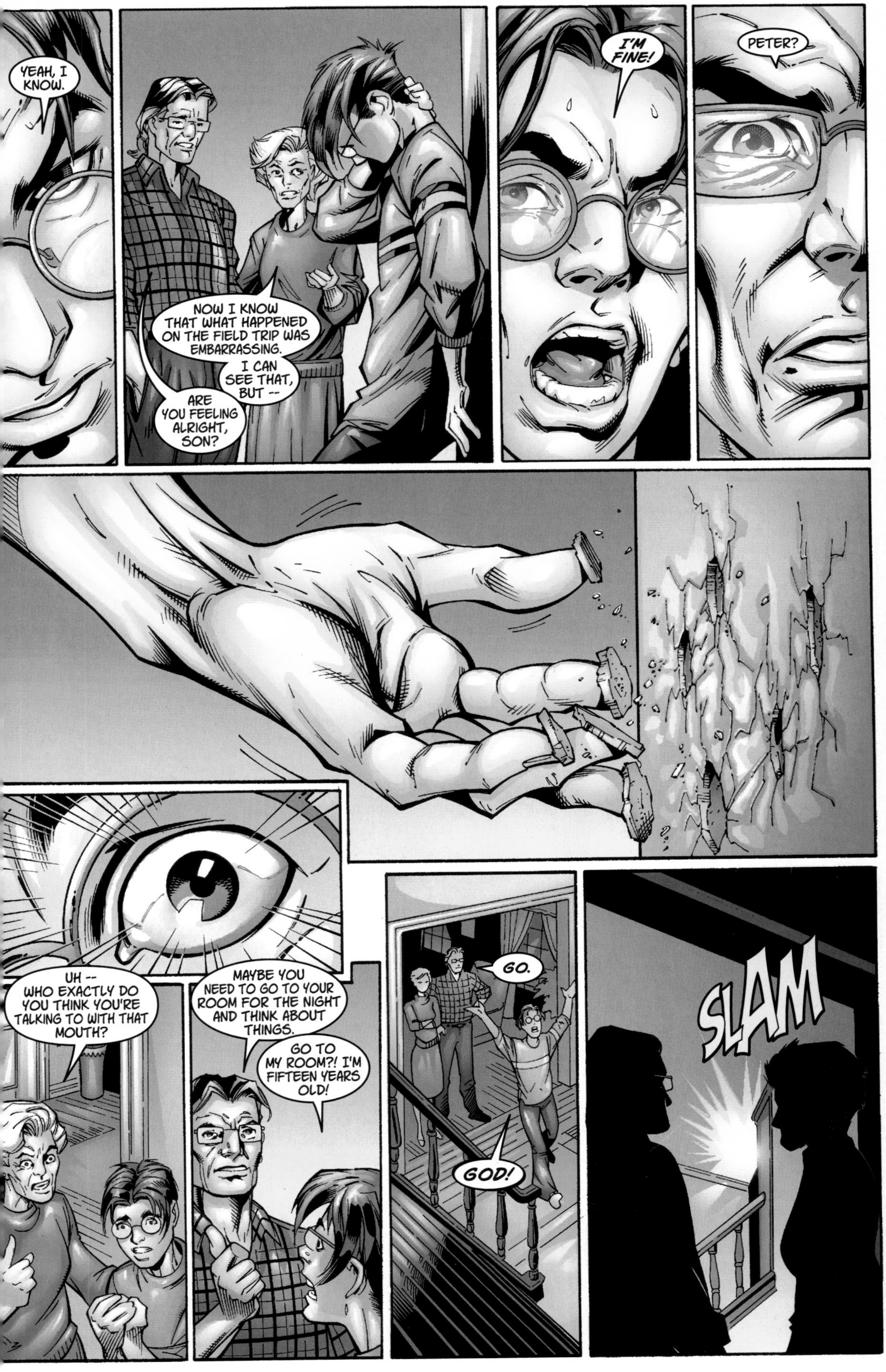

YEAH, I KNOW.
NOW I KNOW THAT WHAT HAPPENED ON THE FIELD TRIP WAS EMBARRASSING.
I CAN SEE THAT, BUT --
ARE YOU FEELING ALRIGHT, SON?
I'M FINE!
PETER?
UH -- WHO EXACTLY DO YOU THINK YOU'RE TALKING TO WITH THAT MOUTH?
MAYBE YOU NEED TO GO TO YOUR ROOM FOR THE NIGHT AND THINK ABOUT THINGS.
GO TO MY ROOM?! I'M FIFTEEN YEARS OLD!
GO.
GOD!
SLAM

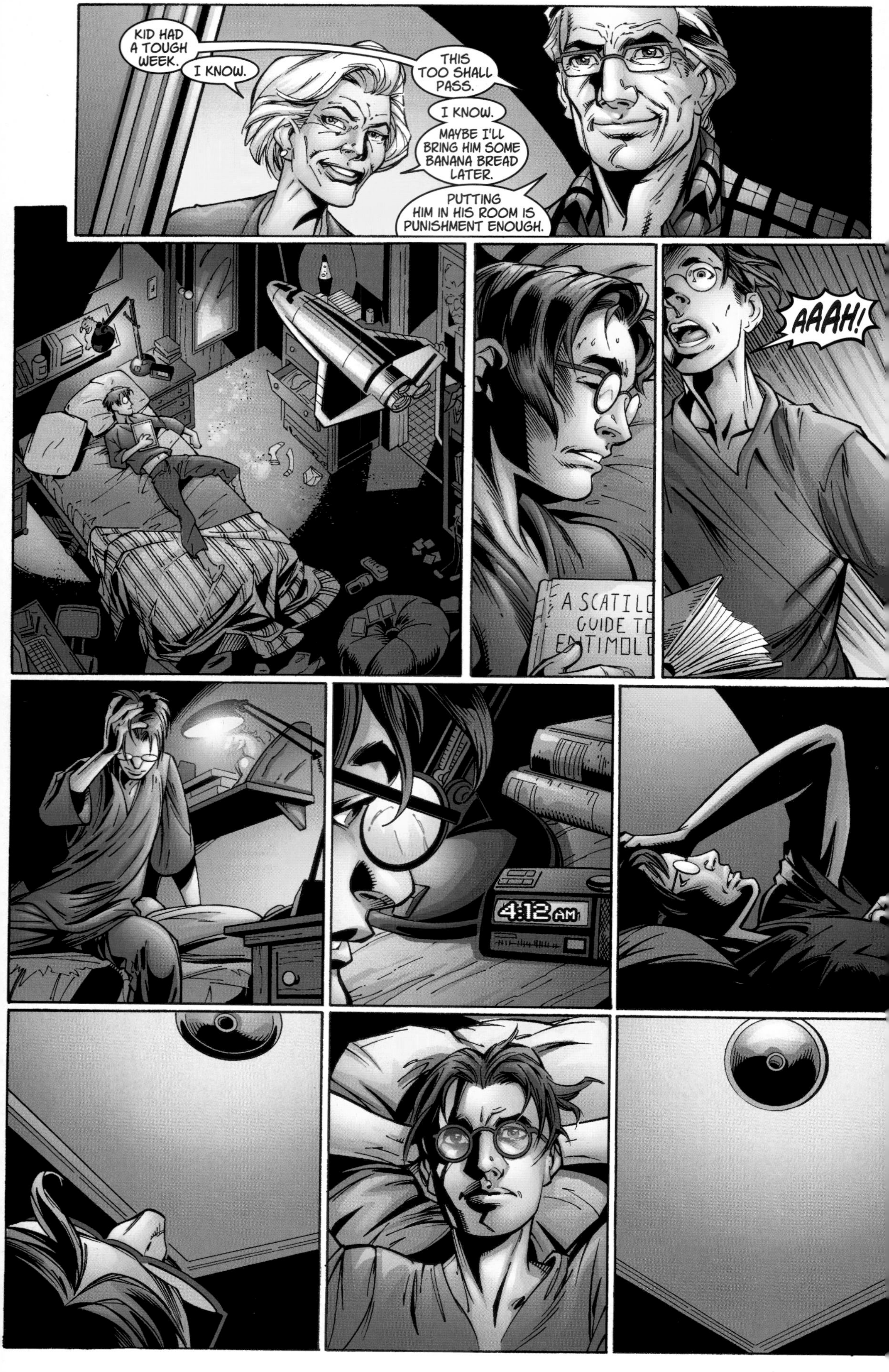
KID HAD A TOUGH WEEK.
I KNOW.
THIS TOO SHALL PASS.
I KNOW.
MAYBE I'LL BRING HIM SOME BANANA BREAD LATER.
PUTTING HIM IN HIS ROOM IS PUNISHMENT ENOUGH.
A SCATILO GUIDE TO ENTIMOLO
AAAH!
4:12 AM

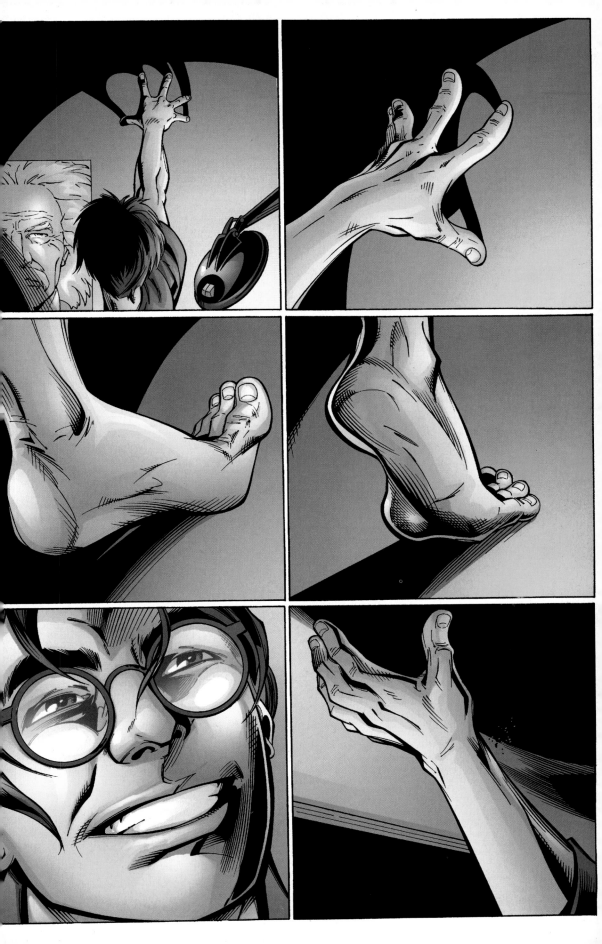

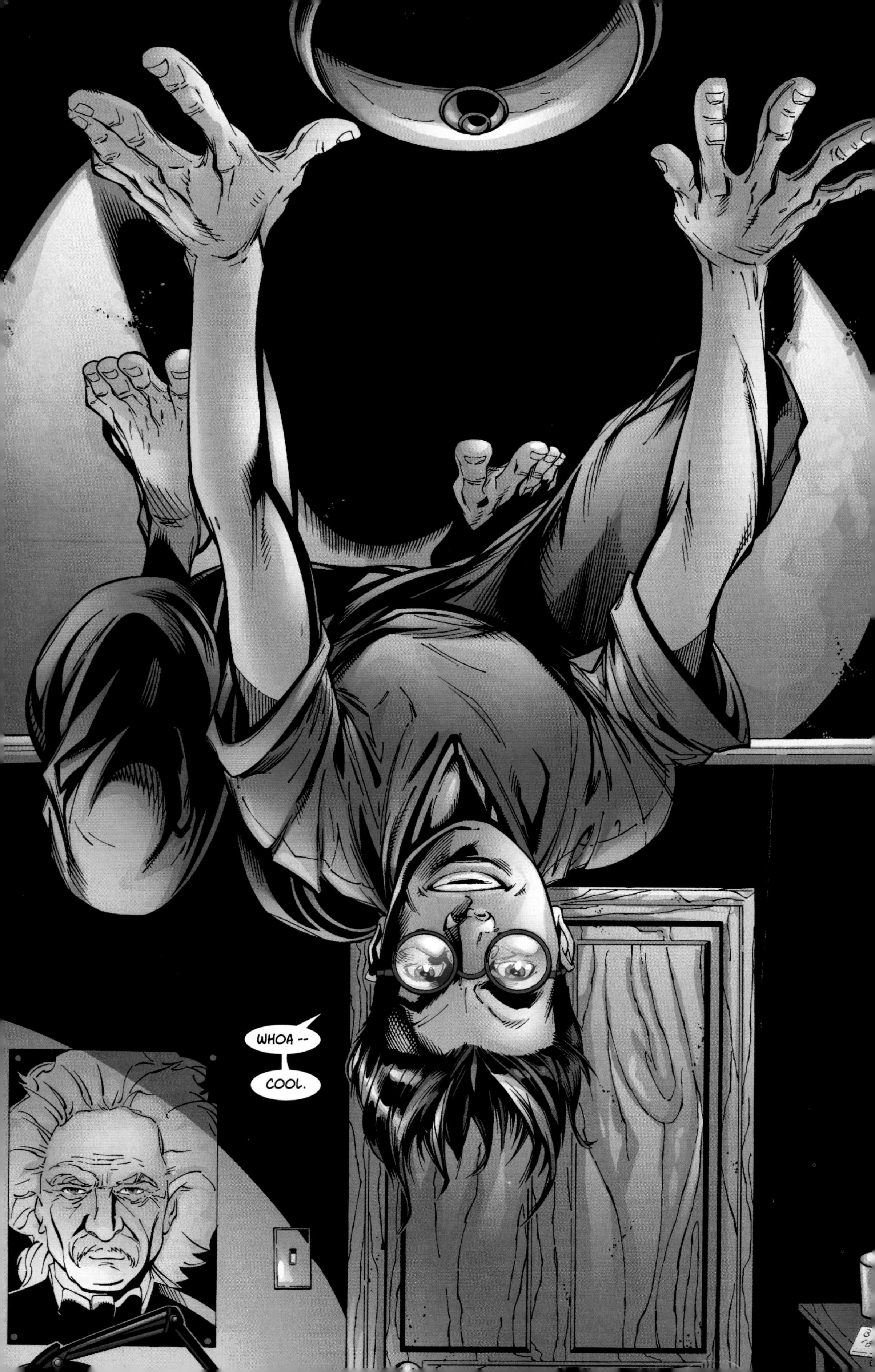
WHOA --
COOL.

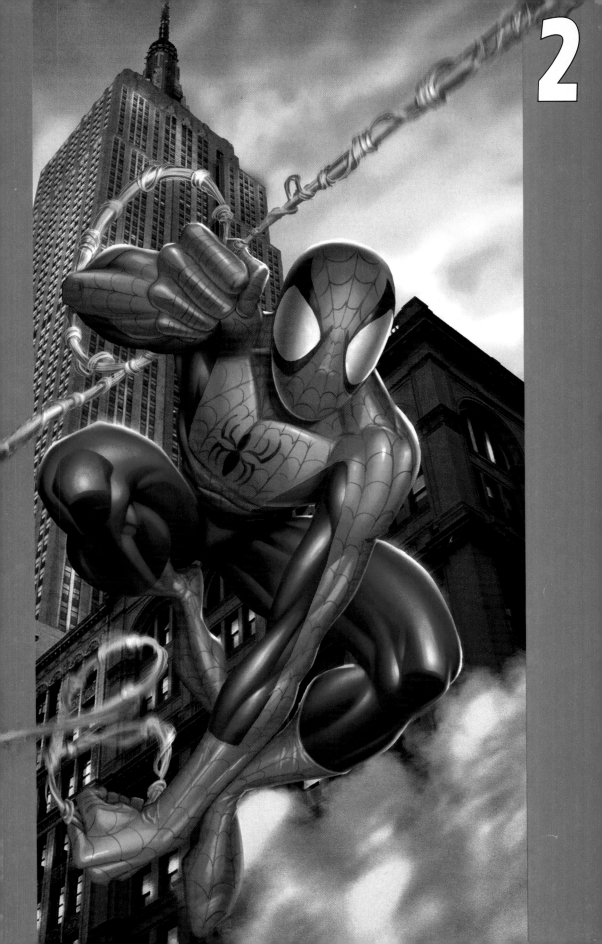

2

IN 1930, THE REPUBLICANS CONTROLLED THE HOUSE OF REPRESENTATIVES IN AN EFFORT TO ELEVATE THE EFFECTS OF THE... ANYONE? ANYONE?

THE GREAT DEPRESSION.

PASSED THE...? ANYONE? ANYONE?

THE TARIFF BILL. THE SMOOT-HAWLEY TARIFF ACT.

ANYONE? RAISED OR LOWERED? RAISED TARIFFS. IN ORDER TO COLLECT MORE REVENUE FOR THE FEDERAL GOVERNMENT.

ANYONE KNOW THE EFFECTS? IT DID NOT WORK AND THE UNITED STATES GOVERNMENT SANK DEEPER INTO THE GREAT DEPRESSION.

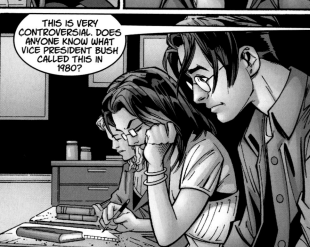

TODAY WE HAVE A SIMILAR DEBATE OVER THIS: ANYONE? ANYONE KNOW WHAT THIS IS?

ANYONE? ANYONE? ANYONE SEEN THIS BEFORE? THE LAFFER ACT. ANYONE KNOW WHAT THIS SAYS?

IT SAYS THAT AT THIS POINT ON THE REVENUE CURVE YOU WILL GET EXACTLY THE SAME AMOUNT OF REVENUE AS THIS POINT.

THIS IS VERY CONTROVERSIAL. DOES ANYONE KNOW WHAT VICE PRESIDENT BUSH CALLED THIS IN 1980?

ANYONE? SOMETHING D-O-O ECONOMICS.

VOODOO ECONOMICS.

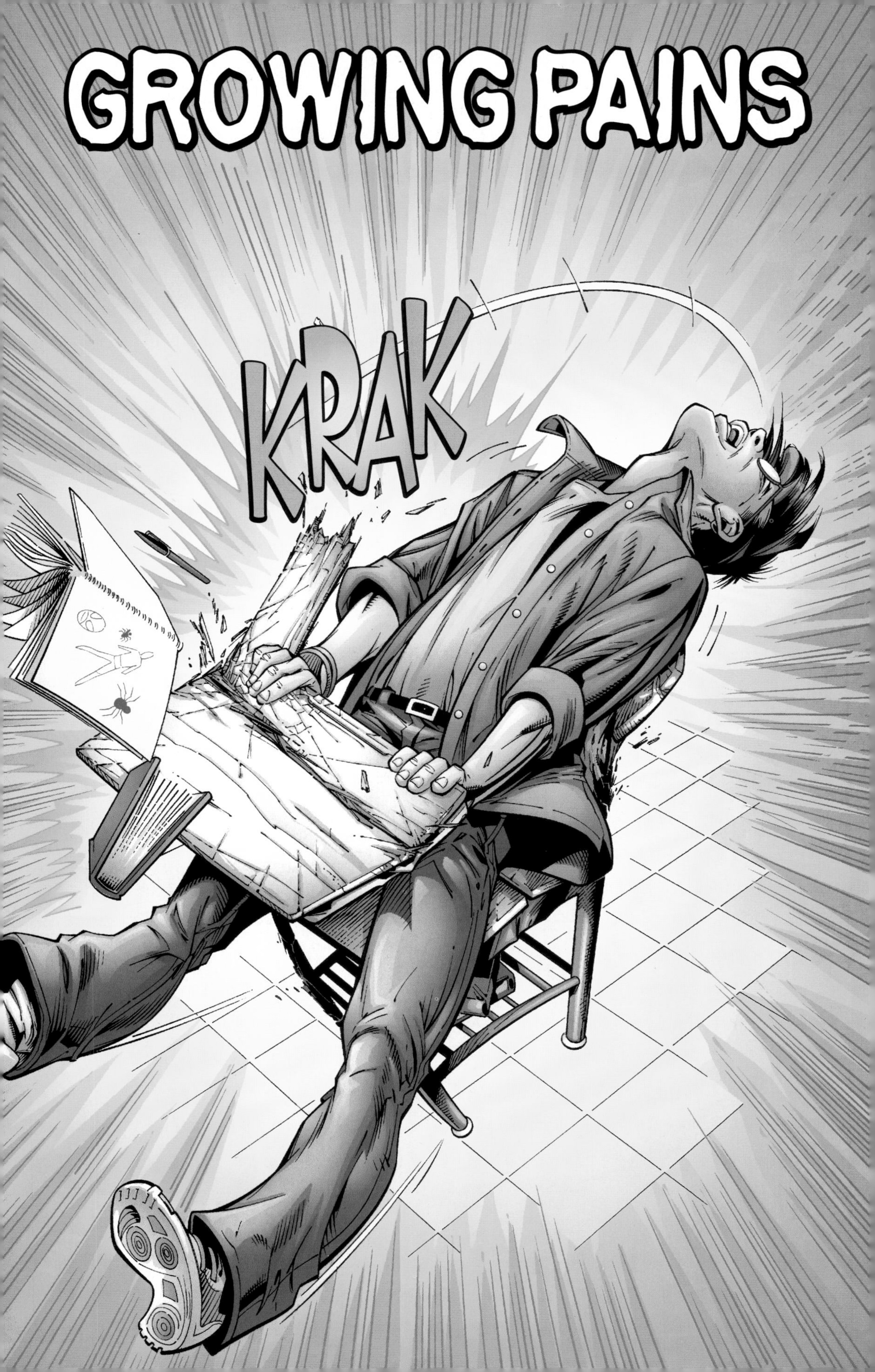
GROWING PAINS
KRAK

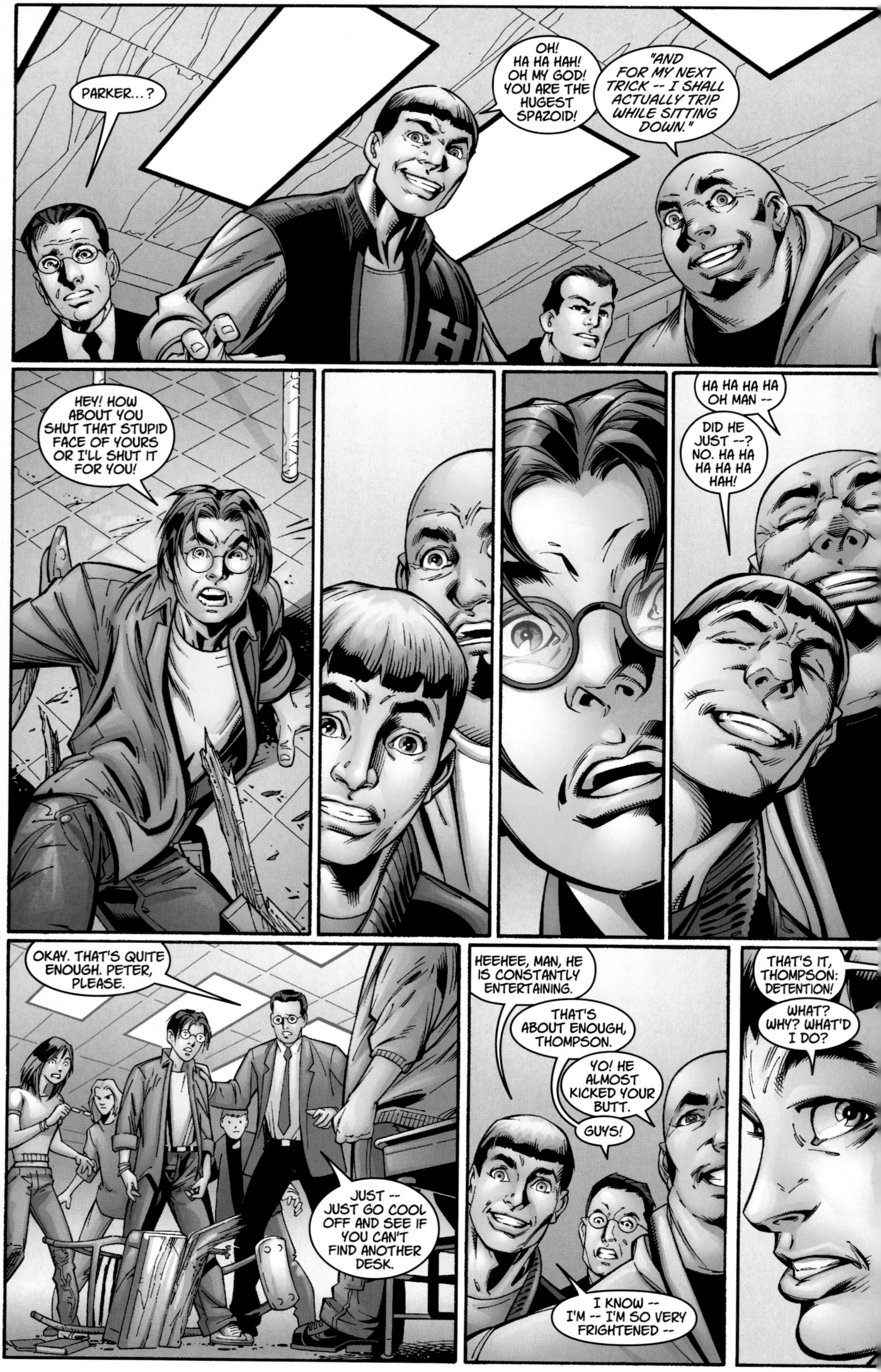
PARKER...?
OH! HA HA HAH! OH MY GOD! YOU ARE THE HUGEST SPAZOID!
"AND FOR MY NEXT TRICK -- I SHALL ACTUALLY TRIP WHILE SITTING DOWN."
HEY! HOW ABOUT YOU SHUT THAT STUPID FACE OF YOURS OR I'LL SHUT IT FOR YOU!
HA HA HA HA OH MAN --
DID HE JUST --? NO. HA HA HA HA HA HAH!
OKAY. THAT'S QUITE ENOUGH. PETER, PLEASE.
JUST -- JUST GO COOL OFF AND SEE IF YOU CAN'T FIND ANOTHER DESK.
HEEHEE, MAN, HE IS CONSTANTLY ENTERTAINING.
THAT'S ABOUT ENOUGH, THOMPSON.
YO! HE ALMOST KICKED YOUR BUTT.
GUYS!
I KNOW -- I'M -- I'M SO VERY FRIGHTENED --
THAT'S IT, THOMPSON: DETENTION!
WHAT? WHY? WHAT'D I DO?

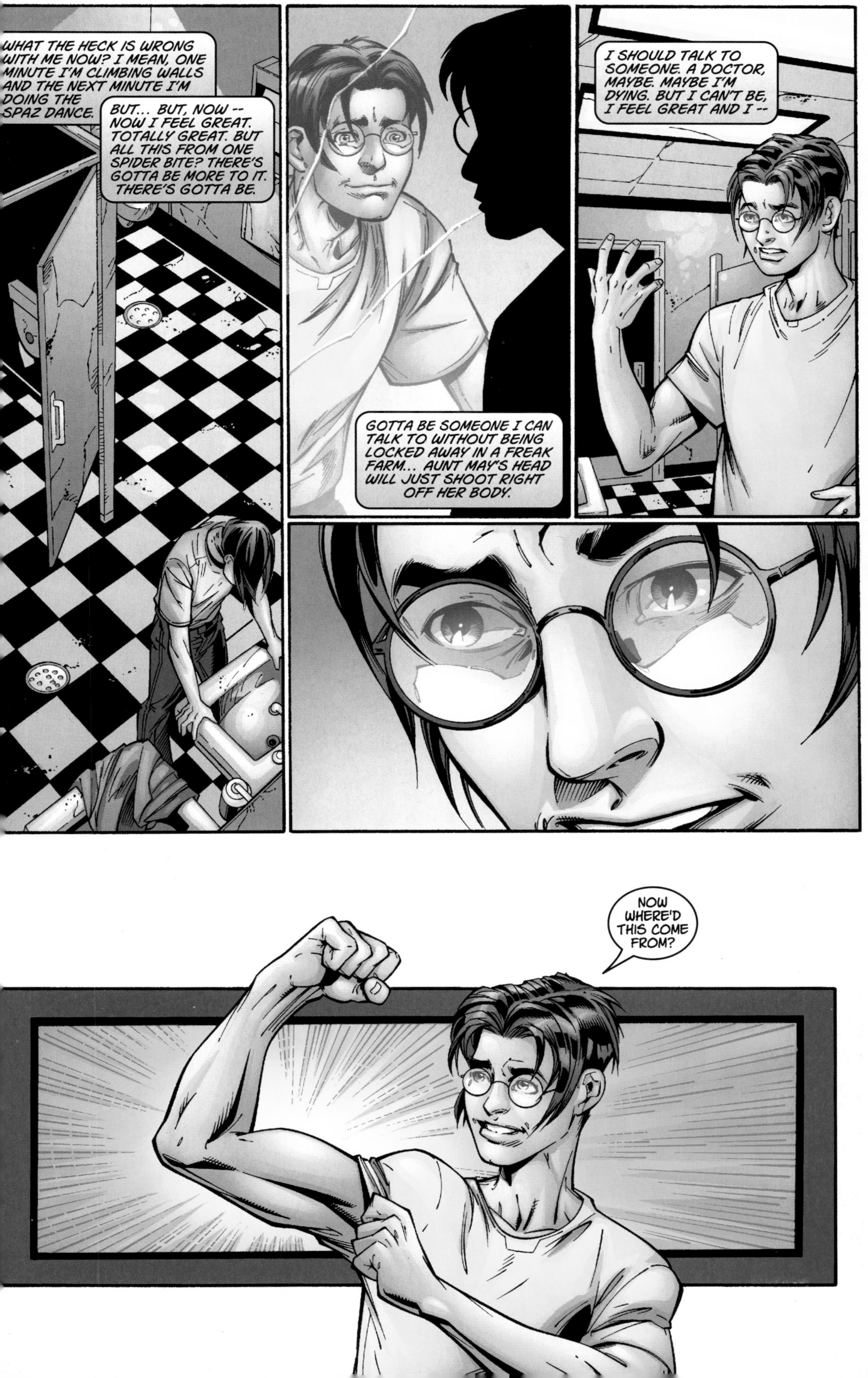
WHAT THE HECK IS WRONG WITH ME NOW? I MEAN, ONE MINUTE I'M CLIMBING WALLS AND THE NEXT MINUTE I'M DOING THE SPAZ DANCE.
BUT... BUT, NOW -- NOW I FEEL GREAT. TOTALLY GREAT. BUT ALL THIS FROM ONE SPIDER BITE? THERE'S GOTTA BE MORE TO IT. THERE'S GOTTA BE.
GOTTA BE SOMEONE I CAN TALK TO WITHOUT BEING LOCKED AWAY IN A FREAK FARM... AUNT MAY'S HEAD WILL JUST SHOOT RIGHT OFF HER BODY.
I SHOULD TALK TO SOMEONE. A DOCTOR, MAYBE. MAYBE I'M DYING. BUT I CAN'T BE, I FEEL GREAT AND I --
NOW WHERE'D THIS COME FROM?

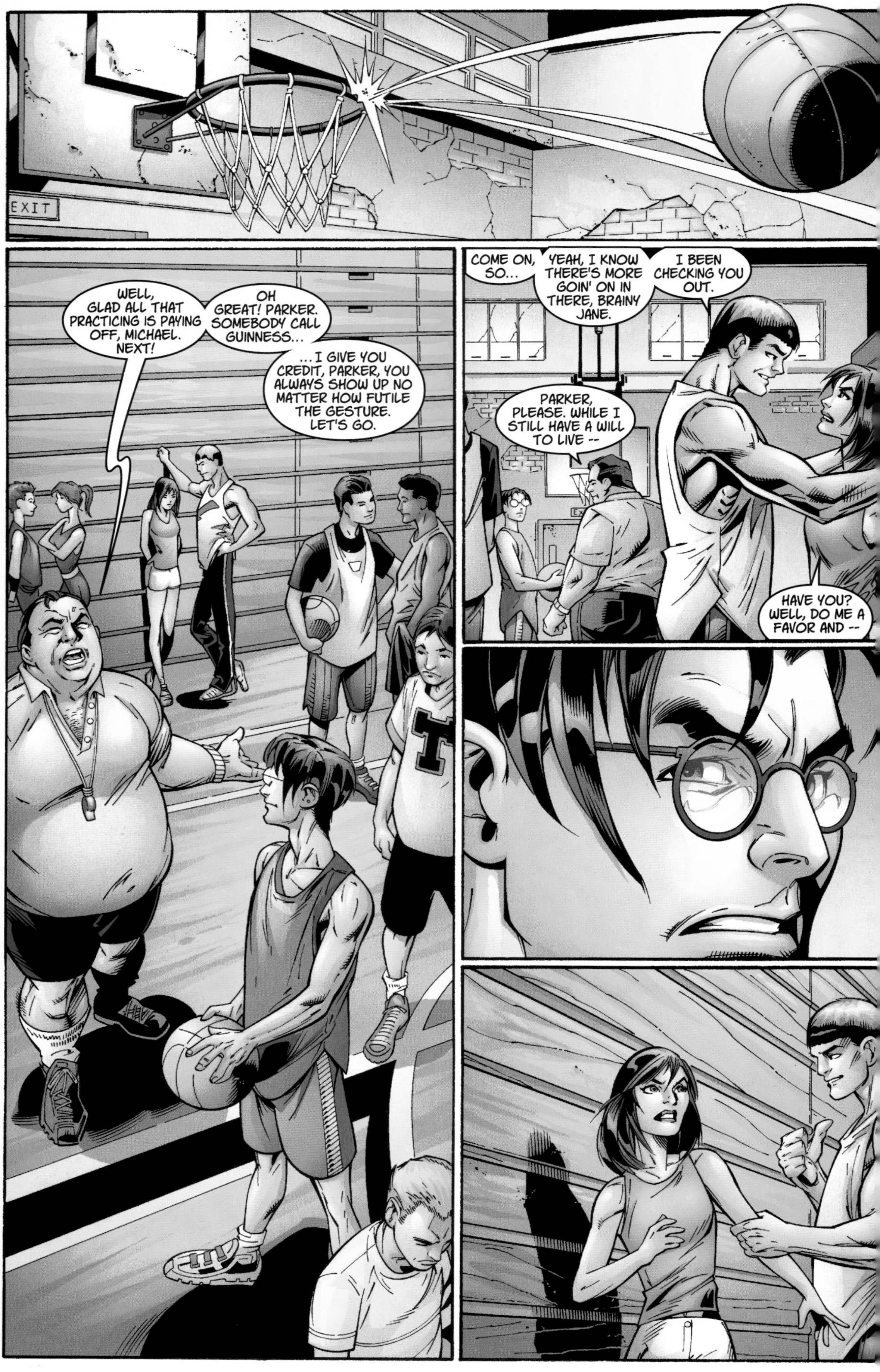

EXIT
WELL, GLAD ALL THAT PRACTICING IS PAYING OFF, MICHAEL. NEXT!
OH GREAT! PARKER. SOMEBODY CALL GUINNESS...
...I GIVE YOU CREDIT, PARKER, YOU ALWAYS SHOW UP NO MATTER HOW FUTILE THE GESTURE. LET'S GO.
COME ON, SO...
YEAH, I KNOW THERE'S MORE GOIN' ON IN THERE, BRAINY JANE.
I BEEN CHECKING YOU OUT.
PARKER, PLEASE. WHILE I STILL HAVE A WILL TO LIVE --
HAVE YOU? WELL, DO ME A FAVOR AND --

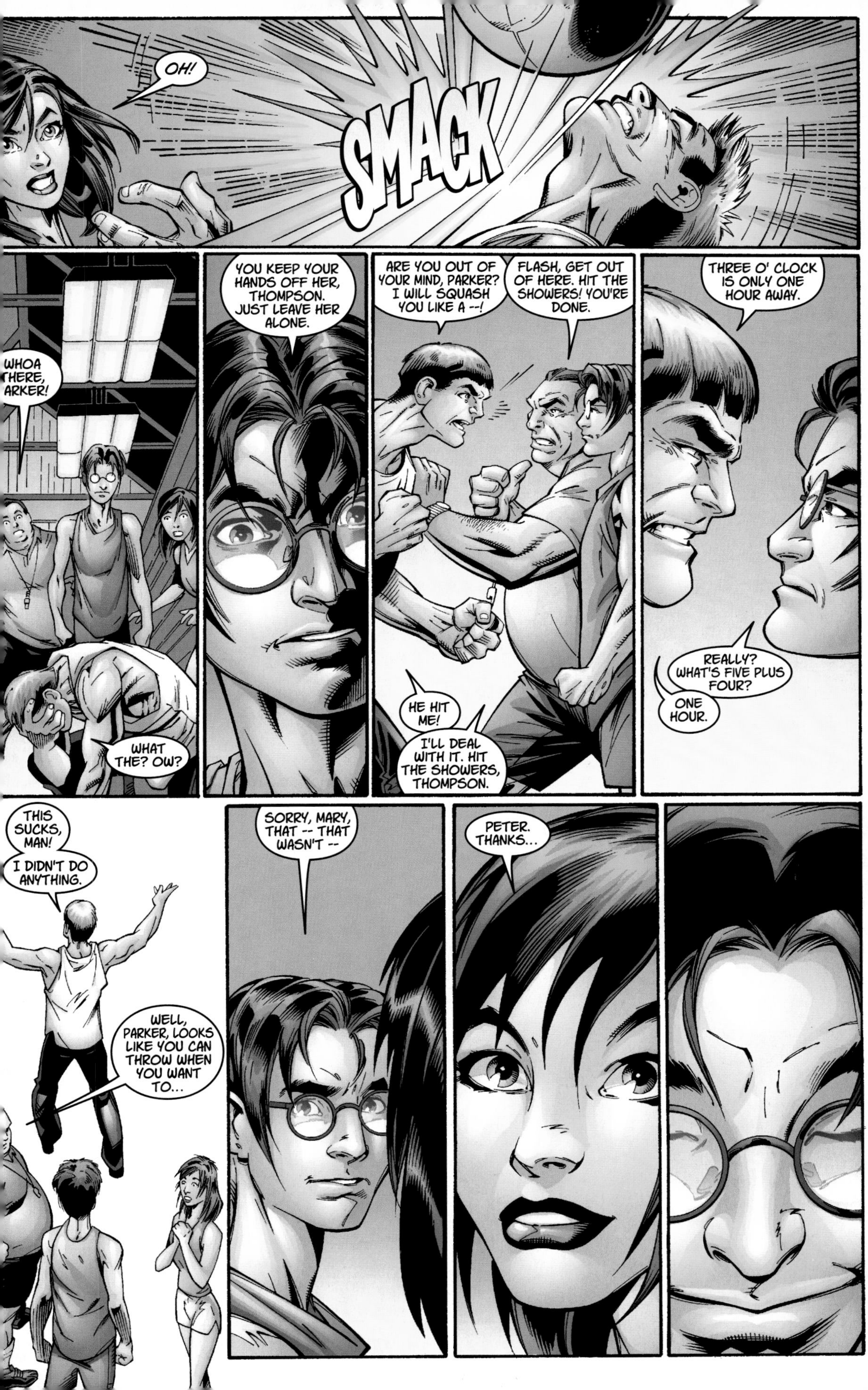
OH!
SMACK
WHOA THERE, ARKER!
WHAT THE? OW?
YOU KEEP YOUR HANDS OFF HER, THOMPSON. JUST LEAVE HER ALONE.
ARE YOU OUT OF YOUR MIND, PARKER? I WILL SQUASH YOU LIKE A --!
FLASH, GET OUT OF HERE. HIT THE SHOWERS! YOU'RE DONE.
HE HIT ME!
I'LL DEAL WITH IT. HIT THE SHOWERS, THOMPSON.
THREE O' CLOCK IS ONLY ONE HOUR AWAY.
REALLY? WHAT'S FIVE PLUS FOUR?
ONE HOUR.
THIS SUCKS, MAN!
I DIDN'T DO ANYTHING.
WELL, PARKER, LOOKS LIKE YOU CAN THROW WHEN YOU WANT TO...
SORRY, MARY, THAT -- THAT WASN'T --
PETER. THANKS...

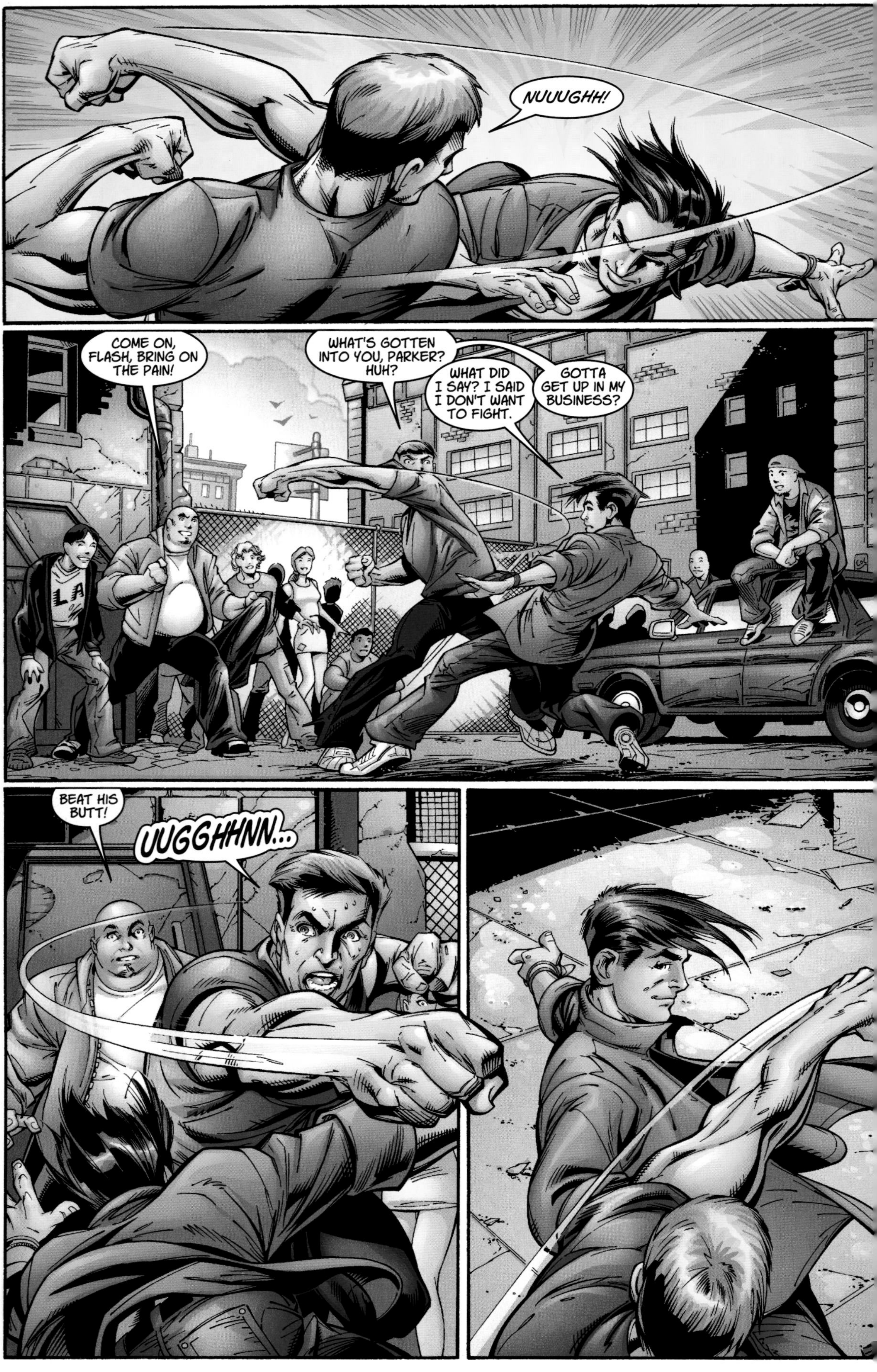
NUUUGHH!
COME ON, FLASH, BRING ON THE PAIN!
WHAT'S GOTTEN INTO YOU, PARKER? HUH?
WHAT DID I SAY? I SAID I DON'T WANT TO FIGHT.
GOTTA GET UP IN MY BUSINESS?
LA
BEAT HIS BUTT!
UUGGHHNN...

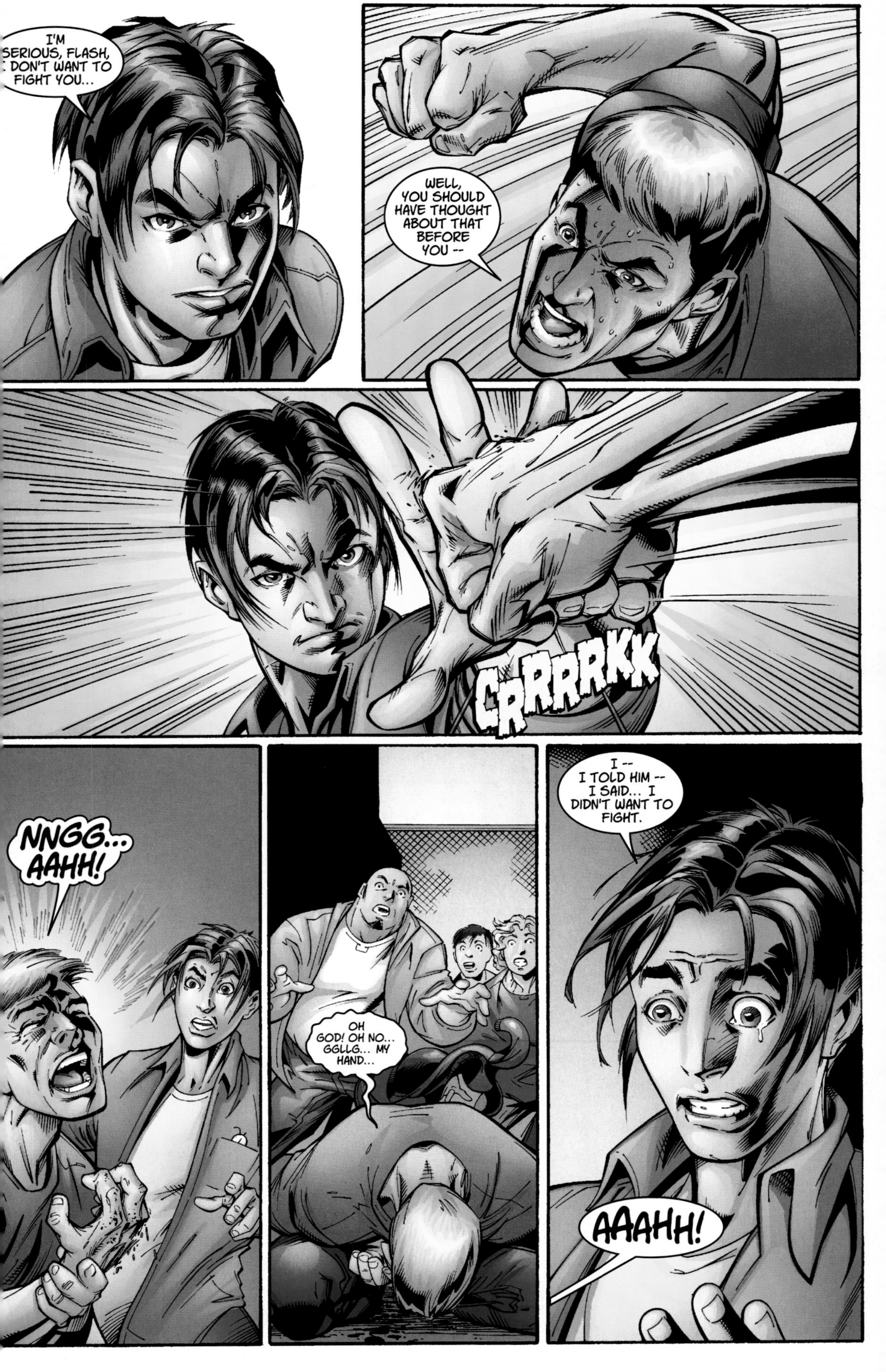
I'M SERIOUS, FLASH, I DON'T WANT TO FIGHT YOU...
WELL, YOU SHOULD HAVE THOUGHT ABOUT THAT BEFORE YOU --
CRRRRKK
NNGG... AAHH!
OH GOD! OH NO... GGLLG... MY HAND...
I -- I TOLD HIM -- I SAID... I DIDN'T WANT TO FIGHT.
AAAHH!

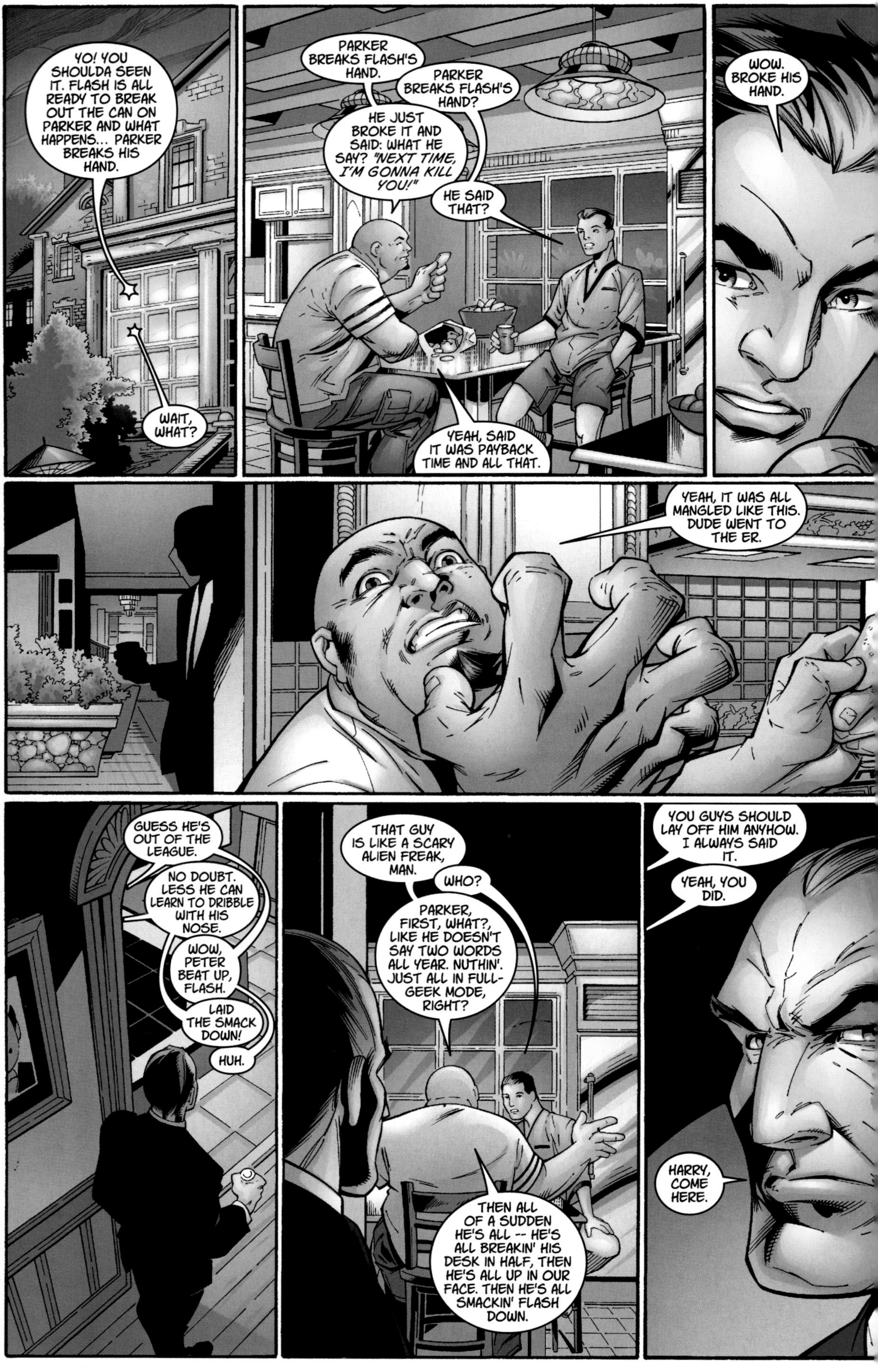
YO! YOU SHOULDA SEEN IT. FLASH IS ALL READY TO BREAK OUT THE CAN ON PARKER AND WHAT HAPPENS... PARKER BREAKS HIS HAND.
WAIT, WHAT?
PARKER BREAKS FLASH'S HAND.
PARKER BREAKS FLASH'S HAND?
HE JUST BROKE IT AND SAID: WHAT HE SAY? "NEXT TIME, I'M GONNA KILL YOU!"
HE SAID THAT?
YEAH, SAID IT WAS PAYBACK TIME AND ALL THAT.
WOW. BROKE HIS HAND.
YEAH, IT WAS ALL MANGLED LIKE THIS. DUDE WENT TO THE ER.
GUESS HE'S OUT OF THE LEAGUE.
NO DOUBT. LESS HE CAN LEARN TO DRIBBLE WITH HIS NOSE.
WOW, PETER BEAT UP, FLASH.
LAID THE SMACK DOWN!
HUH.
THAT GUY IS LIKE A SCARY ALIEN FREAK, MAN.
WHO?
PARKER, FIRST, WHAT?, LIKE HE DOESN'T SAY TWO WORDS ALL YEAR. NUTHIN'. JUST ALL IN FULL-GEEK MODE, RIGHT?
THEN ALL OF A SUDDEN HE'S ALL -- HE'S ALL BREAKIN' HIS DESK IN HALF, THEN HE'S ALL UP IN OUR FACE. THEN HE'S ALL SMACKIN' FLASH DOWN.
YOU GUYS SHOULD LAY OFF HIM ANYHOW. I ALWAYS SAID IT.
YEAH, YOU DID.
HARRY, COME HERE.

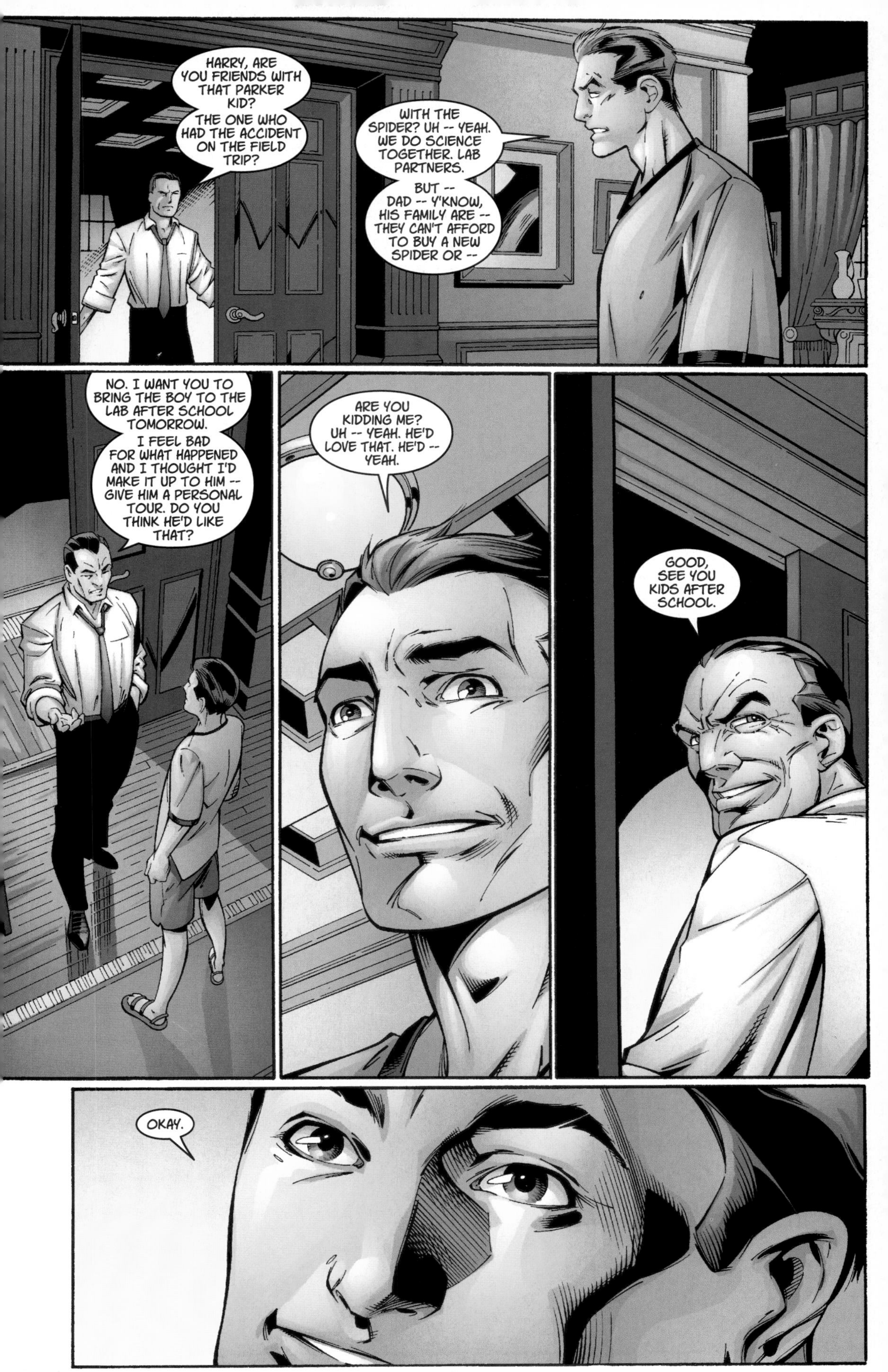
HARRY, ARE YOU FRIENDS WITH THAT PARKER KID?
THE ONE WHO HAD THE ACCIDENT ON THE FIELD TRIP?
WITH THE SPIDER? UH -- YEAH. WE DO SCIENCE TOGETHER. LAB PARTNERS.
BUT -- DAD -- Y'KNOW, HIS FAMILY ARE -- THEY CAN'T AFFORD TO BUY A NEW SPIDER OR --
NO. I WANT YOU TO BRING THE BOY TO THE LAB AFTER SCHOOL TOMORROW.
I FEEL BAD FOR WHAT HAPPENED AND I THOUGHT I'D MAKE IT UP TO HIM -- GIVE HIM A PERSONAL TOUR. DO YOU THINK HE'D LIKE THAT?
ARE YOU KIDDING ME? UH -- YEAH. HE'D LOVE THAT. HE'D -- YEAH.
GOOD, SEE YOU KIDS AFTER SCHOOL.
OKAY.

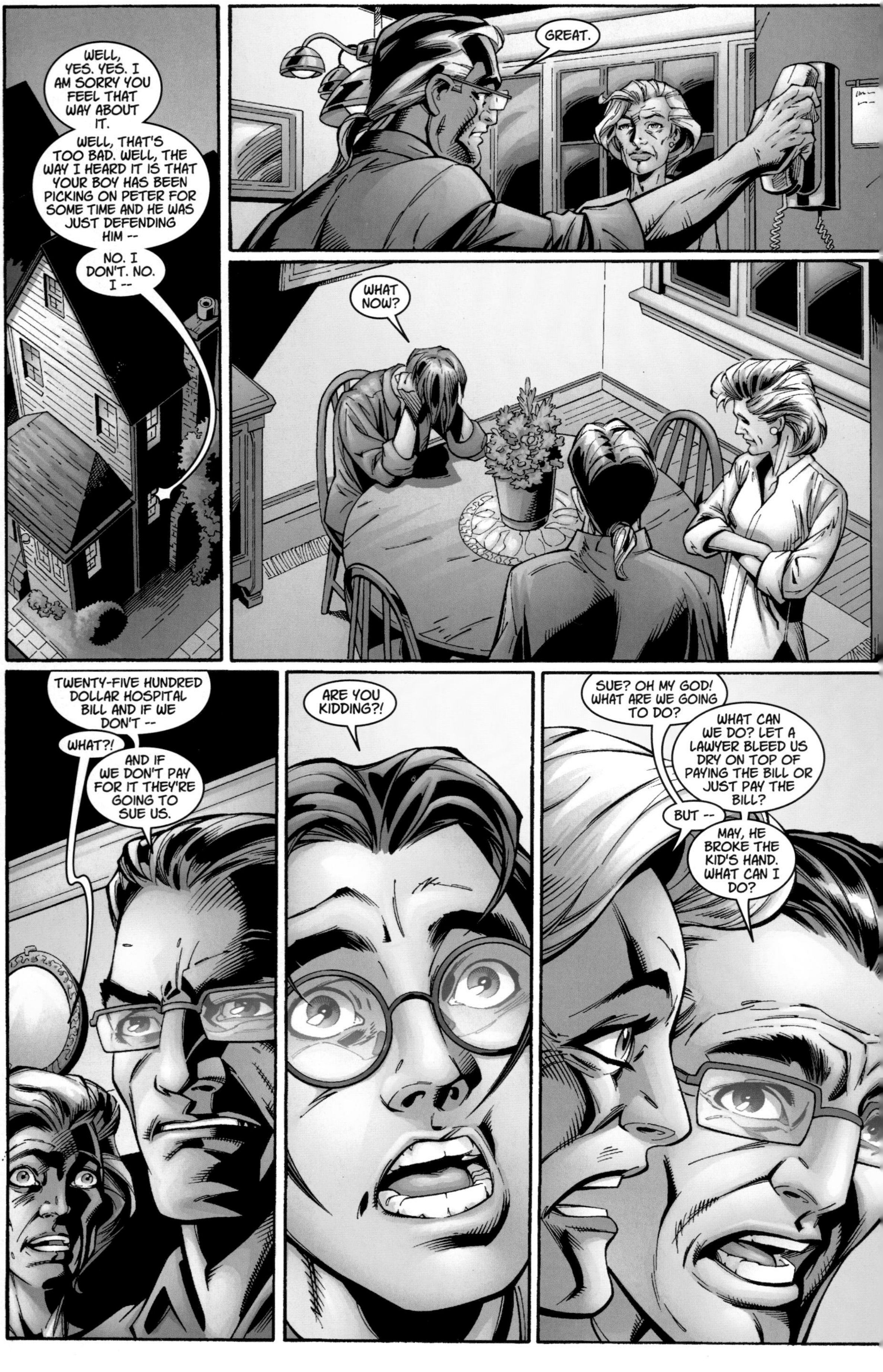
WELL, YES. YES. I AM SORRY YOU FEEL THAT WAY ABOUT IT.
WELL, THAT'S TOO BAD. WELL, THE WAY I HEARD IT IS THAT YOUR BOY HAS BEEN PICKING ON PETER FOR SOME TIME AND HE WAS JUST DEFENDING HIM --
NO. I DON'T. NO. I --
GREAT.
WHAT NOW?
TWENTY-FIVE HUNDRED DOLLAR HOSPITAL BILL AND IF WE DON'T --
WHAT?!
AND IF WE DON'T PAY FOR IT THEY'RE GOING TO SUE US.
ARE YOU KIDDING?!
SUE? OH MY GOD! WHAT ARE WE GOING TO DO?
WHAT CAN WE DO? LET A LAWYER BLEED US DRY ON TOP OF PAYING THE BILL OR JUST PAY THE BILL?
BUT --
MAY, HE BROKE THE KID'S HAND. WHAT CAN I DO?

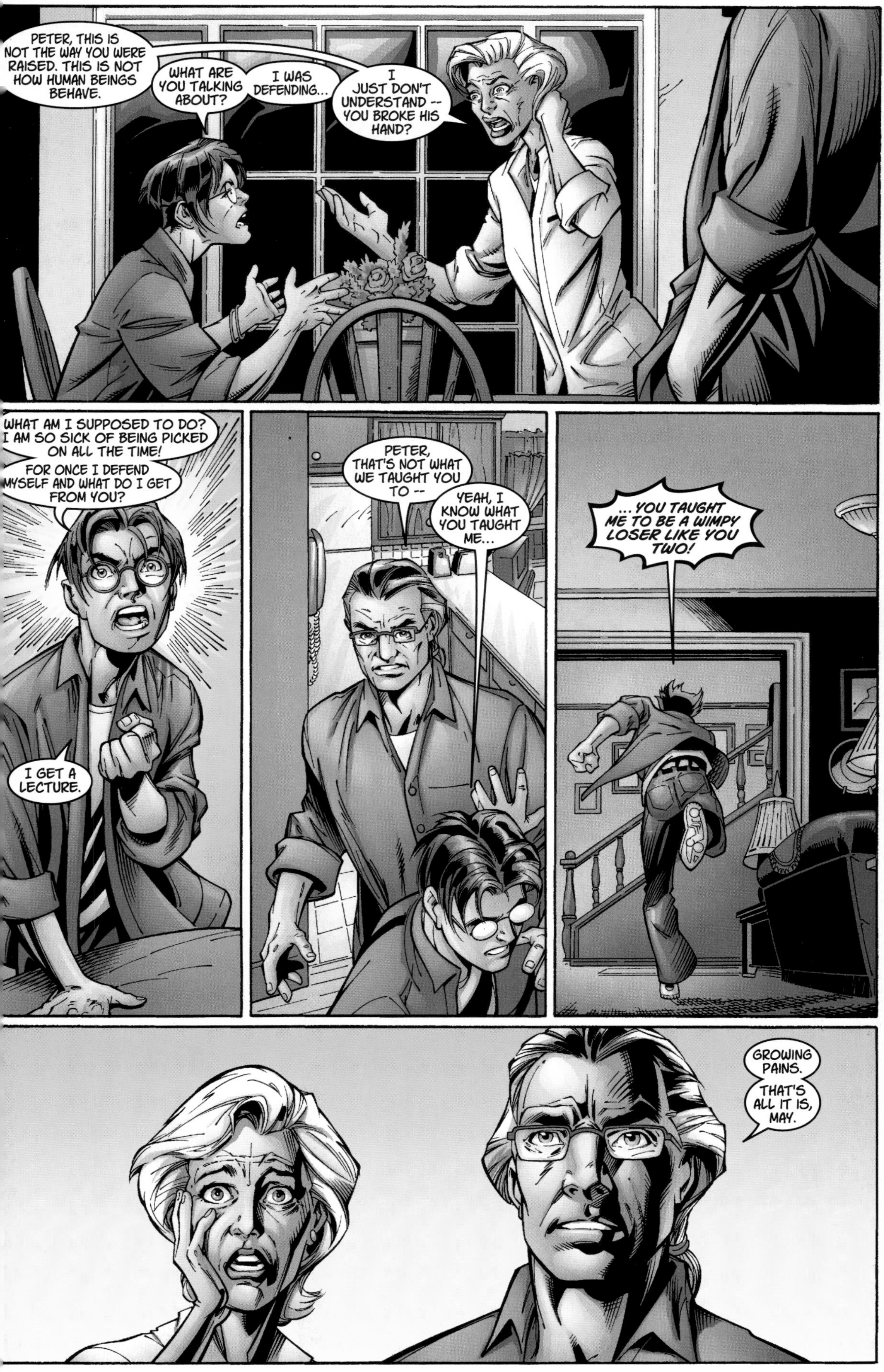

PETER, THIS IS NOT THE WAY YOU WERE RAISED. THIS IS NOT HOW HUMAN BEINGS BEHAVE.
WHAT ARE YOU TALKING ABOUT?
I WAS DEFENDING...
I JUST DON'T UNDERSTAND -- YOU BROKE HIS HAND?
WHAT AM I SUPPOSED TO DO? I AM SO SICK OF BEING PICKED ON ALL THE TIME!
FOR ONCE I DEFEND MYSELF AND WHAT DO I GET FROM YOU?
I GET A LECTURE.
PETER, THAT'S NOT WHAT WE TAUGHT YOU TO --
YEAH, I KNOW WHAT YOU TAUGHT ME...
...YOU TAUGHT ME TO BE A WIMPY LOSER LIKE YOU TWO!
GROWING PAINS.
THAT'S ALL IT IS, MAY.

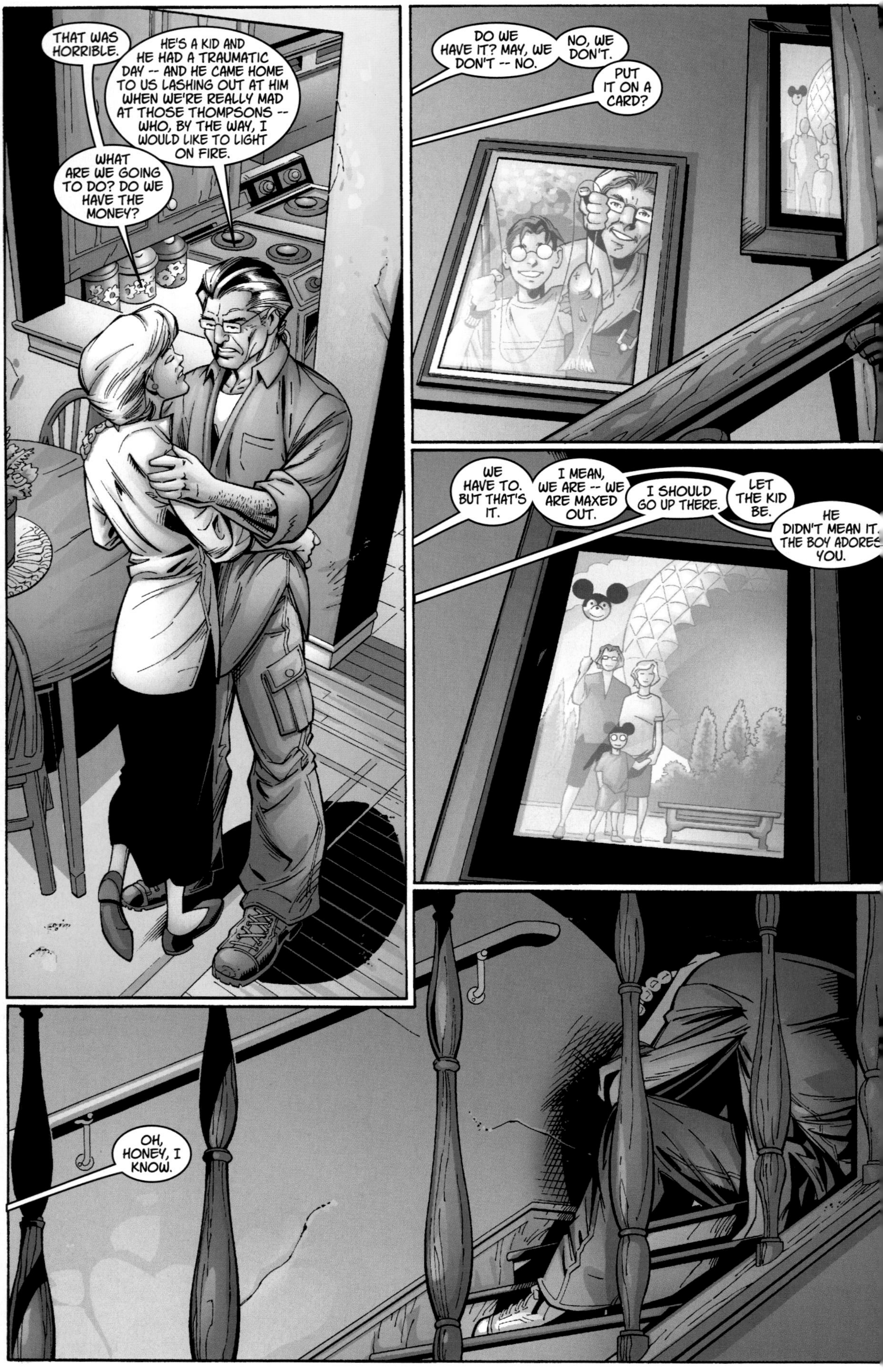
THAT WAS HORRIBLE.
HE'S A KID AND HE HAD A TRAUMATIC DAY -- AND HE CAME HOME TO US LASHING OUT AT HIM WHEN WE'RE REALLY MAD AT THOSE THOMPSONS -- WHO, BY THE WAY, I WOULD LIKE TO LIGHT ON FIRE.
WHAT ARE WE GOING TO DO? DO WE HAVE THE MONEY?
DO WE HAVE IT? MAY, WE DON'T -- NO.
NO, WE DON'T.
PUT IT ON A CARD?
WE HAVE TO. BUT THAT'S IT.
I MEAN, WE ARE -- WE ARE MAXED OUT.
I SHOULD GO UP THERE.
LET THE KID BE.
HE DIDN'T MEAN IT. THE BOY ADORES YOU.
OH, HONEY, I KNOW.

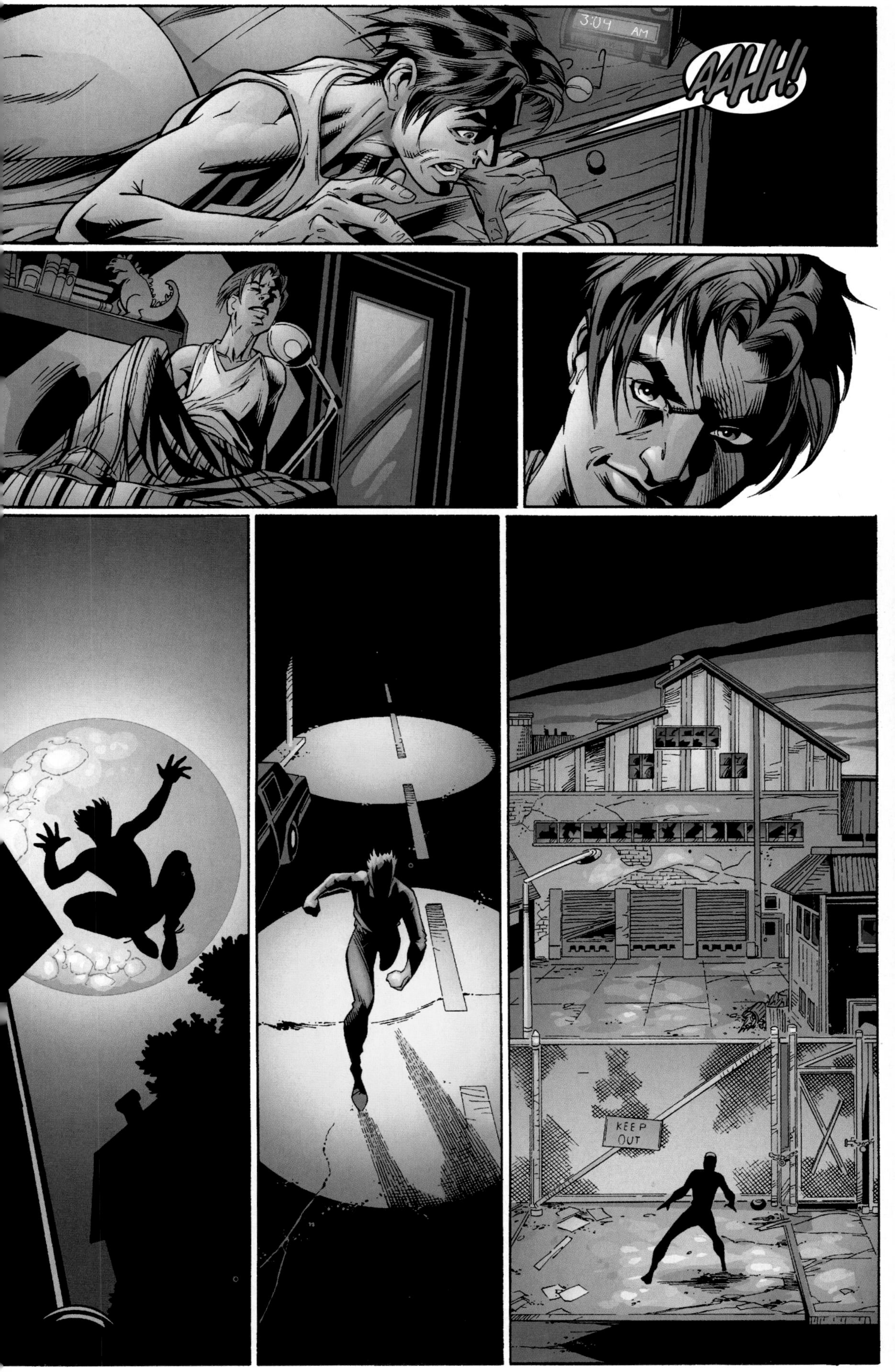
3:04 AM
AAHH!
KEEP OUT

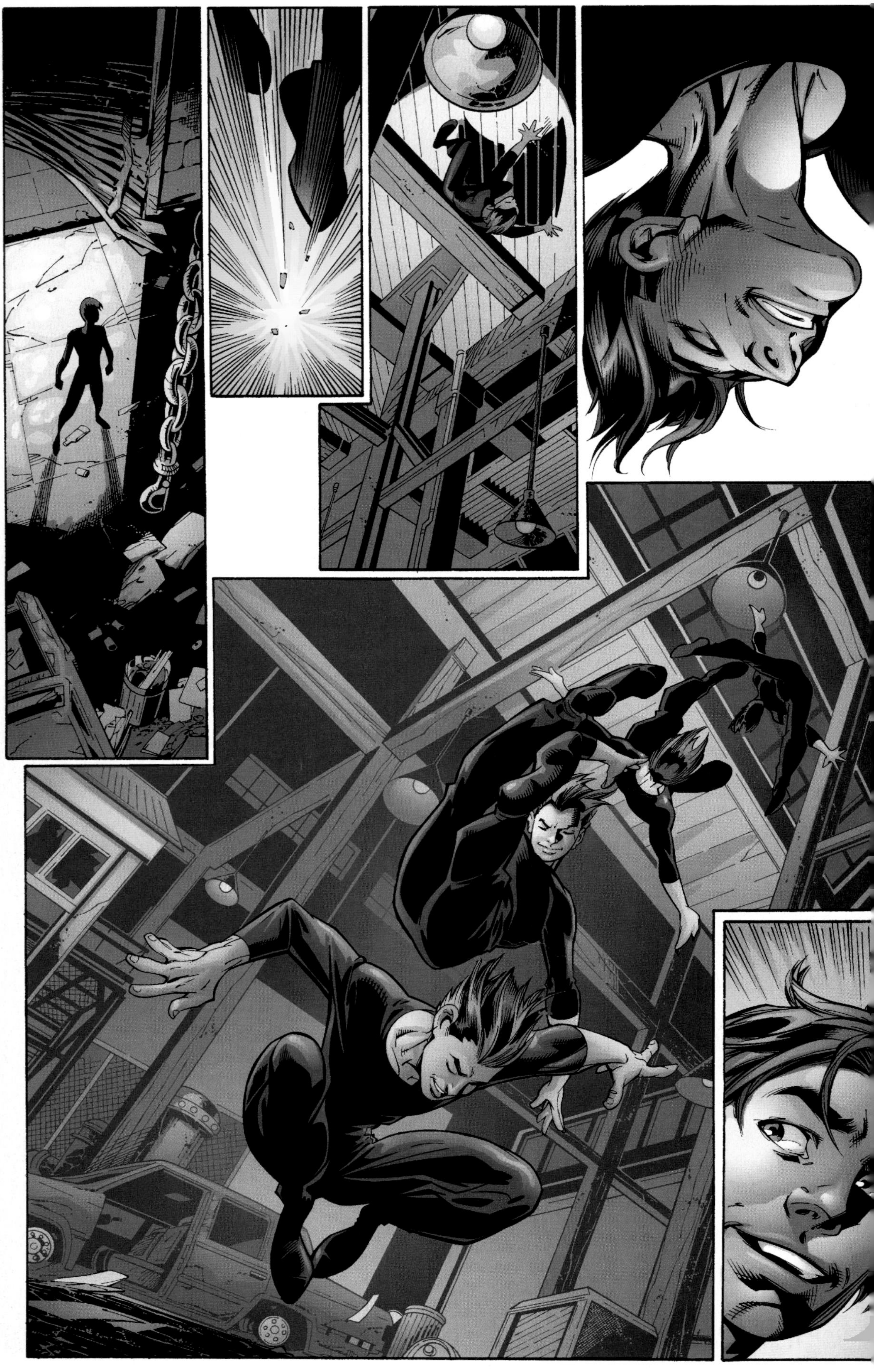

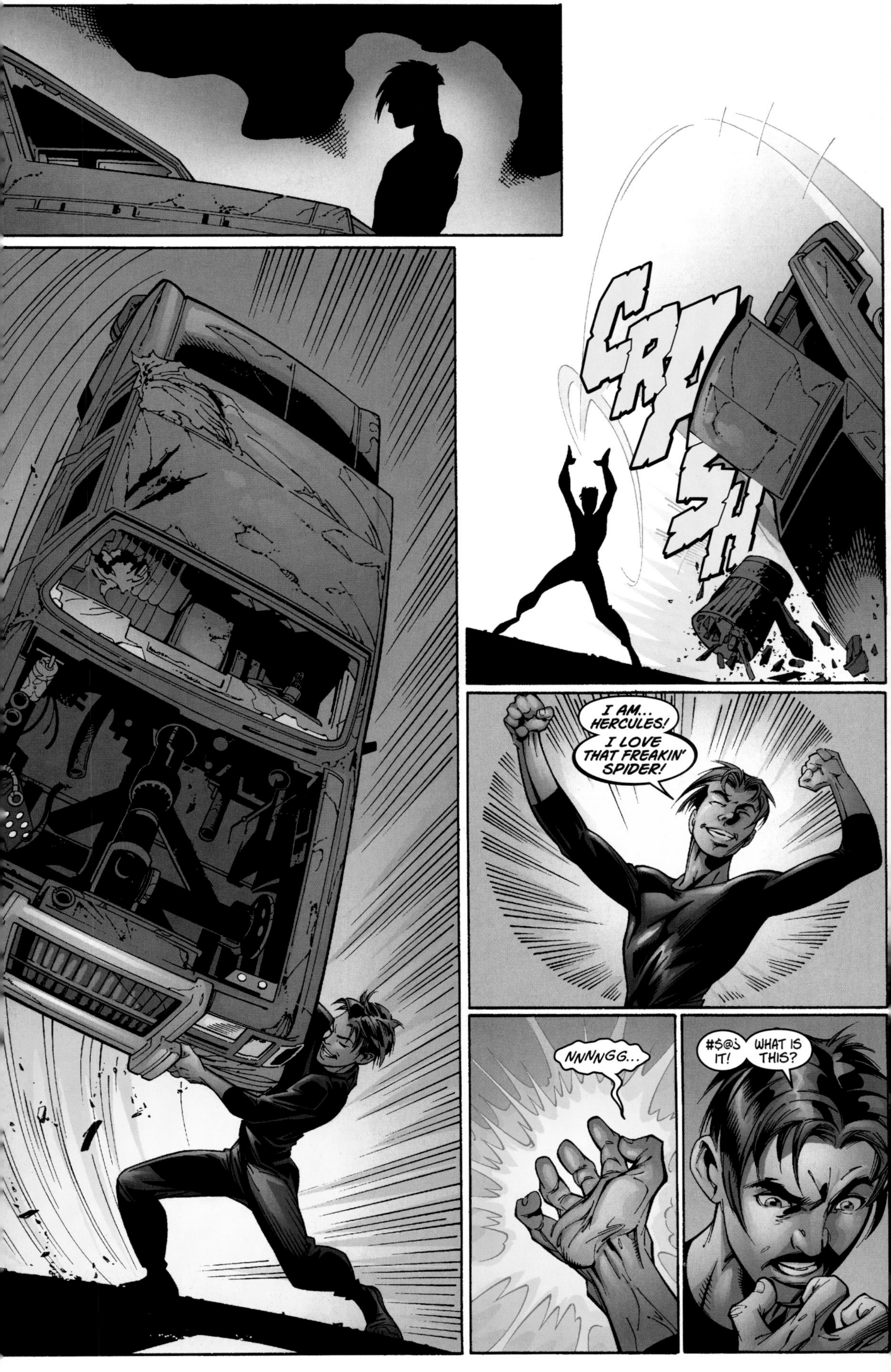
CRASH
I AM... HERCULES! I LOVE THAT FREAKIN' SPIDER!
NNNNGG...
#$@$ IT!
WHAT IS THIS?

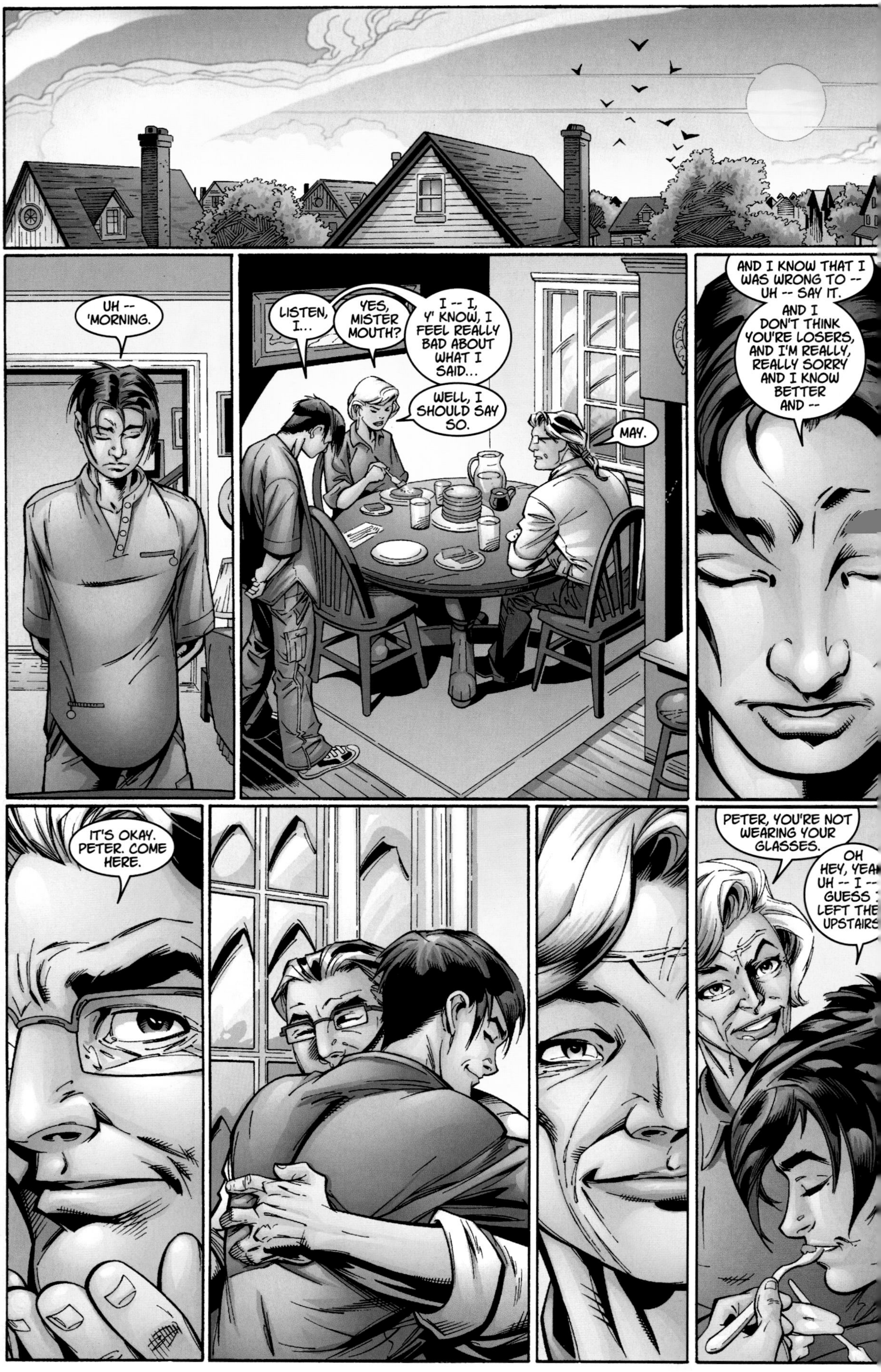
UH -- 'MORNING.
LISTEN, I...
YES, MISTER MOUTH?
I -- I, Y' KNOW, I FEEL REALLY BAD ABOUT WHAT I SAID...
WELL, I SHOULD SAY SO.
MAY.
AND I KNOW THAT I WAS WRONG TO -- UH -- SAY IT.
AND I DON'T THINK YOU'RE LOSERS, AND I'M REALLY, REALLY SORRY AND I KNOW BETTER AND --
IT'S OKAY. PETER. COME HERE.
PETER, YOU'RE NOT WEARING YOUR GLASSES.

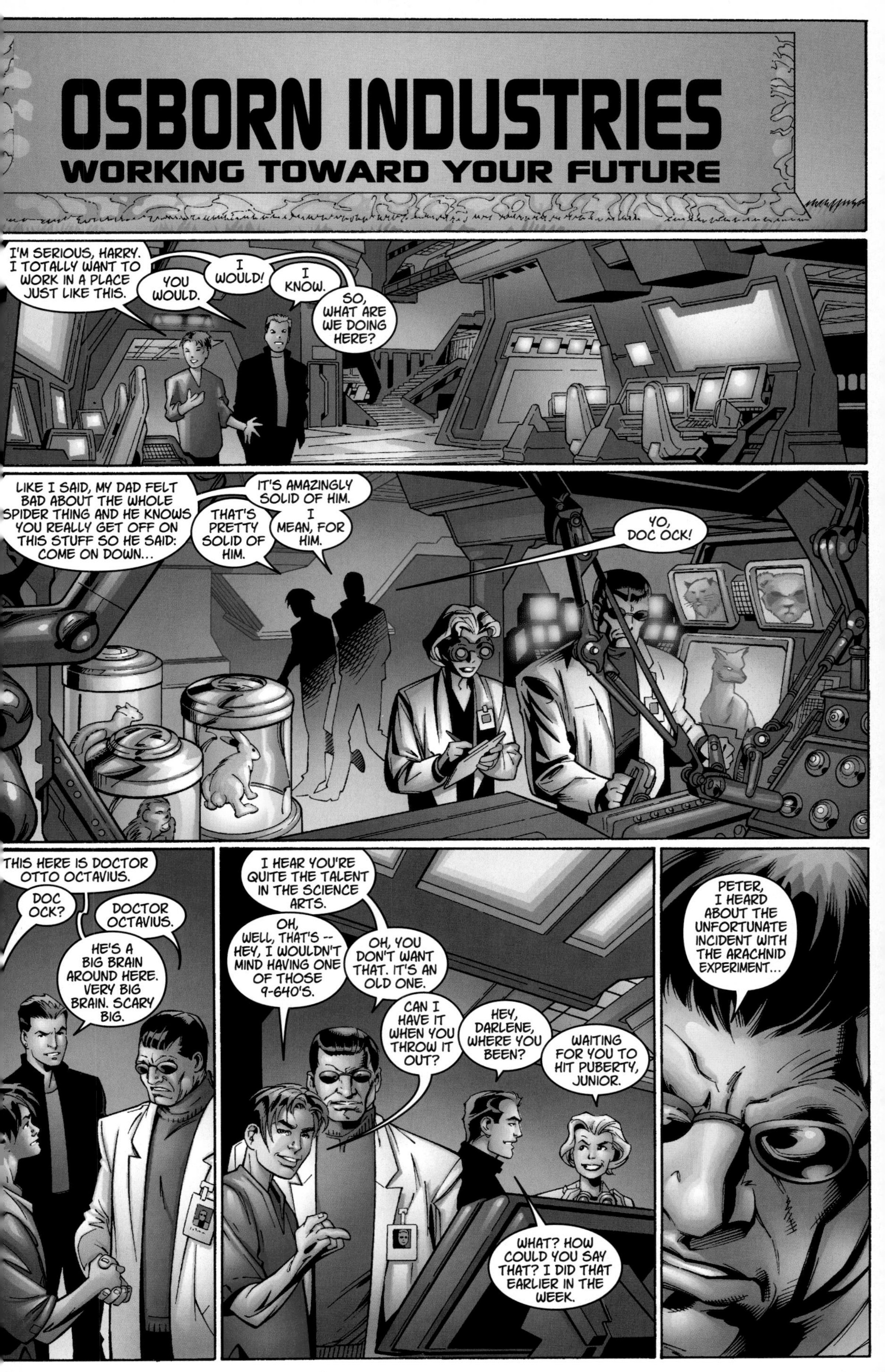
OSBORN INDUSTRIES
WORKING TOWARD YOUR FUTURE
I'M SERIOUS, HARRY. I TOTALLY WANT TO WORK IN A PLACE JUST LIKE THIS.
YOU WOULD.
I WOULD!
I KNOW.
SO, WHAT ARE WE DOING HERE?
LIKE I SAID, MY DAD FELT BAD ABOUT THE WHOLE SPIDER THING AND HE KNOWS YOU REALLY GET OFF ON THIS STUFF SO HE SAID: COME ON DOWN...
THAT'S PRETTY SOLID OF HIM.
IT'S AMAZINGLY SOLID OF HIM.
I MEAN, FOR HIM.
YO, DOC OCK!
THIS HERE IS DOCTOR OTTO OCTAVIUS.
DOC OCK?
DOCTOR OCTAVIUS.
HE'S A BIG BRAIN AROUND HERE. VERY BIG BRAIN. SCARY BIG.
I HEAR YOU'RE QUITE THE TALENT IN THE SCIENCE ARTS.
OH, WELL, THAT'S -- HEY, I WOULDN'T MIND HAVING ONE OF THOSE 9-640'S.
OH, YOU DON'T WANT THAT. IT'S AN OLD ONE.
CAN I HAVE IT WHEN YOU THROW IT OUT?
HEY, DARLENE, WHERE YOU BEEN?
WAITING FOR YOU TO HIT PUBERTY, JUNIOR.
WHAT? HOW COULD YOU SAY THAT? I DID THAT EARLIER IN THE WEEK.
PETER, I HEARD ABOUT THE UNFORTUNATE INCIDENT WITH THE ARACHNID EXPERIMENT...

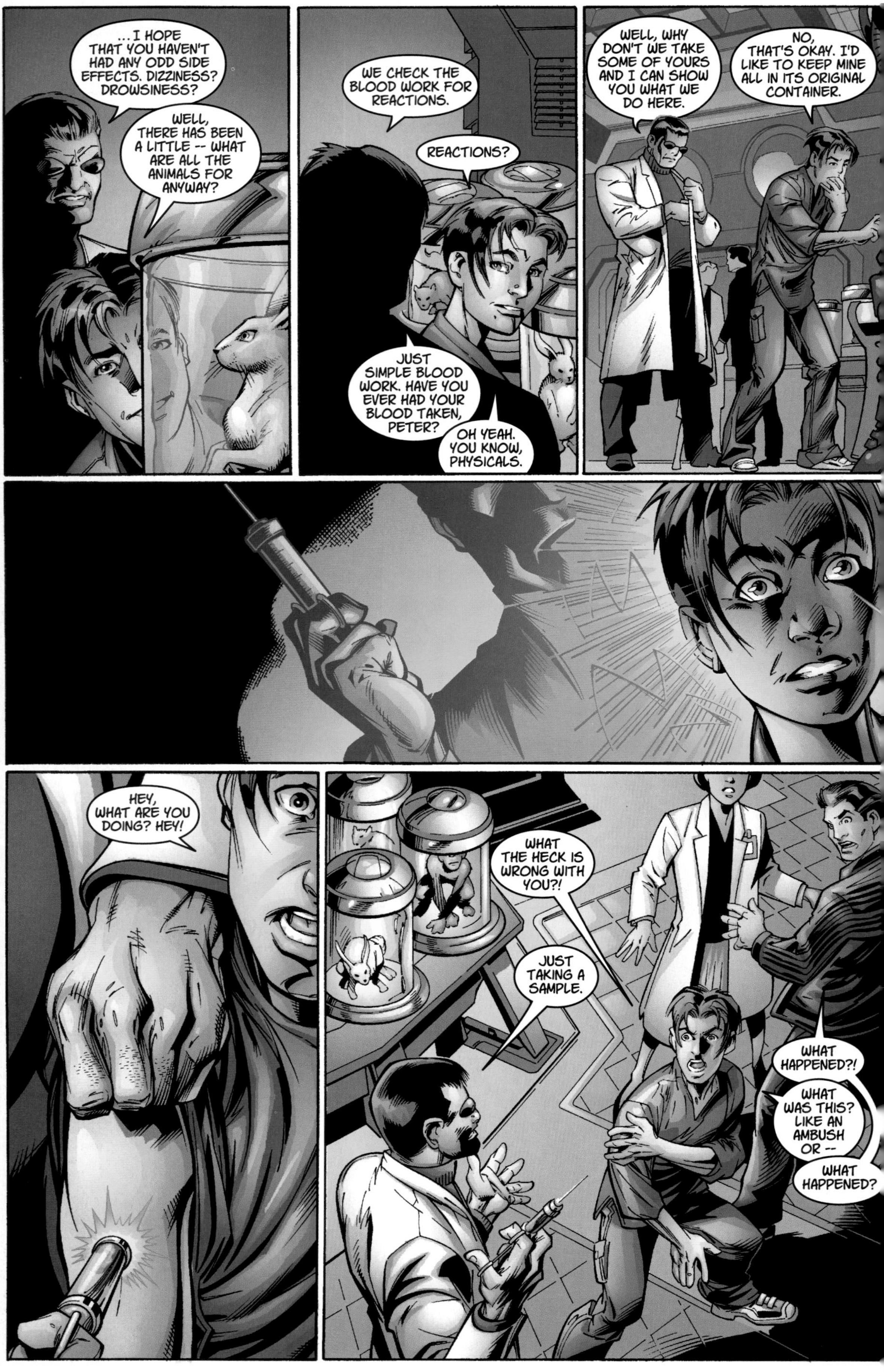
...I HOPE THAT YOU HAVEN'T HAD ANY ODD SIDE EFFECTS. DIZZINESS? DROWSINESS?
WELL, THERE HAS BEEN A LITTLE -- WHAT ARE ALL THE ANIMALS FOR ANYWAY?
WE CHECK THE BLOOD WORK FOR REACTIONS.
REACTIONS?
JUST SIMPLE BLOOD WORK. HAVE YOU EVER HAD YOUR BLOOD TAKEN, PETER?
OH YEAH. YOU KNOW, PHYSICALS.
WELL, WHY DON'T WE TAKE SOME OF YOURS AND I CAN SHOW YOU WHAT WE DO HERE.
NO, THAT'S OKAY. I'D LIKE TO KEEP MINE ALL IN ITS ORIGINAL CONTAINER.
HEY, WHAT ARE YOU DOING? HEY!
WHAT THE HECK IS WRONG WITH YOU?!
JUST TAKING A SAMPLE.
WHAT HAPPENED?!
WHAT WAS THIS? LIKE AN AMBUSH OR --
WHAT HAPPENED?

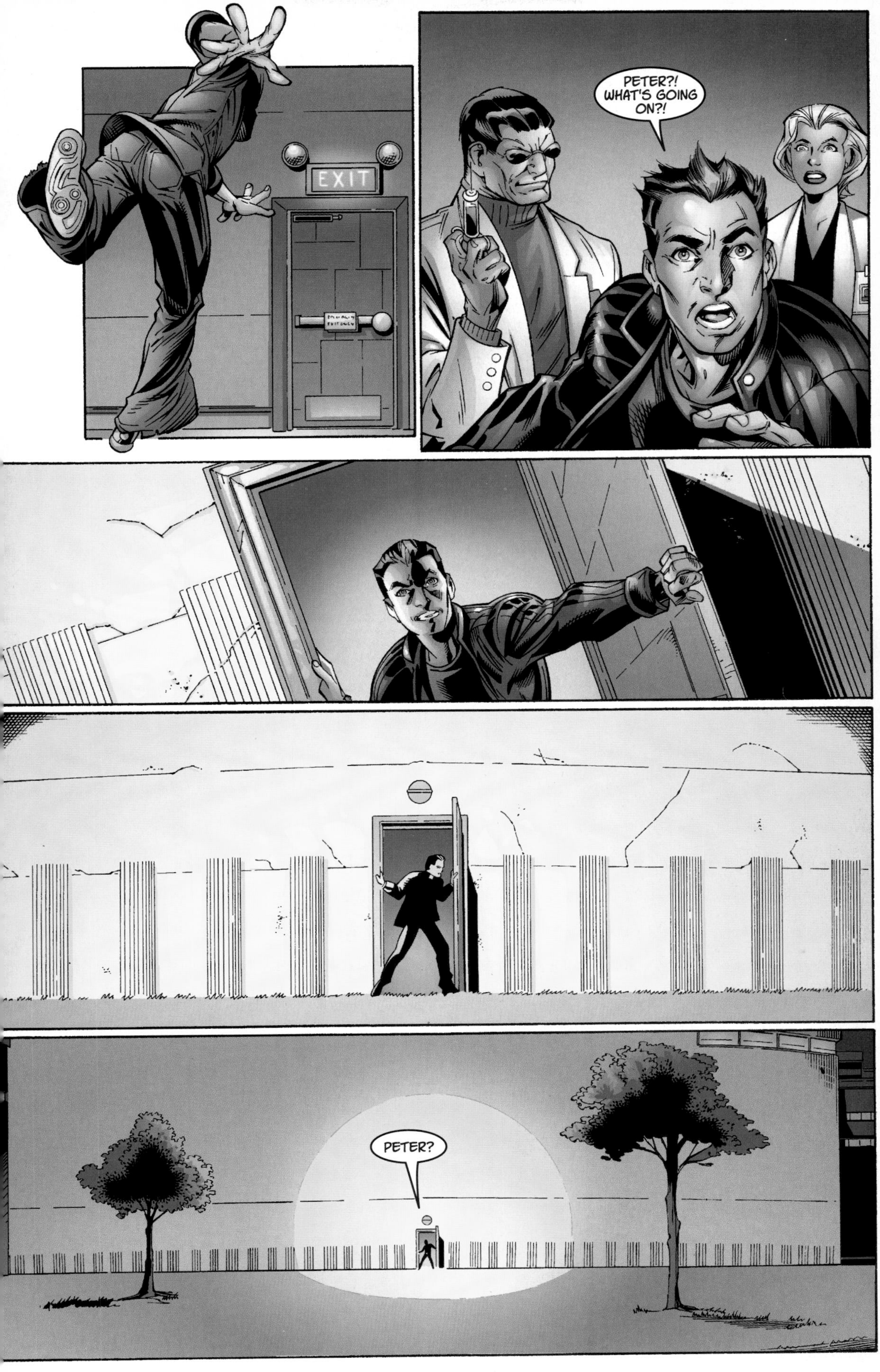
EXIT
PETER?! WHAT'S GOING ON?!
PETER?

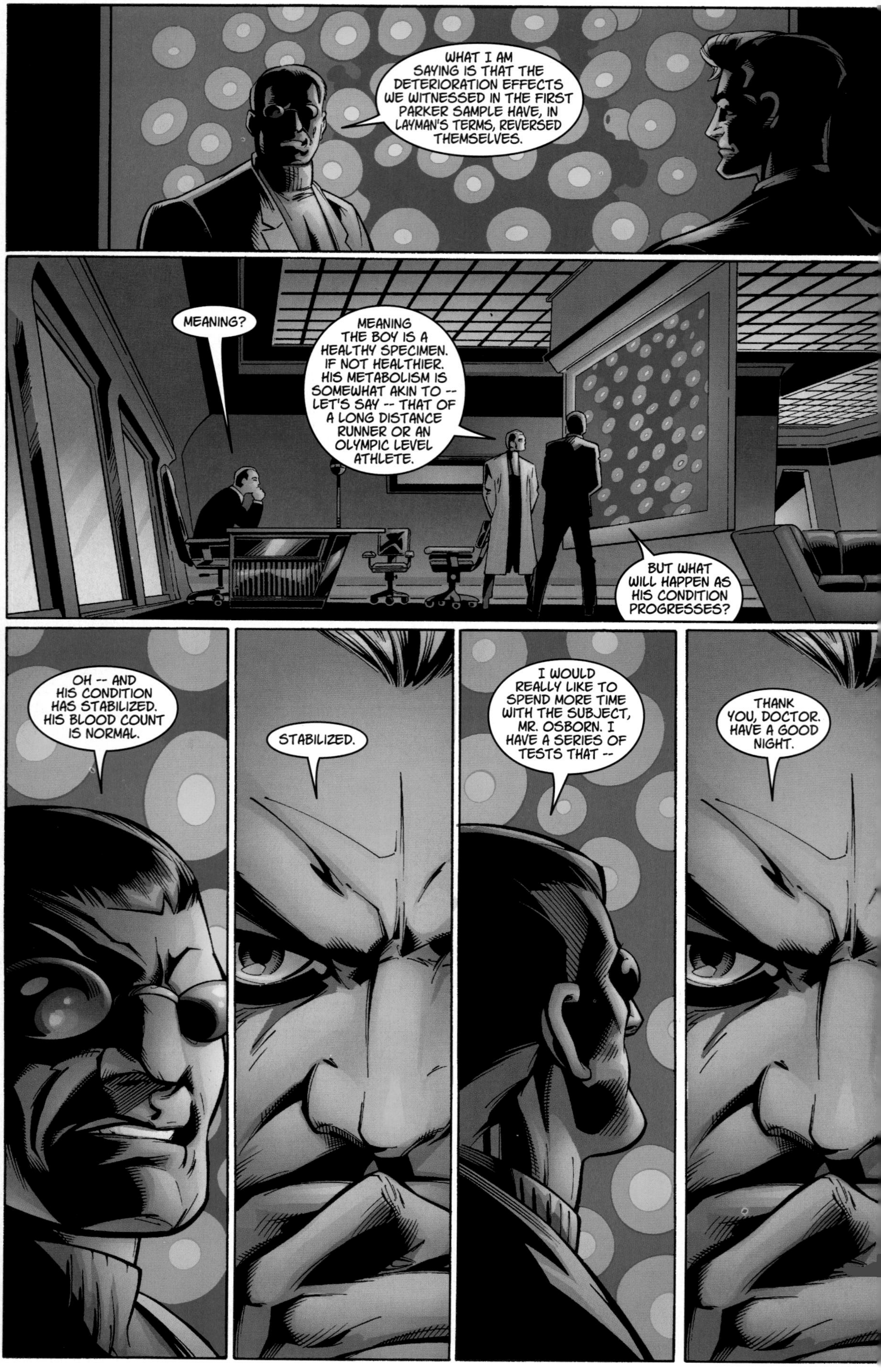
WHAT I AM SAYING IS THAT THE DETERIORATION EFFECTS WE WITNESSED IN THE FIRST PARKER SAMPLE HAVE, IN LAYMAN'S TERMS, REVERSED THEMSELVES.
MEANING?
MEANING THE BOY IS A HEALTHY SPECIMEN. IF NOT HEALTHIER. HIS METABOLISM IS SOMEWHAT AKIN TO -- LET'S SAY -- THAT OF A LONG DISTANCE RUNNER OR AN OLYMPIC LEVEL ATHLETE.
BUT WHAT WILL HAPPEN AS HIS CONDITION PROGRESSES?
OH -- AND HIS CONDITION HAS STABILIZED. HIS BLOOD COUNT IS NORMAL.
STABILIZED.
I WOULD REALLY LIKE TO SPEND MORE TIME WITH THE SUBJECT, MR. OSBORN. I HAVE A SERIES OF TESTS THAT --
THANK YOU, DOCTOR. HAVE A GOOD NIGHT.

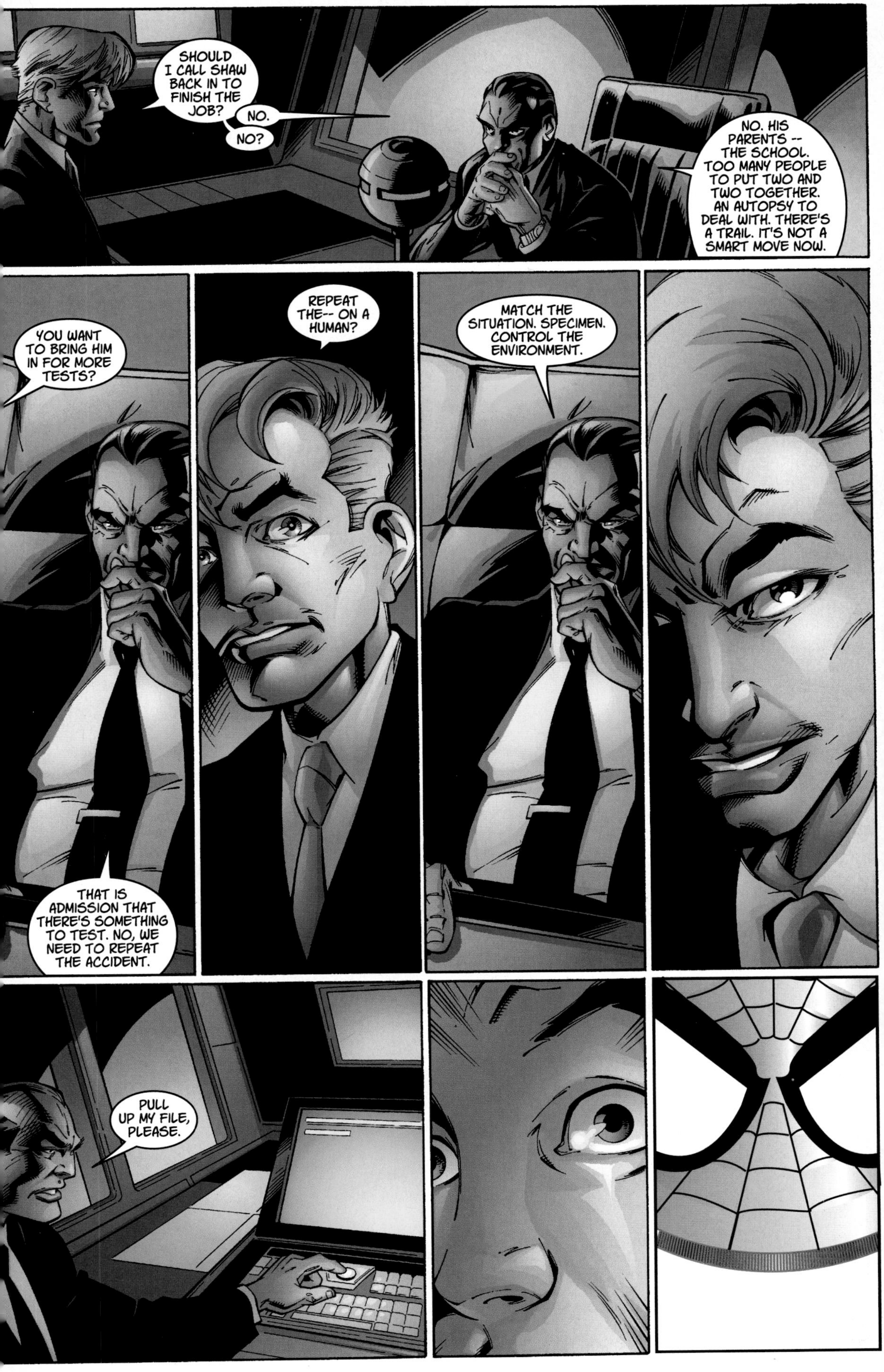
SHOULD I CALL SHAW BACK IN TO FINISH THE JOB?
NO.
NO?
NO. HIS PARENTS -- THE SCHOOL. TOO MANY PEOPLE TO PUT TWO AND TWO TOGETHER. AN AUTOPSY TO DEAL WITH. THERE'S A TRAIL. IT'S NOT A SMART MOVE NOW.
YOU WANT TO BRING HIM IN FOR MORE TESTS?
THAT IS ADMISSION THAT THERE'S SOMETHING TO TEST. NO, WE NEED TO REPEAT THE ACCIDENT.
REPEAT THE-- ON A HUMAN?
MATCH THE SITUATION. SPECIMEN. CONTROL THE ENVIRONMENT.
PULL UP MY FILE, PLEASE.

3

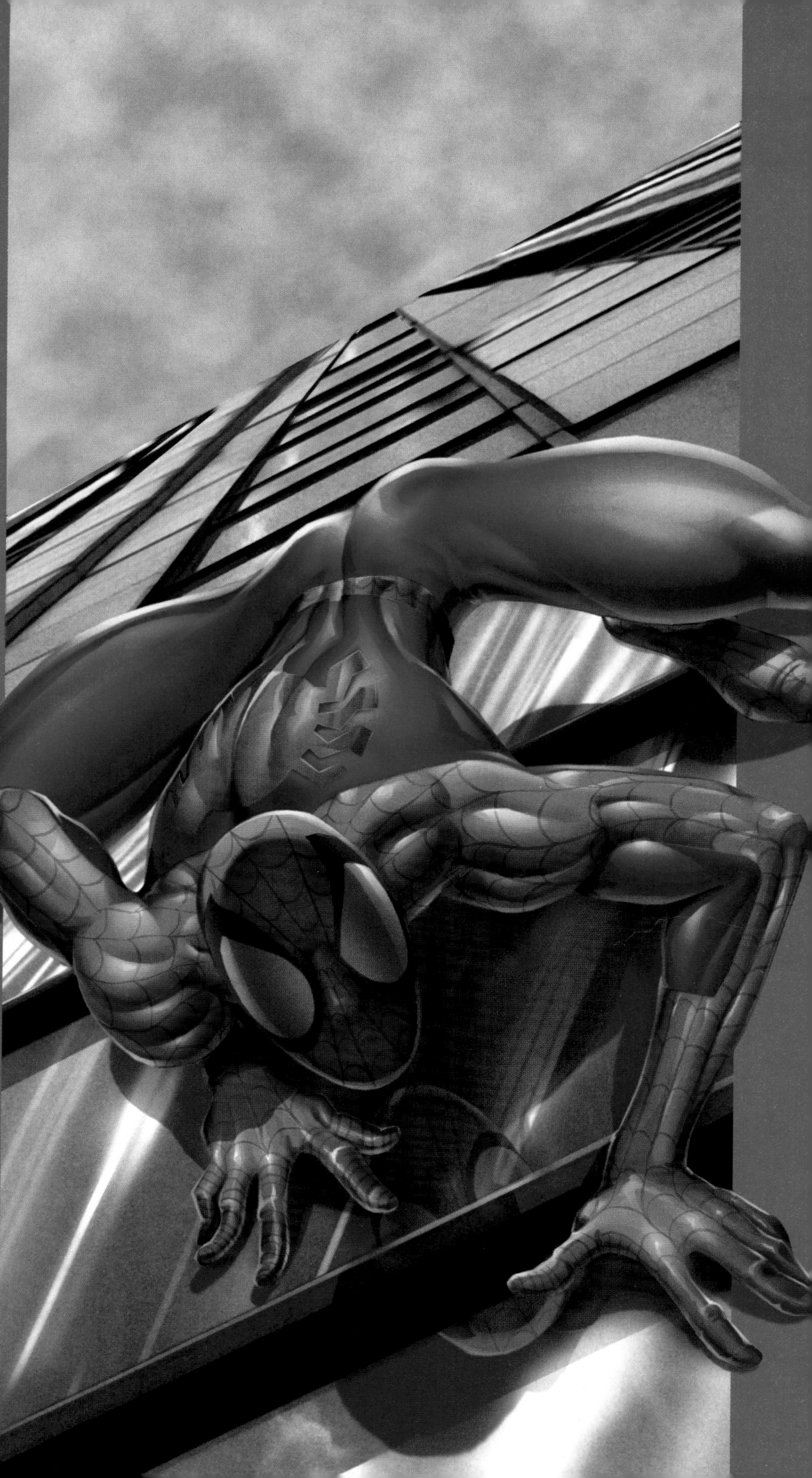

"RIGHT THERE -- YES.

"RIGHT THERE WE CAN SEE WHERE THE ARACHNID OZ EXPERIMENT NUMBER "OO" BIT THAT PARKER BOY.

"INITIALLY, THE BIOLOGICAL EFFECTS TO THE PARKER BOY WERE NEGATIVE. VERY NEGATIVE.

"AND HIS CHANCE FOR SURVIVAL WAS VERY SLIM. FATAL.

"BUT WE NOW BELIEVE THAT IT WAS THE MIXTURE OF SPIDER VENOM WITH THE OZ THAT CREATED THE ADVERSE EFFECTS TO THE BOY'S SYSTEM.

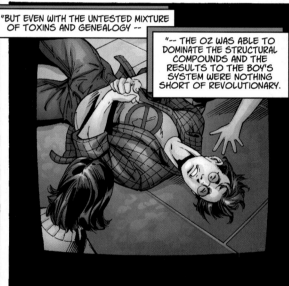

"BUT EVEN WITH THE UNTESTED MIXTURE OF TOXINS AND GENEALOGY --

"-- THE OZ WAS ABLE TO DOMINATE THE STRUCTURAL COMPOUNDS AND THE RESULTS TO THE BOY'S SYSTEM WERE NOTHING SHORT OF REVOLUTIONARY.

"IT WAS AN ACCIDENT, YES, BUT WE HAVE OUR FIRST HUMAN TEST SUBJECT --

"-- AND WHAT HE HAS SHOWN US IS THAT OUR TIME IS NOW.

"TURN IT OFF, PLEASE."

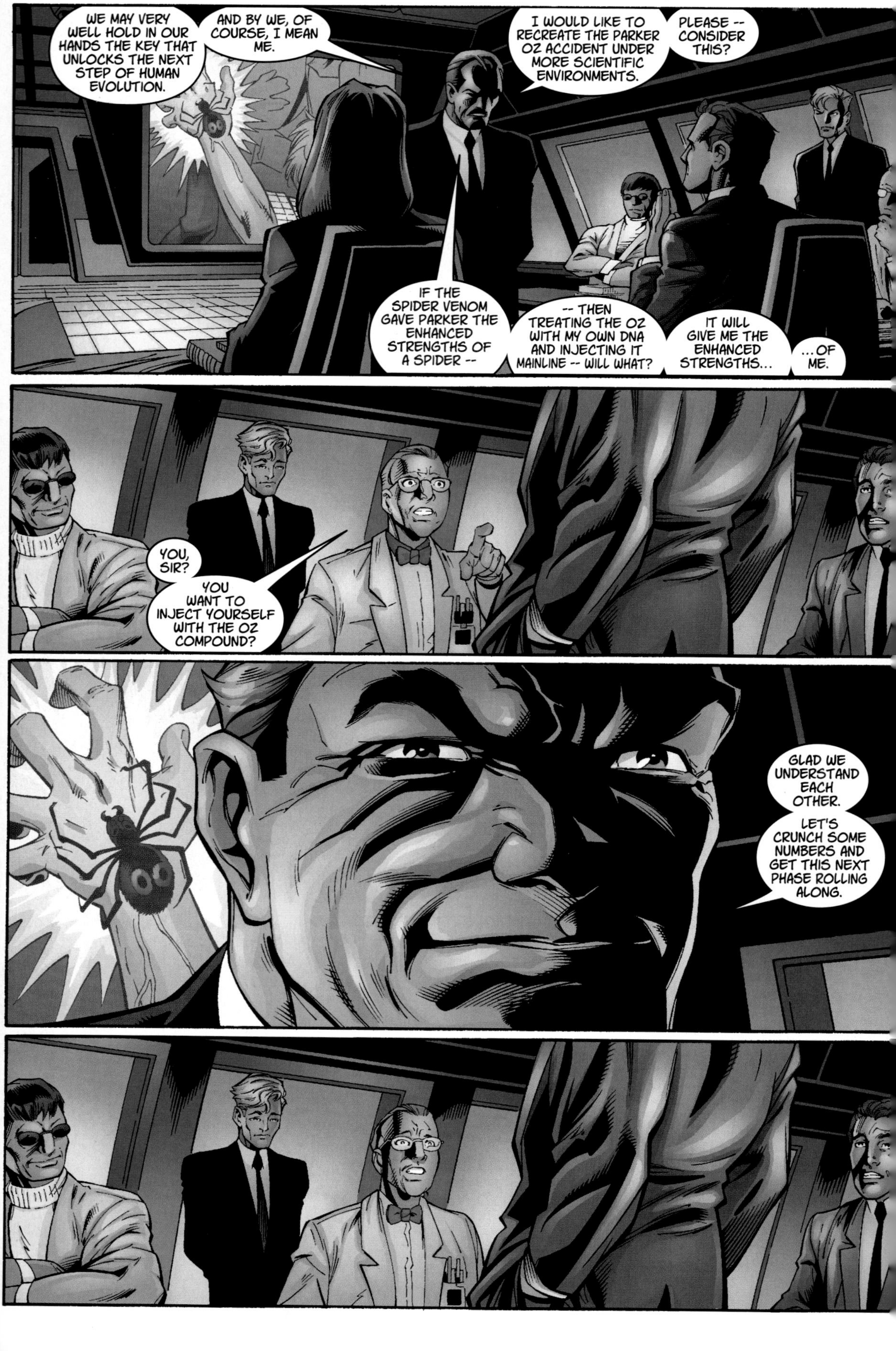
WE MAY VERY WELL HOLD IN OUR HANDS THE KEY THAT UNLOCKS THE NEXT STEP OF HUMAN EVOLUTION.
AND BY WE, OF COURSE, I MEAN ME.
I WOULD LIKE TO RECREATE THE PARKER OZ ACCIDENT UNDER MORE SCIENTIFIC ENVIRONMENTS.
PLEASE -- CONSIDER THIS?
IF THE SPIDER VENOM GAVE PARKER THE ENHANCED STRENGTHS OF A SPIDER --
-- THEN TREATING THE OZ WITH MY OWN DNA AND INJECTING IT MAINLINE -- WILL WHAT?
IT WILL GIVE ME THE ENHANCED STRENGTHS...
...OF ME.
YOU, SIR?
YOU WANT TO INJECT YOURSELF WITH THE OZ COMPOUND?
GLAD WE UNDERSTAND EACH OTHER.
LET'S CRUNCH SOME NUMBERS AND GET THIS NEXT PHASE ROLLING ALONG.

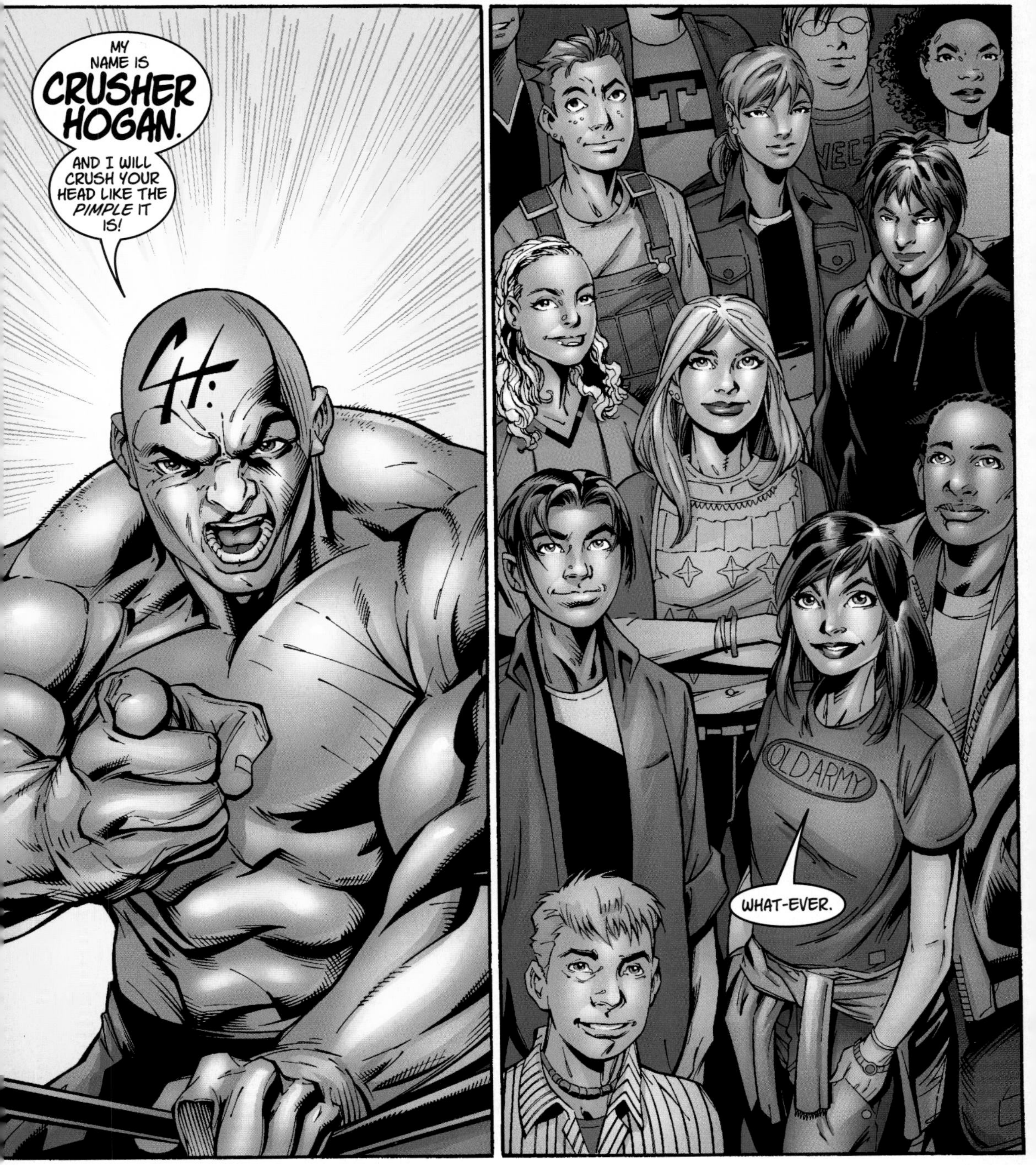
MY NAME IS CRUSHER HOGAN.
AND I WILL CRUSH YOUR HEAD LIKE THE *PIMPLE* IT IS!
OLD ARMY
WHAT-EVER.

WANNABE

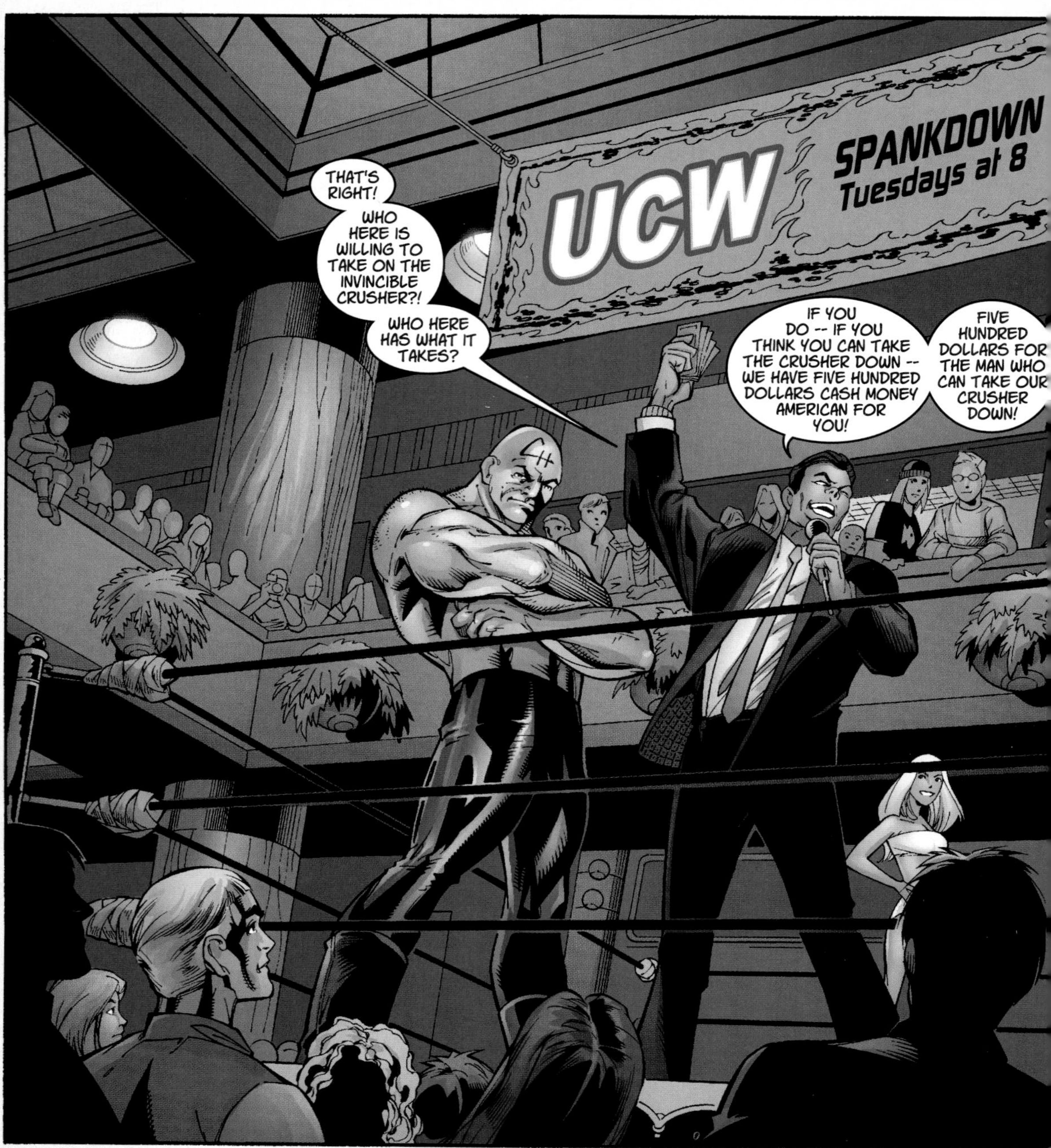
UCW
SPANKDOWN Tuesdays at 8
THAT'S RIGHT!
WHO HERE IS WILLING TO TAKE ON THE INVINCIBLE CRUSHER?!
WHO HERE HAS WHAT IT TAKES?
IF YOU DO -- IF YOU THINK YOU CAN TAKE THE CRUSHER DOWN -- WE HAVE FIVE HUNDRED DOLLARS CASH MONEY AMERICAN FOR YOU!
FIVE HUNDRED DOLLARS FOR THE MAN WHO CAN TAKE OUR CRUSHER DOWN!

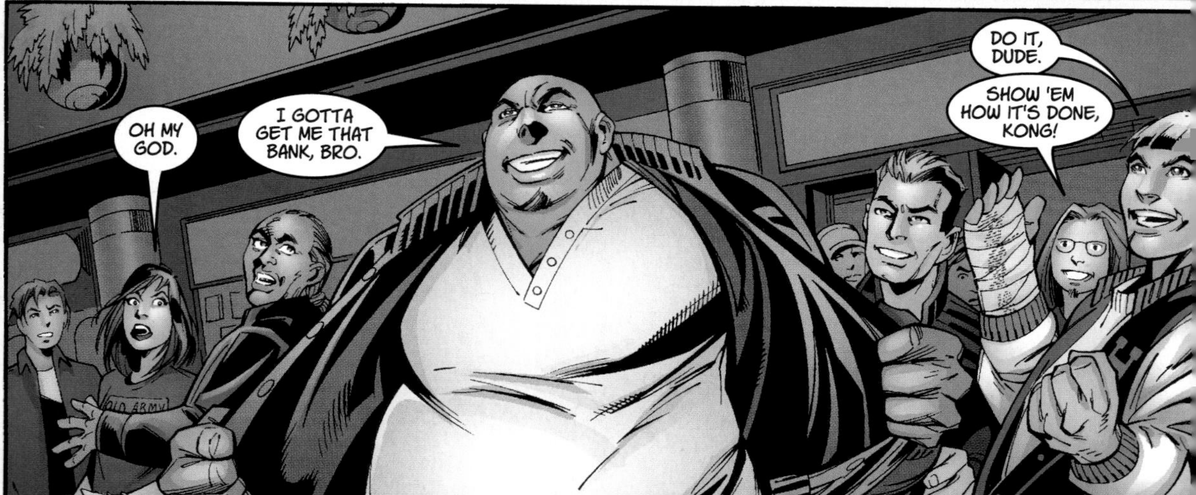
OH MY GOD.
I GOTTA GET ME THAT BANK, BRO.
DO IT, DUDE.
SHOW 'EM HOW IT'S DONE, KONG!
OLD ARMY

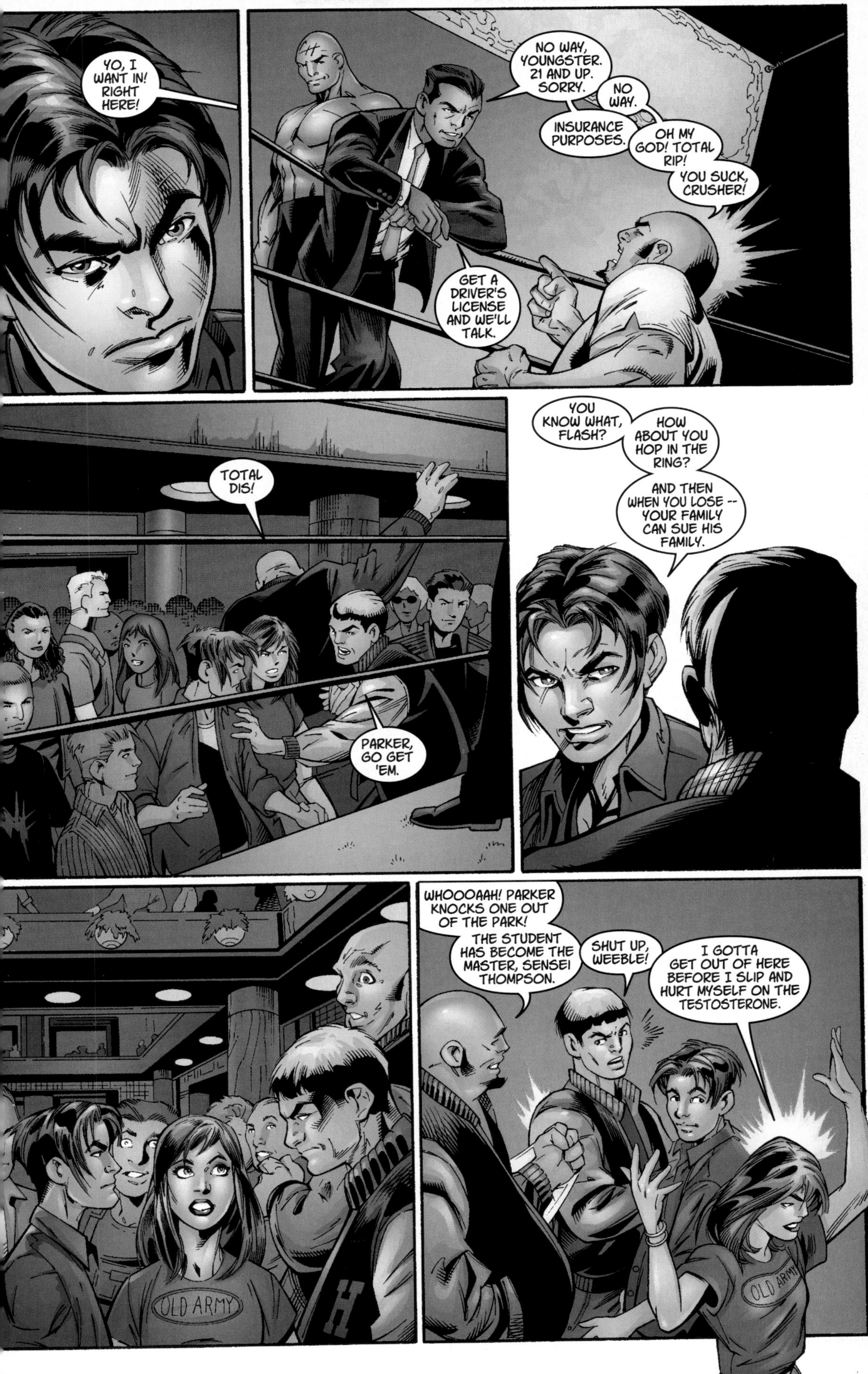
YO, I WANT IN! RIGHT HERE!
NO WAY, YOUNGSTER. 21 AND UP. SORRY.
NO WAY.
INSURANCE PURPOSES.
OH MY GOD! TOTAL RIP!
YOU SUCK, CRUSHER!
GET A DRIVER'S LICENSE AND WE'LL TALK.
TOTAL DIS!
PARKER, GO GET 'EM.
YOU KNOW WHAT, FLASH?
HOW ABOUT YOU HOP IN THE RING?
AND THEN WHEN YOU LOSE -- YOUR FAMILY CAN SUE HIS FAMILY.
WHOOOOAAH! PARKER KNOCKS ONE OUT OF THE PARK!
THE STUDENT HAS BECOME THE MASTER, SENSEI THOMPSON.
SHUT UP, WEEBLE!
I GOTTA GET OUT OF HERE BEFORE I SLIP AND HURT MYSELF ON THE TESTOSTERONE.
OLD ARMY
OLD ARMY

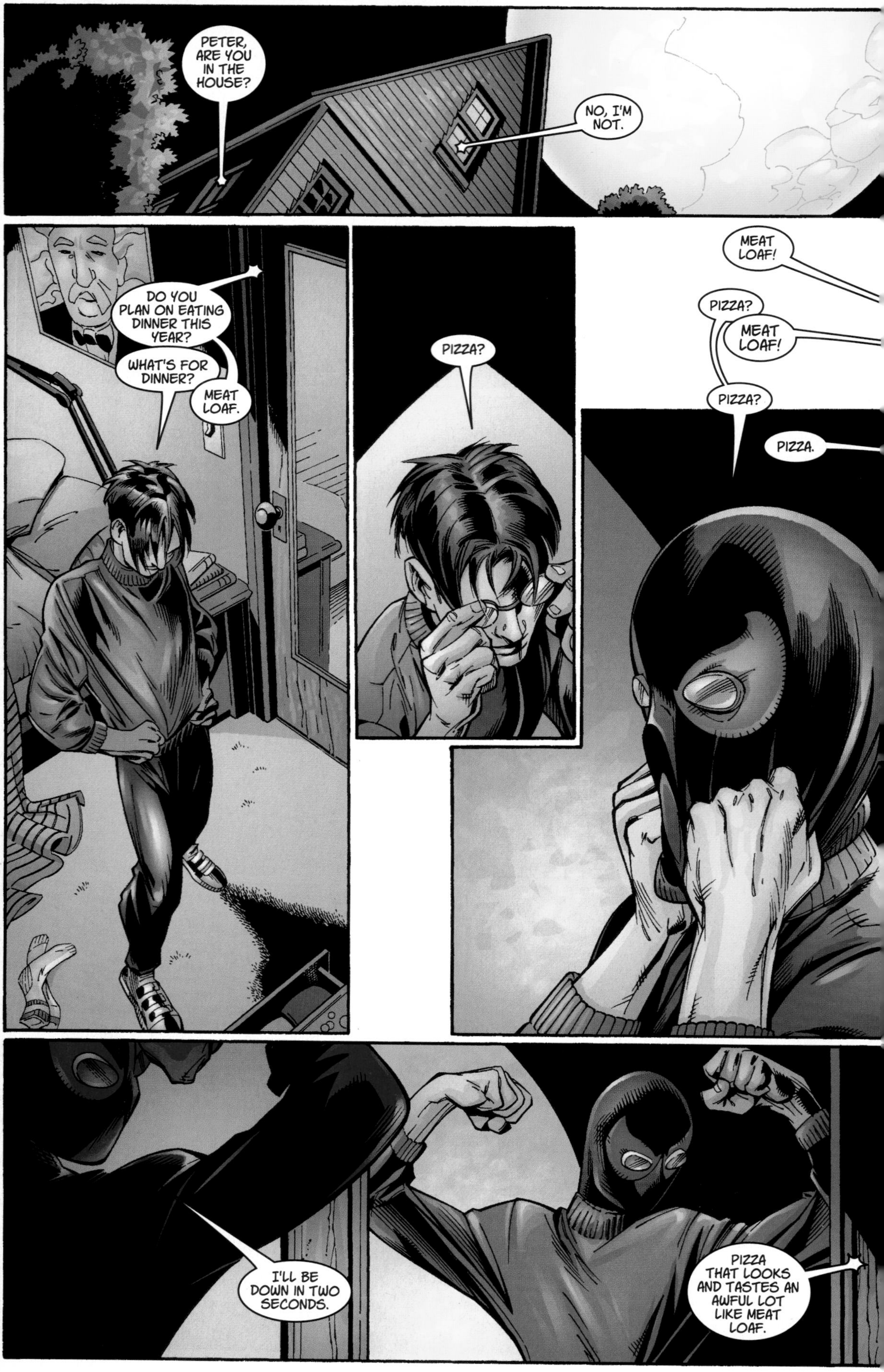
PETER, ARE YOU IN THE HOUSE?
NO, I'M NOT.
DO YOU PLAN ON EATING DINNER THIS YEAR?
WHAT'S FOR DINNER?
MEAT LOAF.
PIZZA?
MEAT LOAF!
PIZZA?
MEAT LOAF!
PIZZA?
PIZZA.
I'LL BE DOWN IN TWO SECONDS.
PIZZA THAT LOOKS AND TASTES AN AWFUL LOT LIKE MEAT LOAF.

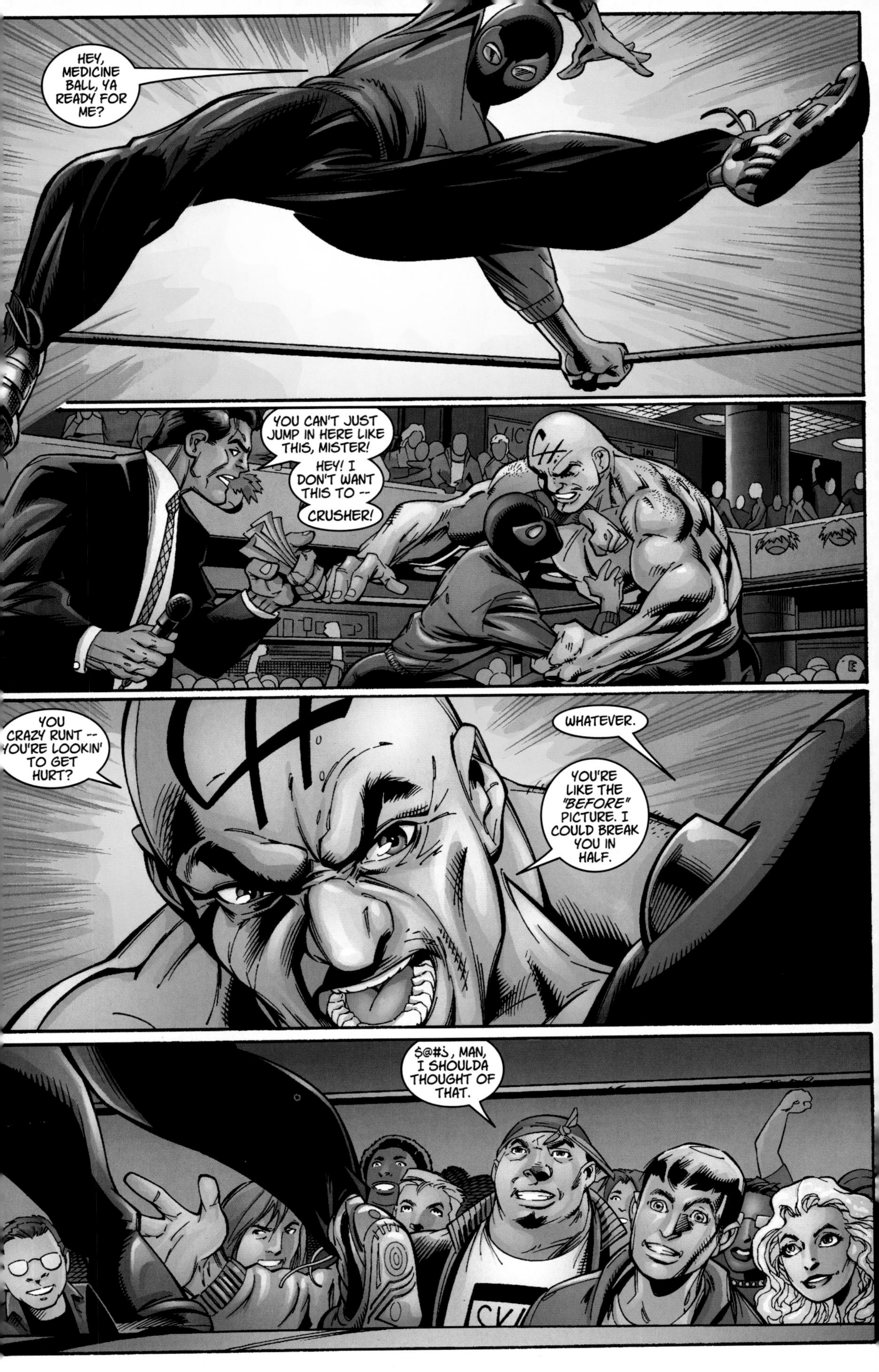
HEY, MEDICINE BALL, YA READY FOR ME?
YOU CAN'T JUST JUMP IN HERE LIKE THIS, MISTER!
HEY! I DON'T WANT THIS TO --
CRUSHER!
YOU CRAZY RUNT -- YOU'RE LOOKIN' TO GET HURT?
WHATEVER.
YOU'RE LIKE THE "BEFORE" PICTURE. I COULD BREAK YOU IN HALF.
$@#¿, MAN, I SHOULDA THOUGHT OF THAT.

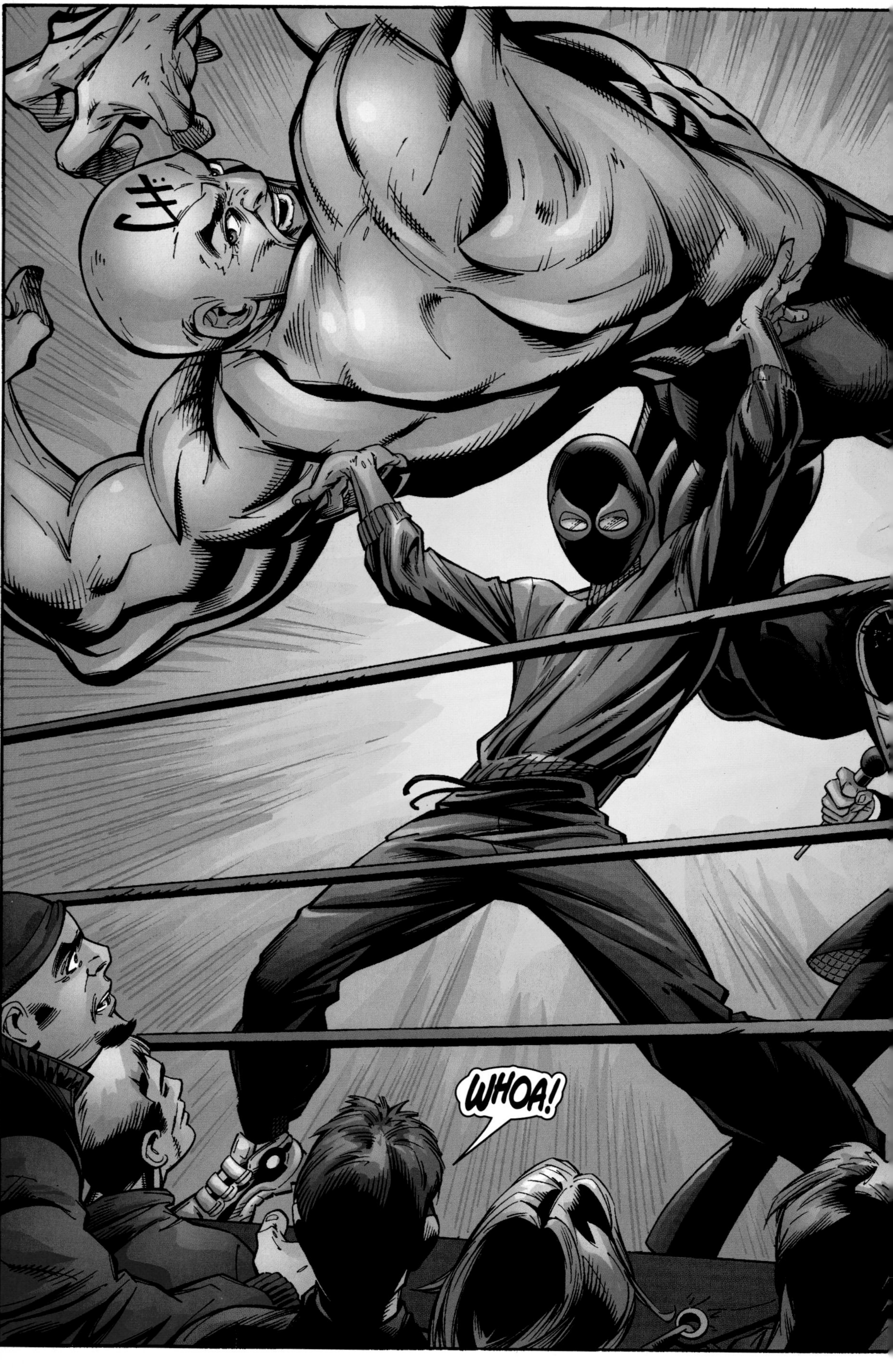
WHOA!

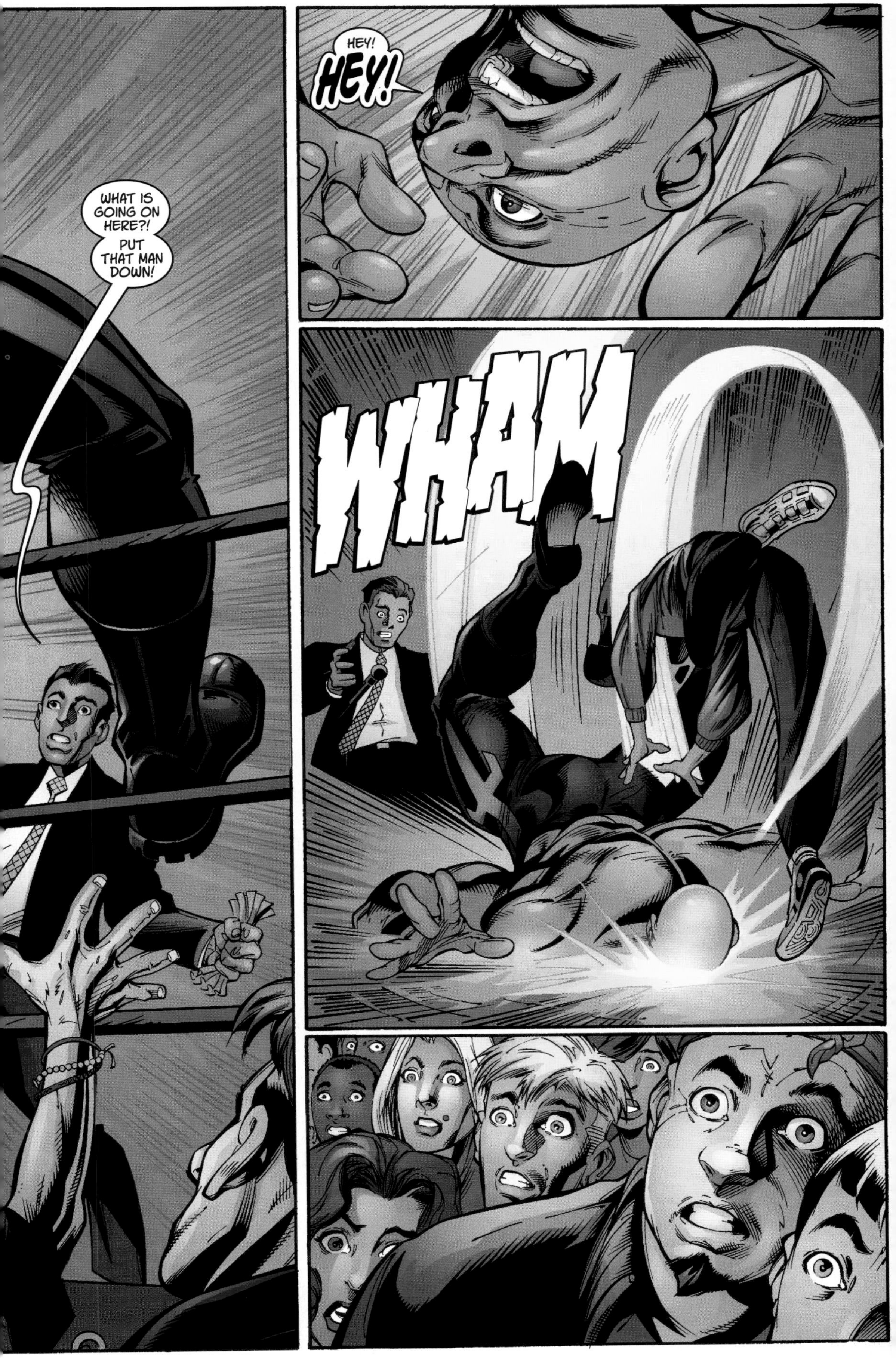
WHAT IS GOING ON HERE?! PUT THAT MAN DOWN!
HEY! HEY!
WHAM

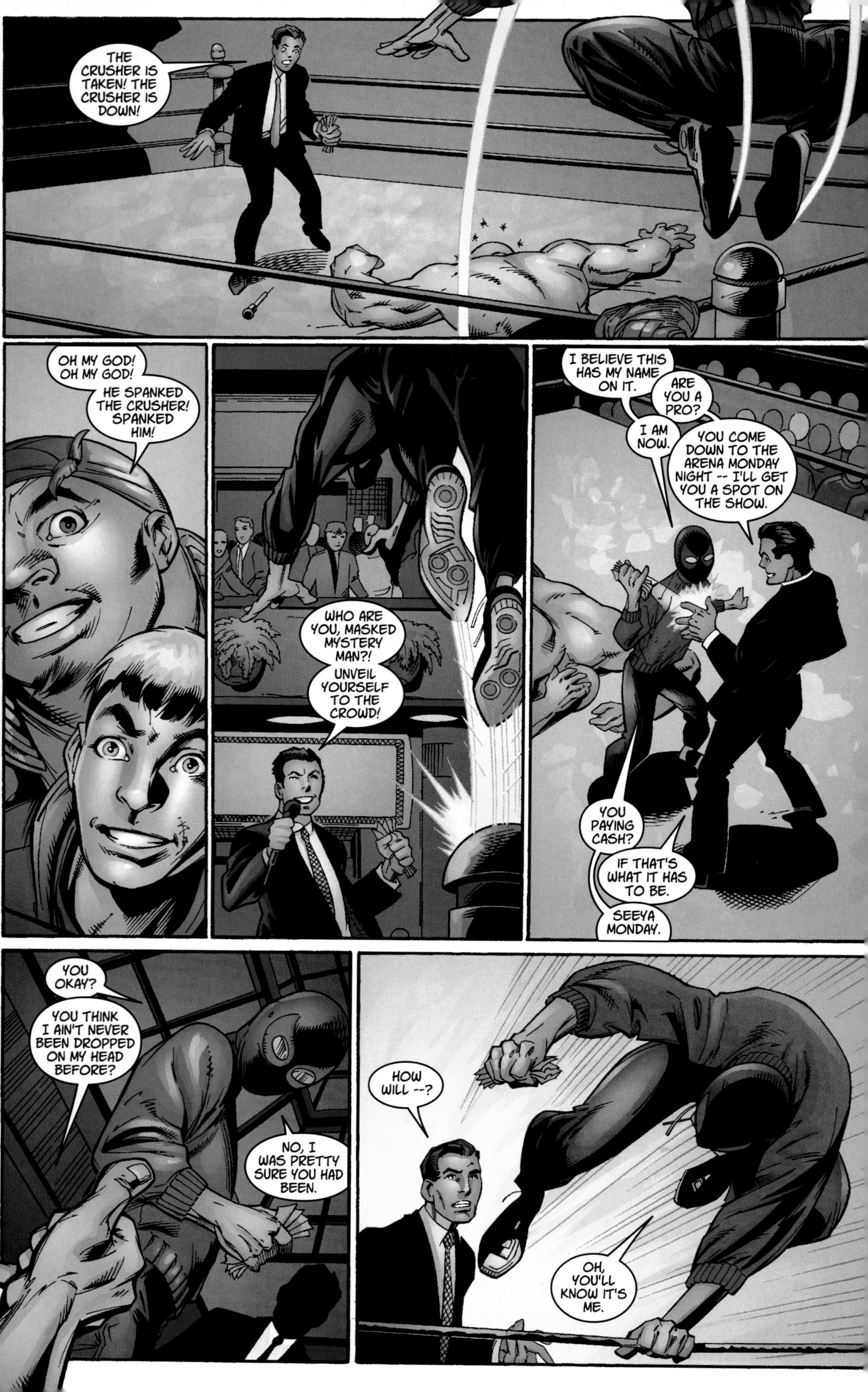
THE CRUSHER IS TAKEN! THE CRUSHER IS DOWN!
OH MY GOD! OH MY GOD!
HE SPANKED THE CRUSHER! SPANKED HIM!
WHO ARE YOU, MASKED MYSTERY MAN?!
UNVEIL YOURSELF TO THE CROWD!
I BELIEVE THIS HAS MY NAME ON IT.
ARE YOU A PRO?
I AM NOW.
YOU COME DOWN TO THE ARENA MONDAY NIGHT -- I'LL GET YOU A SPOT ON THE SHOW.
YOU PAYING CASH?
IF THAT'S WHAT IT HAS TO BE.
SEEYA MONDAY.
YOU OKAY?
YOU THINK I AIN'T NEVER BEEN DROPPED ON MY HEAD BEFORE?
NO, I WAS PRETTY SURE YOU HAD BEEN.
HOW WILL --?
OH, YOU'LL KNOW IT'S ME.

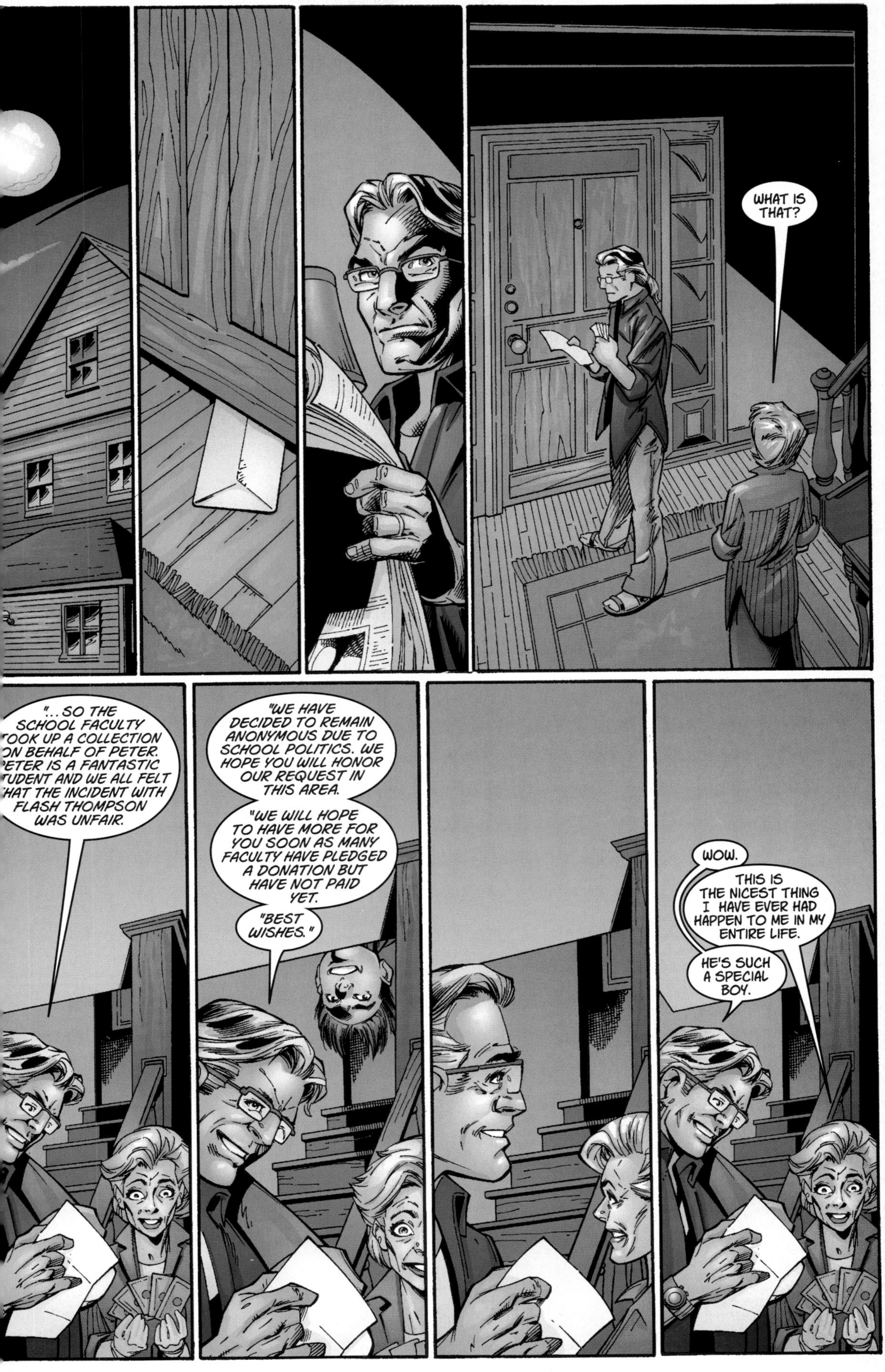
WHAT IS THAT?
"...SO THE SCHOOL FACULTY TOOK UP A COLLECTION ON BEHALF OF PETER. PETER IS A FANTASTIC STUDENT AND WE ALL FELT THAT THE INCIDENT WITH FLASH THOMPSON WAS UNFAIR.
"WE HAVE DECIDED TO REMAIN ANONYMOUS DUE TO SCHOOL POLITICS. WE HOPE YOU WILL HONOR OUR REQUEST IN THIS AREA.
"WE WILL HOPE TO HAVE MORE FOR YOU SOON AS MANY FACULTY HAVE PLEDGED A DONATION BUT HAVE NOT PAID YET.
"BEST WISHES."
WOW.
THIS IS THE NICEST THING I HAVE EVER HAD HAPPEN TO ME IN MY ENTIRE LIFE.
HE'S SUCH A SPECIAL BOY.

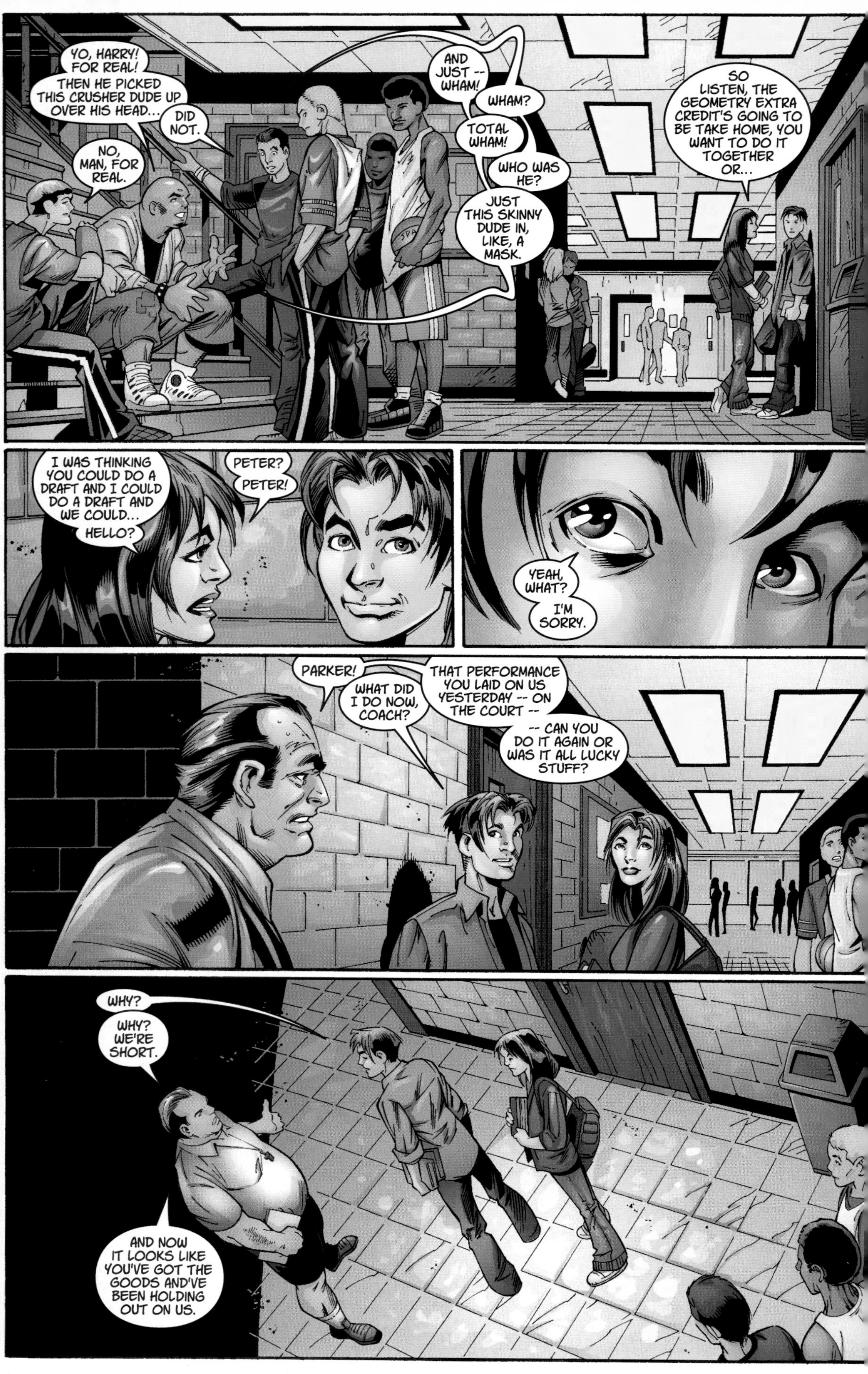
YO, HARRY! FOR REAL! THEN HE PICKED THIS CRUSHER DUDE UP OVER HIS HEAD...
DID NOT.
NO, MAN, FOR REAL.
AND JUST -- WHAM!
WHAM?
TOTAL WHAM!
WHO WAS HE?
JUST THIS SKINNY DUDE IN, LIKE, A MASK.
SO LISTEN, THE GEOMETRY EXTRA CREDIT'S GOING TO BE TAKE HOME, YOU WANT TO DO IT TOGETHER OR...
I WAS THINKING YOU COULD DO A DRAFT AND I COULD DO A DRAFT AND WE COULD...
HELLO?
PETER?
PETER!
YEAH, WHAT?
I'M SORRY.
PARKER!
WHAT DID I DO NOW, COACH?
THAT PERFORMANCE YOU LAID ON US YESTERDAY -- ON THE COURT --
-- CAN YOU DO IT AGAIN OR WAS IT ALL LUCKY STUFF?
WHY?
WHY? WE'RE SHORT.
AND NOW IT LOOKS LIKE YOU'VE GOT THE GOODS AND'VE BEEN HOLDING OUT ON US.

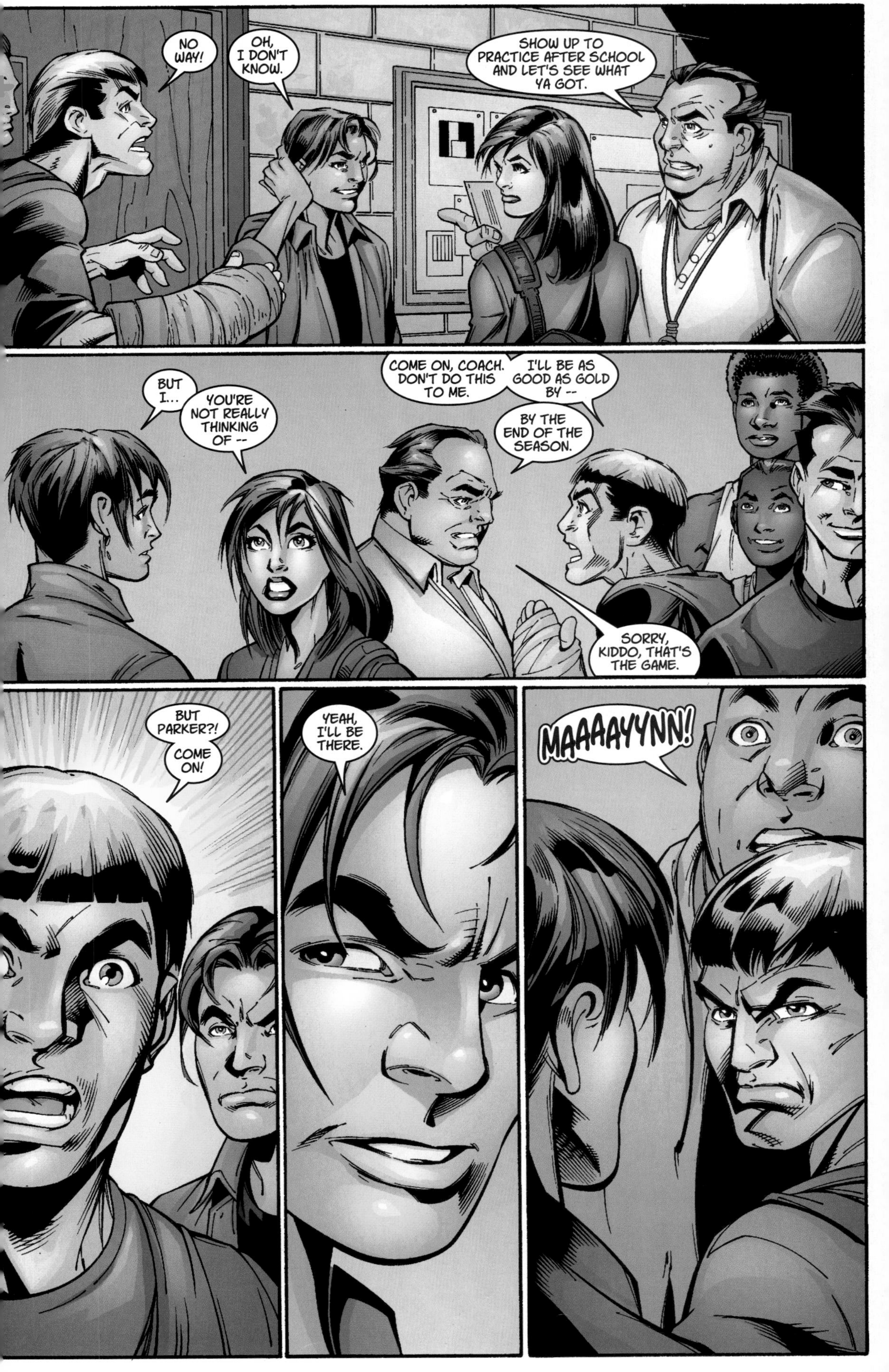
NO WAY!
OH, I DON'T KNOW.
SHOW UP TO PRACTICE AFTER SCHOOL AND LET'S SEE WHAT YA GOT.
BUT I...
YOU'RE NOT REALLY THINKING OF --
COME ON, COACH. DON'T DO THIS TO ME.
I'LL BE AS GOOD AS GOLD BY --
BY THE END OF THE SEASON.
SORRY, KIDDO, THAT'S THE GAME.
BUT PARKER?!
COME ON!
YEAH, I'LL BE THERE.
MAAAAYYNN!

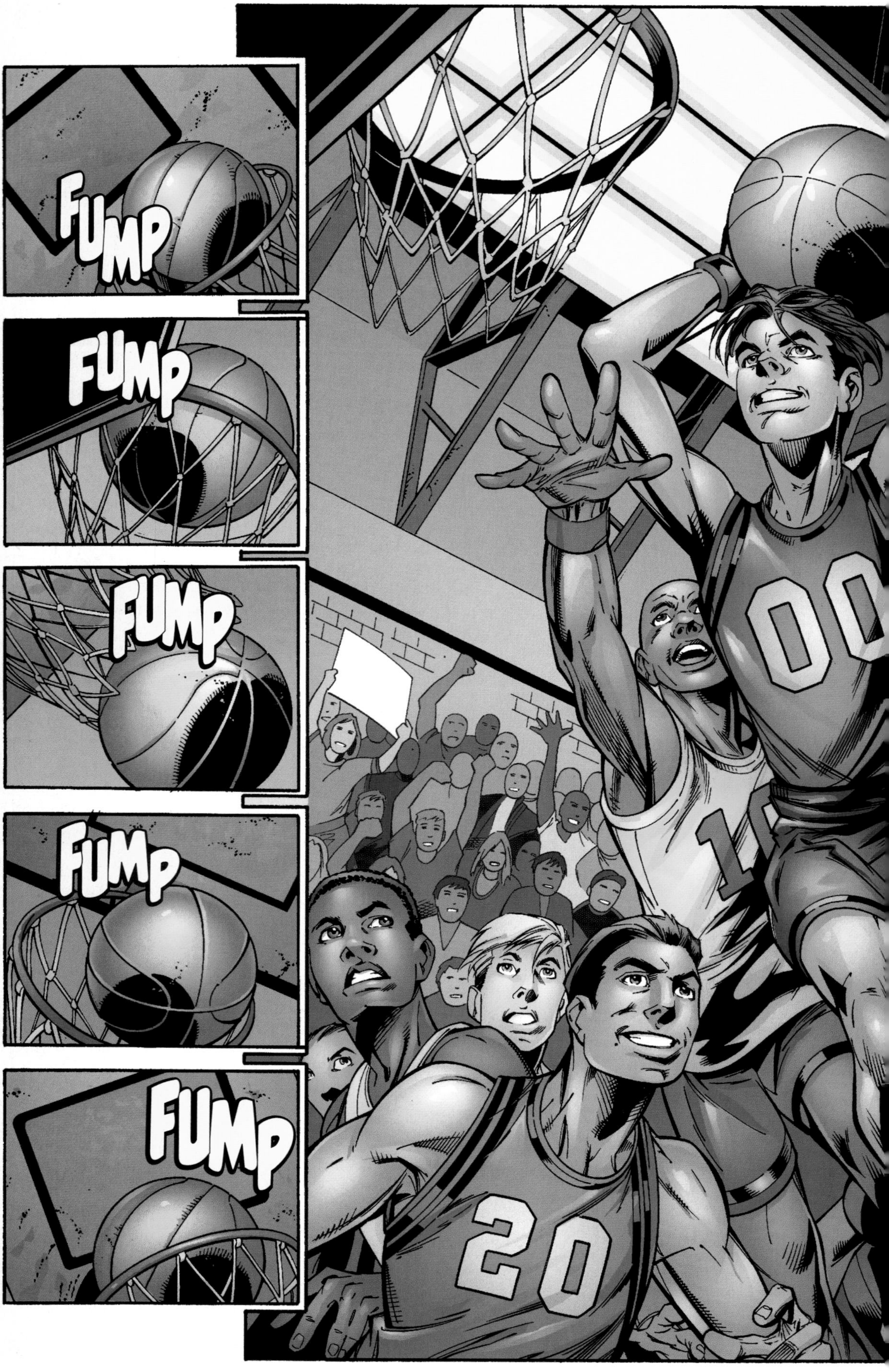
FUMP
FUMP
FUMP
FUMP
FUMP

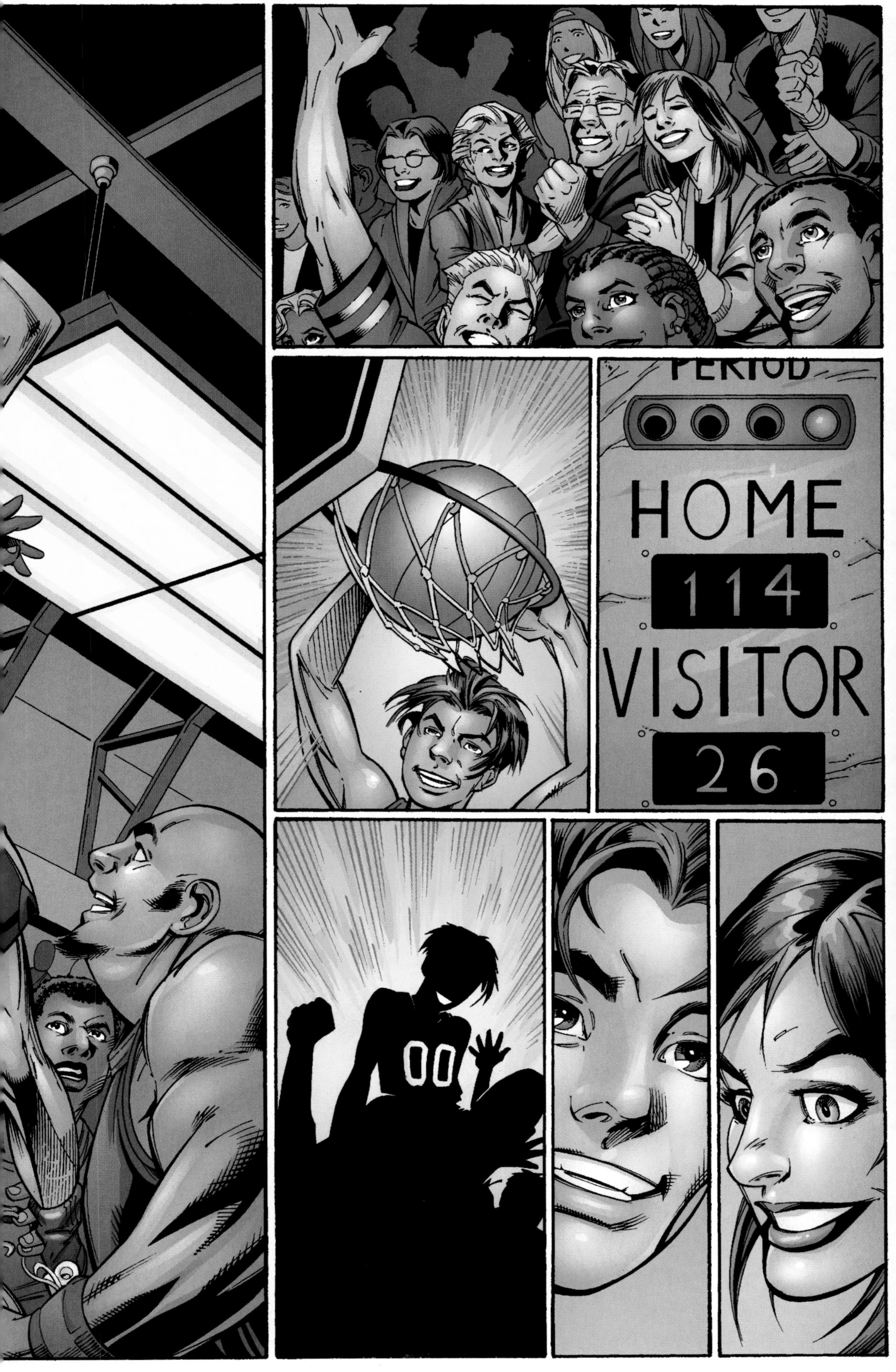
PERIOD
HOME
114
VISITOR
26
00

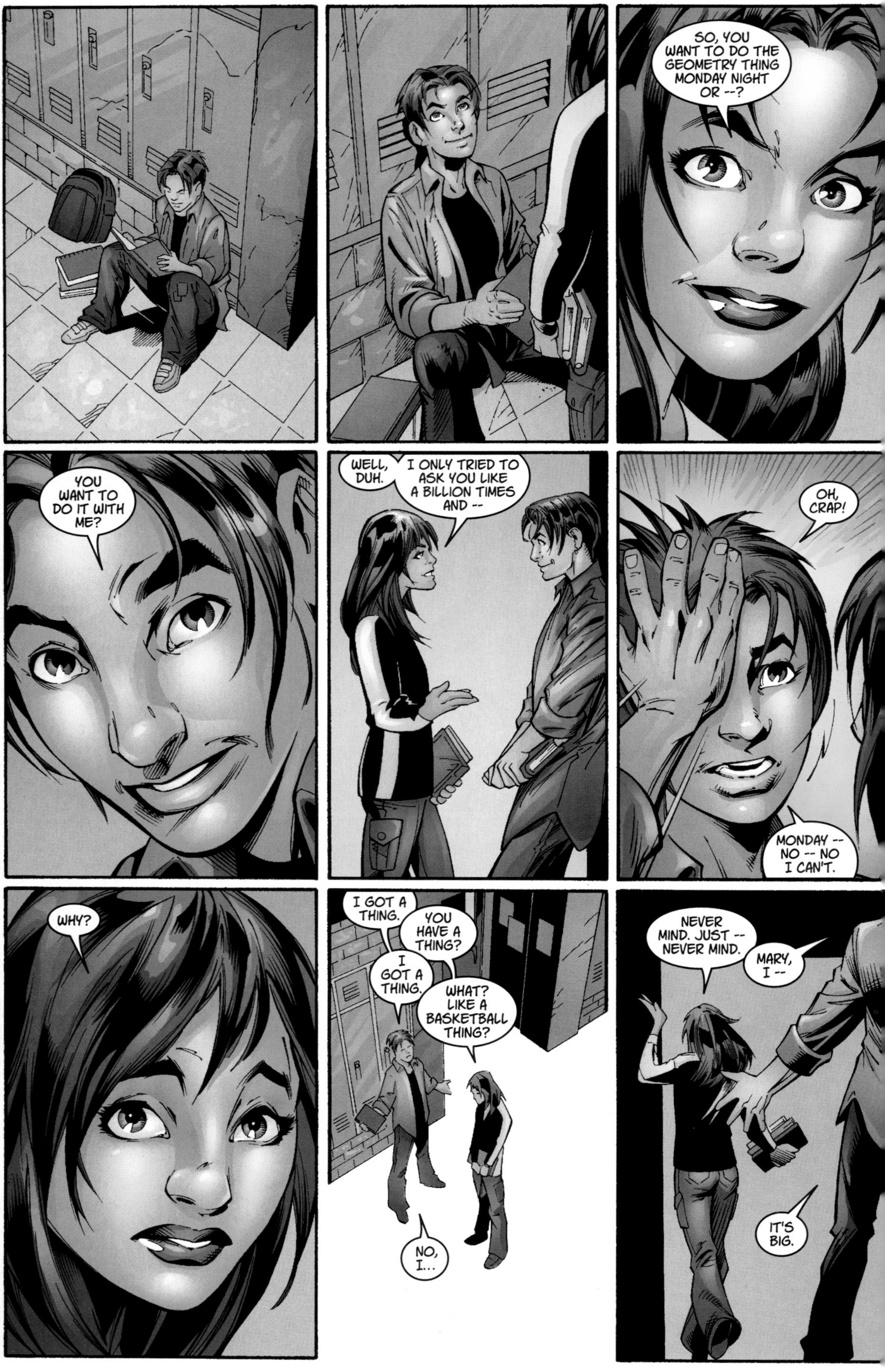
SO, YOU WANT TO DO THE GEOMETRY THING MONDAY NIGHT OR --?
YOU WANT TO DO IT WITH ME?
WELL, DUH.
I ONLY TRIED TO ASK YOU LIKE A BILLION TIMES AND --
OH, CRAP!
MONDAY -- NO -- NO I CAN'T.
WHY?
I GOT A THING.
YOU HAVE A THING?
I GOT A THING.
WHAT? LIKE A BASKETBALL THING?
NO, I...
NEVER MIND. JUST -- NEVER MIND.
MARY, I --
IT'S BIG.

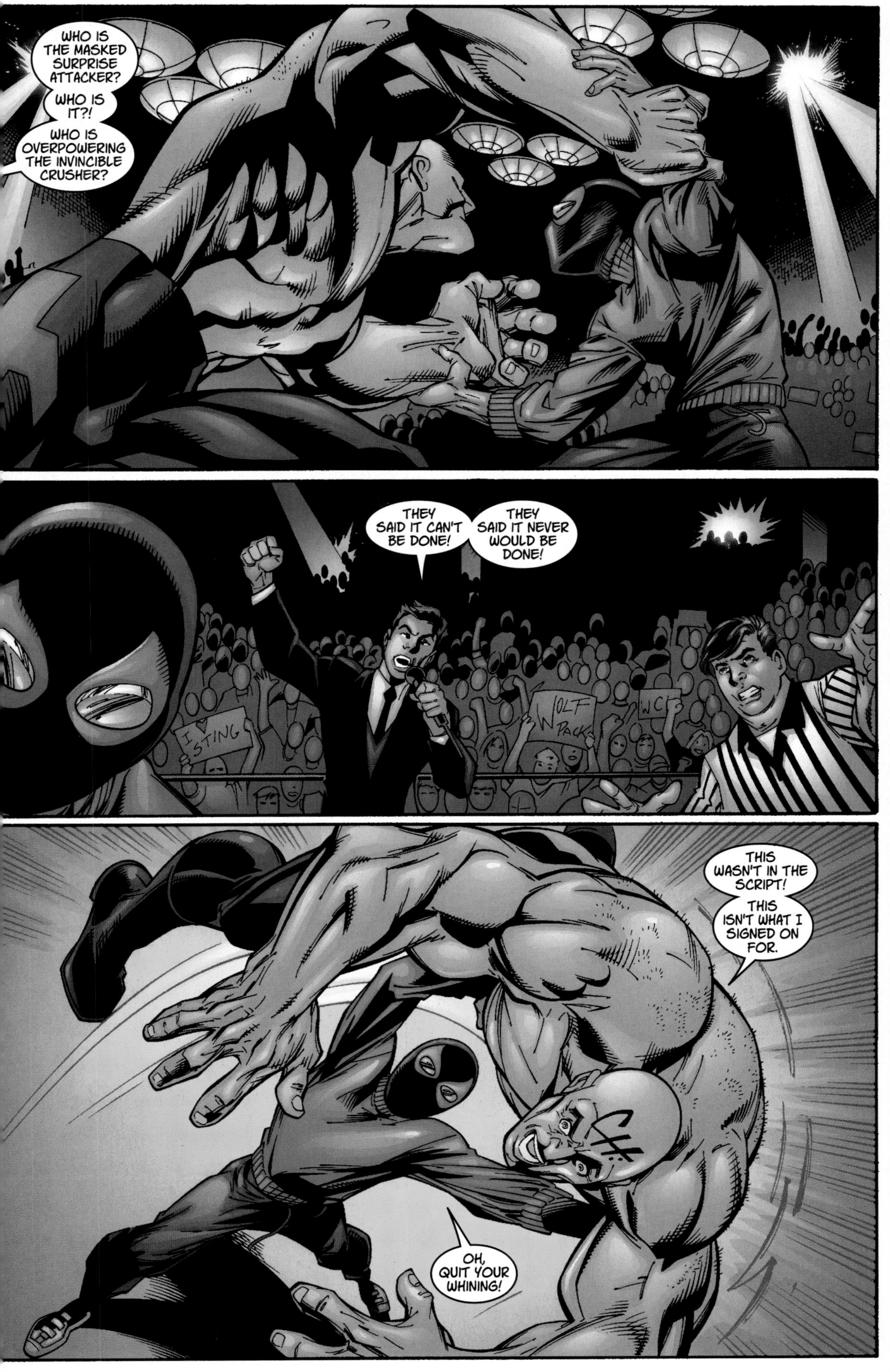
WHO IS THE MASKED SURPRISE ATTACKER?
WHO IS IT?!
WHO IS OVERPOWERING THE INVINCIBLE CRUSHER?
THEY SAID IT CAN'T BE DONE!
THEY SAID IT NEVER WOULD BE DONE!
THIS WASN'T IN THE SCRIPT!
THIS ISN'T WHAT I SIGNED ON FOR.
OH, QUIT YOUR WHINING!

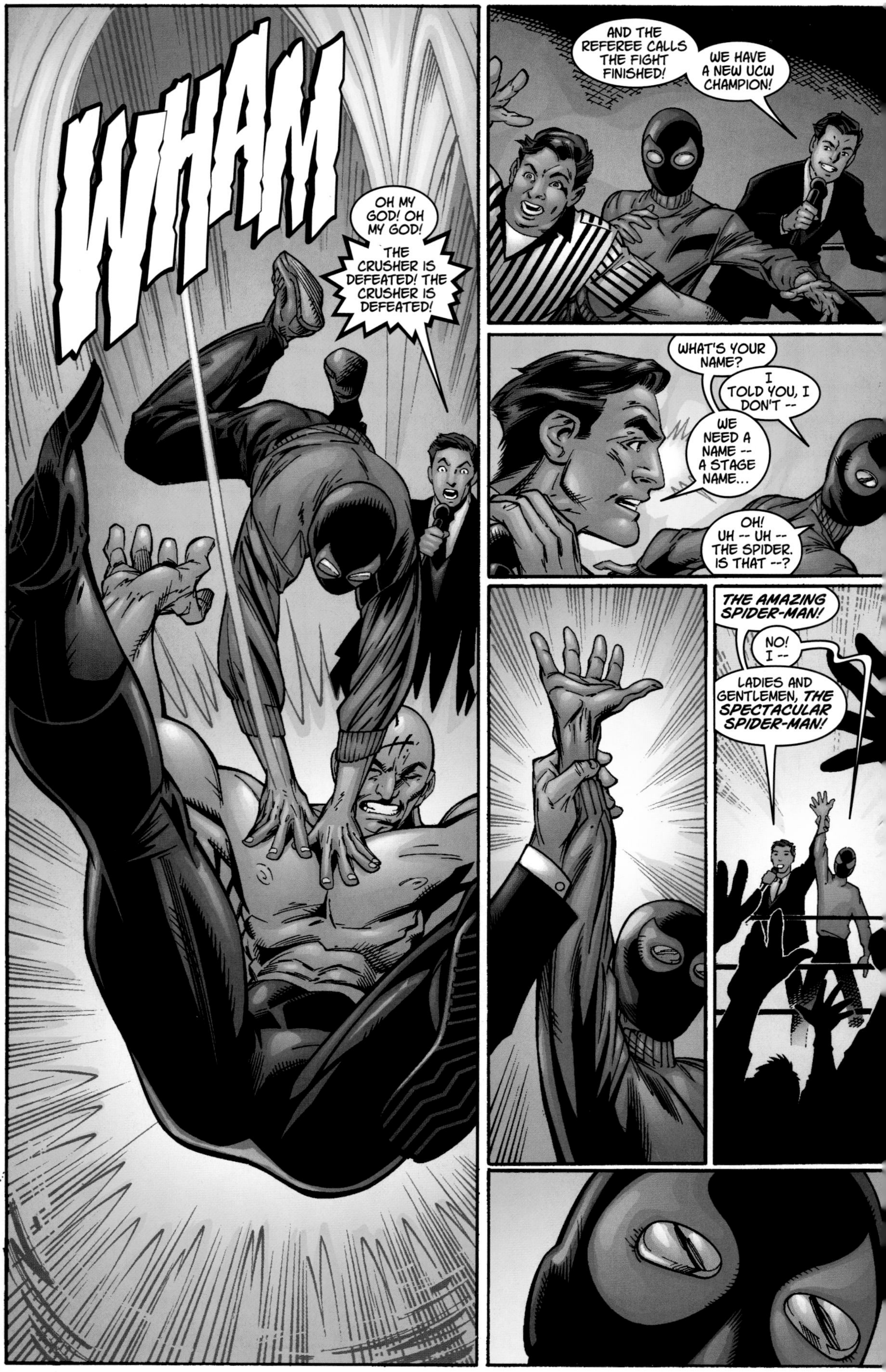
WHAM
OH MY GOD! OH MY GOD!
THE CRUSHER IS DEFEATED! THE CRUSHER IS DEFEATED!
AND THE REFEREE CALLS THE FIGHT FINISHED!
WE HAVE A NEW UCW CHAMPION!
WHAT'S YOUR NAME?
I TOLD YOU, I DON'T --
WE NEED A NAME -- A STAGE NAME...
OH! UH -- UH -- THE SPIDER. IS THAT --?
THE AMAZING SPIDER-MAN!
NO! I --
LADIES AND GENTLEMEN, THE SPECTACULAR SPIDER-MAN!

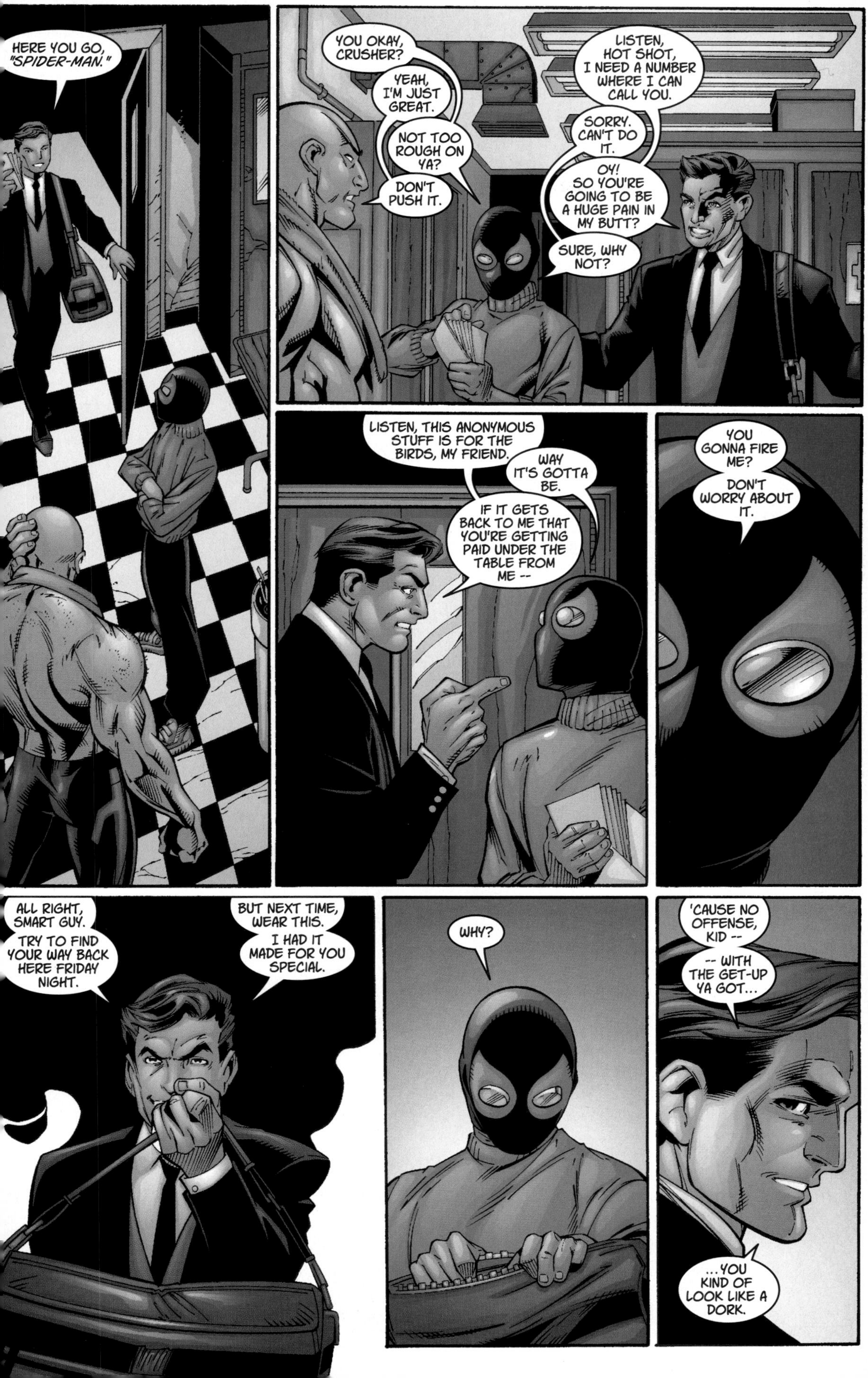
HERE YOU GO, "SPIDER-MAN."
YOU OKAY, CRUSHER?
YEAH, I'M JUST GREAT.
NOT TOO ROUGH ON YA?
DON'T PUSH IT.
LISTEN, HOT SHOT, I NEED A NUMBER WHERE I CAN CALL YOU.
SORRY. CAN'T DO IT.
OY! SO YOU'RE GOING TO BE A HUGE PAIN IN MY BUTT?
SURE, WHY NOT?
LISTEN, THIS ANONYMOUS STUFF IS FOR THE BIRDS, MY FRIEND.
WAY IT'S GOTTA BE.
IF IT GETS BACK TO ME THAT YOU'RE GETTING PAID UNDER THE TABLE FROM ME --
YOU GONNA FIRE ME?
DON'T WORRY ABOUT IT.
ALL RIGHT, SMART GUY.
TRY TO FIND YOUR WAY BACK HERE FRIDAY NIGHT.
BUT NEXT TIME, WEAR THIS.
I HAD IT MADE FOR YOU SPECIAL.
WHY?
'CAUSE NO OFFENSE, KID --
-- WITH THE GET-UP YA GOT...
...YOU KIND OF LOOK LIKE A DORK.

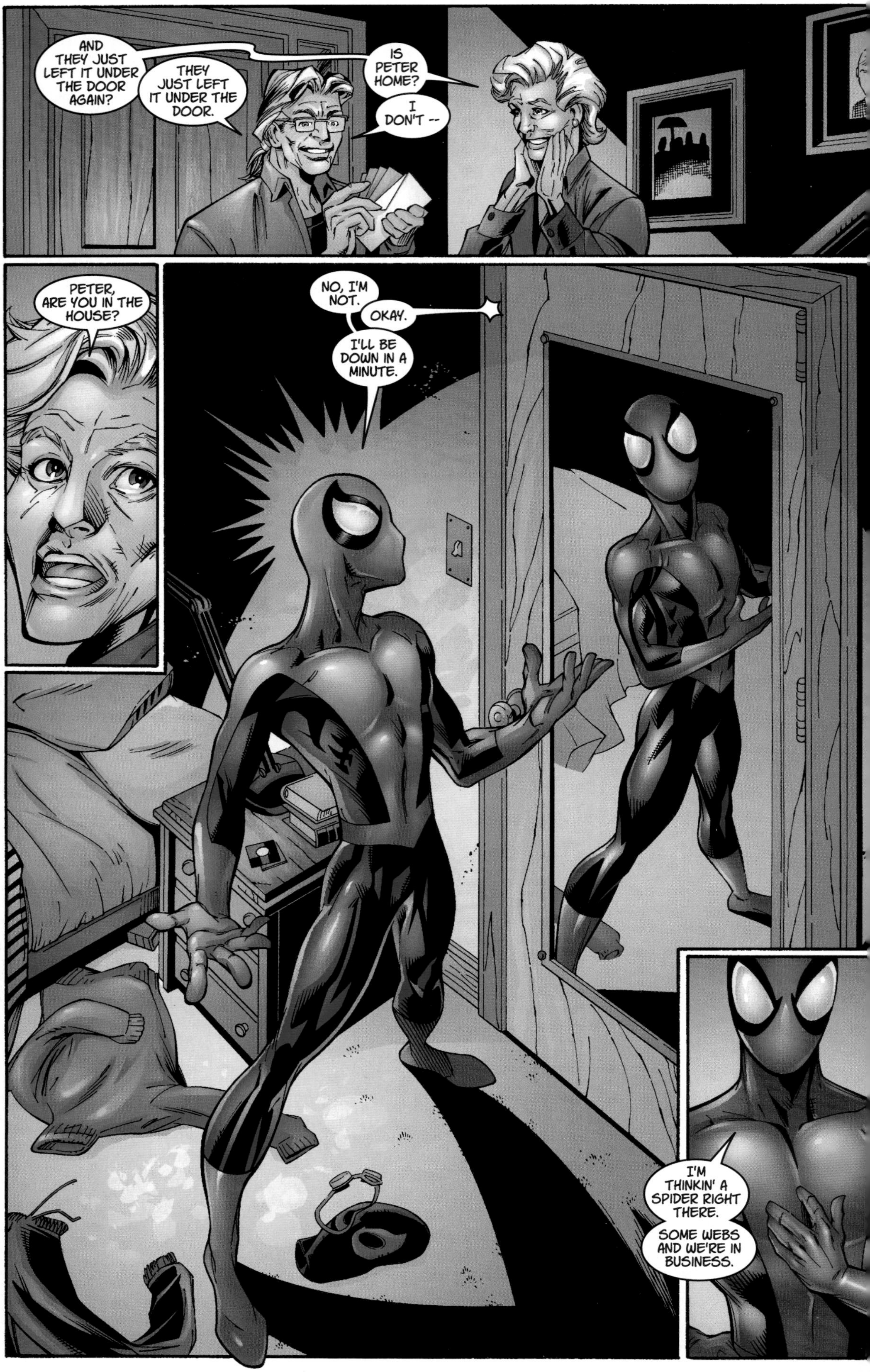

AND THEY JUST LEFT IT UNDER THE DOOR AGAIN?
THEY JUST LEFT IT UNDER THE DOOR.
IS PETER HOME?
I DON'T --
PETER, ARE YOU IN THE HOUSE?
NO, I'M NOT.
OKAY.
I'LL BE DOWN IN A MINUTE.
I'M THINKIN' A SPIDER RIGHT THERE.
SOME WEBS AND WE'RE IN BUSINESS.

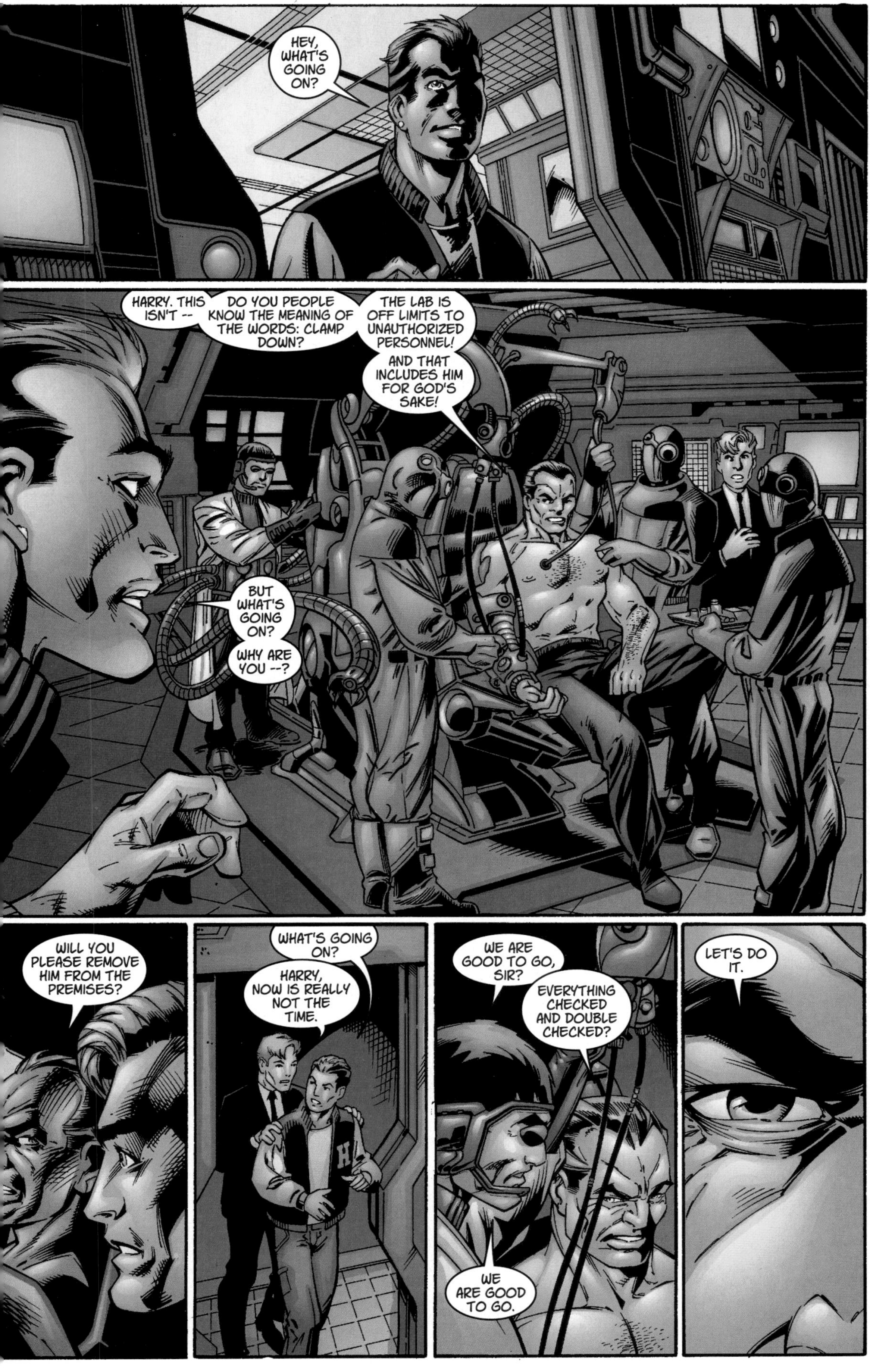
HEY, WHAT'S GOING ON?
HARRY. THIS ISN'T --
DO YOU PEOPLE KNOW THE MEANING OF THE WORDS: CLAMP DOWN?
THE LAB IS OFF LIMITS TO UNAUTHORIZED PERSONNEL!
AND THAT INCLUDES HIM FOR GOD'S SAKE!
BUT WHAT'S GOING ON?
WHY ARE YOU --?
WILL YOU PLEASE REMOVE HIM FROM THE PREMISES?
WHAT'S GOING ON?
HARRY, NOW IS REALLY NOT THE TIME.
WE ARE GOOD TO GO, SIR?
EVERYTHING CHECKED AND DOUBLE CHECKED?
WE ARE GOOD TO GO.
LET'S DO IT.

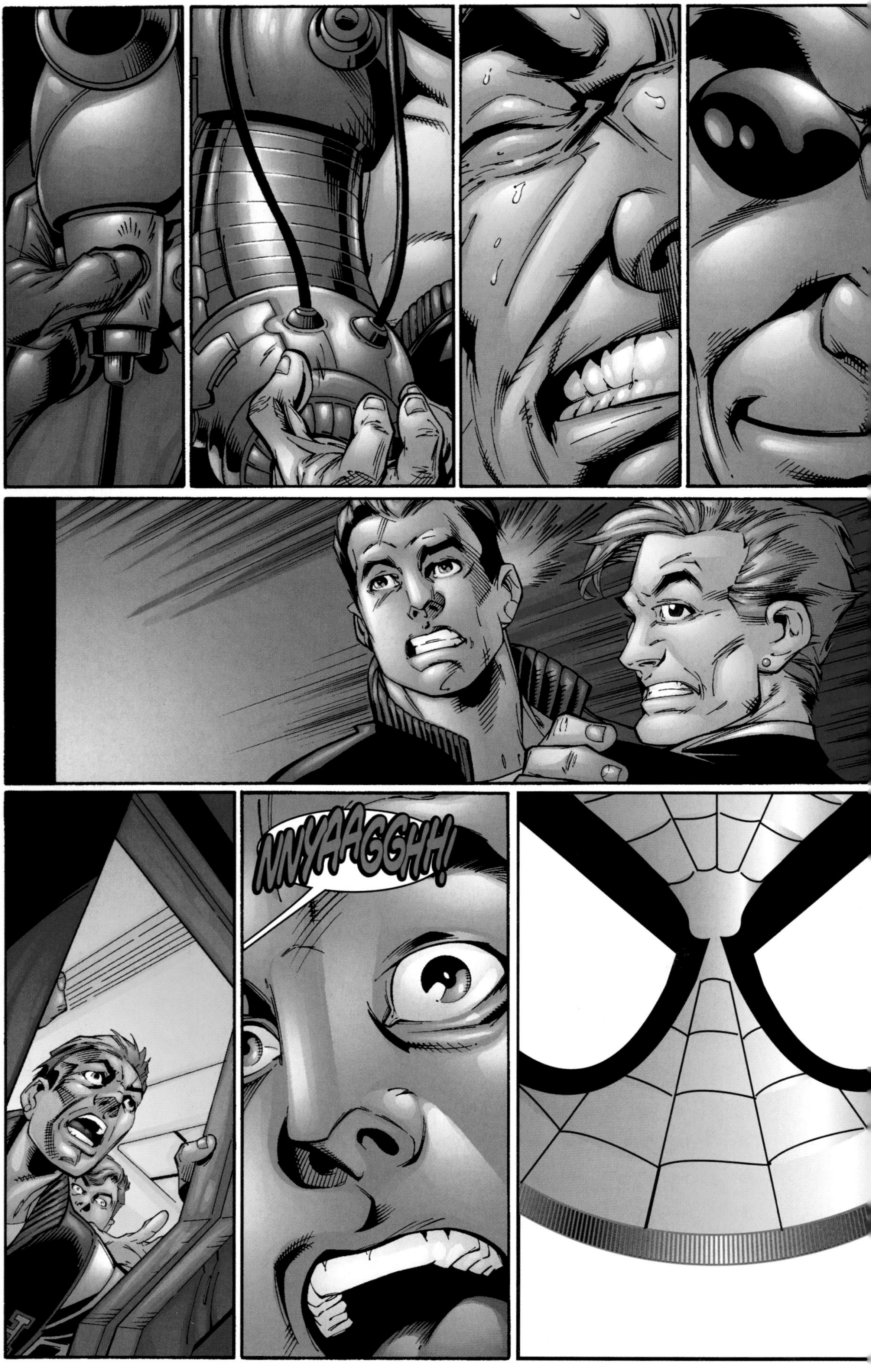
NNYAAGGHH!

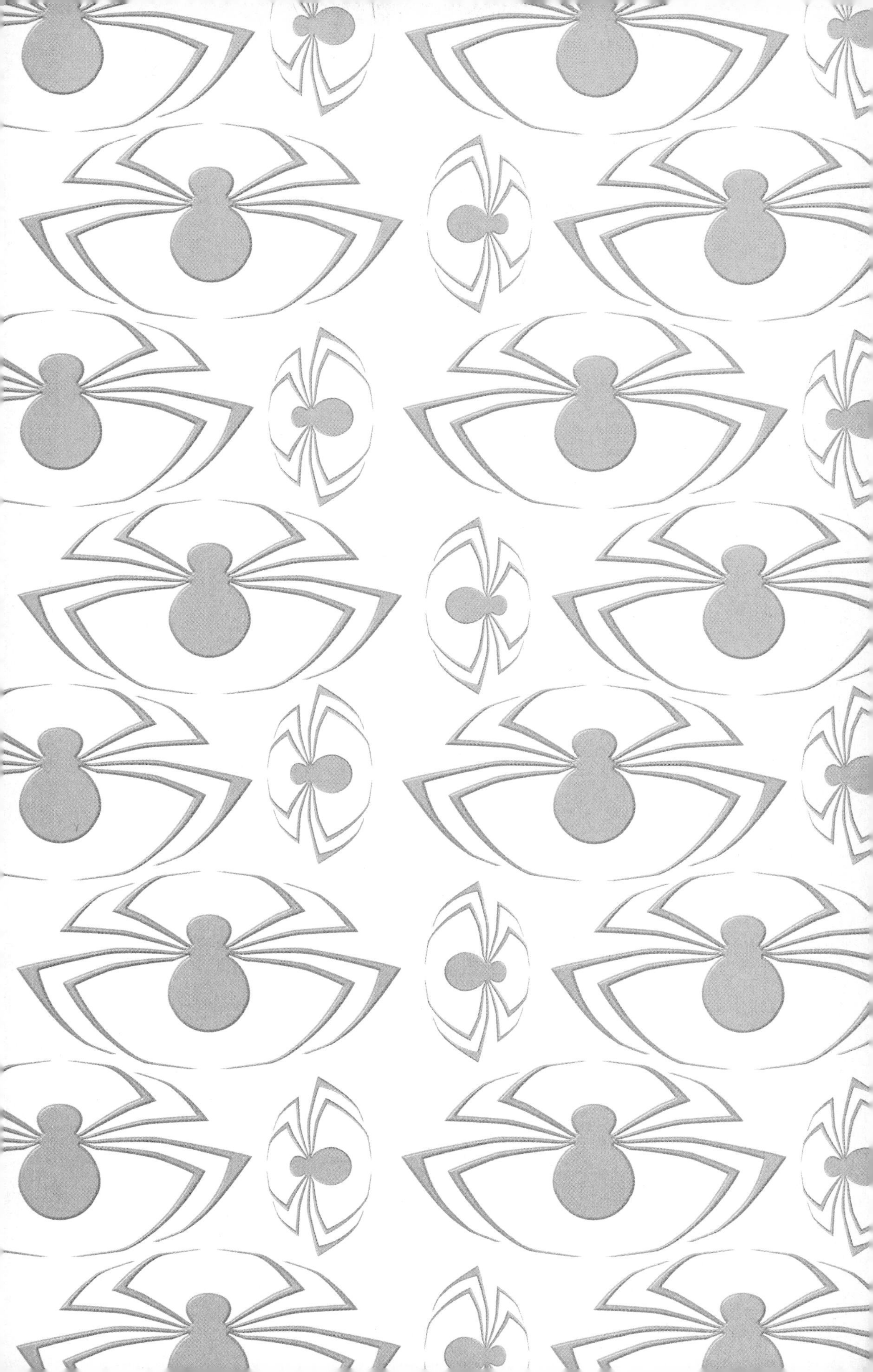

4

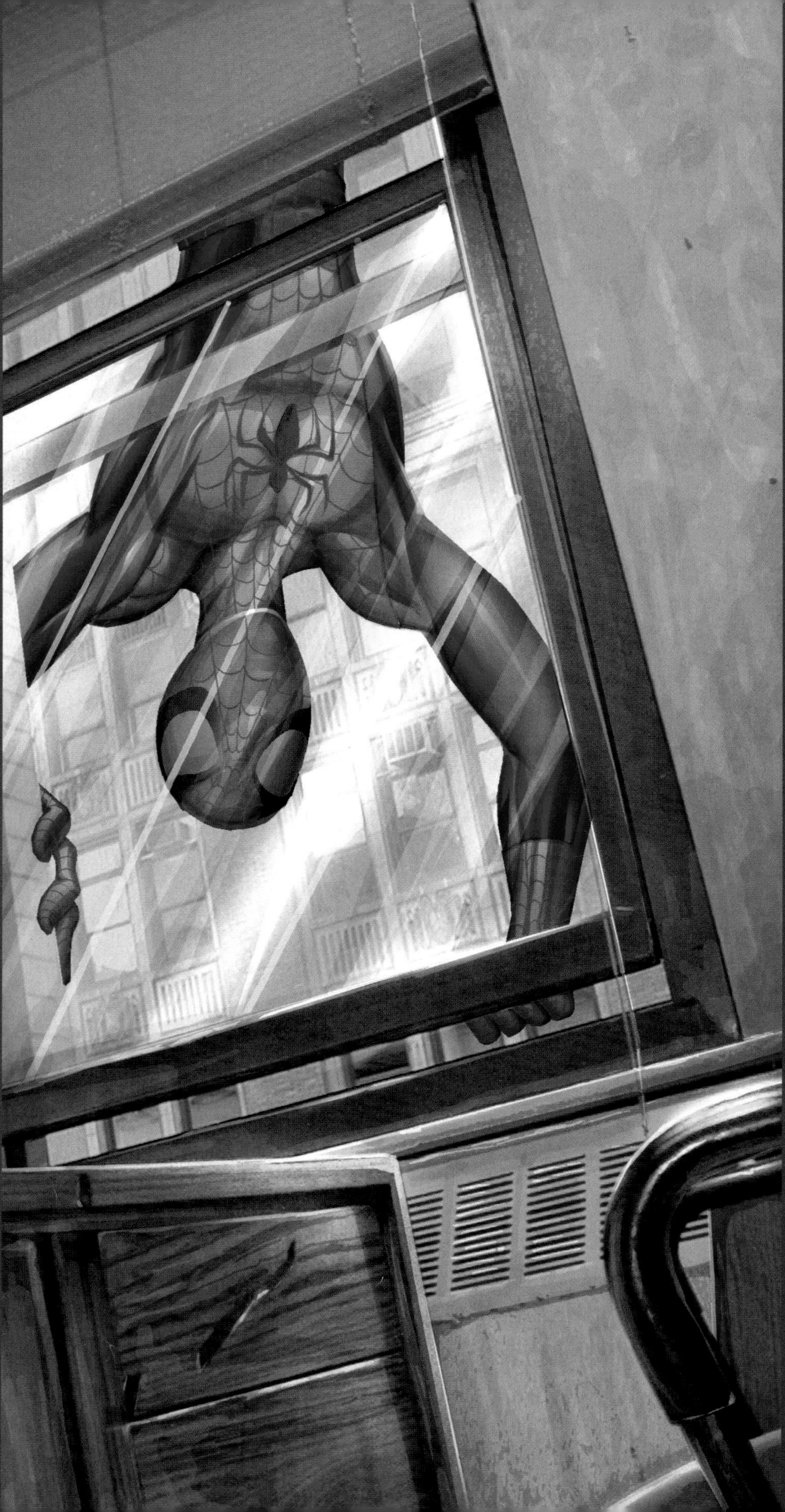

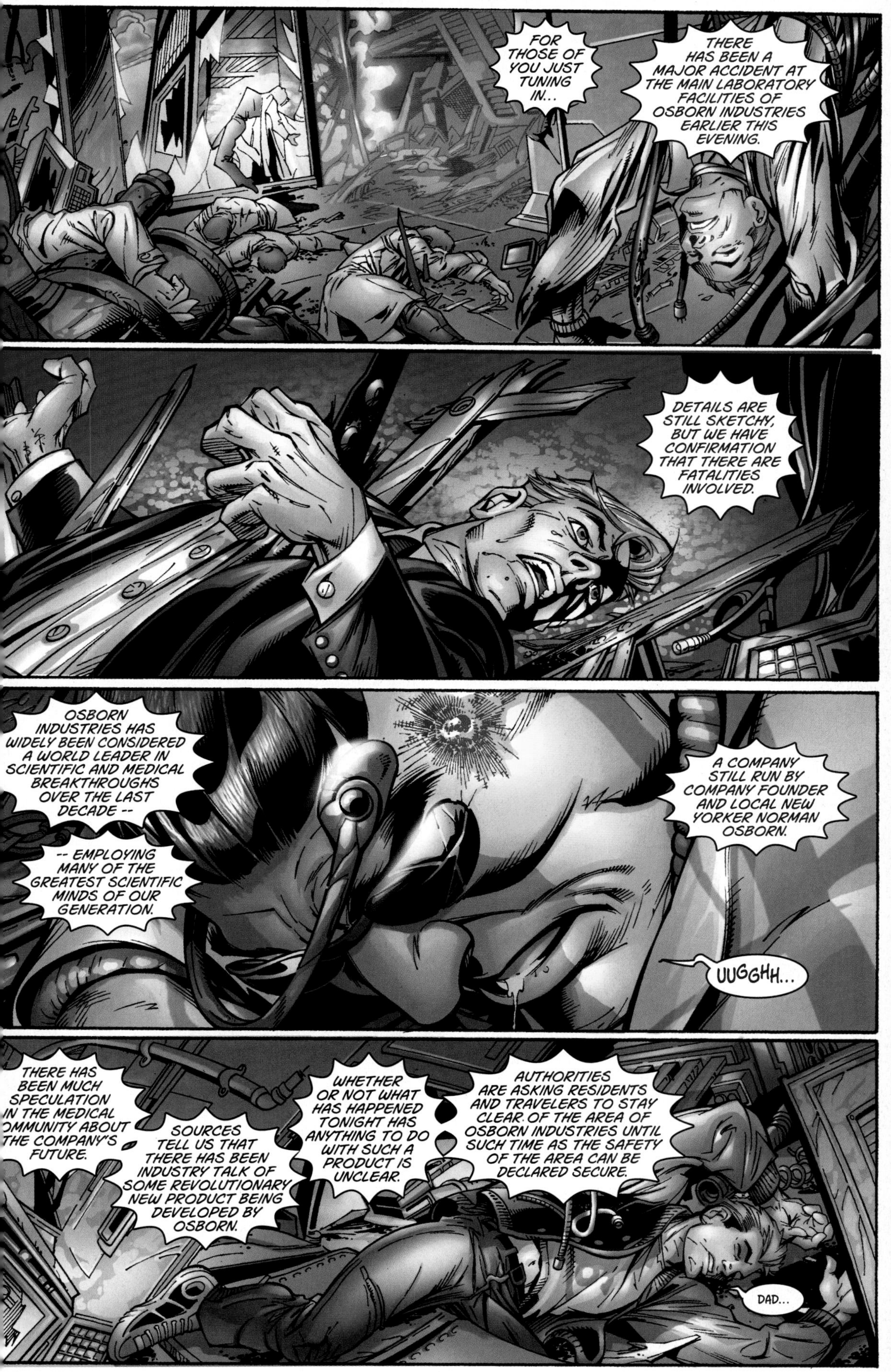
FOR THOSE OF YOU JUST TUNING IN...
THERE HAS BEEN A MAJOR ACCIDENT AT THE MAIN LABORATORY FACILITIES OF OSBORN INDUSTRIES EARLIER THIS EVENING.
DETAILS ARE STILL SKETCHY, BUT WE HAVE CONFIRMATION THAT THERE ARE FATALITIES INVOLVED.
OSBORN INDUSTRIES HAS WIDELY BEEN CONSIDERED A WORLD LEADER IN SCIENTIFIC AND MEDICAL BREAKTHROUGHS OVER THE LAST DECADE --
-- EMPLOYING MANY OF THE GREATEST SCIENTIFIC MINDS OF OUR GENERATION.
A COMPANY STILL RUN BY COMPANY FOUNDER AND LOCAL NEW YORKER NORMAN OSBORN.
UUGGHH...
THERE HAS BEEN MUCH SPECULATION IN THE MEDICAL COMMUNITY ABOUT THE COMPANY'S FUTURE.
SOURCES TELL US THAT THERE HAS BEEN INDUSTRY TALK OF SOME REVOLUTIONARY NEW PRODUCT BEING DEVELOPED BY OSBORN.
WHETHER OR NOT WHAT HAS HAPPENED TONIGHT HAS ANYTHING TO DO WITH SUCH A PRODUCT IS UNCLEAR.
AUTHORITIES ARE ASKING RESIDENTS AND TRAVELERS TO STAY CLEAR OF THE AREA OF OSBORN INDUSTRIES UNTIL SUCH TIME AS THE SAFETY OF THE AREA CAN BE DECLARED SECURE.
DAD...

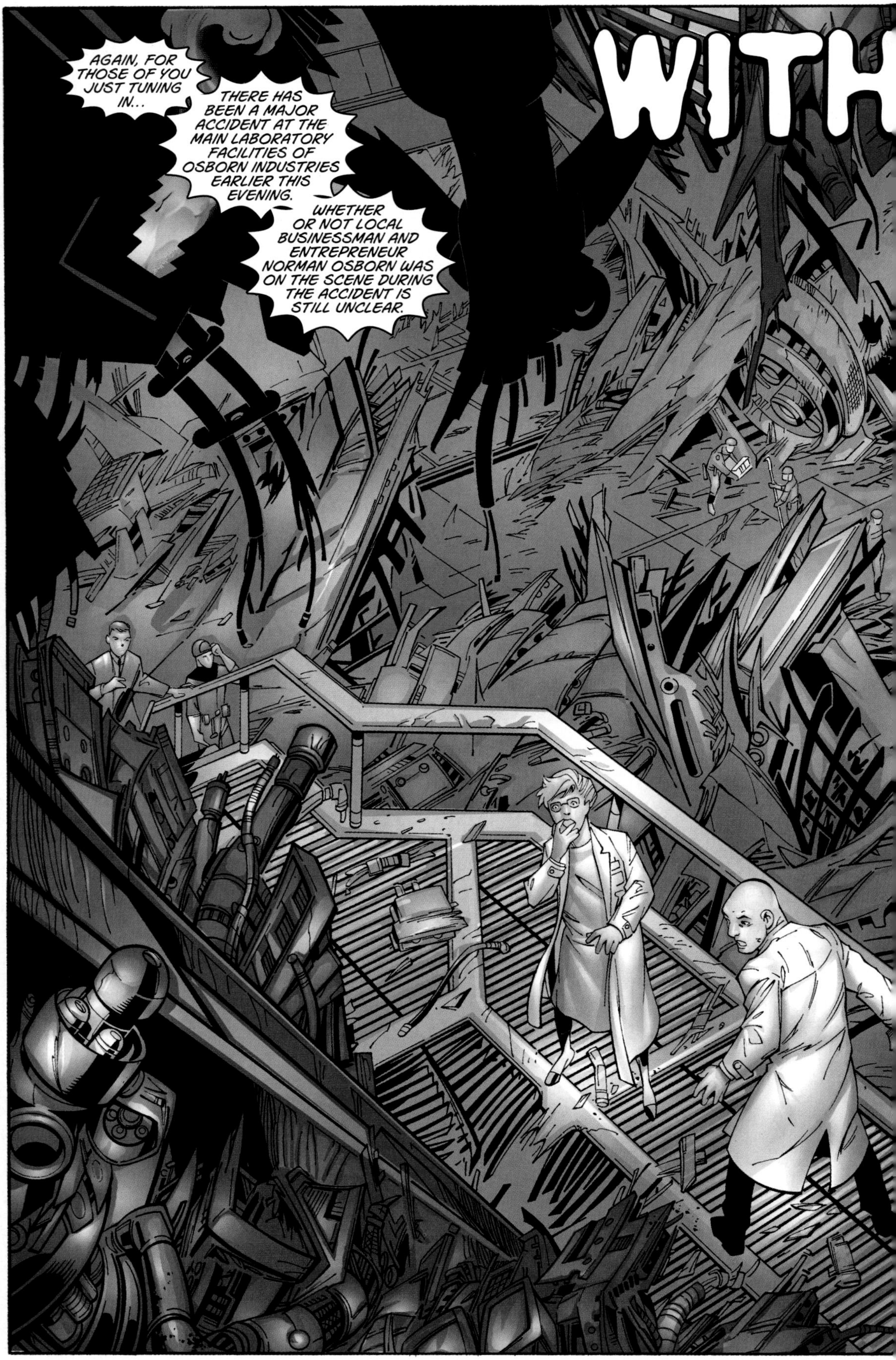
WITH
AGAIN, FOR THOSE OF YOU JUST TUNING IN...
THERE HAS BEEN A MAJOR ACCIDENT AT THE MAIN LABORATORY FACILITIES OF OSBORN INDUSTRIES EARLIER THIS EVENING.
WHETHER OR NOT LOCAL BUSINESSMAN AND ENTREPRENEUR NORMAN OSBORN WAS ON THE SCENE DURING THE ACCIDENT IS STILL UNCLEAR.

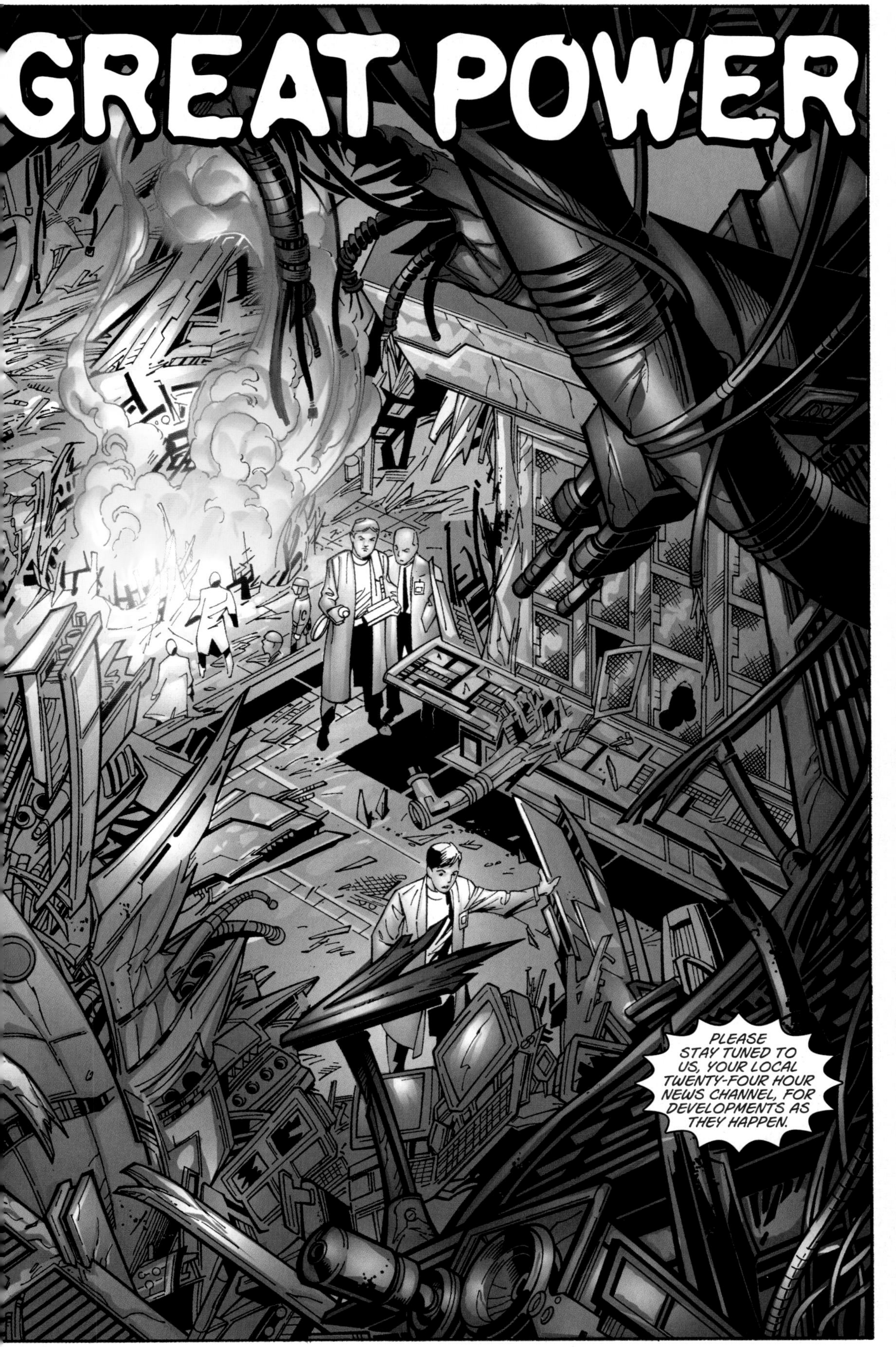
GREAT POWER
PLEASE STAY TUNED TO US, YOUR LOCAL TWENTY-FOUR HOUR NEWS CHANNEL, FOR DEVELOPMENTS AS THEY HAPPEN.

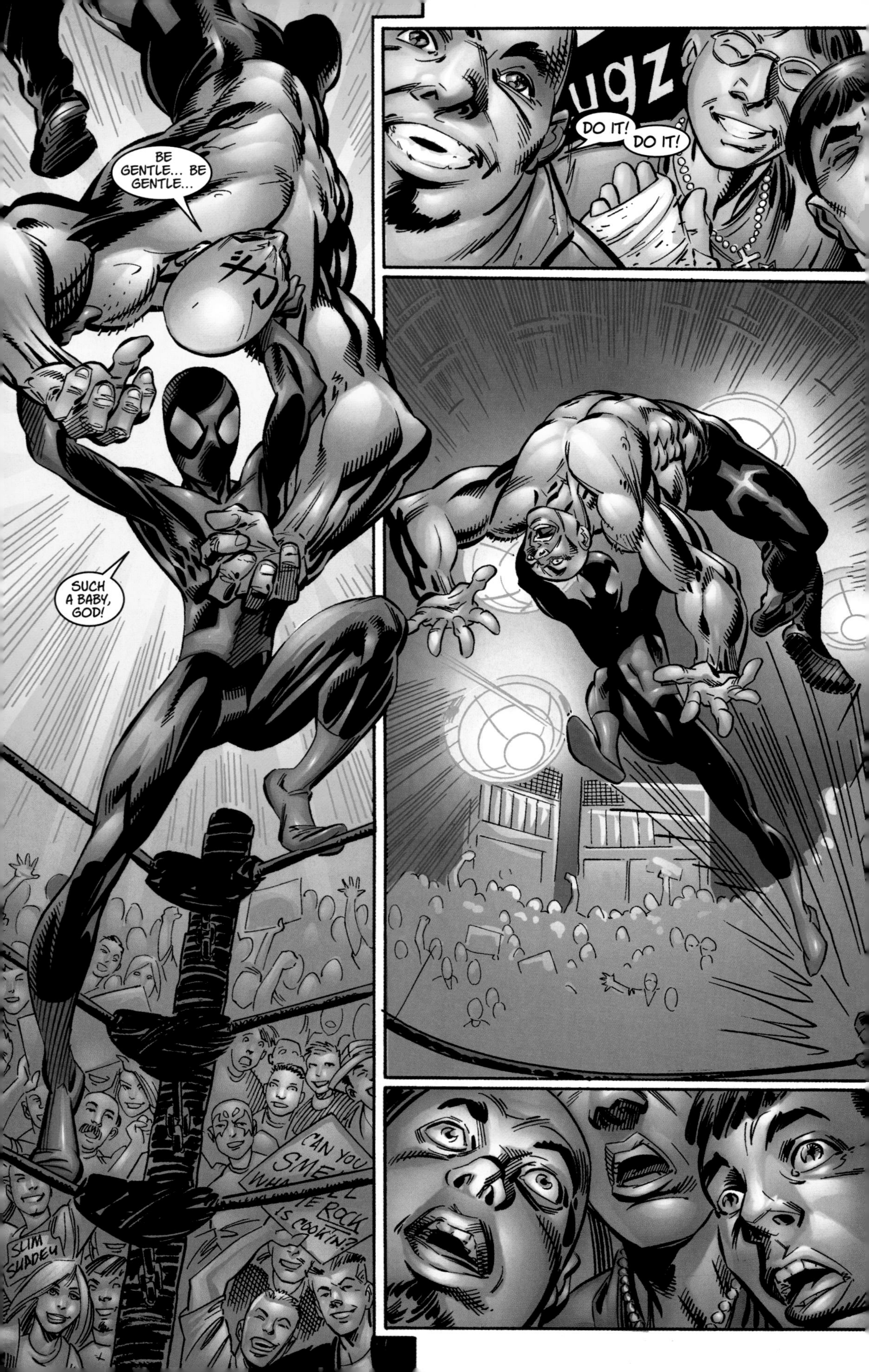
BE GENTLE... BE GENTLE...
SUCH A BABY, GOD!
DO IT!
DO IT!
SLIM SUDDEN
CAN YOU SMELL WHAT THE ROCK IS COOKIN'?

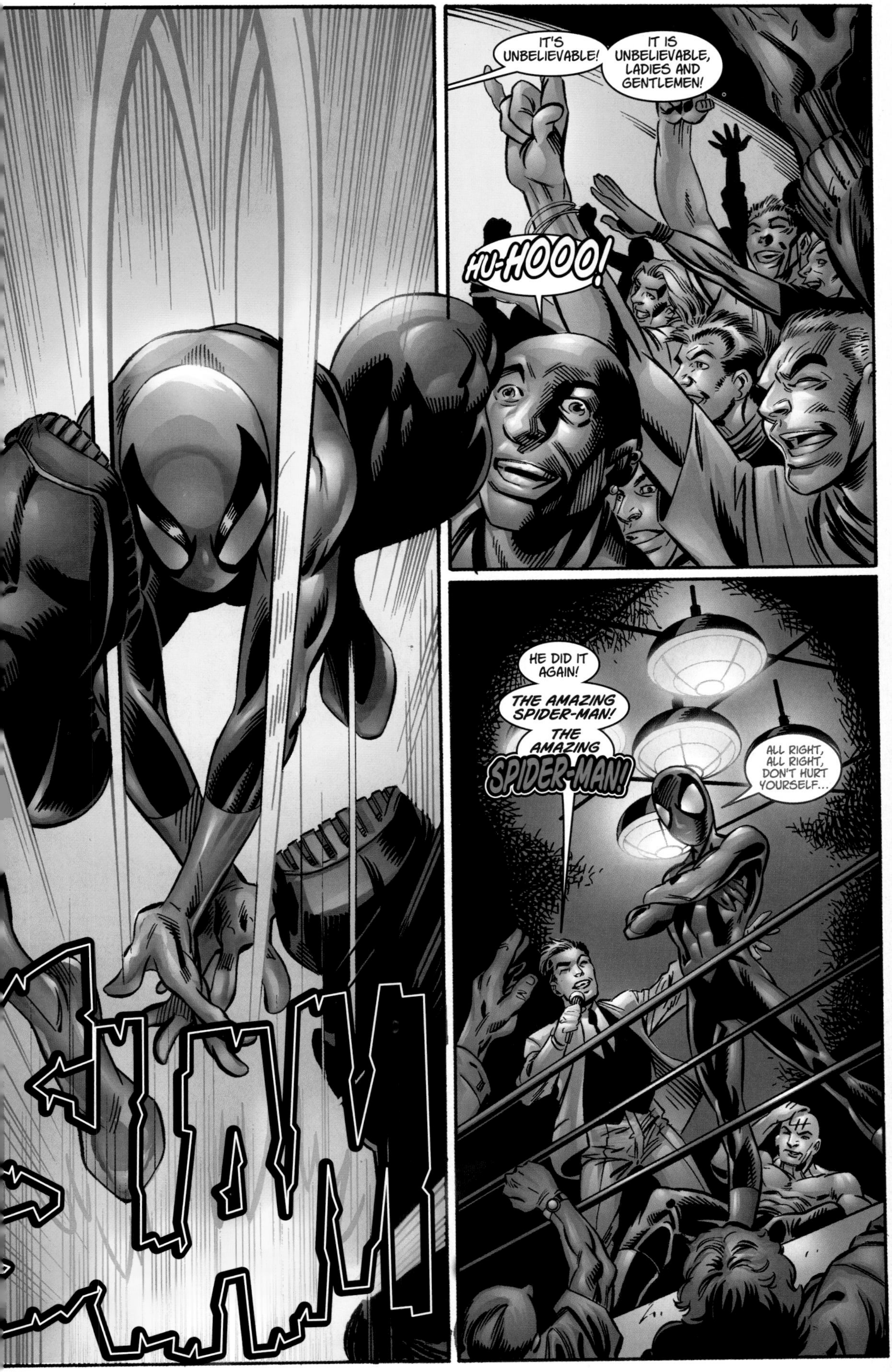
IT'S UNBELIEVABLE!
IT IS UNBELIEVABLE, LADIES AND GENTLEMEN!
HU-HOOO!
HE DID IT AGAIN!
THE AMAZING SPIDER-MAN!
THE AMAZING SPIDER-MAN!
ALL RIGHT, ALL RIGHT, DON'T HURT YOURSELF...

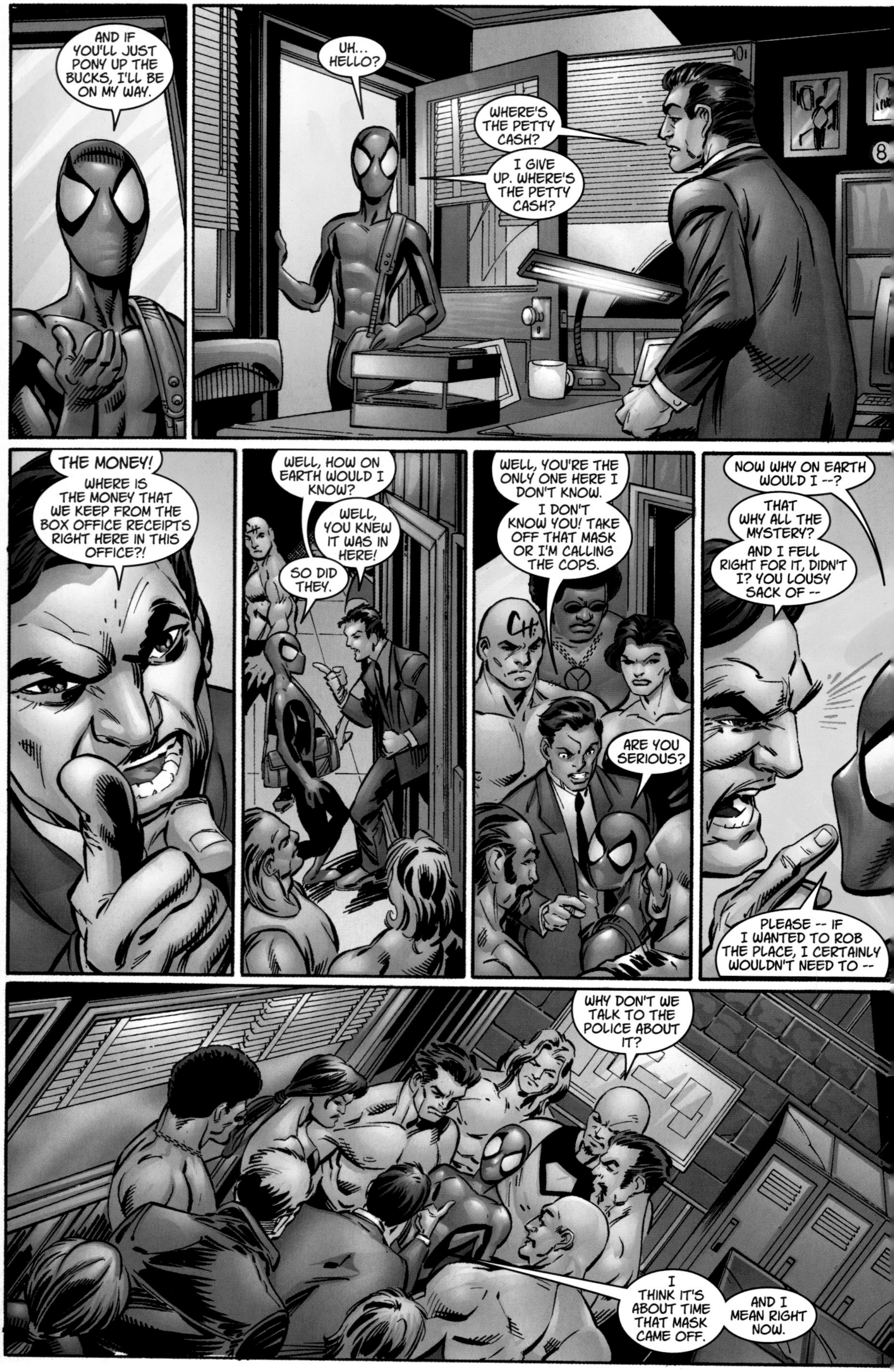
AND IF YOU'LL JUST PONY UP THE BUCKS, I'LL BE ON MY WAY.
UH... HELLO?
WHERE'S THE PETTY CASH?
I GIVE UP. WHERE'S THE PETTY CASH?
8
THE MONEY! WHERE IS THE MONEY THAT WE KEEP FROM THE BOX OFFICE RECEIPTS RIGHT HERE IN THIS OFFICE?!
WELL, HOW ON EARTH WOULD I KNOW?
WELL, YOU KNEW IT WAS IN HERE!
SO DID THEY.
WELL, YOU'RE THE ONLY ONE HERE I DON'T KNOW.
I DON'T KNOW YOU! TAKE OFF THAT MASK OR I'M CALLING THE COPS.
ARE YOU SERIOUS?
NOW WHY ON EARTH WOULD I --?
THAT WHY ALL THE MYSTERY?
AND I FELL RIGHT FOR IT, DIDN'T I? YOU LOUSY SACK OF --
PLEASE -- IF I WANTED TO ROB THE PLACE, I CERTAINLY WOULDN'T NEED TO --
WHY DON'T WE TALK TO THE POLICE ABOUT IT?
I THINK IT'S ABOUT TIME THAT MASK CAME OFF.
AND I MEAN RIGHT NOW.

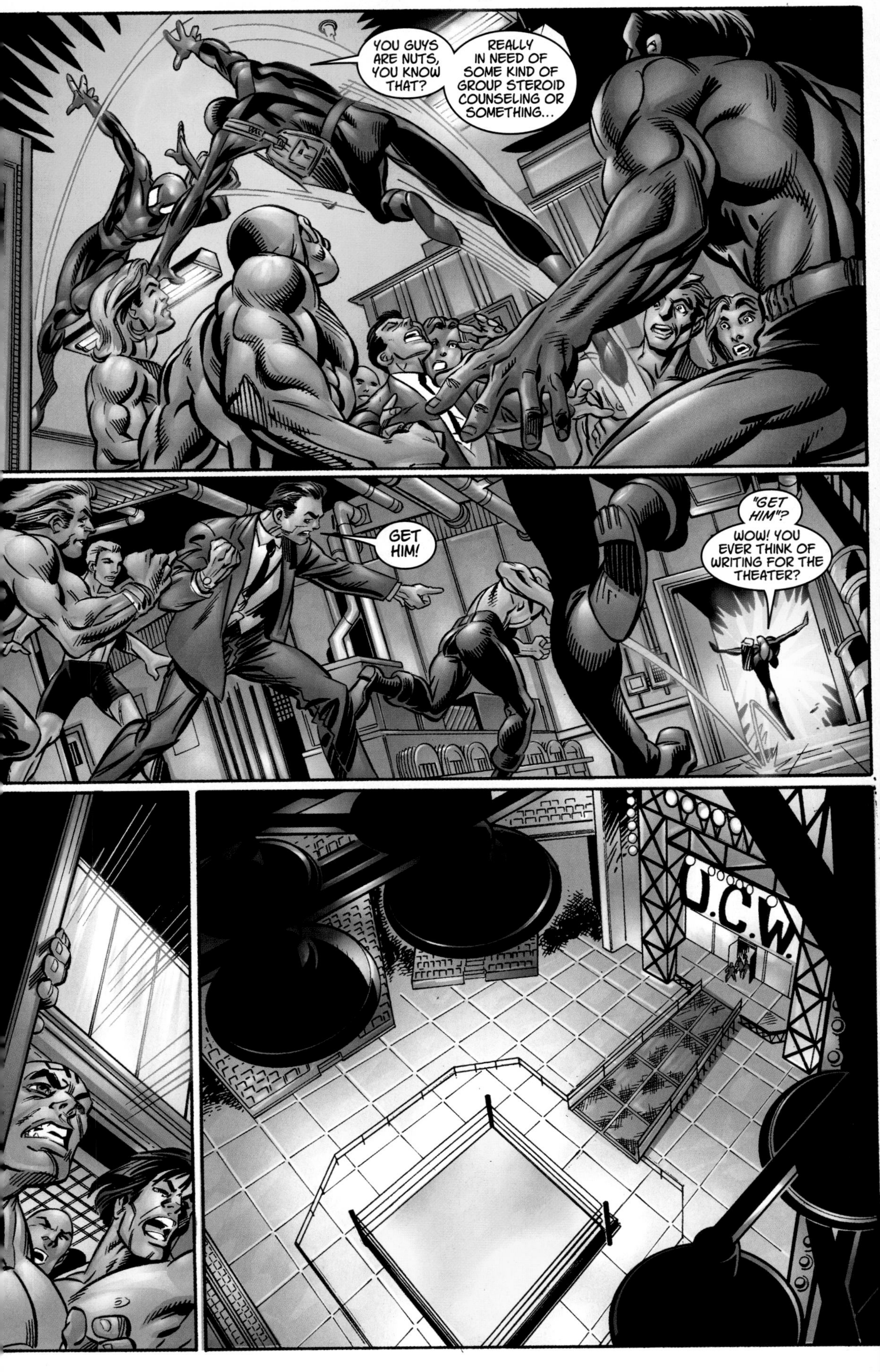
YOU GUYS ARE NUTS, YOU KNOW THAT?
REALLY IN NEED OF SOME KIND OF GROUP STEROID COUNSELING OR SOMETHING...
GET HIM!
"GET HIM"?
WOW! YOU EVER THINK OF WRITING FOR THE THEATER?
U.C.W.

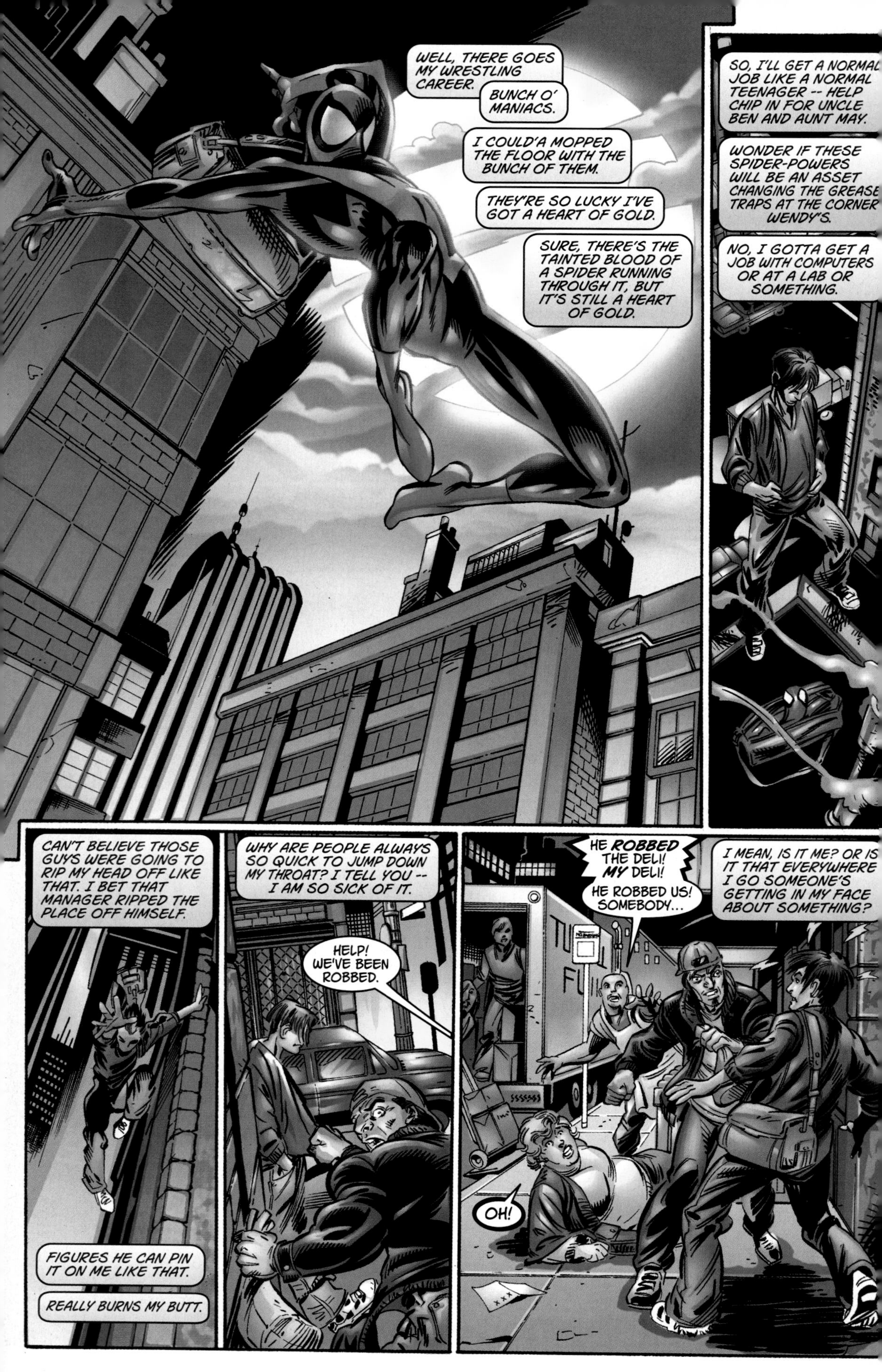

WELL, THERE GOES MY WRESTLING CAREER.
BUNCH O' MANIACS.
I COULD'A MOPPED THE FLOOR WITH THE BUNCH OF THEM.
THEY'RE SO LUCKY I'VE GOT A HEART OF GOLD.
SURE, THERE'S THE TAINTED BLOOD OF A SPIDER RUNNING THROUGH IT, BUT IT'S STILL A HEART OF GOLD.
SO, I'LL GET A NORMAL JOB LIKE A NORMAL TEENAGER -- HELP CHIP IN FOR UNCLE BEN AND AUNT MAY.
WONDER IF THESE SPIDER-POWERS WILL BE AN ASSET CHANGING THE GREASE TRAPS AT THE CORNER WENDY'S.
NO, I GOTTA GET A JOB WITH COMPUTERS OR AT A LAB OR SOMETHING.
CAN'T BELIEVE THOSE GUYS WERE GOING TO RIP MY HEAD OFF LIKE THAT. I BET THAT MANAGER RIPPED THE PLACE OFF HIMSELF.
FIGURES HE CAN PIN IT ON ME LIKE THAT.
REALLY BURNS MY BUTT.
WHY ARE PEOPLE ALWAYS SO QUICK TO JUMP DOWN MY THROAT? I TELL YOU -- I AM SO SICK OF IT.
HELP! WE'VE BEEN ROBBED.
HE ROBBED THE DELI! MY DELI!
HE ROBBED US! SOMEBODY...
I MEAN, IS IT ME? OR IS IT THAT EVERYWHERE I GO SOMEONE'S GETTING IN MY FACE ABOUT SOMETHING?
OH!

HEY! GET...

GET OUTTA MY WAY! OUT!

SHALL WE DANCE?

JEEZ! CAN YOU BELIEVE THAT GUY?

"RESERVOIR DORK!"

WHAT?

WHAT WAS THAT?

WHAT WAS WHAT?

WHY DIDN'T YOU STOP HIM?

ALL YOU HAD TO DO WAS TRIP HIM.

STICK YOUR FOOT OUT AND HE'S KISSING PAVEMENT!

WHATEVER...

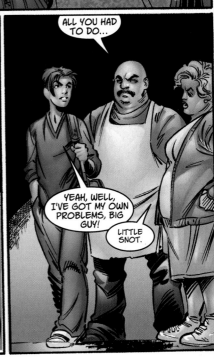

ALL YOU HAD TO DO...

YEAH, WELL, I'VE GOT MY OWN PROBLEMS, BIG GUY!

LITTLE SNOT.

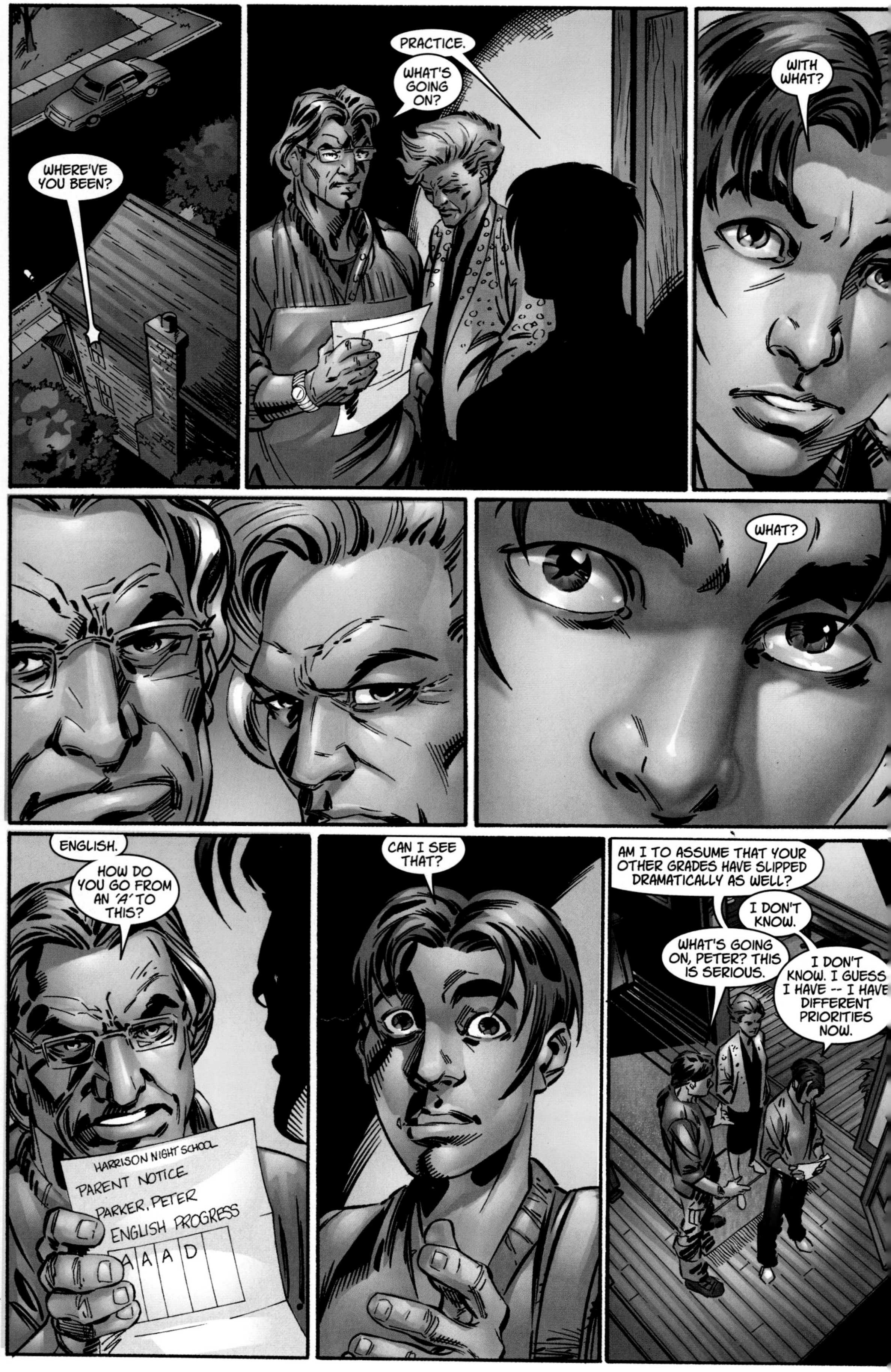
WHERE'VE YOU BEEN?
PRACTICE.
WHAT'S GOING ON?
WITH WHAT?
WHAT?
ENGLISH.
HOW DO YOU GO FROM AN 'A' TO THIS?
HARRISON NIGHT SCHOOL
PARENT NOTICE
PARKER, PETER
ENGLISH PROGRESS
A A A D
CAN I SEE THAT?
AM I TO ASSUME THAT YOUR OTHER GRADES HAVE SLIPPED DRAMATICALLY AS WELL?
I DON'T KNOW.
WHAT'S GOING ON, PETER? THIS IS SERIOUS.
I DON'T KNOW. I GUESS I HAVE -- I HAVE DIFFERENT PRIORITIES NOW.

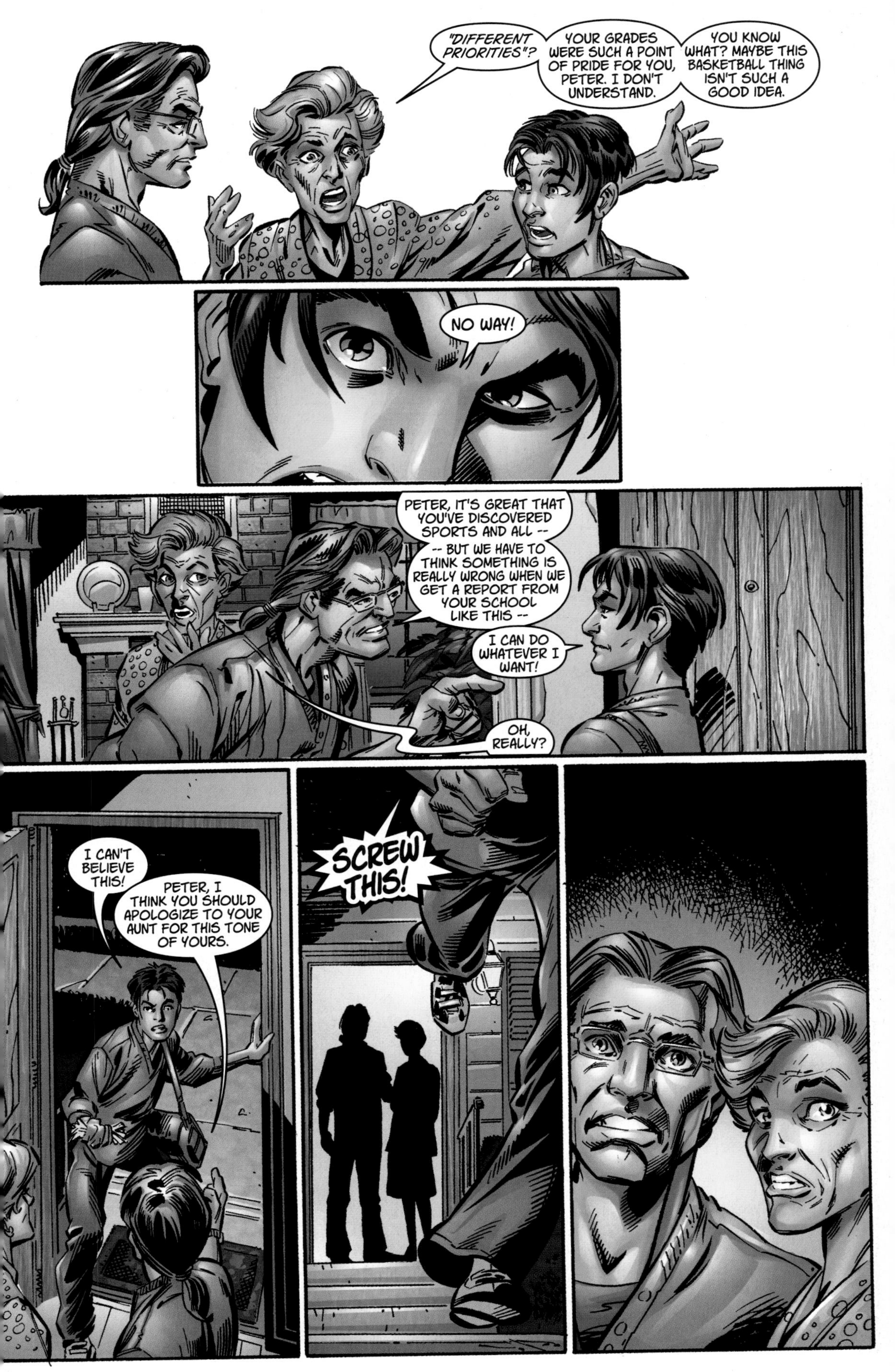
"DIFFERENT PRIORITIES"?
YOUR GRADES WERE SUCH A POINT OF PRIDE FOR YOU, PETER. I DON'T UNDERSTAND.
YOU KNOW WHAT? MAYBE THIS BASKETBALL THING ISN'T SUCH A GOOD IDEA.
NO WAY!
PETER, IT'S GREAT THAT YOU'VE DISCOVERED SPORTS AND ALL --
-- BUT WE HAVE TO THINK SOMETHING IS REALLY WRONG WHEN WE GET A REPORT FROM YOUR SCHOOL LIKE THIS --
I CAN DO WHATEVER I WANT!
OH, REALLY?
I CAN'T BELIEVE THIS!
PETER, I THINK YOU SHOULD APOLOGIZE TO YOUR AUNT FOR THIS TONE OF YOURS.
SCREW THIS!

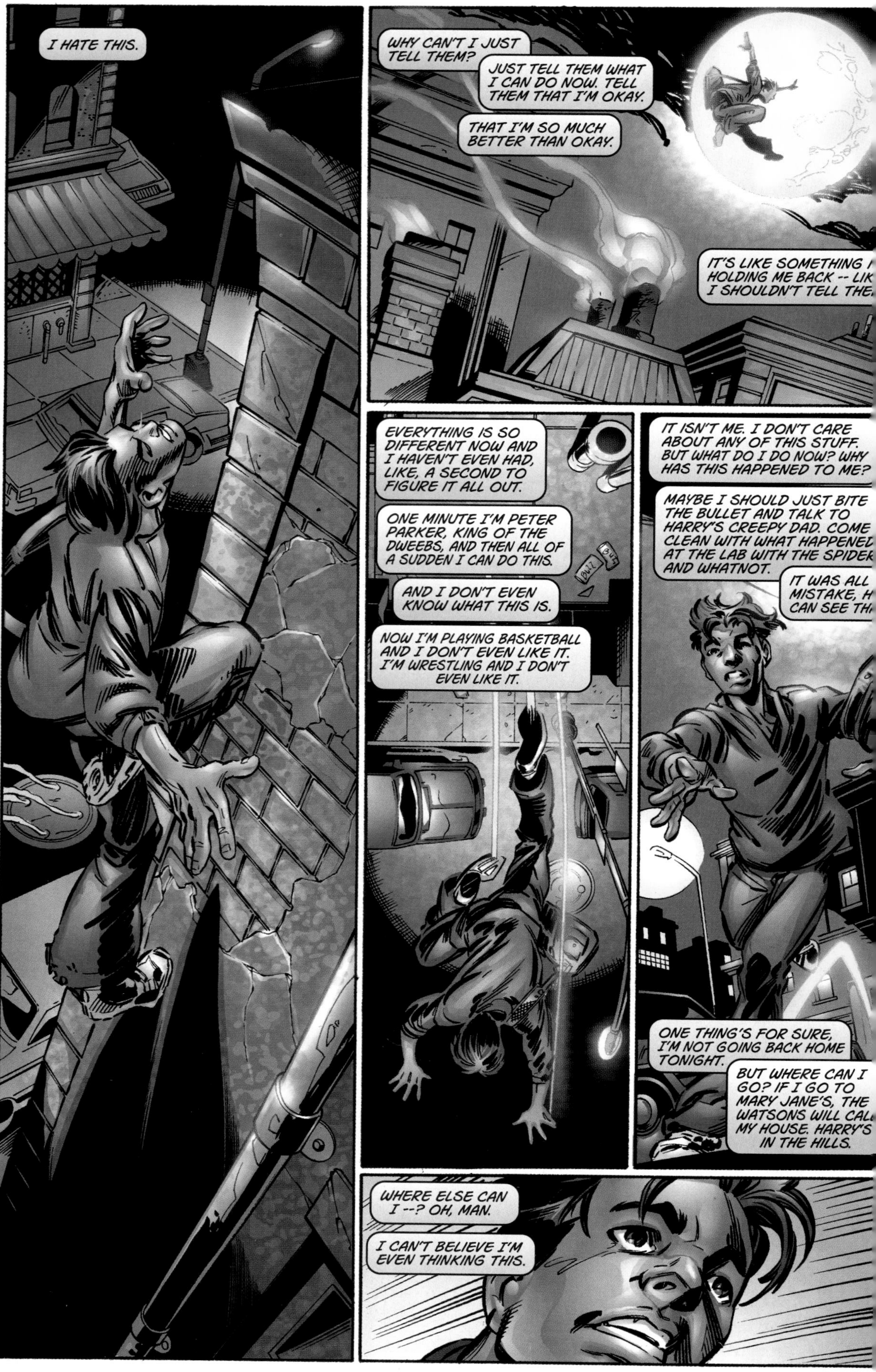

I HATE THIS.
WHY CAN'T I JUST TELL THEM?
JUST TELL THEM WHAT I CAN DO NOW. TELL THEM THAT I'M OKAY.
THAT I'M SO MUCH BETTER THAN OKAY.
IT'S LIKE SOMETHING I HOLDING ME BACK -- LIK I SHOULDN'T TELL THE
EVERYTHING IS SO DIFFERENT NOW AND I HAVEN'T EVEN HAD, LIKE, A SECOND TO FIGURE IT ALL OUT.
ONE MINUTE I'M PETER PARKER, KING OF THE DWEEBS, AND THEN ALL OF A SUDDEN I CAN DO THIS.
AND I DON'T EVEN KNOW WHAT THIS IS.
NOW I'M PLAYING BASKETBALL AND I DON'T EVEN LIKE IT. I'M WRESTLING AND I DON'T EVEN LIKE IT.
IT ISN'T ME. I DON'T CARE ABOUT ANY OF THIS STUFF. BUT WHAT DO I DO NOW? WHY HAS THIS HAPPENED TO ME?
MAYBE I SHOULD JUST BITE THE BULLET AND TALK TO HARRY'S CREEPY DAD. COME CLEAN WITH WHAT HAPPENED AT THE LAB WITH THE SPIDER AND WHATNOT.
IT WAS ALL MISTAKE, H CAN SEE TH
ONE THING'S FOR SURE, I'M NOT GOING BACK HOME TONIGHT.
BUT WHERE CAN I GO? IF I GO TO MARY JANE'S, THE WATSONS WILL CAL MY HOUSE. HARRY'S IN THE HILLS.
WHERE ELSE CAN I --? OH, MAN.
I CAN'T BELIEVE I'M EVEN THINKING THIS.

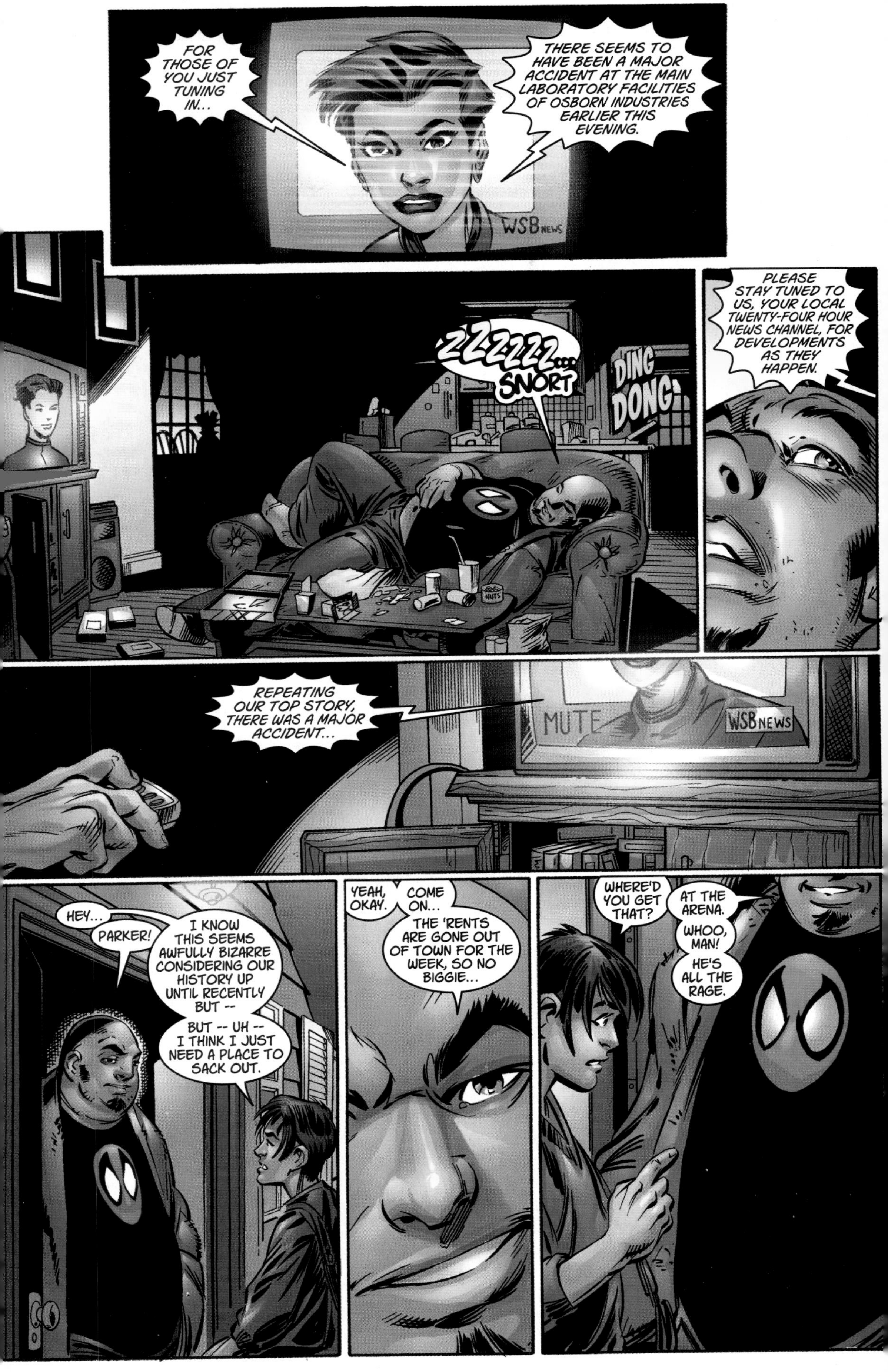
FOR THOSE OF YOU JUST TUNING IN...
THERE SEEMS TO HAVE BEEN A MAJOR ACCIDENT AT THE MAIN LABORATORY FACILITIES OF OSBORN INDUSTRIES EARLIER THIS EVENING.
WSB NEWS
ZZZZZZ... SNORT
DING DONG
NUTS
PLEASE STAY TUNED TO US, YOUR LOCAL TWENTY-FOUR HOUR NEWS CHANNEL, FOR DEVELOPMENTS AS THEY HAPPEN.
REPEATING OUR TOP STORY, THERE WAS A MAJOR ACCIDENT...
MUTE
WSB NEWS
HEY...
PARKER!
I KNOW THIS SEEMS AWFULLY BIZARRE CONSIDERING OUR HISTORY UP UNTIL RECENTLY BUT --
BUT -- UH -- I THINK I JUST NEED A PLACE TO SACK OUT.
YEAH, OKAY.
COME ON...
THE 'RENTS ARE GONE OUT OF TOWN FOR THE WEEK, SO NO BIGGIE...
WHERE'D YOU GET THAT?
AT THE ARENA.
WHOO, MAN!
HE'S ALL THE RAGE.

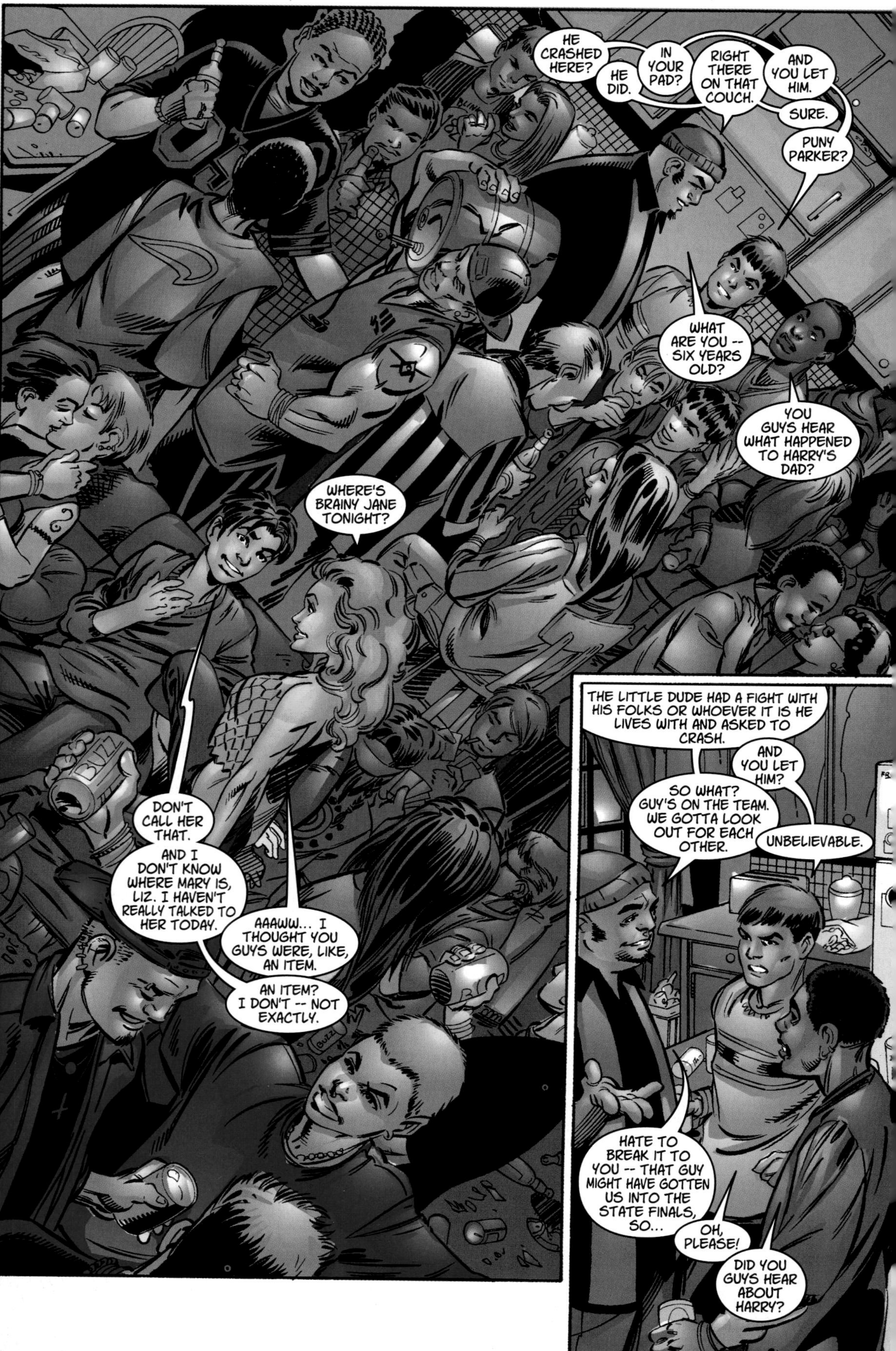
HE CRASHED HERE?
IN YOUR PAD?
HE DID.
RIGHT THERE ON THAT COUCH.
AND YOU LET HIM.
SURE.
PUNY PARKER?
WHAT ARE YOU -- SIX YEARS OLD?
YOU GUYS HEAR WHAT HAPPENED TO HARRY'S DAD?
WHERE'S BRAINY JANE TONIGHT?
DON'T CALL HER THAT.
AND I DON'T KNOW WHERE MARY IS, LIZ. I HAVEN'T REALLY TALKED TO HER TODAY.
AAAWW... I THOUGHT YOU GUYS WERE, LIKE, AN ITEM.
AN ITEM? I DON'T -- NOT EXACTLY.
THE LITTLE DUDE HAD A FIGHT WITH HIS FOLKS OR WHOEVER IT IS HE LIVES WITH AND ASKED TO CRASH.
AND YOU LET HIM?
SO WHAT? GUY'S ON THE TEAM. WE GOTTA LOOK OUT FOR EACH OTHER.
UNBELIEVABLE.
HATE TO BREAK IT TO YOU -- THAT GUY MIGHT HAVE GOTTEN US INTO THE STATE FINALS, SO...
OH, PLEASE!
DID YOU GUYS HEAR ABOUT HARRY?

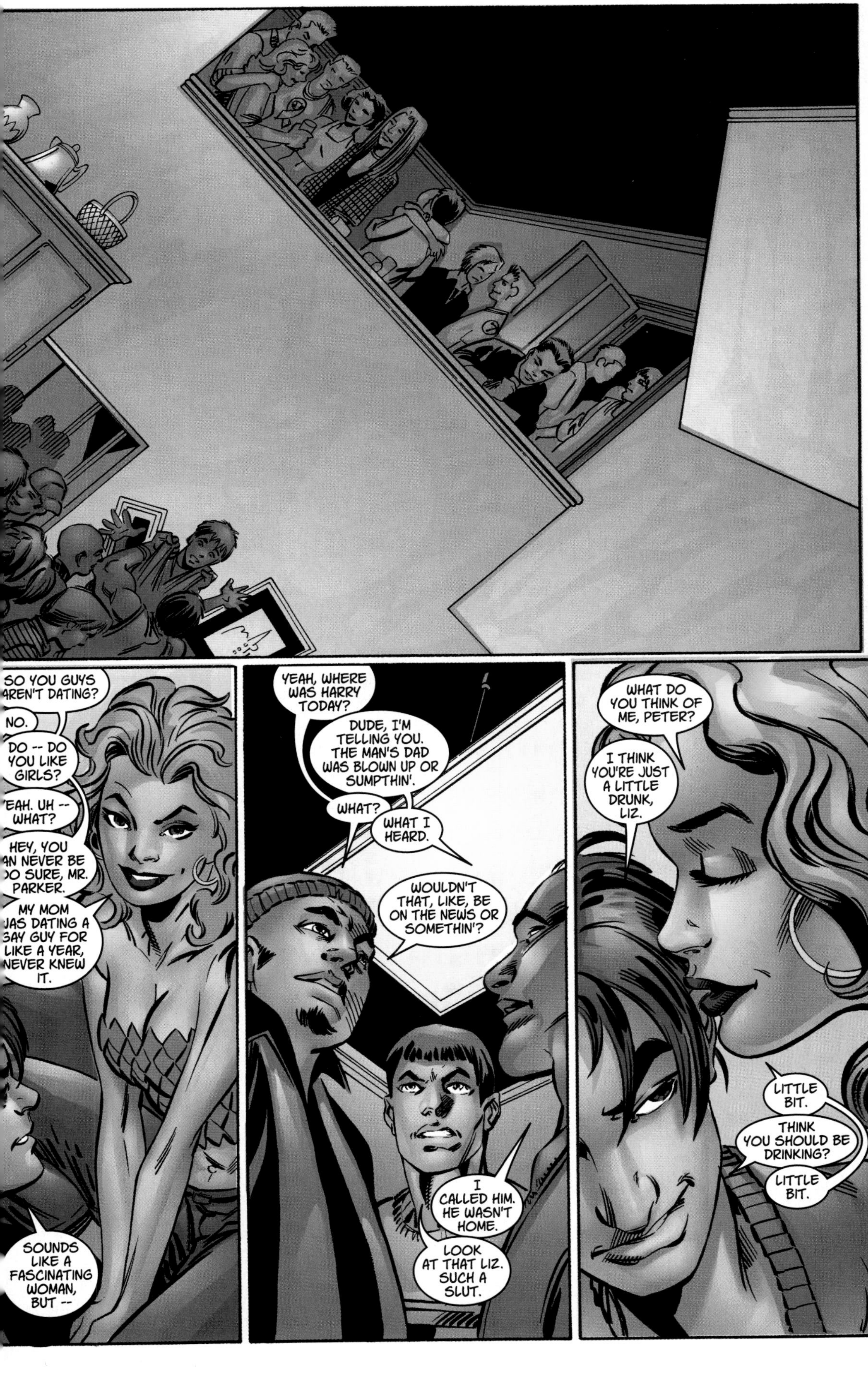
SO YOU GUYS
AREN'T DATING?
NO.
DO -- DO YOU LIKE GIRLS?
YEAH. UH -- WHAT?
HEY, YOU AN NEVER BE O SURE, MR. PARKER.
MY MOM WAS DATING A GAY GUY FOR LIKE A YEAR, NEVER KNEW IT.
SOUNDS LIKE A FASCINATING WOMAN, BUT --
YEAH, WHERE WAS HARRY TODAY?
DUDE, I'M TELLING YOU. THE MAN'S DAD WAS BLOWN UP OR SUMPTHIN'.
WHAT?
WHAT I HEARD.
WOULDN'T THAT, LIKE, BE ON THE NEWS OR SOMETHIN'?
I CALLED HIM. HE WASN'T HOME.
LOOK AT THAT LIZ. SUCH A SLUT.
WHAT DO YOU THINK OF ME, PETER?
I THINK YOU'RE JUST A LITTLE DRUNK, LIZ.
LITTLE BIT.
THINK YOU SHOULD BE DRINKING?
LITTLE BIT.

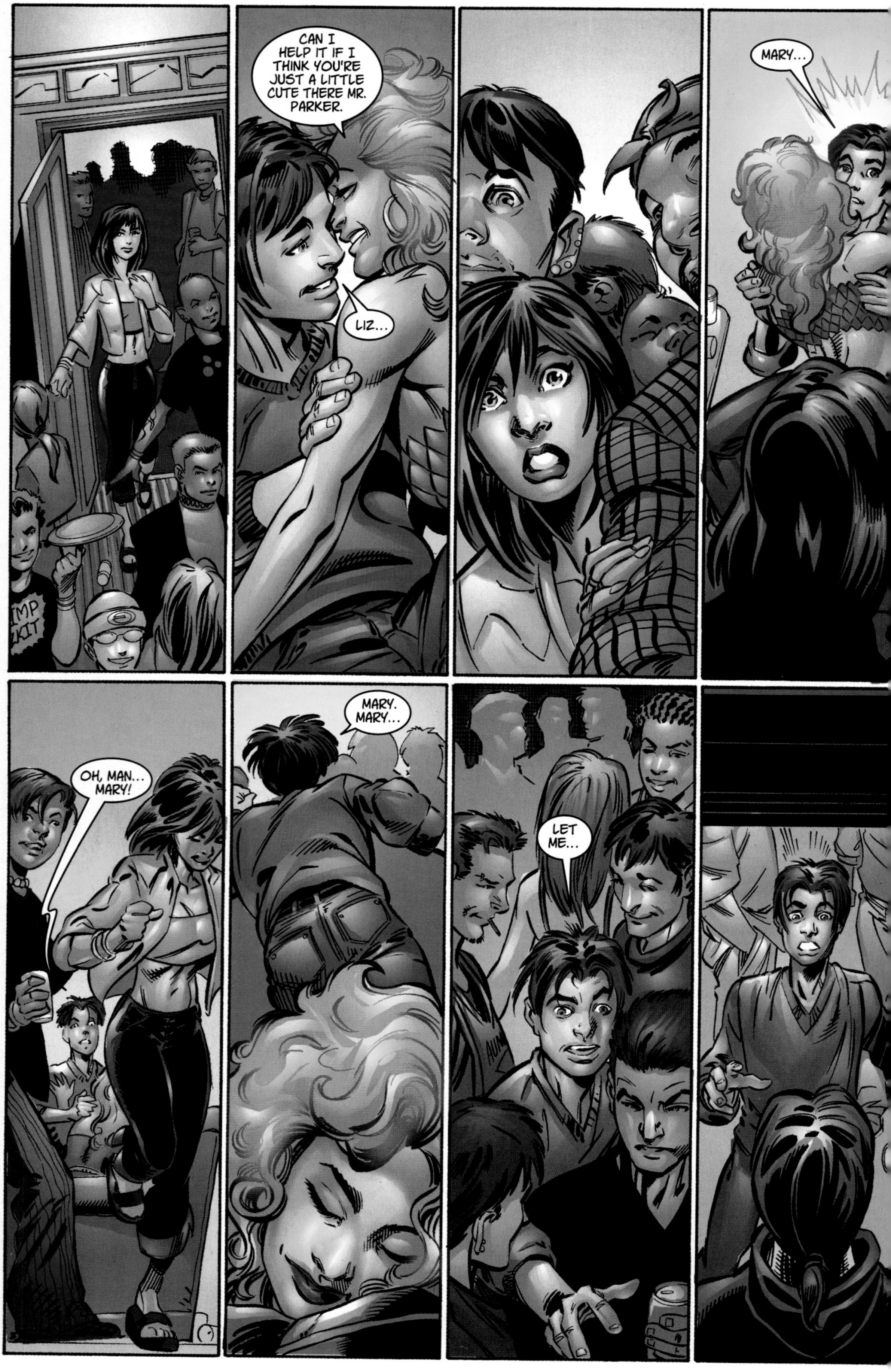
CAN I HELP IT IF I THINK YOU'RE JUST A LITTLE CUTE THERE MR. PARKER.
LIZ...
MARY...
OH, MAN... MARY!
MARY. MARY...
LET ME...

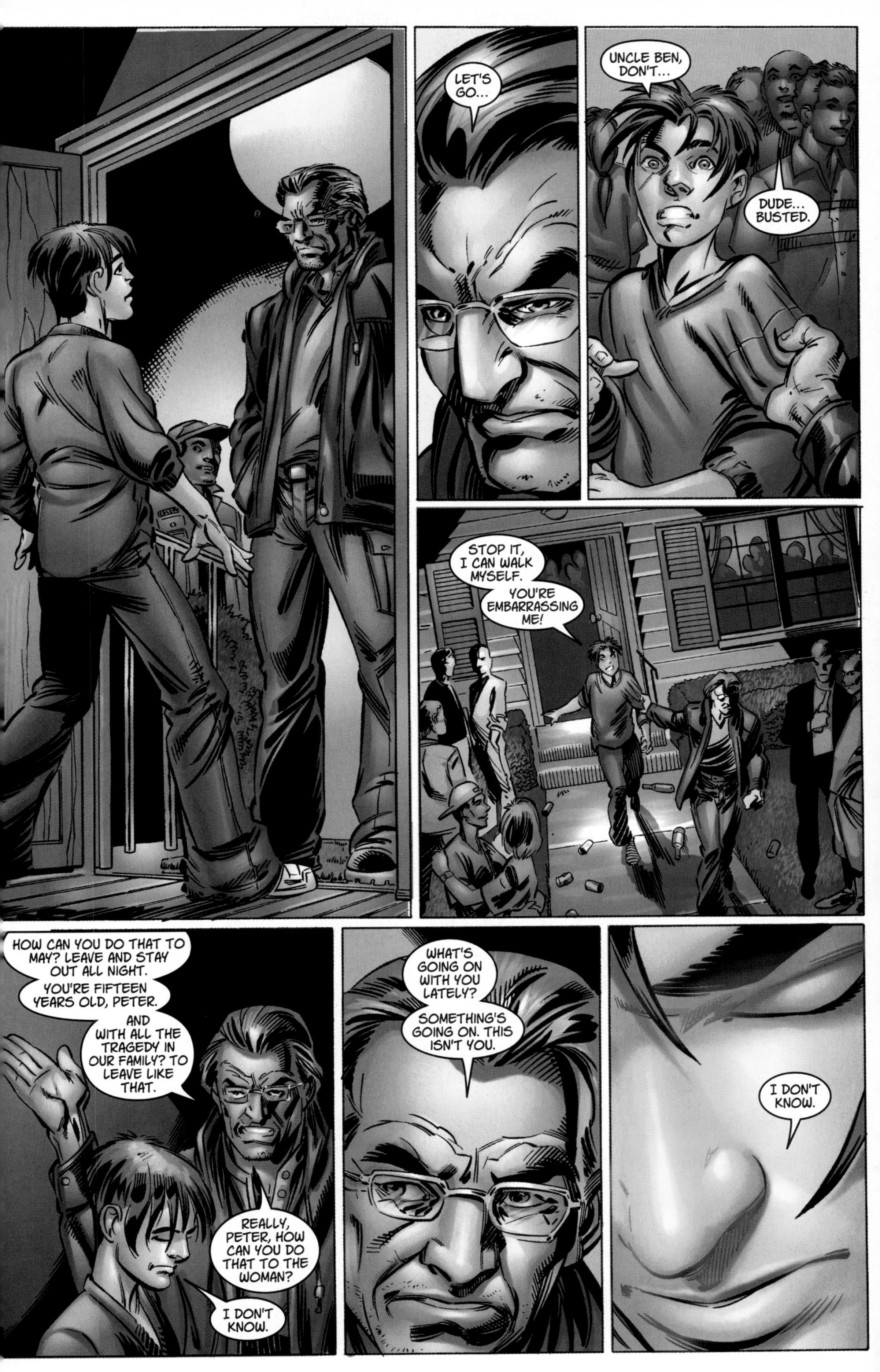
LET'S GO...
UNCLE BEN, DON'T...
DUDE... BUSTED.
STOP IT, I CAN WALK MYSELF.
YOU'RE EMBARRASSING ME!
HOW CAN YOU DO THAT TO MAY? LEAVE AND STAY OUT ALL NIGHT.
YOU'RE FIFTEEN YEARS OLD, PETER.
AND WITH ALL THE TRAGEDY IN OUR FAMILY? TO LEAVE LIKE THAT.
REALLY, PETER, HOW CAN YOU DO THAT TO THE WOMAN?
I DON'T KNOW.
WHAT'S GOING ON WITH YOU LATELY?
SOMETHING'S GOING ON. THIS ISN'T YOU.
I DON'T KNOW.

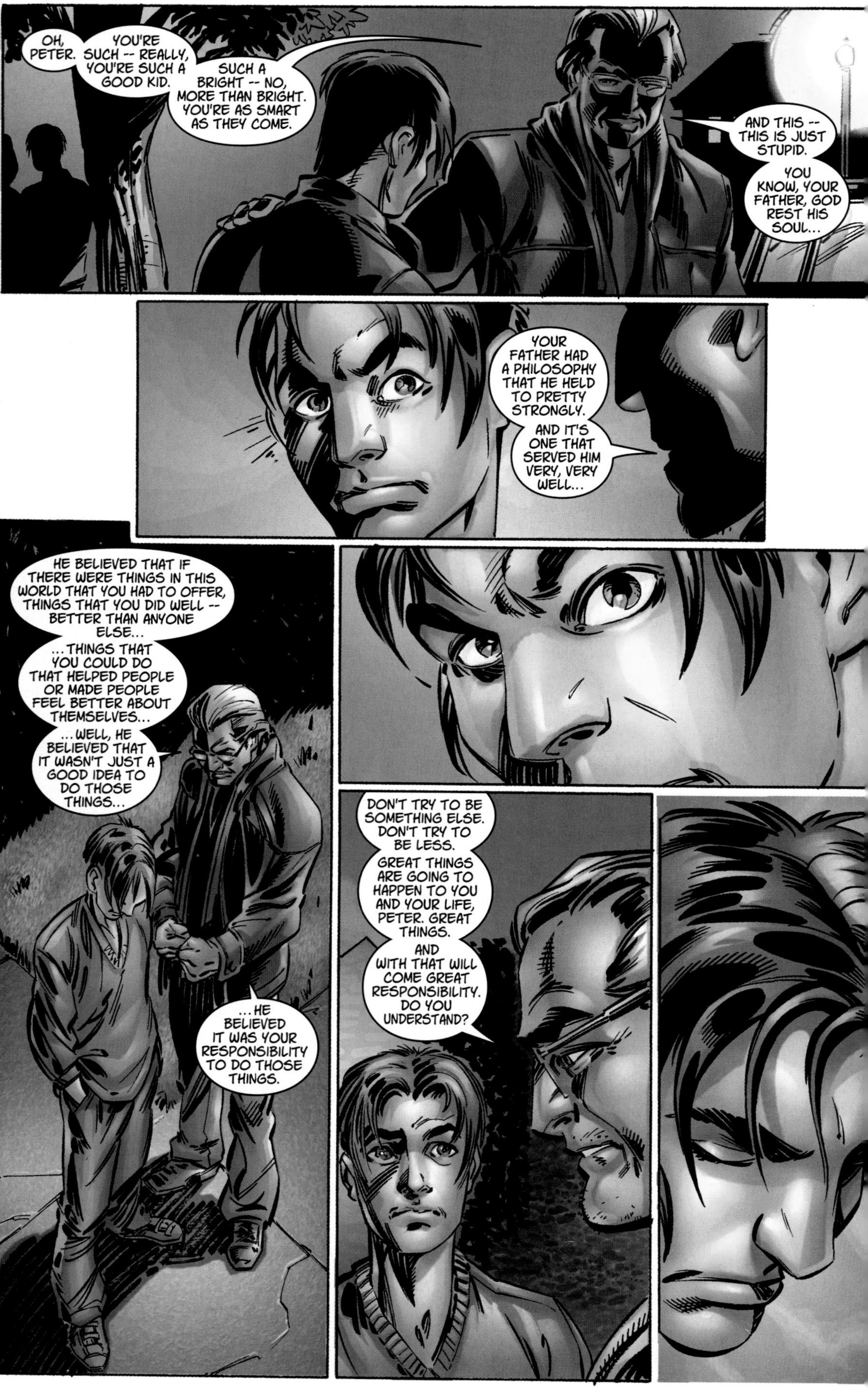
OH, PETER.
YOU'RE SUCH -- REALLY, YOU'RE SUCH A GOOD KID.
SUCH A BRIGHT -- NO, MORE THAN BRIGHT. YOU'RE AS SMART AS THEY COME.
AND THIS -- THIS IS JUST STUPID.
YOU KNOW, YOUR FATHER, GOD REST HIS SOUL...
YOUR FATHER HAD A PHILOSOPHY THAT HE HELD TO PRETTY STRONGLY.
AND IT'S ONE THAT SERVED HIM VERY, VERY WELL...
HE BELIEVED THAT IF THERE WERE THINGS IN THIS WORLD THAT YOU HAD TO OFFER, THINGS THAT YOU DID WELL -- BETTER THAN ANYONE ELSE...
...THINGS THAT YOU COULD DO THAT HELPED PEOPLE OR MADE PEOPLE FEEL BETTER ABOUT THEMSELVES...
...WELL, HE BELIEVED THAT IT WASN'T JUST A GOOD IDEA TO DO THOSE THINGS...
...HE BELIEVED IT WAS YOUR RESPONSIBILITY TO DO THOSE THINGS.
DON'T TRY TO BE SOMETHING ELSE. DON'T TRY TO BE LESS.
GREAT THINGS ARE GOING TO HAPPEN TO YOU AND YOUR LIFE, PETER. GREAT THINGS.
AND WITH THAT WILL COME GREAT RESPONSIBILITY. DO YOU UNDERSTAND?

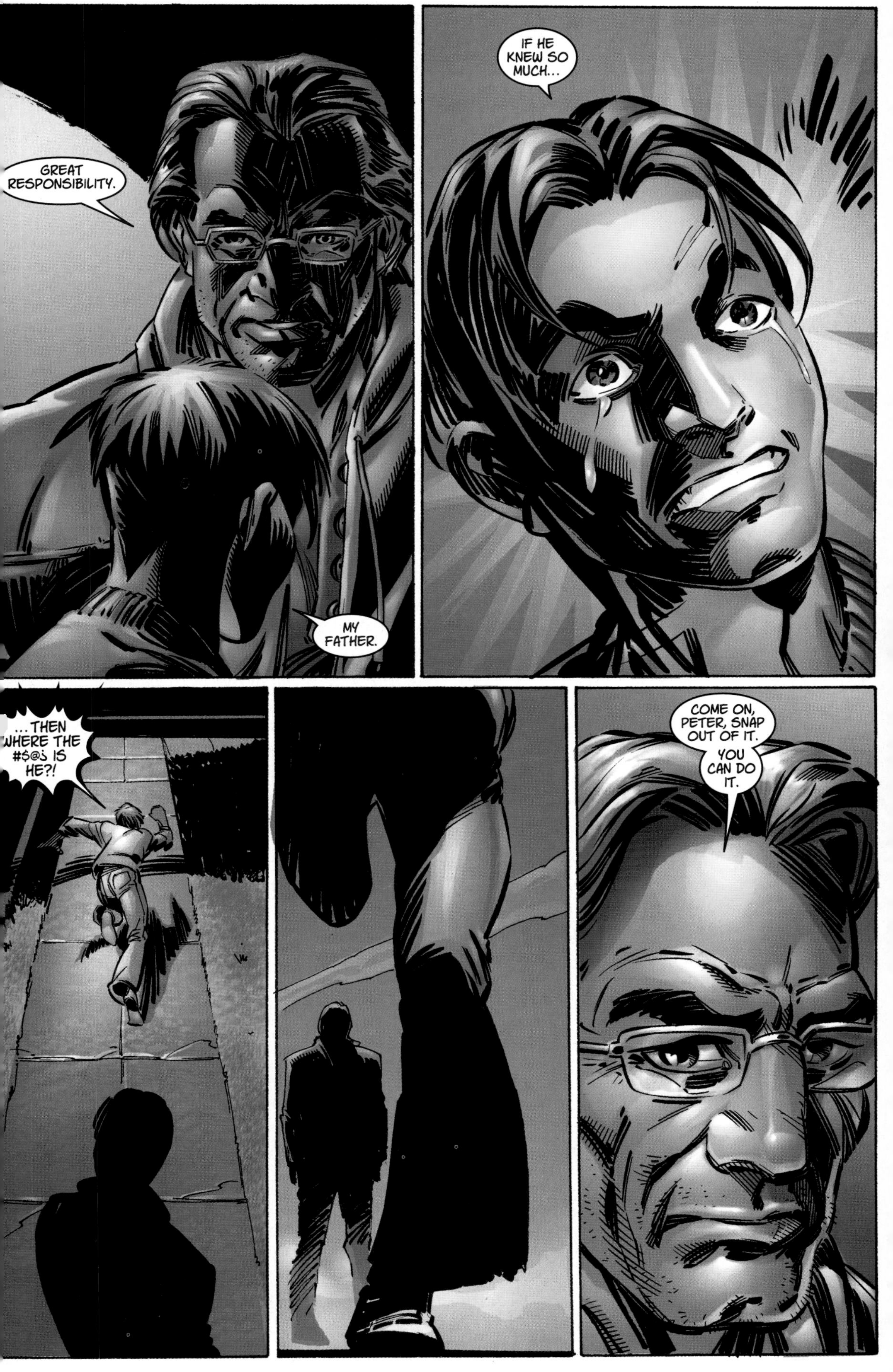
GREAT RESPONSIBILITY.
MY FATHER.
IF HE KNEW SO MUCH...
...THEN WHERE THE #$@¿ IS HE?!
COME ON, PETER, SNAP OUT OF IT.
YOU CAN DO IT.

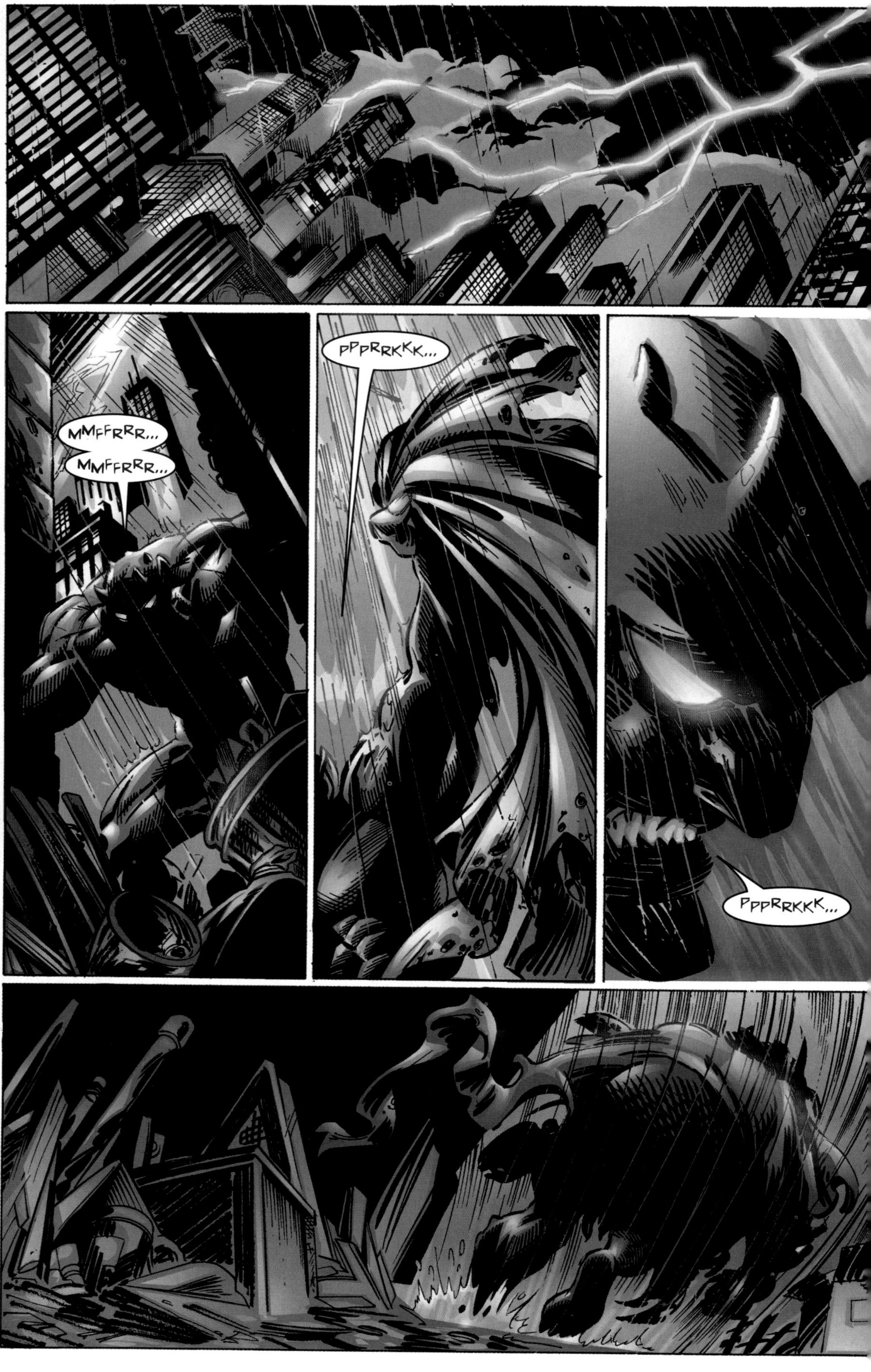
MMFFRRR...
MMFFRRR...
PPPRRKKK...
PPPRRKKK...

SO STUPID.

CRYING LIKE A GIRL. HE DIDN'T DESERVE THAT. HE DOESN'T KNOW.

HE DOESN'T KNOW THAT EVER SINCE THIS WHOLE SPIDER-MAN THING BEGAN ALL I CAN THINK IS THAT THE ONE PERSON WHO WOULD KNOW WHAT TO DO WAS MY DAD.

MY DAD WOULD HAVE KNOWN WHAT TO MAKE OF ALL THIS -- MY POWERS -- WHAT THEY MEAN.

BUT I'M WRONG. AND I'M SICK OF BEING WRONG.

UNCLE BEN AND AUNT MAY ARE MY FAMILY AND IT'S WAY PAST TIME FOR ME TO GROW UP.

IT'S TIME I TOLD THEM WHAT IS GOING ON WITH ME AND WHATEVER HAPPENS, HAPPENS.

IF I'M A FREAK -- I'M A FREAK.

THEY LOVE ME NO MATTER WHAT.

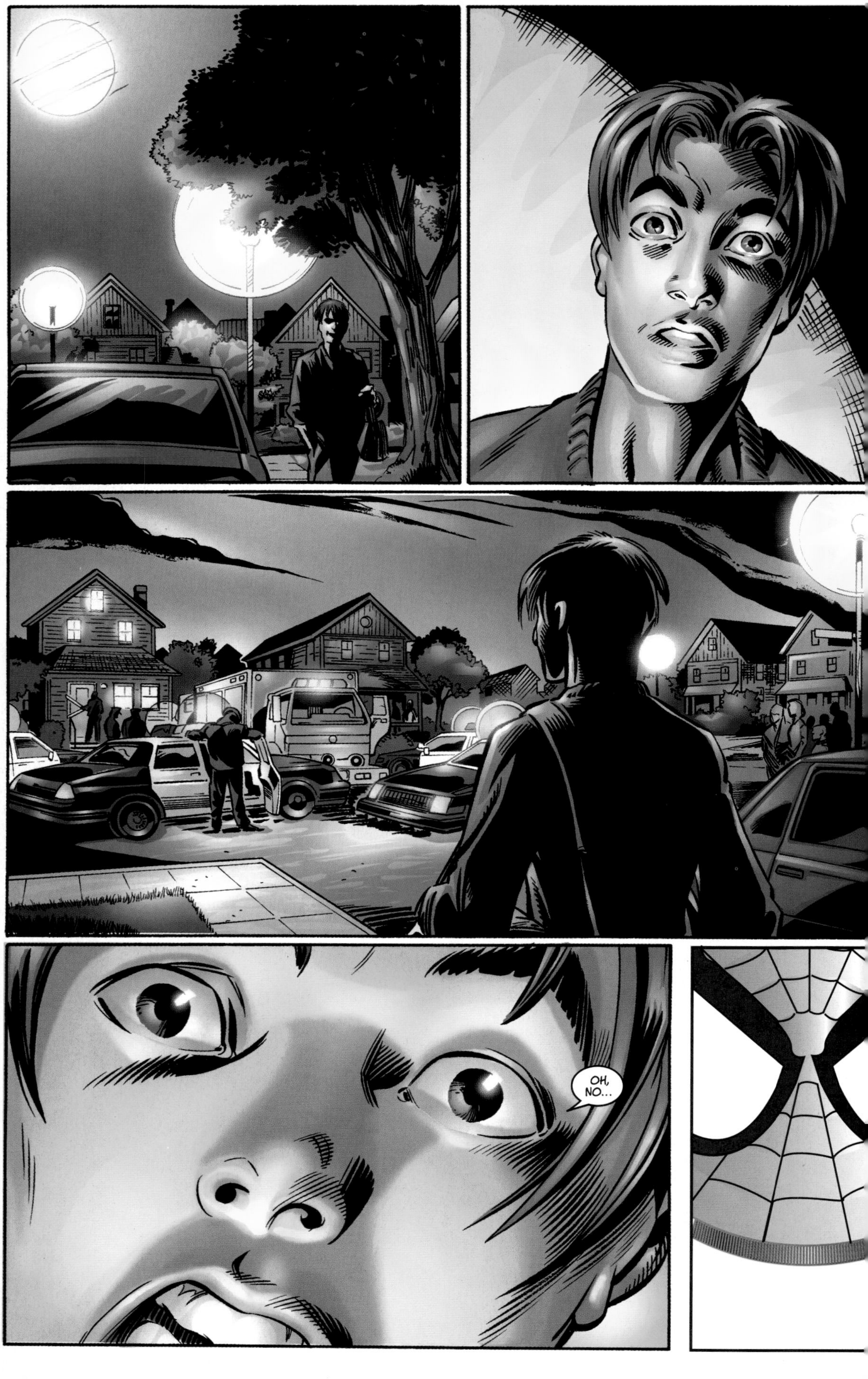
OH, NO...

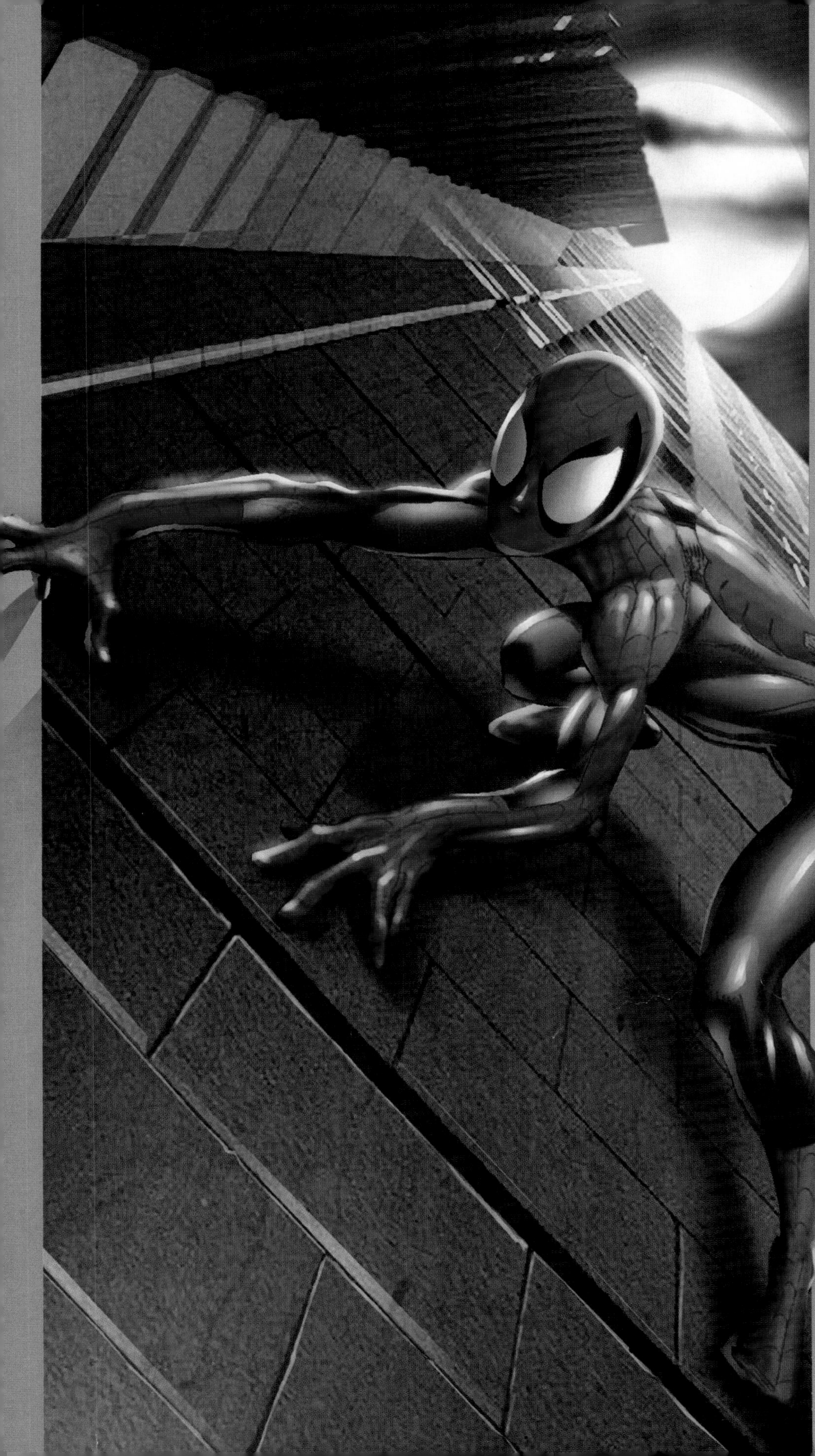

5

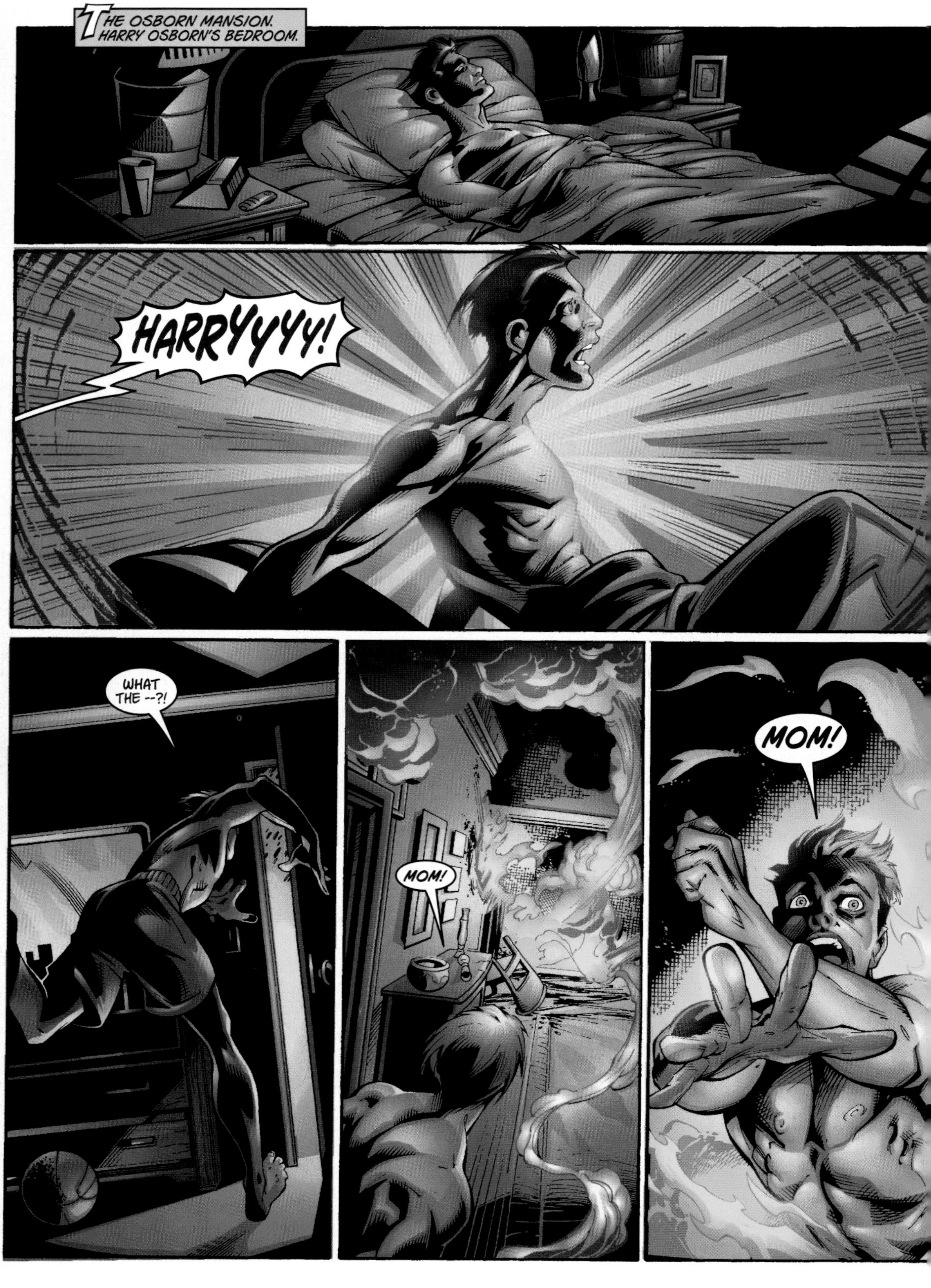
THE OSBORN MANSION. HARRY OSBORN'S BEDROOM.
HARRYYYY!
WHAT THE --?!
MOM!
MOM!

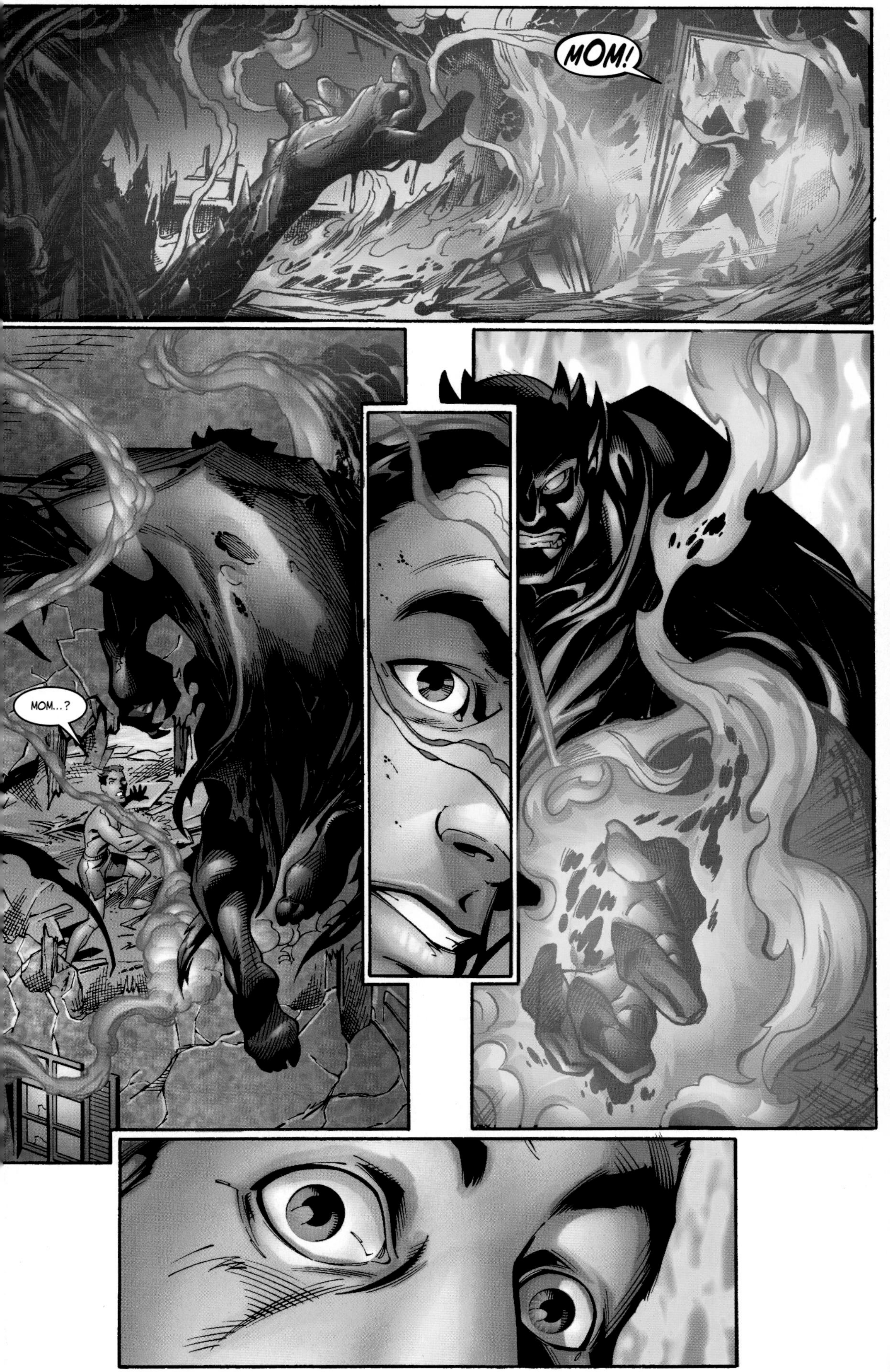
MOM!
MOM...?

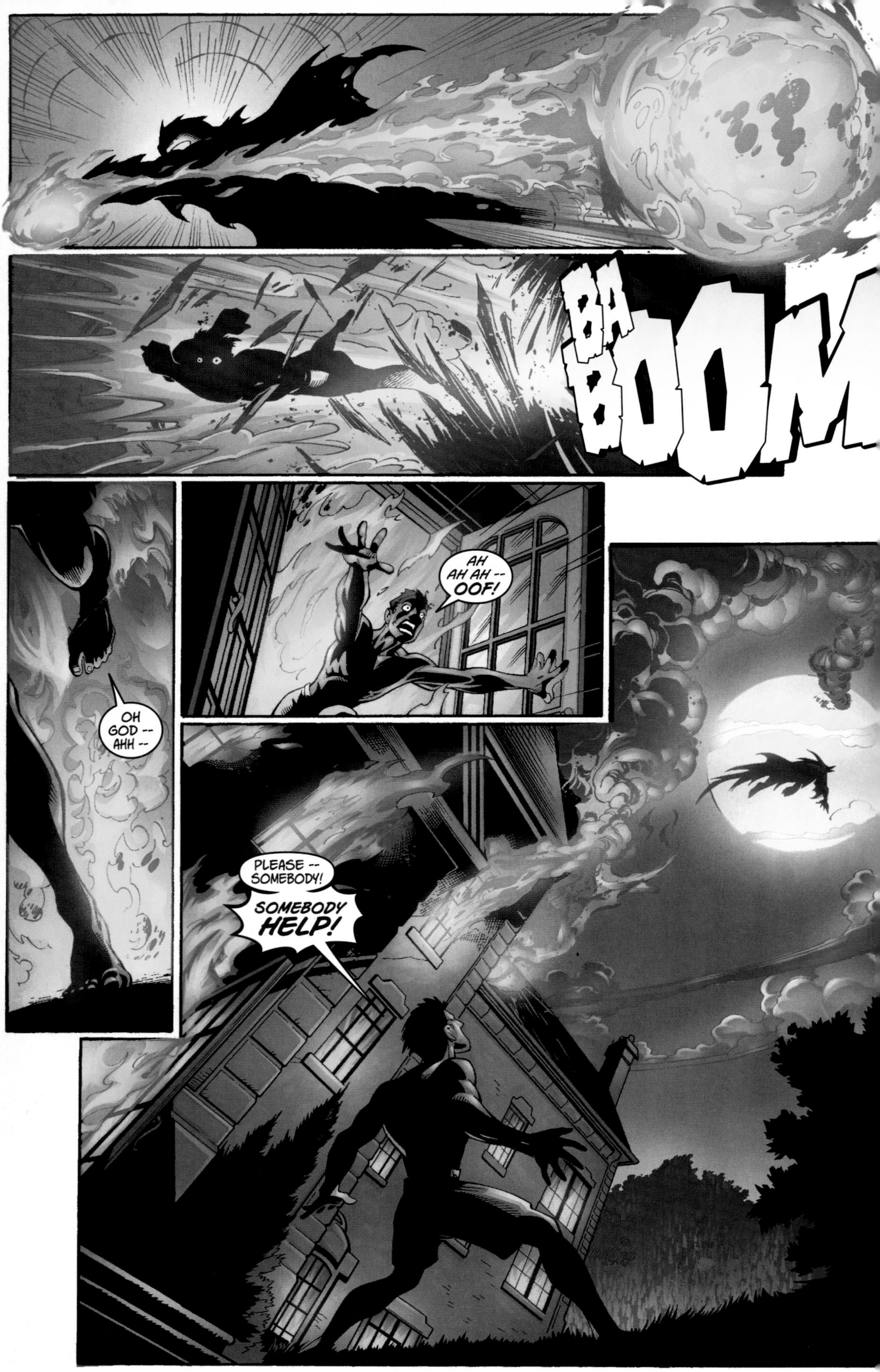
BA BOOM
AH AH AH -- OOF!
OH GOD -- AHH --
PLEASE -- SOMEBODY!
SOMEBODY HELP!

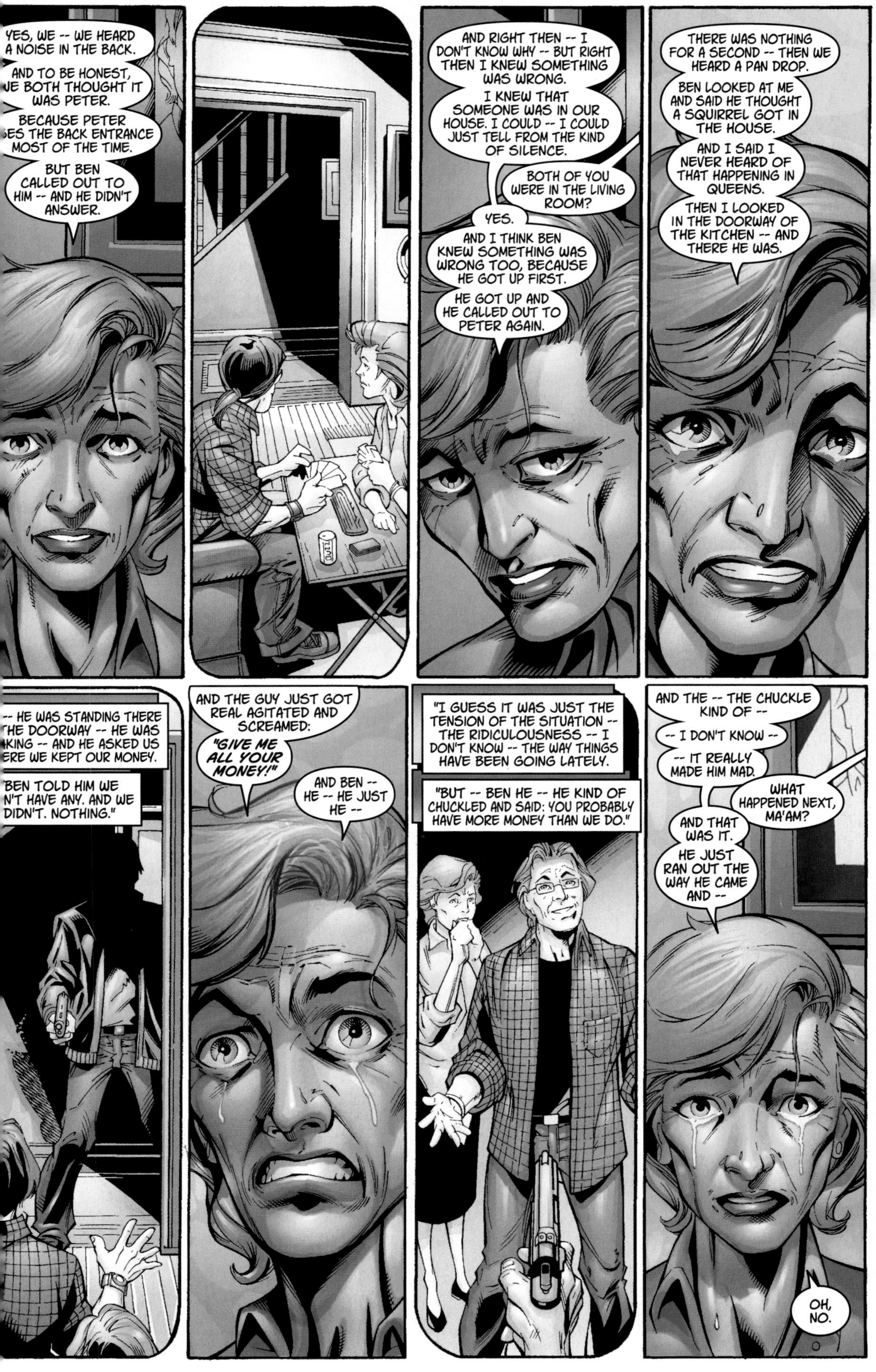

YES, WE -- WE HEARD A NOISE IN THE BACK.
AND TO BE HONEST, WE BOTH THOUGHT IT WAS PETER.
BECAUSE PETER USES THE BACK ENTRANCE MOST OF THE TIME.
BUT BEN CALLED OUT TO HIM -- AND HE DIDN'T ANSWER.
AND RIGHT THEN -- I DON'T KNOW WHY -- BUT RIGHT THEN I KNEW SOMETHING WAS WRONG.
I KNEW THAT SOMEONE WAS IN OUR HOUSE. I COULD -- I COULD JUST TELL FROM THE KIND OF SILENCE.
BOTH OF YOU WERE IN THE LIVING ROOM?
YES.
AND I THINK BEN KNEW SOMETHING WAS WRONG TOO, BECAUSE HE GOT UP FIRST.
HE GOT UP AND HE CALLED OUT TO PETER AGAIN.
THERE WAS NOTHING FOR A SECOND -- THEN WE HEARD A PAN DROP.
BEN LOOKED AT ME AND SAID HE THOUGHT A SQUIRREL GOT IN THE HOUSE.
AND I SAID I NEVER HEARD OF THAT HAPPENING IN QUEENS.
THEN I LOOKED IN THE DOORWAY OF THE KITCHEN -- AND THERE HE WAS.
-- HE WAS STANDING THERE THE DOORWAY -- HE WAS KING -- AND HE ASKED US ERE WE KEPT OUR MONEY.
"BEN TOLD HIM WE N'T HAVE ANY. AND WE DIDN'T. NOTHING."
AND THE GUY JUST GOT REAL AGITATED AND SCREAMED:
"GIVE ME ALL YOUR MONEY!"
AND BEN -- HE -- HE JUST HE --
"I GUESS IT WAS JUST THE TENSION OF THE SITUATION -- THE RIDICULOUSNESS -- I DON'T KNOW -- THE WAY THINGS HAVE BEEN GOING LATELY.
"BUT -- BEN HE -- HE KIND OF CHUCKLED AND SAID: YOU PROBABLY HAVE MORE MONEY THAN WE DO."
AND THE -- THE CHUCKLE KIND OF --
-- I DON'T KNOW --
-- IT REALLY MADE HIM MAD.
WHAT HAPPENED NEXT, MA'AM?
AND THAT WAS IT.
HE JUST RAN OUT THE WAY HE CAME AND --
OH, NO.

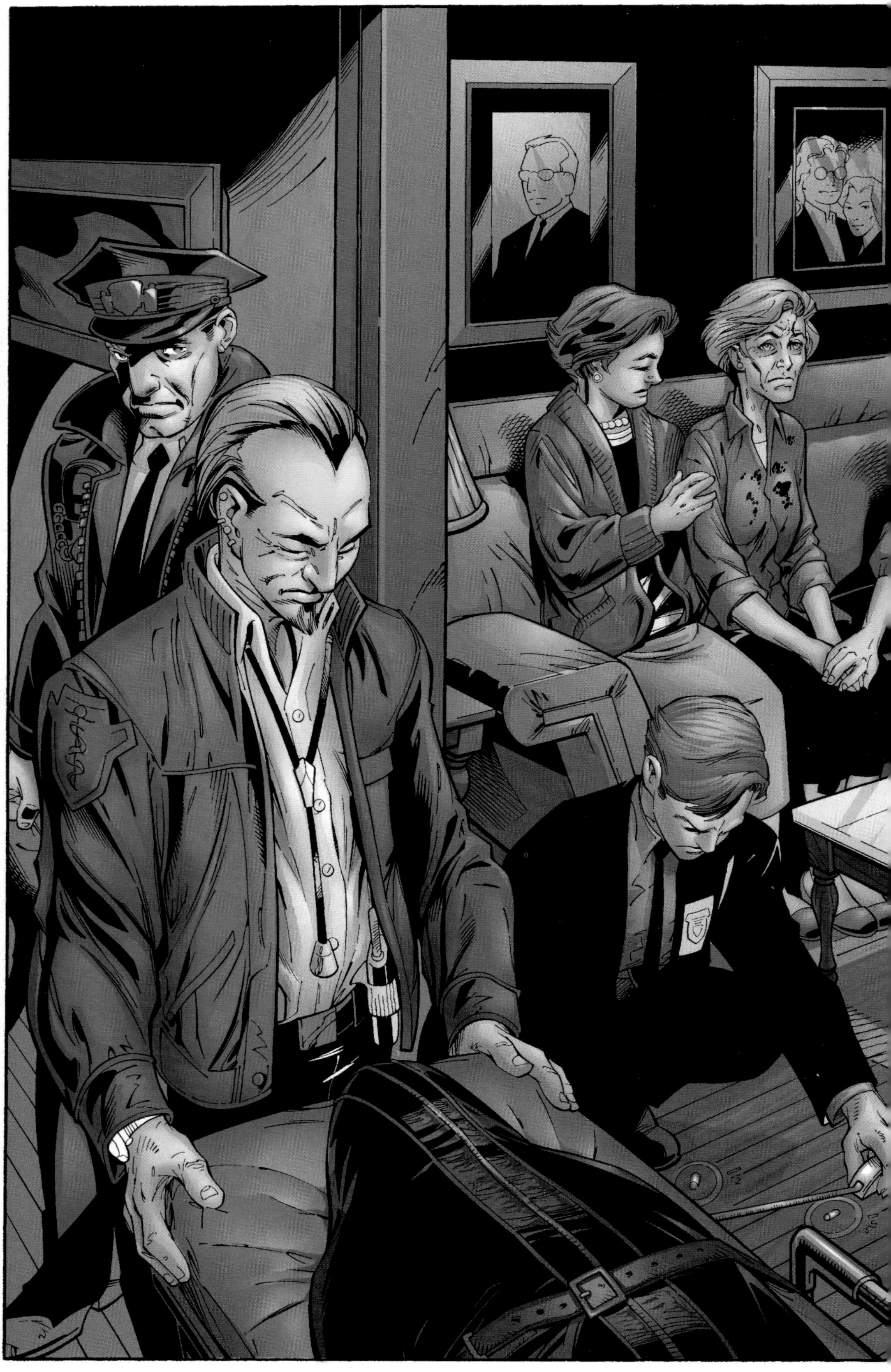

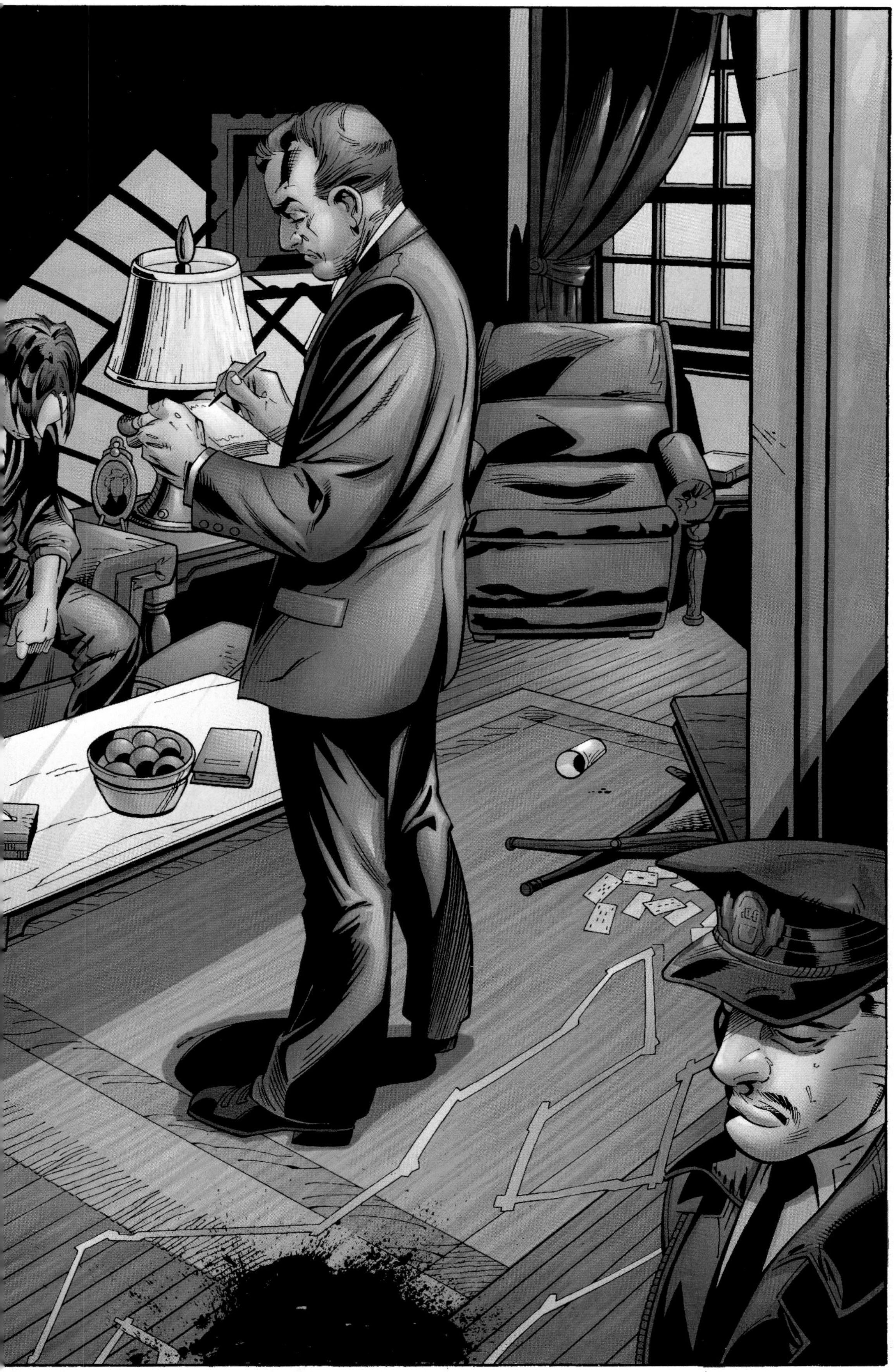

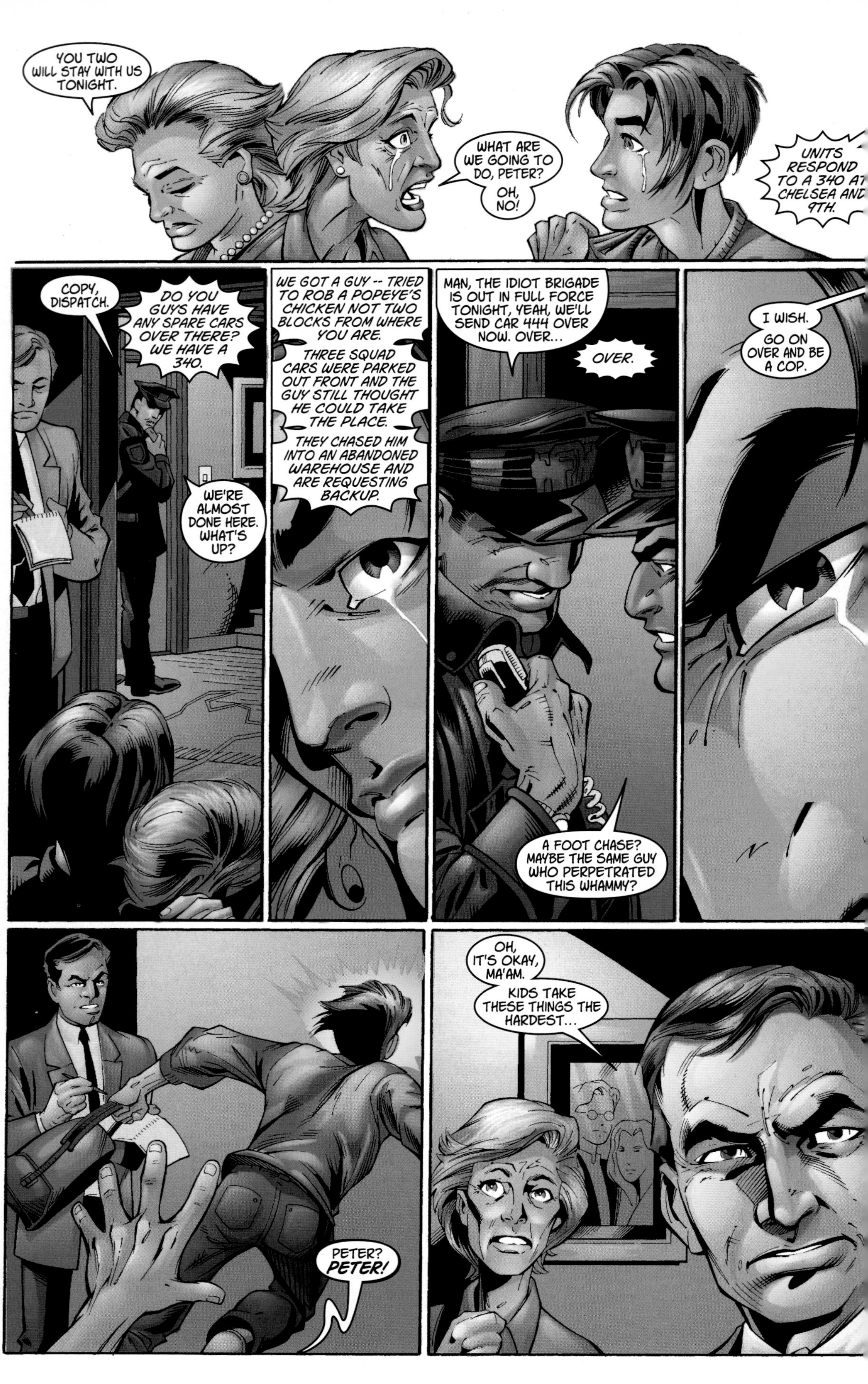
YOU TWO WILL STAY WITH US TONIGHT.
WHAT ARE WE GOING TO DO, PETER?
OH, NO!
UNITS RESPOND TO A 340 AT CHELSEA AND 9TH.
COPY, DISPATCH.
DO YOU GUYS HAVE ANY SPARE CARS OVER THERE? WE HAVE A 340.
WE'RE ALMOST DONE HERE. WHAT'S UP?
WE GOT A GUY -- TRIED TO ROB A POPEYE'S CHICKEN NOT TWO BLOCKS FROM WHERE YOU ARE.
THREE SQUAD CARS WERE PARKED OUT FRONT AND THE GUY STILL THOUGHT HE COULD TAKE THE PLACE.
THEY CHASED HIM INTO AN ABANDONED WAREHOUSE AND ARE REQUESTING BACKUP.
MAN, THE IDIOT BRIGADE IS OUT IN FULL FORCE TONIGHT, YEAH, WE'LL SEND CAR 444 OVER NOW. OVER...
OVER.
A FOOT CHASE? MAYBE THE SAME GUY WHO PERPETRATED THIS WHAMMY?
I WISH.
GO ON OVER AND BE A COP.
PETER? PETER!
OH, IT'S OKAY, MA'AM.
KIDS TAKE THESE THINGS THE HARDEST...

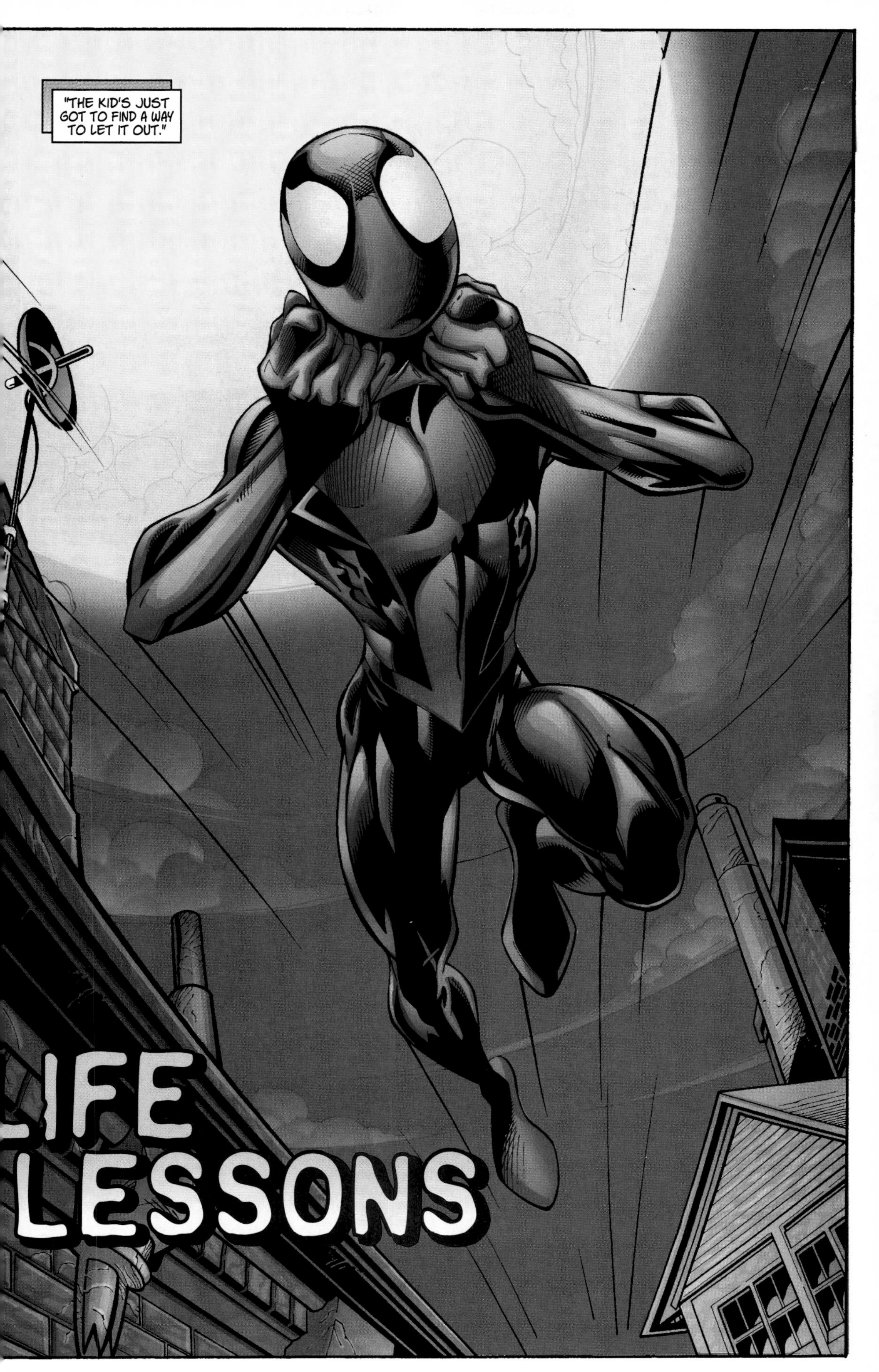
"THE KID'S JUST GOT TO FIND A WAY TO LET IT OUT."
LIFE LESSONS

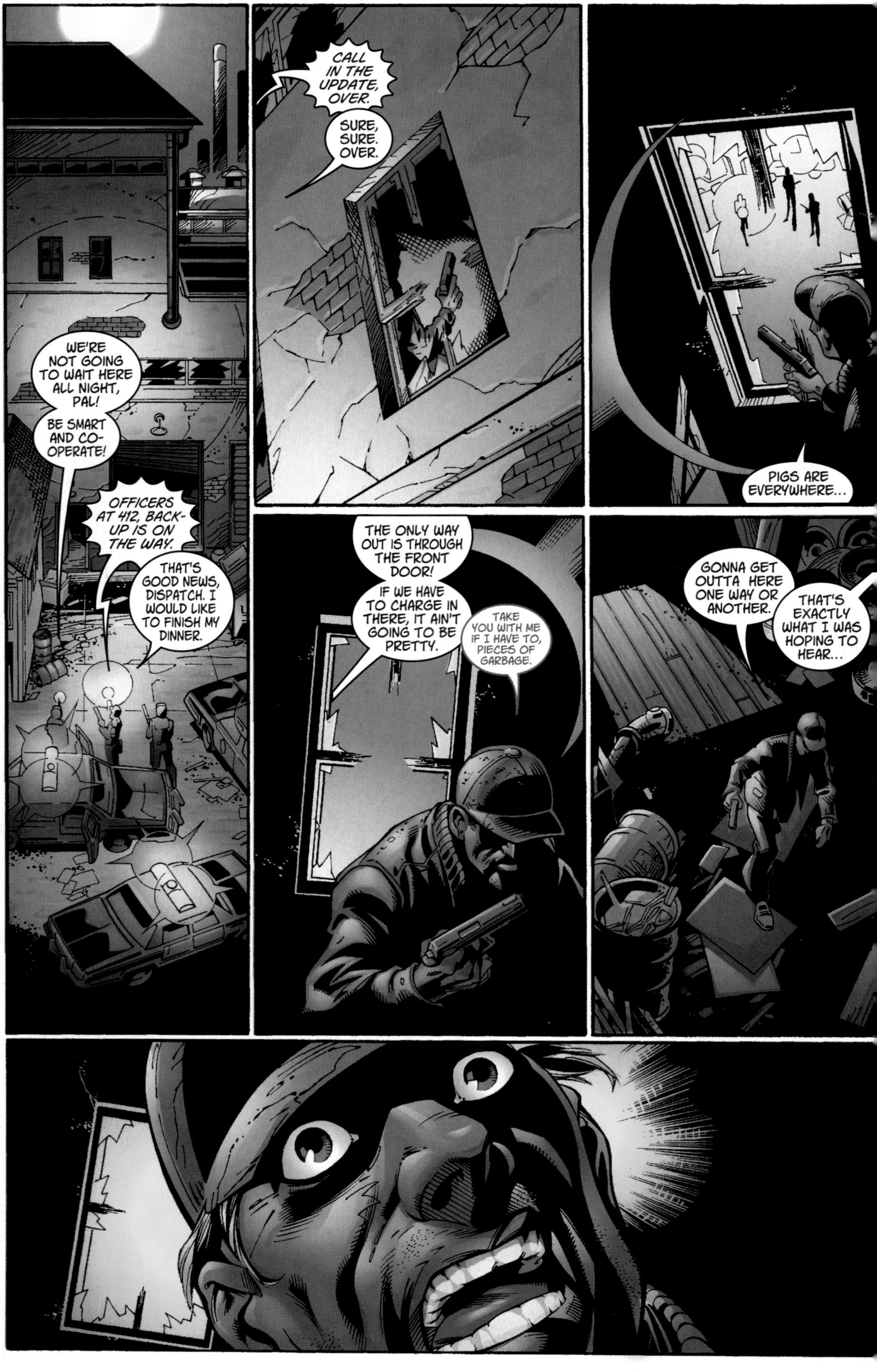
WE'RE NOT GOING TO WAIT HERE ALL NIGHT, PAL!
BE SMART AND CO-OPERATE!
OFFICERS AT 412, BACK-UP IS ON THE WAY.
THAT'S GOOD NEWS, DISPATCH. I WOULD LIKE TO FINISH MY DINNER.
CALL IN THE UPDATE, OVER.
SURE, SURE. OVER.
PIGS ARE EVERYWHERE...
THE ONLY WAY OUT IS THROUGH THE FRONT DOOR!
IF WE HAVE TO CHARGE IN THERE, IT AIN'T GOING TO BE PRETTY.
TAKE YOU WITH ME IF I HAVE TO, PIECES OF GARBAGE.
GONNA GET OUTTA HERE ONE WAY OR ANOTHER.
THAT'S EXACTLY WHAT I WAS HOPING TO HEAR...

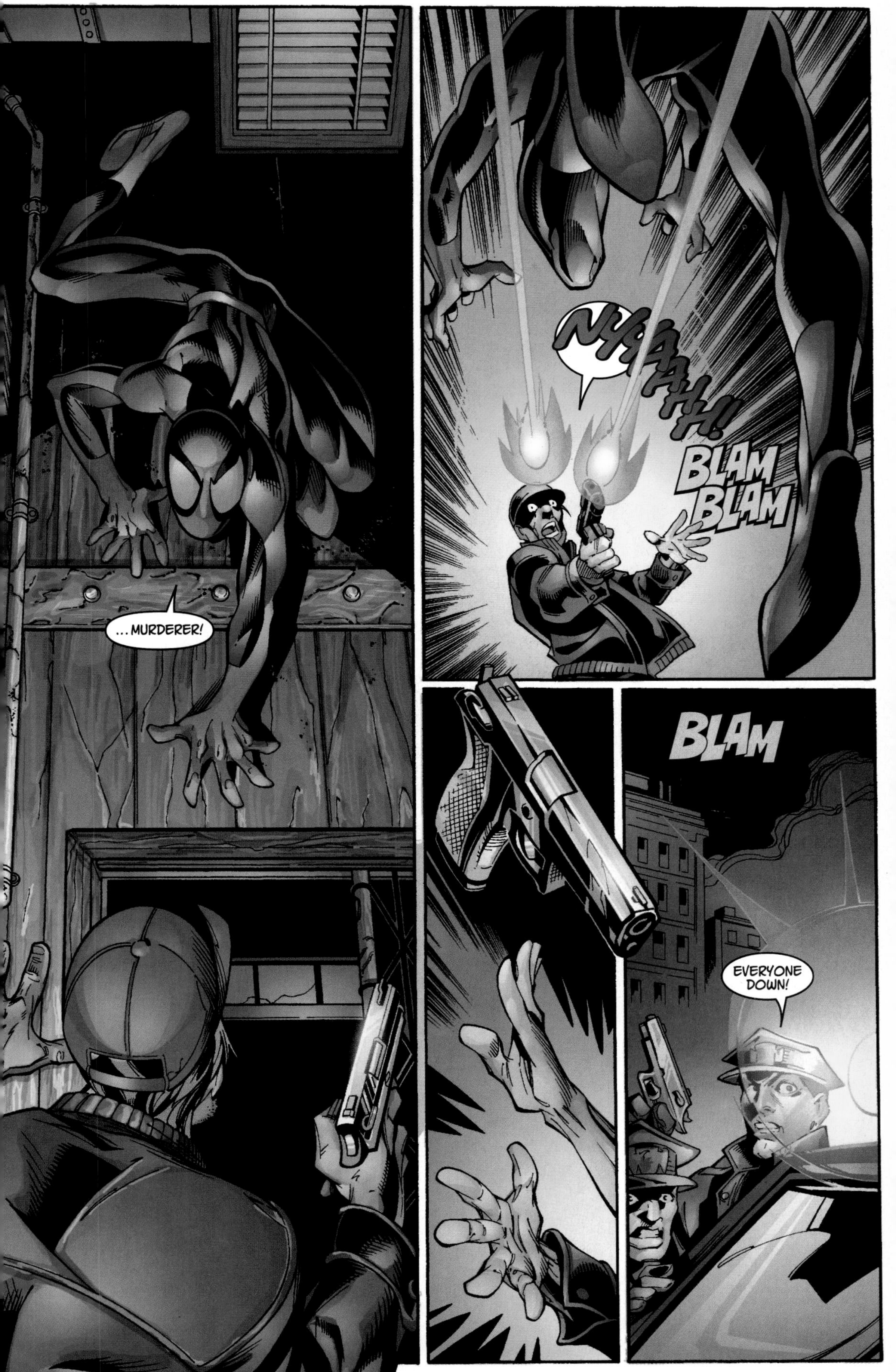
...MURDERER!
NYAAAHH!
BLAM
BLAM
BLAM
EVERYONE DOWN!

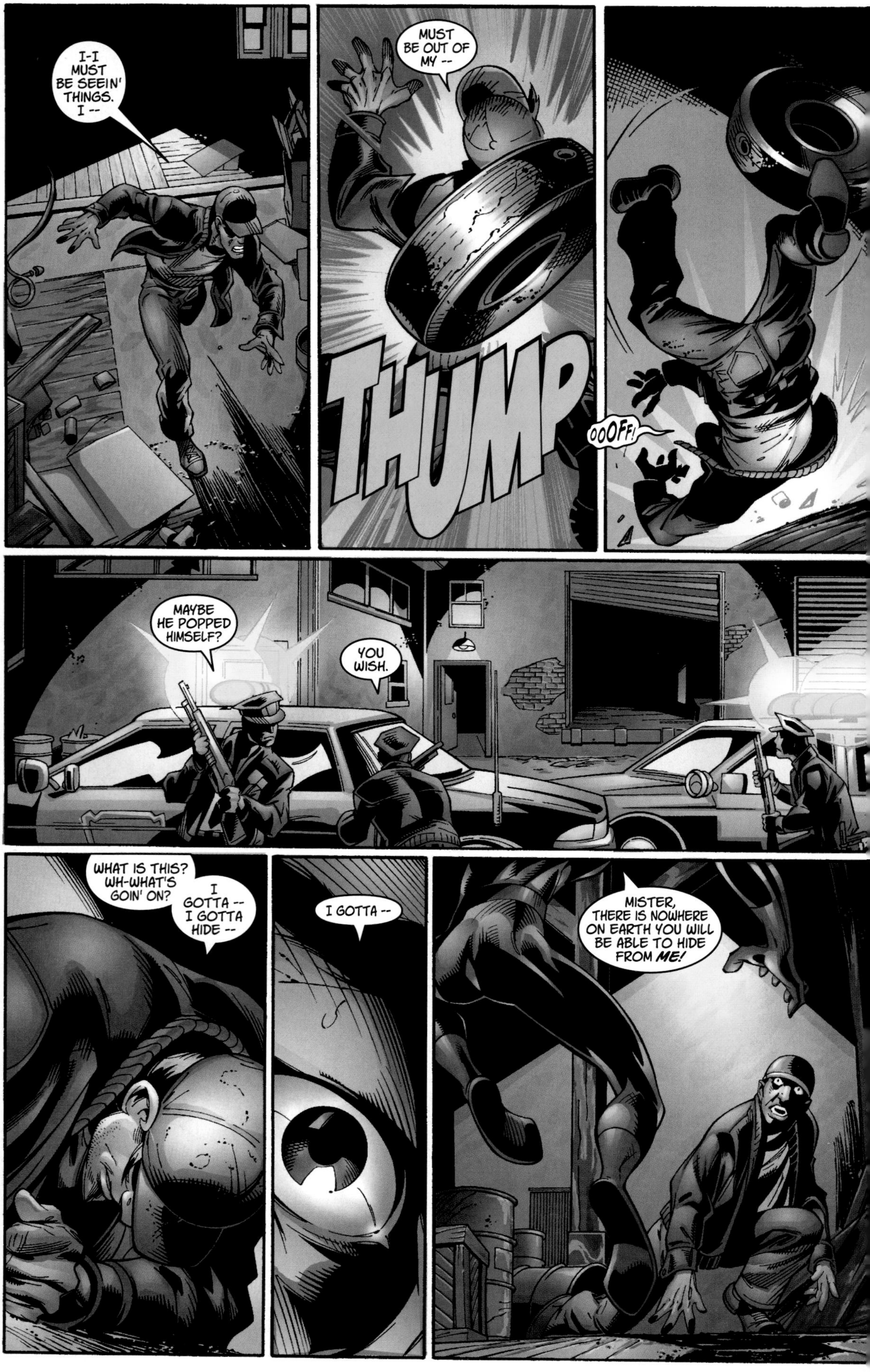
I-I MUST BE SEEIN' THINGS. I --
MUST BE OUT OF MY --
THUMP
OOOFF!
MAYBE HE POPPED HIMSELF?
YOU WISH.
WHAT IS THIS? WH-WHAT'S GOIN' ON?
I GOTTA -- I GOTTA HIDE --
I GOTTA --
MISTER, THERE IS NOWHERE ON EARTH YOU WILL BE ABLE TO HIDE FROM *ME!*

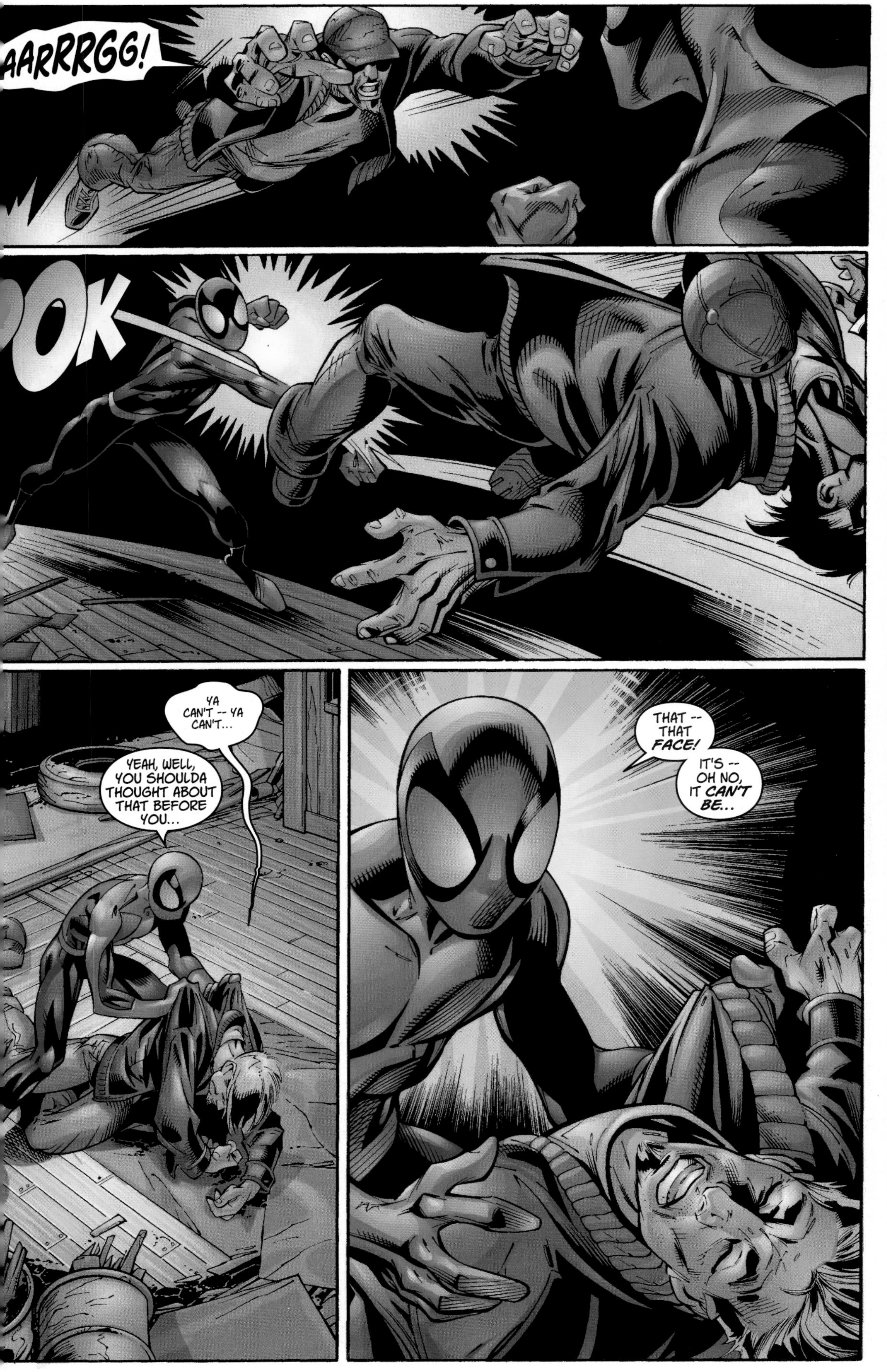

AARRRGG!
OOK
YA CAN'T -- YA CAN'T...
YEAH, WELL, YOU SHOULDA THOUGHT ABOUT THAT BEFORE YOU...
THAT -- THAT FACE!
IT'S -- OH NO, IT CAN'T BE...

GET OUTTA MY WAY!

OUT!

WHY DIDN'T YOU STOP HIM?

NOT MY JOB.

"NOT YOUR JOB?"

ALL YOU HAD TO DO WAS TRIP HIM. STICK YOUR FOOT OUT AND HE'S KISSING PAVEMENT!

WELL, SORR-EE. BUT THAT REALLY ISN'T MY DEPARTMENT, IS IT?

I'VE GOT MY OWN PROBLEMS, BIG GUY.

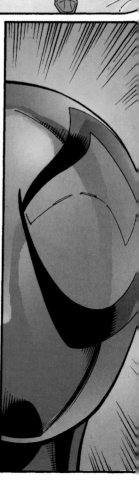

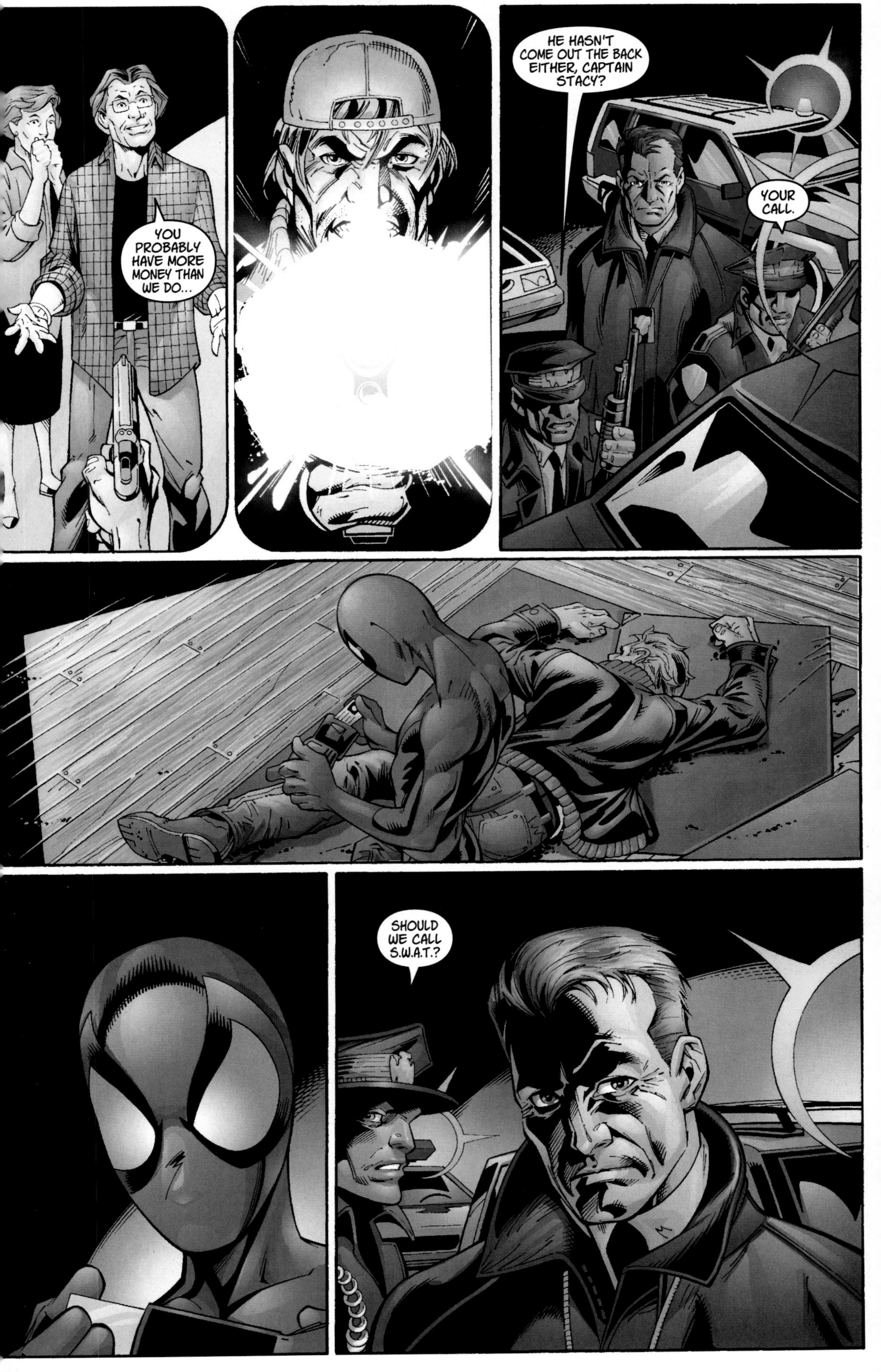
YOU PROBABLY HAVE MORE MONEY THAN WE DO...
HE HASN'T COME OUT THE BACK EITHER, CAPTAIN STACY?
YOUR CALL.
SHOULD WE CALL S.W.A.T.?

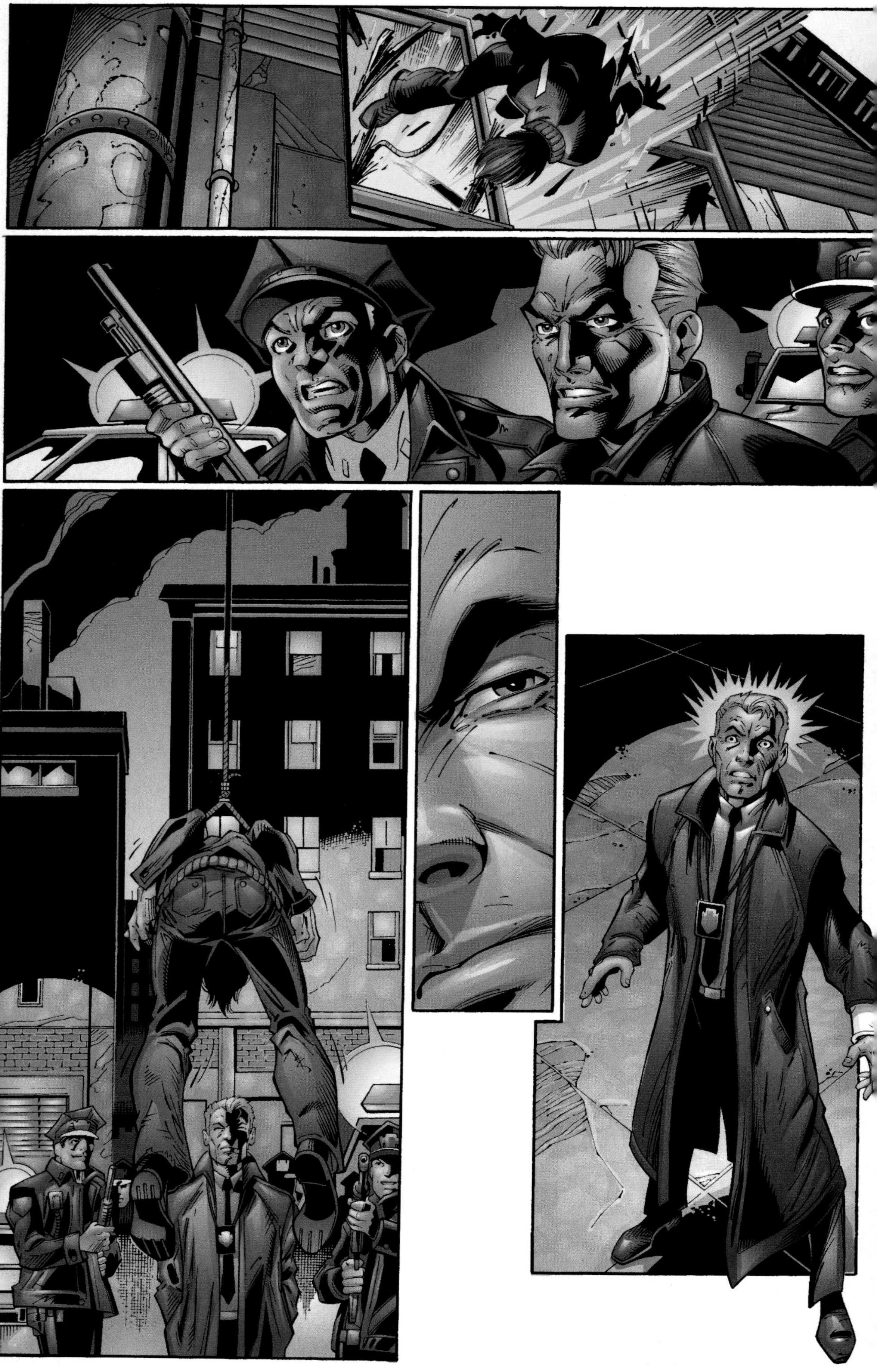

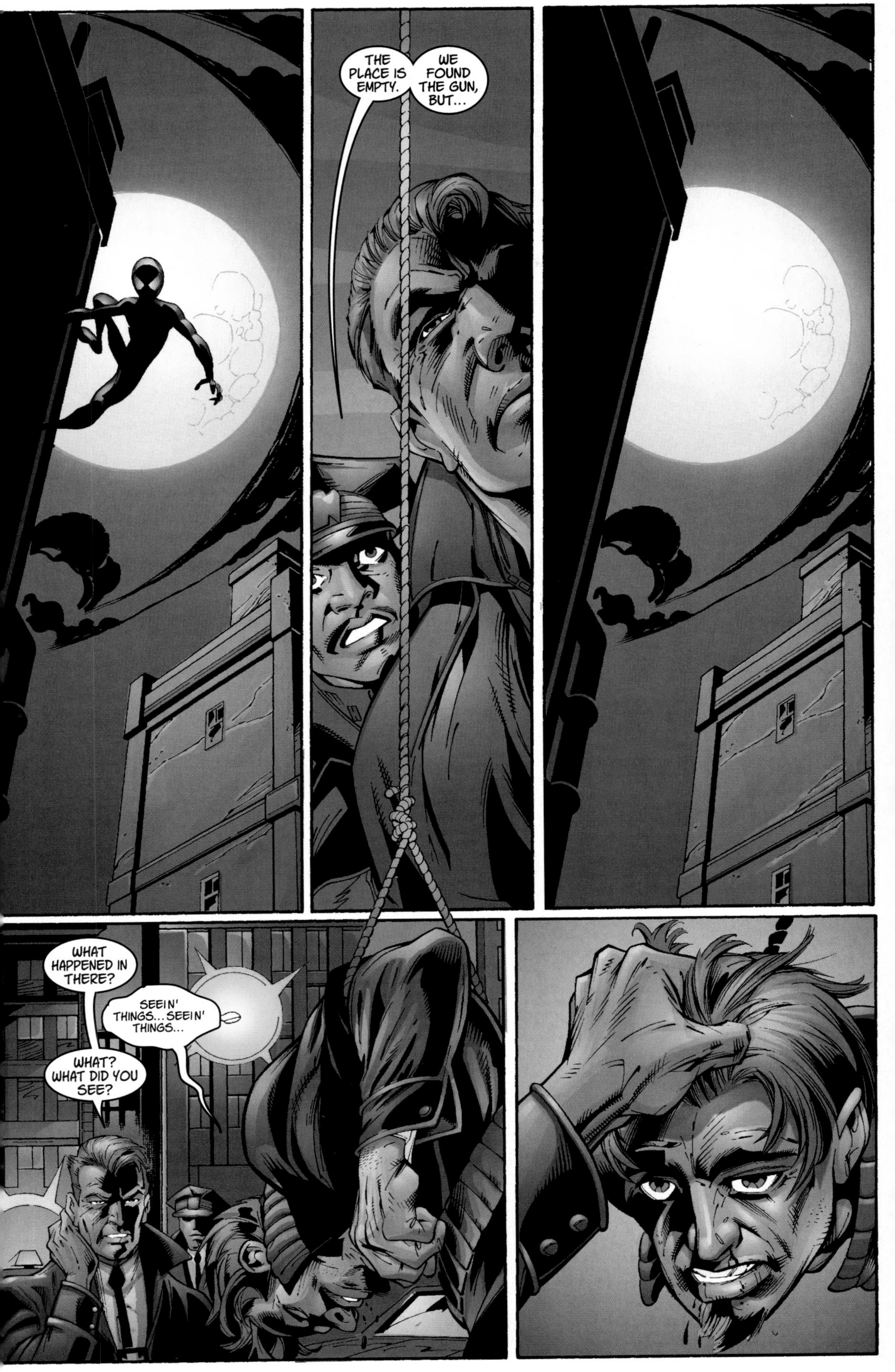
THE PLACE IS EMPTY.
WE FOUND THE GUN, BUT...
WHAT HAPPENED IN THERE?
SEEIN' THINGS... SEEIN' THINGS...
WHAT? WHAT DID YOU SEE?

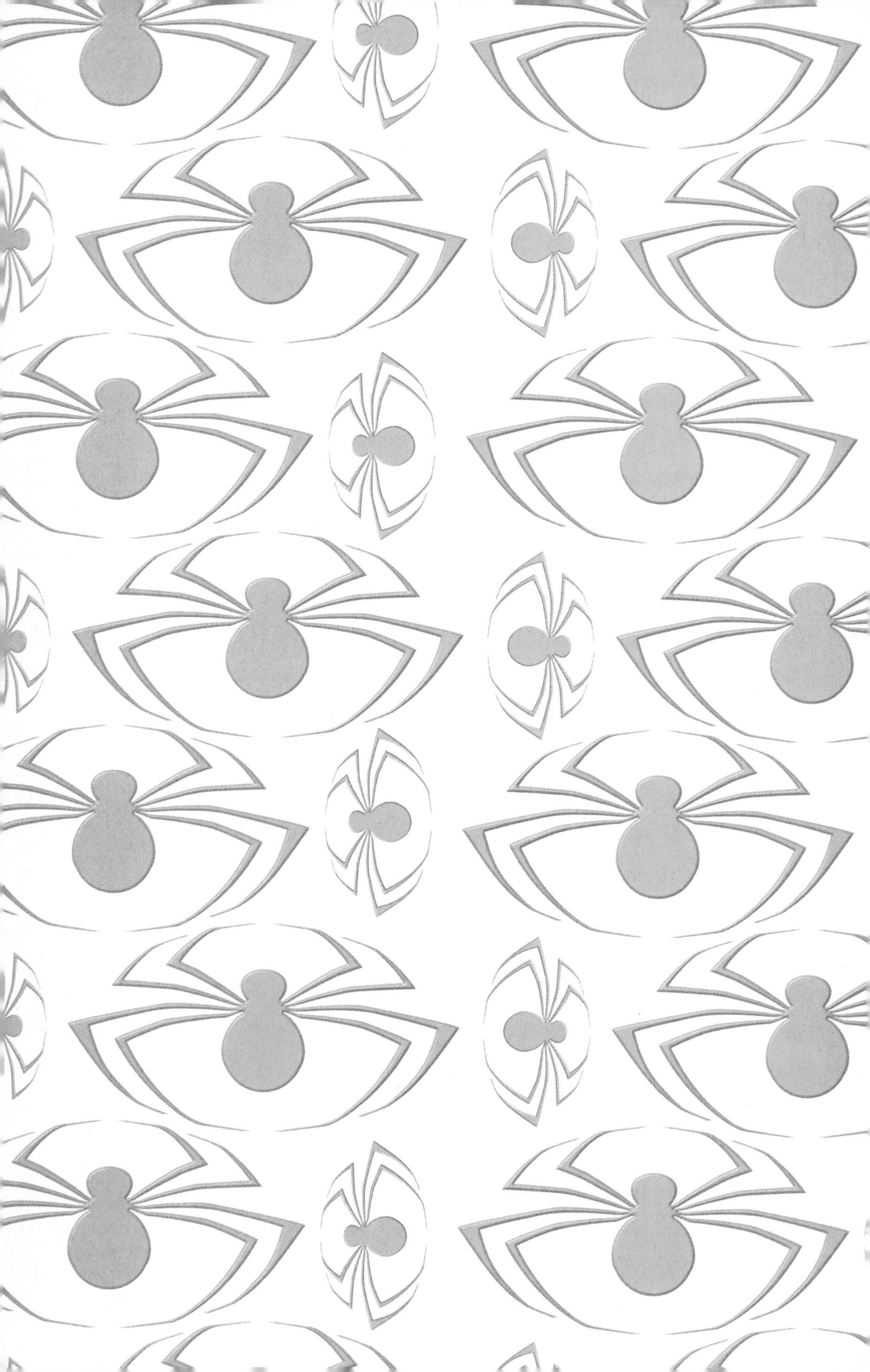

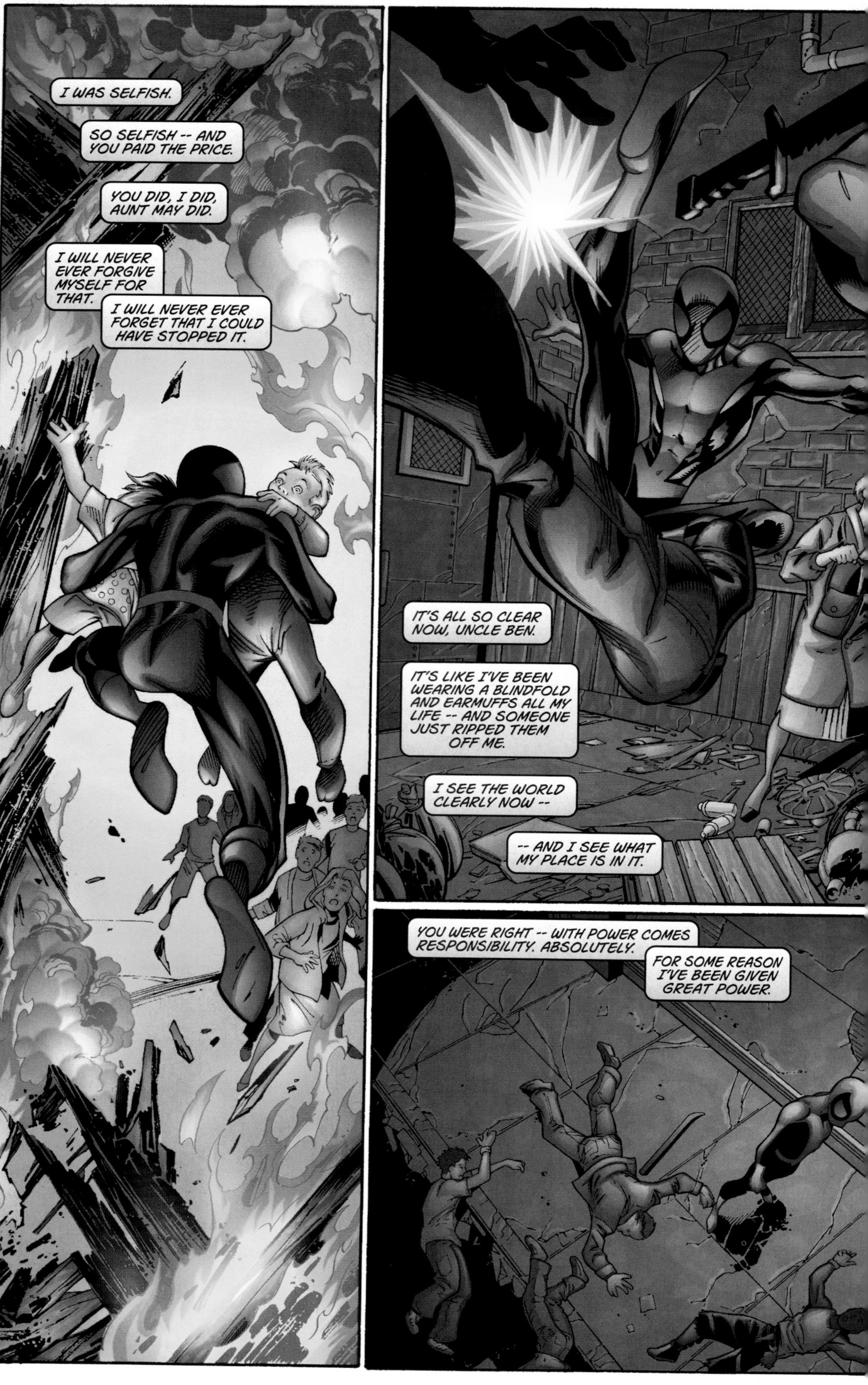
I WAS SELFISH.
SO SELFISH -- AND YOU PAID THE PRICE.
YOU DID, I DID, AUNT MAY DID.
I WILL NEVER EVER FORGIVE MYSELF FOR THAT.
I WILL NEVER EVER FORGET THAT I COULD HAVE STOPPED IT.
IT'S ALL SO CLEAR NOW, UNCLE BEN.
IT'S LIKE I'VE BEEN WEARING A BLINDFOLD AND EARMUFFS ALL MY LIFE -- AND SOMEONE JUST RIPPED THEM OFF ME.
I SEE THE WORLD CLEARLY NOW --
-- AND I SEE WHAT MY PLACE IS IN IT.
YOU WERE RIGHT -- WITH POWER COMES RESPONSIBILITY. ABSOLUTELY.
FOR SOME REASON I'VE BEEN GIVEN GREAT POWER.

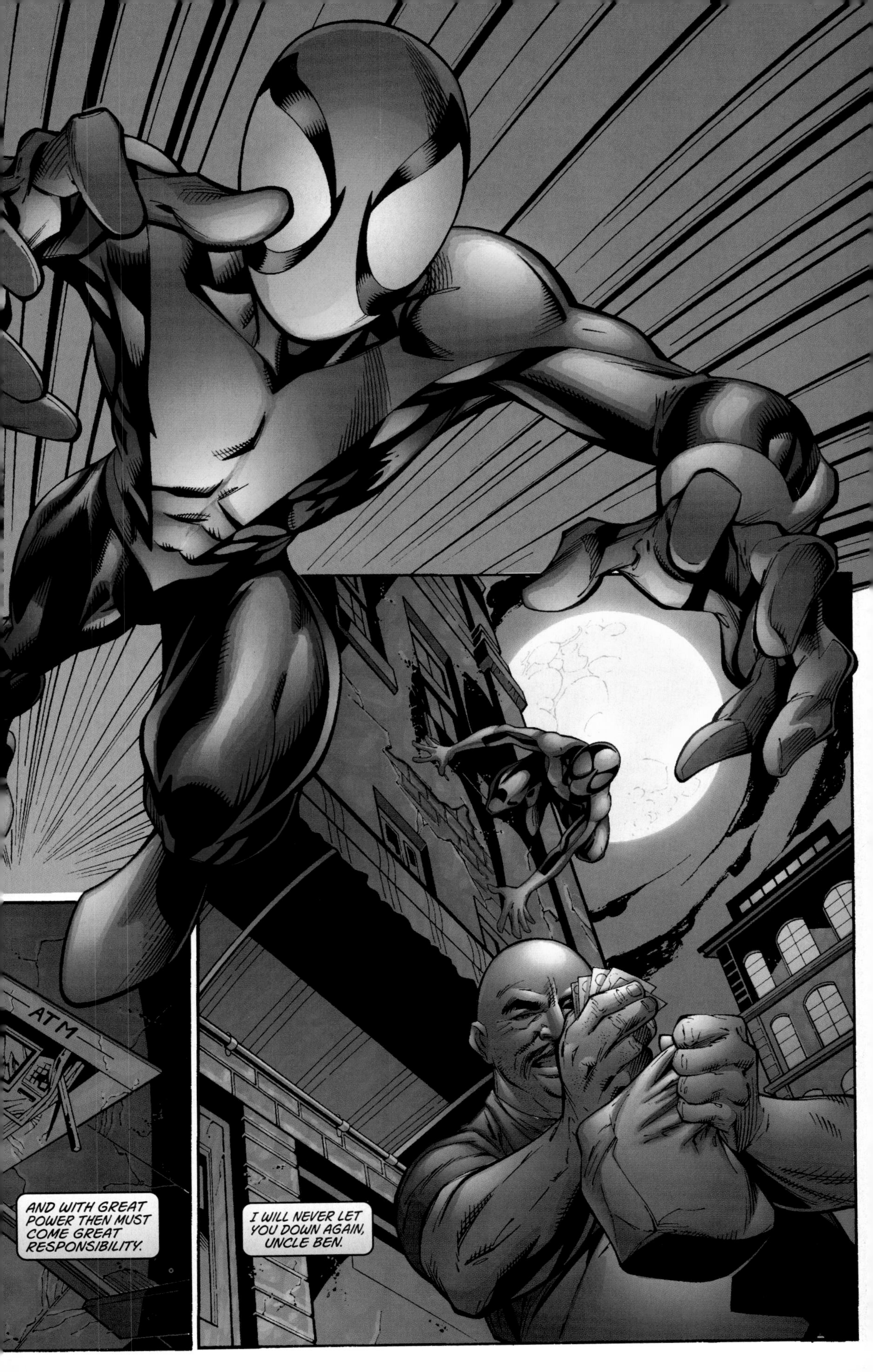
ATM
AND WITH GREAT POWER THEN MUST COME GREAT RESPONSIBILITY.
I WILL NEVER LET YOU DOWN AGAIN, UNCLE BEN.

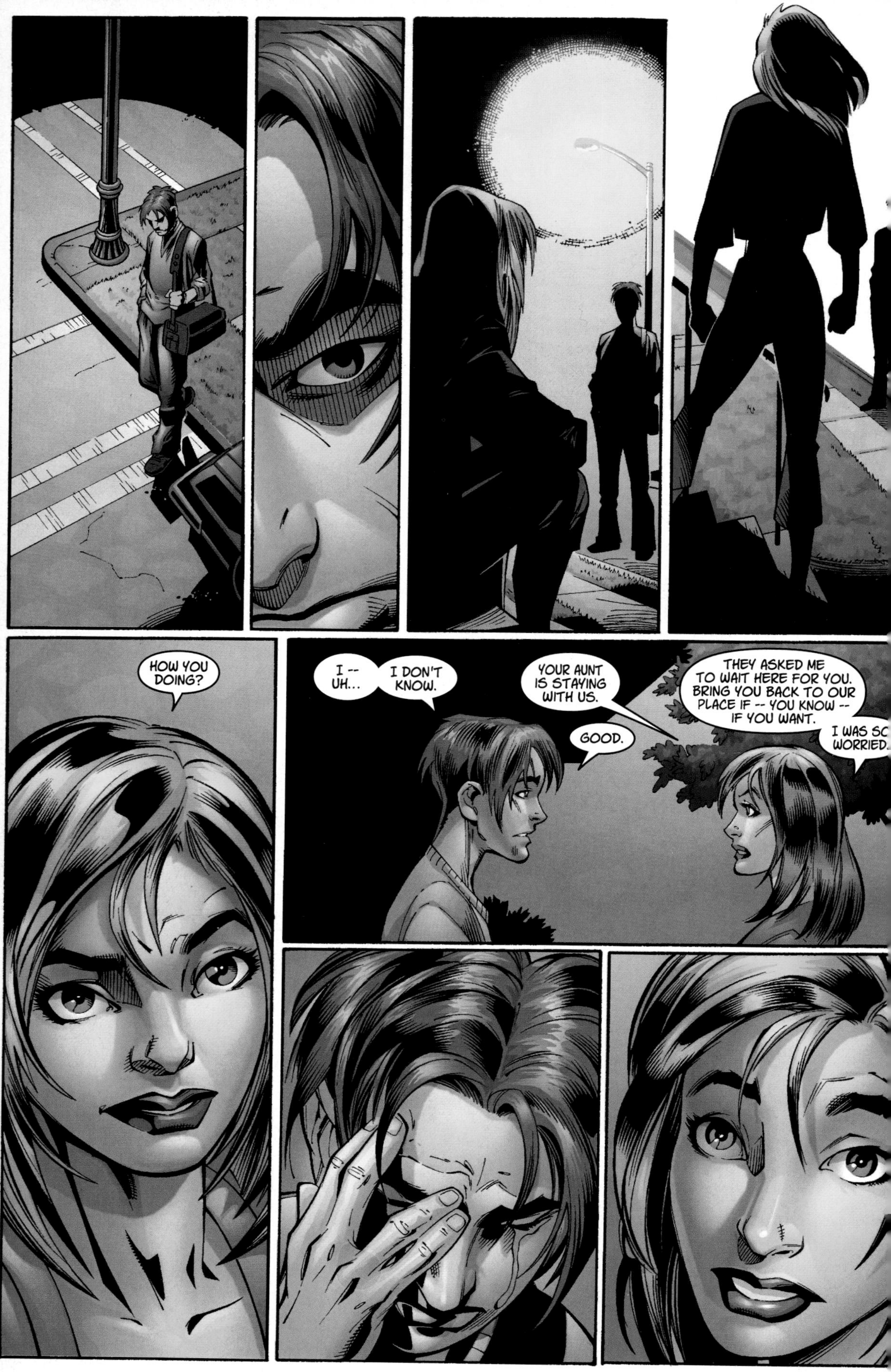
HOW YOU DOING?
I -- UH...
I DON'T KNOW.
YOUR AUNT IS STAYING WITH US.
GOOD.
THEY ASKED ME TO WAIT HERE FOR YOU. BRING YOU BACK TO OUR PLACE IF -- YOU KNOW -- IF YOU WANT.

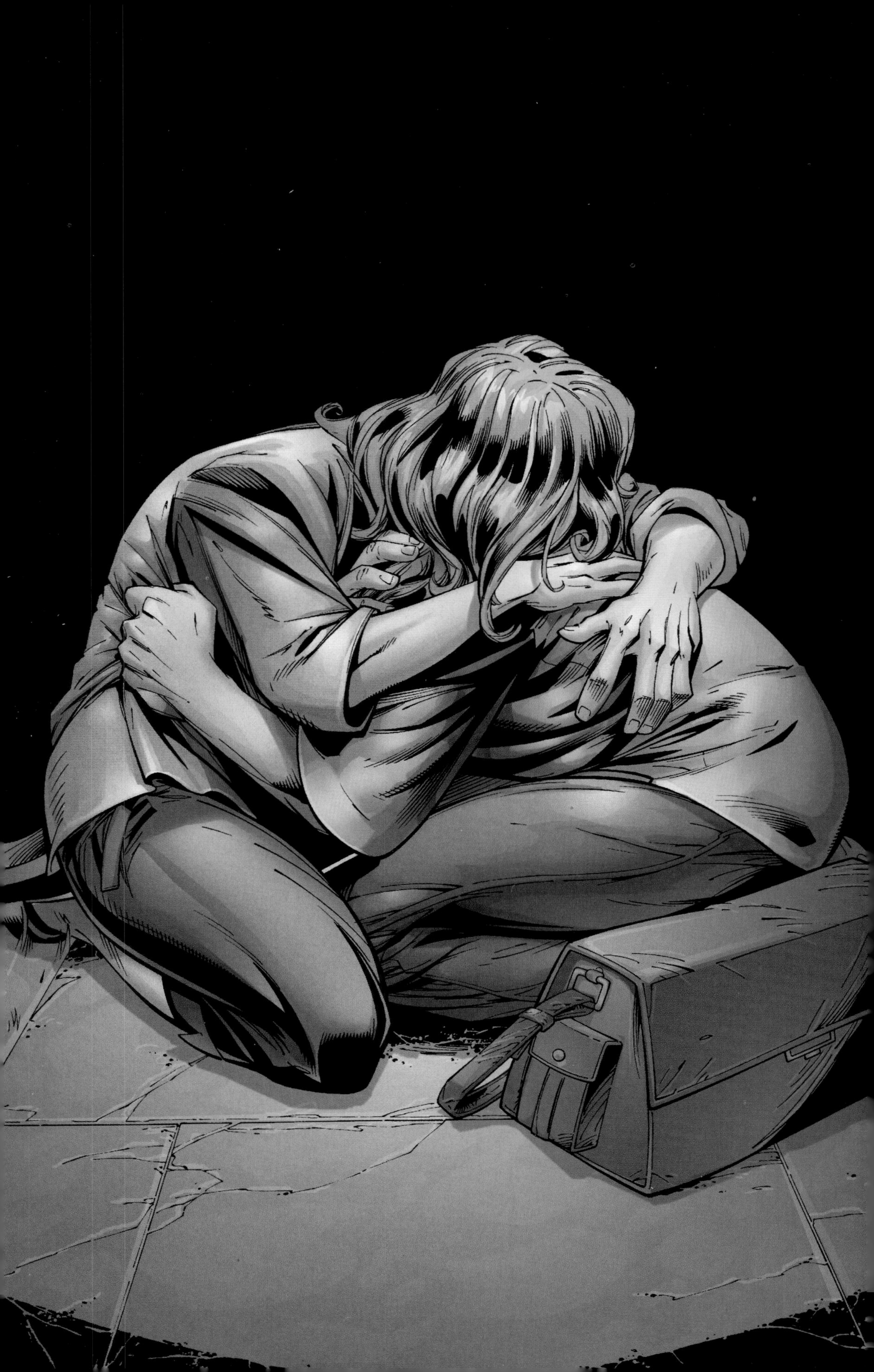

6

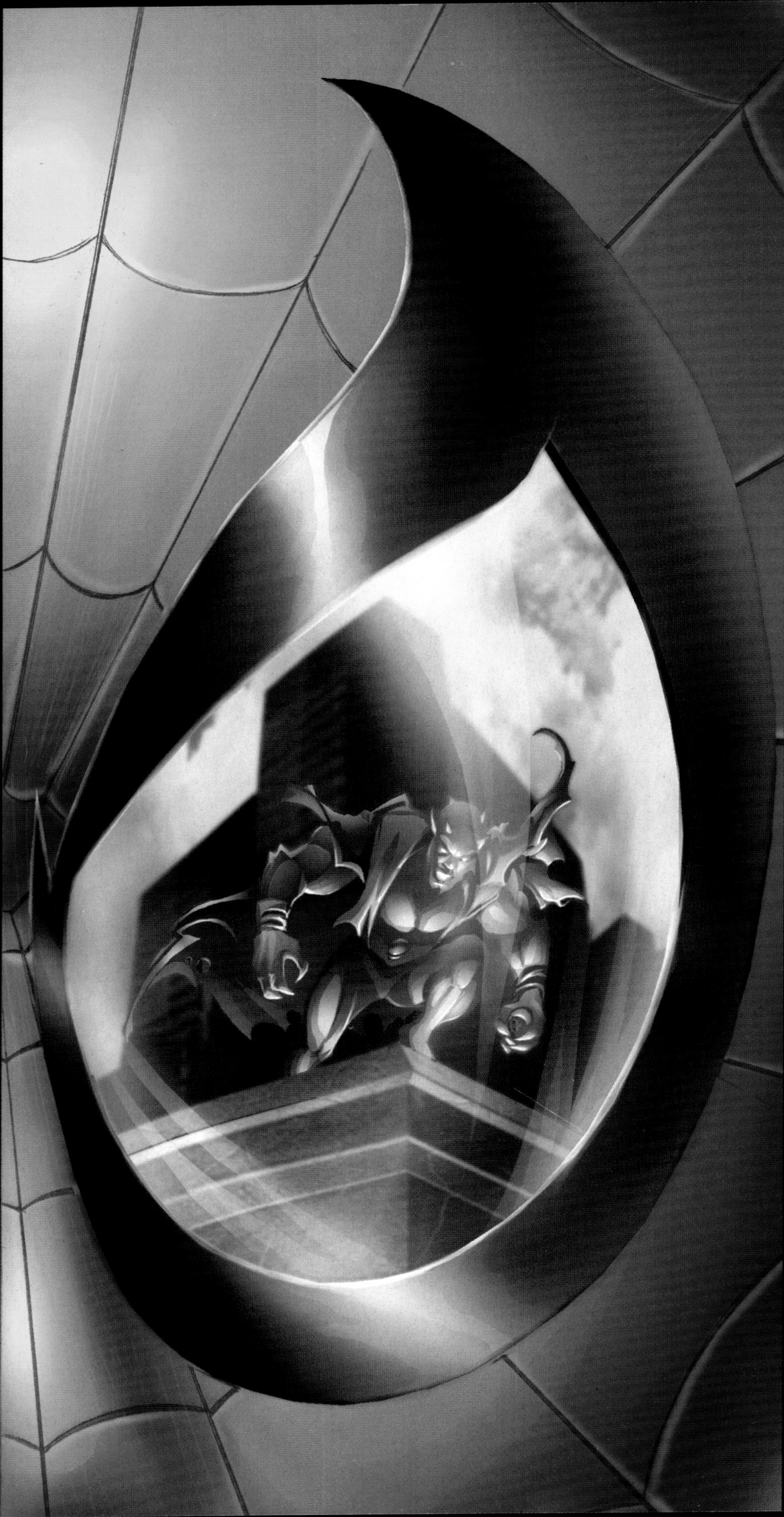

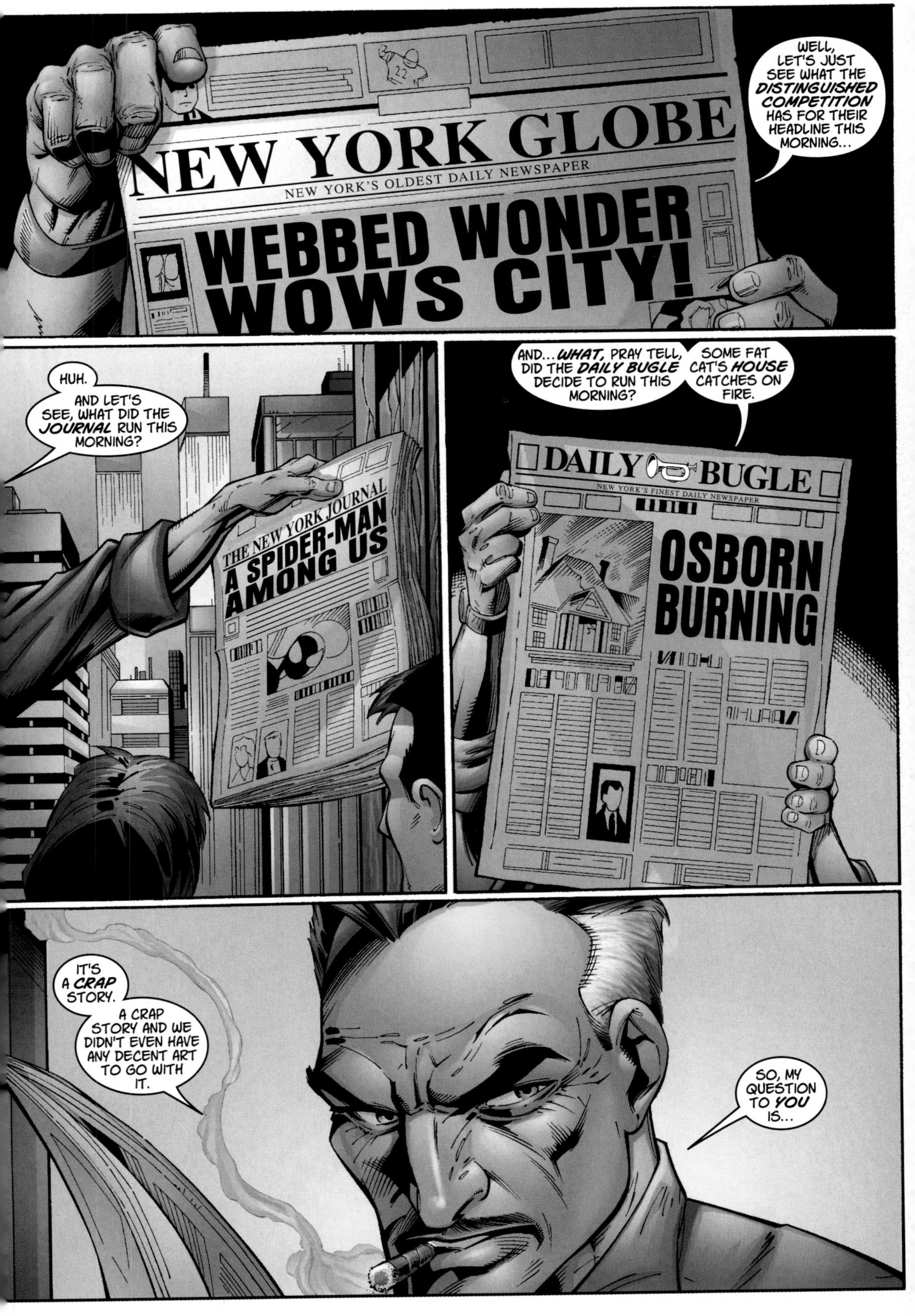
NEW YORK GLOBE
NEW YORK'S OLDEST DAILY NEWSPAPER
WEBBED WONDER WOWS CITY!
WELL, LET'S JUST SEE WHAT THE DISTINGUISHED COMPETITION HAS FOR THEIR HEADLINE THIS MORNING...
HUH.
AND LET'S SEE, WHAT DID THE JOURNAL RUN THIS MORNING?
THE NEW YORK JOURNAL
A SPIDER-MAN AMONG US
AND... WHAT, PRAY TELL, DID THE DAILY BUGLE DECIDE TO RUN THIS MORNING?
SOME FAT CAT'S HOUSE CATCHES ON FIRE.
DAILY BUGLE
NEW YORK'S FINEST DAILY NEWSPAPER
OSBORN BURNING
IT'S A CRAP STORY.
A CRAP STORY AND WE DIDN'T EVEN HAVE ANY DECENT ART TO GO WITH IT.
SO, MY QUESTION TO YOU IS...

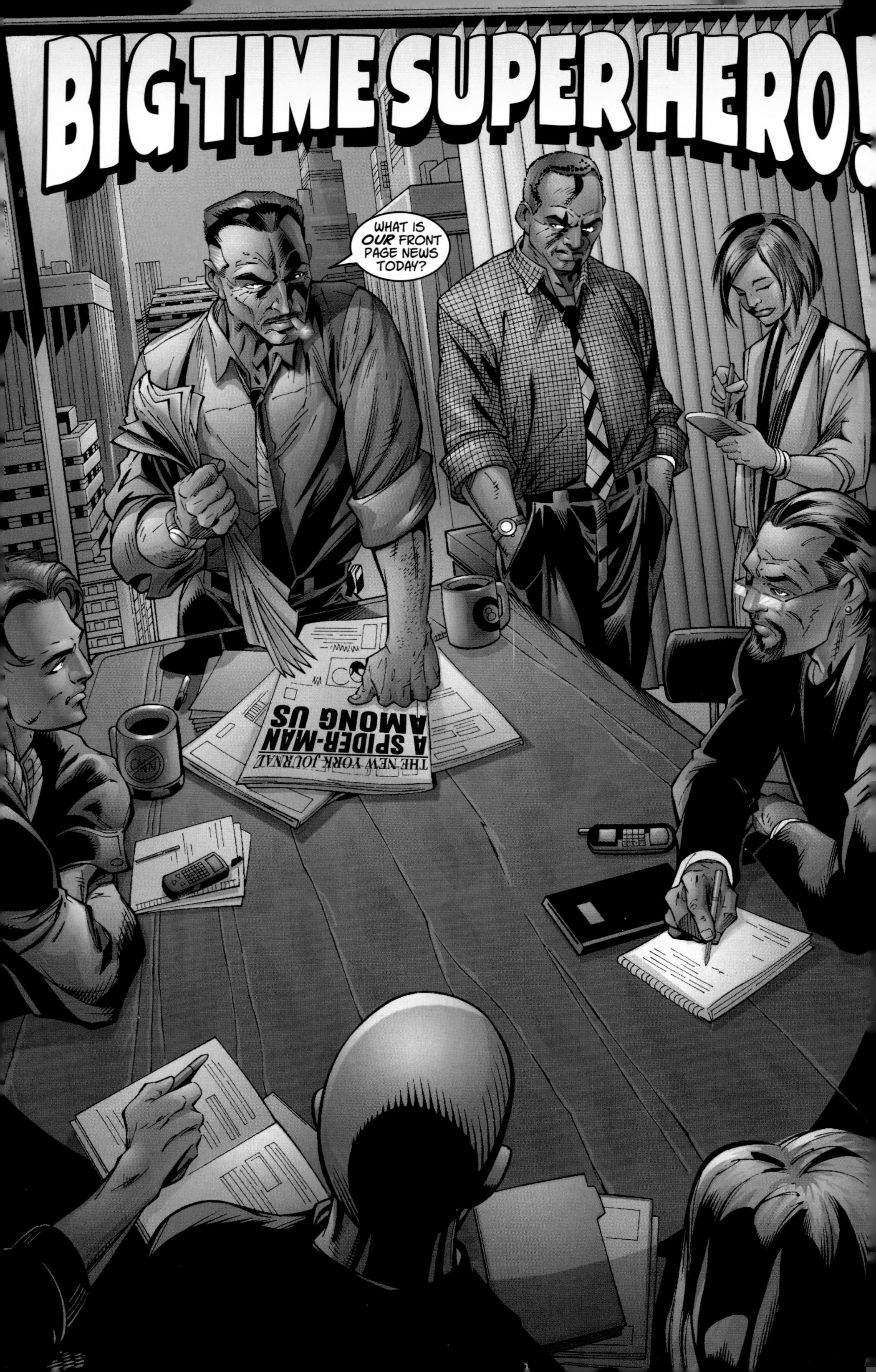
BIG TIME SUPER HERO!
WHAT IS OUR FRONT PAGE NEWS TODAY?
THE NEW YORK JOURNAL
A SPIDER-MAN AMONG US

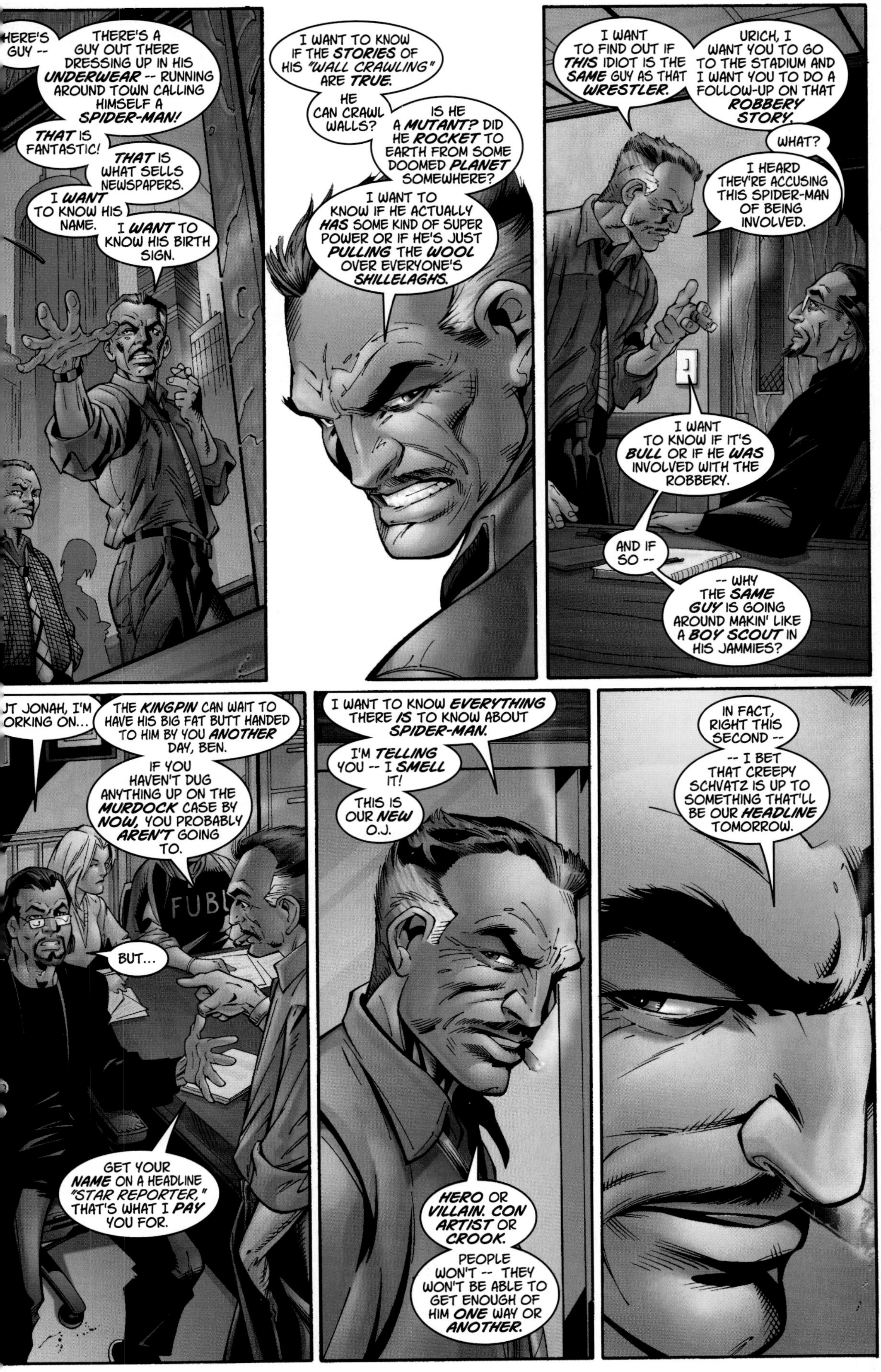
HERE'S GUY --
THERE'S A GUY OUT THERE DRESSING UP IN HIS UNDERWEAR -- RUNNING AROUND TOWN CALLING HIMSELF A SPIDER-MAN!
THAT IS FANTASTIC!
THAT IS WHAT SELLS NEWSPAPERS.
I WANT TO KNOW HIS NAME.
I WANT TO KNOW HIS BIRTH SIGN.
I WANT TO KNOW IF THE STORIES OF HIS "WALL CRAWLING" ARE TRUE.
HE CAN CRAWL WALLS?
IS HE A MUTANT? DID HE ROCKET TO EARTH FROM SOME DOOMED PLANET SOMEWHERE?
I WANT TO KNOW IF HE ACTUALLY HAS SOME KIND OF SUPER POWER OR IF HE'S JUST PULLING THE WOOL OVER EVERYONE'S SHILLELAGHS.
I WANT TO FIND OUT IF THIS IDIOT IS THE SAME GUY AS THAT WRESTLER.
URICH, I WANT YOU TO GO TO THE STADIUM AND I WANT YOU TO DO A FOLLOW-UP ON THAT ROBBERY STORY.
WHAT?
I HEARD THEY'RE ACCUSING THIS SPIDER-MAN OF BEING INVOLVED.
I WANT TO KNOW IF IT'S BULL OR IF HE WAS INVOLVED WITH THE ROBBERY.
AND IF SO --
-- WHY THE SAME GUY IS GOING AROUND MAKIN' LIKE A BOY SCOUT IN HIS JAMMIES?
UT JONAH, I'M ORKING ON...
THE KINGPIN CAN WAIT TO HAVE HIS BIG FAT BUTT HANDED TO HIM BY YOU ANOTHER DAY, BEN.
IF YOU HAVEN'T DUG ANYTHING UP ON THE MURDOCK CASE BY NOW, YOU PROBABLY AREN'T GOING TO.
BUT...
GET YOUR NAME ON A HEADLINE "STAR REPORTER," THAT'S WHAT I PAY YOU FOR.
I WANT TO KNOW EVERYTHING THERE IS TO KNOW ABOUT SPIDER-MAN.
I'M TELLING YOU -- I SMELL IT!
THIS IS OUR NEW O.J.
HERO OR VILLAIN. CON ARTIST OR CROOK.
PEOPLE WON'T -- THEY WON'T BE ABLE TO GET ENOUGH OF HIM ONE WAY OR ANOTHER.
IN FACT, RIGHT THIS SECOND --
-- I BET THAT CREEPY SCHVATZ IS UP TO SOMETHING THAT'LL BE OUR HEADLINE TOMORROW.

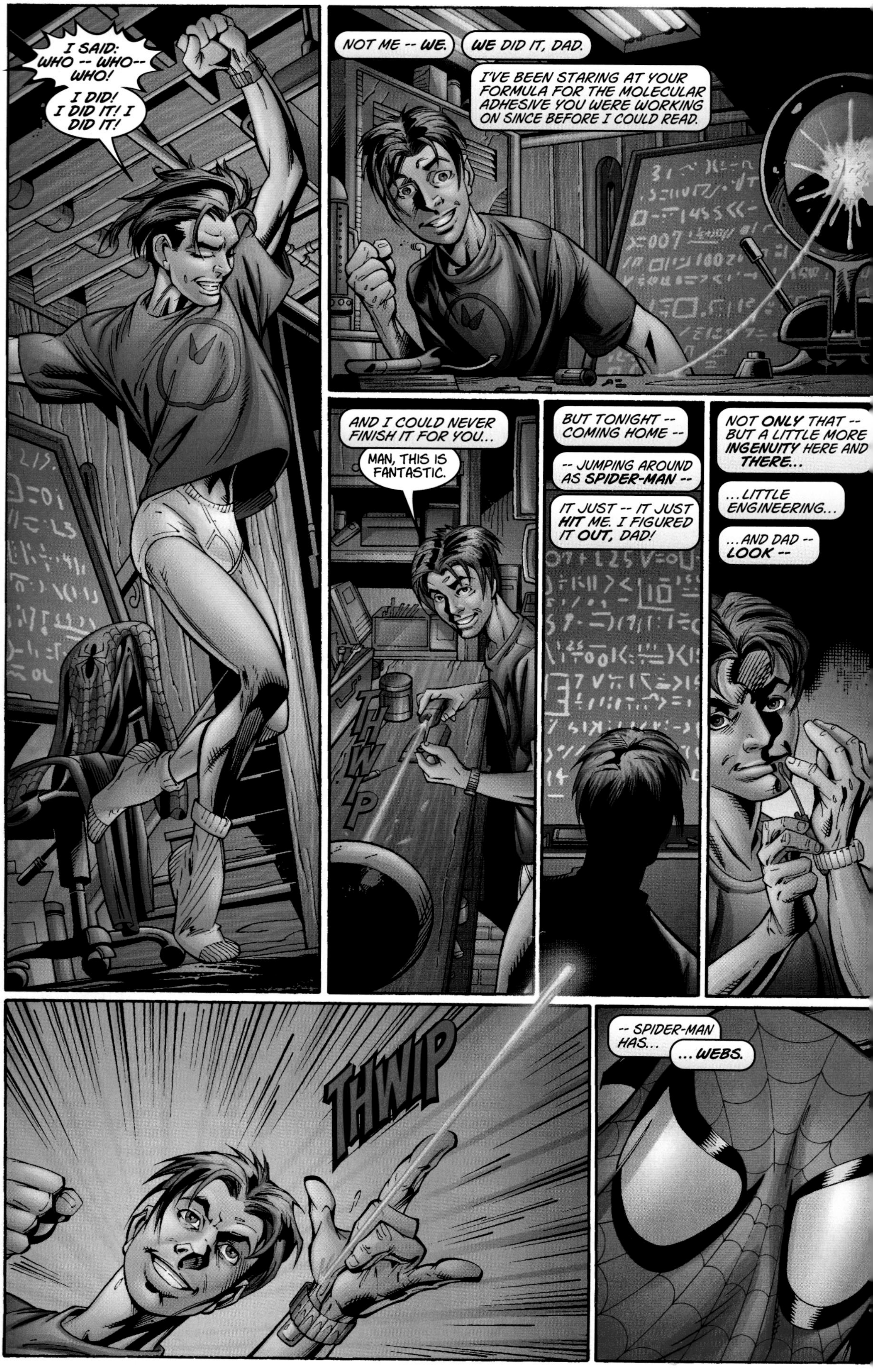
I SAID: WHO -- WHO-- WHO!
I DID! I DID IT! I DID IT!
NOT ME -- WE.
WE DID IT, DAD.
I'VE BEEN STARING AT YOUR FORMULA FOR THE MOLECULAR ADHESIVE YOU WERE WORKING ON SINCE BEFORE I COULD READ.
AND I COULD NEVER FINISH IT FOR YOU...
MAN, THIS IS FANTASTIC.
THWIP
BUT TONIGHT -- COMING HOME --
-- JUMPING AROUND AS SPIDER-MAN --
IT JUST -- IT JUST HIT ME. I FIGURED IT OUT, DAD!
NOT ONLY THAT -- BUT A LITTLE MORE INGENUITY HERE AND THERE...
...LITTLE ENGINEERING...
...AND DAD -- LOOK --
THWIP
-- SPIDER-MAN HAS...
...WEBS.

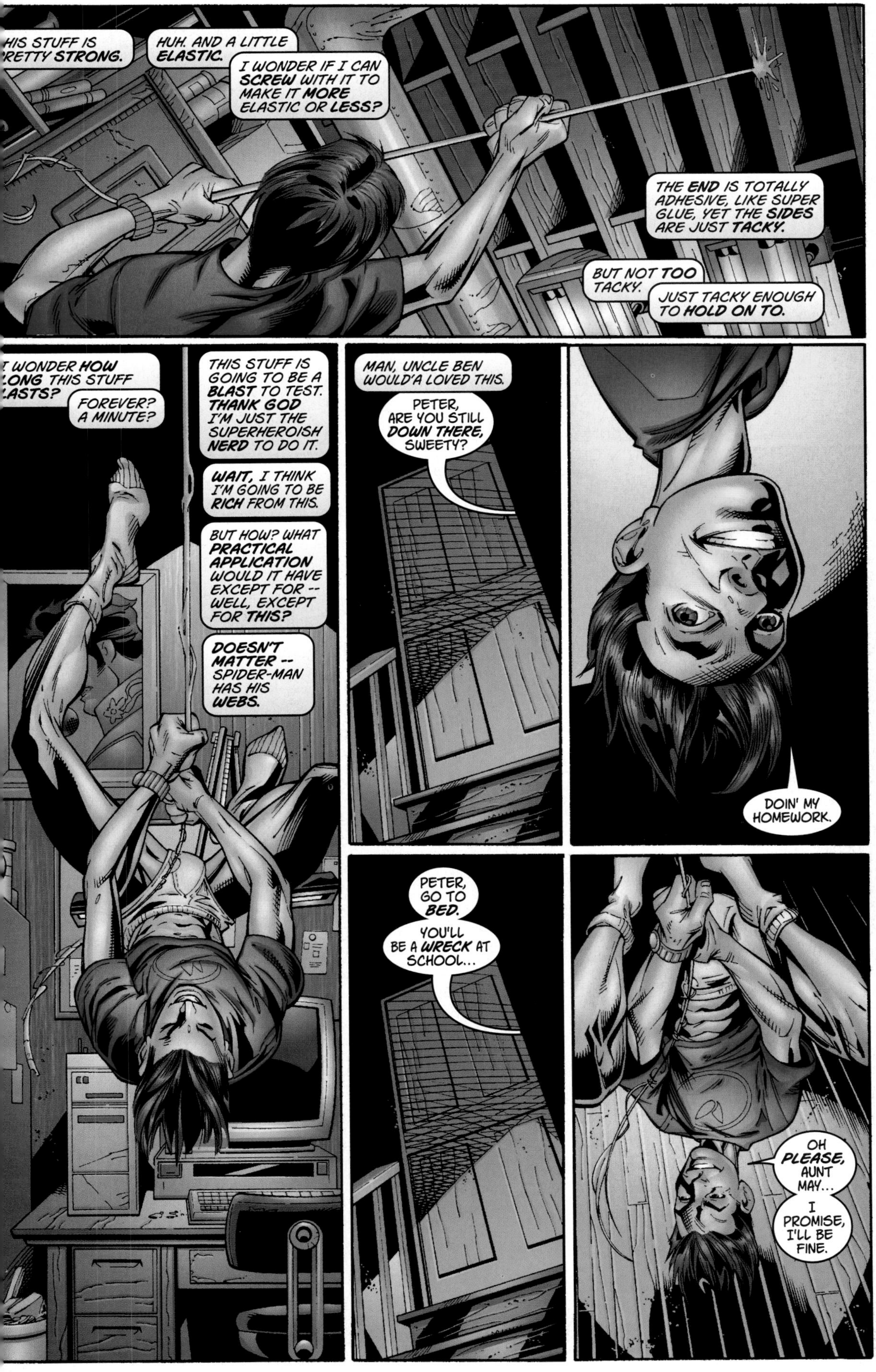
HIS STUFF IS RETTY STRONG.
HUH. AND A LITTLE ELASTIC.
I WONDER IF I CAN SCREW WITH IT TO MAKE IT MORE ELASTIC OR LESS?
THE END IS TOTALLY ADHESIVE, LIKE SUPER GLUE, YET THE SIDES ARE JUST TACKY.
BUT NOT TOO TACKY.
JUST TACKY ENOUGH TO HOLD ON TO.
I WONDER HOW LONG THIS STUFF LASTS?
FOREVER? A MINUTE?
THIS STUFF IS GOING TO BE A BLAST TO TEST. THANK GOD I'M JUST THE SUPERHEROISH NERD TO DO IT.
WAIT, I THINK I'M GOING TO BE RICH FROM THIS.
BUT HOW? WHAT PRACTICAL APPLICATION WOULD IT HAVE EXCEPT FOR -- WELL, EXCEPT FOR THIS?
DOESN'T MATTER -- SPIDER-MAN HAS HIS WEBS.
MAN, UNCLE BEN WOULD'A LOVED THIS.
PETER, ARE YOU STILL DOWN THERE, SWEETY?
DOIN' MY HOMEWORK.
PETER, GO TO BED.
YOU'LL BE A WRECK AT SCHOOL...
OH PLEASE, AUNT MAY...
I PROMISE, I'LL BE FINE.

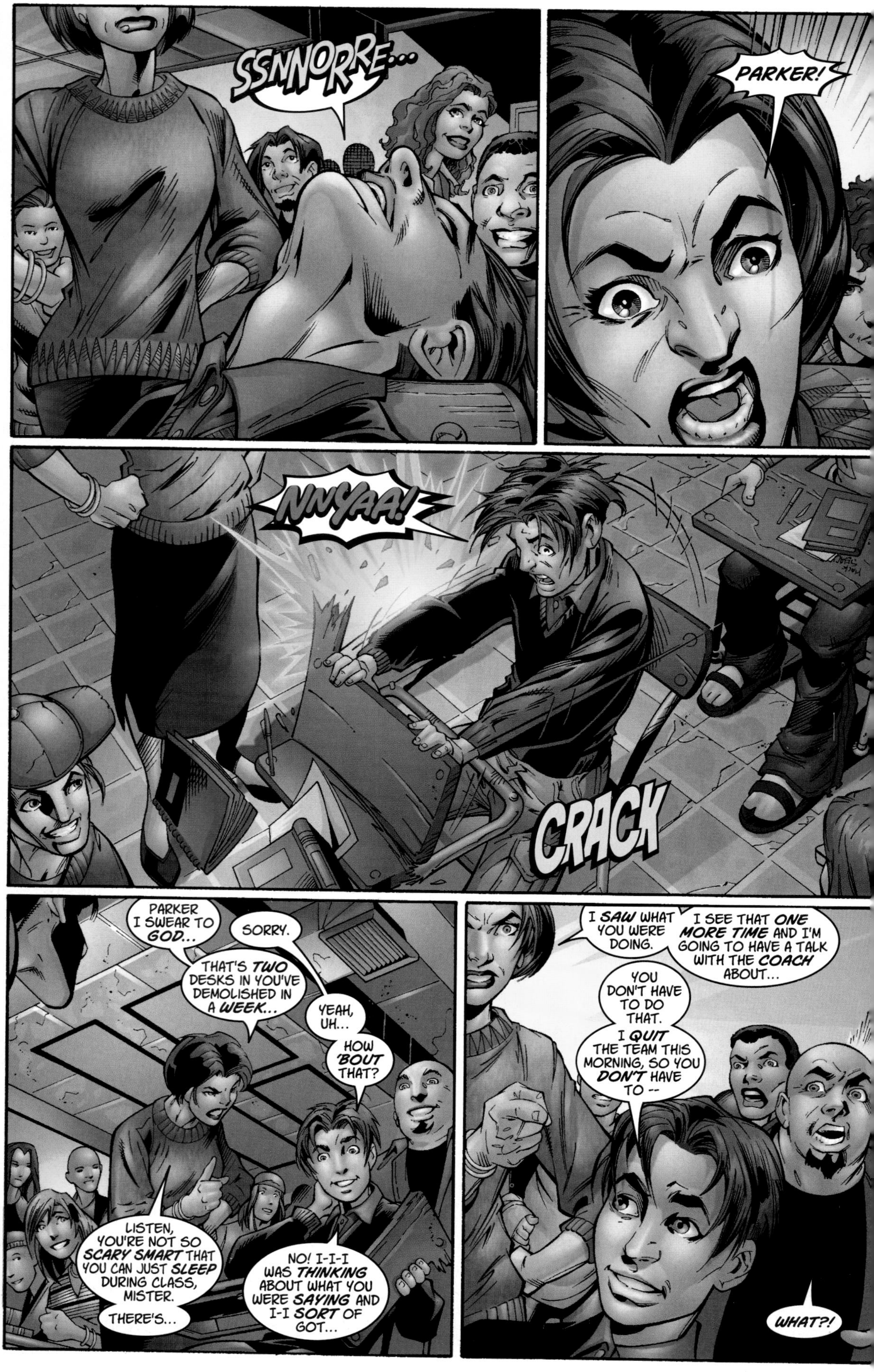
SSNNORRE...
PARKER!
NNYAA!
CRACK
PARKER I SWEAR TO GOD...
SORRY.
THAT'S TWO DESKS IN YOU'VE DEMOLISHED IN A WEEK...
YEAH, UH...
HOW 'BOUT THAT?
LISTEN, YOU'RE NOT SO SCARY SMART THAT YOU CAN JUST SLEEP DURING CLASS, MISTER.
THERE'S...
NO! I-I-I WAS THINKING ABOUT WHAT YOU WERE SAYING AND I-I SORT OF GOT...
I SAW WHAT YOU WERE DOING.
I SEE THAT ONE MORE TIME AND I'M GOING TO HAVE A TALK WITH THE COACH ABOUT...
YOU DON'T HAVE TO DO THAT.
I QUIT THE TEAM THIS MORNING, SO YOU DON'T HAVE TO --
WHAT?!

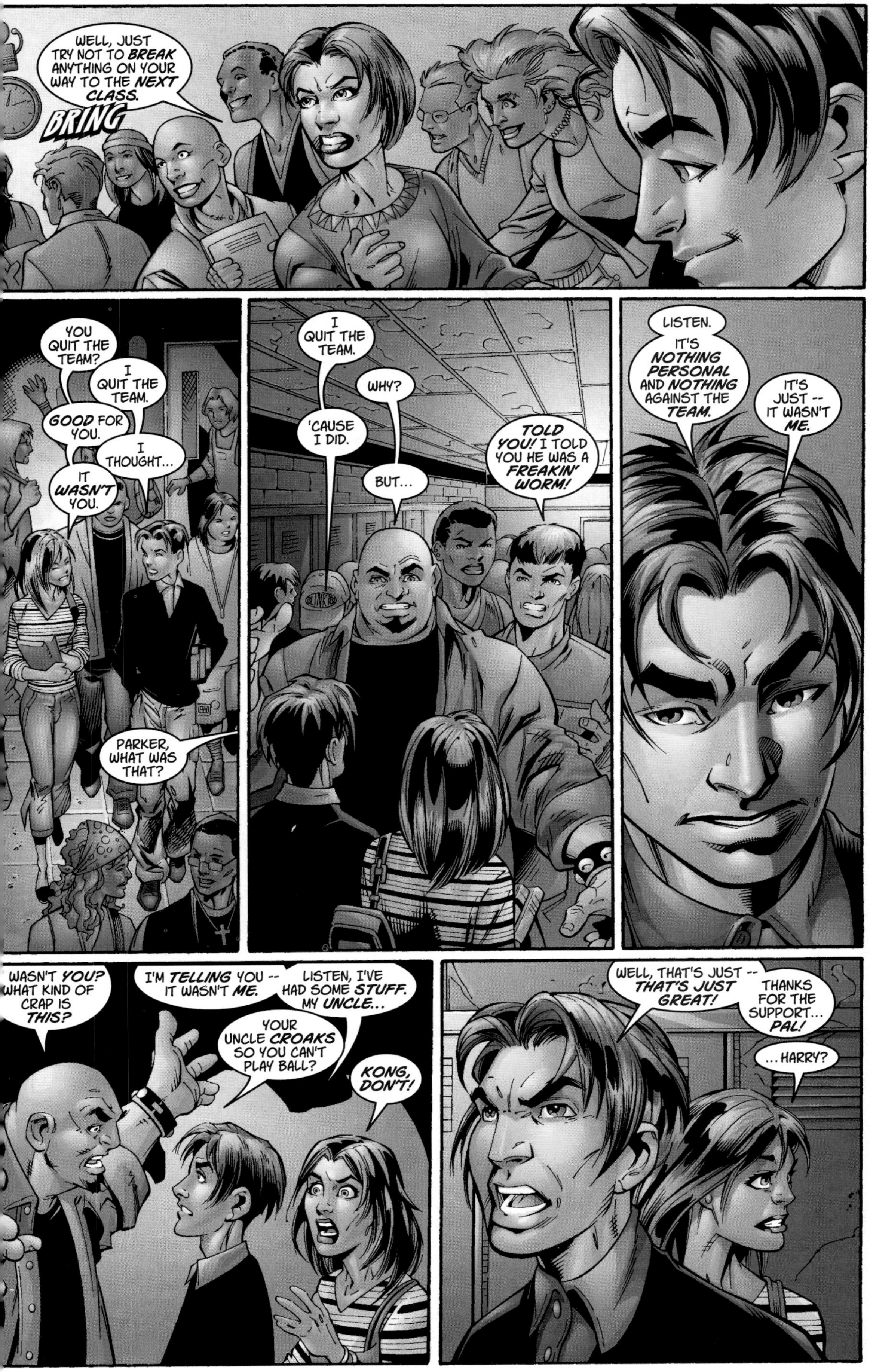

WELL, JUST TRY NOT TO BREAK ANYTHING ON YOUR WAY TO THE NEXT CLASS.
BRING
YOU QUIT THE TEAM?
I QUIT THE TEAM.
GOOD FOR YOU.
I THOUGHT...
IT WASN'T YOU.
PARKER, WHAT WAS THAT?
I QUIT THE TEAM.
WHY?
'CAUSE I DID.
BUT...
TOLD YOU! I TOLD YOU HE WAS A FREAKIN' WORM!
LISTEN.
IT'S NOTHING PERSONAL AND NOTHING AGAINST THE TEAM.
IT'S JUST -- IT WASN'T ME.
WASN'T YOU? WHAT KIND OF CRAP IS THIS?
I'M TELLING YOU -- IT WASN'T ME.
LISTEN, I'VE HAD SOME STUFF. MY UNCLE...
YOUR UNCLE CROAKS SO YOU CAN'T PLAY BALL?
KONG, DON'T!
WELL, THAT'S JUST -- THAT'S JUST GREAT!
THANKS FOR THE SUPPORT... PAL!
...HARRY?

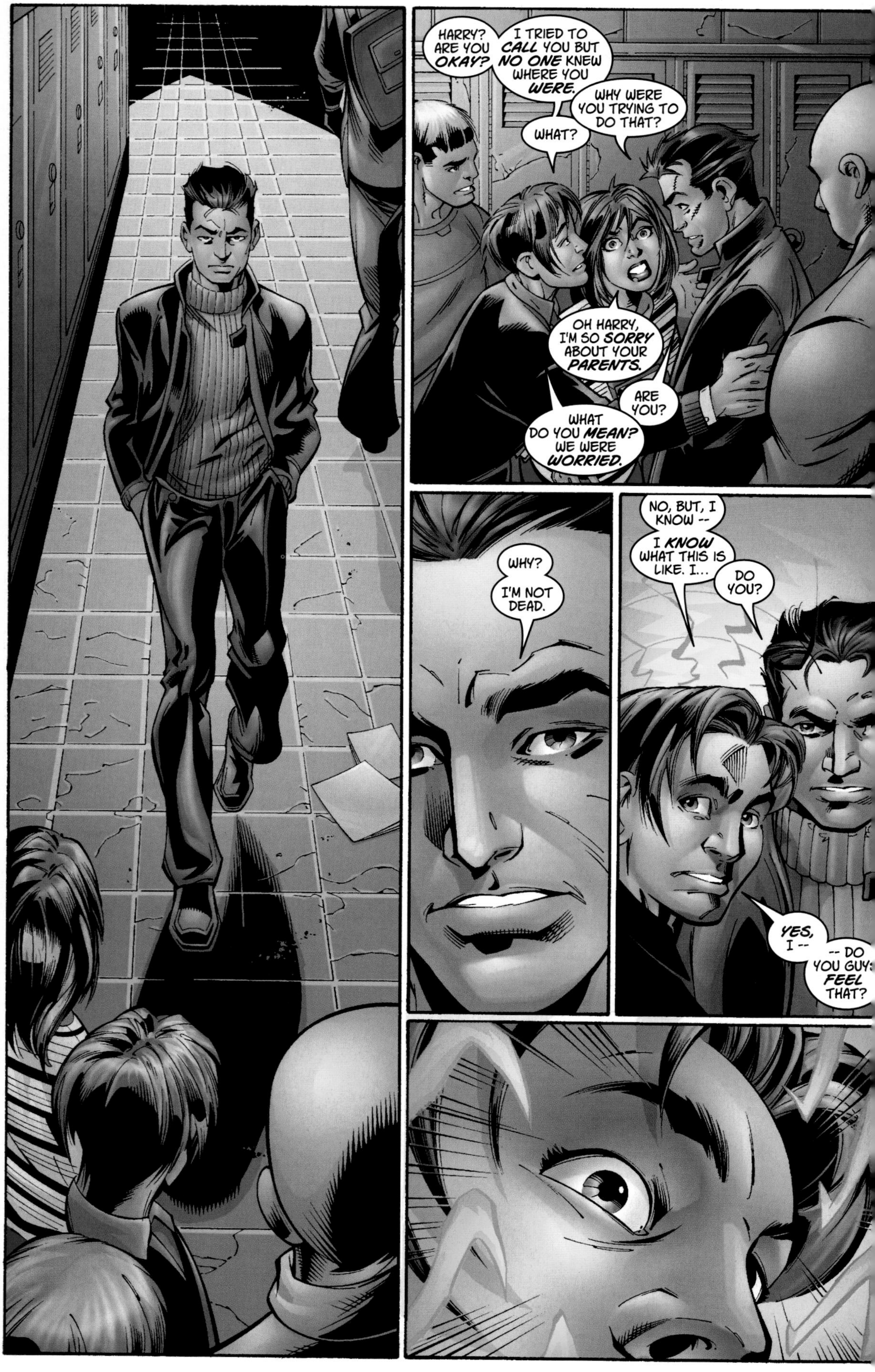
HARRY? ARE YOU OKAY?
I TRIED TO CALL YOU BUT NO ONE KNEW WHERE YOU WERE.
WHAT?
WHY WERE YOU TRYING TO DO THAT?
OH HARRY, I'M SO SORRY ABOUT YOUR PARENTS.
ARE YOU?
WHAT DO YOU MEAN? WE WERE WORRIED.
WHY?
I'M NOT DEAD.
NO, BUT, I KNOW --
I KNOW WHAT THIS IS LIKE. I...
DO YOU?
YES, I --
-- DO YOU GUY FEEL THAT?

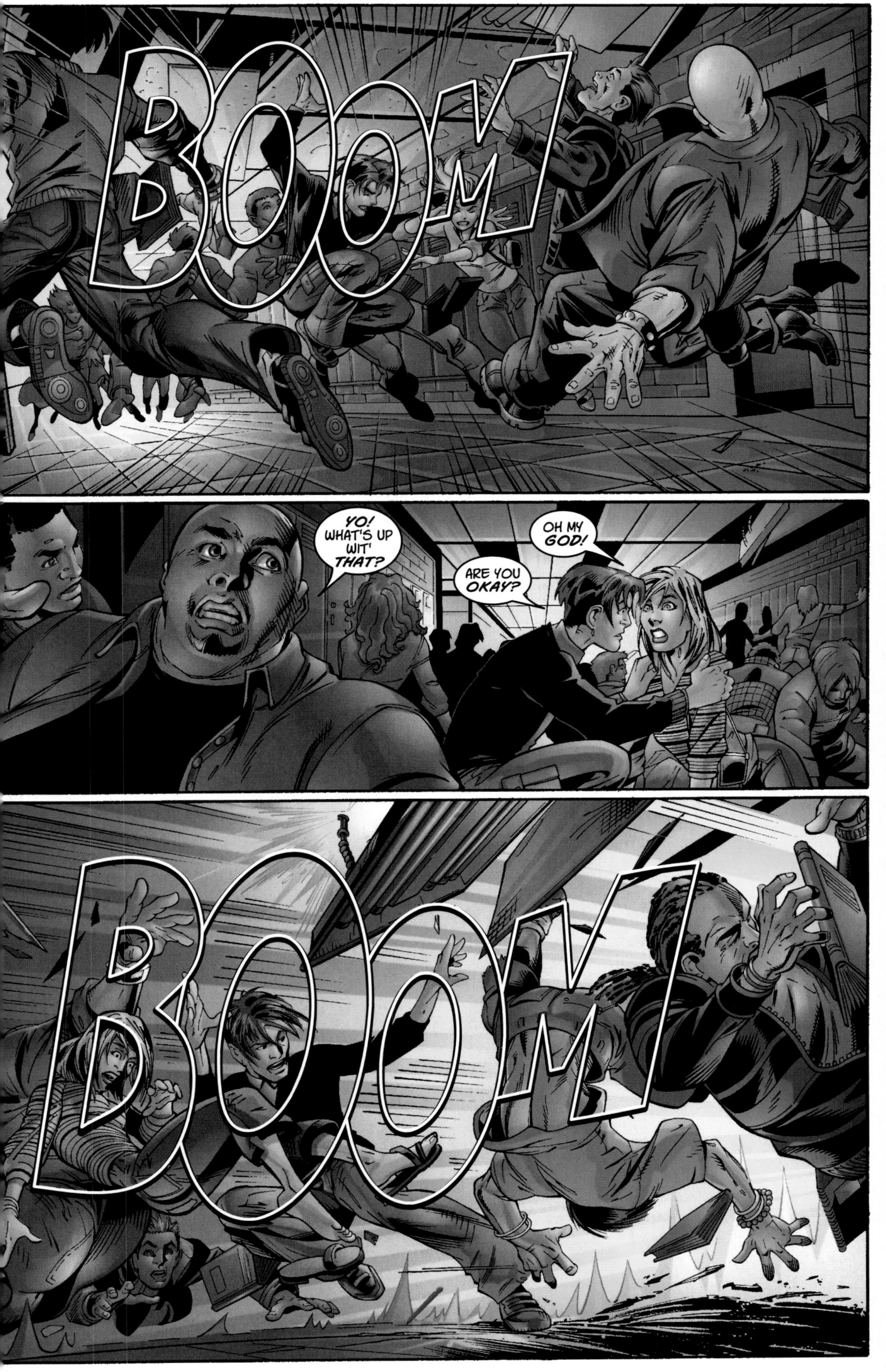
BOOM
YO! WHAT'S UP WIT' THAT?
OH MY GOD!
ARE YOU OKAY?
BOOM

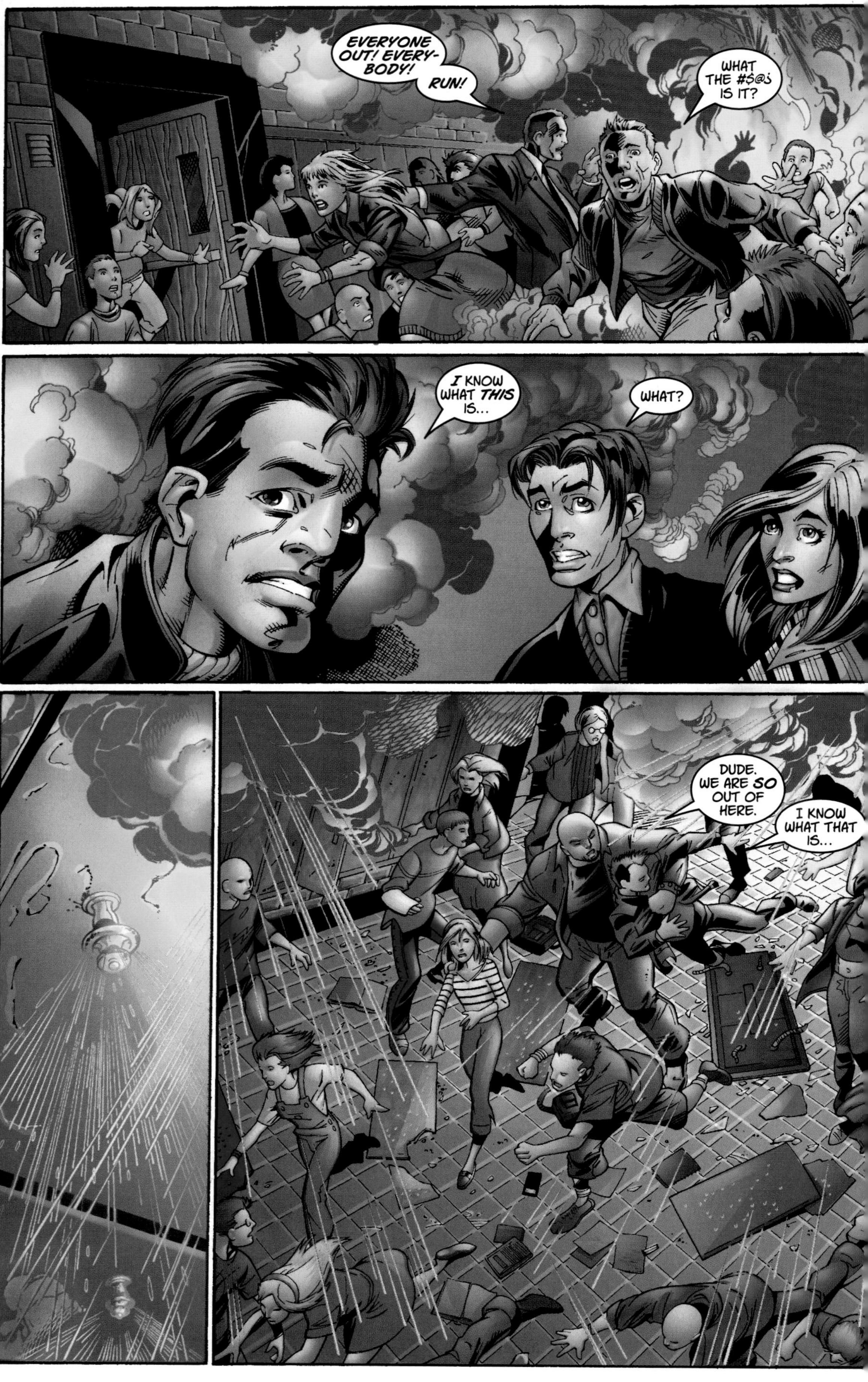
EVERYONE OUT! EVERY-BODY!
RUN!
WHAT THE #$@¡ IS IT?
I KNOW WHAT THIS IS...
WHAT?
DUDE. WE ARE SO OUT OF HERE.
I KNOW WHAT THAT IS...

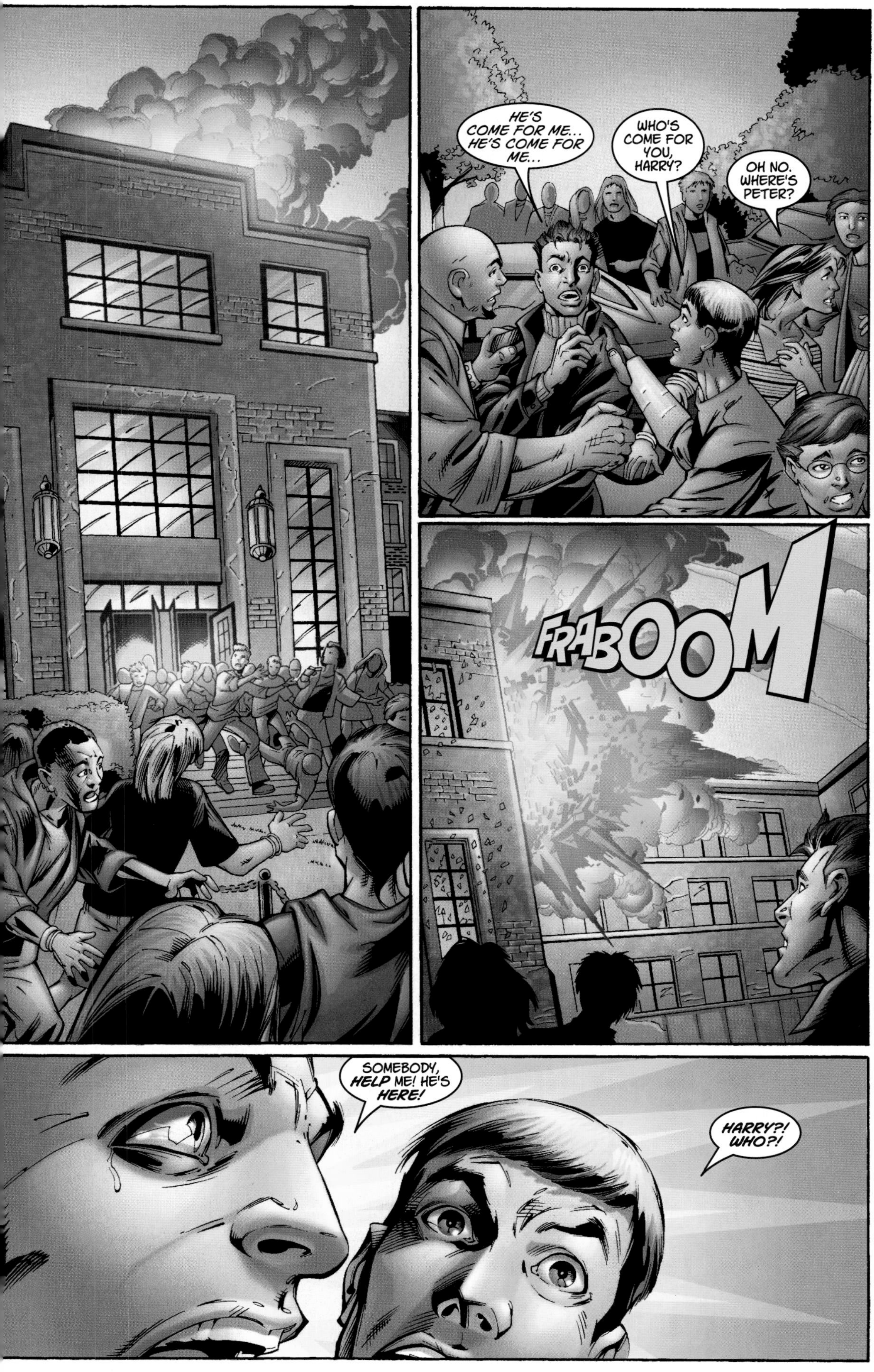
HE'S COME FOR ME... HE'S COME FOR ME...
WHO'S COME FOR YOU, HARRY?
OH NO. WHERE'S PETER?
FRABOOOM
SOMEBODY, HELP ME! HE'S HERE!
HARRY?! WHO?!

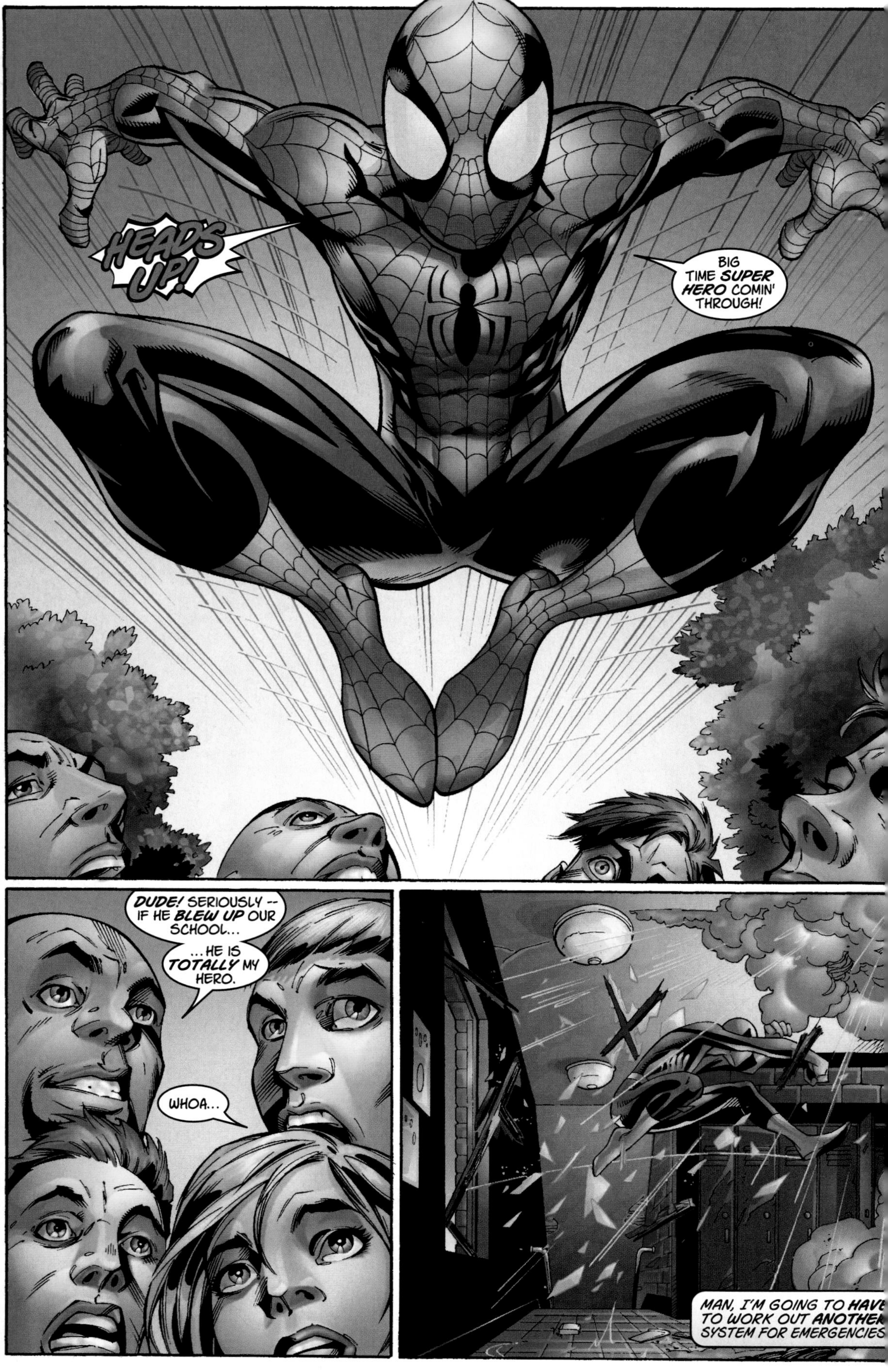
HEAD'S UP!
BIG TIME SUPER HERO COMIN' THROUGH!
DUDE! SERIOUSLY -- IF HE BLEW UP OUR SCHOOL...
...HE IS TOTALLY MY HERO.
WHOA...
MAN, I'M GOING TO HAVE TO WORK OUT ANOTHER SYSTEM FOR EMERGENCIES

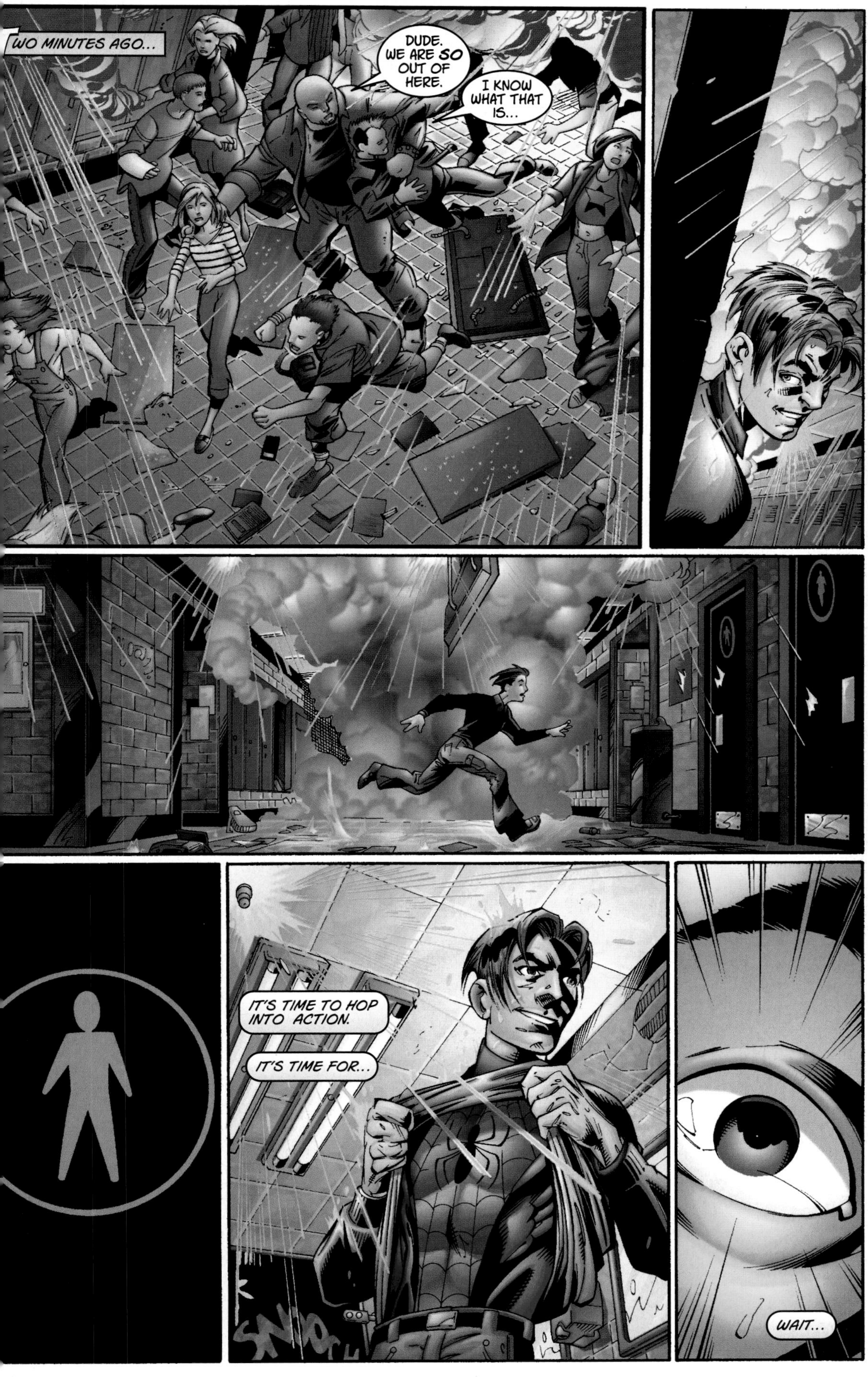
WO MINUTES AGO...
DUDE. WE ARE SO OUT OF HERE.
I KNOW WHAT THAT IS...
IT'S TIME TO HOP INTO ACTION.
IT'S TIME FOR...
WAIT...

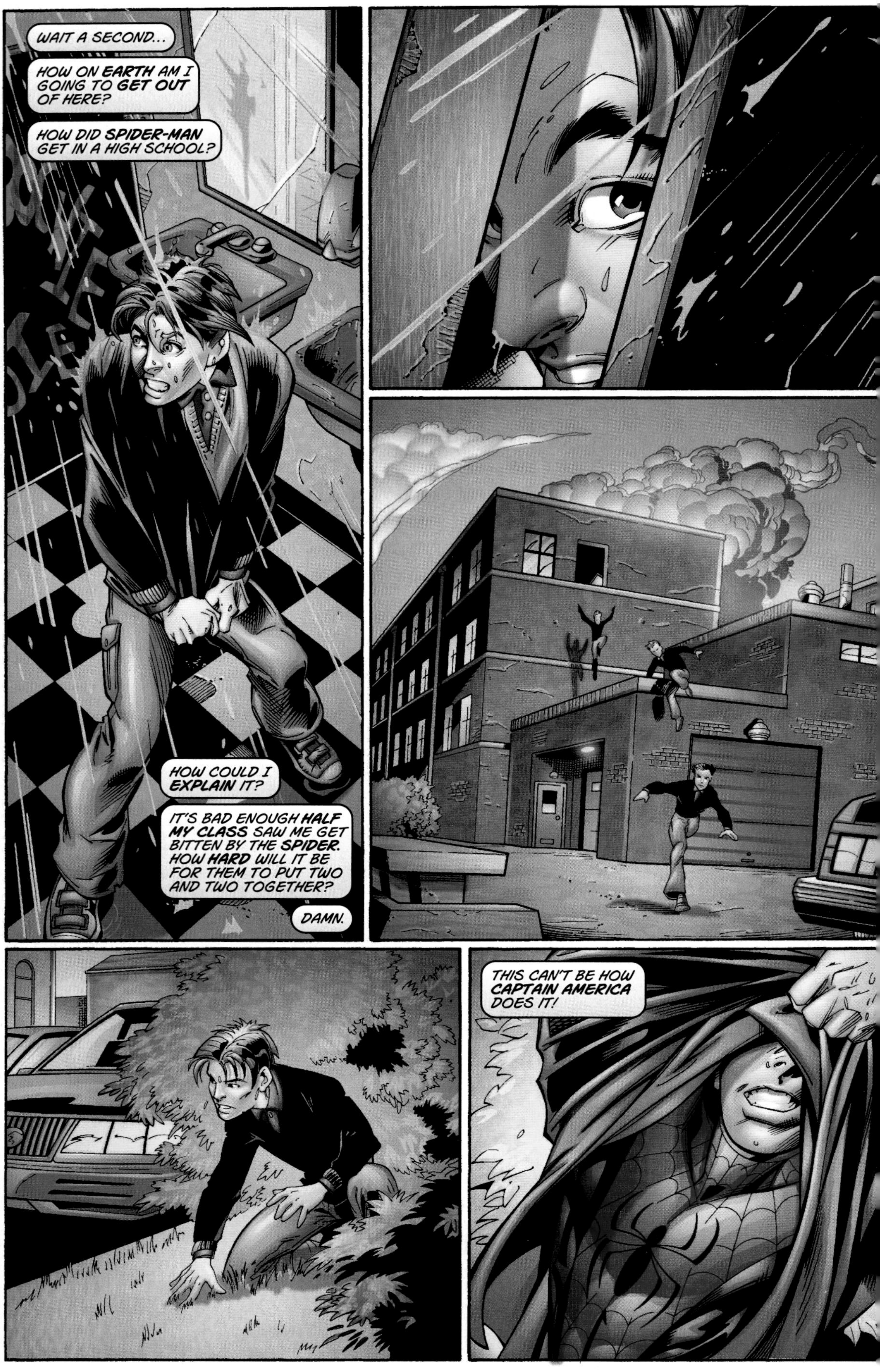
WAIT A SECOND...
HOW ON EARTH AM I GOING TO GET OUT OF HERE?
HOW DID SPIDER-MAN GET IN A HIGH SCHOOL?
HOW COULD I EXPLAIN IT?
IT'S BAD ENOUGH HALF MY CLASS SAW ME GET BITTEN BY THE SPIDER. HOW HARD WILL IT BE FOR THEM TO PUT TWO AND TWO TOGETHER?
DAMN.
THIS CAN'T BE HOW CAPTAIN AMERICA DOES IT!

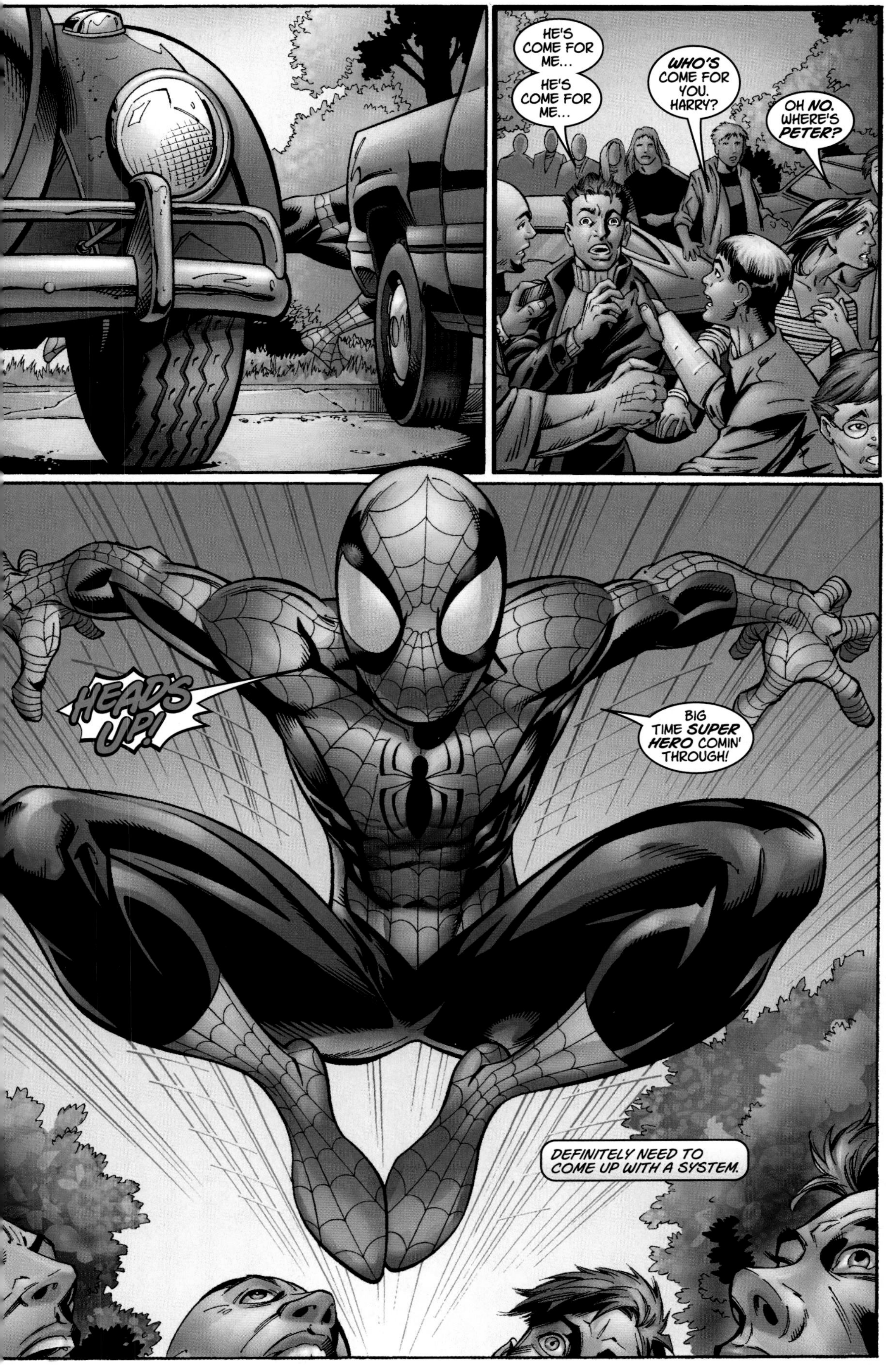
HE'S COME FOR ME...
HE'S COME FOR ME...
WHO'S COME FOR YOU. HARRY?
OH NO. WHERE'S PETER?
HEADS UP!
BIG TIME SUPER HERO COMIN' THROUGH!
DEFINITELY NEED TO COME UP WITH A SYSTEM.

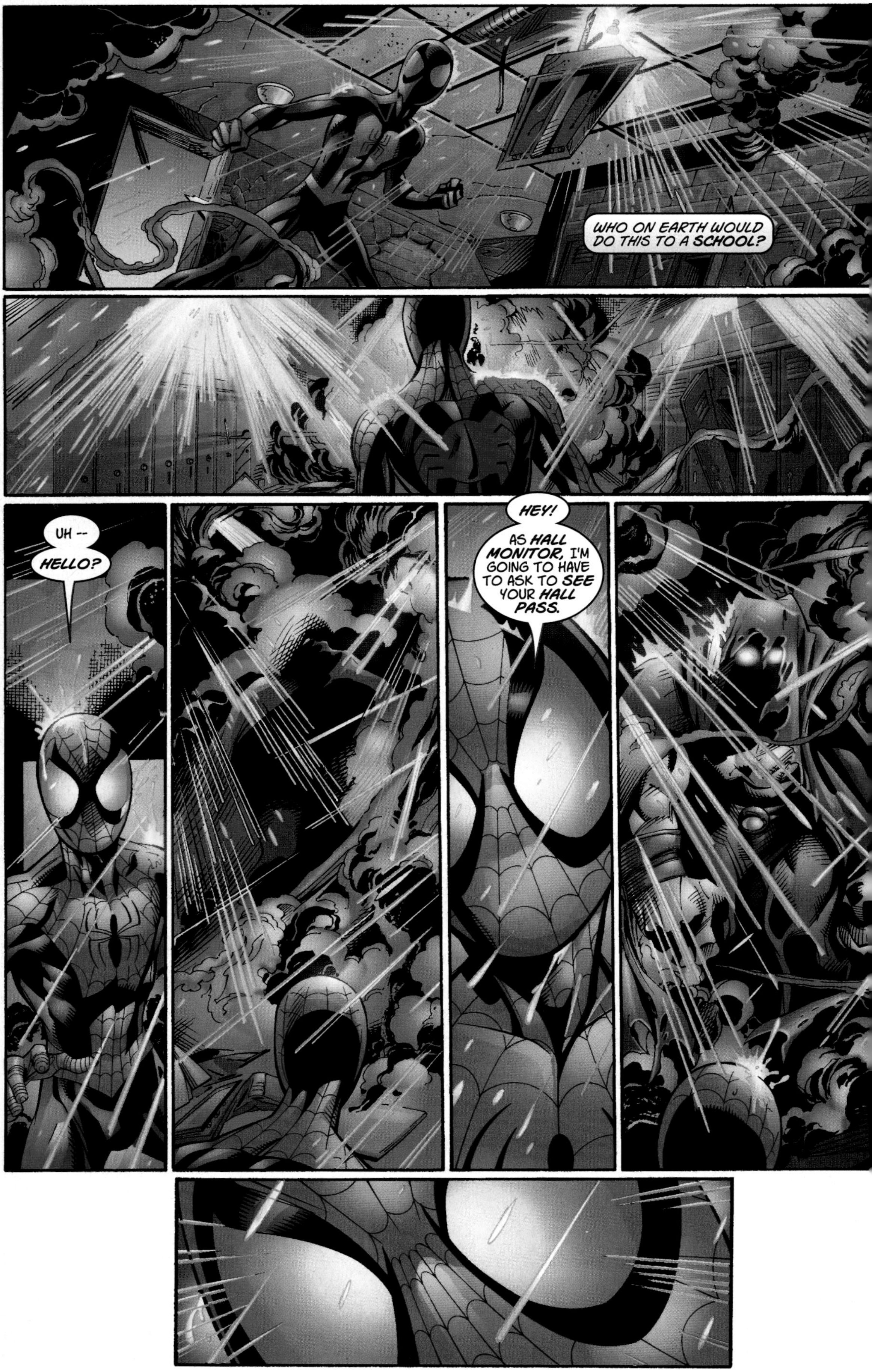
WHO ON EARTH WOULD DO THIS TO A SCHOOL?
UH --
HELLO?
HEY!
AS HALL MONITOR, I'M GOING TO HAVE TO ASK TO SEE YOUR HALL PASS.

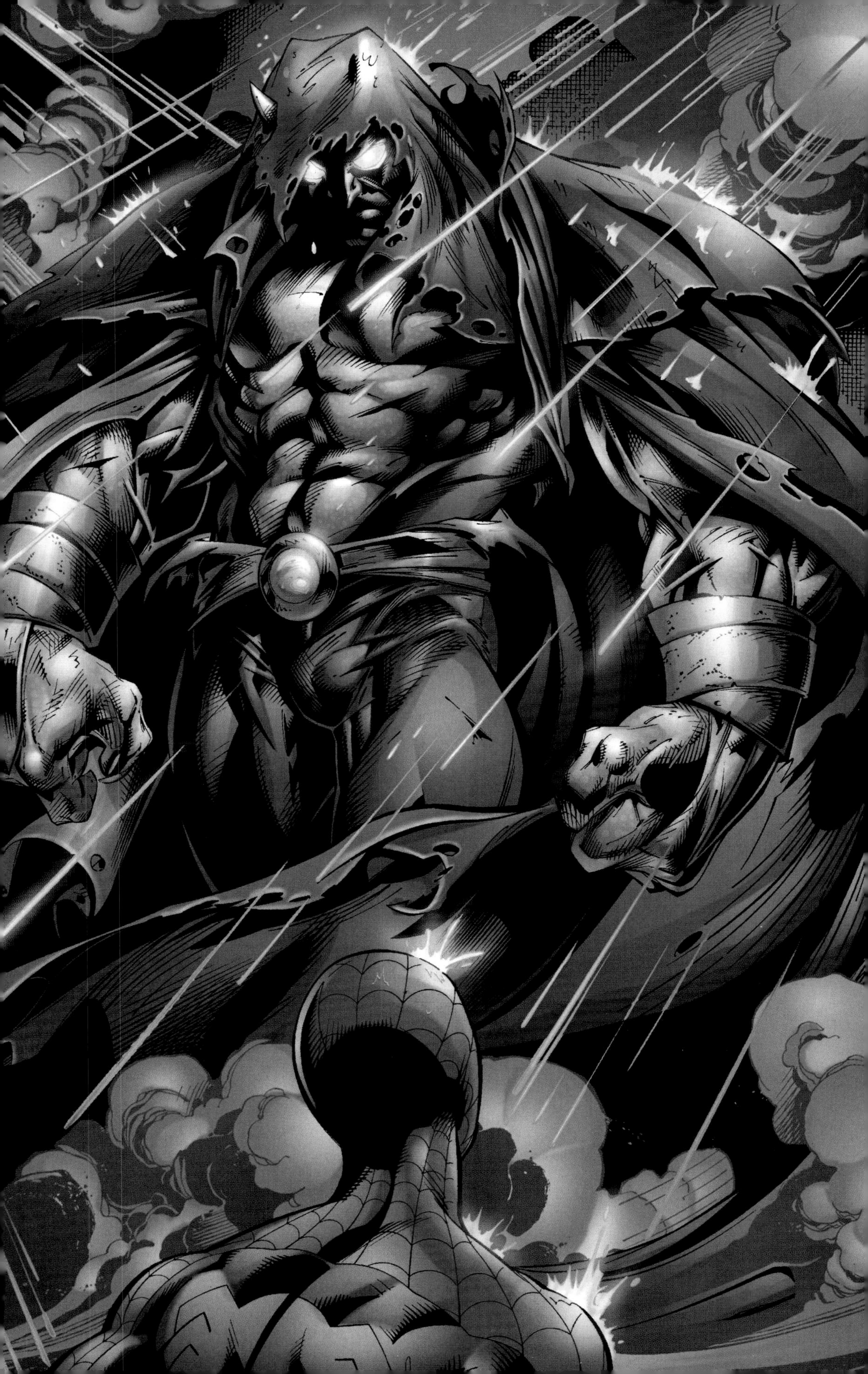

UH... YOU WOULDN'T HAPPEN TO BE THE NEW *HOME EC TEACHER*, WOULD YOU?

LISTEN, I DON'T WANT TO TELL YOU YOUR BUSINESS...

NYYYRR!

...BUT THAT'S KIND OF A *FIRE HAZARD.*

FUMP

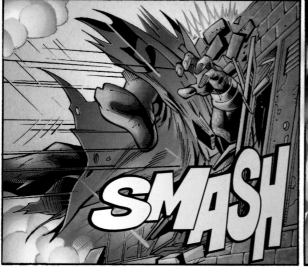

SMASH

I HOPE YOU DON'T THINK I'M GOING TO HELP YOU CLEAN THIS UP... BECAUSE *YOU -- ARE -- ON -- YOUR -- OWN.*

LOOK AT ME BEIN[G] THE *SMART-MOUT[H]* WHEN I'M *SCARED* OUT OF MY MIND.

I GUESS IT'S EITHER THA[T] OR I PEE IN MY TIGHT[S].

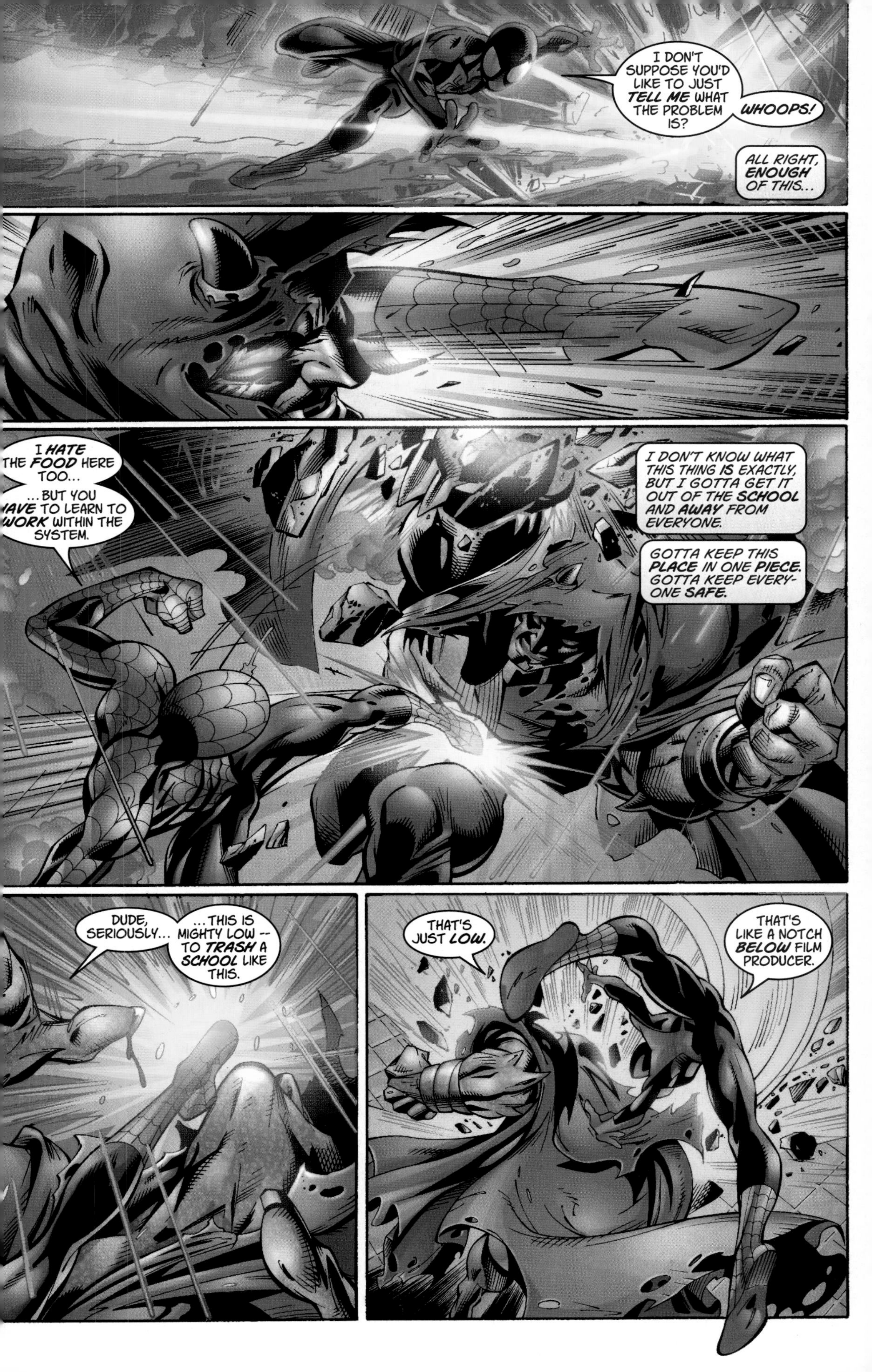
I DON'T SUPPOSE YOU'D LIKE TO JUST TELL ME WHAT THE PROBLEM IS?
WHOOPS!
ALL RIGHT, ENOUGH OF THIS...
I HATE THE FOOD HERE TOO...
...BUT YOU HAVE TO LEARN TO WORK WITHIN THE SYSTEM.
I DON'T KNOW WHAT THIS THING IS EXACTLY, BUT I GOTTA GET IT OUT OF THE SCHOOL AND AWAY FROM EVERYONE.
GOTTA KEEP THIS PLACE IN ONE PIECE. GOTTA KEEP EVERY-ONE SAFE.
DUDE, SERIOUSLY...
...THIS IS MIGHTY LOW -- TO TRASH A SCHOOL LIKE THIS.
THAT'S JUST LOW.
THAT'S LIKE A NOTCH BELOW FILM PRODUCER.

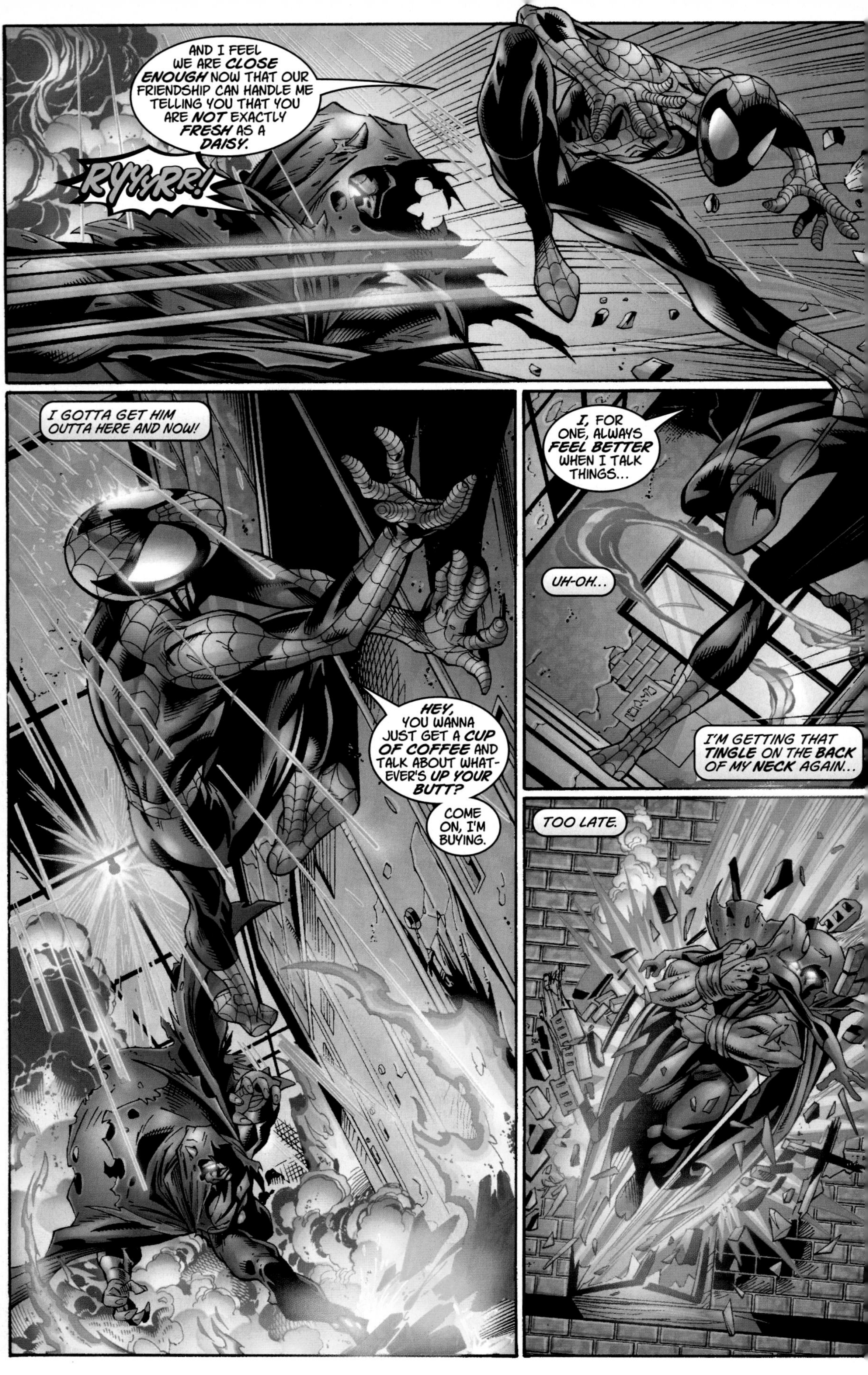
AND I FEEL WE ARE CLOSE ENOUGH NOW THAT OUR FRIENDSHIP CAN HANDLE ME TELLING YOU THAT YOU ARE NOT EXACTLY FRESH AS A DAISY.
RYYYRR!
I GOTTA GET HIM OUTTA HERE AND NOW!
HEY, YOU WANNA JUST GET A CUP OF COFFEE AND TALK ABOUT WHATEVER'S UP YOUR BUTT?
COME ON, I'M BUYING.
I, FOR ONE, ALWAYS FEEL BETTER WHEN I TALK THINGS...
UH-OH...
I'M GETTING THAT TINGLE ON THE BACK OF MY NECK AGAIN...
TOO LATE.

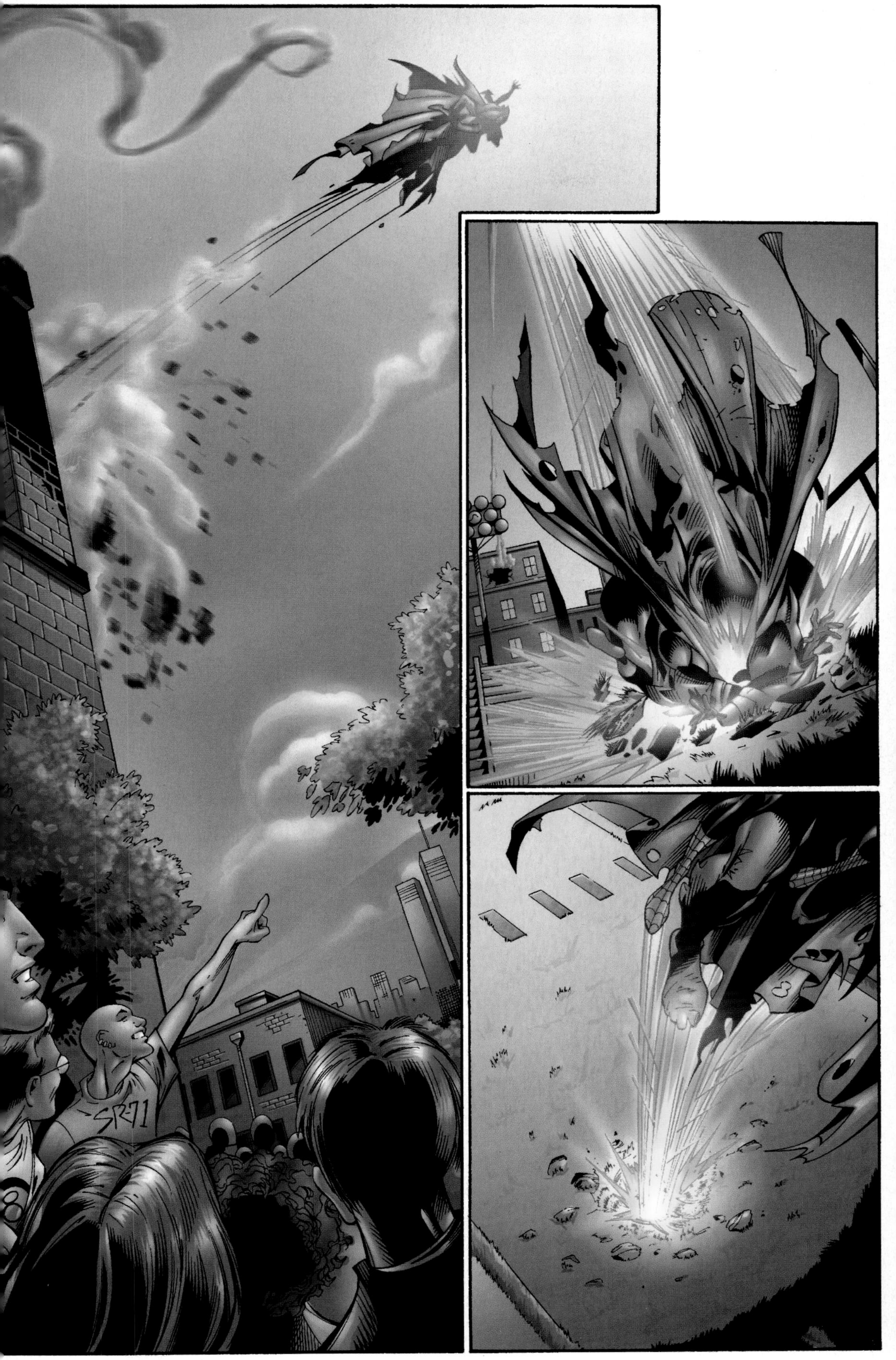
SR-71

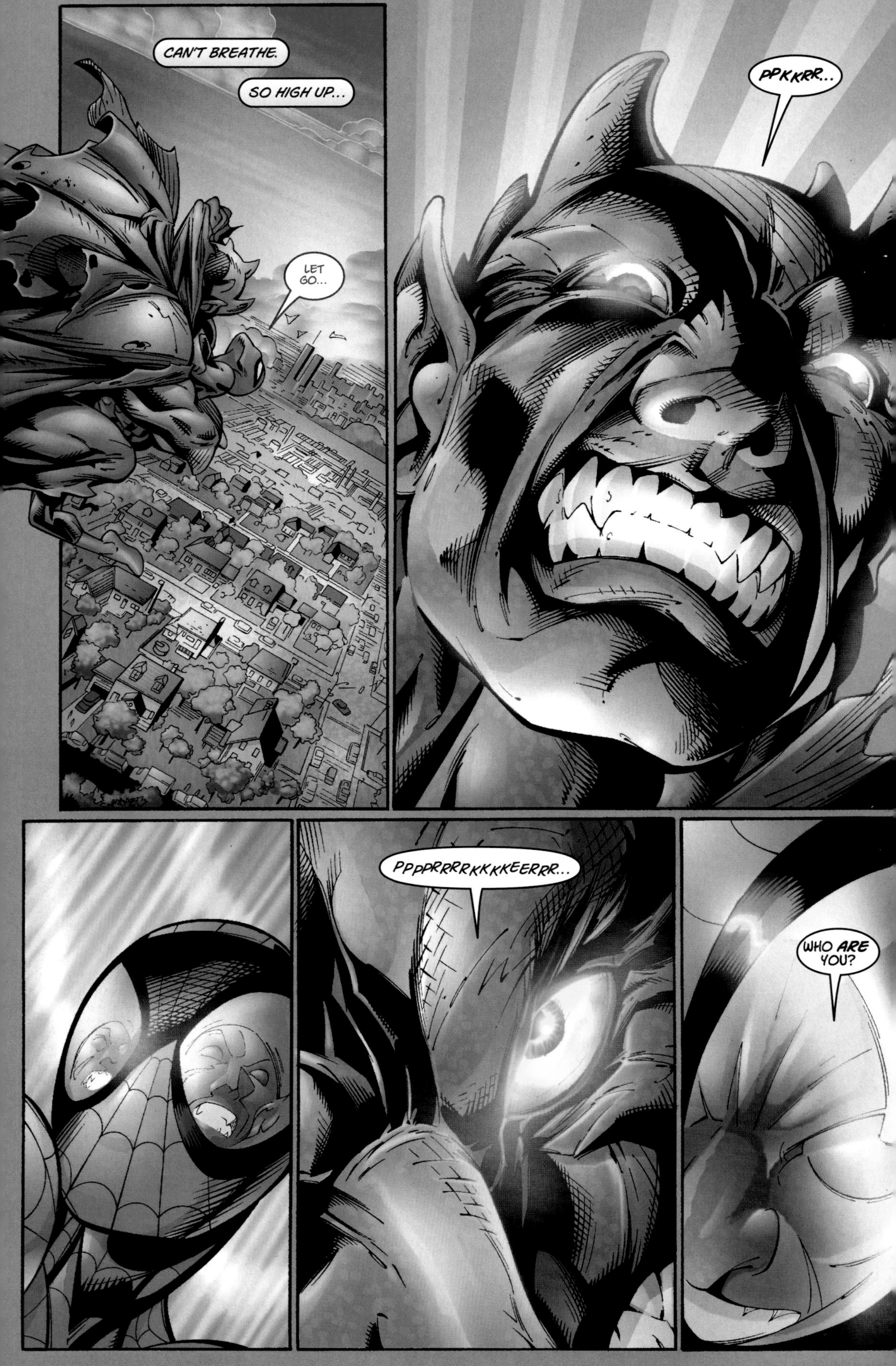
CAN'T BREATHE.
SO HIGH UP...
LET GO...
PPKKRR...
PPPPRRRRKKKKEERRR...
WHO ARE YOU?

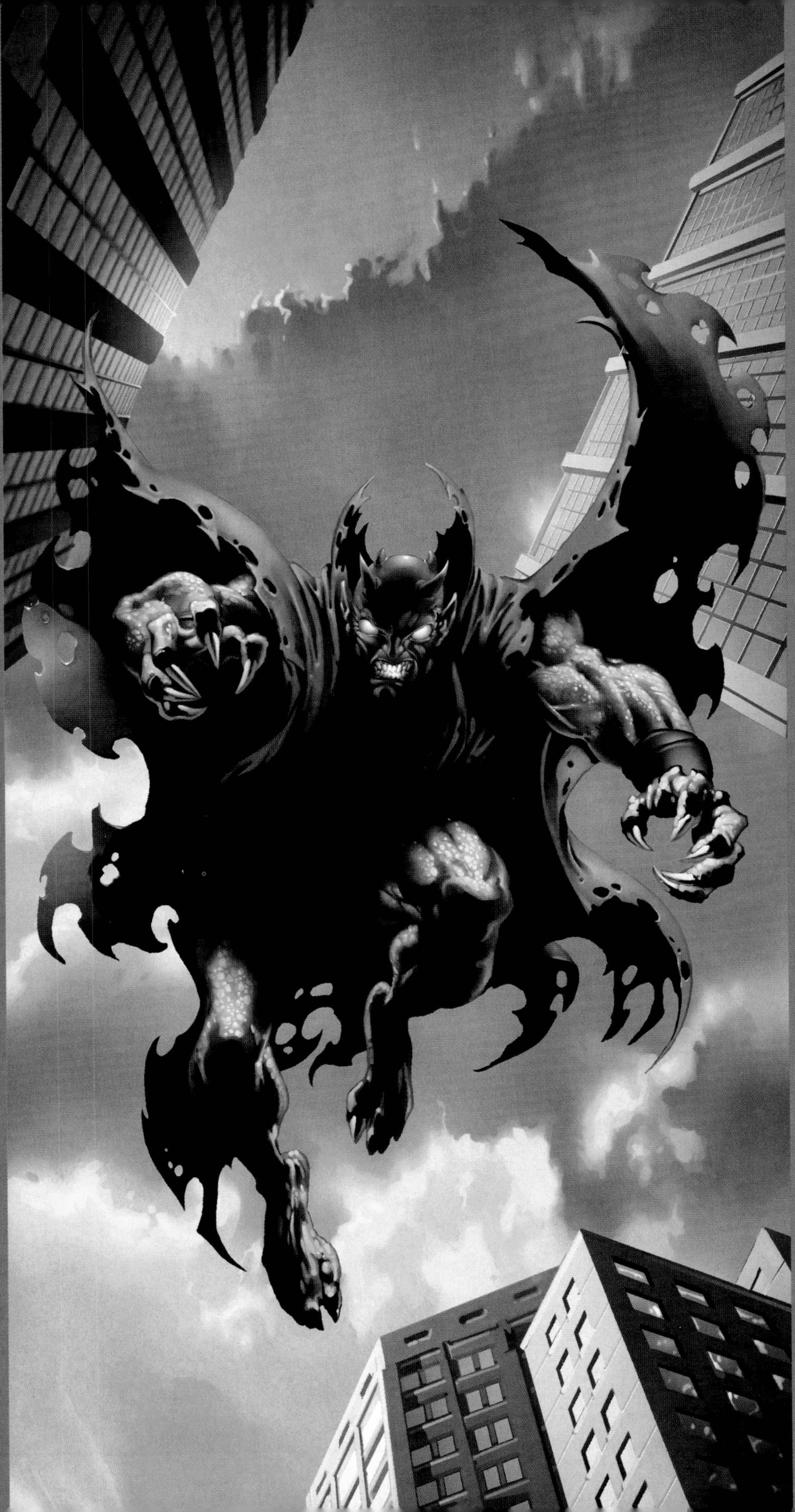

7

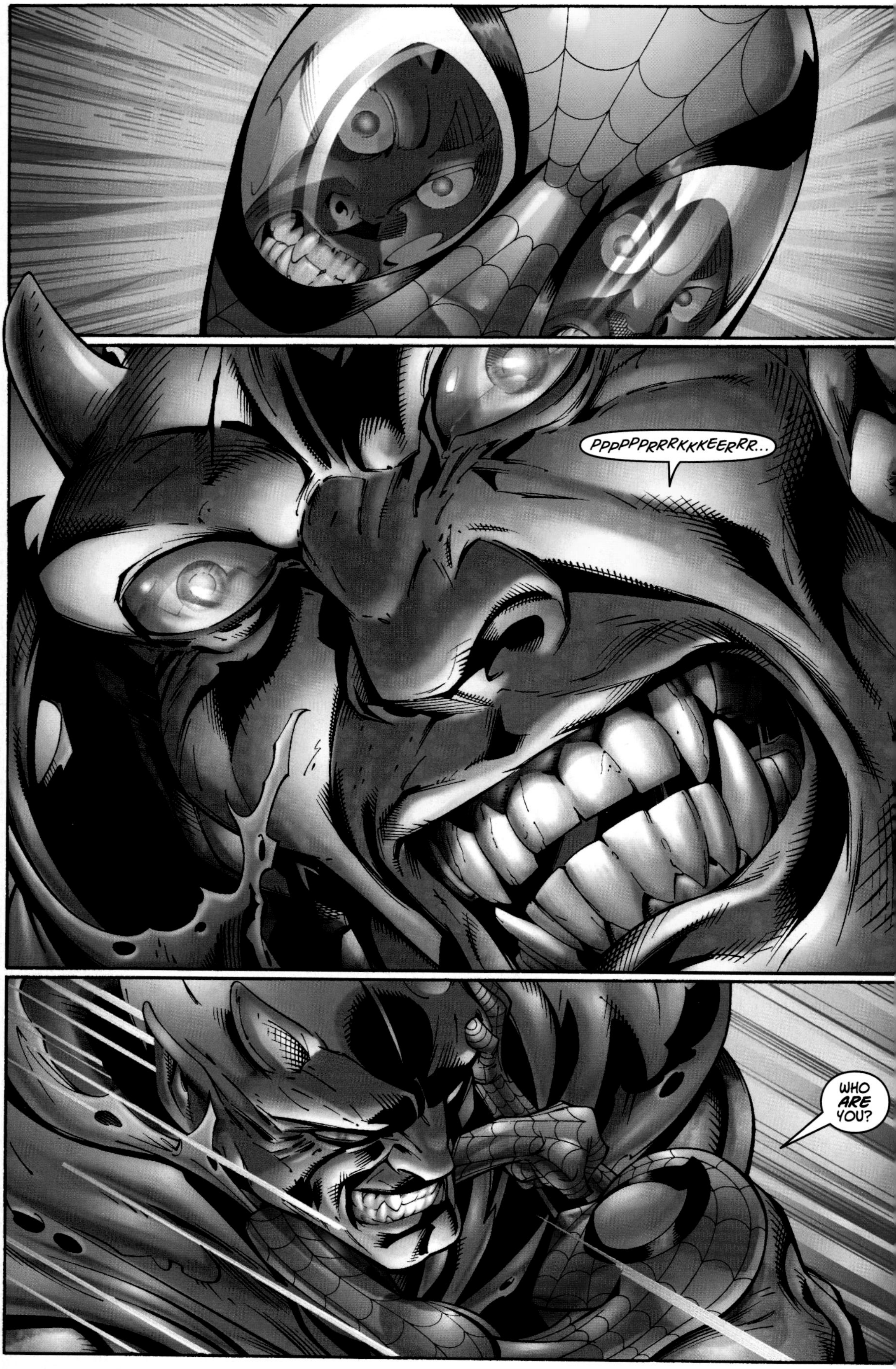
PPPPPPRRRKKKEERRR...
WHO ARE YOU?

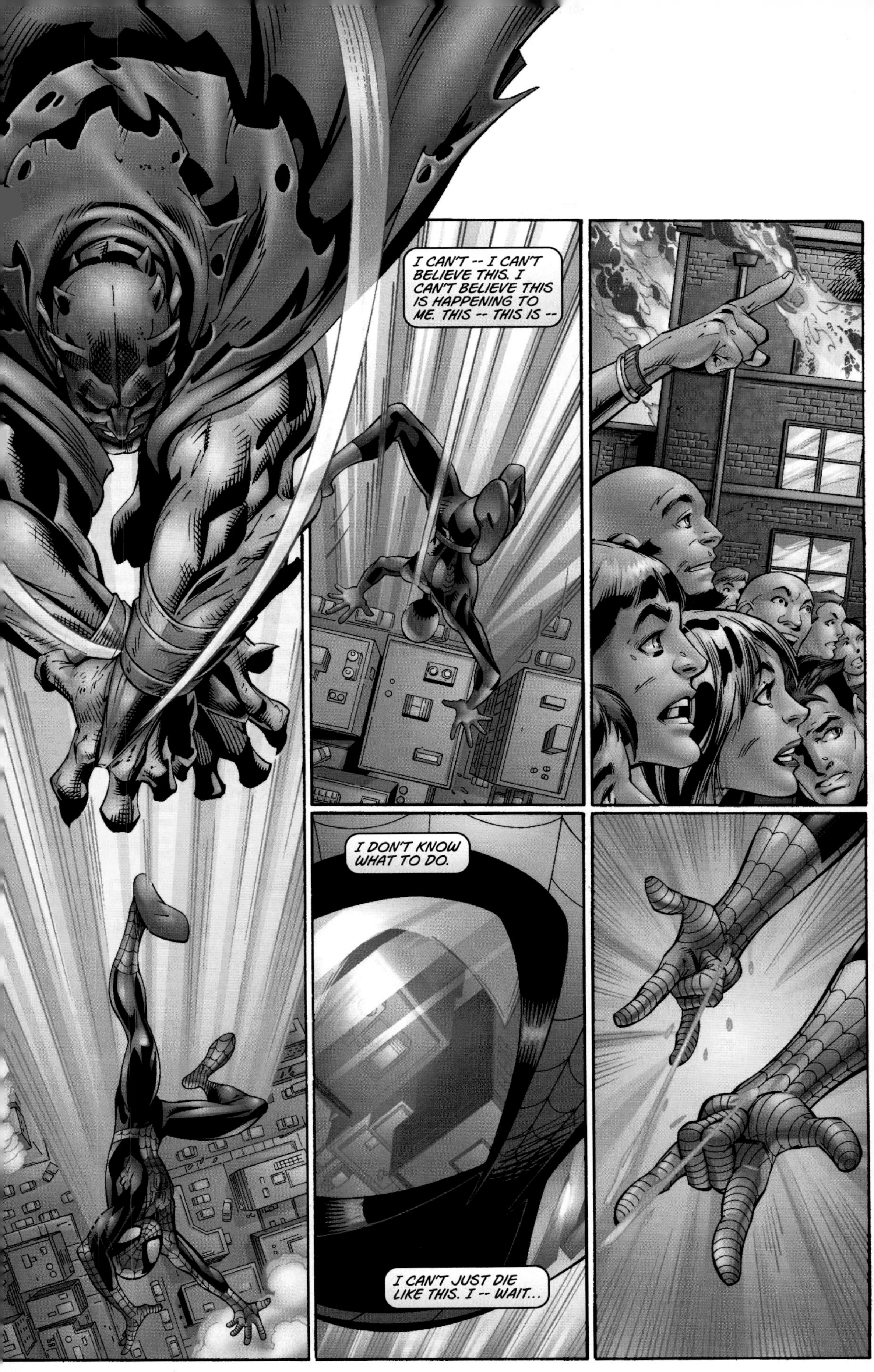
I CAN'T -- I CAN'T BELIEVE THIS. I CAN'T BELIEVE THIS IS HAPPENING TO ME. THIS -- THIS IS --
I DON'T KNOW WHAT TO DO.
I CAN'T JUST DIE LIKE THIS. I -- WAIT...

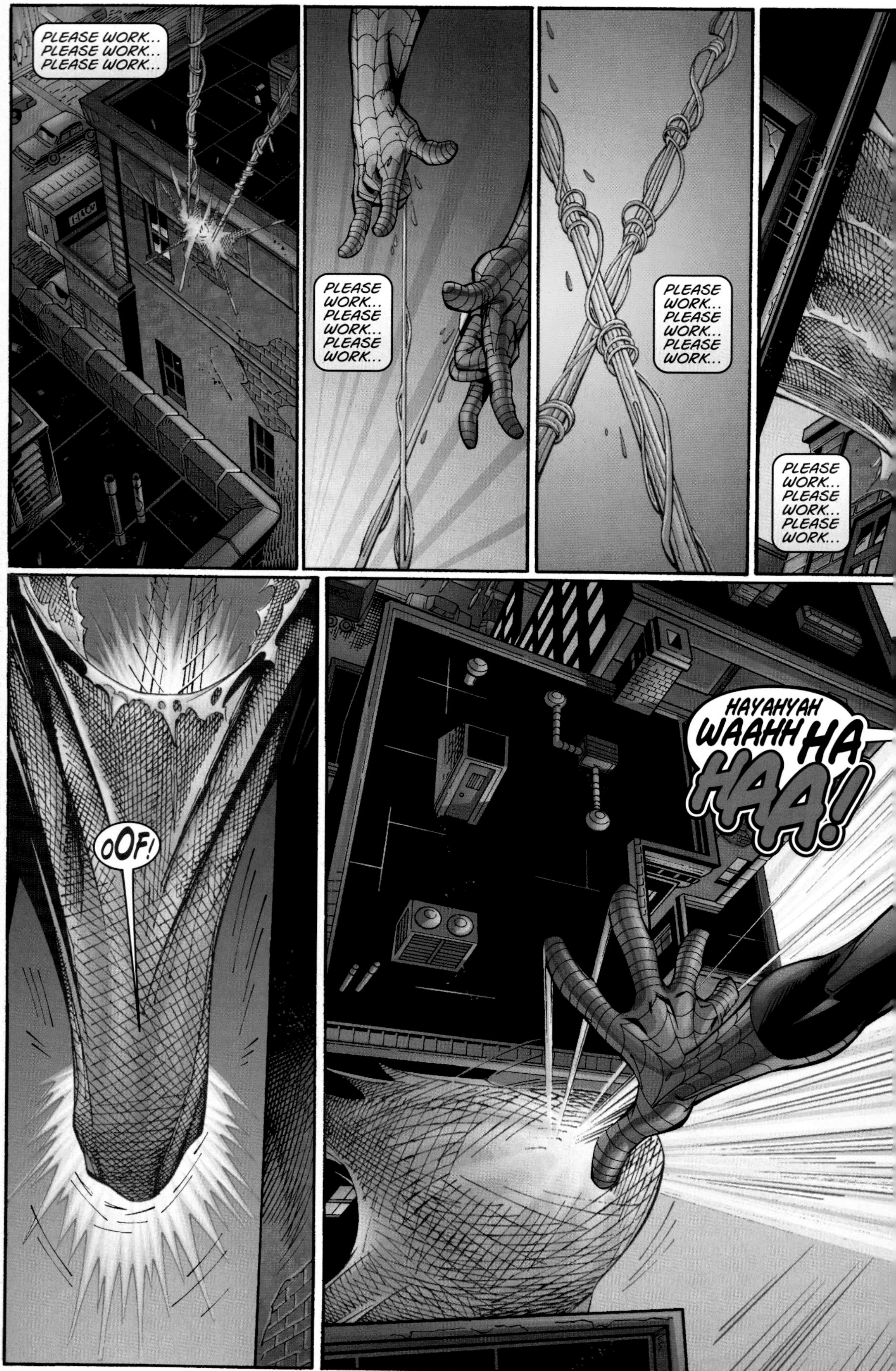
PLEASE WORK...
PLEASE WORK...
PLEASE WORK...
PLEASE WORK...
PLEASE WORK...
PLEASE WORK...
PLEASE WORK...
PLEASE WORK...
PLEASE WORK...
PLEASE WORK...
PLEASE WORK...
PLEASE WORK...
OOF!
HAYAHYAH WAAHH HA HAA!

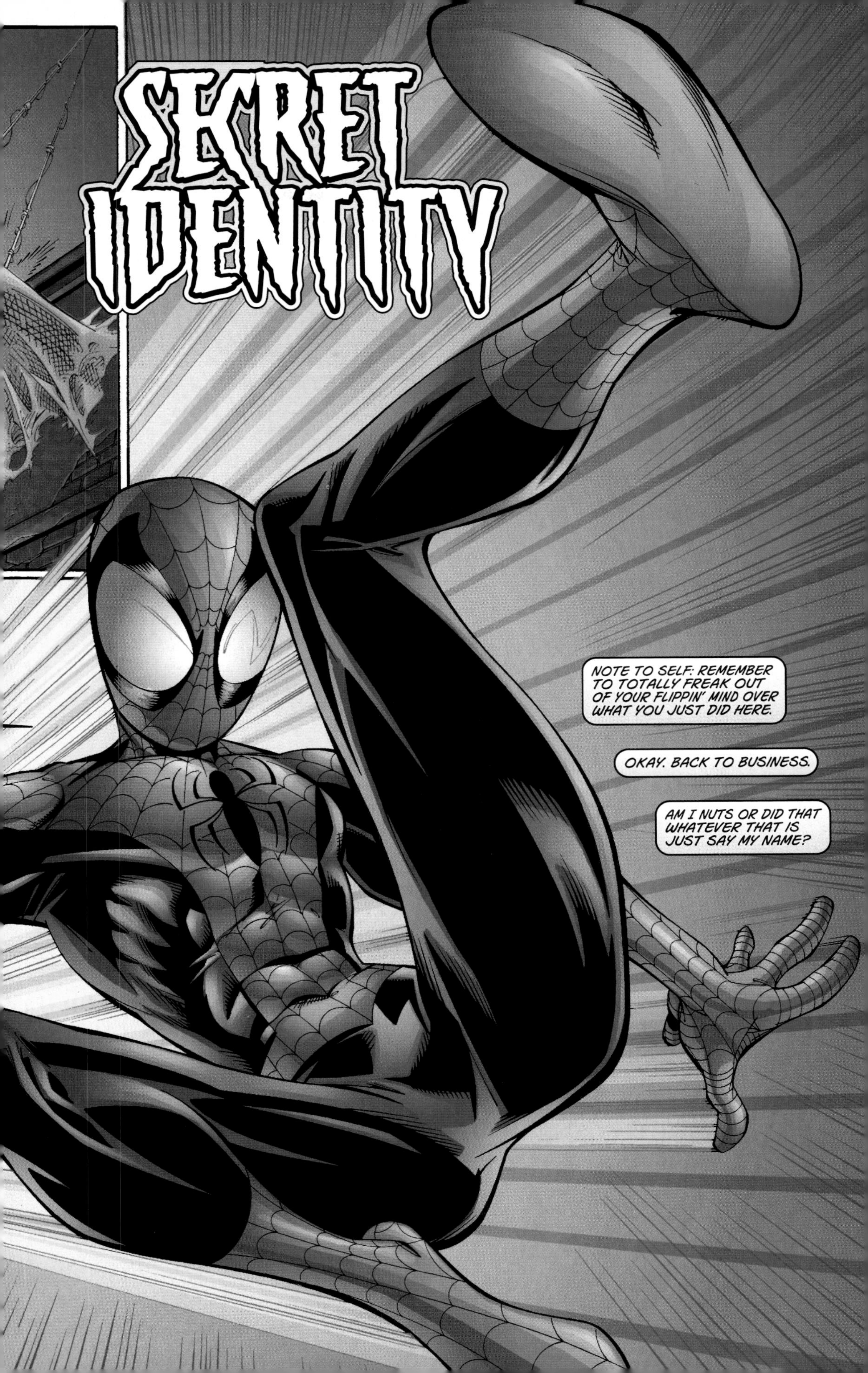
SECRET IDENTITY
NOTE TO SELF: REMEMBER TO TOTALLY FREAK OUT OF YOUR FLIPPIN' MIND OVER WHAT YOU JUST DID HERE.
OKAY. BACK TO BUSINESS.
AM I NUTS OR DID THAT WHATEVER THAT IS JUST SAY MY NAME?

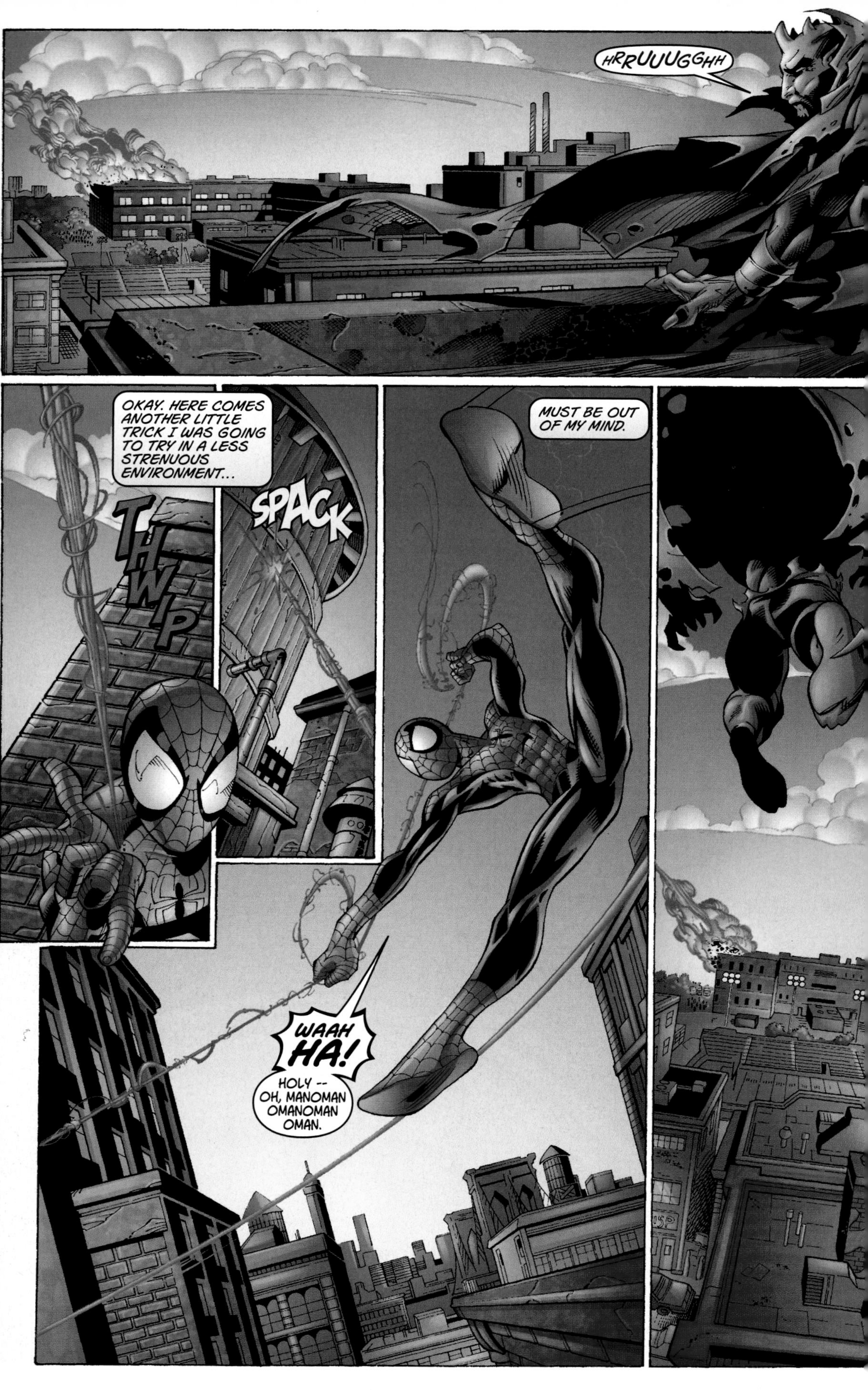
HRRUUUGGHH
OKAY. HERE COMES ANOTHER LITTLE TRICK I WAS GOING TO TRY IN A LESS STRENUOUS ENVIRONMENT...
THWIP
SPACK
MUST BE OUT OF MY MIND.
WAAH HA!
HOLY -- OH, MANOMAN OMANOMAN OMAN.

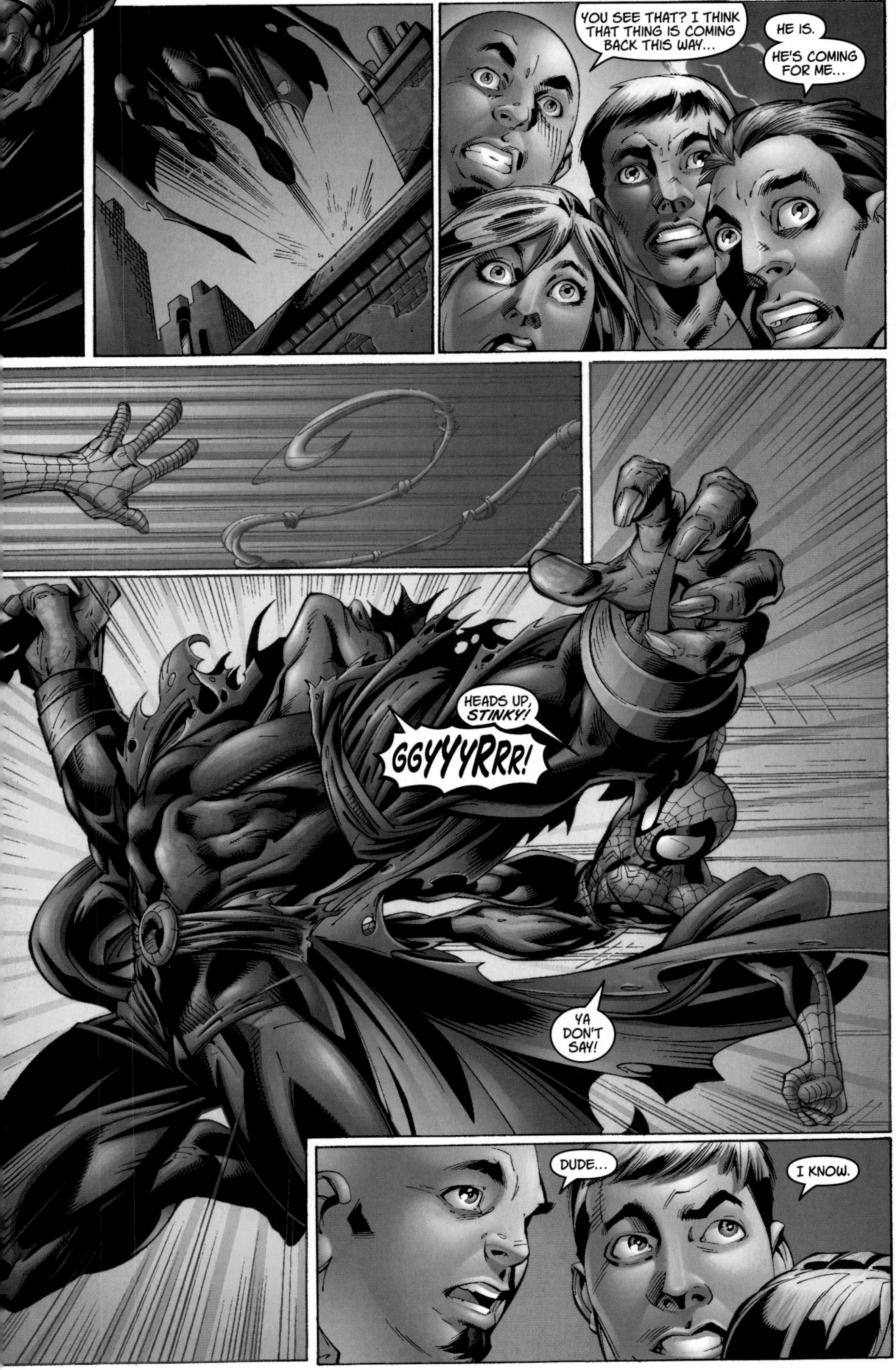
YOU SEE THAT? I THINK THAT THING IS COMING BACK THIS WAY...
HE IS.
HE'S COMING FOR ME...
HEADS UP, STINKY!
GGYYYRRR!
YA DON'T SAY!
DUDE...
I KNOW.

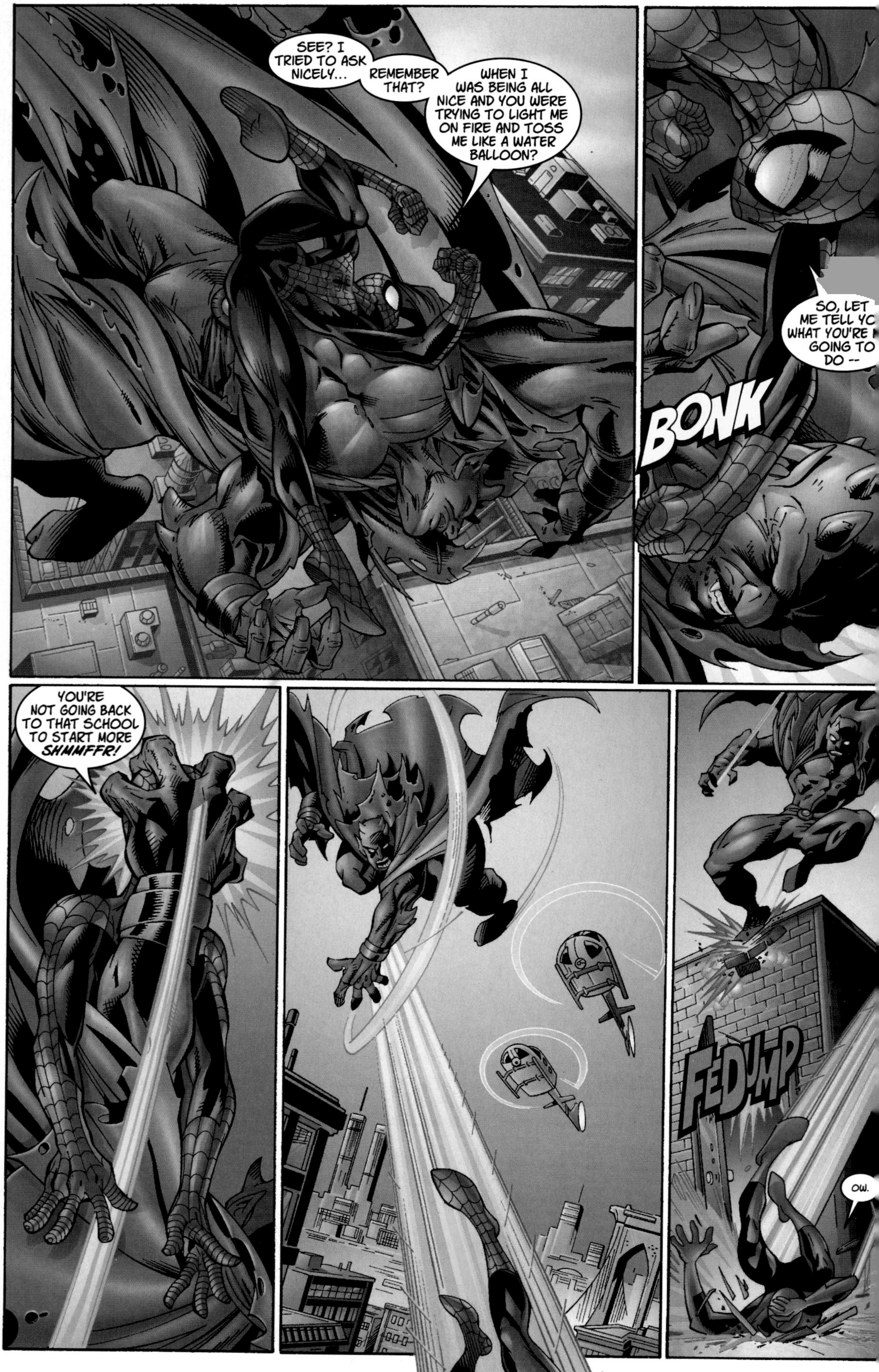
SEE? I TRIED TO ASK NICELY...
REMEMBER THAT?
WHEN I WAS BEING ALL NICE AND YOU WERE TRYING TO LIGHT ME ON FIRE AND TOSS ME LIKE A WATER BALLOON?
BONK
YOU'RE NOT GOING BACK TO THAT SCHOOL TO START MORE SHMMFFR!
FEDUMP
OW.

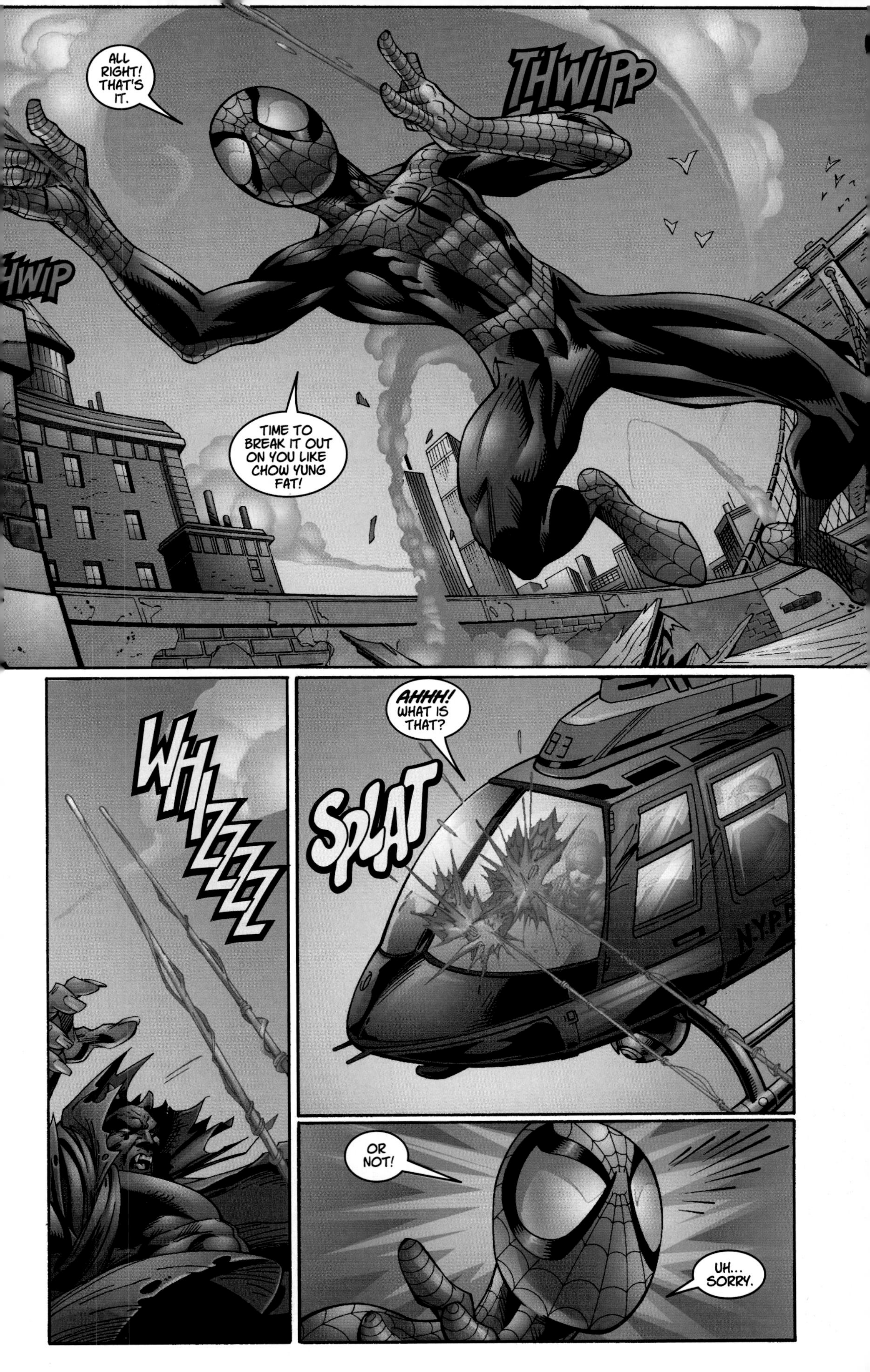
ALL RIGHT! THAT'S IT.
THWIPP
THWIP
TIME TO BREAK IT OUT ON YOU LIKE CHOW YUNG FAT!
WHIZZZZ
AHHH! WHAT IS THAT?
SPLAT
N.Y.P.D.
OR NOT!
UH... SORRY.

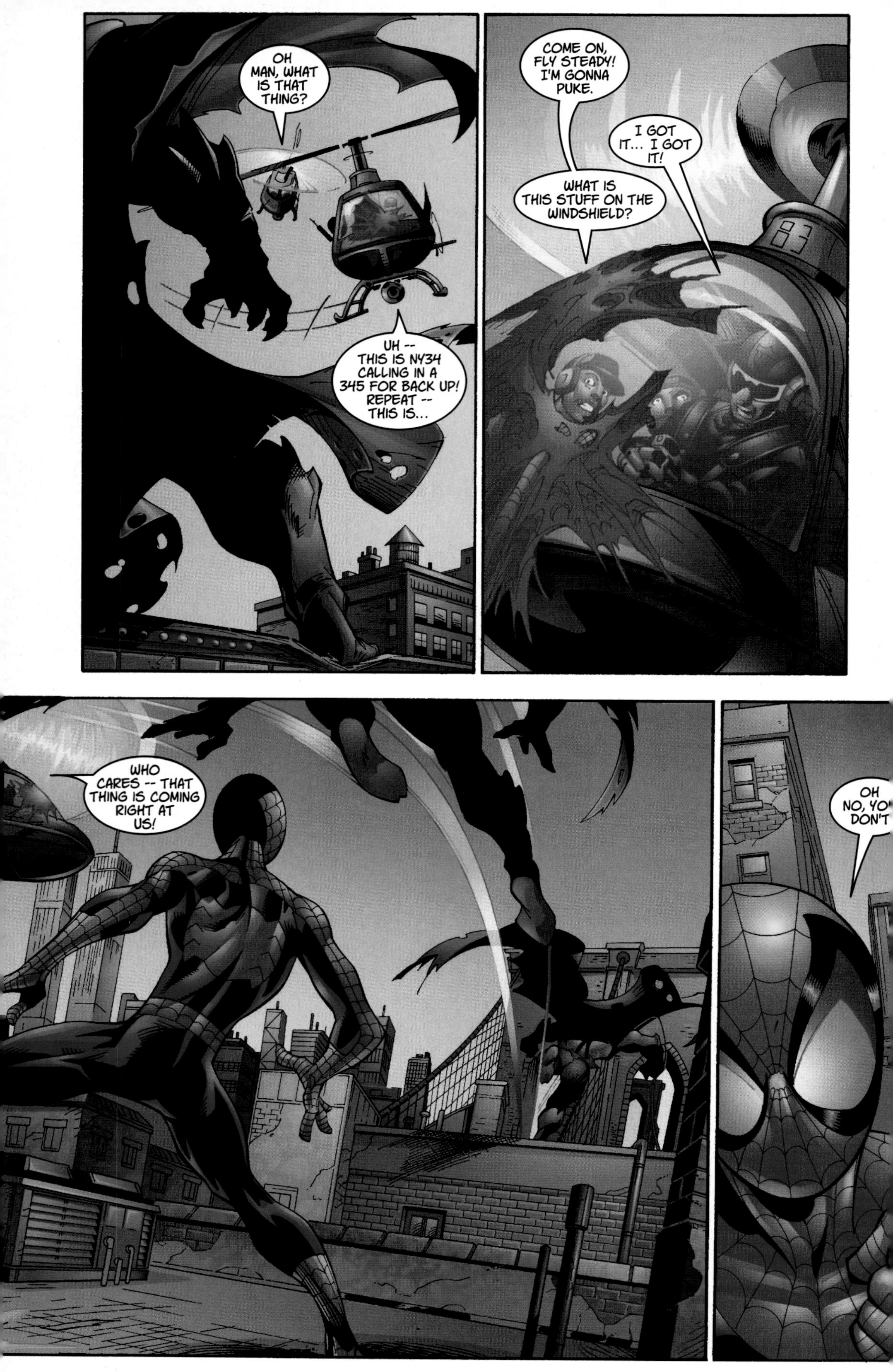
OH MAN, WHAT IS THAT THING?
UH -- THIS IS NY34 CALLING IN A 345 FOR BACK UP! REPEAT -- THIS IS...
COME ON, FLY STEADY! I'M GONNA PUKE.
WHAT IS THIS STUFF ON THE WINDSHIELD?
I GOT IT... I GOT IT!
83
WHO CARES -- THAT THING IS COMING RIGHT AT US!
OH NO, YO DON'T

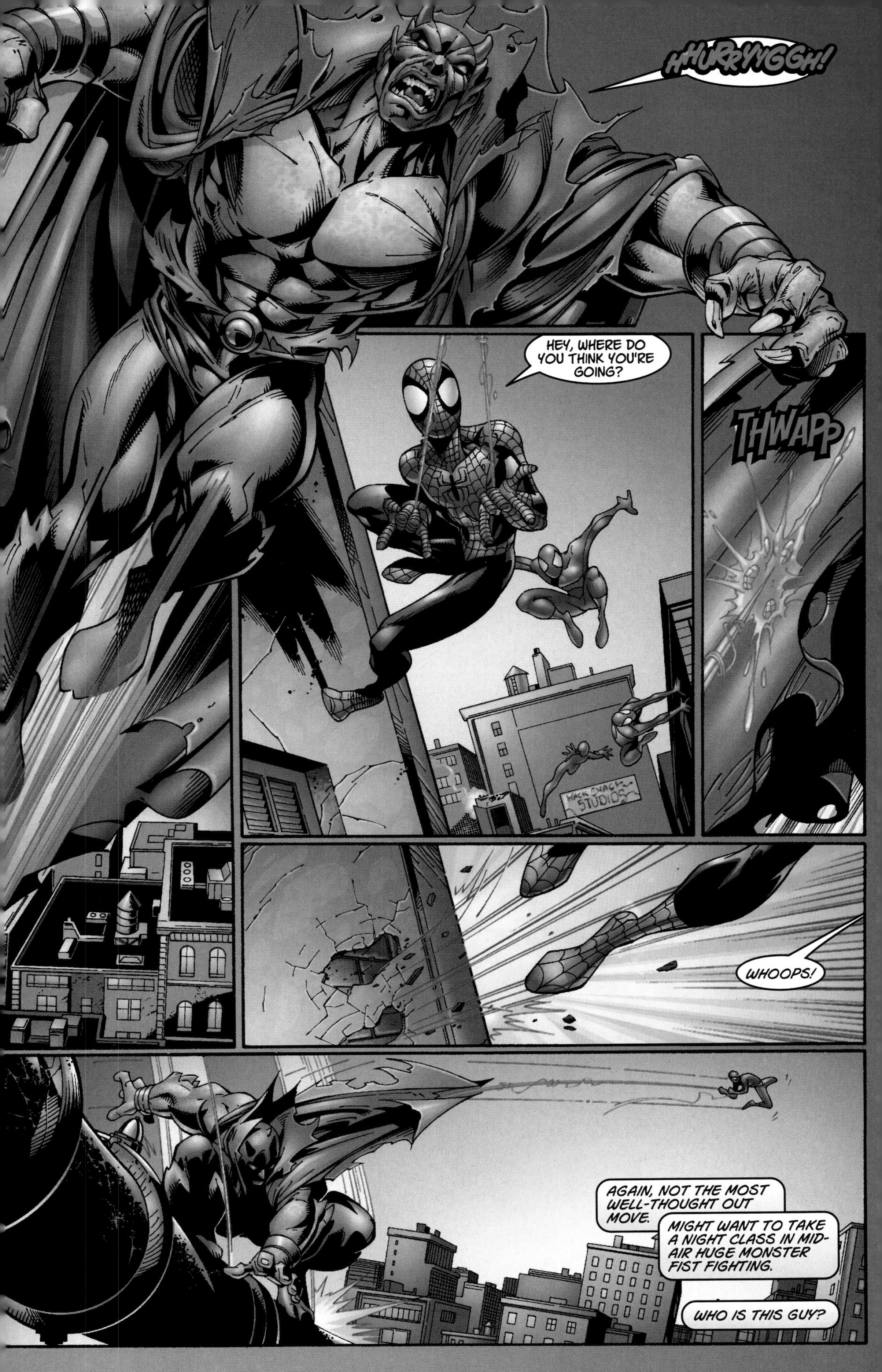
HHURRYYGGH!
HEY, WHERE DO YOU THINK YOU'RE GOING?
THWAPP
WHOOPS!
AGAIN, NOT THE MOST WELL-THOUGHT OUT MOVE.
MIGHT WANT TO TAKE A NIGHT CLASS IN MID-AIR HUGE MONSTER FIST FIGHTING.
WHO IS THIS GUY?

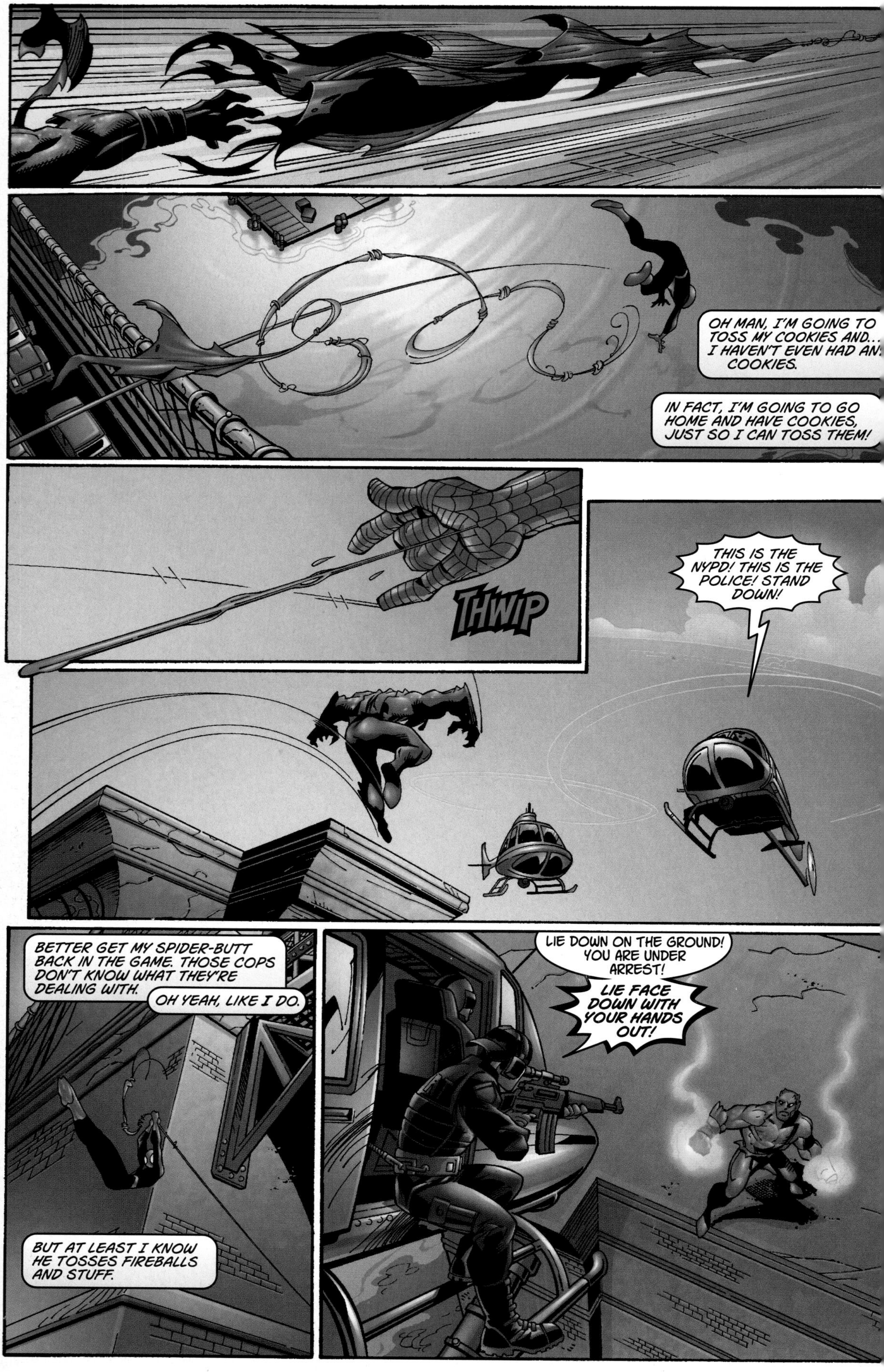

OH MAN, I'M GOING TO TOSS MY COOKIES AND... I HAVEN'T EVEN HAD AN COOKIES.
IN FACT, I'M GOING TO GO HOME AND HAVE COOKIES, JUST SO I CAN TOSS THEM!
THWIP
THIS IS THE NYPD! THIS IS THE POLICE! STAND DOWN!
BETTER GET MY SPIDER-BUTT BACK IN THE GAME. THOSE COPS DON'T KNOW WHAT THEY'RE DEALING WITH.
OH YEAH, LIKE I DO.
BUT AT LEAST I KNOW HE TOSSES FIREBALLS AND STUFF.
LIE DOWN ON THE GROUND! YOU ARE UNDER ARREST!
LIE FACE DOWN WITH YOUR HANDS OUT!

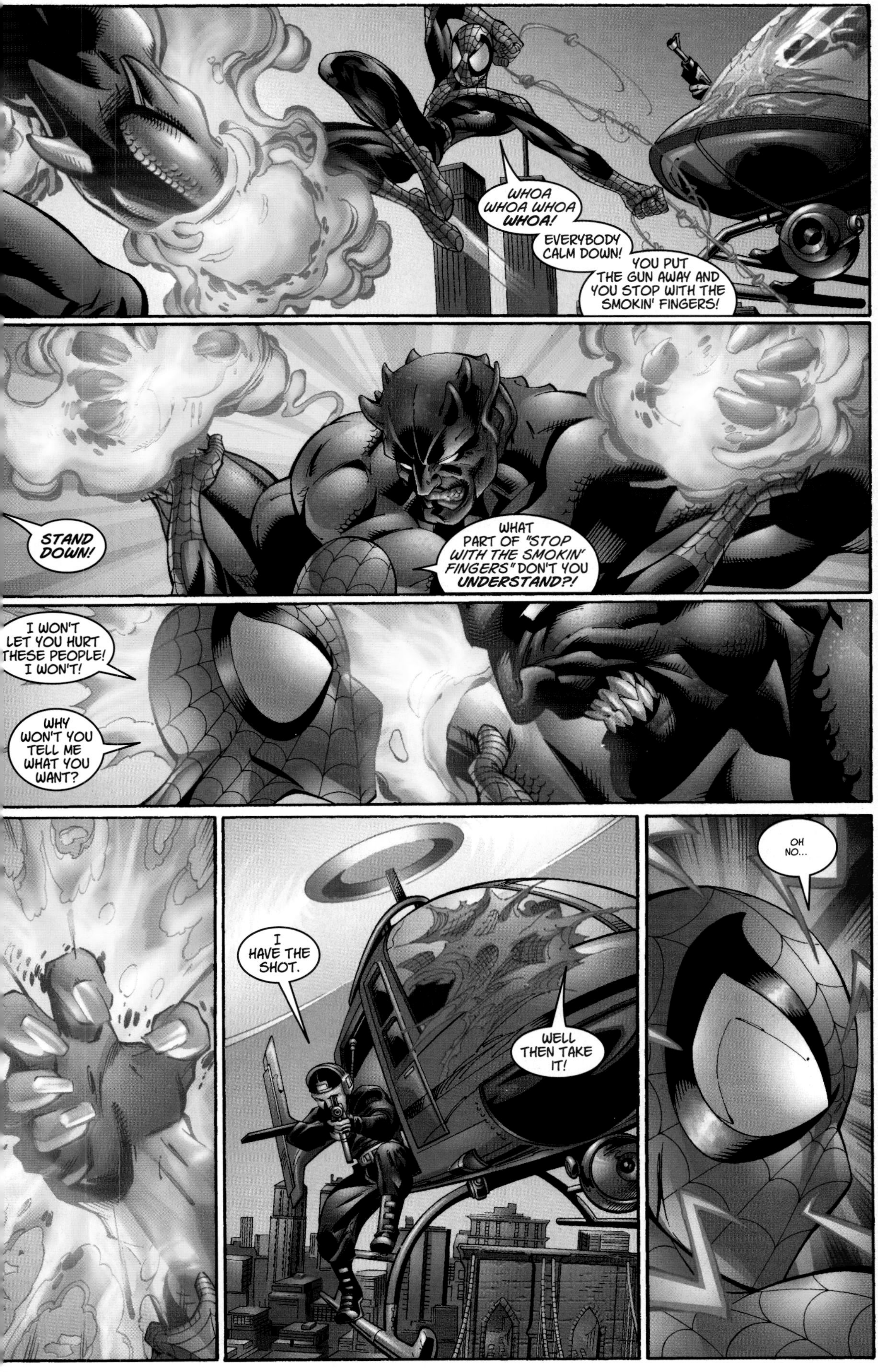
WHOA WHOA WHOA WHOA!
EVERYBODY CALM DOWN!
YOU PUT THE GUN AWAY AND YOU STOP WITH THE SMOKIN' FINGERS!
STAND DOWN!
WHAT PART OF "STOP WITH THE SMOKIN' FINGERS" DON'T YOU UNDERSTAND?!
I WON'T LET YOU HURT THESE PEOPLE! I WON'T!
WHY WON'T YOU TELL ME WHAT YOU WANT?
I HAVE THE SHOT.
WELL THEN TAKE IT!
OH NO...

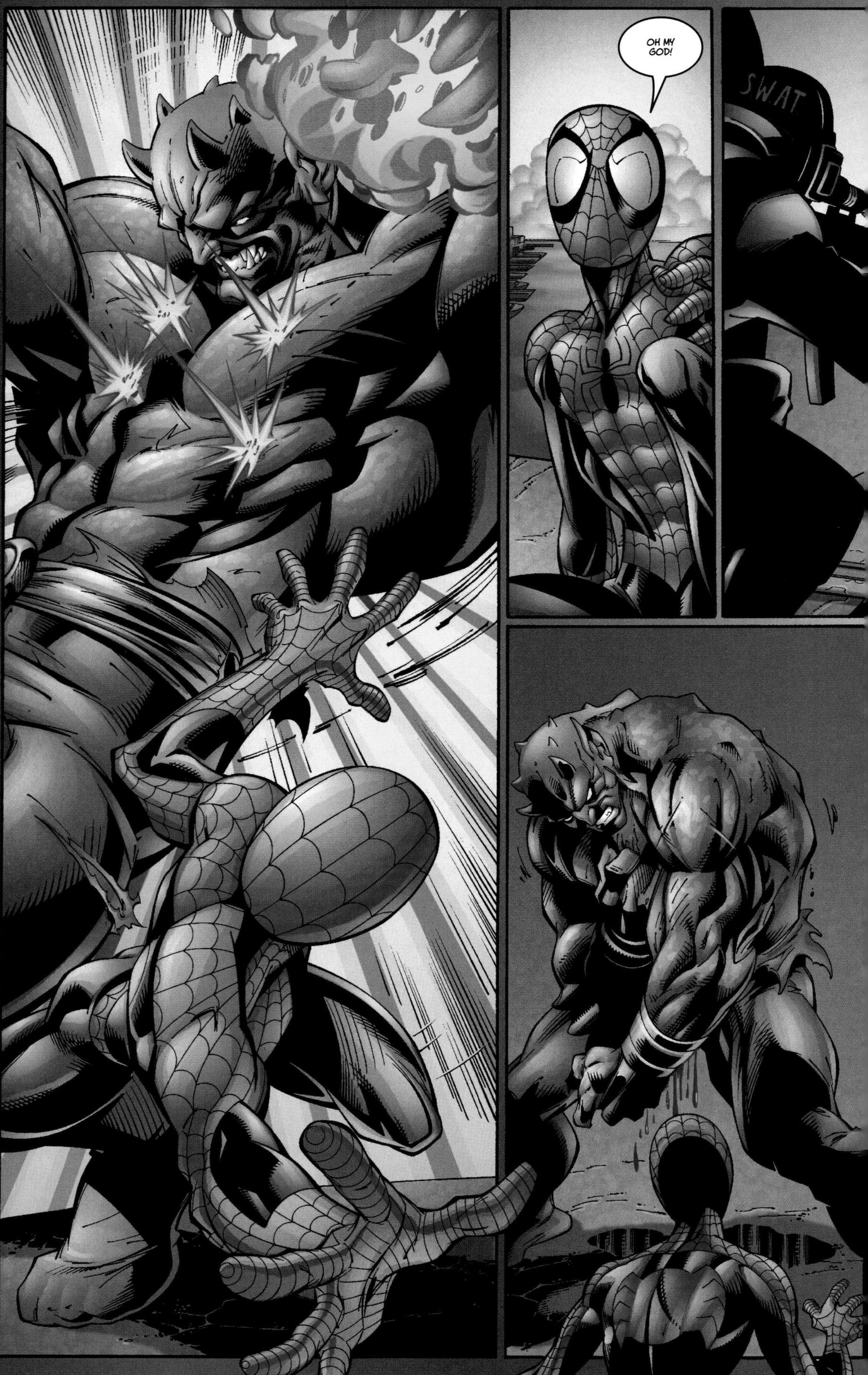
OH MY GOD!
S.W.A.T.

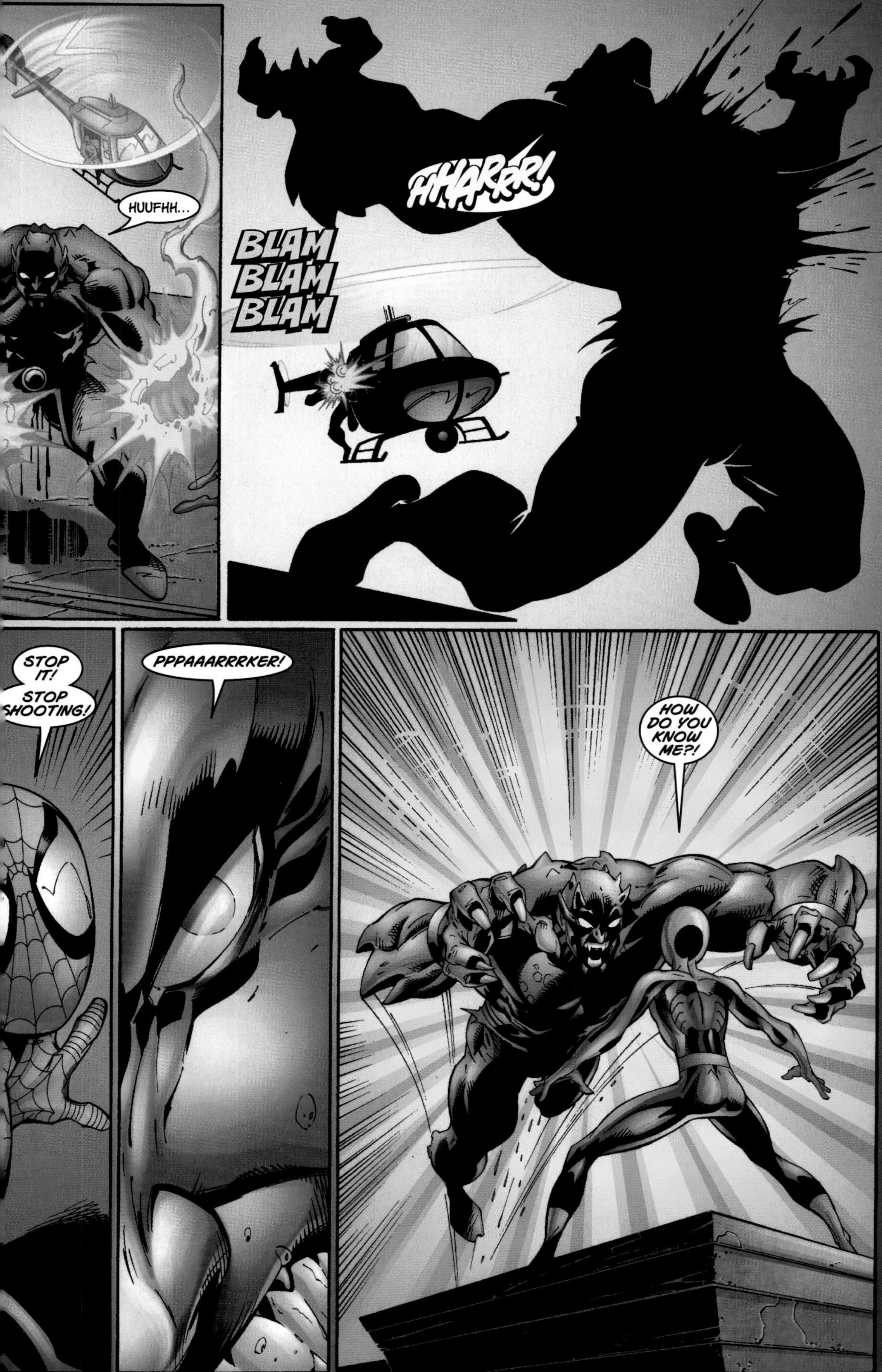
HUUFHH...
BLAM
BLAM
BLAM
HHARRR!
STOP IT! STOP SHOOTING!
PPPAAARRRKER!
HOW DO YOU KNOW ME?!

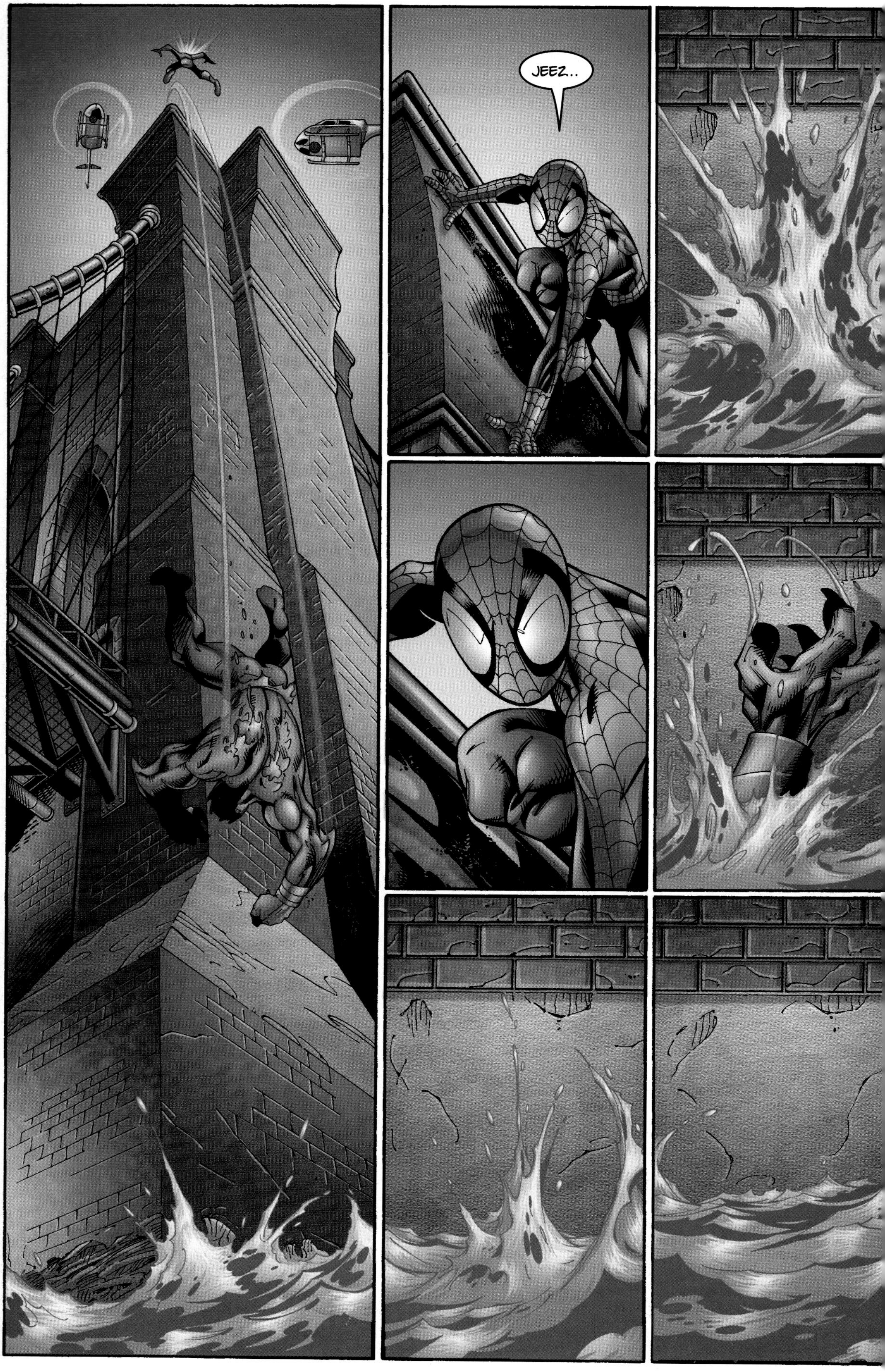
JEEZ..

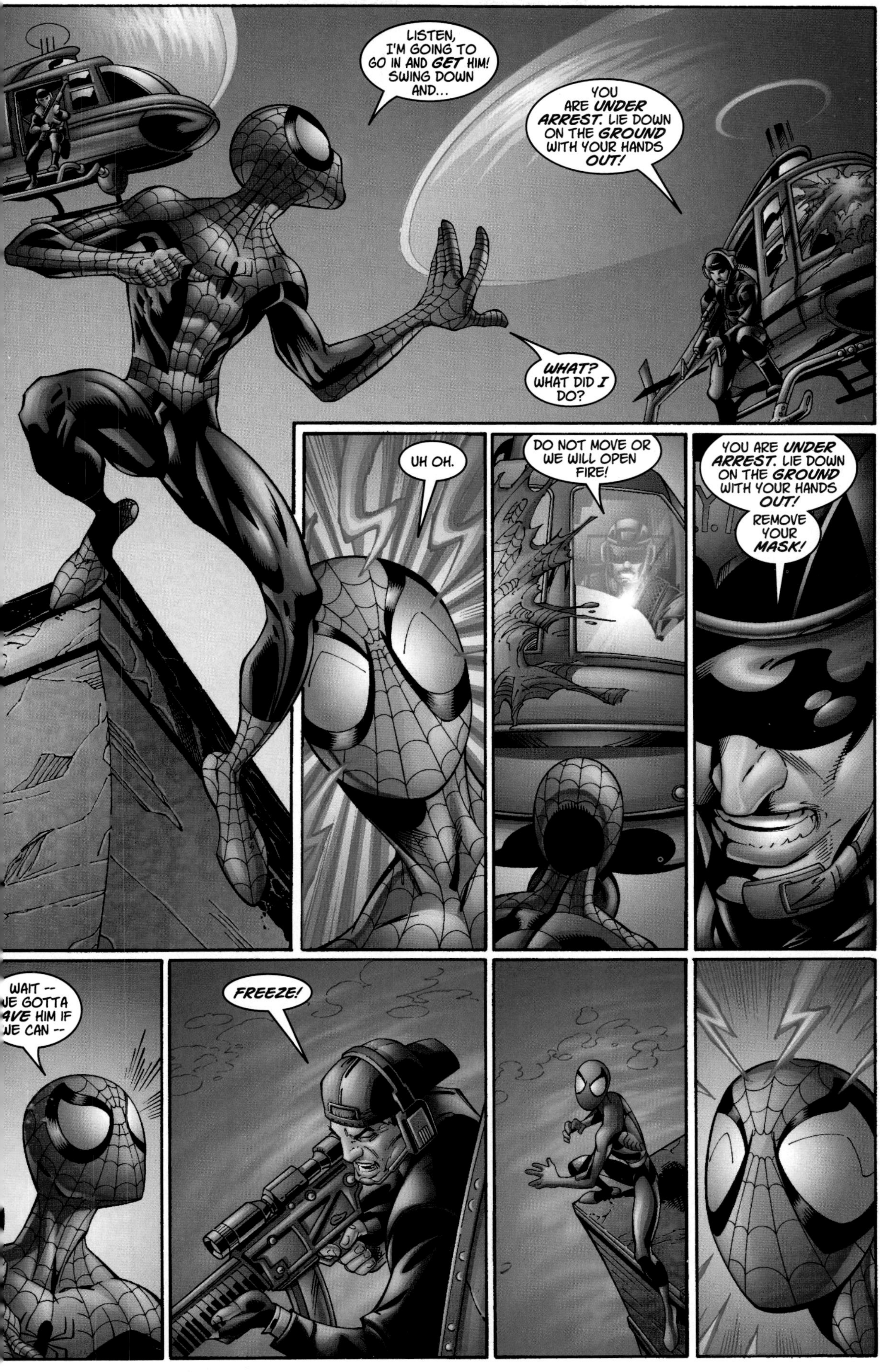
LISTEN, I'M GOING TO GO IN AND GET HIM! SWING DOWN AND...
YOU ARE UNDER ARREST. LIE DOWN ON THE GROUND WITH YOUR HANDS OUT!
WHAT? WHAT DID I DO?
UH OH.
DO NOT MOVE OR WE WILL OPEN FIRE!
YOU ARE UNDER ARREST. LIE DOWN ON THE GROUND WITH YOUR HANDS OUT!
REMOVE YOUR MASK!
WAIT -- WE GOTTA SAVE HIM IF WE CAN --
FREEZE!

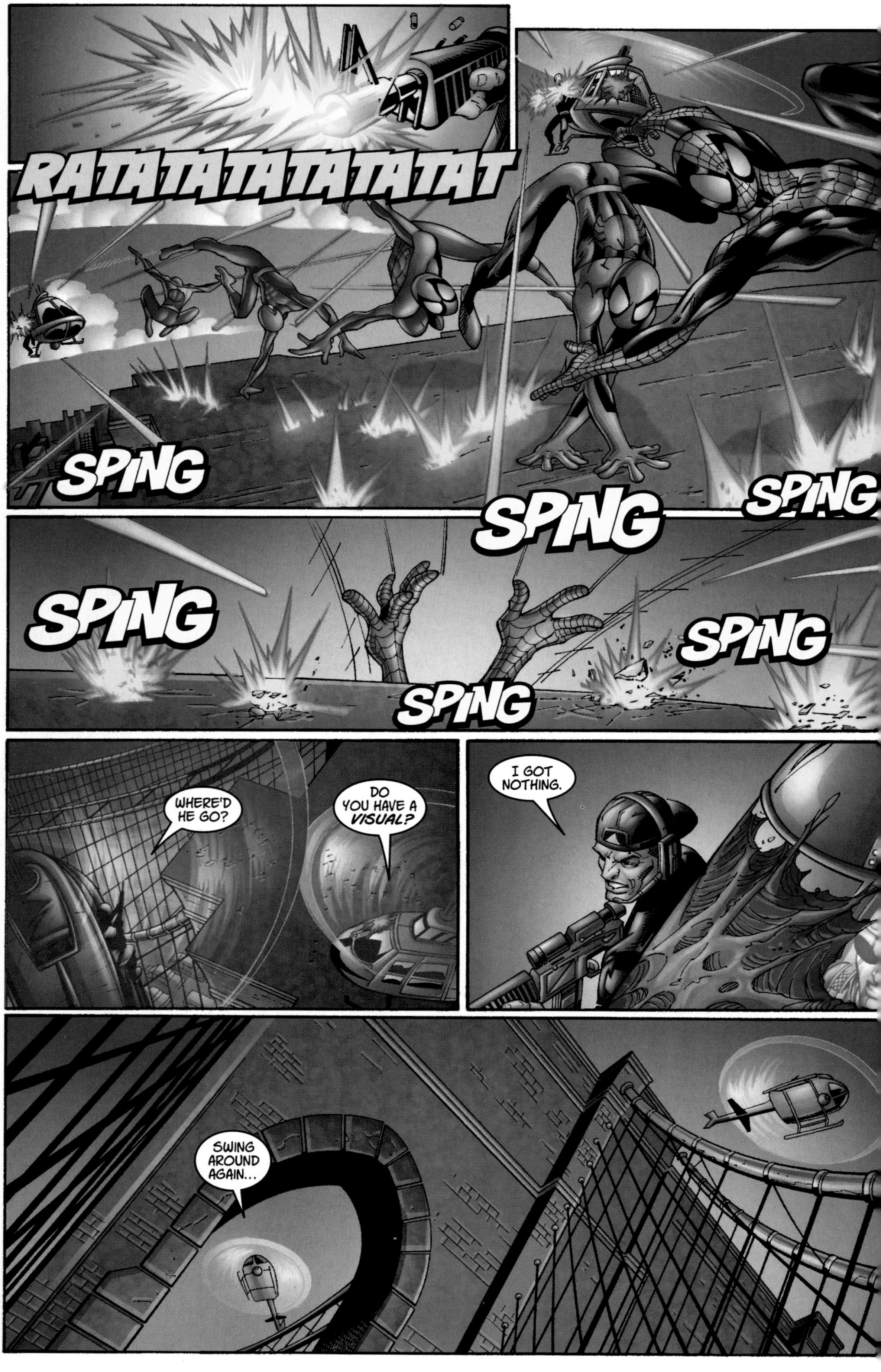
RATATATATATATAT
SPING
SPING
SPING
SPING
SPING
SPING
WHERE'D HE GO?
DO YOU HAVE A *VISUAL?*
I GOT NOTHING.
SWING AROUND AGAIN...

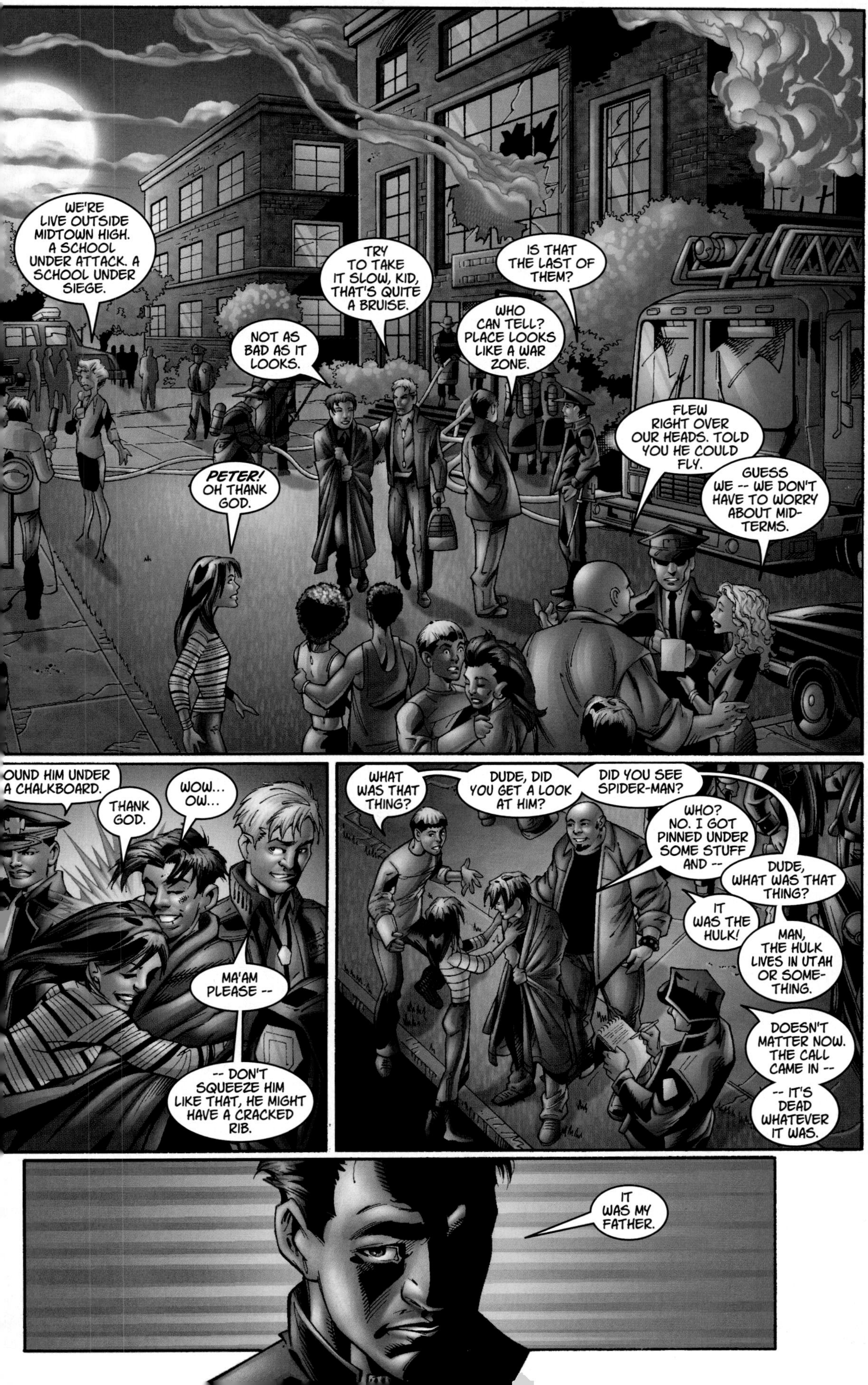
WE'RE LIVE OUTSIDE MIDTOWN HIGH. A SCHOOL UNDER ATTACK. A SCHOOL UNDER SIEGE.
TRY TO TAKE IT SLOW, KID, THAT'S QUITE A BRUISE.
NOT AS BAD AS IT LOOKS.
IS THAT THE LAST OF THEM?
WHO CAN TELL? PLACE LOOKS LIKE A WAR ZONE.
PETER! OH THANK GOD.
FLEW RIGHT OVER OUR HEADS. TOLD YOU HE COULD FLY.
GUESS WE -- WE DON'T HAVE TO WORRY ABOUT MID-TERMS.
OUND HIM UNDER A CHALKBOARD.
THANK GOD.
WOW... OW...
MA'AM PLEASE --
-- DON'T SQUEEZE HIM LIKE THAT, HE MIGHT HAVE A CRACKED RIB.
WHAT WAS THAT THING?
DUDE, DID YOU GET A LOOK AT HIM?
DID YOU SEE SPIDER-MAN?
WHO? NO. I GOT PINNED UNDER SOME STUFF AND --
DUDE, WHAT WAS THAT THING?
IT WAS THE HULK!
MAN, THE HULK LIVES IN UTAH OR SOME-THING.
DOESN'T MATTER NOW. THE CALL CAME IN --
-- IT'S DEAD WHATEVER IT WAS.
IT WAS MY FATHER.

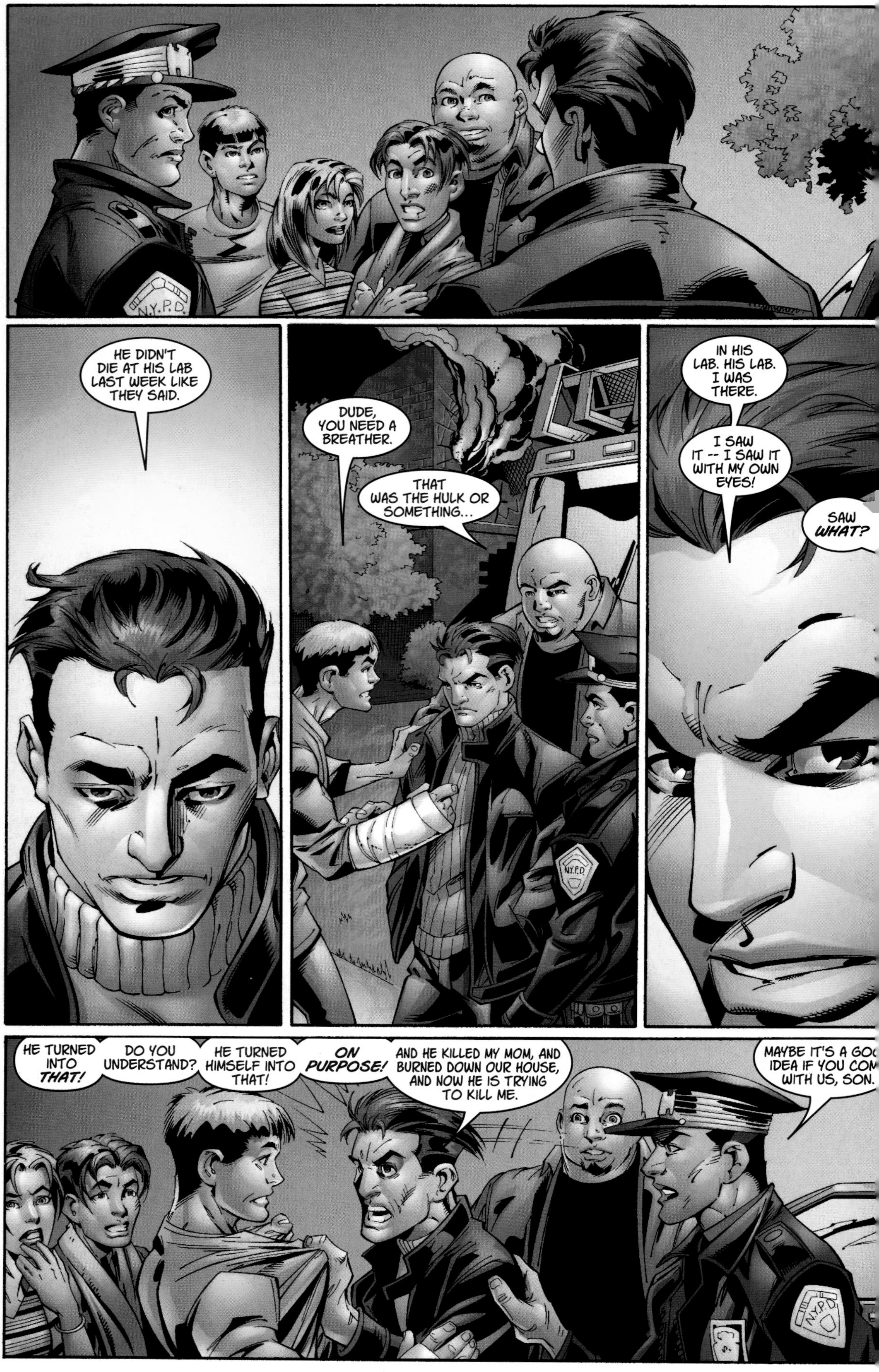
HE DIDN'T DIE AT HIS LAB LAST WEEK LIKE THEY SAID.
DUDE, YOU NEED A BREATHER.
THAT WAS THE HULK OR SOMETHING...
IN HIS LAB. HIS LAB. I WAS THERE.
I SAW IT -- I SAW IT WITH MY OWN EYES!
SAW *WHAT?*
HE TURNED INTO *THAT!*
DO YOU UNDERSTAND?
HE TURNED HIMSELF INTO THAT!
ON PURPOSE!
AND HE KILLED MY MOM, AND BURNED DOWN OUR HOUSE, AND NOW HE IS TRYING TO KILL ME.
MAYBE IT'S A GOO IDEA IF YOU COM WITH US, SON.

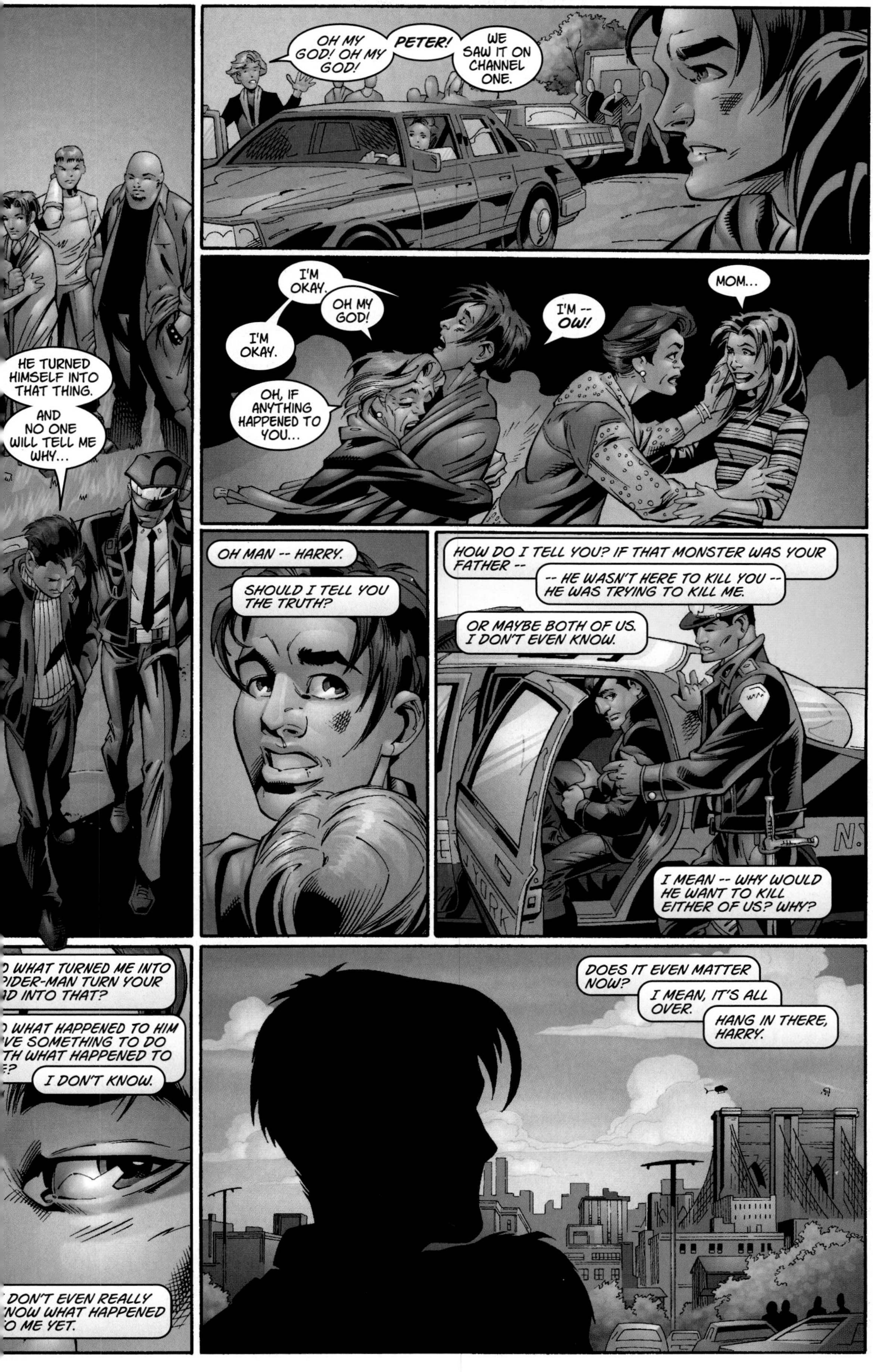
OH MY GOD! OH MY GOD!
PETER!
WE SAW IT ON CHANNEL ONE.
HE TURNED HIMSELF INTO THAT THING.
AND NO ONE WILL TELL ME WHY...
I'M OKAY.
I'M OKAY.
OH MY GOD!
OH, IF ANYTHING HAPPENED TO YOU...
I'M -- OW!
MOM...
OH MAN -- HARRY.
SHOULD I TELL YOU THE TRUTH?
HOW DO I TELL YOU? IF THAT MONSTER WAS YOUR FATHER --
-- HE WASN'T HERE TO KILL YOU -- HE WAS TRYING TO KILL ME.
OR MAYBE BOTH OF US. I DON'T EVEN KNOW.
I MEAN -- WHY WOULD HE WANT TO KILL EITHER OF US? WHY?
D WHAT TURNED ME INTO PIDER-MAN TURN YOUR D INTO THAT?
D WHAT HAPPENED TO HIM VE SOMETHING TO DO TH WHAT HAPPENED TO E?
I DON'T KNOW.
DON'T EVEN REALLY NOW WHAT HAPPENED O ME YET.
DOES IT EVEN MATTER NOW?
I MEAN, IT'S ALL OVER.
HANG IN THERE, HARRY.

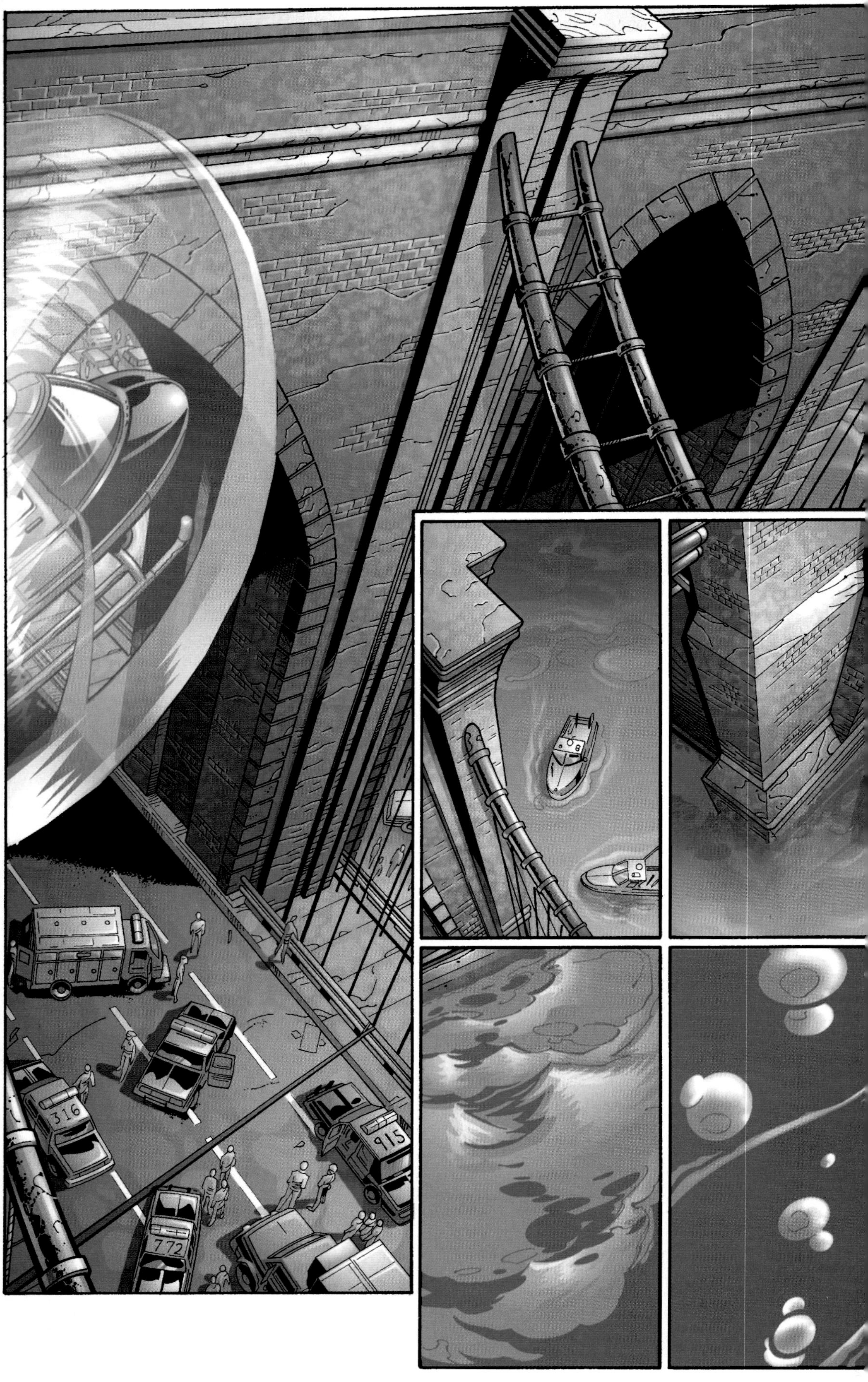
316
915
772

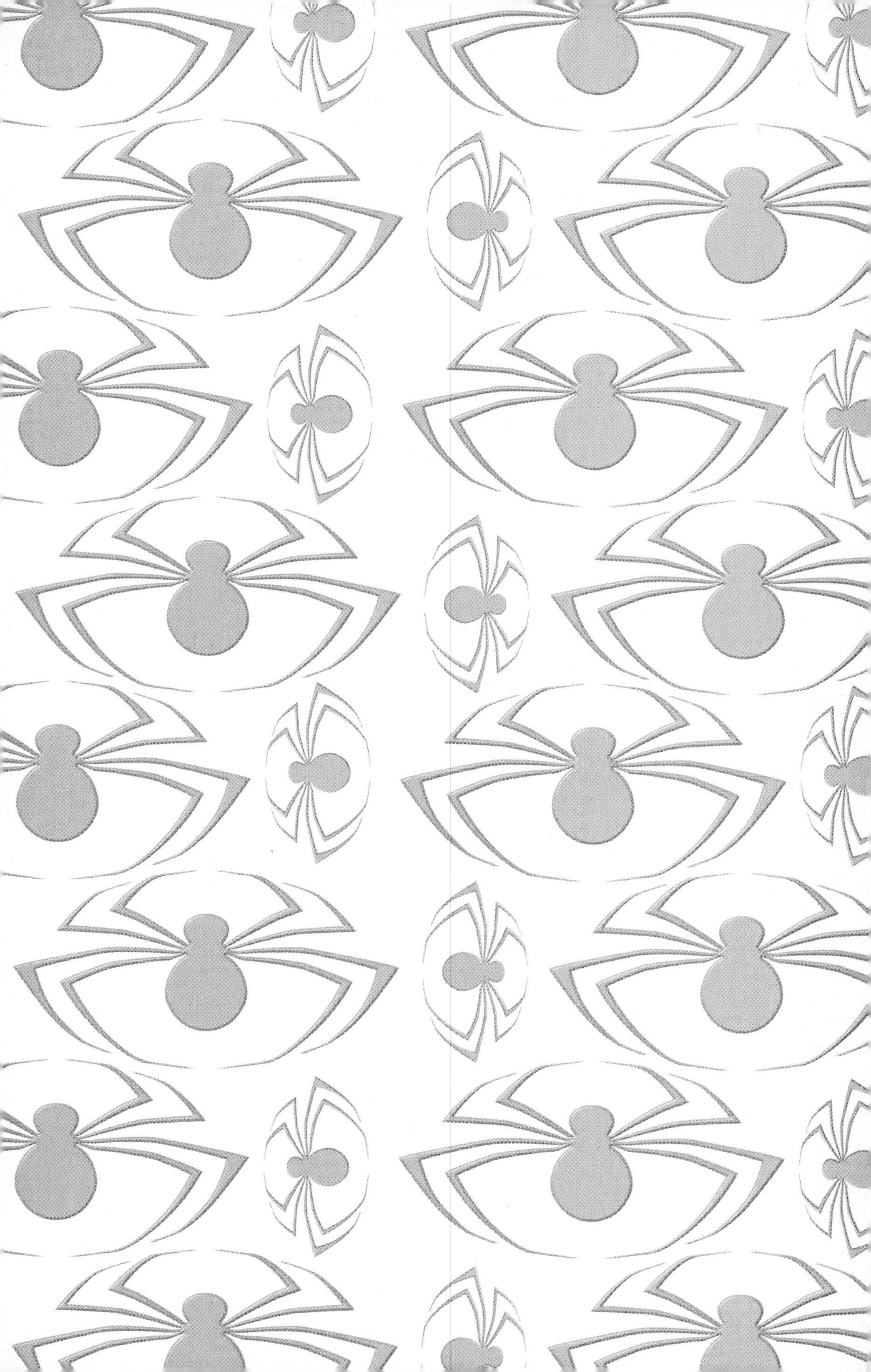

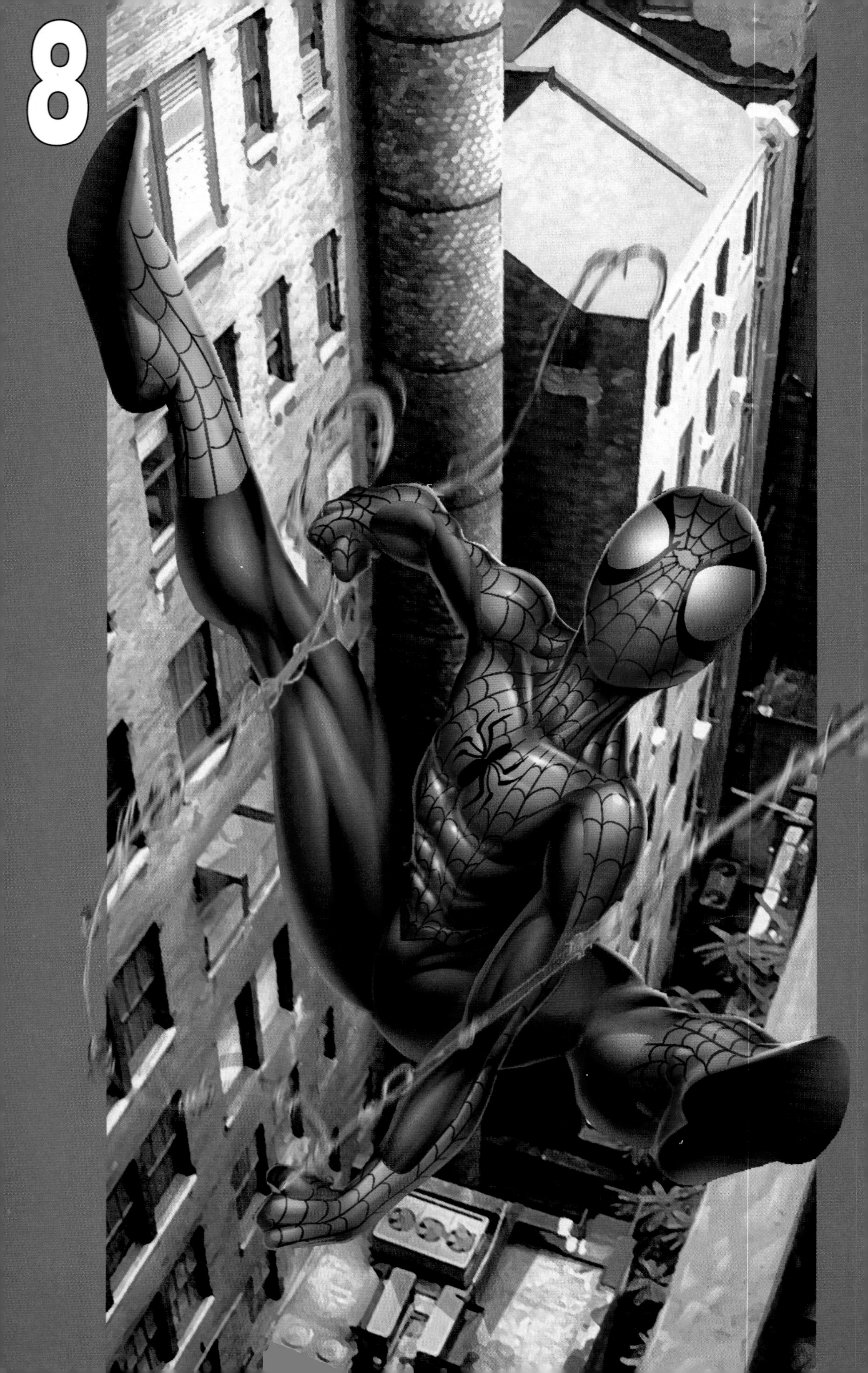
8

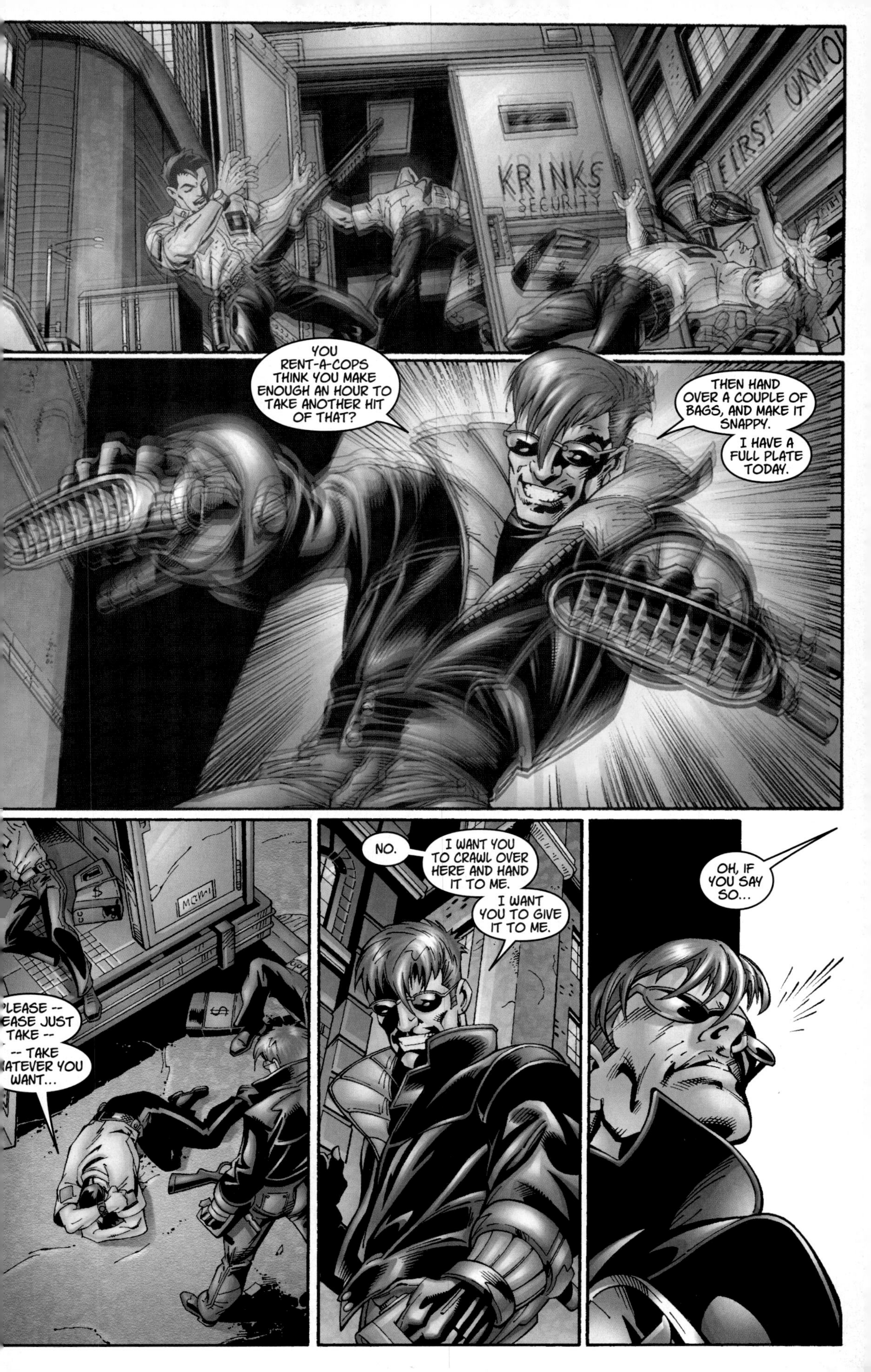
FIRST UNION
KRINKS SECURITY
YOU RENT-A-COPS THINK YOU MAKE ENOUGH AN HOUR TO TAKE ANOTHER HIT OF THAT?
THEN HAND OVER A COUPLE OF BAGS, AND MAKE IT SNAPPY.
I HAVE A FULL PLATE TODAY.
-- TAKE
WANT...
NO.
I WANT YOU TO CRAWL OVER HERE AND HAND IT TO ME.
I WANT YOU TO GIVE IT TO ME.
OH, IF YOU SAY SO...

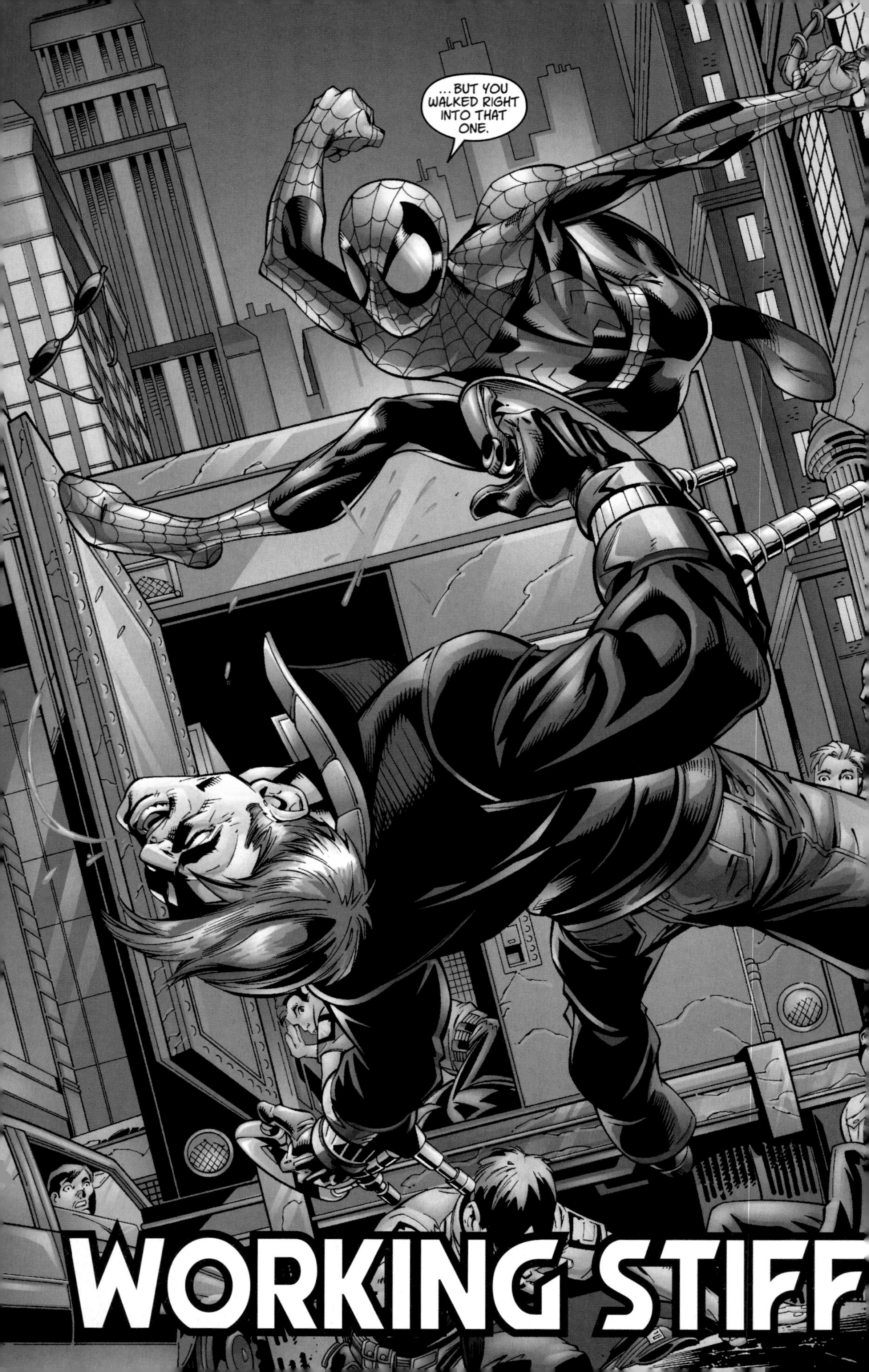
...BUT YOU WALKED RIGHT INTO THAT ONE.
WORKING STIFF

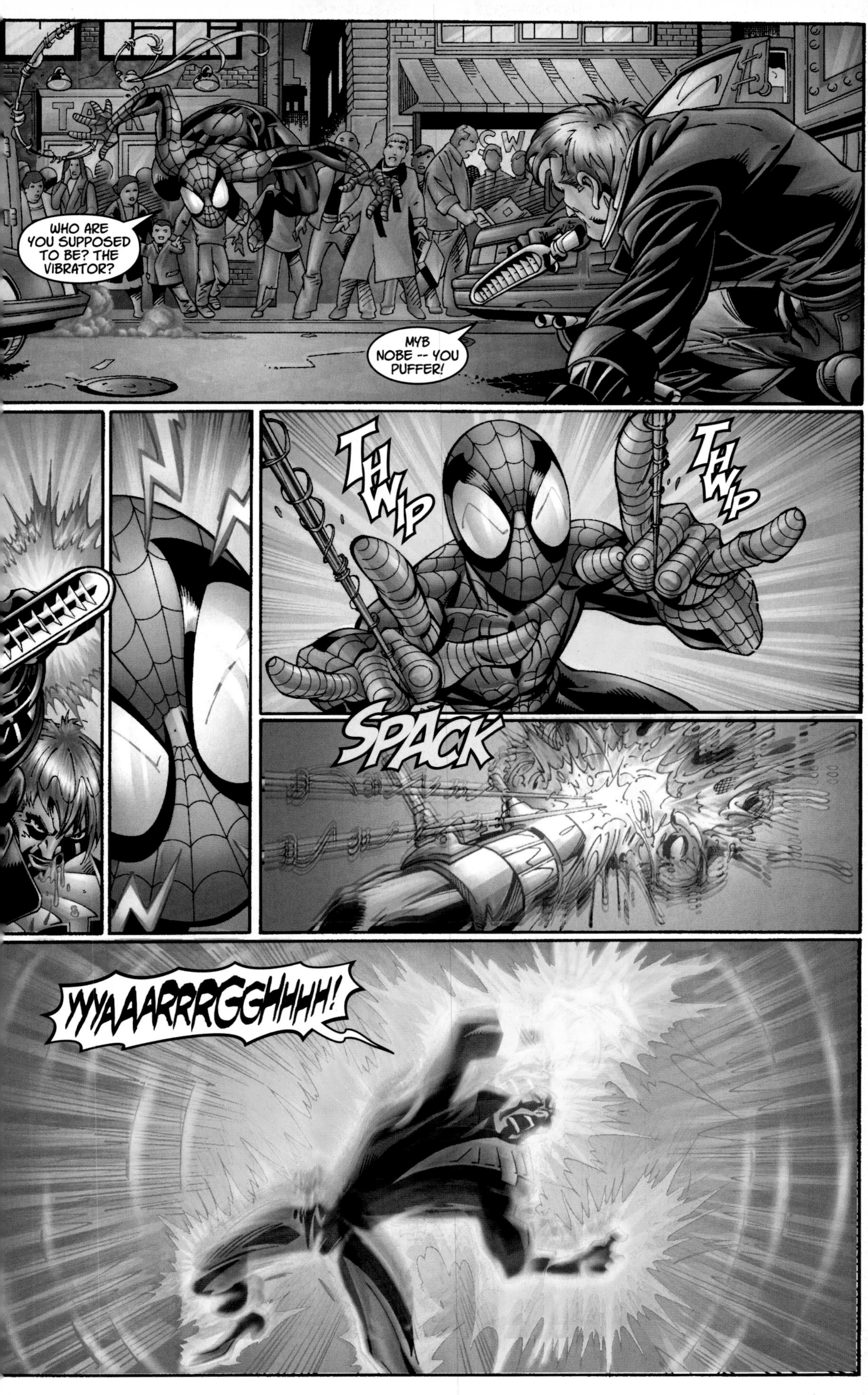
WHO ARE YOU SUPPOSED TO BE? THE VIBRATOR?
MYB NOBE -- YOU PUFFER!
THWIP
THWIP
SPACK
YYYAAARRRGGHHHH!

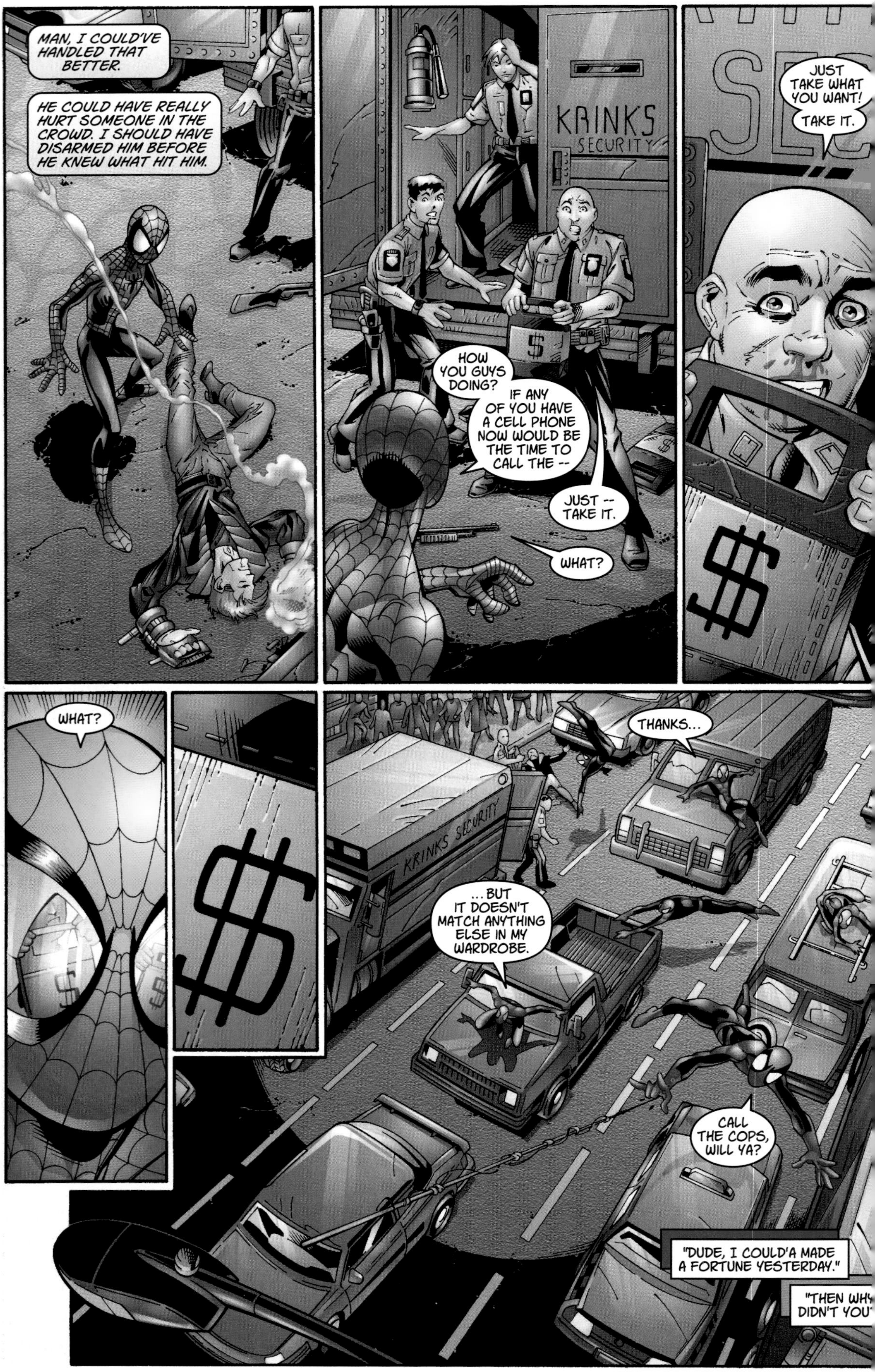
MAN, I COULD'VE HANDLED THAT BETTER.
HE COULD HAVE REALLY HURT SOMEONE IN THE CROWD. I SHOULD HAVE DISARMED HIM BEFORE HE KNEW WHAT HIT HIM.
KRINKS SECURITY
HOW YOU GUYS DOING?
IF ANY OF YOU HAVE A CELL PHONE NOW WOULD BE THE TIME TO CALL THE --
JUST -- TAKE IT.
WHAT?
JUST TAKE WHAT YOU WANT!
TAKE IT.
WHAT?
KRINKS SECURITY
THANKS...
...BUT IT DOESN'T MATCH ANYTHING ELSE IN MY WARDROBE.
CALL THE COPS, WILL YA?
"DUDE, I COULD'A MADE A FORTUNE YESTERDAY."
"THEN WHY DIDN'T YOU

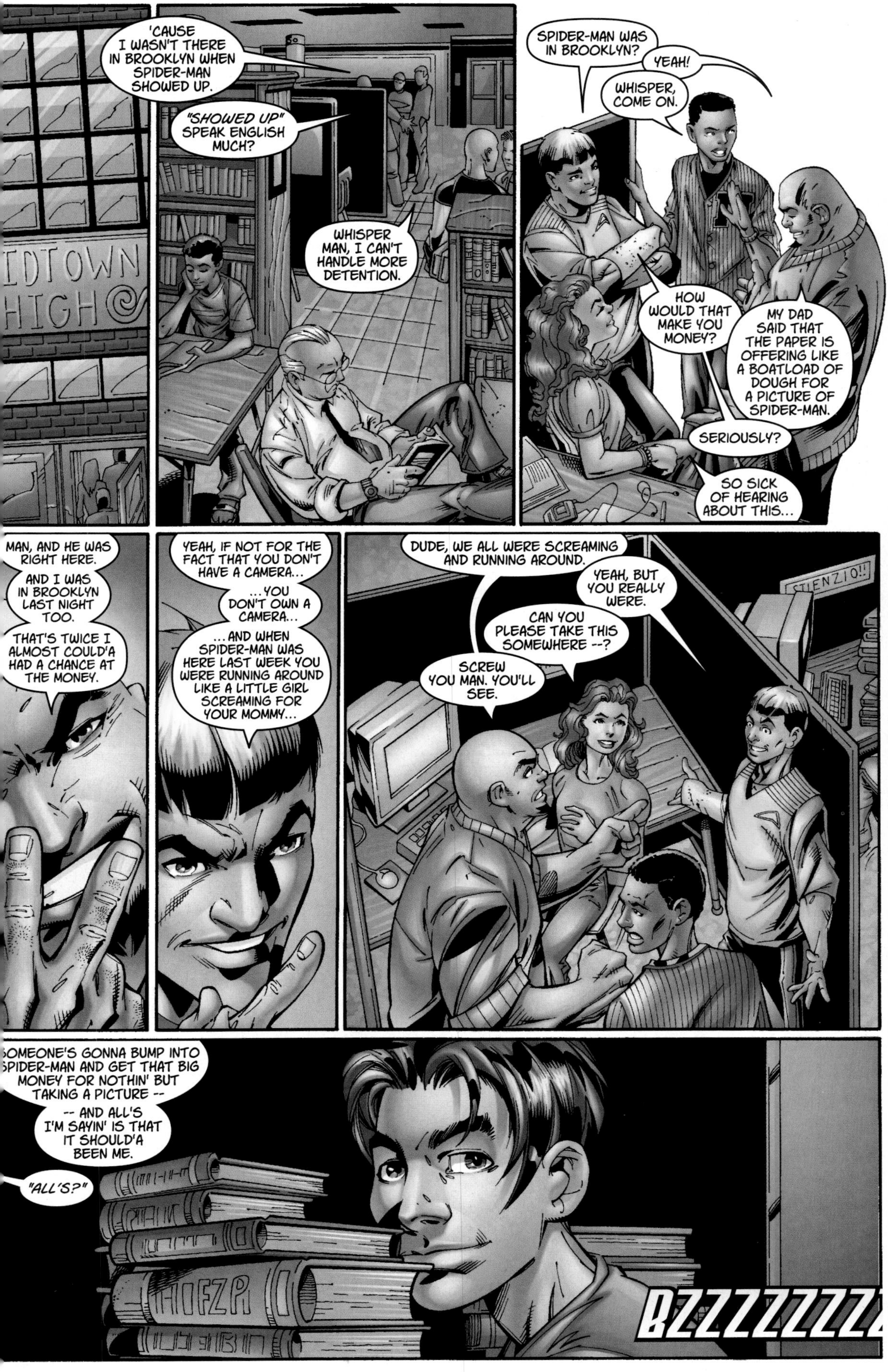
'CAUSE I WASN'T THERE IN BROOKLYN WHEN SPIDER-MAN SHOWED UP.
"SHOWED UP" SPEAK ENGLISH MUCH?
WHISPER MAN, I CAN'T HANDLE MORE DETENTION.
IDTOWN HIGH
SPIDER-MAN WAS IN BROOKLYN?
YEAH!
WHISPER, COME ON.
HOW WOULD THAT MAKE YOU MONEY?
MY DAD SAID THAT THE PAPER IS OFFERING LIKE A BOATLOAD OF DOUGH FOR A PICTURE OF SPIDER-MAN.
SERIOUSLY?
SO SICK OF HEARING ABOUT THIS...
MAN, AND HE WAS RIGHT HERE.
AND I WAS IN BROOKLYN LAST NIGHT TOO.
THAT'S TWICE I ALMOST COULD'A HAD A CHANCE AT THE MONEY.
YEAH, IF NOT FOR THE FACT THAT YOU DON'T HAVE A CAMERA...
...YOU DON'T OWN A CAMERA...
...AND WHEN SPIDER-MAN WAS HERE LAST WEEK YOU WERE RUNNING AROUND LIKE A LITTLE GIRL SCREAMING FOR YOUR MOMMY...
DUDE, WE ALL WERE SCREAMING AND RUNNING AROUND.
YEAH, BUT YOU REALLY WERE.
CAN YOU PLEASE TAKE THIS SOMEWHERE --?
SCREW YOU MAN. YOU'LL SEE.
SILENZIO!!
SOMEONE'S GONNA BUMP INTO SPIDER-MAN AND GET THAT BIG MONEY FOR NOTHIN' BUT TAKING A PICTURE --
-- AND ALL'S I'M SAYIN' IS THAT IT SHOULD'A BEEN ME.
"ALL'S?"
BZZZZZZZZ

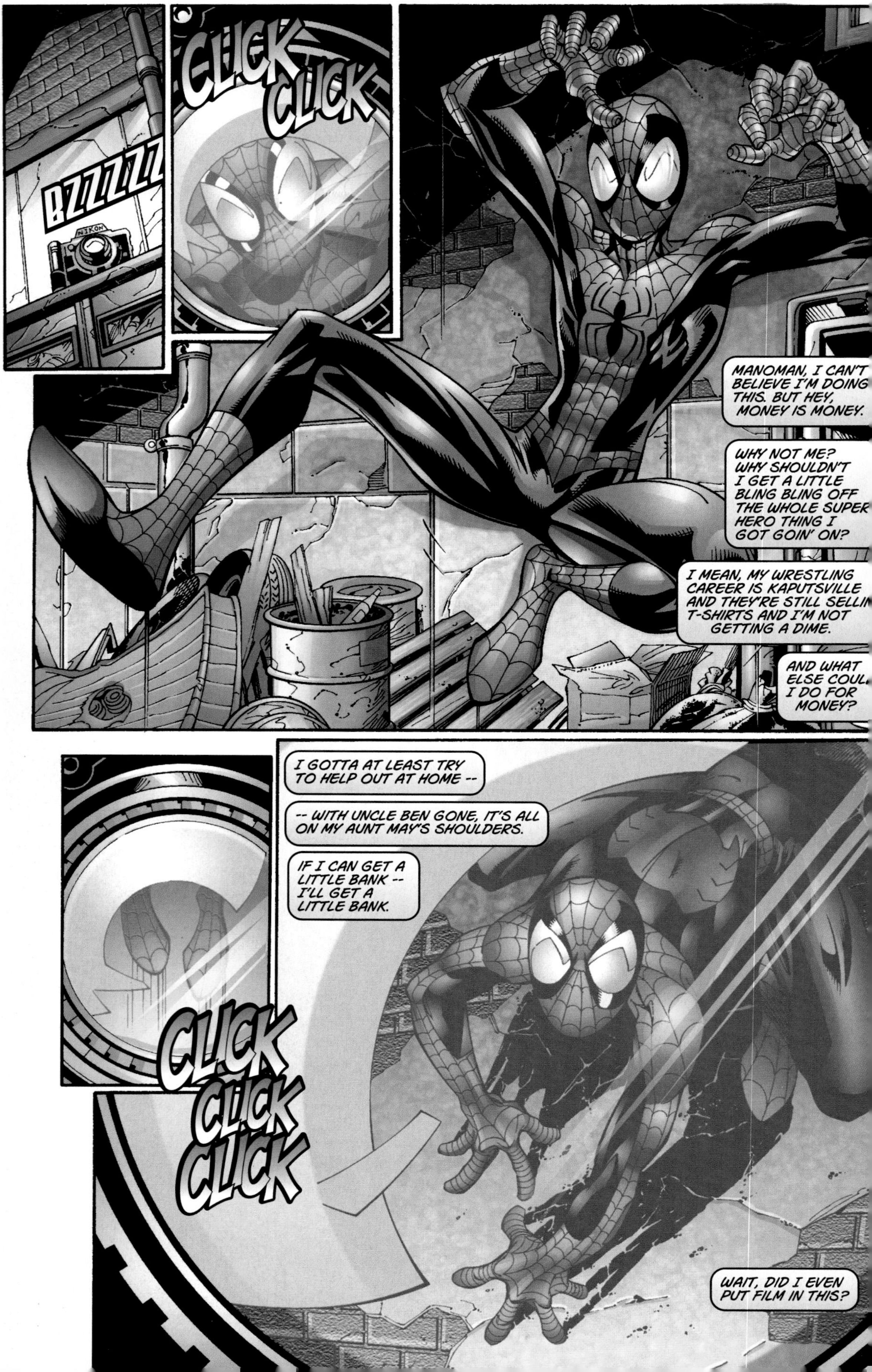
BZZZZZ
CLICK CLICK
MANOMAN, I CAN'T BELIEVE I'M DOING THIS. BUT HEY, MONEY IS MONEY.
WHY NOT ME? WHY SHOULDN'T I GET A LITTLE BLING BLING OFF THE WHOLE SUPER HERO THING I GOT GOIN' ON?
I MEAN, MY WRESTLING CAREER IS KAPUTSVILLE AND THEY'RE STILL SELLIN' T-SHIRTS AND I'M NOT GETTING A DIME.
AND WHAT ELSE COULD I DO FOR MONEY?
I GOTTA AT LEAST TRY TO HELP OUT AT HOME --
-- WITH UNCLE BEN GONE, IT'S ALL ON MY AUNT MAY'S SHOULDERS.
IF I CAN GET A LITTLE BANK -- I'LL GET A LITTLE BANK.
CLICK CLICK CLICK
WAIT, DID I EVEN PUT FILM IN THIS?

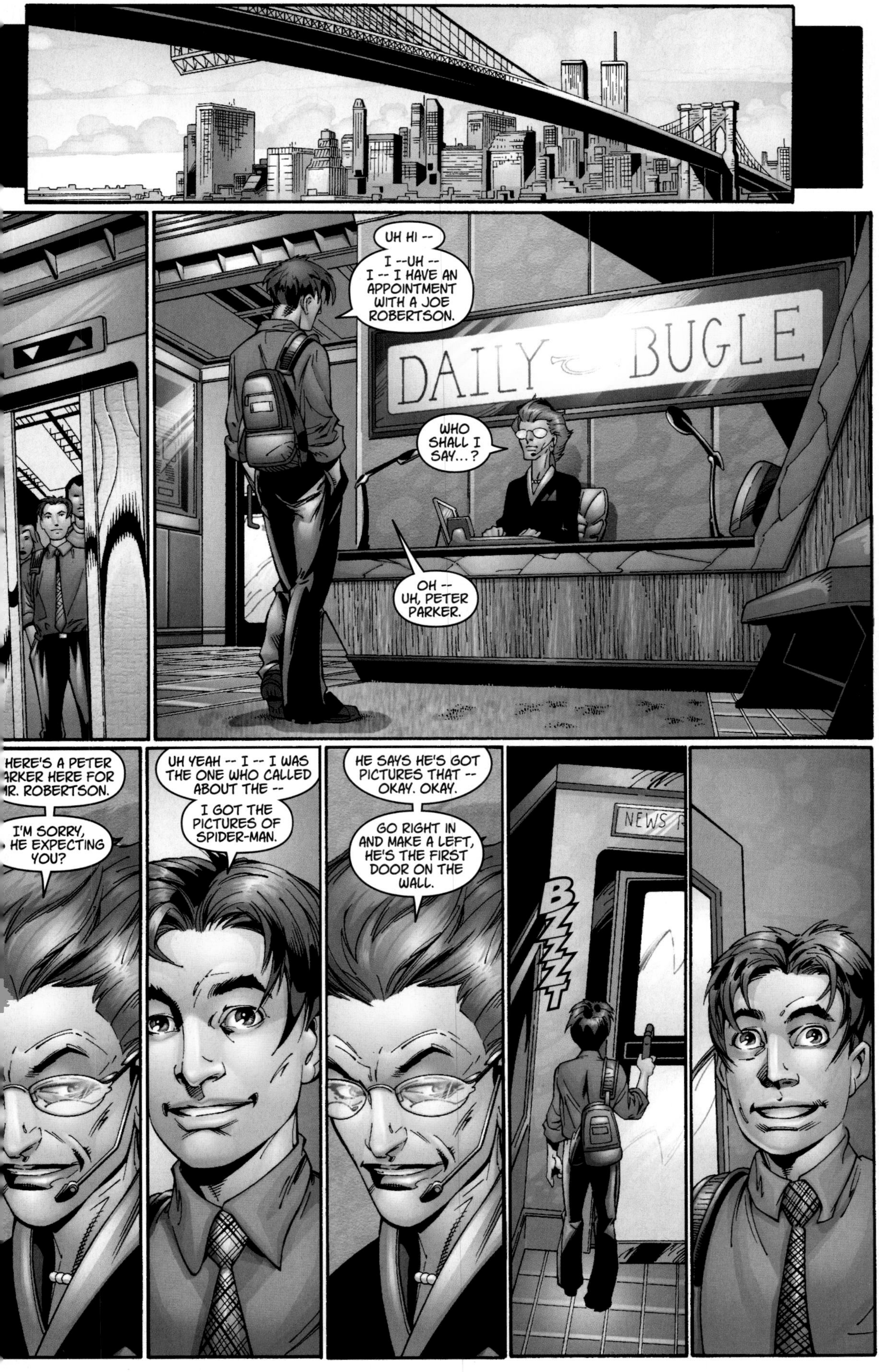
UH HI --
I --UH --
I -- I HAVE AN APPOINTMENT WITH A JOE ROBERTSON.
DAILY BUGLE
WHO SHALL I SAY...?
OH -- UH, PETER PARKER.
HERE'S A PETER ARKER HERE FOR R. ROBERTSON.
I'M SORRY, HE EXPECTING YOU?
UH YEAH -- I -- I WAS THE ONE WHO CALLED ABOUT THE --
I GOT THE PICTURES OF SPIDER-MAN.
HE SAYS HE'S GOT PICTURES THAT -- OKAY. OKAY.
GO RIGHT IN AND MAKE A LEFT, HE'S THE FIRST DOOR ON THE WALL.
BZZZT

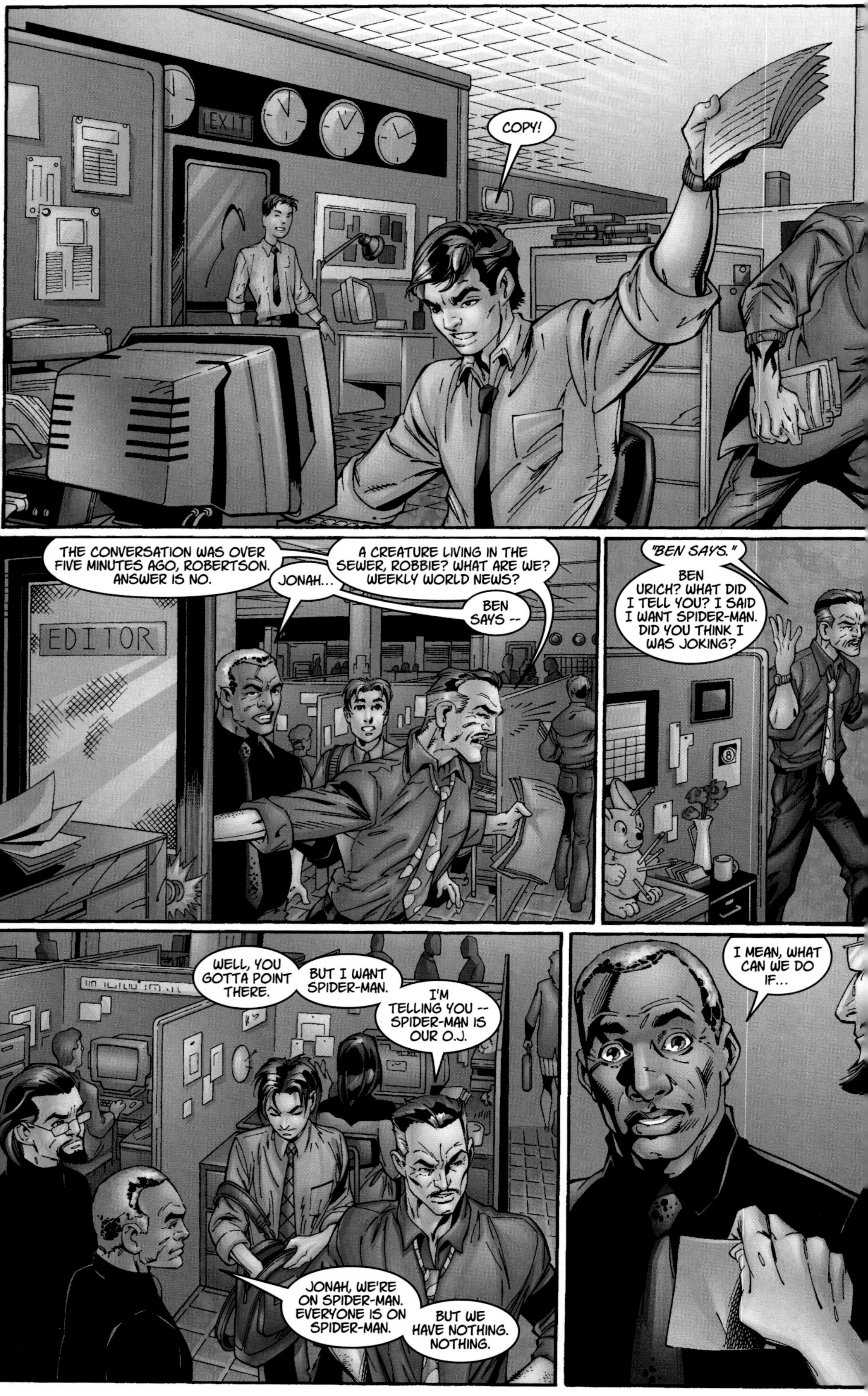
COPY!
THE CONVERSATION WAS OVER FIVE MINUTES AGO, ROBERTSON. ANSWER IS NO.
JONAH...
A CREATURE LIVING IN THE SEWER, ROBBIE? WHAT ARE WE? WEEKLY WORLD NEWS?
BEN SAYS --
"BEN SAYS."
BEN URICH? WHAT DID I TELL YOU? I SAID I WANT SPIDER-MAN. DID YOU THINK I WAS JOKING?
WELL, YOU GOTTA POINT THERE.
BUT I WANT SPIDER-MAN.
I'M TELLING YOU -- SPIDER-MAN IS OUR O.J.
JONAH, WE'RE ON SPIDER-MAN. EVERYONE IS ON SPIDER-MAN.
BUT WE HAVE NOTHING. NOTHING.
I MEAN, WHAT CAN WE DO IF...

I'M WORKING ON IT.

"WORKING ON IT."

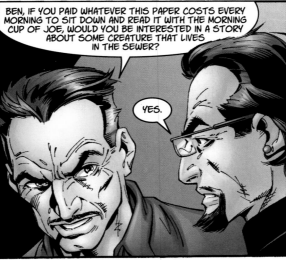

BEN, IF YOU PAID WHATEVER THIS PAPER COSTS EVERY MORNING TO SIT DOWN AND READ IT WITH THE MORNING CUP OF JOE, WOULD YOU BE INTERESTED IN A STORY ABOUT SOME CREATURE THAT LIVES IN THE SEWER?

YES.

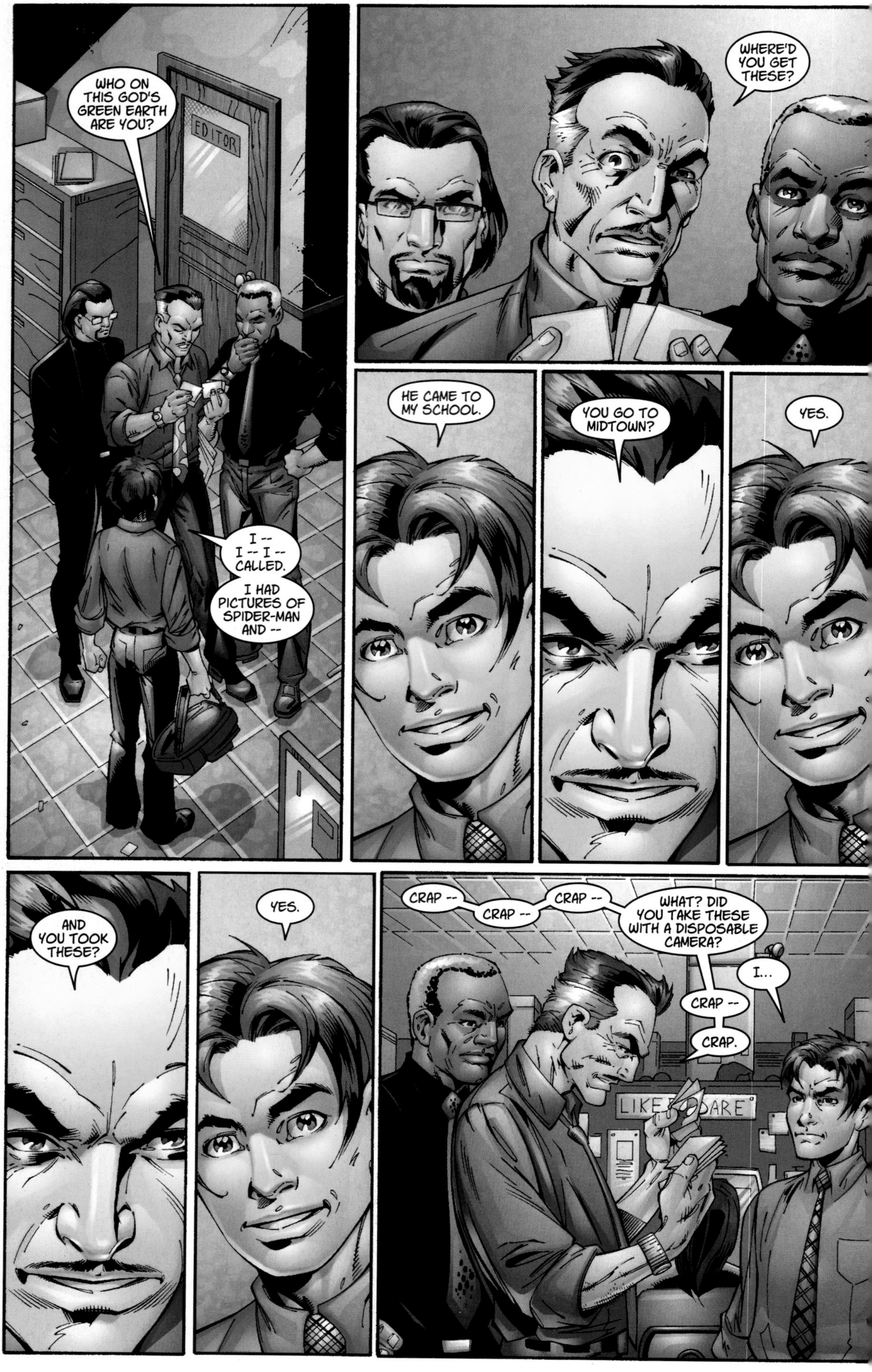
WHO ON THIS GOD'S GREEN EARTH ARE YOU?
EDITOR
I -- I -- I -- CALLED.
I HAD PICTURES OF SPIDER-MAN AND --
WHERE'D YOU GET THESE?
HE CAME TO MY SCHOOL.
YOU GO TO MIDTOWN?
YES.
AND YOU TOOK THESE?
YES.
CRAP --
CRAP --
CRAP --
WHAT? DID YOU TAKE THESE WITH A DISPOSABLE CAMERA?
I...
CRAP --
CRAP.

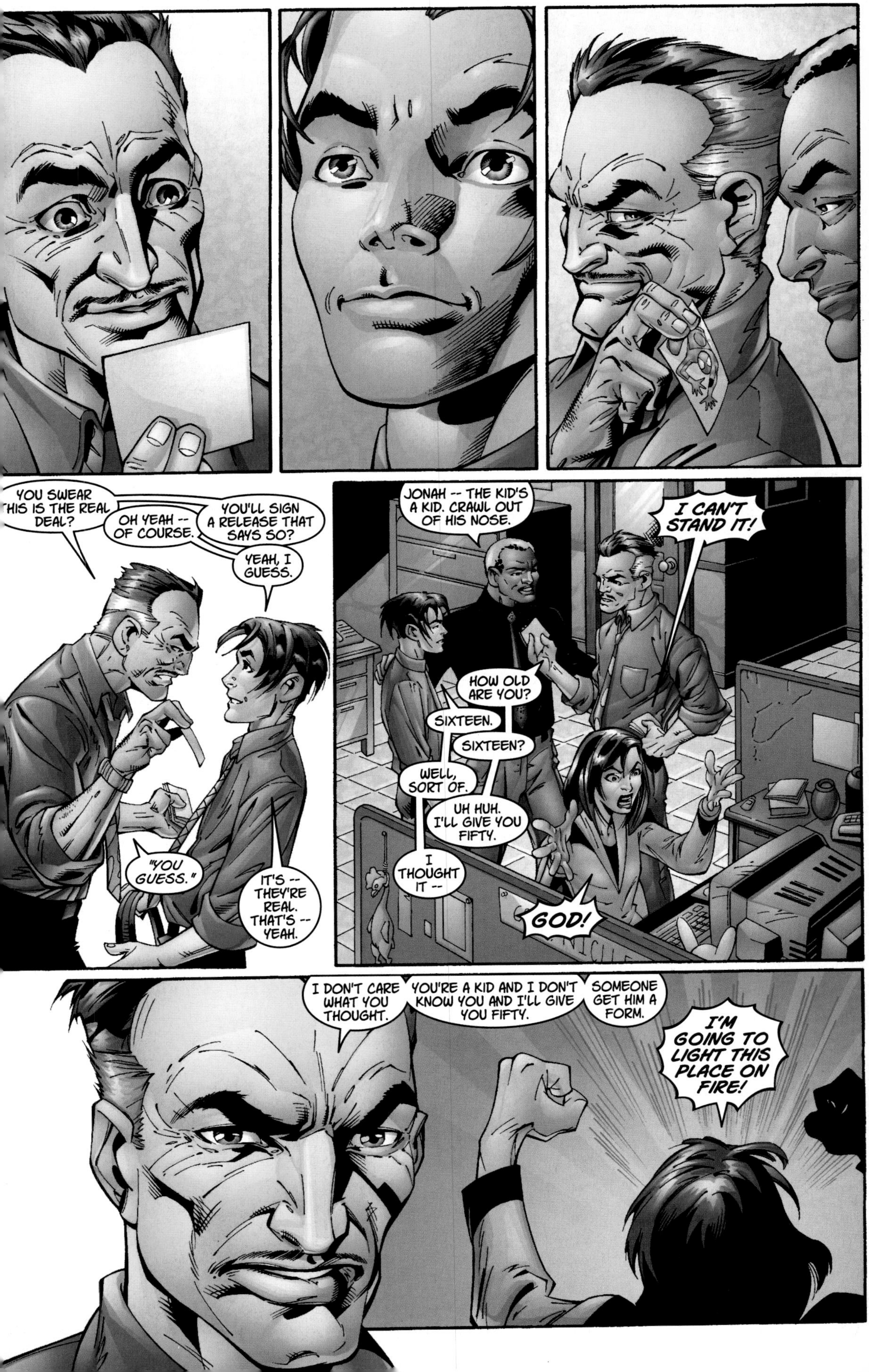
YOU SWEAR THIS IS THE REAL DEAL?
OH YEAH -- OF COURSE.
YOU'LL SIGN A RELEASE THAT SAYS SO?
YEAH, I GUESS.
"YOU GUESS."
IT'S -- THEY'RE REAL. THAT'S -- YEAH.
JONAH -- THE KID'S A KID. CRAWL OUT OF HIS NOSE.
I CAN'T STAND IT!
HOW OLD ARE YOU?
SIXTEEN.
SIXTEEN?
WELL, SORT OF.
UH HUH. I'LL GIVE YOU FIFTY.
I THOUGHT IT --
GOD!
I DON'T CARE WHAT YOU THOUGHT.
YOU'RE A KID AND I DON'T KNOW YOU AND I'LL GIVE YOU FIFTY.
SOMEONE GET HIM A FORM.
I'M GOING TO LIGHT THIS PLACE ON FIRE!

WHAT NOW, MS. BRANT?

I CAN'T -- I'M NOT DOING THIS ANYMORE, JONAH.

YOU'LL DO WHAT I --

NO. NO. I'M THE ASSOCIATE BOOK EDITOR.

I'M NOT A FREAKIN' WEB DESIGNER. I CAN'T GET THIS FREAKIN' THING TO WORK!

IT FREEZES UP ON ME EVERY TIME I TAKE A DEEP BREATH AND I CAN'T I CAN'T -- I CAN'T -- FORGET IT. NOPE.

BUT WE PAID FOR YOU TO TAKE THAT CLASS.

IT WAS A ONE DAY CLASS, JONAH. IF I TOOK A ONE DAY CLASS IN CHINESE -- I WOULDN'T KNOW CHINESE BY THE END OF THE DAY.

I DON'T -- ARRRGH!

HEY, WHAT HAPPENED TO OUR WEB SITE?! IT'S NOT COMING UP ON THE FREAKIN' BROWSER!

I DON'T KNOW! YOU SIT!

YOU CRASHED IT!

YOU SIT!

UH -- IT LOOKS LIKE THE SCRIPT'S IN A RECURSIVE LOOP.

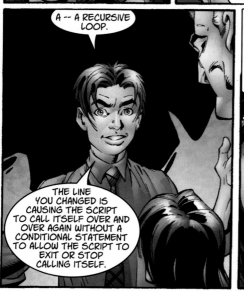

A -- A RECURSIVE LOOP.

THE LINE YOU CHANGED IS CAUSING THE SCRIPT TO CALL ITSELF OVER AND OVER AGAIN WITHOUT A CONDITIONAL STATEMENT TO ALLOW THE SCRIPT TO EXIT OR STOP CALLING ITSELF.

NONE OF THE PAGES ON THE SITE ARE RENDERED BECAUSE THE RESULTS OF THE SCRIPT ARE NEEDED, BUT SINCE THE SCRIPT IS RECURSIVELY CALLING ITSELF, YOU'LL NEVER GET RESULTS AND THE PAGES WILL NEVER RENDER.

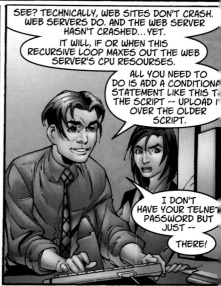

SEE? TECHNICALLY, WEB SITES DON'T CRASH. WEB SERVERS DO. AND THE WEB SERVER HASN'T CRASHED...YET.

IT WILL, IF OR WHEN THIS RECURSIVE LOOP MAXES OUT THE WEB SERVER'S CPU RESOURSES.

ALL YOU NEED TO DO IS ADD A CONDITIONAL STATEMENT LIKE THIS T THE SCRIPT -- UPLOAD I OVER THE OLDER SCRIPT.

I DON'T HAVE YOUR TELNE PASSWORD BUT JUST --

THERE!

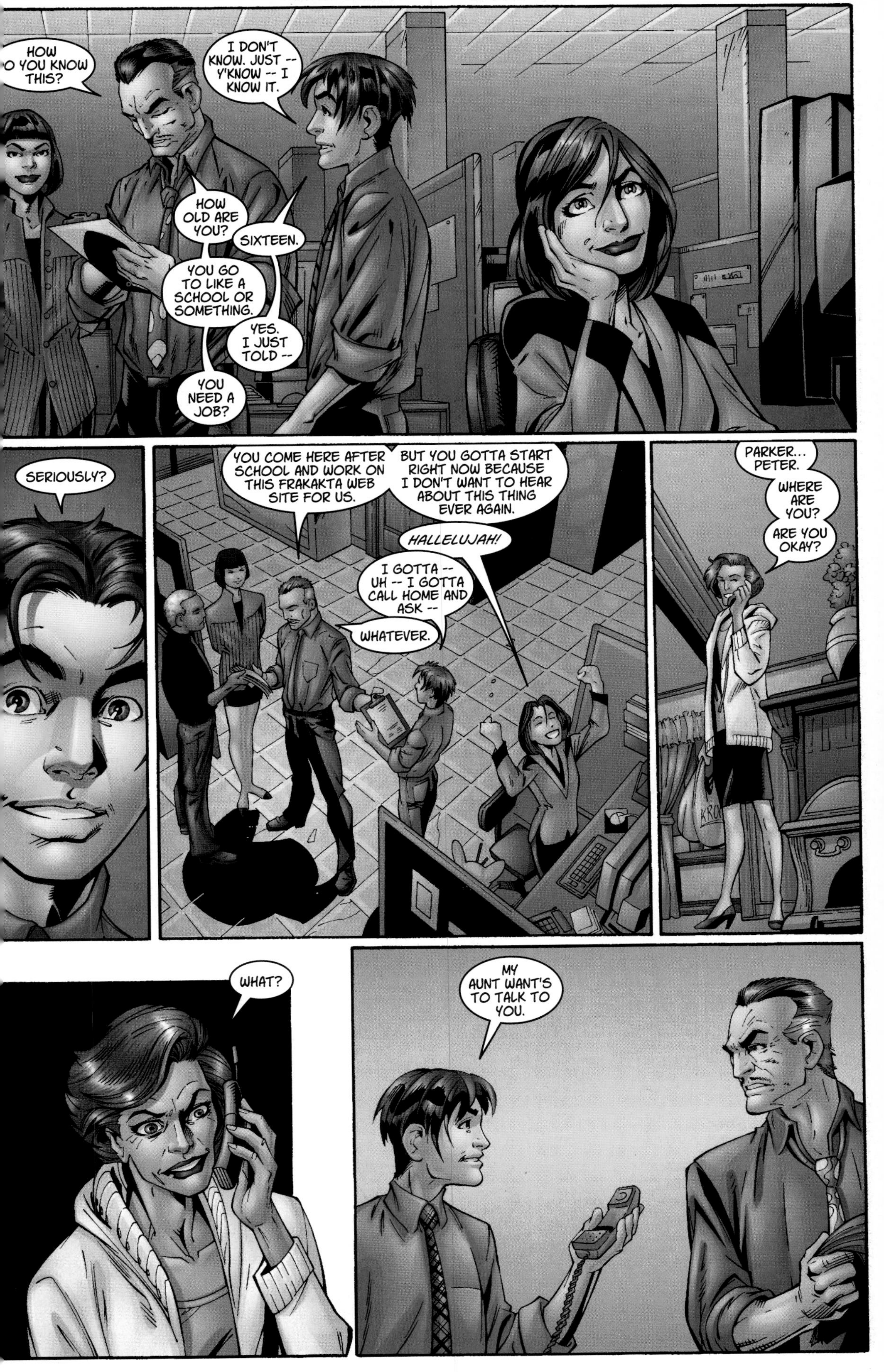
HOW DO YOU KNOW THIS?
I DON'T KNOW. JUST -- Y'KNOW -- I KNOW IT.
HOW OLD ARE YOU?
SIXTEEN.
YOU GO TO LIKE A SCHOOL OR SOMETHING.
YES. I JUST TOLD --
YOU NEED A JOB?
SERIOUSLY?
YOU COME HERE AFTER SCHOOL AND WORK ON THIS FRAKAKTA WEB SITE FOR US.
BUT YOU GOTTA START RIGHT NOW BECAUSE I DON'T WANT TO HEAR ABOUT THIS THING EVER AGAIN.
HALLELUJAH!
I GOTTA -- UH -- I GOTTA CALL HOME AND ASK --
WHATEVER.
PARKER... PETER.
WHERE ARE YOU?
ARE YOU OKAY?
WHAT?
MY AUNT WANT'S TO TALK TO YOU.

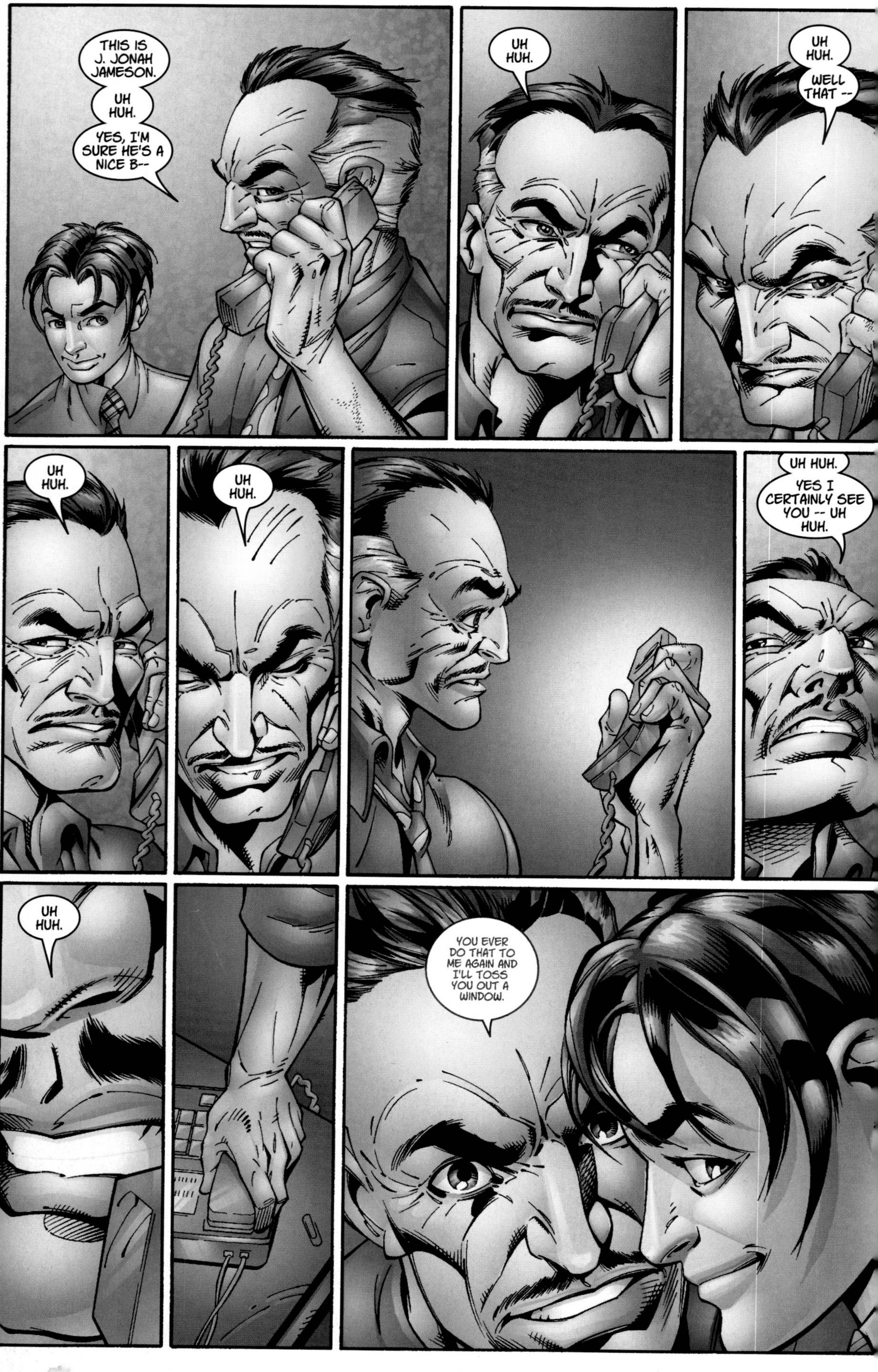
THIS IS J. JONAH JAMESON.
UH HUH.
YES, I'M SURE HE'S A NICE B--
UH HUH.
UH HUH.
WELL THAT --
UH HUH.
UH HUH.
UH HUH.
YES I CERTAINLY SEE YOU -- UH HUH.
UH HUH.
YOU EVER DO THAT TO ME AGAIN AND I'LL TOSS YOU OUT A WINDOW.

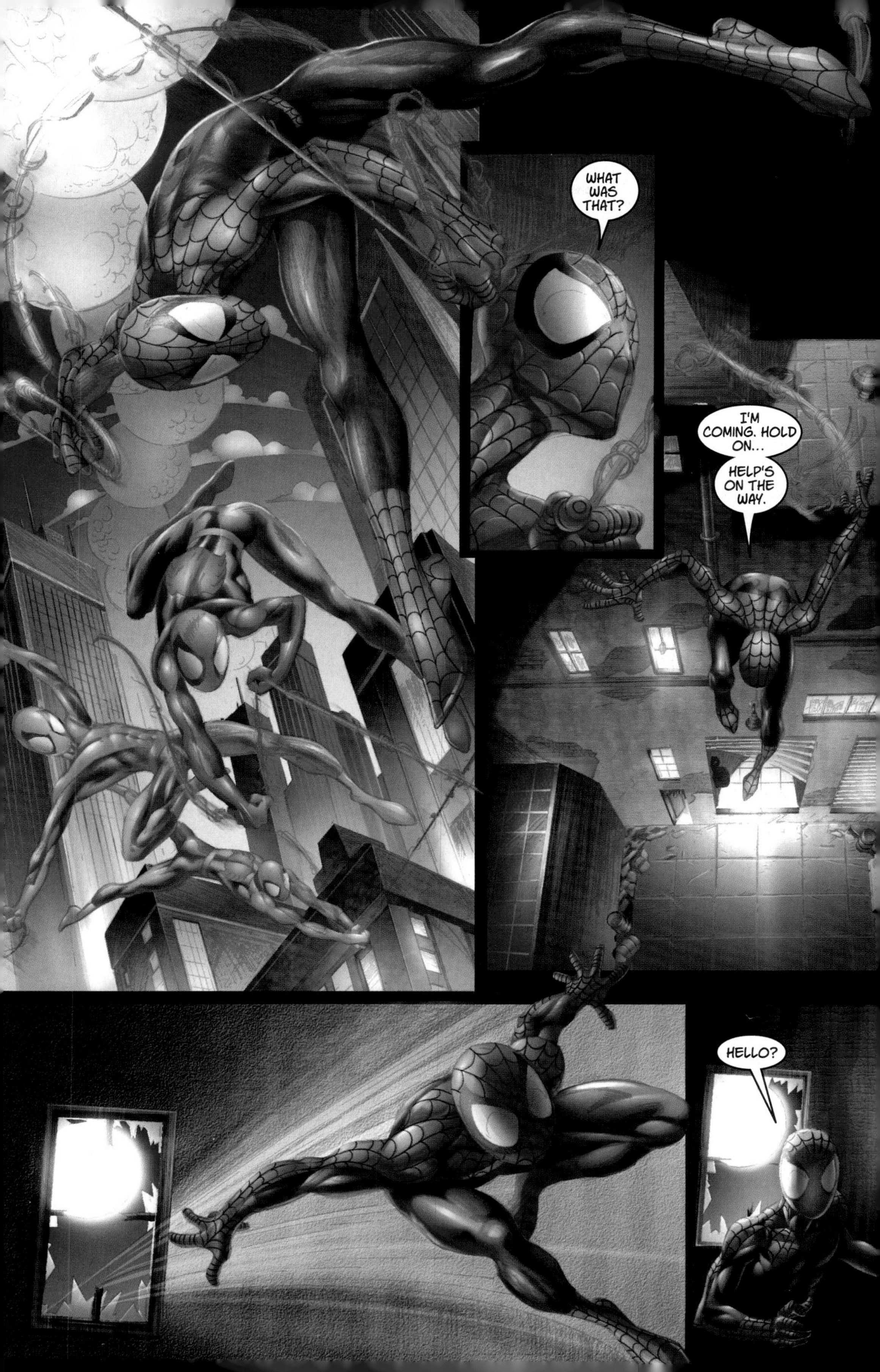
WHAT WAS THAT?
I'M COMING. HOLD ON...
HELP'S ON THE WAY.
HELLO?

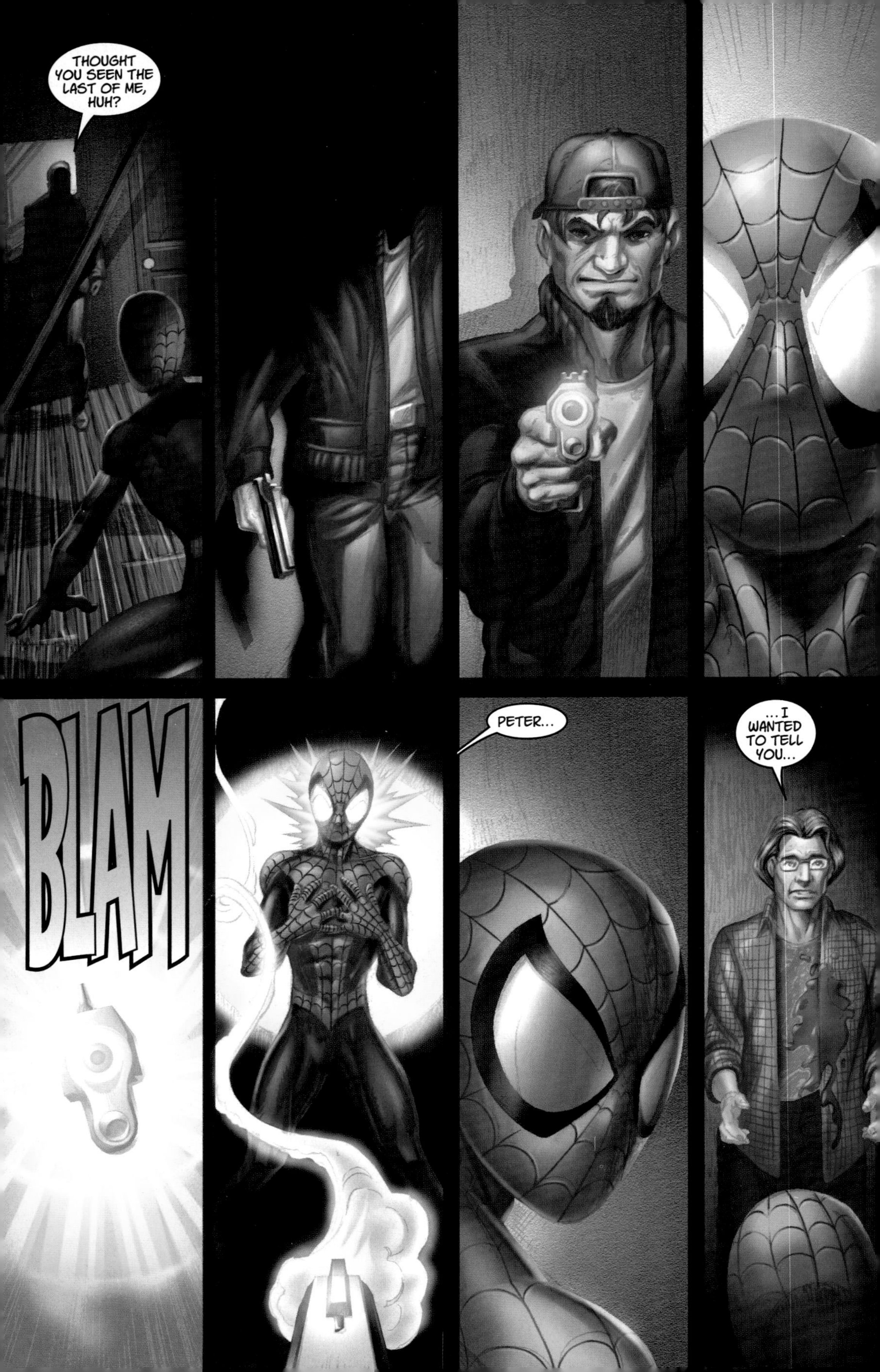
THOUGHT YOU SEEN THE LAST OF ME, HUH?
BLAM
PETER...
...I WANTED TO TELL YOU...

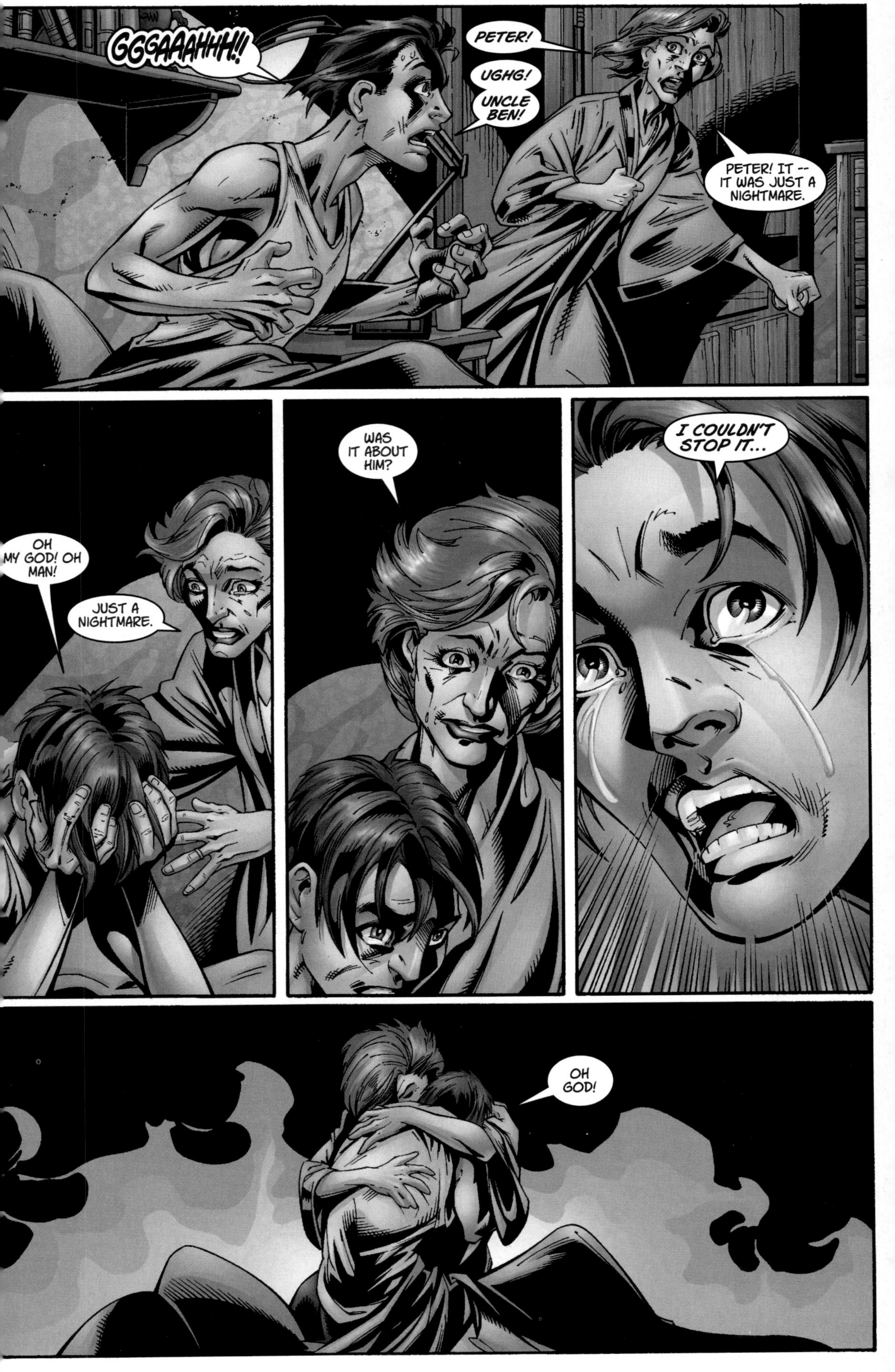
GGGAAAHHH!!
PETER!
UGHG!
UNCLE BEN!
PETER! IT -- IT WAS JUST A NIGHTMARE.
OH MY GOD! OH MAN!
JUST A NIGHTMARE.
WAS IT ABOUT HIM?
I COULDN'T STOP IT...
OH GOD!

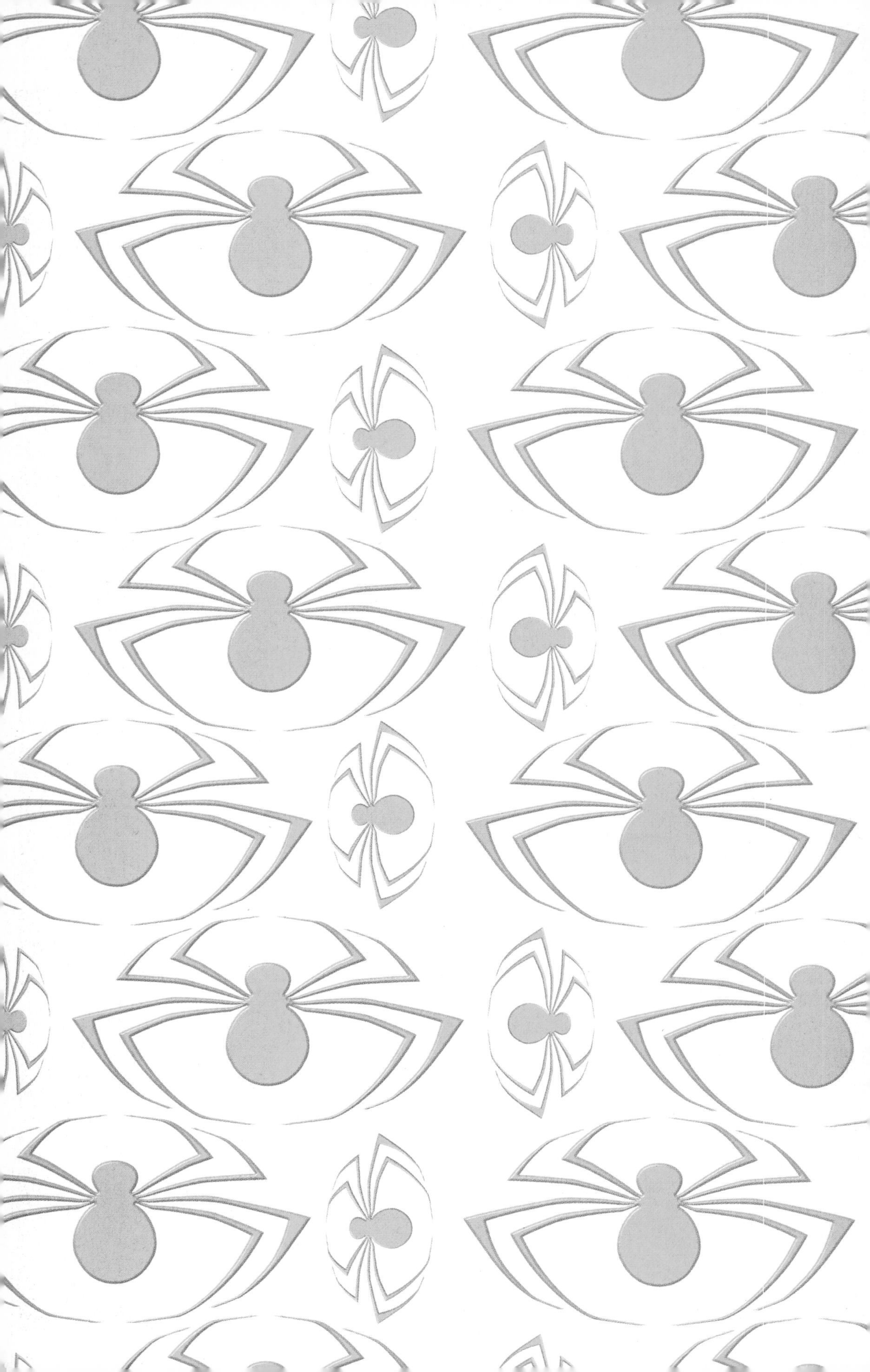

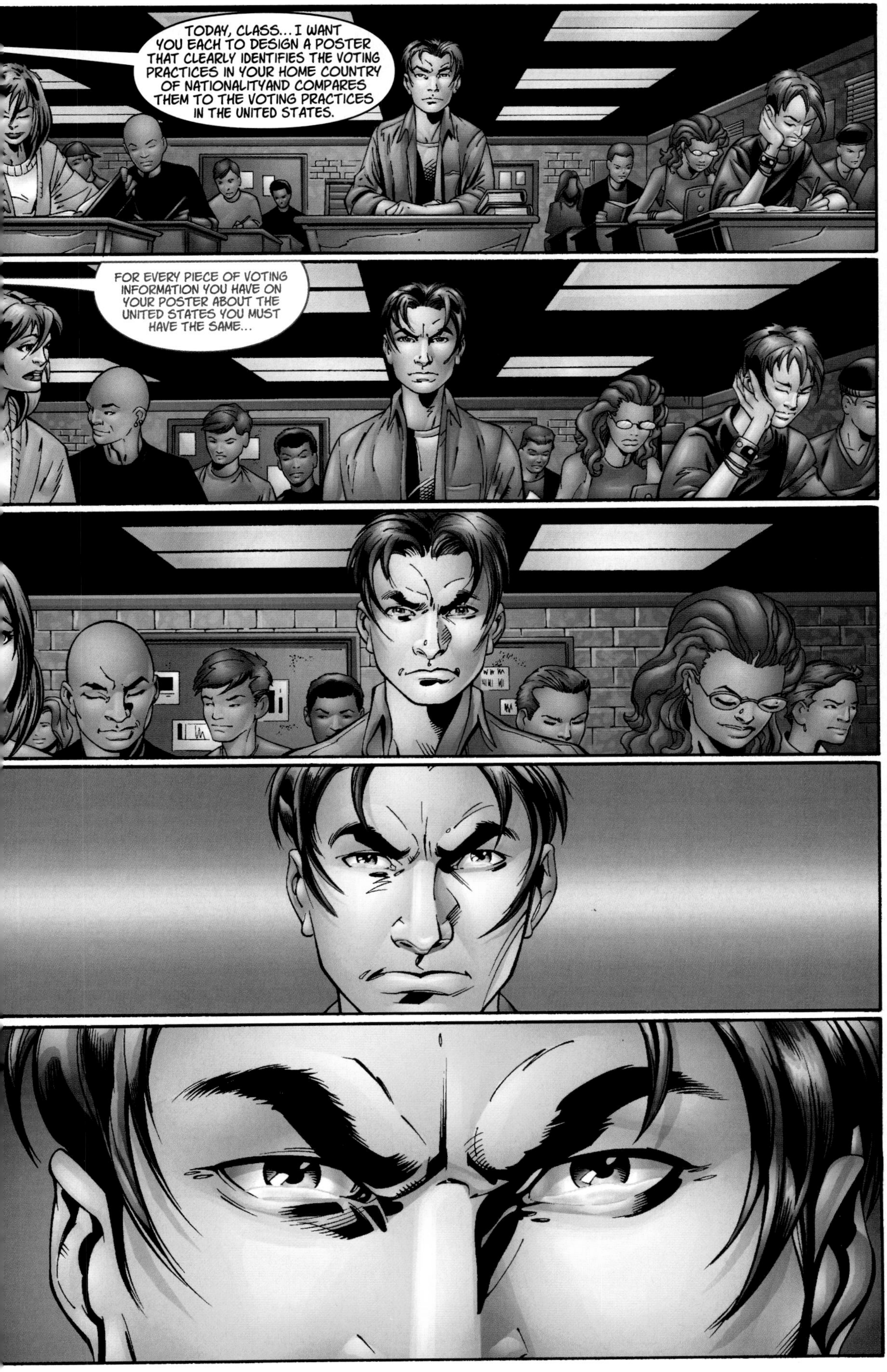
TODAY, CLASS... I WANT YOU EACH TO DESIGN A POSTER THAT CLEARLY IDENTIFIES THE VOTING PRACTICES IN YOUR HOME COUNTRY OF NATIONALITYAND COMPARES THEM TO THE VOTING PRACTICES IN THE UNITED STATES.
FOR EVERY PIECE OF VOTING INFORMATION YOU HAVE ON YOUR POSTER ABOUT THE UNITED STATES YOU MUST HAVE THE SAME...

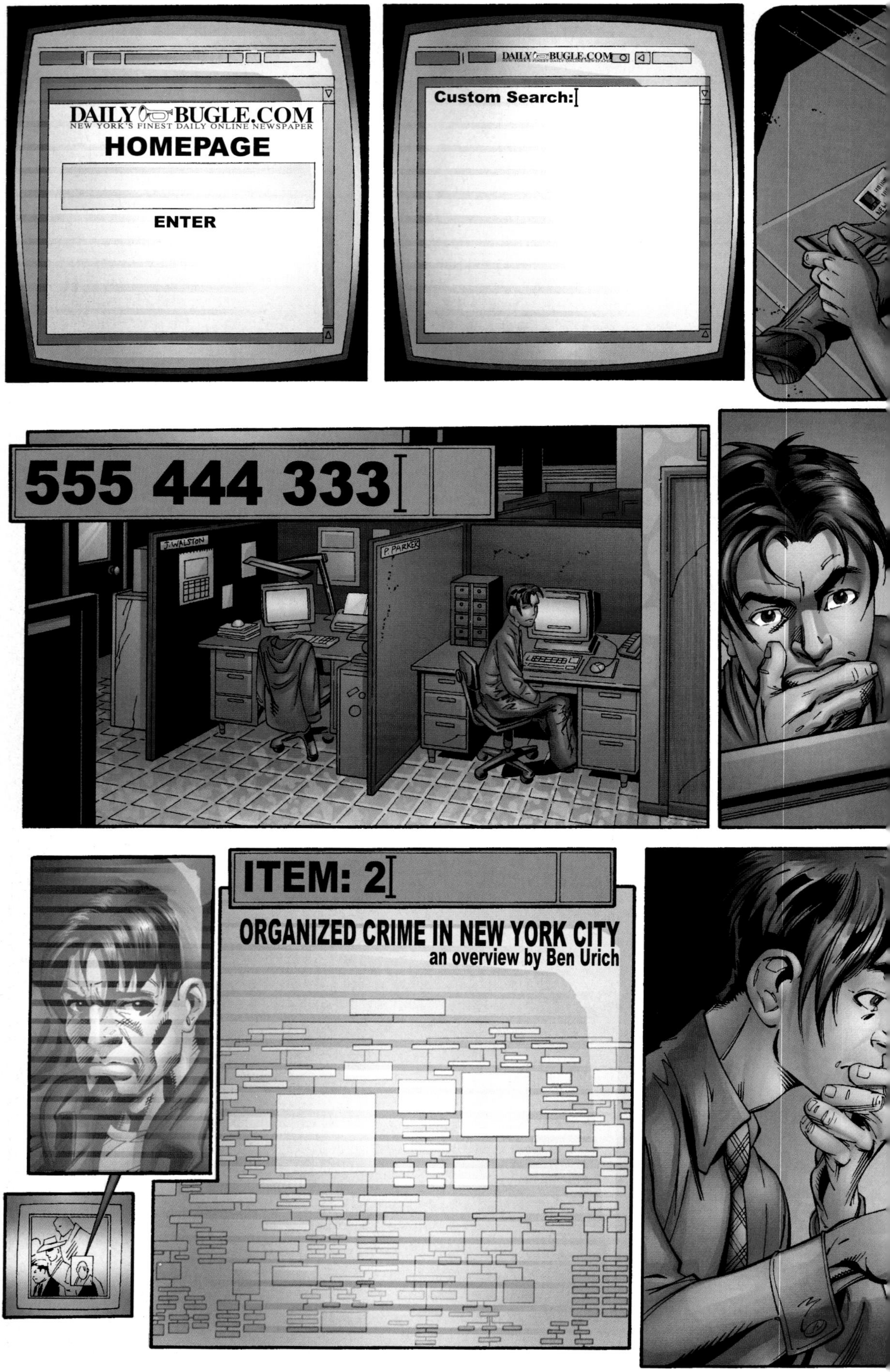

DAILY BUGLE.COM
NEW YORK'S FINEST DAILY ONLINE NEWSPAPER
HOMEPAGE
ENTER
DAILY BUGLE.COM
Custom Search:
555 444 333
J. WALSTON
P. PARKER
ITEM: 2
ORGANIZED CRIME IN NEW YORK CITY
an overview by Ben Urich

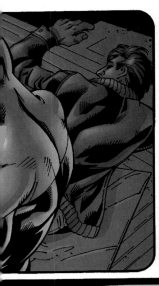

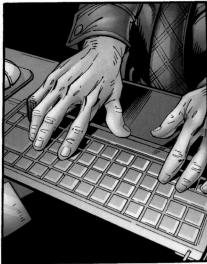

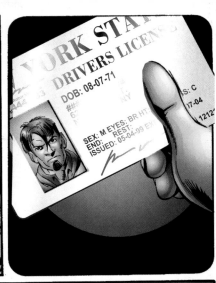

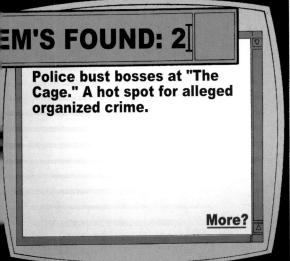

DRIVERS LICE
DOB: 08-07-71
SEX: M EYES: BR
END: REST:
ISSUED: 05-04-99
EM'S FOUND: 2
Police bust bosses at "The Cage." A hot spot for alleged organized crime.
More?
REVENGE EXTRACTION
OONER
BILLI
ONE
WILSON FISK
THE KINGPIN
ENFORCEN

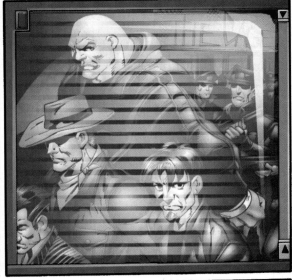

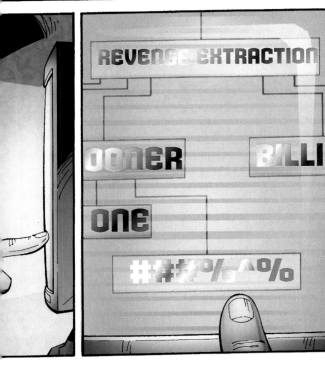

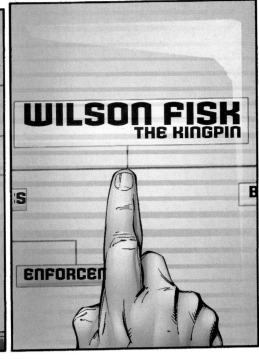

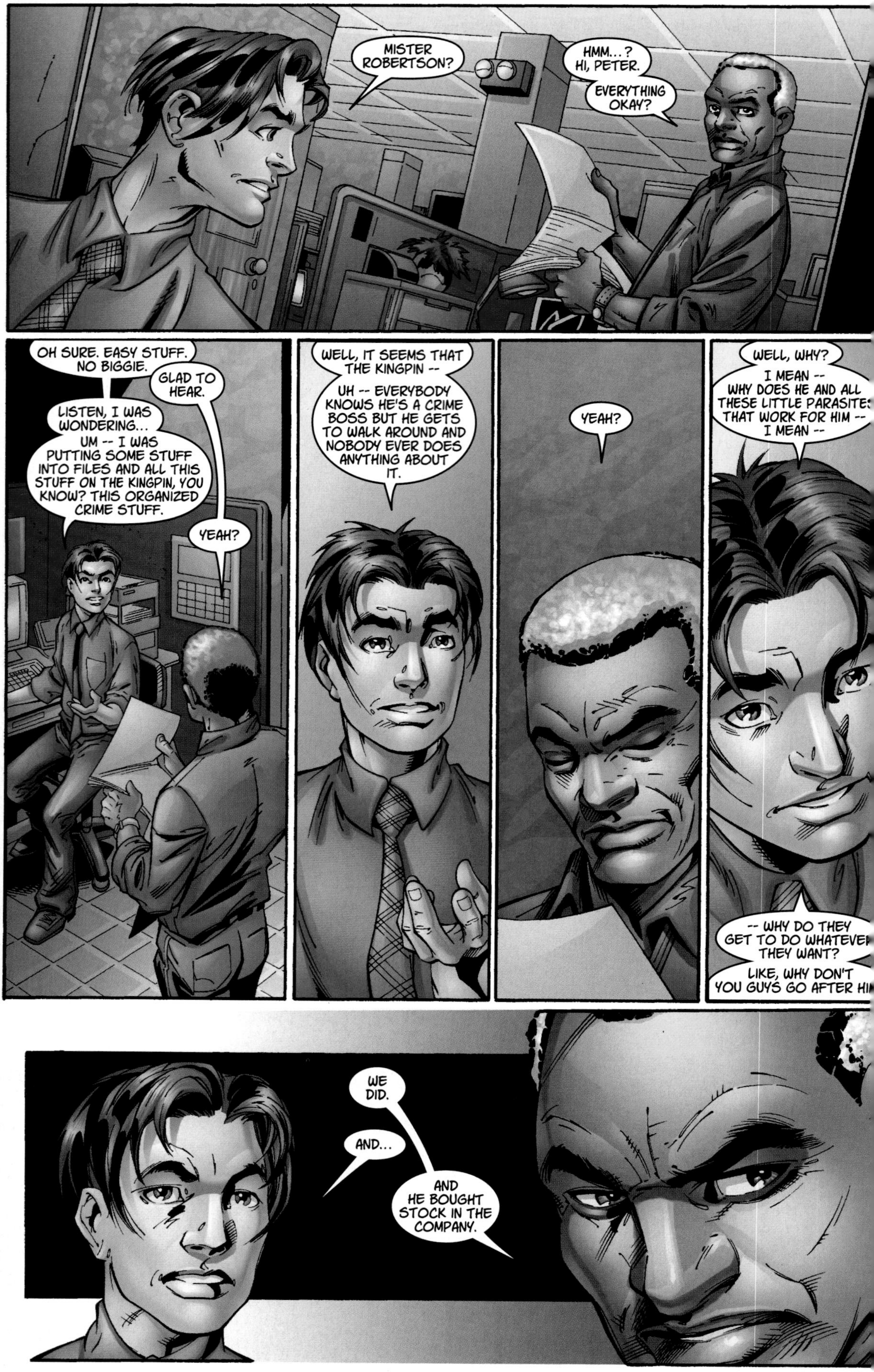

MISTER ROBERTSON?
HMM...? HI, PETER.
EVERYTHING OKAY?
OH SURE. EASY STUFF. NO BIGGIE.
GLAD TO HEAR.
LISTEN, I WAS WONDERING...
UM -- I WAS PUTTING SOME STUFF INTO FILES AND ALL THIS STUFF ON THE KINGPIN, YOU KNOW? THIS ORGANIZED CRIME STUFF.
YEAH?
WELL, IT SEEMS THAT THE KINGPIN --
UH -- EVERYBODY KNOWS HE'S A CRIME BOSS BUT HE GETS TO WALK AROUND AND NOBODY EVER DOES ANYTHING ABOUT IT.
YEAH?
WELL, WHY?
I MEAN -- WHY DOES HE AND ALL THESE LITTLE PARASITES THAT WORK FOR HIM -- I MEAN --
-- WHY DO THEY GET TO DO WHATEVER THEY WANT?
LIKE, WHY DON'T YOU GUYS GO AFTER HI
WE DID.
AND...
AND HE BOUGHT STOCK IN THE COMPANY.

LISTEN...

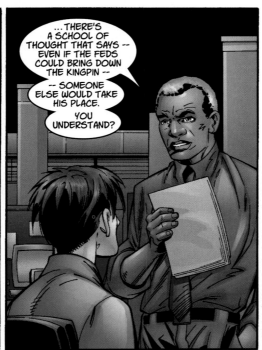

...THERE'S A SCHOOL OF THOUGHT THAT SAYS -- EVEN IF THE FEDS COULD BRING DOWN THE KINGPIN --

-- SOMEONE ELSE WOULD TAKE HIS PLACE.

YOU UNDERSTAND?

JUST THE WAY IT IS.

WILSON FISK
THE KINGPIN

OH YEAH? WELL, WE'LL SEE.

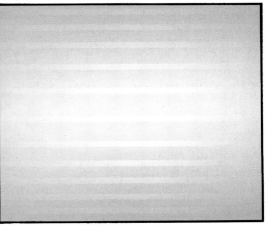

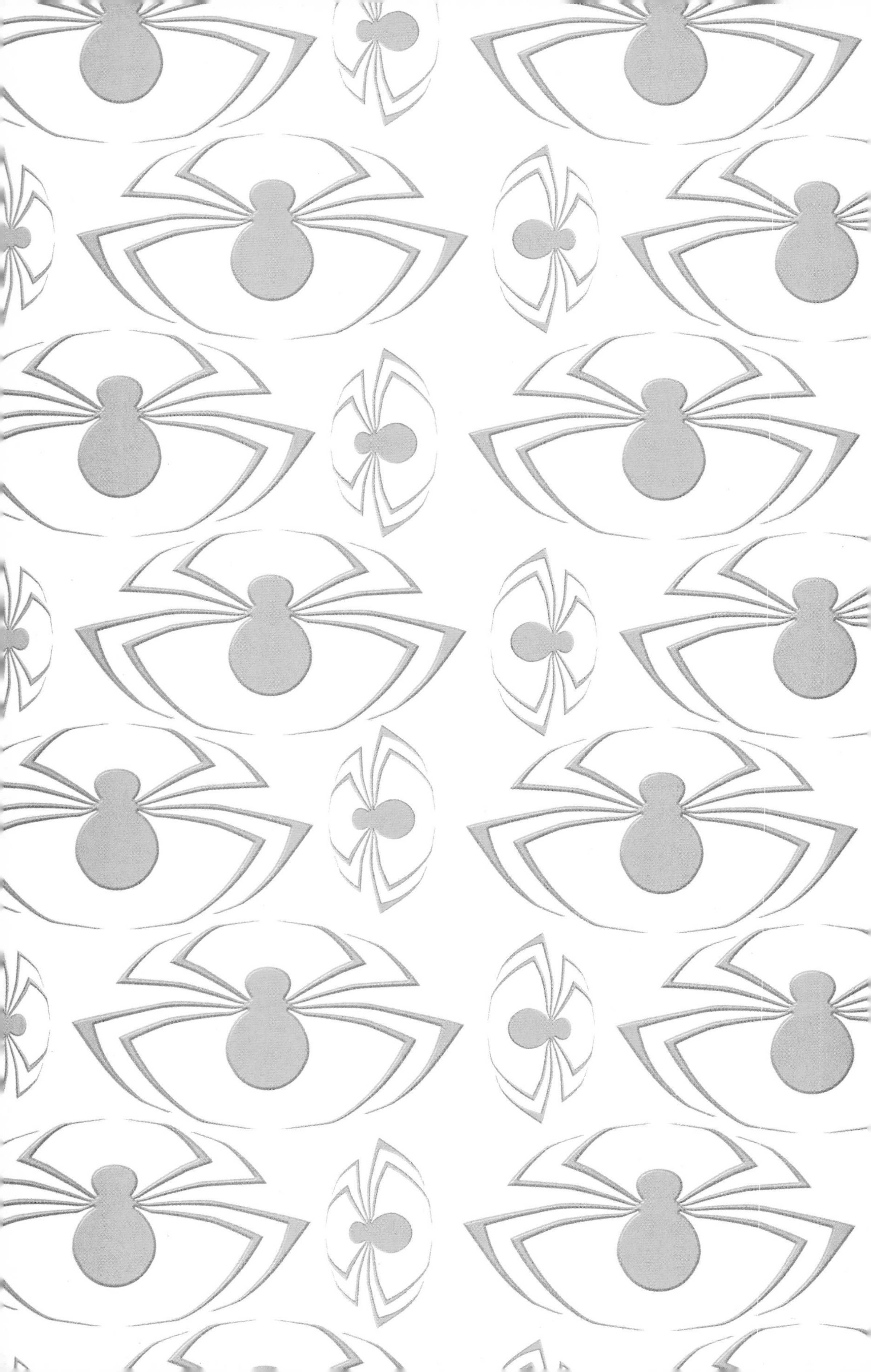

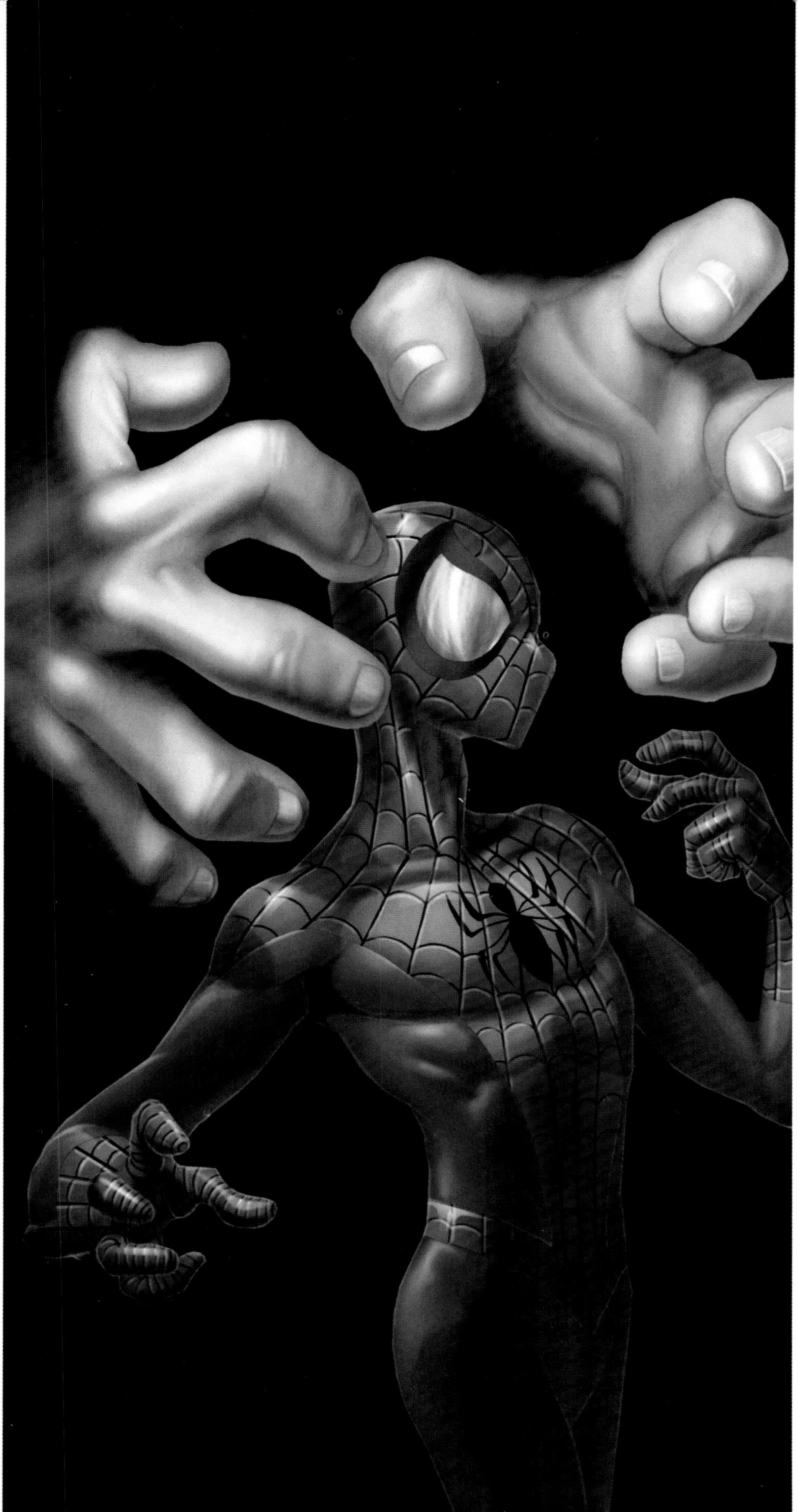

9

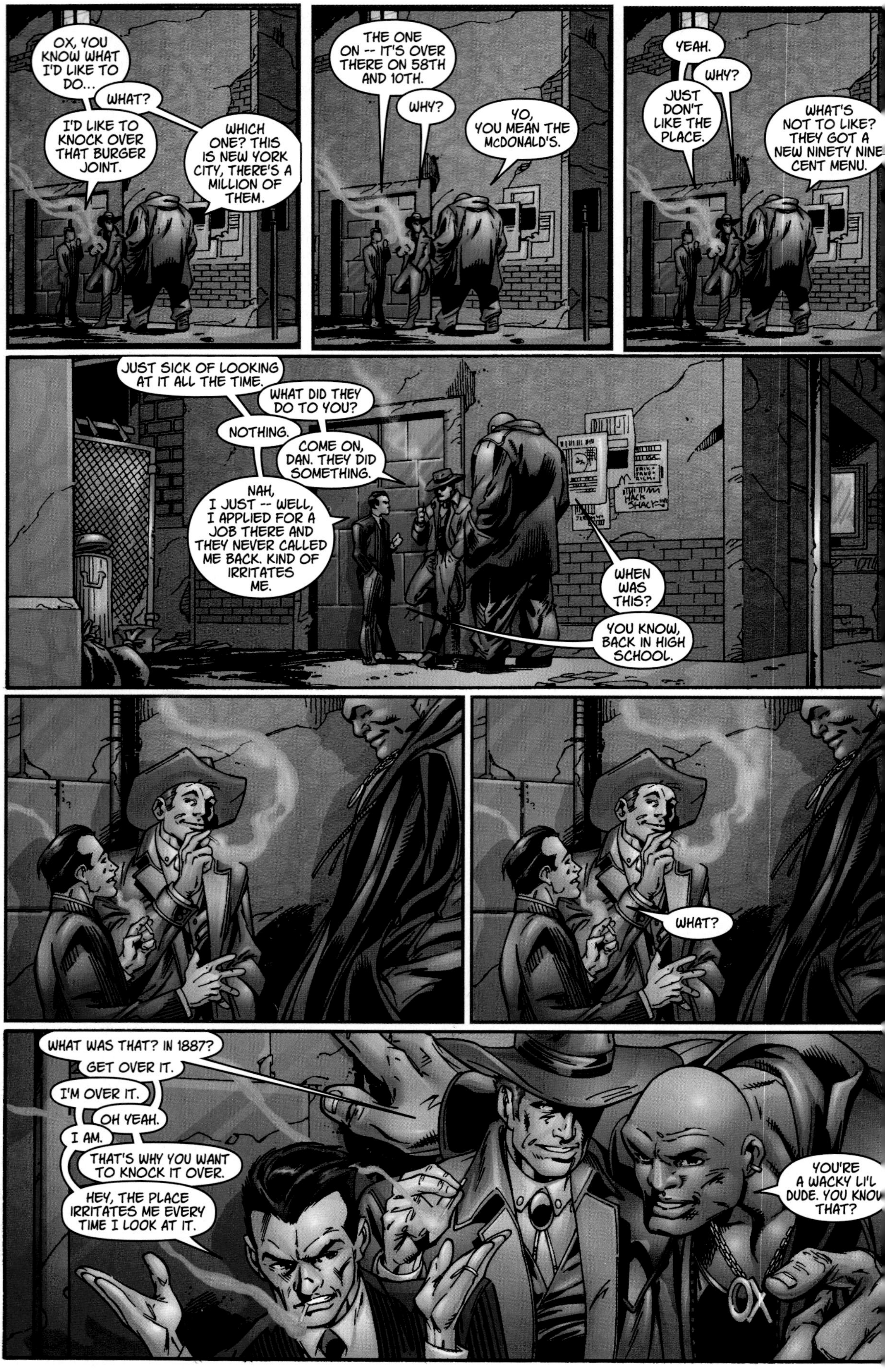
OX, YOU KNOW WHAT I'D LIKE TO DO...
WHAT?
I'D LIKE TO KNOCK OVER THAT BURGER JOINT.
WHICH ONE? THIS IS NEW YORK CITY, THERE'S A MILLION OF THEM.
THE ONE ON -- IT'S OVER THERE ON 58TH AND 10TH.
WHY?
YO, YOU MEAN THE McDONALD'S.
YEAH.
WHY?
JUST DON'T LIKE THE PLACE.
WHAT'S NOT TO LIKE? THEY GOT A NEW NINETY NINE CENT MENU.
JUST SICK OF LOOKING AT IT ALL THE TIME.
WHAT DID THEY DO TO YOU?
NOTHING.
COME ON, DAN. THEY DID SOMETHING.
NAH, I JUST -- WELL, I APPLIED FOR A JOB THERE AND THEY NEVER CALLED ME BACK. KIND OF IRRITATES ME.
WHEN WAS THIS?
YOU KNOW, BACK IN HIGH SCHOOL.
WHAT?
WHAT WAS THAT? IN 1887?
GET OVER IT.
I'M OVER IT.
OH YEAH.
I AM.
THAT'S WHY YOU WANT TO KNOCK IT OVER.
HEY, THE PLACE IRRITATES ME EVERY TIME I LOOK AT IT.
YOU'RE A WACKY LI'L DUDE. YOU KNOW THAT?

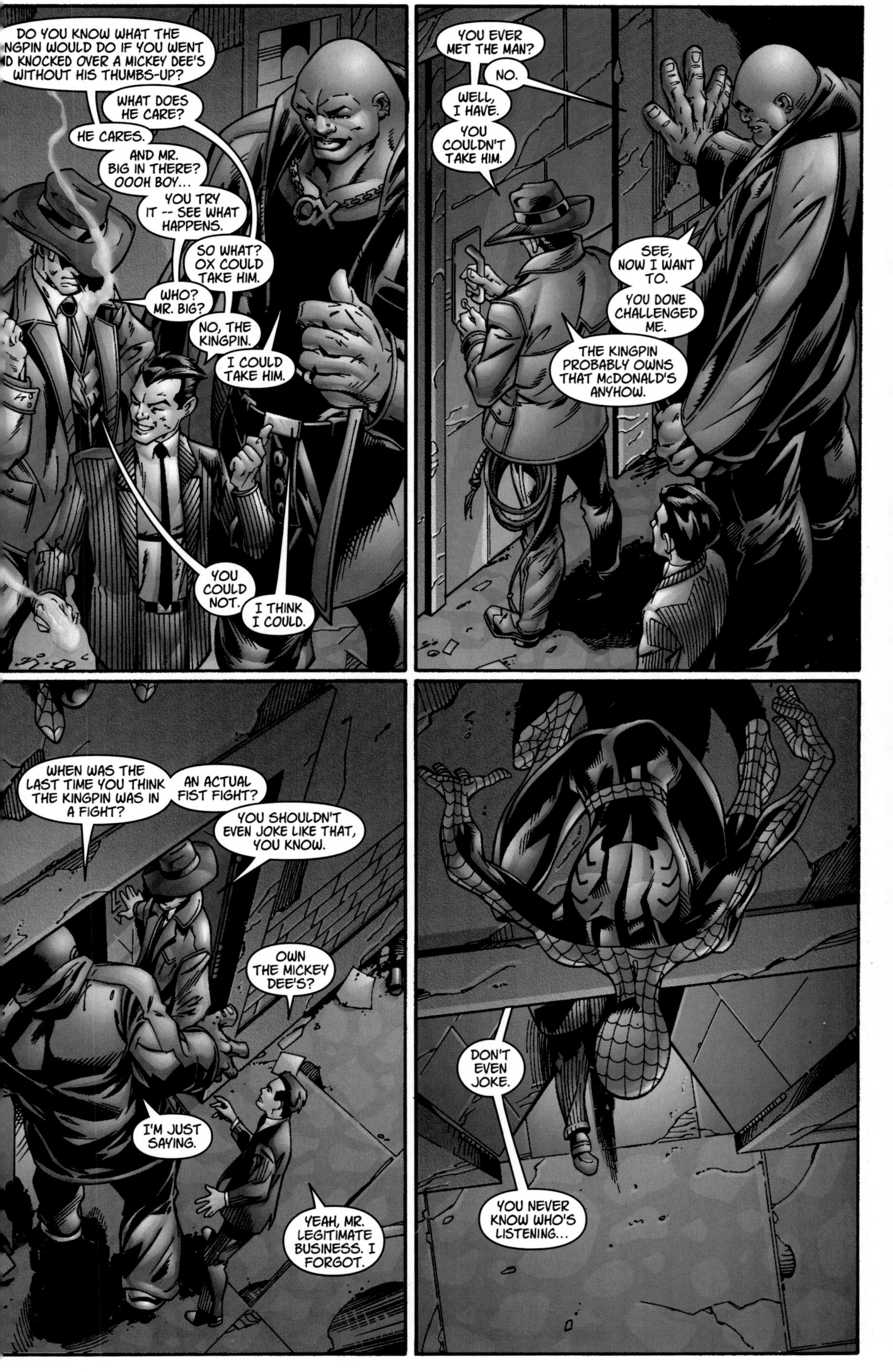
DO YOU KNOW WHAT THE KINGPIN WOULD DO IF YOU WENT AND KNOCKED OVER A MICKEY DEE'S WITHOUT HIS THUMBS-UP?
WHAT DOES HE CARE?
HE CARES.
AND MR. BIG IN THERE? OOOH BOY...
YOU TRY IT -- SEE WHAT HAPPENS.
SO WHAT? OX COULD TAKE HIM.
WHO? MR. BIG?
NO, THE KINGPIN.
I COULD TAKE HIM.
YOU COULD NOT.
I THINK I COULD.
YOU EVER MET THE MAN?
NO.
WELL, I HAVE.
YOU COULDN'T TAKE HIM.
SEE, NOW I WANT TO.
YOU DONE CHALLENGED ME.
THE KINGPIN PROBABLY OWNS THAT McDONALD'S ANYHOW.
WHEN WAS THE LAST TIME YOU THINK THE KINGPIN WAS IN A FIGHT?
AN ACTUAL FIST FIGHT?
YOU SHOULDN'T EVEN JOKE LIKE THAT, YOU KNOW.
OWN THE MICKEY DEE'S?
I'M JUST SAYING.
YEAH, MR. LEGITIMATE BUSINESS. I FORGOT.
DON'T EVEN JOKE.
YOU NEVER KNOW WHO'S LISTENING...

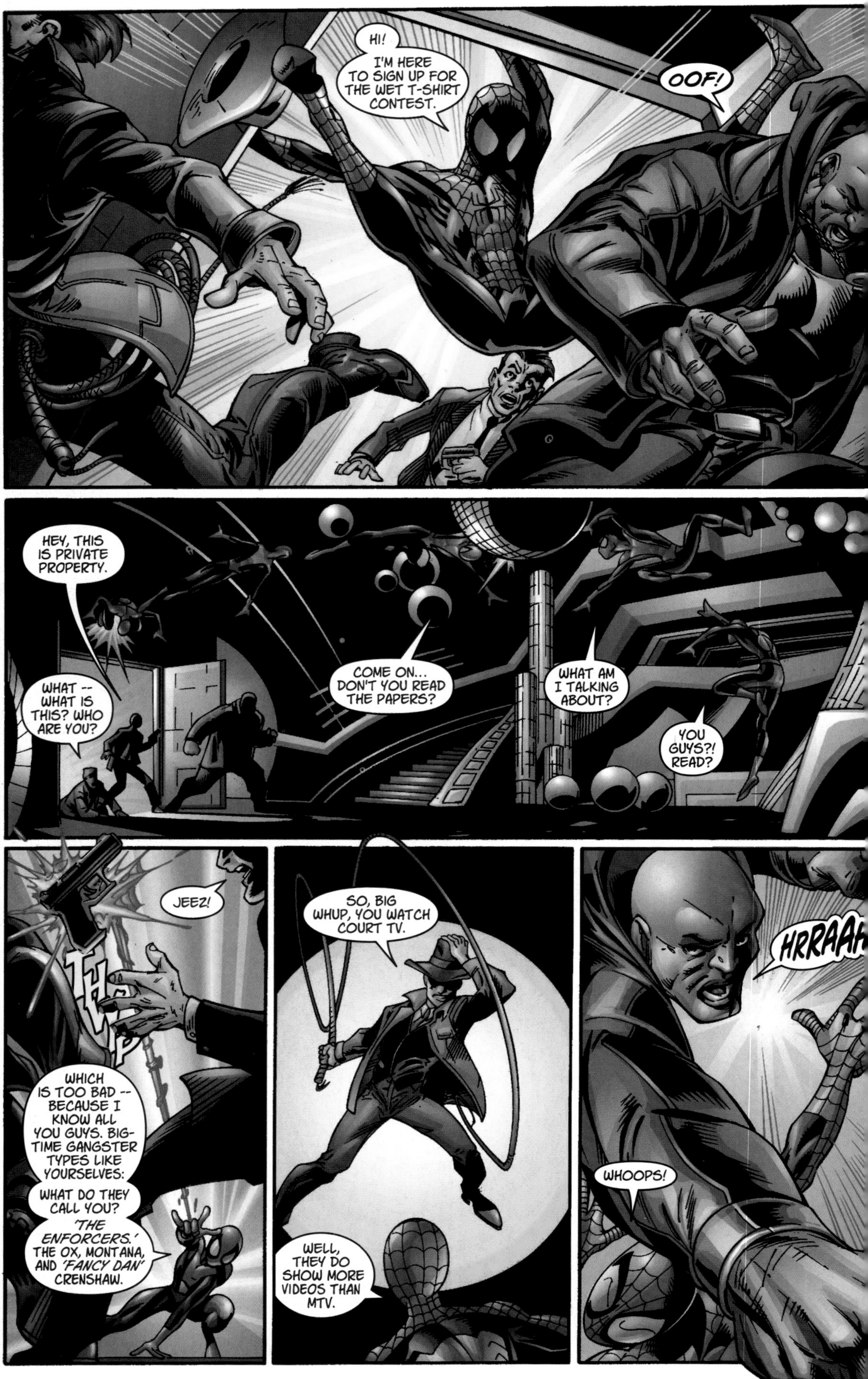

HI! I'M HERE TO SIGN UP FOR THE WET T-SHIRT CONTEST.
OOF!
HEY, THIS IS PRIVATE PROPERTY.
WHAT -- WHAT IS THIS? WHO ARE YOU?
COME ON... DON'T YOU READ THE PAPERS?
WHAT AM I TALKING ABOUT?
YOU GUYS?! READ?
JEEZ!
WHICH IS TOO BAD -- BECAUSE I KNOW ALL YOU GUYS. BIG-TIME GANGSTER TYPES LIKE YOURSELVES:
WHAT DO THEY CALL YOU? 'THE ENFORCERS.' THE OX, MONTANA, AND 'FANCY DAN' CRENSHAW.
SO, BIG WHUP, YOU WATCH COURT TV.
WELL, THEY DO SHOW MORE VIDEOS THAN MTV.
WHOOPS!

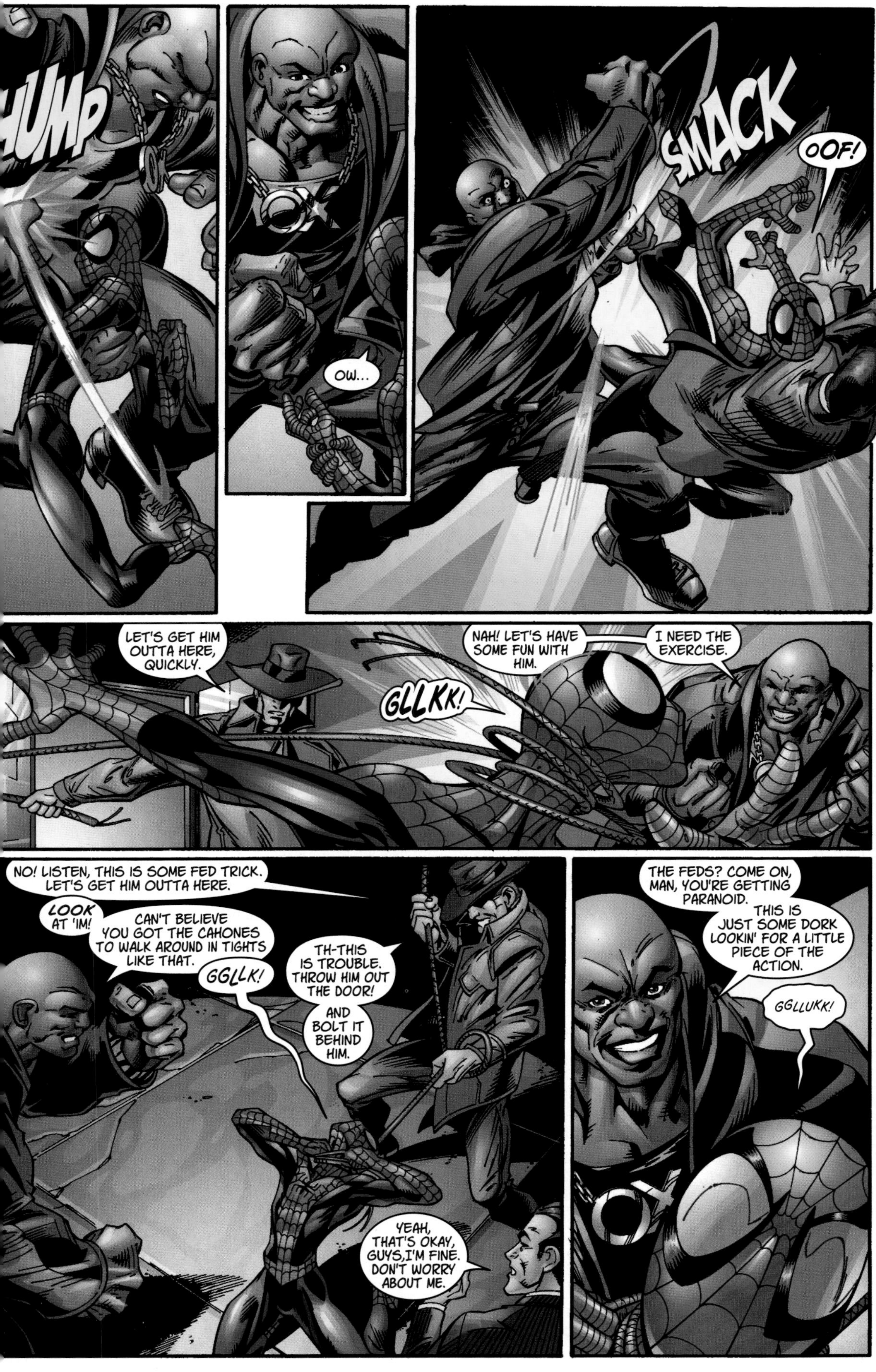
THUMP
OW...
SMACK
OOF!
LET'S GET HIM OUTTA HERE, QUICKLY.
NAH! LET'S HAVE SOME FUN WITH HIM.
I NEED THE EXERCISE.
GLLKK!
NO! LISTEN, THIS IS SOME FED TRICK. LET'S GET HIM OUTTA HERE.
LOOK AT 'IM!
CAN'T BELIEVE YOU GOT THE CAHONES TO WALK AROUND IN TIGHTS LIKE THAT.
GGLLK!
TH-THIS IS TROUBLE. THROW HIM OUT THE DOOR!
AND BOLT IT BEHIND HIM.
YEAH, THAT'S OKAY, GUYS, I'M FINE. DON'T WORRY ABOUT ME.
THE FEDS? COME ON, MAN, YOU'RE GETTING PARANOID.
THIS IS JUST SOME DORK LOOKIN' FOR A LITTLE PIECE OF THE ACTION.
GGLLUKK!

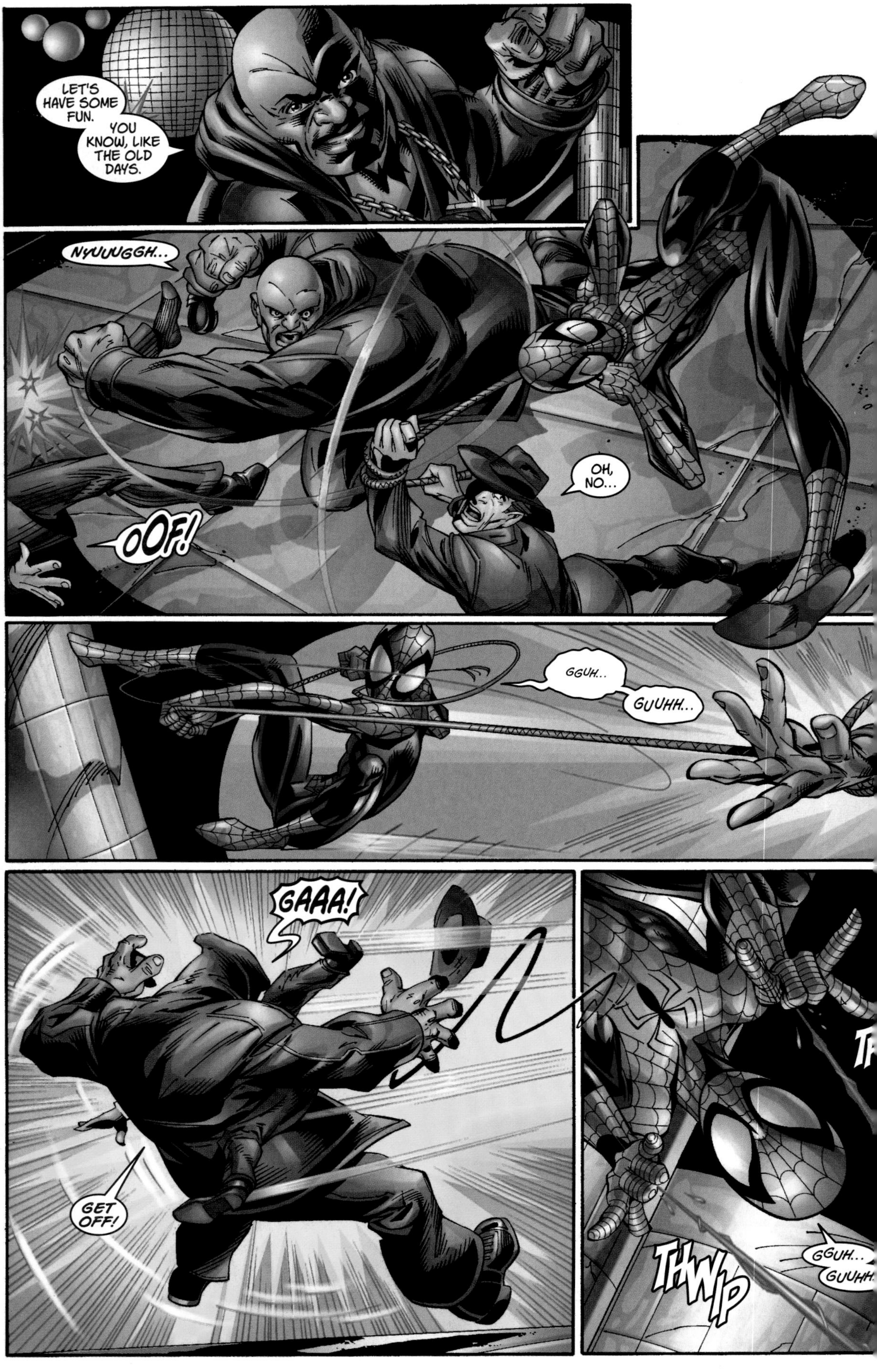
LET'S HAVE SOME FUN.
YOU KNOW, LIKE THE OLD DAYS.
NYUUUGGH...
OH, NO...
OOF!
GGUH...
GUUHH...
GAAA!
GET OFF!
THWIP
GGUH... GUUHH...

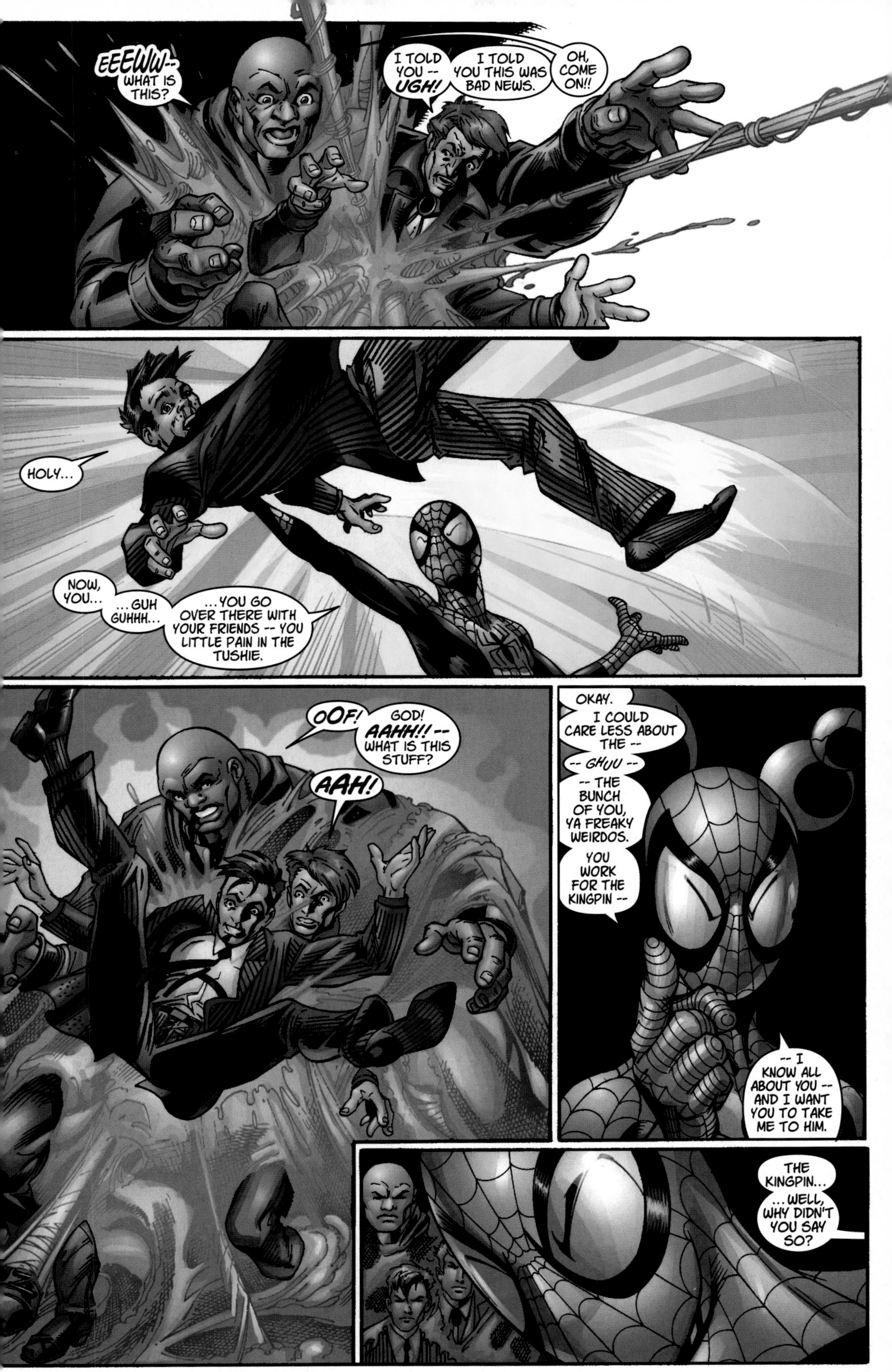
EEEWW-- WHAT IS THIS?
I TOLD YOU -- UGH!
I TOLD YOU THIS WAS BAD NEWS.
OH, COME ON!!
HOLY...
NOW, YOU...
...GUH GUHHH...
...YOU GO OVER THERE WITH YOUR FRIENDS -- YOU LITTLE PAIN IN THE TUSHIE.
OOF!
GOD! AAHH!! -- WHAT IS THIS STUFF?
AAH!
OKAY.
I COULD CARE LESS ABOUT THE --
-- GHUU --
-- THE BUNCH OF YOU, YA FREAKY WEIRDOS.
YOU WORK FOR THE KINGPIN --
-- I KNOW ALL ABOUT YOU -- AND I WANT YOU TO TAKE ME TO HIM.
THE KINGPIN...
...WELL, WHY DIDN'T YOU SAY SO?

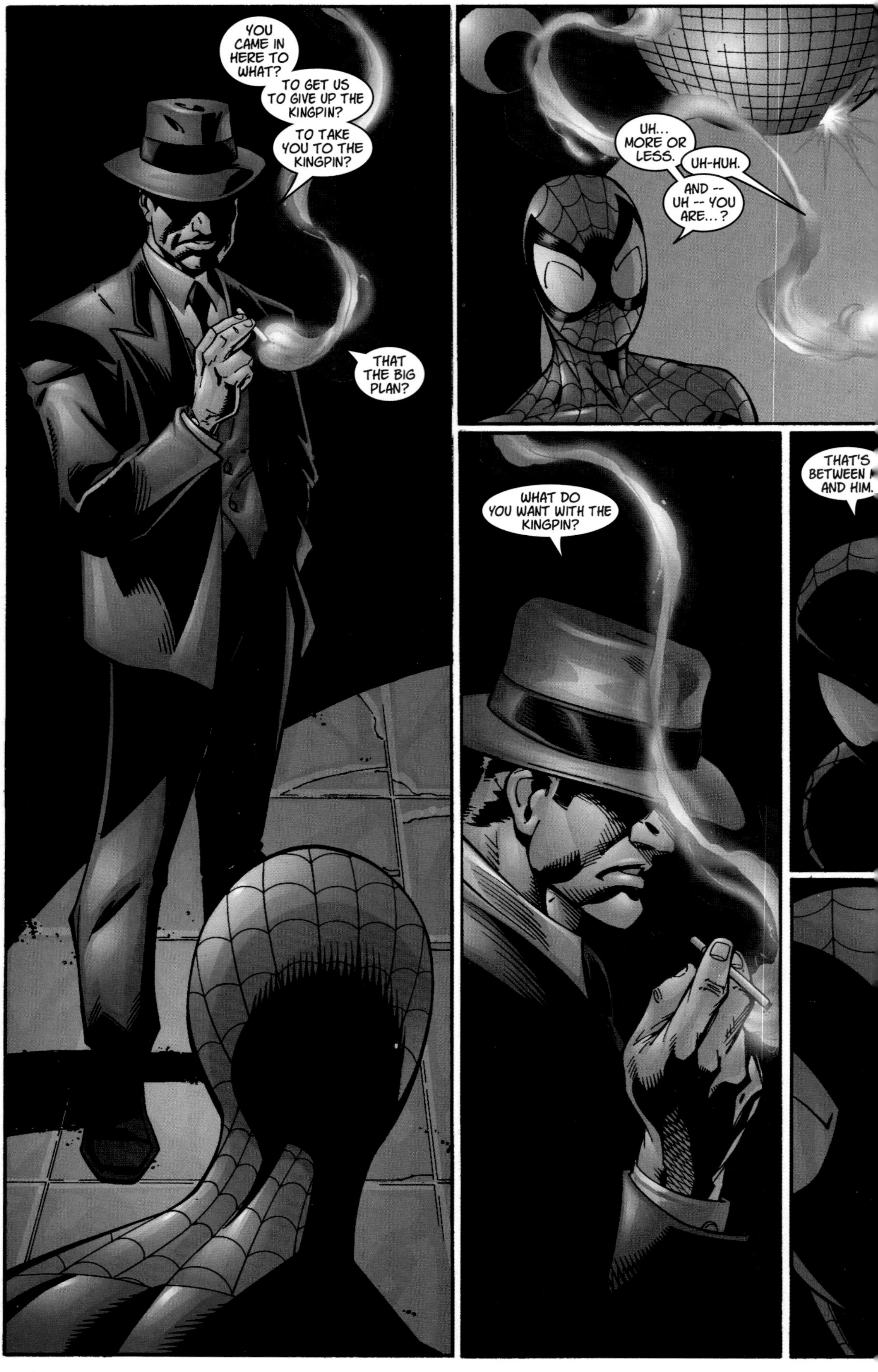
YOU CAME IN HERE TO WHAT?
TO GET US TO GIVE UP THE KINGPIN?
TO TAKE YOU TO THE KINGPIN?
THAT THE BIG PLAN?
UH... MORE OR LESS.
UH-HUH.
AND -- UH -- YOU ARE...?
WHAT DO YOU WANT WITH THE KINGPIN?
AND HIM.

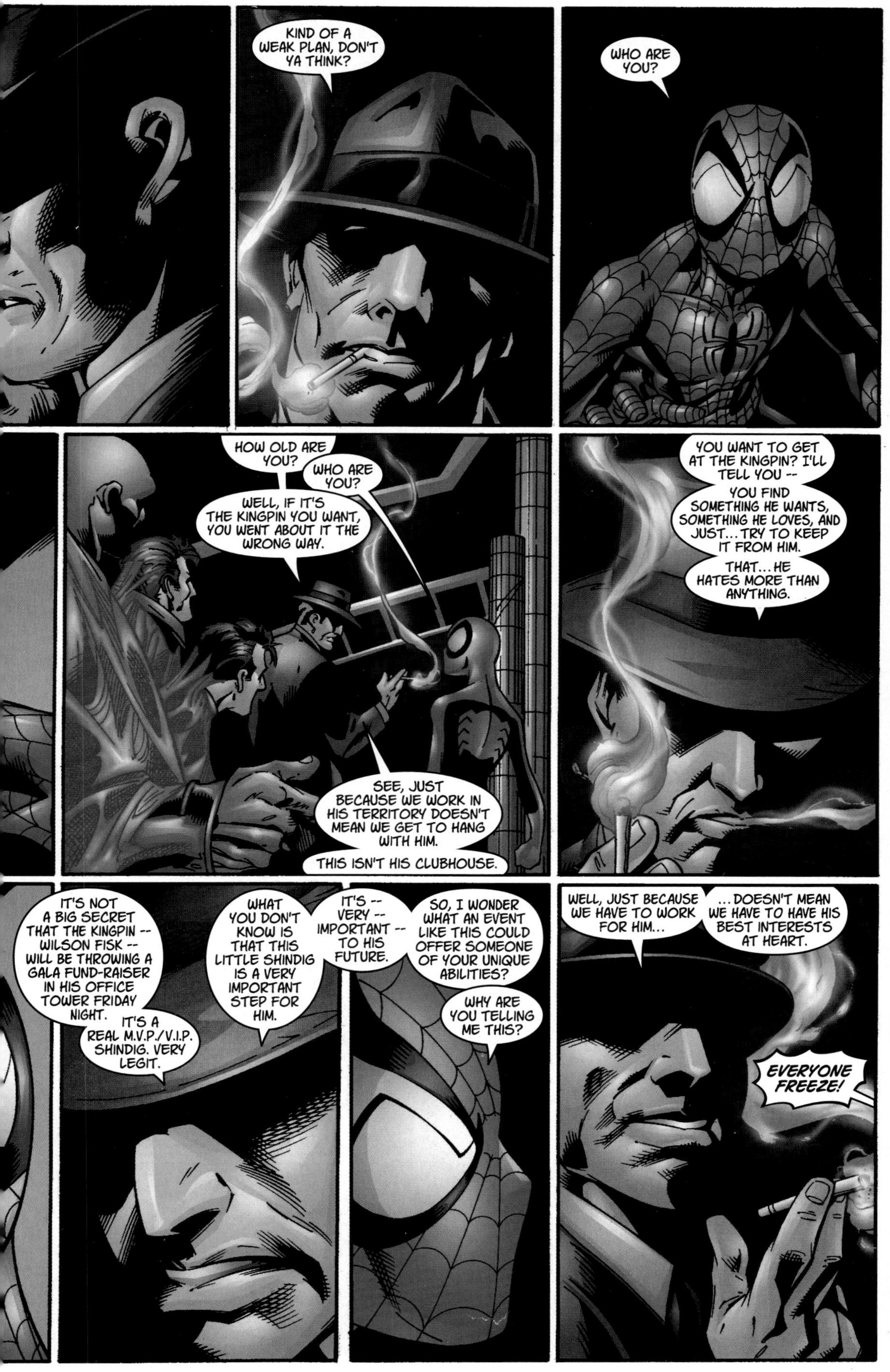
KIND OF A WEAK PLAN, DON'T YA THINK?
WHO ARE YOU?
HOW OLD ARE YOU?
WHO ARE YOU?
WELL, IF IT'S THE KINGPIN YOU WANT, YOU WENT ABOUT IT THE WRONG WAY.
SEE, JUST BECAUSE WE WORK IN HIS TERRITORY DOESN'T MEAN WE GET TO HANG WITH HIM.
THIS ISN'T HIS CLUBHOUSE.
YOU WANT TO GET AT THE KINGPIN? I'LL TELL YOU --
YOU FIND SOMETHING HE WANTS, SOMETHING HE LOVES, AND JUST... TRY TO KEEP IT FROM HIM.
THAT... HE HATES MORE THAN ANYTHING.
IT'S NOT A BIG SECRET THAT THE KINGPIN -- WILSON FISK -- WILL BE THROWING A GALA FUND-RAISER IN HIS OFFICE TOWER FRIDAY NIGHT.
IT'S A REAL M.V.P./V.I.P. SHINDIG. VERY LEGIT.
WHAT YOU DON'T KNOW IS THAT THIS LITTLE SHINDIG IS A VERY IMPORTANT STEP FOR HIM.
IT'S -- VERY -- IMPORTANT -- TO HIS FUTURE.
SO, I WONDER WHAT AN EVENT LIKE THIS COULD OFFER SOMEONE OF YOUR UNIQUE ABILITIES?
WHY ARE YOU TELLING ME THIS?
WELL, JUST BECAUSE WE HAVE TO WORK FOR HIM...
...DOESN'T MEAN WE HAVE TO HAVE HIS BEST INTERESTS AT HEART.
EVERYONE FREEZE!

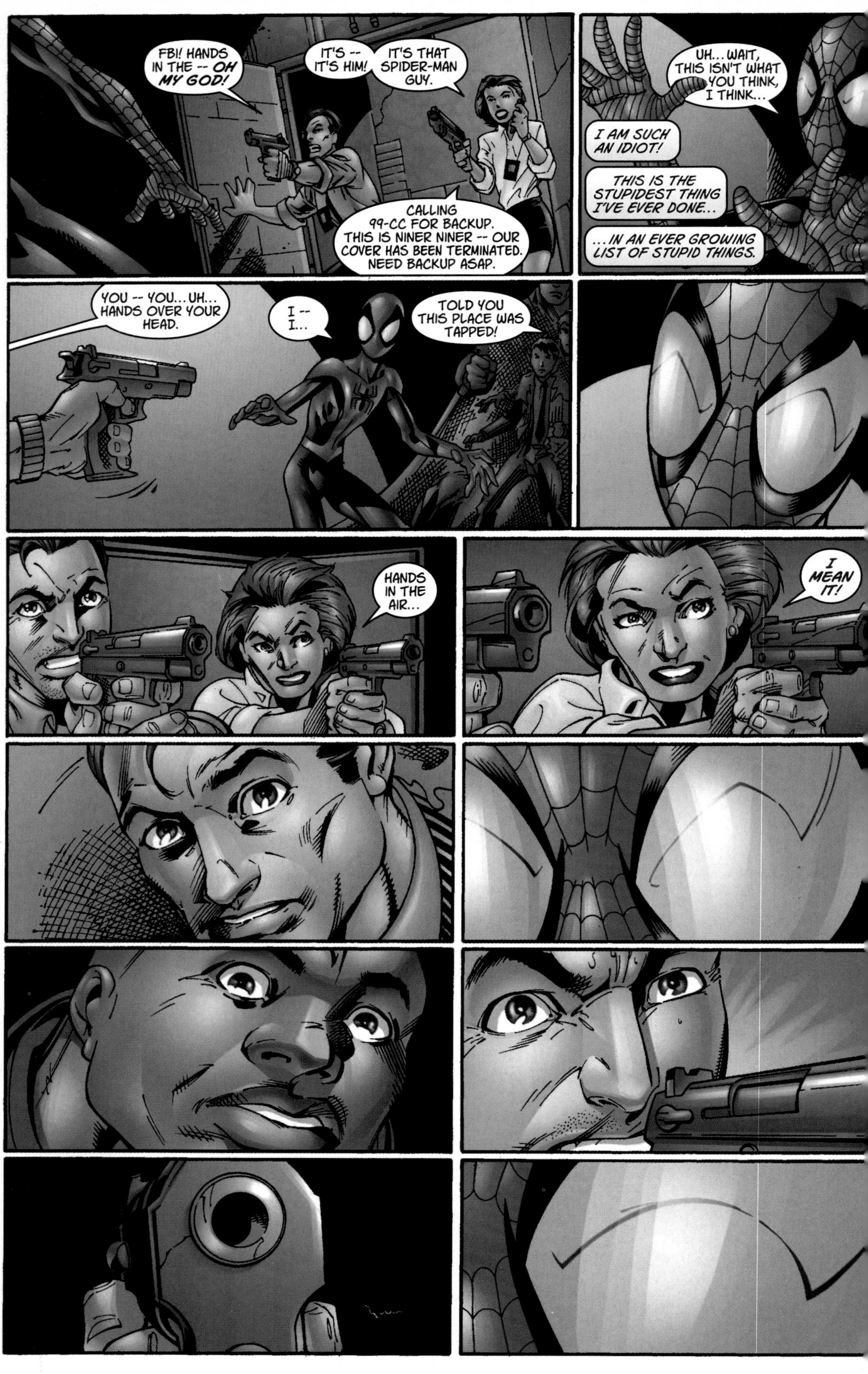
FBI! HANDS IN THE -- OH MY GOD!
IT'S -- IT'S HIM!
IT'S THAT SPIDER-MAN GUY.
CALLING 99-CC FOR BACKUP. THIS IS NINER NINER -- OUR COVER HAS BEEN TERMINATED. NEED BACKUP ASAP.
UH... WAIT, THIS ISN'T WHAT YOU THINK, I THINK...
I AM SUCH AN IDIOT!
THIS IS THE STUPIDEST THING I'VE EVER DONE...
...IN AN EVER GROWING LIST OF STUPID THINGS.
YOU -- YOU... UH... HANDS OVER YOUR HEAD.
I -- I...
TOLD YOU THIS PLACE WAS TAPPED!
HANDS IN THE AIR...
I MEAN IT!

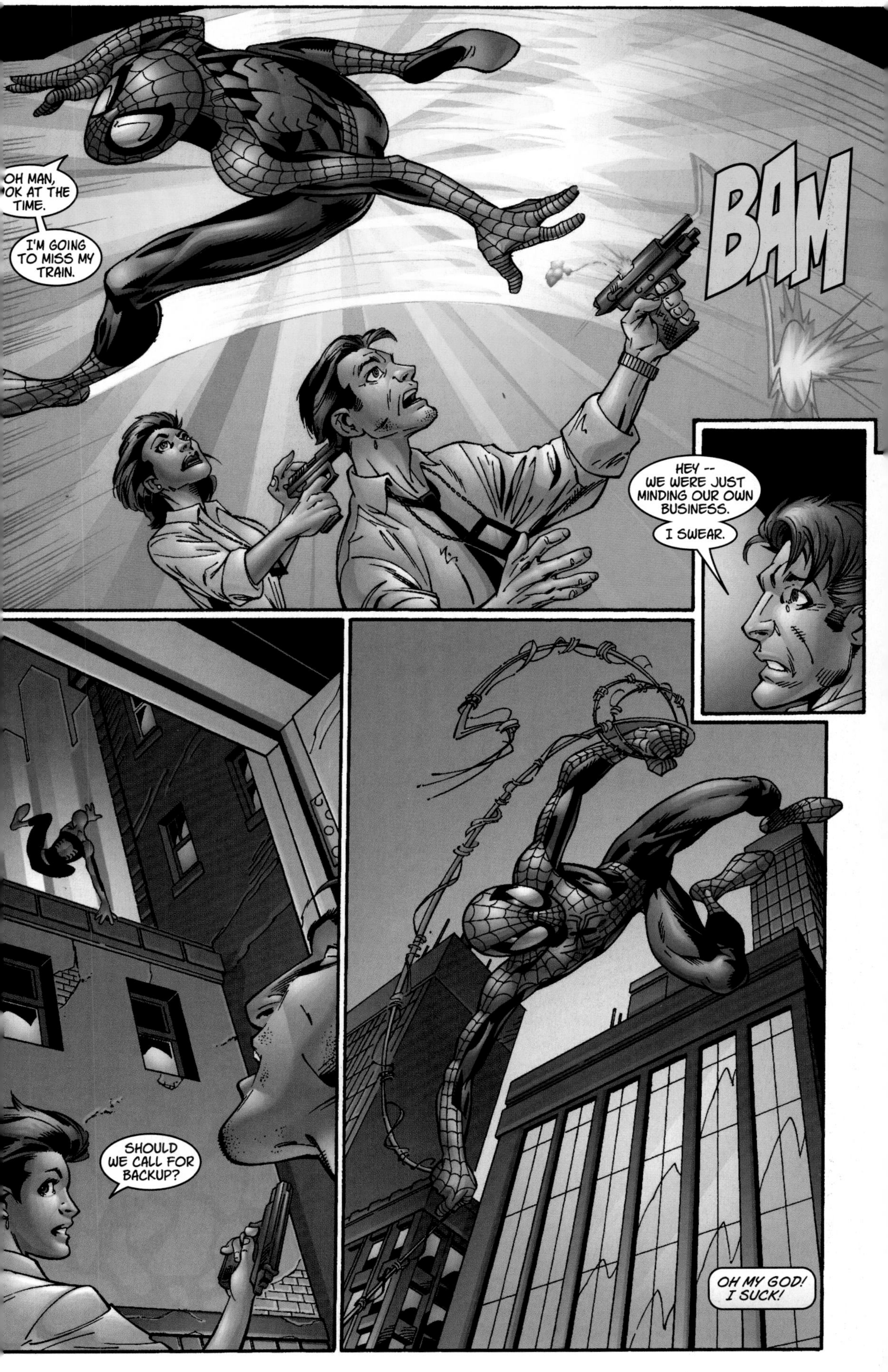
OH MAN, OK AT THE TIME.
I'M GOING TO MISS MY TRAIN.
BAM
HEY -- WE WERE JUST MINDING OUR OWN BUSINESS.
I SWEAR.
SHOULD WE CALL FOR BACKUP?
OH MY GOD! I SUCK!

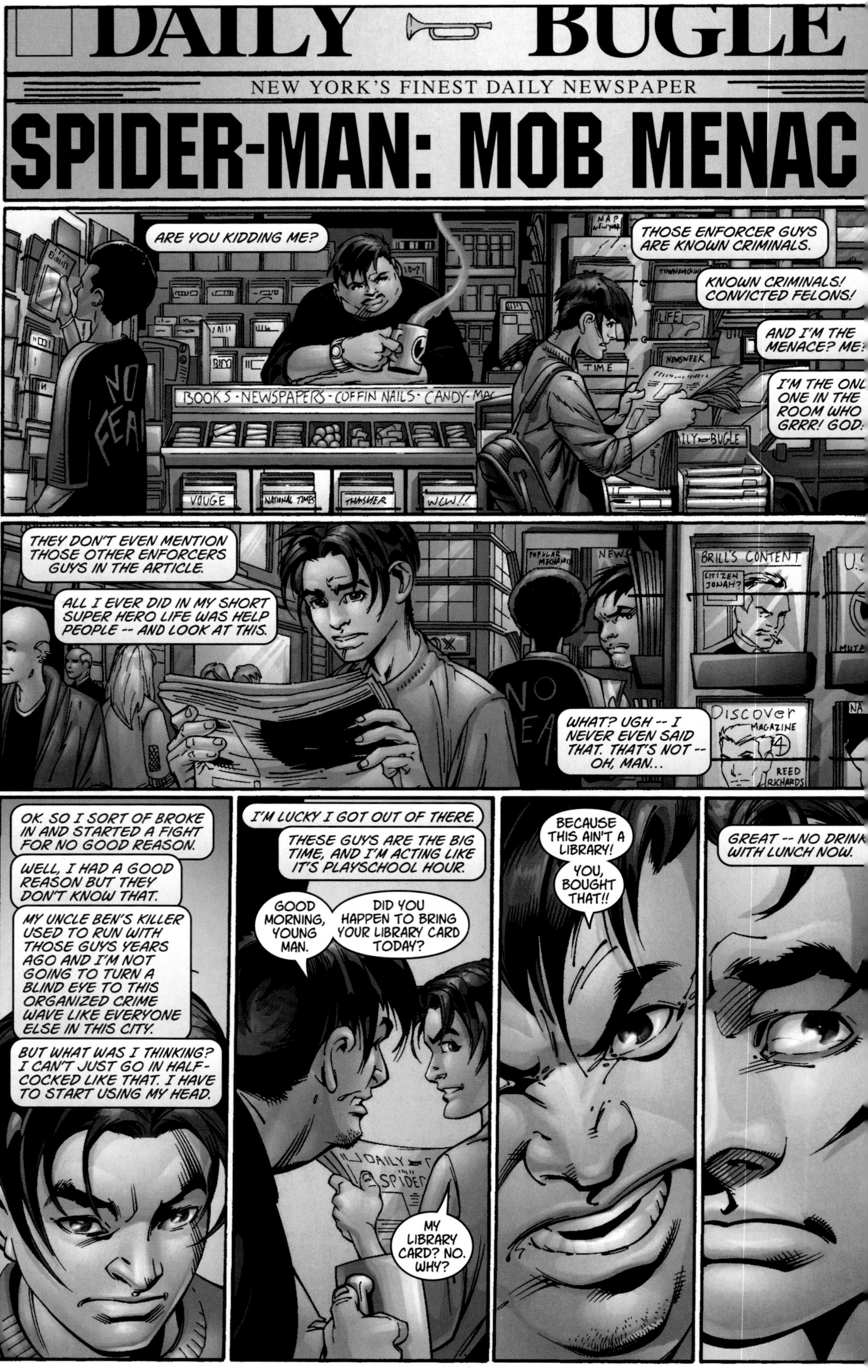

DAILY BUGLE
NEW YORK'S FINEST DAILY NEWSPAPER
SPIDER-MAN: MOB MENAC
ARE YOU KIDDING ME?
THOSE ENFORCER GUYS ARE KNOWN CRIMINALS.
KNOWN CRIMINALS! CONVICTED FELONS!
AND I'M THE MENACE? ME?
I'M THE ONL ONE IN THE ROOM WHO GRRR! GOD.
BOOKS - NEWSPAPERS - COFFIN NAILS - CANDY - MAG
VOUGE
NATIONAL TIMES
THASHER
WCW!!
THEY DON'T EVEN MENTION THOSE OTHER ENFORCERS GUYS IN THE ARTICLE.
ALL I EVER DID IN MY SHORT SUPER HERO LIFE WAS HELP PEOPLE -- AND LOOK AT THIS.
BRILL'S CONTENT
CITIZEN JONAH?
WHAT? UGH -- I NEVER EVEN SAID THAT. THAT'S NOT -- OH, MAN...
Discover MAGAZINE
REED RICHARDS
OK. SO I SORT OF BROKE IN AND STARTED A FIGHT FOR NO GOOD REASON.
WELL, I HAD A GOOD REASON BUT THEY DON'T KNOW THAT.
MY UNCLE BEN'S KILLER USED TO RUN WITH THOSE GUYS YEARS AGO AND I'M NOT GOING TO TURN A BLIND EYE TO THIS ORGANIZED CRIME WAVE LIKE EVERYONE ELSE IN THIS CITY.
BUT WHAT WAS I THINKING? I CAN'T JUST GO IN HALF-COCKED LIKE THAT. I HAVE TO START USING MY HEAD.
I'M LUCKY I GOT OUT OF THERE.
THESE GUYS ARE THE BIG TIME, AND I'M ACTING LIKE IT'S PLAYSCHOOL HOUR.
GOOD MORNING, YOUNG MAN.
DID YOU HAPPEN TO BRING YOUR LIBRARY CARD TODAY?
MY LIBRARY CARD? NO. WHY?
BECAUSE THIS AIN'T A LIBRARY!
YOU, BOUGHT THAT!!
GREAT -- NO DRINK WITH LUNCH NOW.

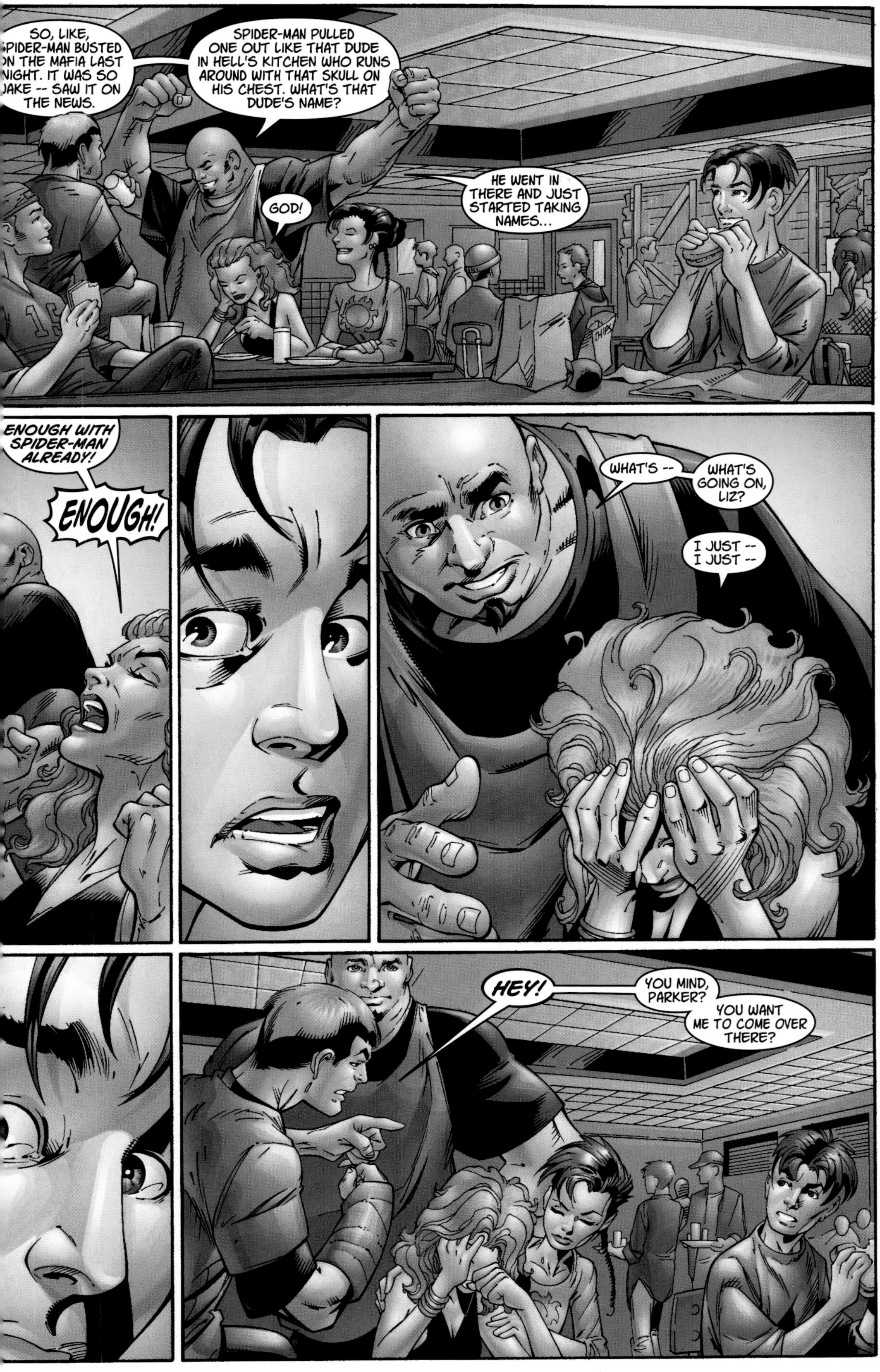
SO, LIKE, SPIDER-MAN BUSTED ON THE MAFIA LAST NIGHT. IT WAS SO JAKE -- SAW IT ON THE NEWS.
SPIDER-MAN PULLED ONE OUT LIKE THAT DUDE IN HELL'S KITCHEN WHO RUNS AROUND WITH THAT SKULL ON HIS CHEST. WHAT'S THAT DUDE'S NAME?
GOD!
HE WENT IN THERE AND JUST STARTED TAKING NAMES...
CHIPS
ENOUGH WITH SPIDER-MAN ALREADY!
ENOUGH!
WHAT'S --
WHAT'S GOING ON, LIZ?
I JUST -- I JUST --
HEY!
YOU MIND, PARKER?
YOU WANT ME TO COME OVER THERE?

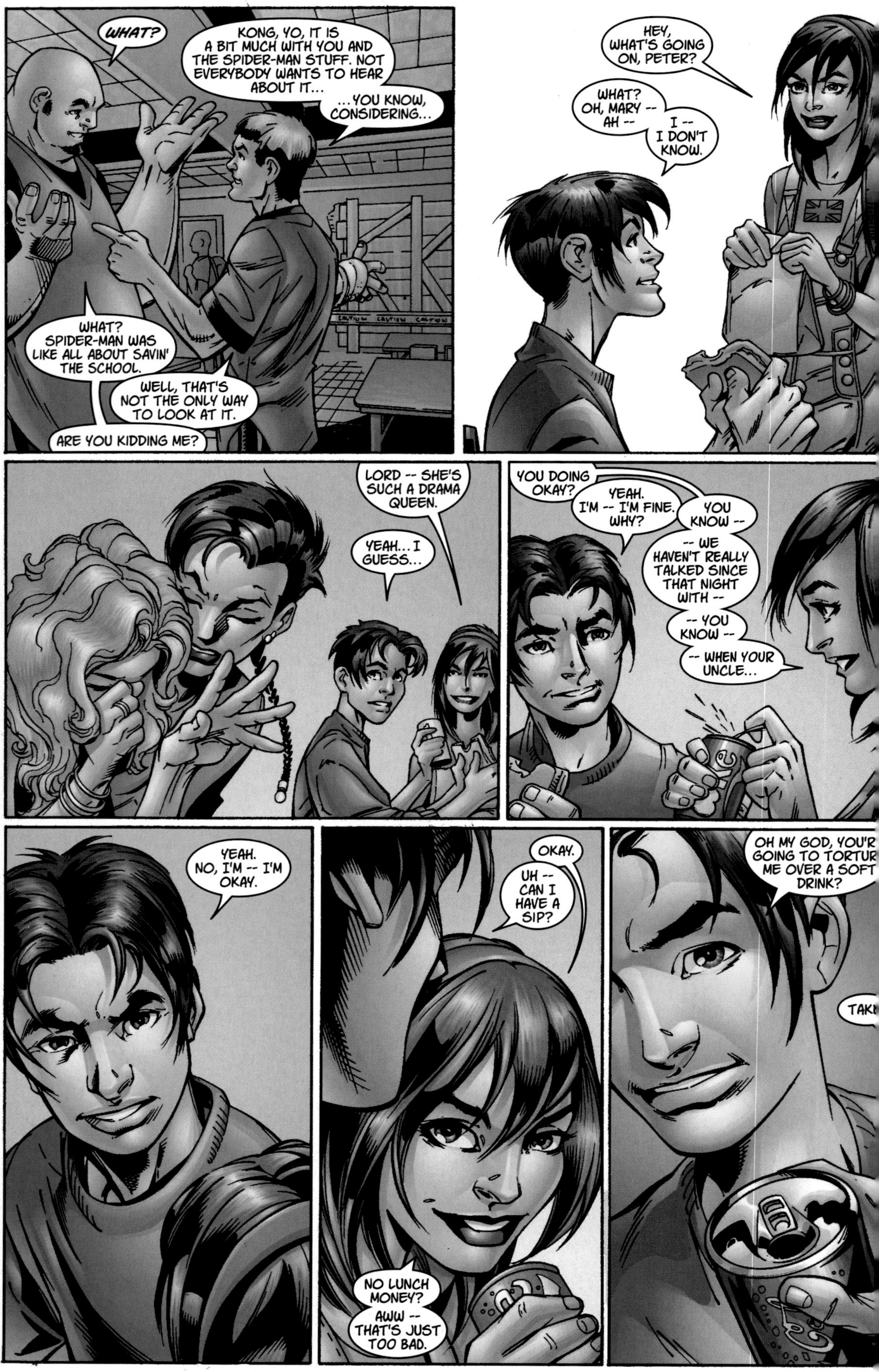
WHAT?
KONG, YO, IT IS A BIT MUCH WITH YOU AND THE SPIDER-MAN STUFF. NOT EVERYBODY WANTS TO HEAR ABOUT IT...
...YOU KNOW, CONSIDERING...
WHAT? SPIDER-MAN WAS LIKE ALL ABOUT SAVIN' THE SCHOOL.
WELL, THAT'S NOT THE ONLY WAY TO LOOK AT IT.
ARE YOU KIDDING ME?
HEY, WHAT'S GOING ON, PETER?
WHAT? OH, MARY -- AH --
I -- I DON'T KNOW.
LORD -- SHE'S SUCH A DRAMA QUEEN.
YEAH... I GUESS...
YOU DOING OKAY?
YEAH. I'M -- I'M FINE. WHY?
YOU KNOW --
-- WE HAVEN'T REALLY TALKED SINCE THAT NIGHT WITH --
-- YOU KNOW --
-- WHEN YOUR UNCLE...
YEAH. NO, I'M -- I'M OKAY.
OKAY.
UH -- CAN I HAVE A SIP?
NO LUNCH MONEY? AWW -- THAT'S JUST TOO BAD.
OH MY GOD, YOU'R GOING TO TORTUR ME OVER A SOFT DRINK?
CAUTION CAUTION CAUTION

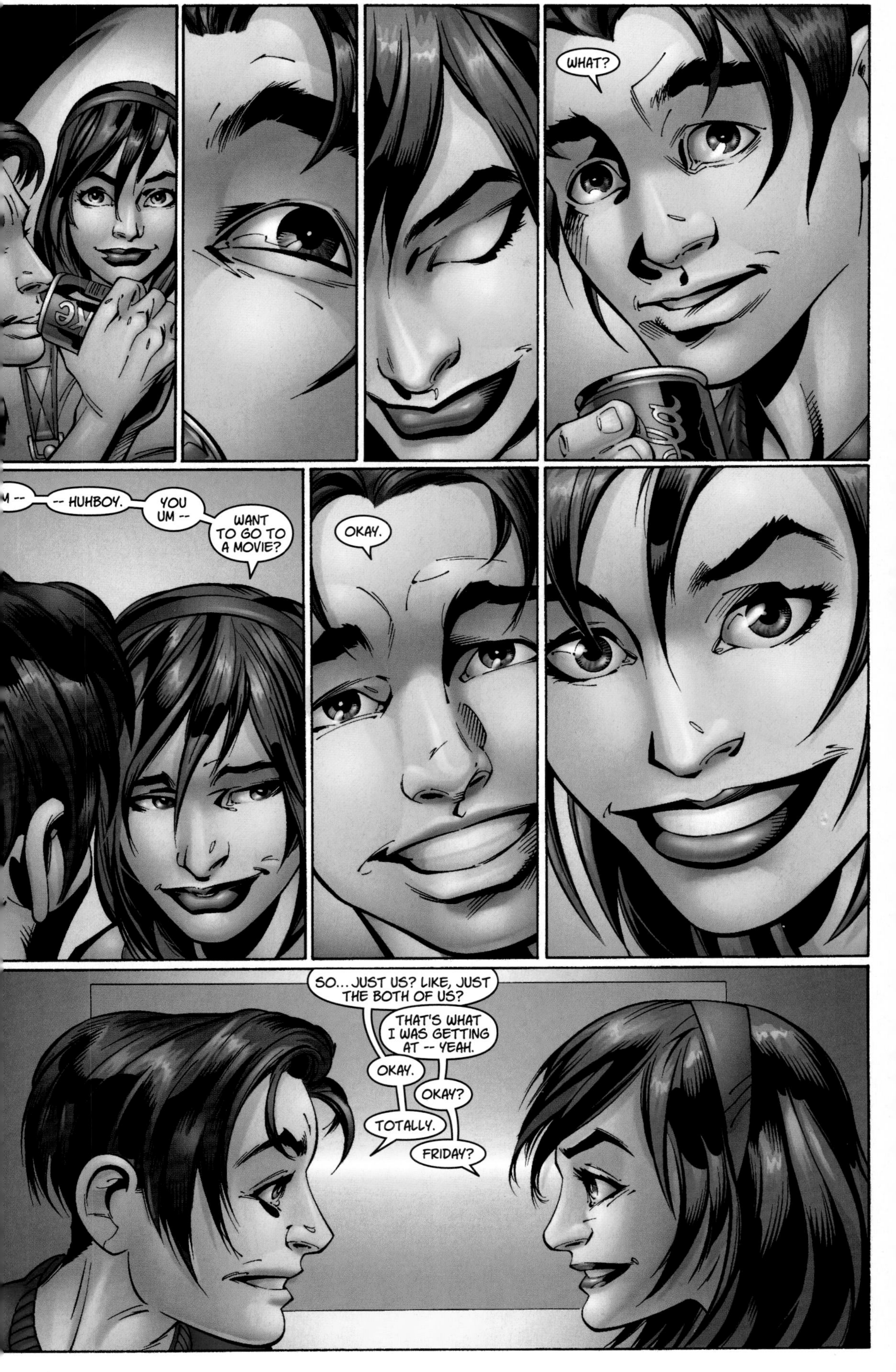
WHAT?
UM --
-- HUHBOY.
YOU UM --
WANT TO GO TO A MOVIE?
OKAY.
SO... JUST US? LIKE, JUST THE BOTH OF US?
THAT'S WHAT I WAS GETTING AT -- YEAH.
OKAY.
OKAY?
TOTALLY.
FRIDAY?

IT'S NOT A BIG SECRET THAT THE KINGPIN -- WILSON FISK -- WILL BE THROWING A GALA FUND-RAISER IN HIS OFFICE TOWER FRIDAY NIGHT.

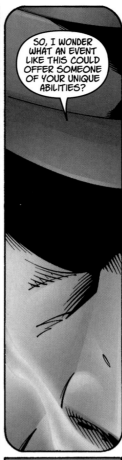

SO, I WONDER WHAT AN EVENT LIKE THIS COULD OFFER SOMEONE OF YOUR UNIQUE ABILITIES?

LET'S SAY SATURDAY.

WHAT'S GOING ON FRIDAY?

UH -- WORK.

I -- YEAH -- HAVE TO WORK AT THE PAPER.

OH YEAH -- DUH.

SO, YOU CAN DO SATURDAY?

I CAN DO SATURDAY.

COOL. IT'LL BE FUN.

IF I PICK THE MOVIE.

I KNEW THAT WAS COMING.

JUST AS LONG AS WE BOT[H] KNOW WHO'S I[N] CHARGE.

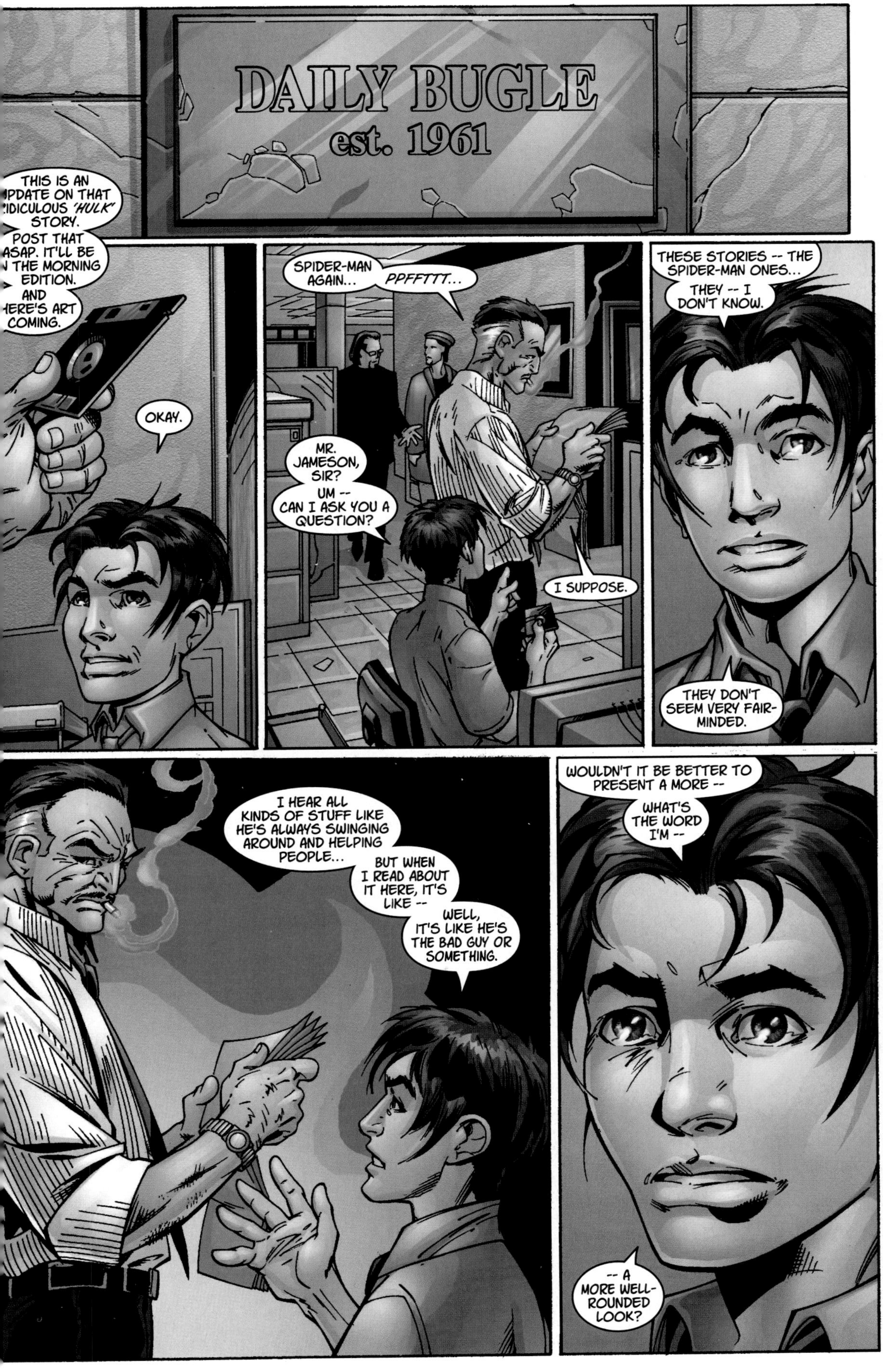
DAILY BUGLE
est. 1961
THIS IS AN UPDATE ON THAT RIDICULOUS 'HULK' STORY.
POST THAT ASAP. IT'LL BE IN THE MORNING EDITION.
AND HERE'S ART COMING.
OKAY.
SPIDER-MAN AGAIN...
PPFFTTT...
MR. JAMESON, SIR?
UM -- CAN I ASK YOU A QUESTION?
I SUPPOSE.
THESE STORIES -- THE SPIDER-MAN ONES...
THEY -- I DON'T KNOW.
THEY DON'T SEEM VERY FAIR-MINDED.
I HEAR ALL KINDS OF STUFF LIKE HE'S ALWAYS SWINGING AROUND AND HELPING PEOPLE...
BUT WHEN I READ ABOUT IT HERE, IT'S LIKE --
WELL, IT'S LIKE HE'S THE BAD GUY OR SOMETHING.
WOULDN'T IT BE BETTER TO PRESENT A MORE --
WHAT'S THE WORD I'M --
-- A MORE WELL-ROUNDED LOOK?

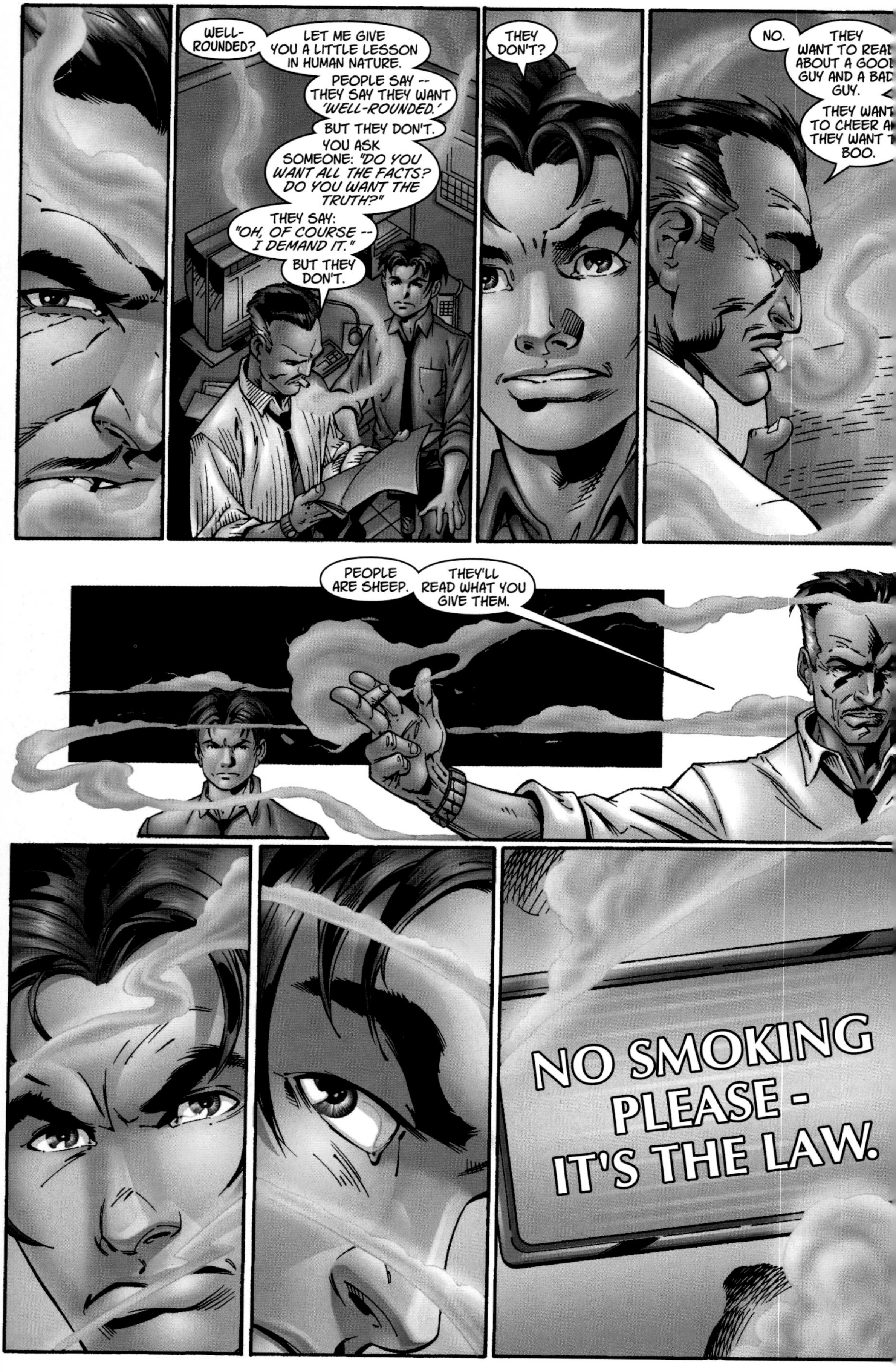
WELL-ROUNDED?
LET ME GIVE YOU A LITTLE LESSON IN HUMAN NATURE.
PEOPLE SAY -- THEY SAY THEY WANT *'WELL-ROUNDED.'*
BUT THEY DON'T.
YOU ASK SOMEONE: *"DO YOU WANT ALL THE FACTS? DO YOU WANT THE TRUTH?"*
THEY SAY: *"OH, OF COURSE -- I DEMAND IT."*
BUT THEY DON'T.
THEY DON'T?
NO.
PEOPLE ARE SHEEP.
THEY'LL READ WHAT YOU GIVE THEM.
NO SMOKING PLEASE - IT'S THE LAW.

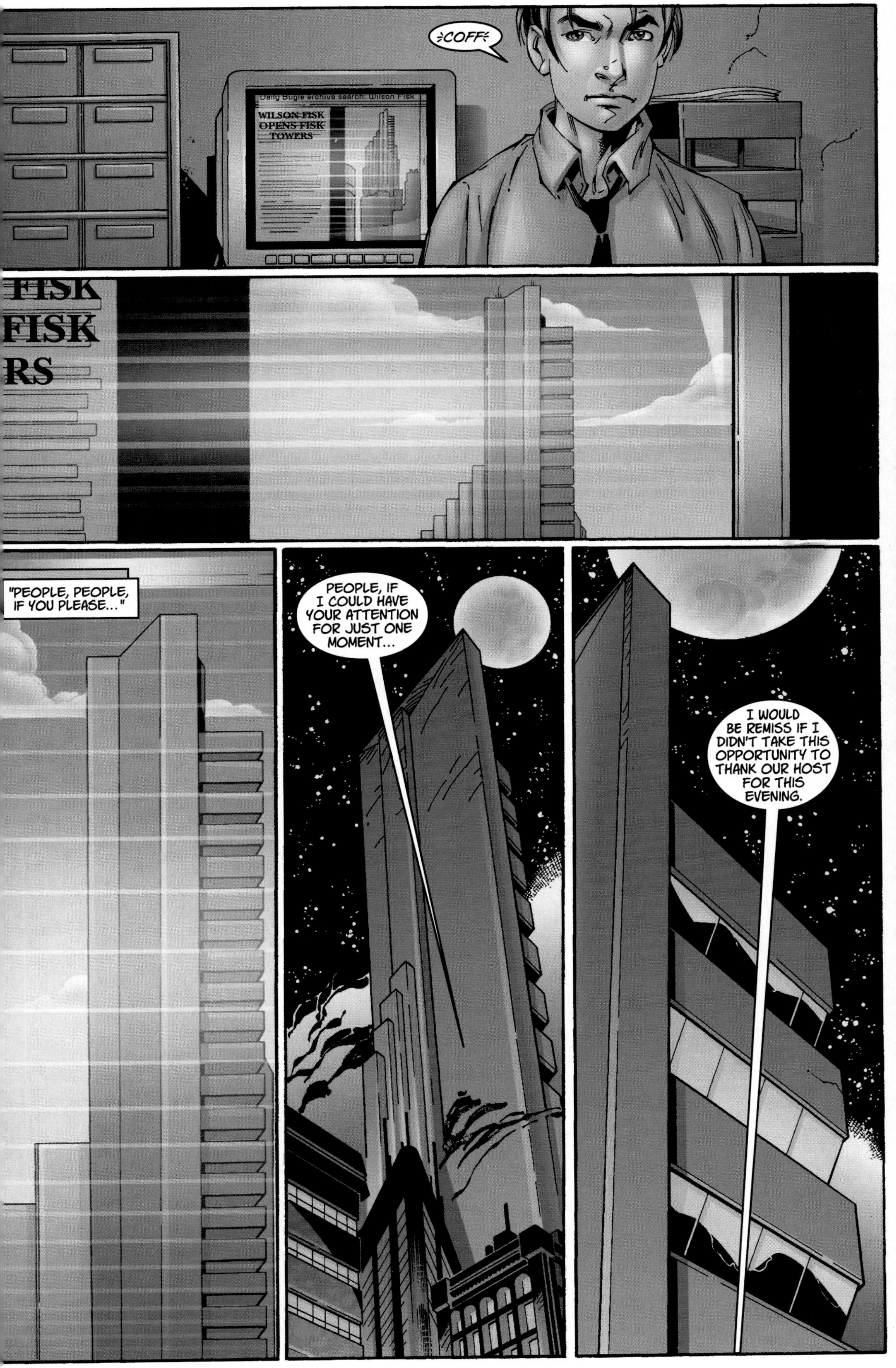

COFF
Daily Bugle archive search: Wilson Fisk
WILSON FISK OPENS FISK TOWERS
"PEOPLE, PEOPLE, IF YOU PLEASE..."
PEOPLE, IF I COULD HAVE YOUR ATTENTION FOR JUST ONE MOMENT...
I WOULD BE REMISS IF I DIDN'T TAKE THIS OPPORTUNITY TO THANK OUR HOST FOR THIS EVENING.

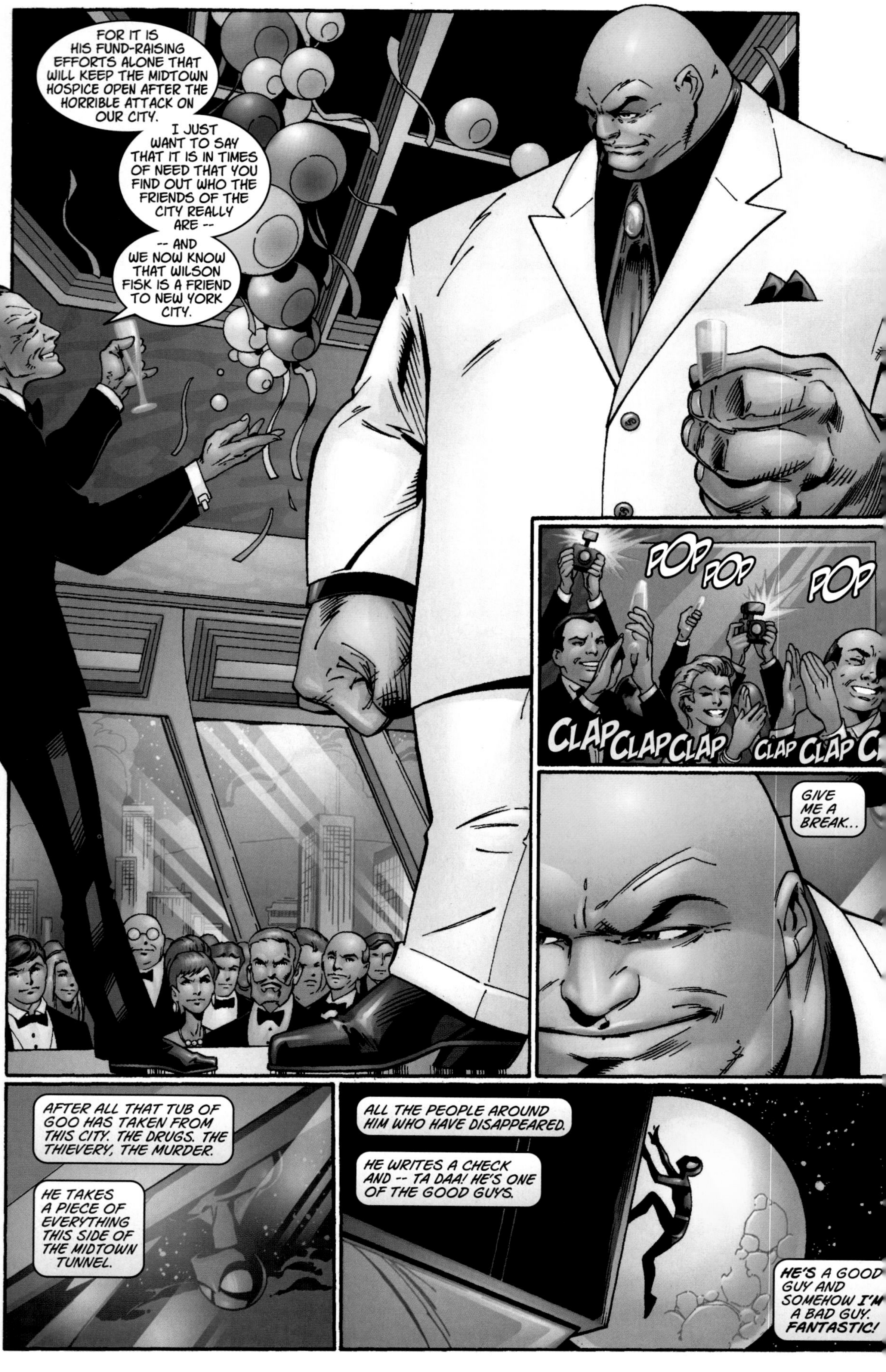
FOR IT IS HIS FUND-RAISING EFFORTS ALONE THAT WILL KEEP THE MIDTOWN HOSPICE OPEN AFTER THE HORRIBLE ATTACK ON OUR CITY.
I JUST WANT TO SAY THAT IT IS IN TIMES OF NEED THAT YOU FIND OUT WHO THE FRIENDS OF THE CITY REALLY ARE --
-- AND WE NOW KNOW THAT WILSON FISK IS A FRIEND TO NEW YORK CITY.
POP POP POP
CLAP CLAP CLAP CLAP CLAP
GIVE ME A BREAK...
AFTER ALL THAT TUB OF GOO HAS TAKEN FROM THIS CITY. THE DRUGS. THE THIEVERY, THE MURDER.
HE TAKES A PIECE OF EVERYTHING THIS SIDE OF THE MIDTOWN TUNNEL.
ALL THE PEOPLE AROUND HIM WHO HAVE DISAPPEARED.
HE WRITES A CHECK AND -- TA DAA! HE'S ONE OF THE GOOD GUYS.
HE'S A GOOD GUY AND SOMEHOW I'M A BAD GUY. FANTASTIC!

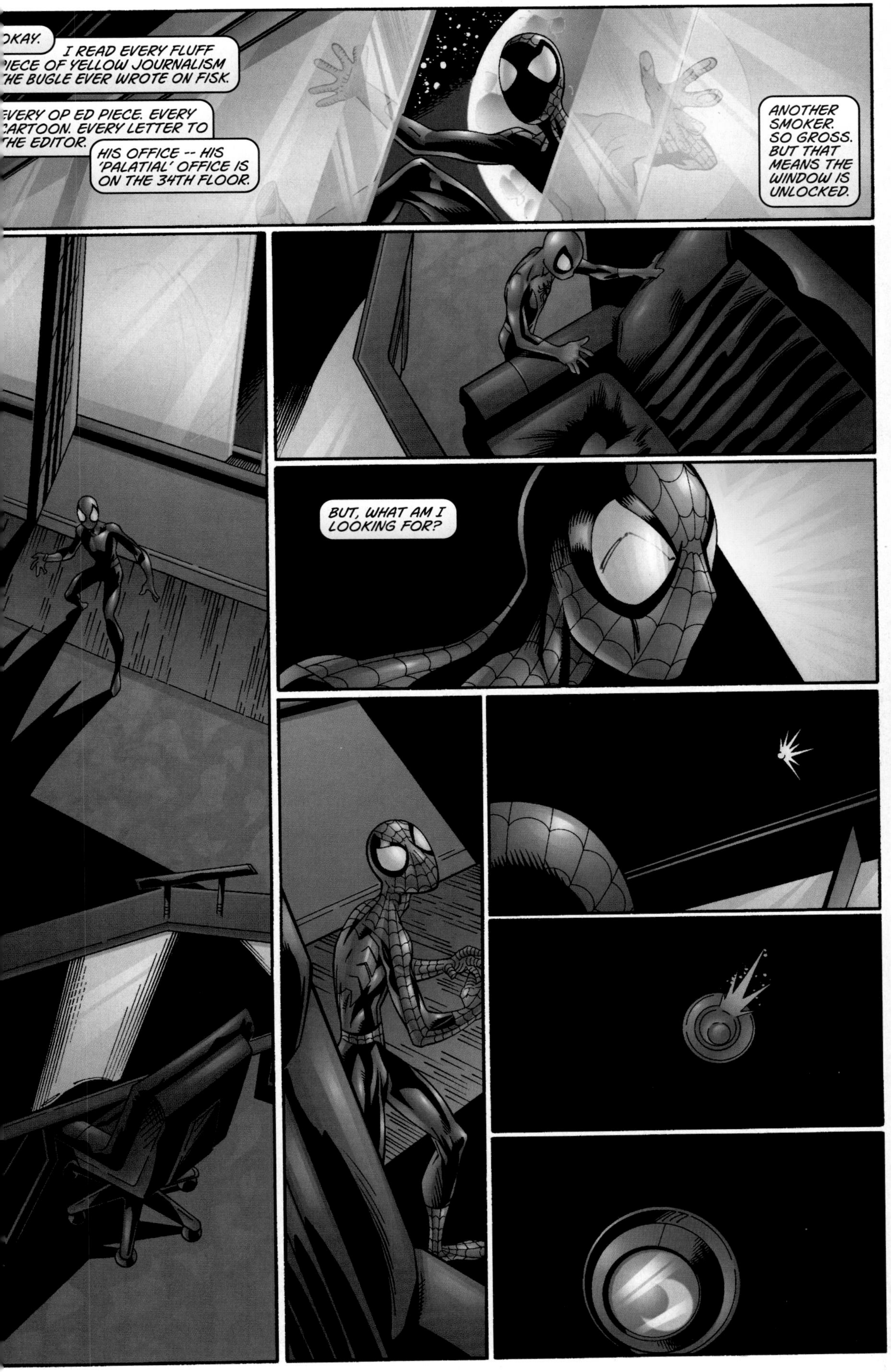
OKAY.
I READ EVERY FLUFF PIECE OF YELLOW JOURNALISM THE BUGLE EVER WROTE ON FISK.
EVERY OP ED PIECE. EVERY CARTOON. EVERY LETTER TO THE EDITOR.
HIS OFFICE -- HIS 'PALATIAL' OFFICE IS ON THE 34TH FLOOR.
ANOTHER SMOKER. SO GROSS. BUT THAT MEANS THE WINDOW IS UNLOCKED.
BUT, WHAT AM I LOOKING FOR?

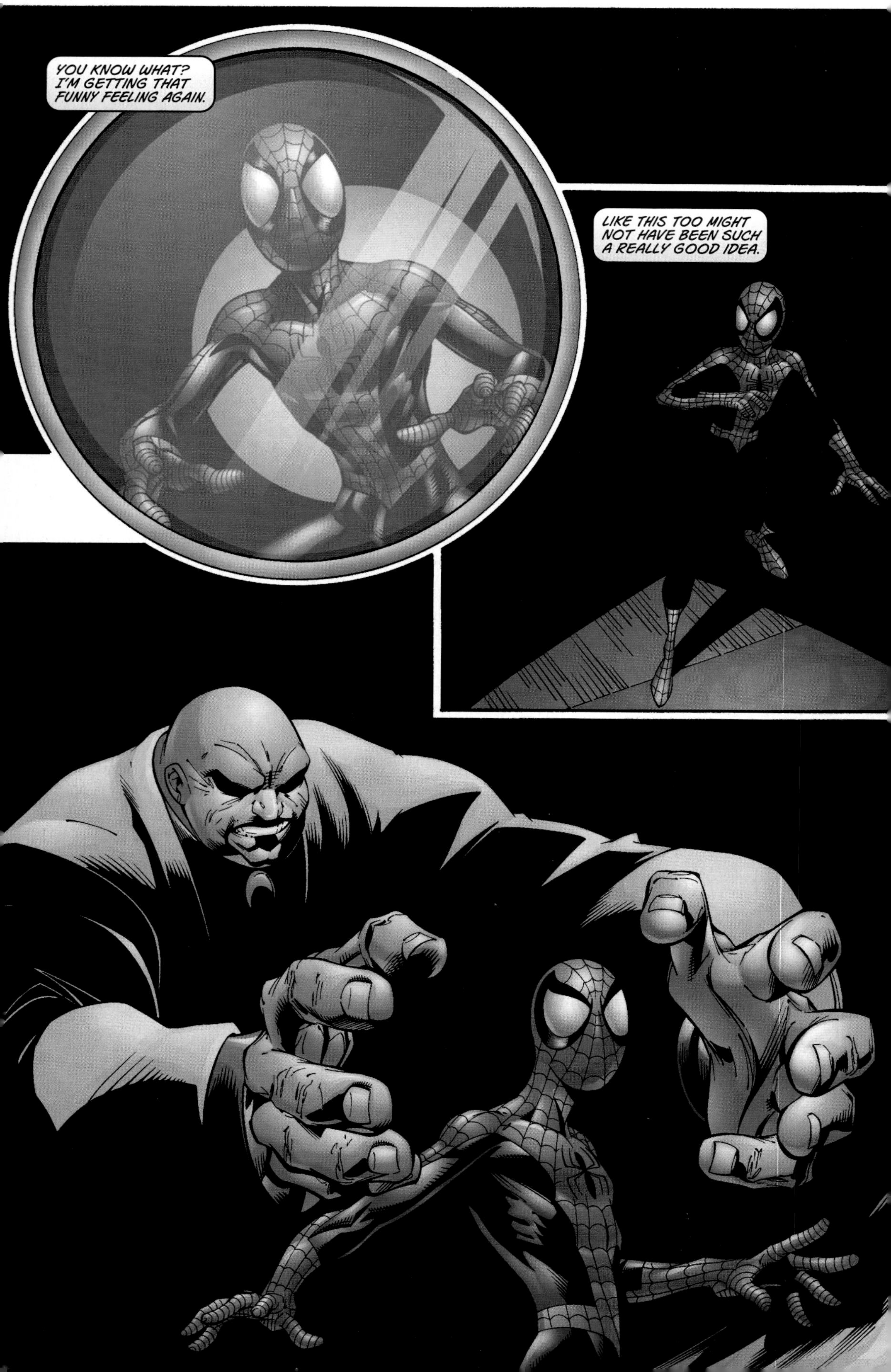
YOU KNOW WHAT? I'M GETTING THAT FUNNY FEELING AGAIN.
LIKE THIS TOO MIGHT NOT HAVE BEEN SUCH A REALLY GOOD IDEA.

10

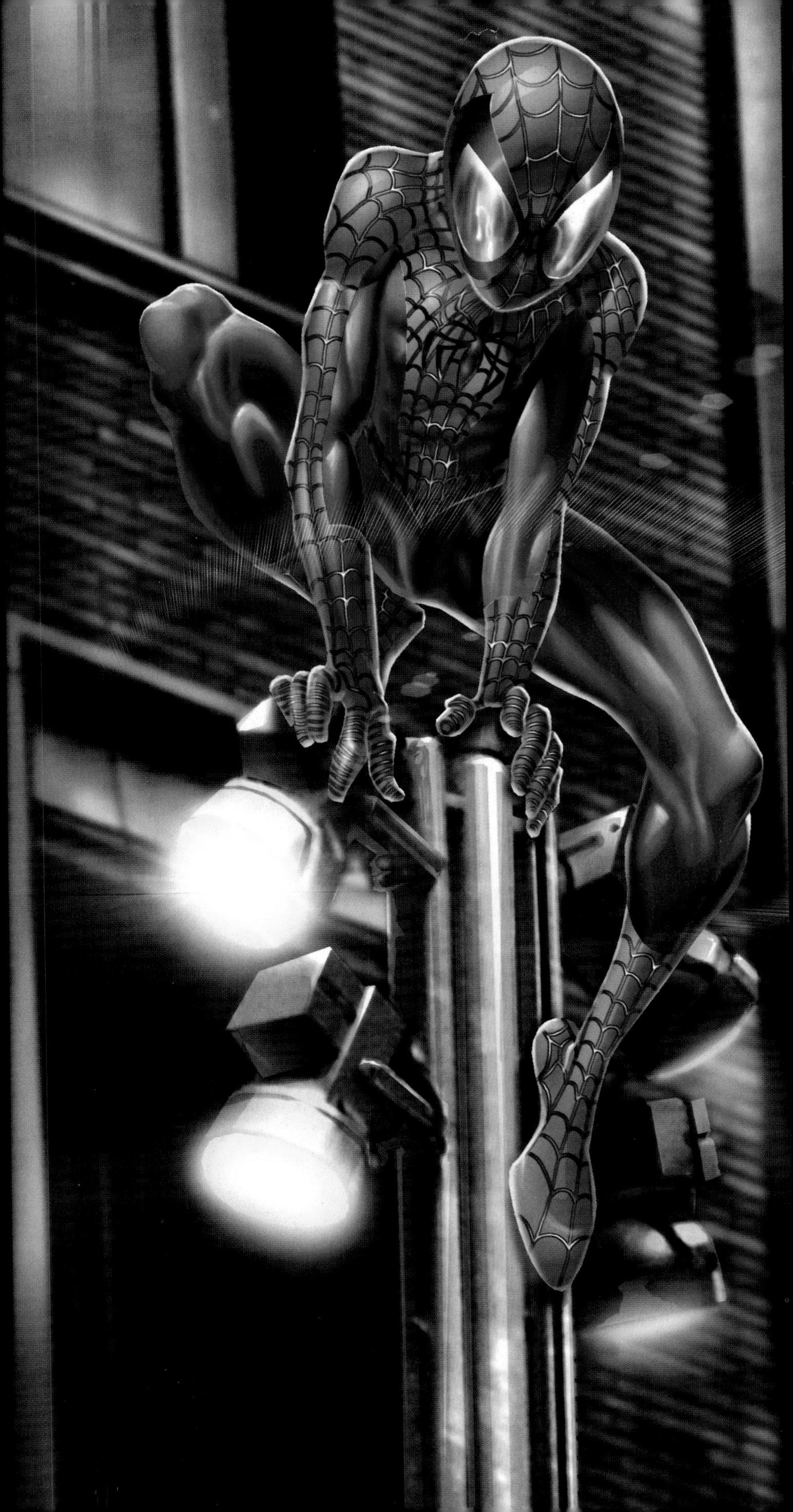

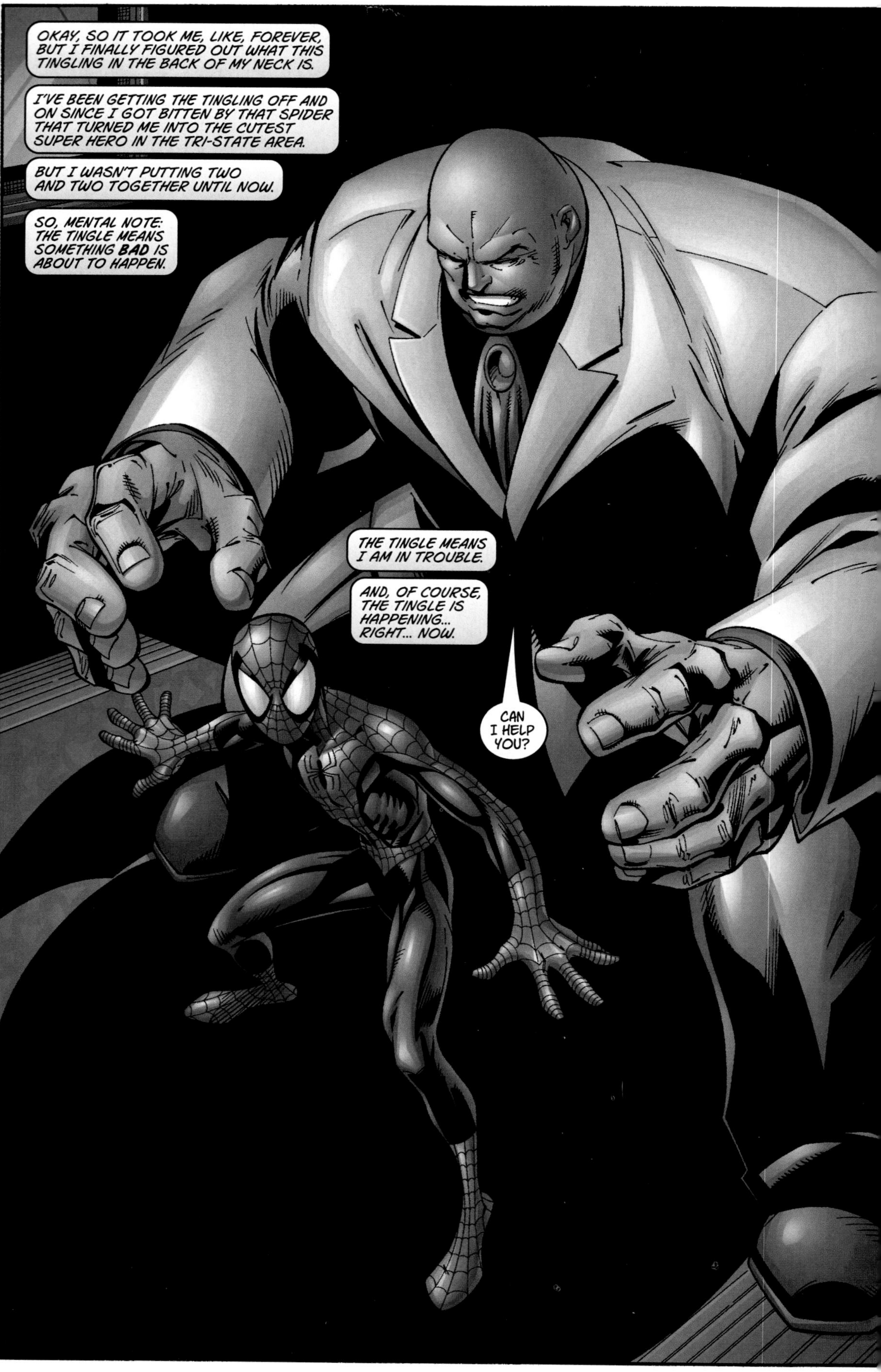
OKAY, SO IT TOOK ME, LIKE, FOREVER, BUT I FINALLY FIGURED OUT WHAT THIS TINGLING IN THE BACK OF MY NECK IS.
I'VE BEEN GETTING THE TINGLING OFF AND ON SINCE I GOT BITTEN BY THAT SPIDER THAT TURNED ME INTO THE CUTEST SUPER HERO IN THE TRI-STATE AREA.
BUT I WASN'T PUTTING TWO AND TWO TOGETHER UNTIL NOW.
SO, MENTAL NOTE: THE TINGLE MEANS SOMETHING BAD IS ABOUT TO HAPPEN.
THE TINGLE MEANS I AM IN TROUBLE.
AND, OF COURSE, THE TINGLE IS HAPPENING... RIGHT... NOW.
CAN I HELP YOU?

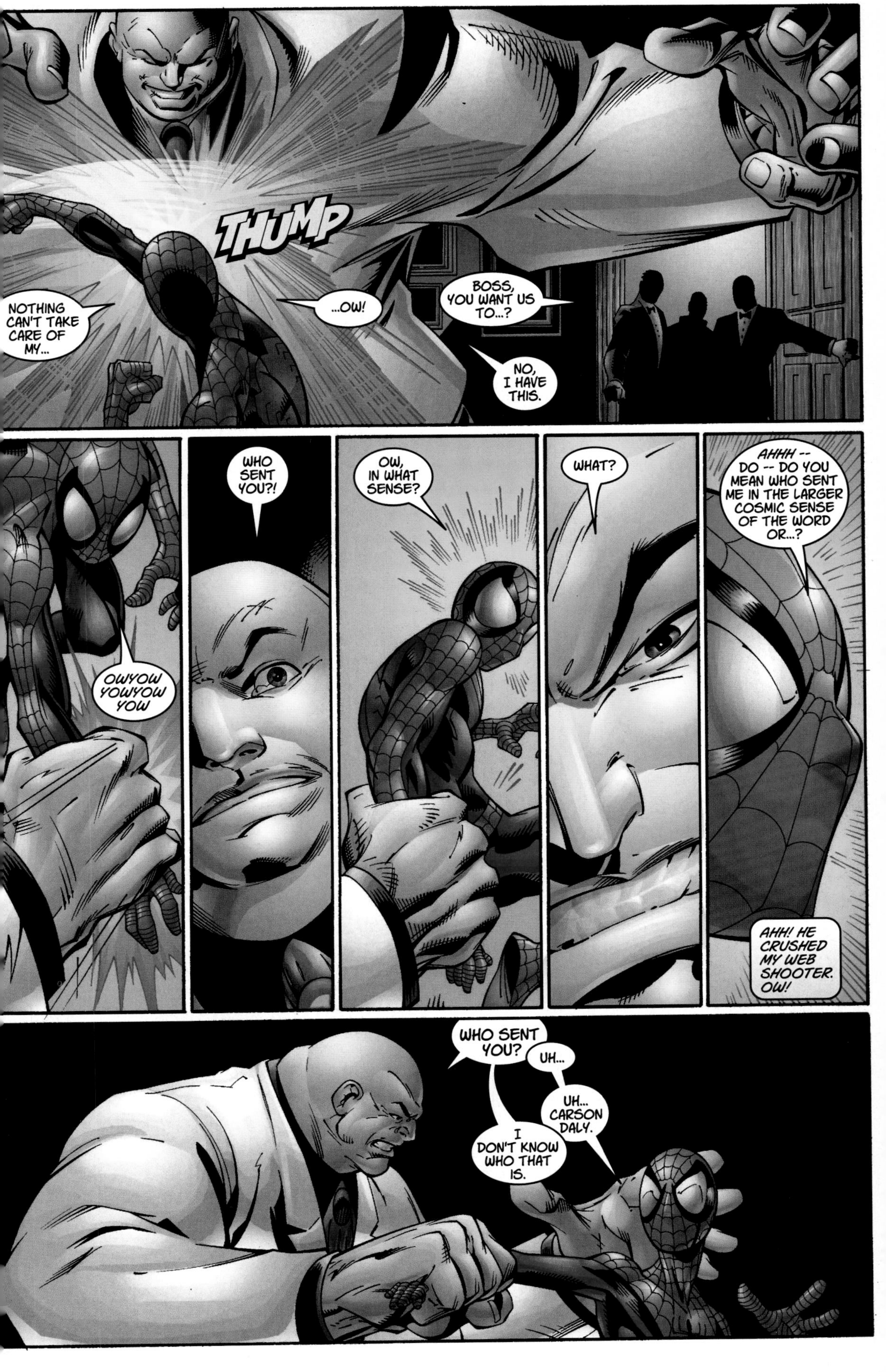
THUMP
NOTHING CAN'T TAKE CARE OF MY...
...OW!
BOSS, YOU WANT US TO...?
NO, I HAVE THIS.
OWYOW YOWYOW YOW
WHO SENT YOU?!
OW, IN WHAT SENSE?
WHAT?
AHHH -- DO -- DO YOU MEAN WHO SENT ME IN THE LARGER COSMIC SENSE OF THE WORD OR...?
AHH! HE CRUSHED MY WEB SHOOTER. OW!
WHO SENT YOU?
UH...
UH... CARSON DALY.
I DON'T KNOW WHO THAT IS.

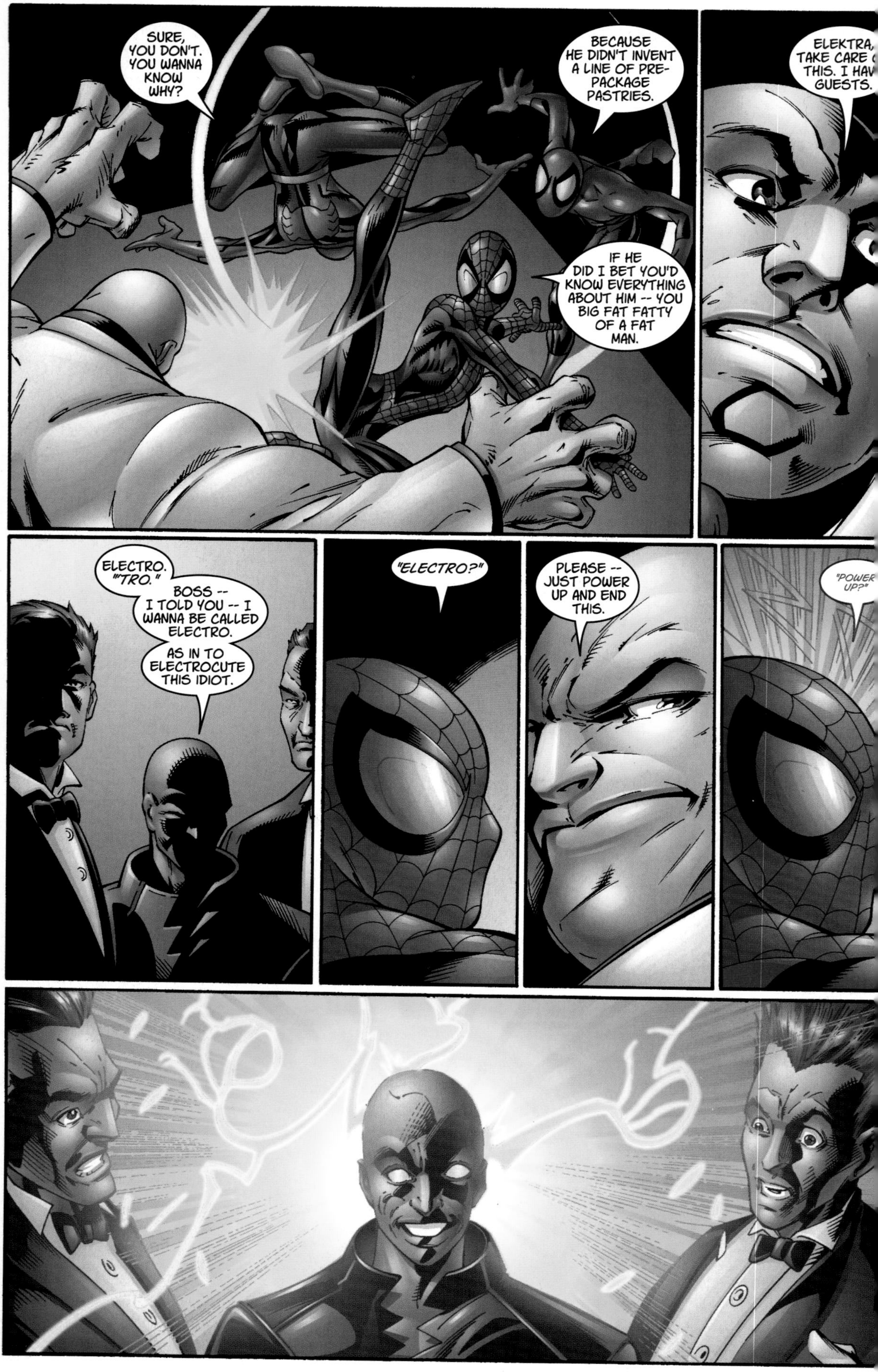
SURE, YOU DON'T. YOU WANNA KNOW WHY?
BECAUSE HE DIDN'T INVENT A LINE OF PRE-PACKAGE PASTRIES.
IF HE DID I BET YOU'D KNOW EVERYTHING ABOUT HIM -- YOU BIG FAT FATTY OF A FAT MAN.
ELEKTRA, TAKE CARE OF THIS. I HAVE GUESTS.
ELECTRO. "TRO."
BOSS -- I TOLD YOU -- I WANNA BE CALLED ELECTRO.
AS IN TO ELECTROCUTE THIS IDIOT.
"ELECTRO?"
PLEASE -- JUST POWER UP AND END THIS.
"POWER UP?"

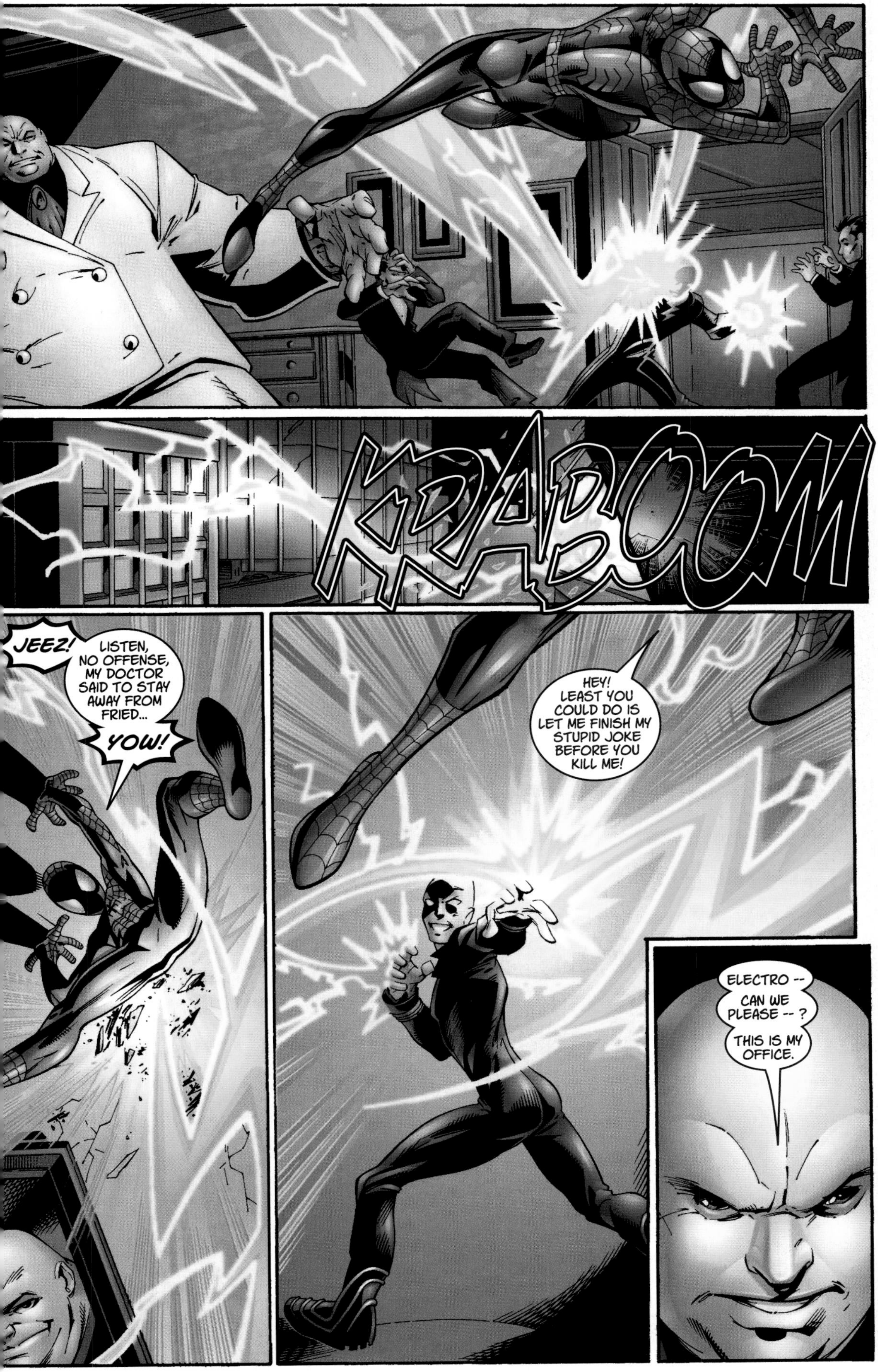
KRABOOM
JEEZ!
LISTEN, NO OFFENSE, MY DOCTOR SAID TO STAY AWAY FROM FRIED...
YOW!
HEY! LEAST YOU COULD DO IS LET ME FINISH MY STUPID JOKE BEFORE YOU KILL ME!
ELECTRO --
CAN WE PLEASE -- ?
THIS IS MY OFFICE.

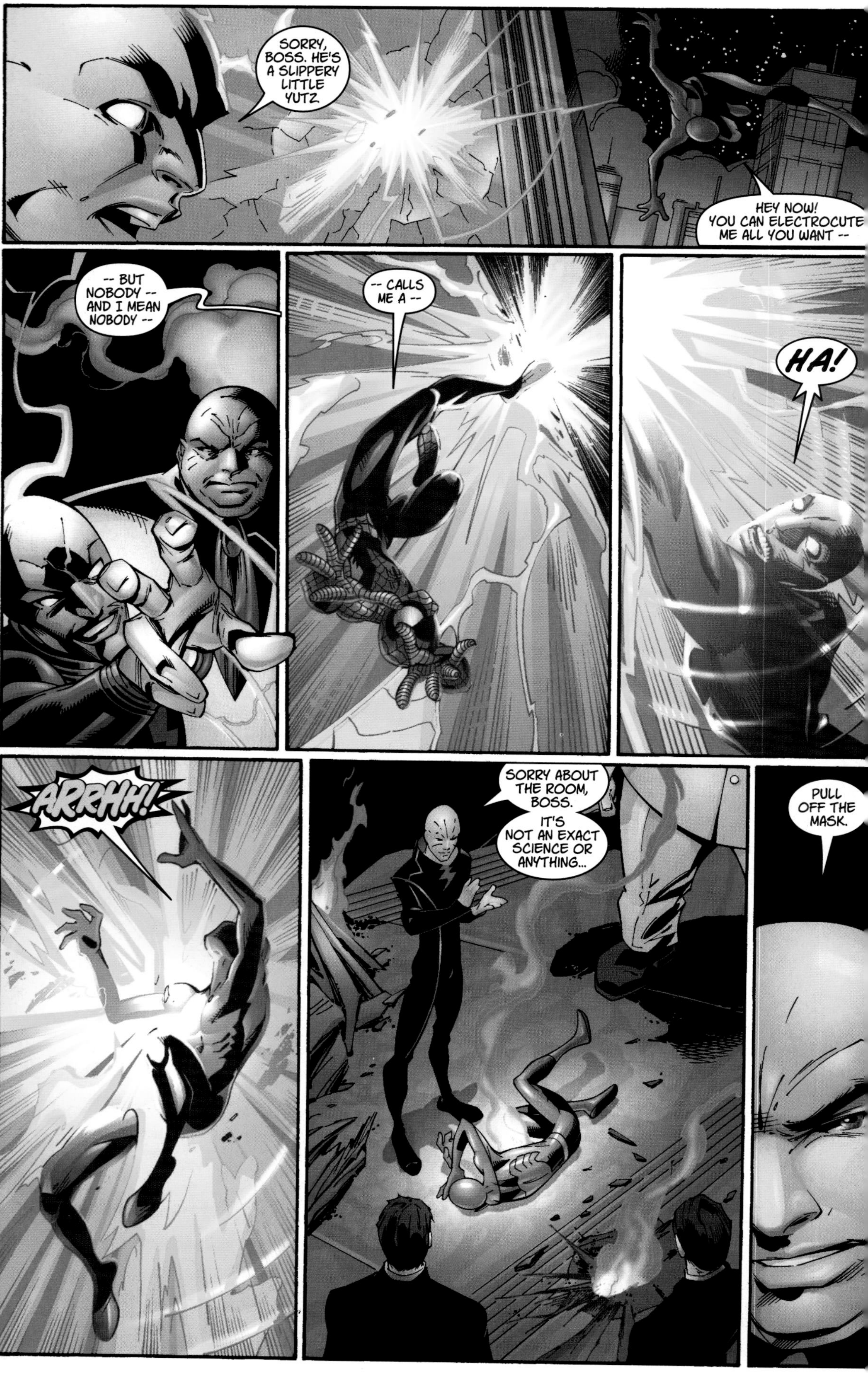
SORRY, BOSS. HE'S A SLIPPERY LITTLE YUTZ.
HEY NOW! YOU CAN ELECTROCUTE ME ALL YOU WANT --
-- BUT NOBODY -- AND I MEAN NOBODY --
-- CALLS ME A --
HA!
ARRHH!
SORRY ABOUT THE ROOM, BOSS.
IT'S NOT AN EXACT SCIENCE OR ANYTHING...
PULL OFF THE MASK.

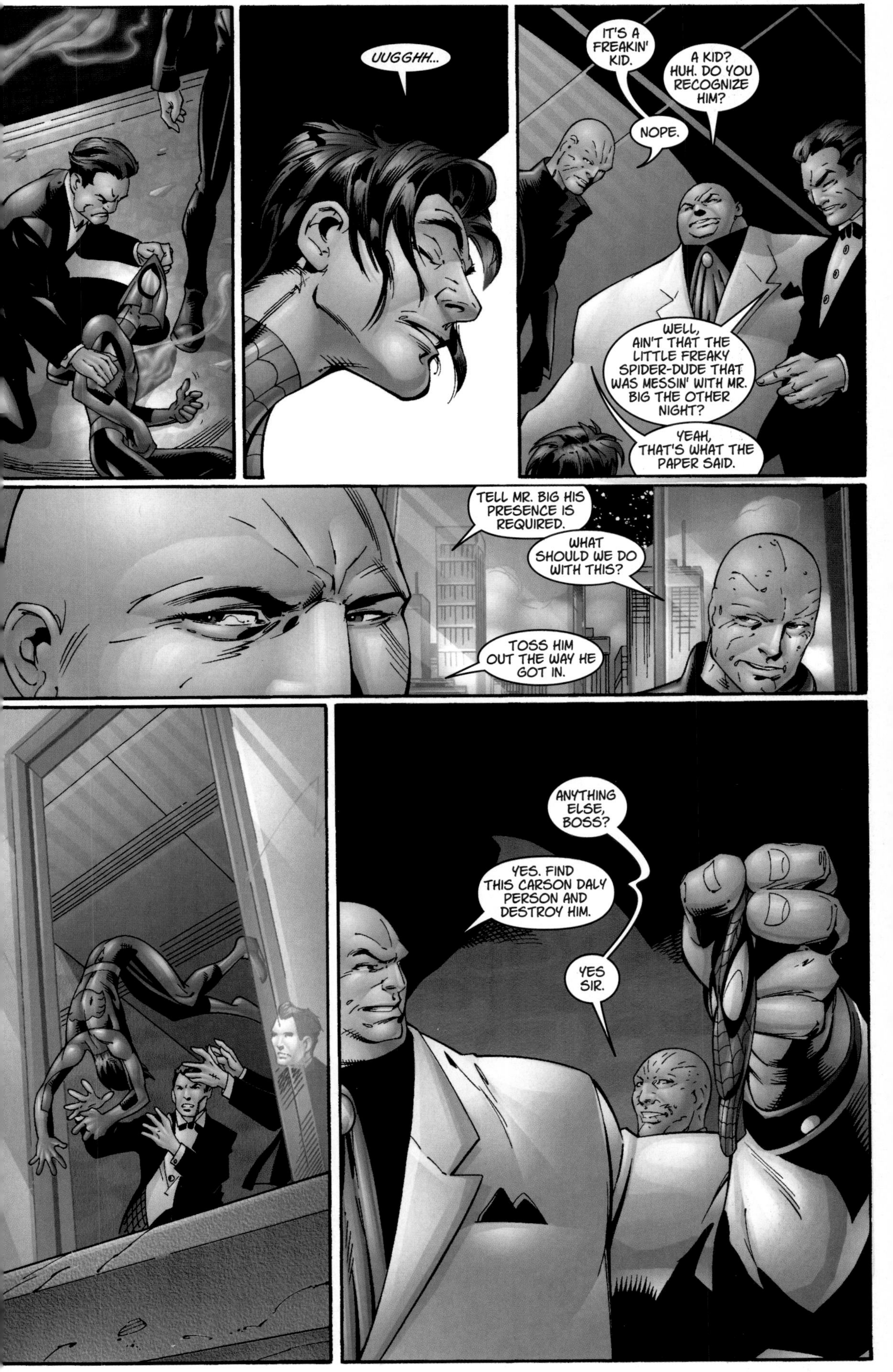
UUGGHH...
IT'S A FREAKIN' KID.
A KID? HUH. DO YOU RECOGNIZE HIM?
NOPE.
WELL, AIN'T THAT THE LITTLE FREAKY SPIDER-DUDE THAT WAS MESSIN' WITH MR. BIG THE OTHER NIGHT?
YEAH, THAT'S WHAT THE PAPER SAID.
TELL MR. BIG HIS PRESENCE IS REQUIRED.
WHAT SHOULD WE DO WITH THIS?
TOSS HIM OUT THE WAY HE GOT IN.
ANYTHING ELSE, BOSS?
YES. FIND THIS CARSON DALY PERSON AND DESTROY HIM.
YES SIR.

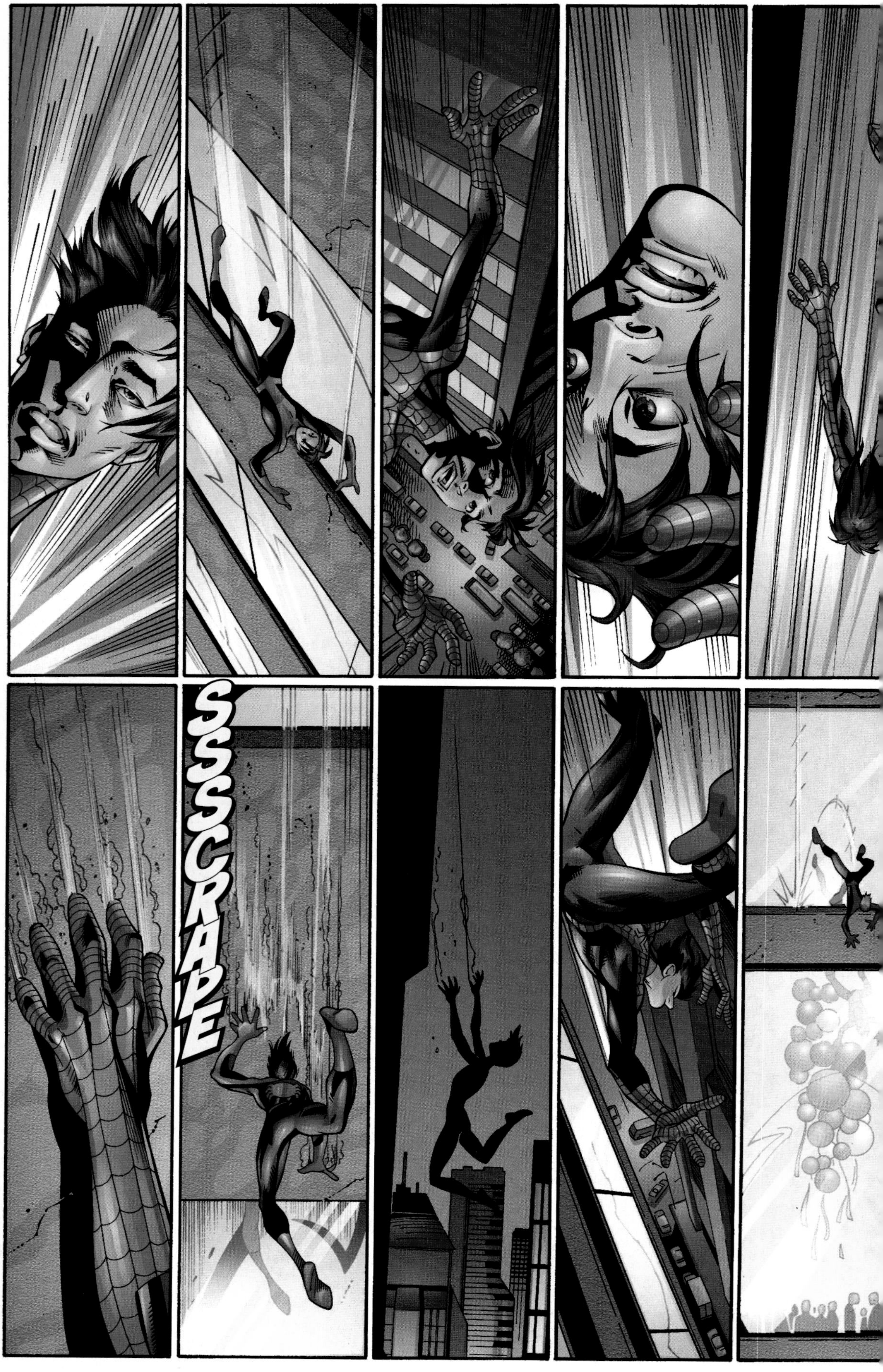
SSSCRAPE

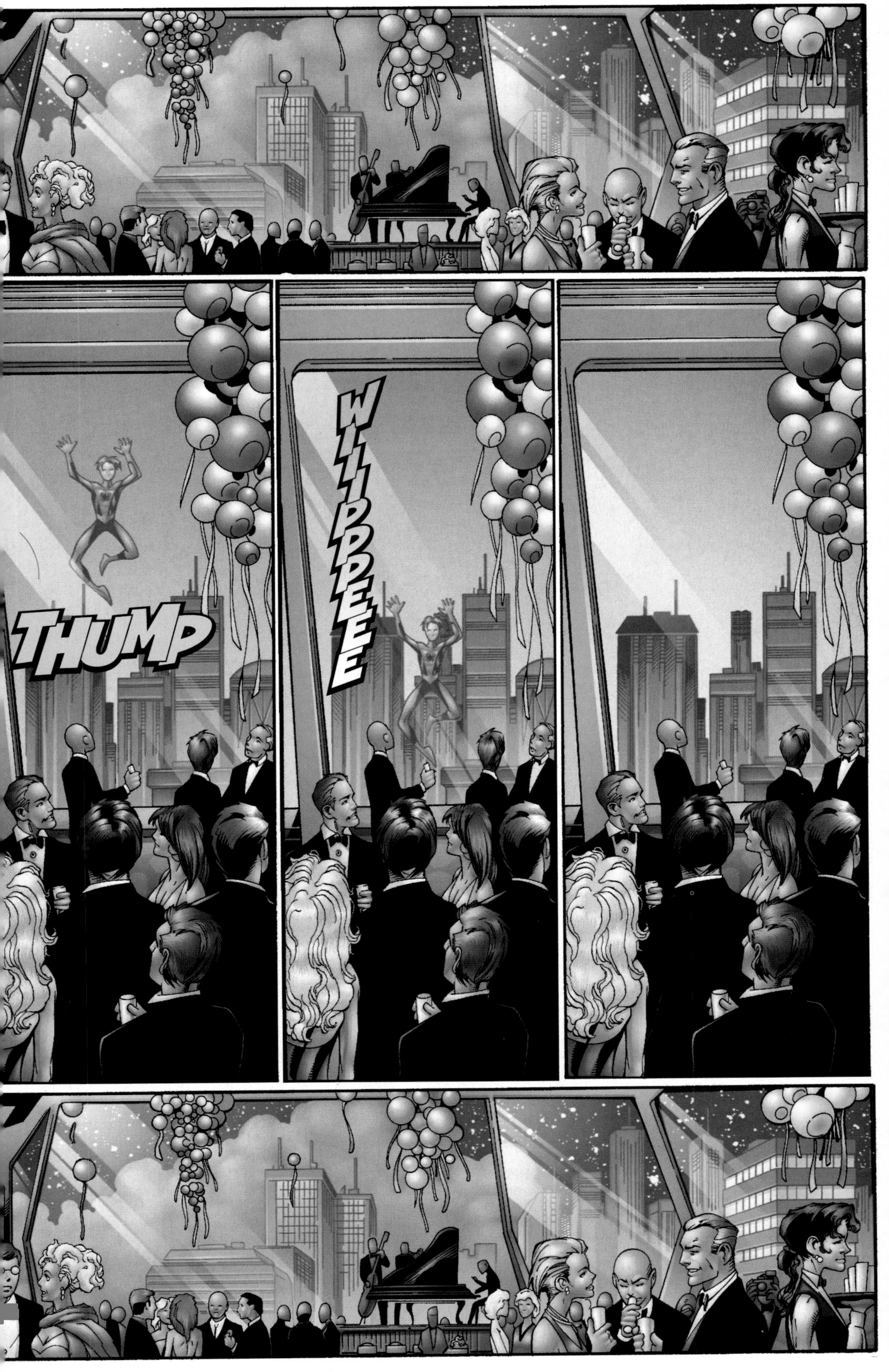
THUMP
WIIIPPEEE

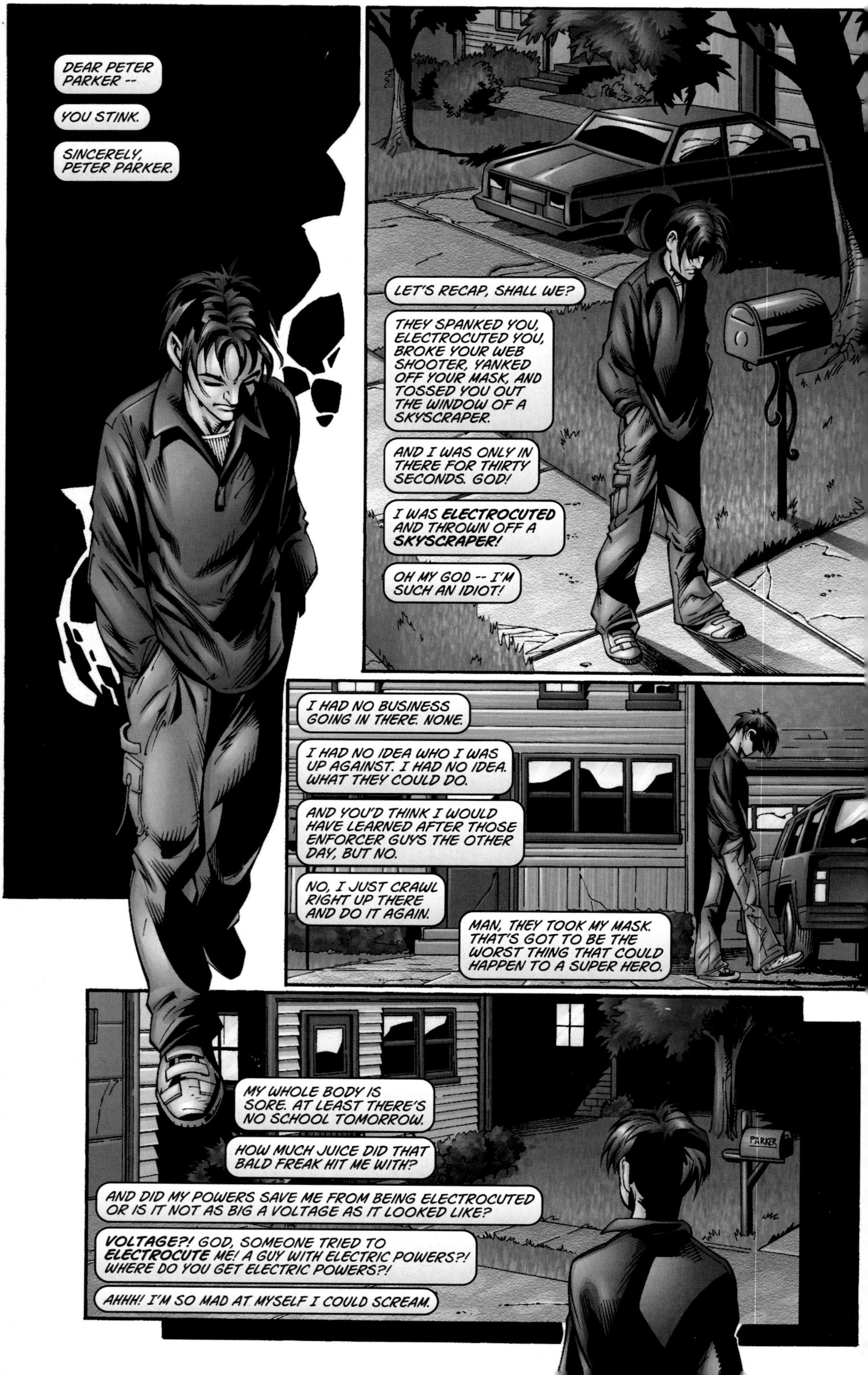
DEAR PETER PARKER --
YOU STINK.
SINCERELY, PETER PARKER.
LET'S RECAP, SHALL WE?
THEY SPANKED YOU, ELECTROCUTED YOU, BROKE YOUR WEB SHOOTER, YANKED OFF YOUR MASK, AND TOSSED YOU OUT THE WINDOW OF A SKYSCRAPER.
AND I WAS ONLY IN THERE FOR THIRTY SECONDS. GOD!
I WAS **ELECTROCUTED** AND THROWN OFF A **SKYSCRAPER!**
OH MY GOD -- I'M SUCH AN IDIOT!
I HAD NO BUSINESS GOING IN THERE. NONE.
I HAD NO IDEA WHO I WAS UP AGAINST. I HAD NO IDEA. WHAT THEY COULD DO.
AND YOU'D THINK I WOULD HAVE LEARNED AFTER THOSE ENFORCER GUYS THE OTHER DAY, BUT NO.
NO, I JUST CRAWL RIGHT UP THERE AND DO IT AGAIN.
MAN, THEY TOOK MY MASK. THAT'S GOT TO BE THE WORST THING THAT COULD HAPPEN TO A SUPER HERO.
MY WHOLE BODY IS SORE. AT LEAST THERE'S NO SCHOOL TOMORROW.
HOW MUCH JUICE DID THAT BALD FREAK HIT ME WITH?
AND DID MY POWERS SAVE ME FROM BEING ELECTROCUTED OR IS IT NOT AS BIG A VOLTAGE AS IT LOOKED LIKE?
VOLTAGE?! GOD, SOMEONE TRIED TO **ELECTROCUTE** ME! A GUY WITH ELECTRIC POWERS?! WHERE DO YOU GET ELECTRIC POWERS?!
AHHH! I'M SO MAD AT MYSELF I COULD SCREAM.
PARKER

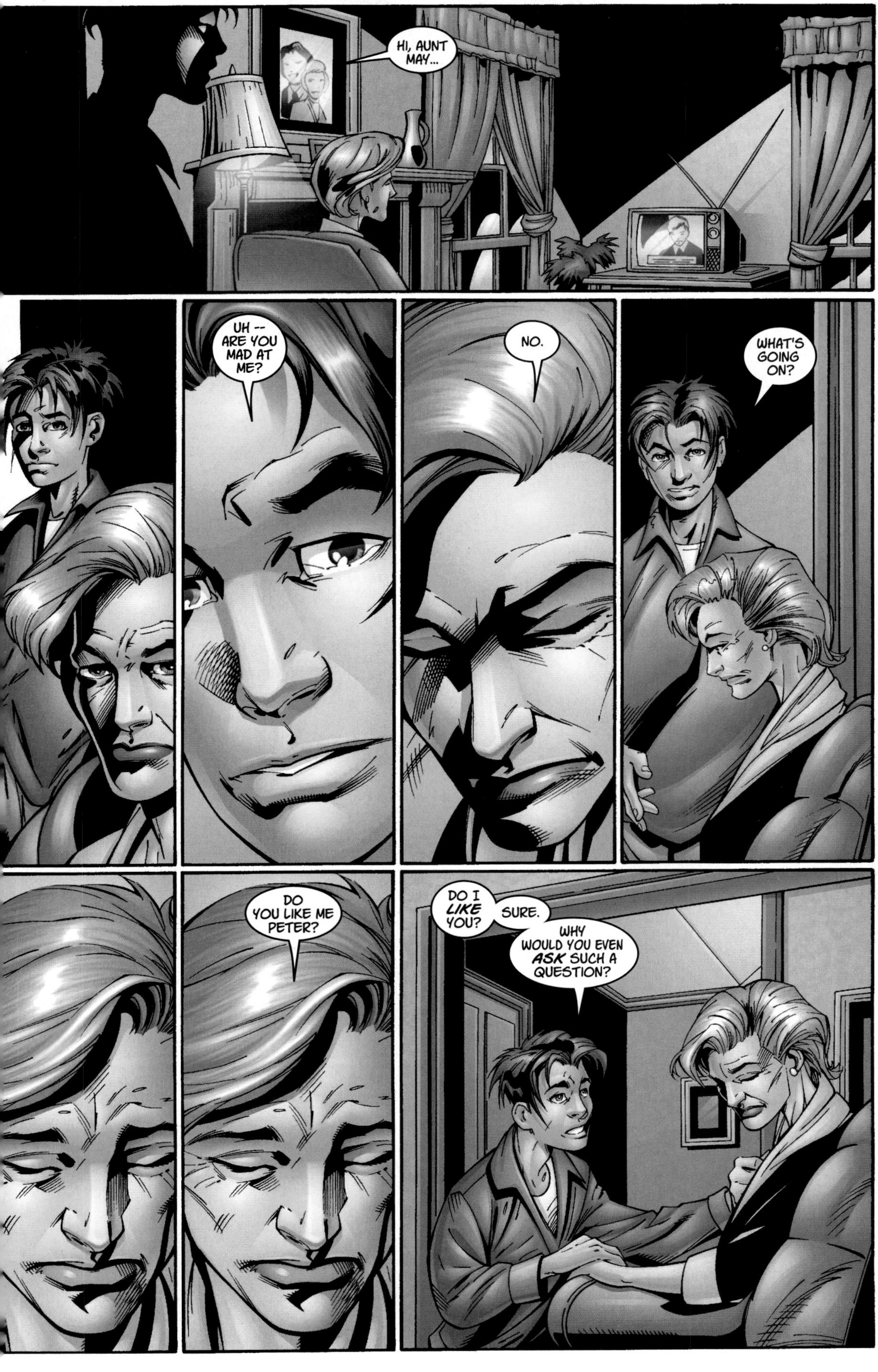
HI, AUNT MAY...
UH -- ARE YOU MAD AT ME?
NO.
WHAT'S GOING ON?
DO YOU LIKE ME PETER?
DO I *LIKE* YOU?
SURE.
WHY WOULD YOU EVEN ***ASK*** SUCH A QUESTION?

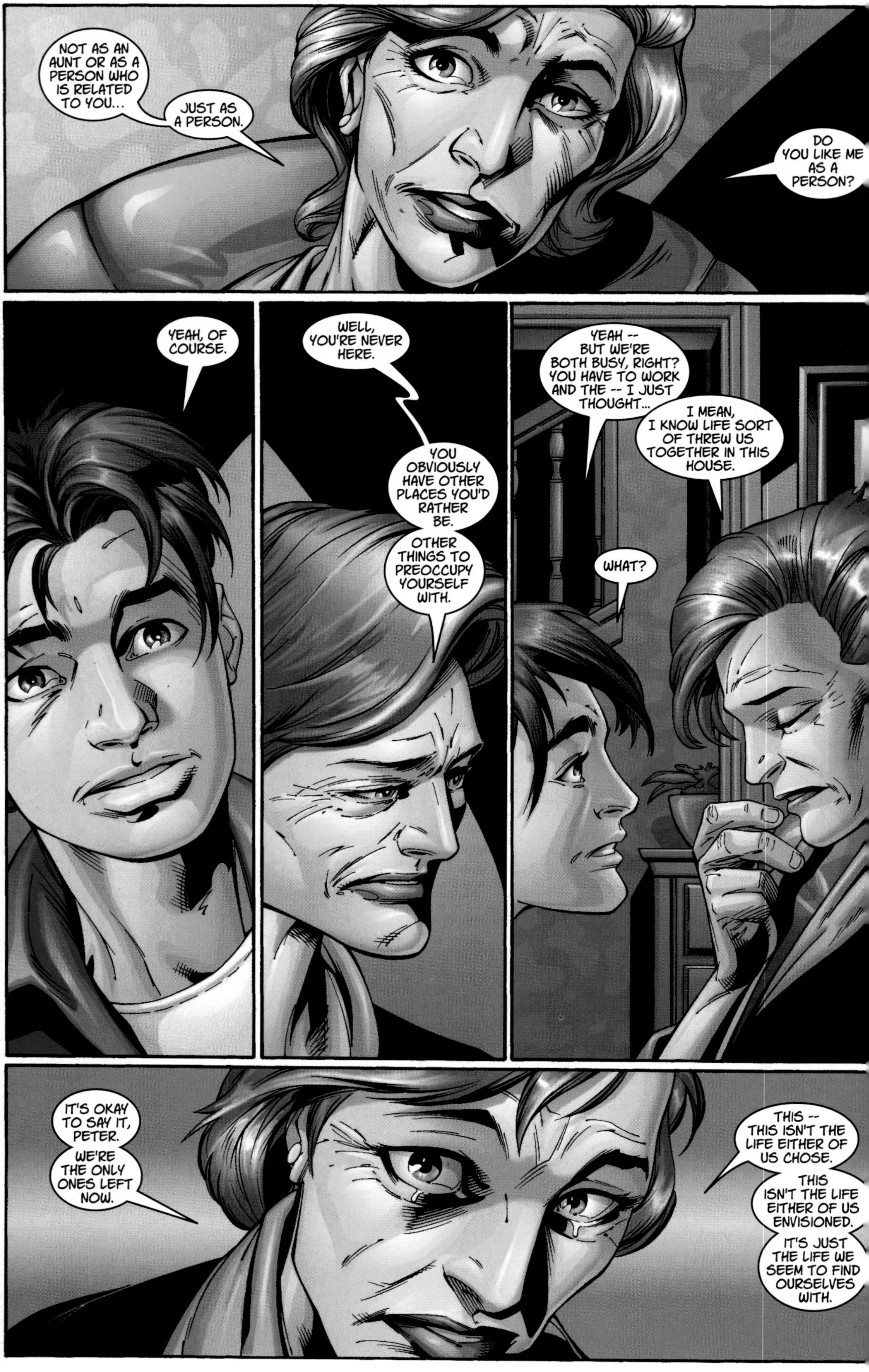
NOT AS AN AUNT OR AS A PERSON WHO IS RELATED TO YOU...
JUST AS A PERSON.
DO YOU LIKE ME AS A PERSON?
YEAH, OF COURSE.
WELL, YOU'RE NEVER HERE.
YOU OBVIOUSLY HAVE OTHER PLACES YOU'D RATHER BE.
OTHER THINGS TO PREOCCUPY YOURSELF WITH.
YEAH -- BUT WE'RE BOTH BUSY, RIGHT? YOU HAVE TO WORK AND THE -- I JUST THOUGHT...
I MEAN, I KNOW LIFE SORT OF THREW US TOGETHER IN THIS HOUSE.
WHAT?
IT'S OKAY TO SAY IT, PETER.
WE'RE THE ONLY ONES LEFT NOW.
THIS -- THIS ISN'T THE LIFE EITHER OF US CHOSE.
THIS ISN'T THE LIFE EITHER OF US ENVISIONED.
IT'S JUST THE LIFE WE SEEM TO FIND OURSELVES WITH.

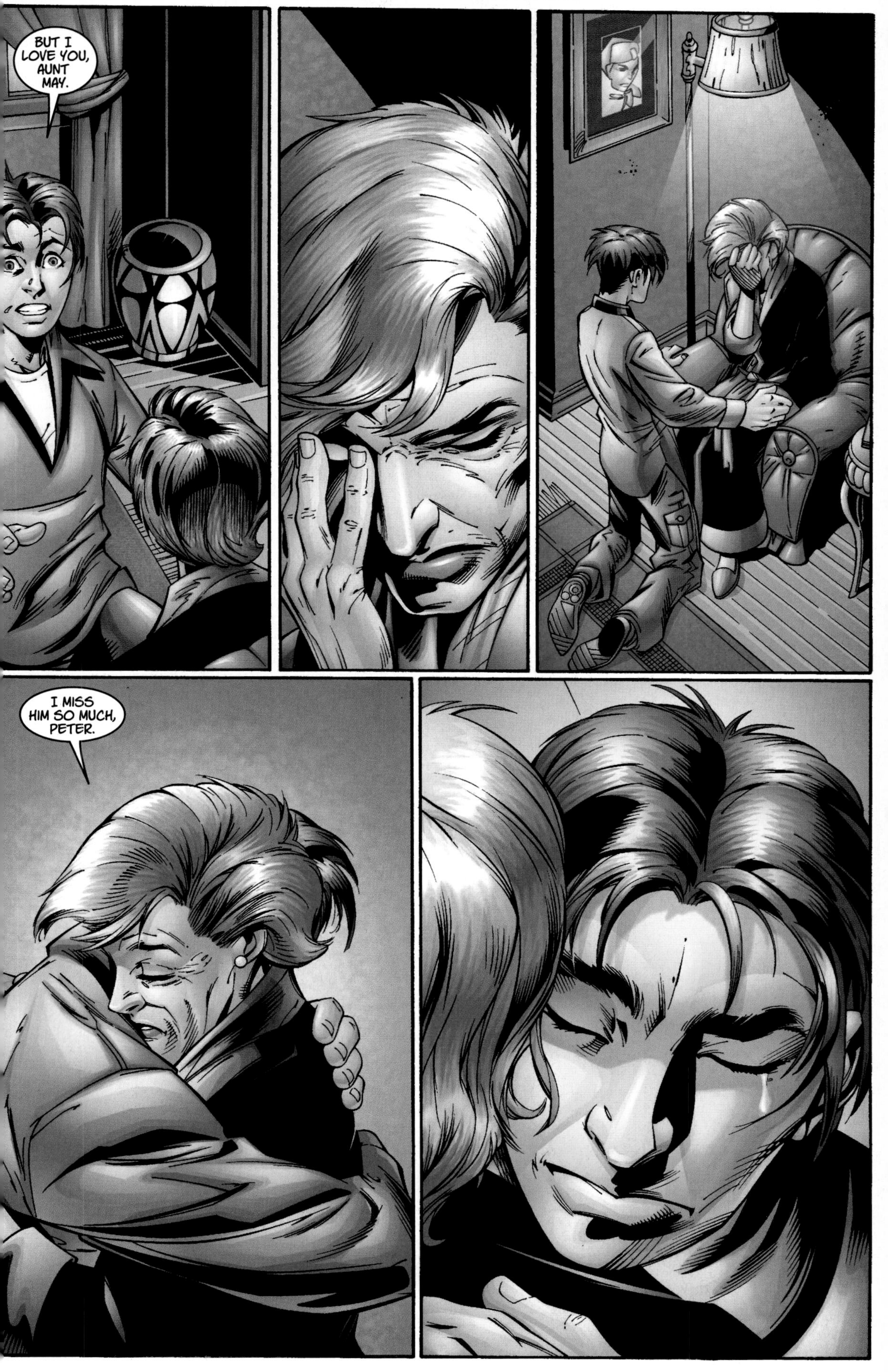
BUT I LOVE YOU, AUNT MAY.
I MISS HIM SO MUCH, PETER.

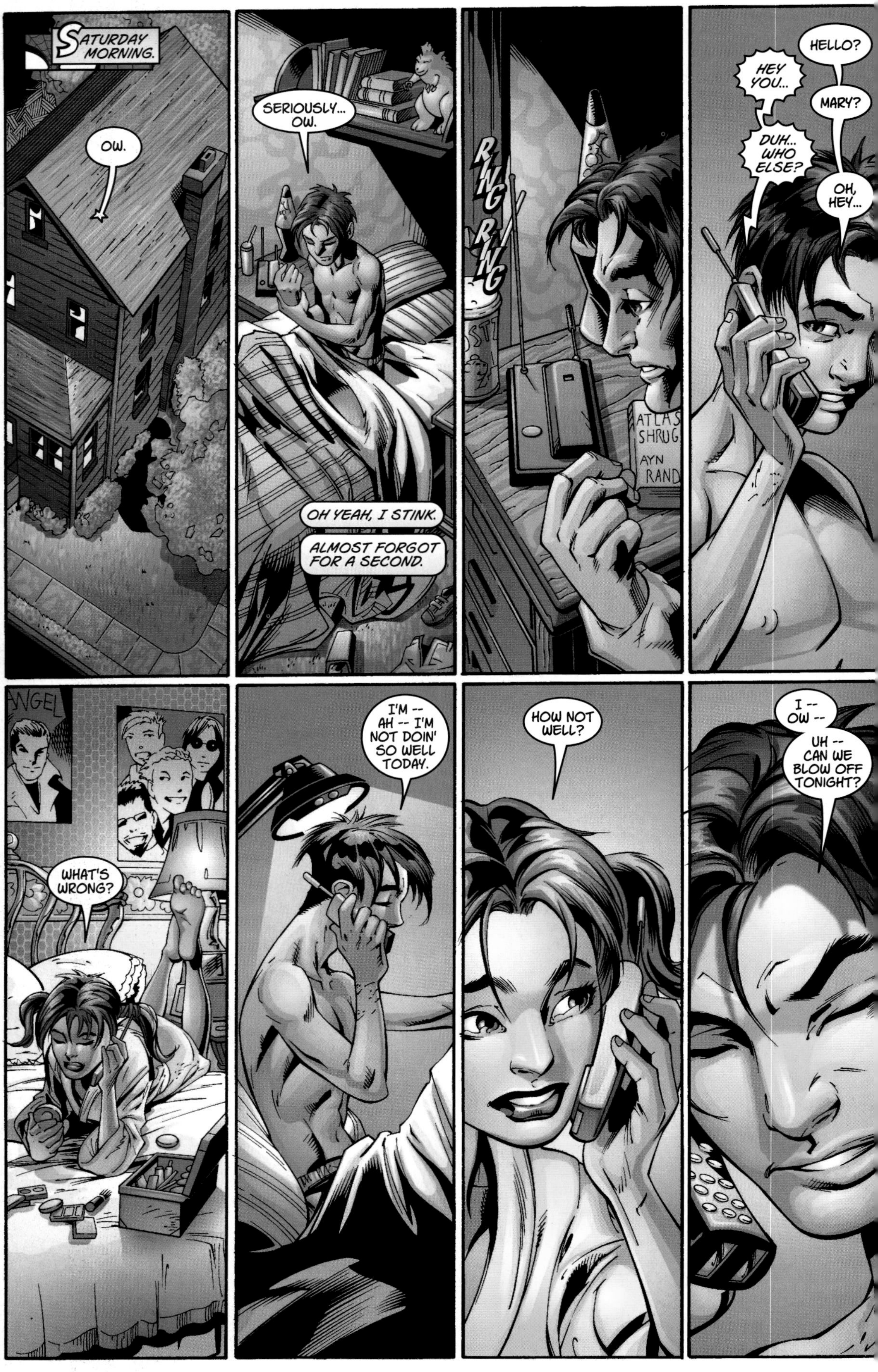
SATURDAY MORNING.
OW.
SERIOUSLY... OW.
OH YEAH, I STINK.
ALMOST FORGOT FOR A SECOND.
RING RING
ATLAS SHRUG AYN RAND
HELLO?
HEY YOU...
MARY?
DUH... WHO ELSE?
OH, HEY...
ANGEL
WHAT'S WRONG?
I'M -- AH -- I'M NOT DOIN' SO WELL TODAY.
HOW NOT WELL?
I -- OW --
UH -- CAN WE BLOW OFF TONIGHT?

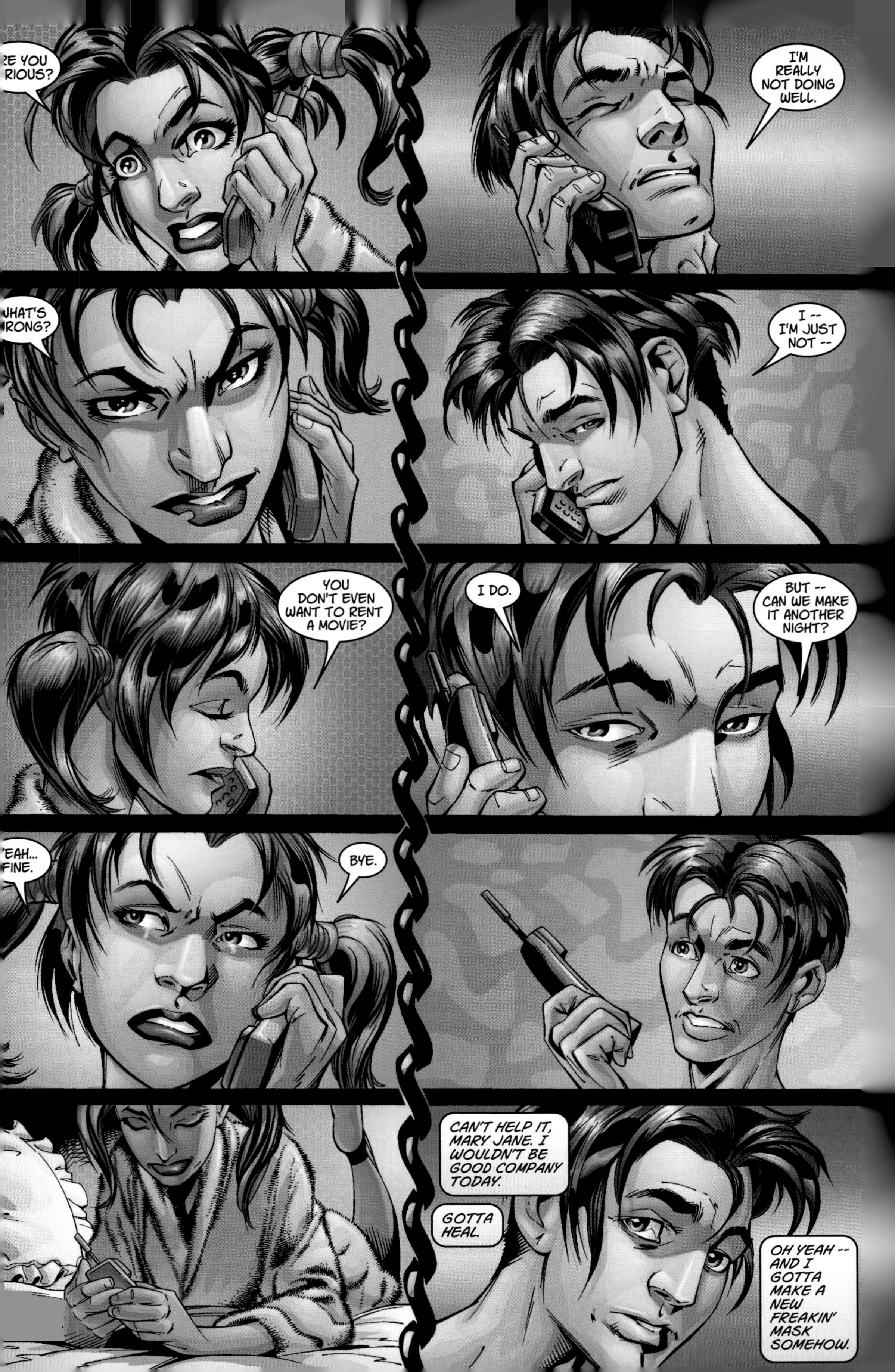
RE YOU
RIOUS?
I'M REALLY NOT DOING WELL.
WHAT'S
RONG?
I -- I'M JUST NOT --
YOU DON'T EVEN WANT TO RENT A MOVIE?
I DO.
BUT -- CAN WE MAKE IT ANOTHER NIGHT?
EAH...
FINE.
BYE.
CAN'T HELP IT, MARY JANE. I WOULDN'T BE GOOD COMPANY TODAY.
GOTTA HEAL.
OH YEAH -- AND I GOTTA MAKE A NEW FREAKIN' MASK SOMEHOW.

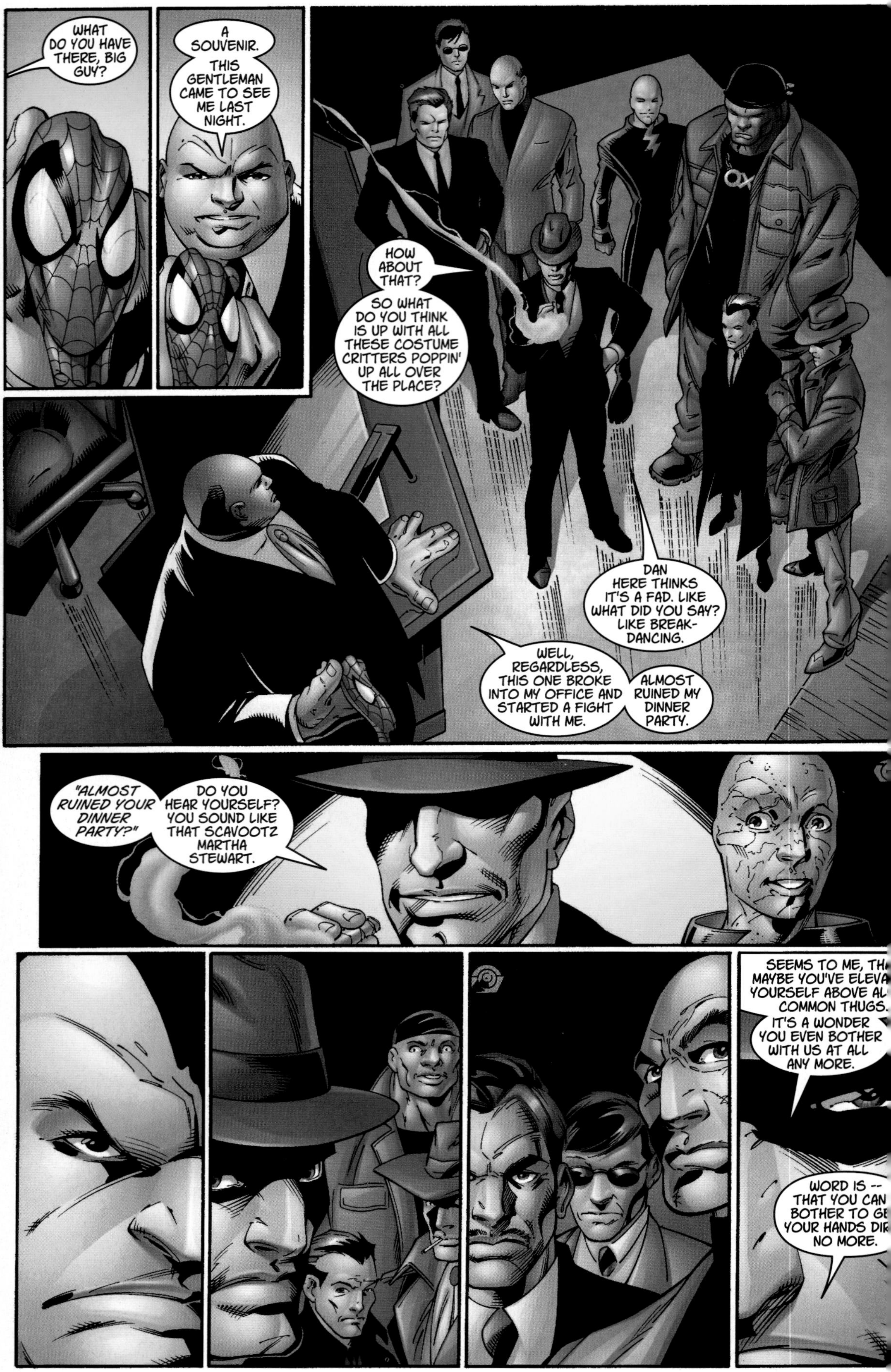
WHAT DO YOU HAVE THERE, BIG GUY?
A SOUVENIR.
THIS GENTLEMAN CAME TO SEE ME LAST NIGHT.
HOW ABOUT THAT?
SO WHAT DO YOU THINK IS UP WITH ALL THESE COSTUME CRITTERS POPPIN' UP ALL OVER THE PLACE?
DAN HERE THINKS IT'S A FAD. LIKE WHAT DID YOU SAY? LIKE BREAK-DANCING.
WELL, REGARDLESS, THIS ONE BROKE INTO MY OFFICE AND STARTED A FIGHT WITH ME.
ALMOST RUINED MY DINNER PARTY.
"ALMOST RUINED YOUR DINNER PARTY?"
DO YOU HEAR YOURSELF? YOU SOUND LIKE THAT SCAVOOTZ MARTHA STEWART.
SEEMS TO ME, TH MAYBE YOU'VE ELEVA YOURSELF ABOVE AL COMMON THUGS.
IT'S A WONDER YOU EVEN BOTHER WITH US AT ALL ANY MORE.
WORD IS -- THAT YOU CAN BOTHER TO GE YOUR HANDS DIR NO MORE.

AHH. FINALLY! HE TAKES A STAND.

I WAS WONDERING WHEN AND IF YOU'D EVER MUSTER THE GUTS TO DO IT.

MONTANA, OX, IF YOU'D BE SO KIND AS TO HOLD YOUR UNDERBOSS STEADY FOR ME, PLEASE.

TIME TO PICK A SIDE, BOYS.

NO.

COME ON, BOSS YOU UNDERSTAND...

YOU'RE RIGHT.

I DO HAVE A RATHER STRICT POLICY ABOUT GETTING MY HANDS DIRTY WITH THE SORDID NASTINESS OF THE DAY-TO-DAY.

THIS IS TRUE.

NO!

SO THIS IS HOW IT IS?! THIS IS HOW IT IS?!

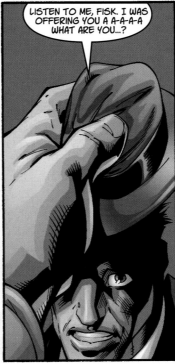

LISTEN TO ME, FISK. I WAS OFFERING YOU A A-A-A WHAT ARE YOU...?

WHAT -- WHAT ARE YOU DOING?!

WHAT ARE -- ? COME ON, FISK -- THIS -- THIS ISN'T WHAT I...

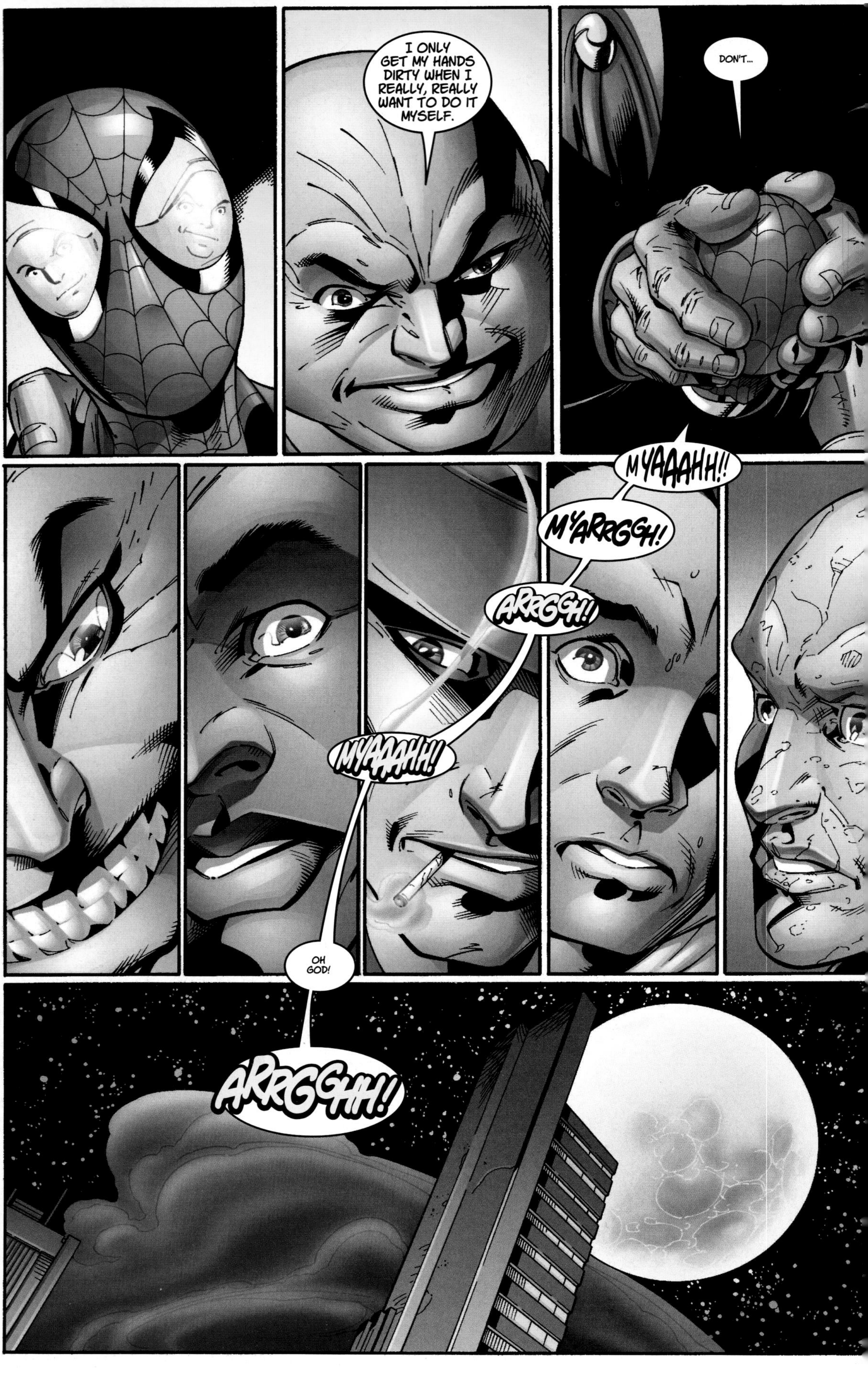

I ONLY GET MY HANDS DIRTY WHEN I REALLY, REALLY WANT TO DO IT MYSELF.
DON'T...
MYAAAHH!!
MYARRGGH!
ARRGGH!
MYAAAHH!
OH GOD!
ARRGGHH!

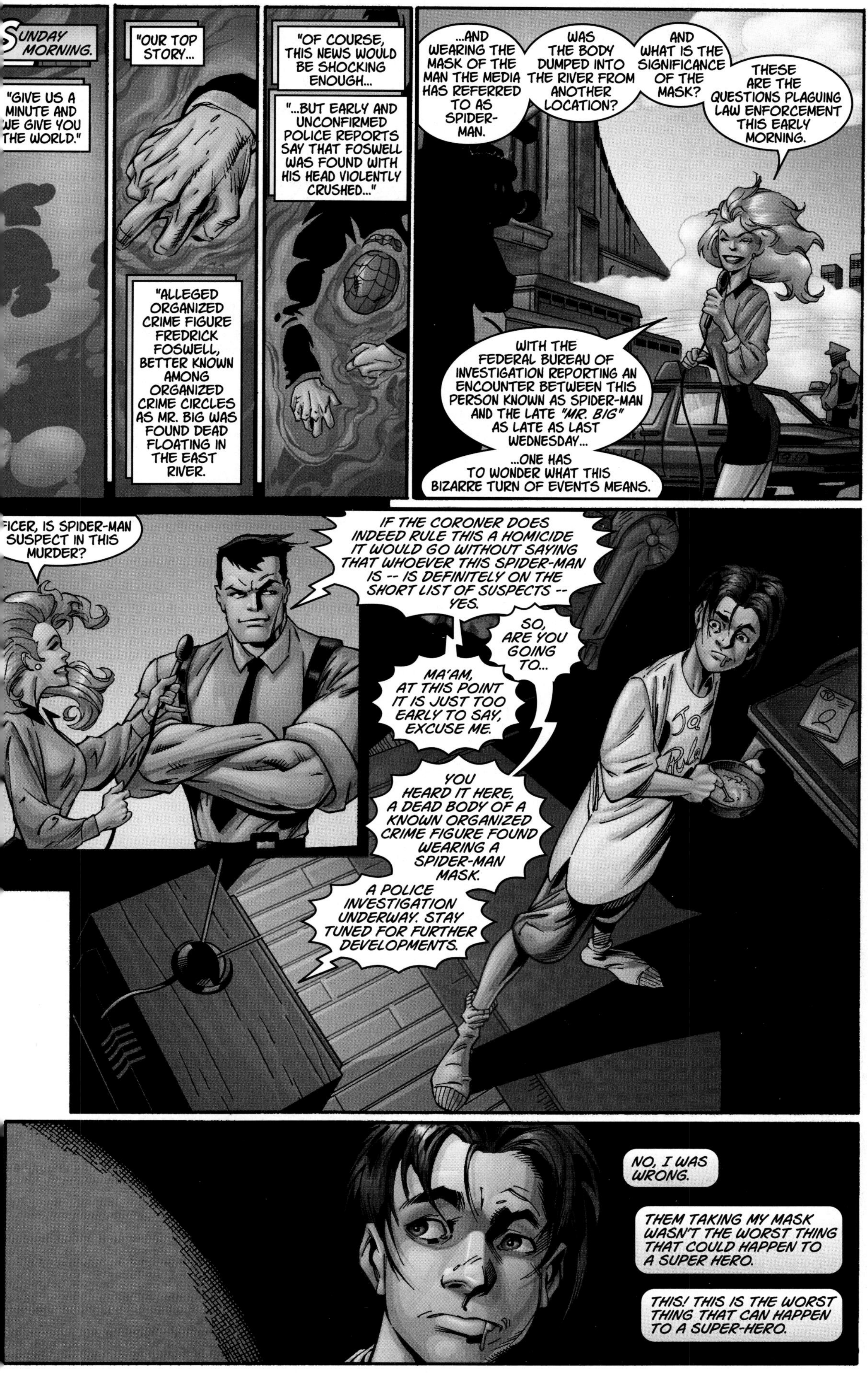
SUNDAY MORNING.
"GIVE US A MINUTE AND WE GIVE YOU THE WORLD."
"OUR TOP STORY...
"ALLEGED ORGANIZED CRIME FIGURE FREDRICK FOSWELL, BETTER KNOWN AMONG ORGANIZED CRIME CIRCLES AS MR. BIG WAS FOUND DEAD FLOATING IN THE EAST RIVER.
"OF COURSE, THIS NEWS WOULD BE SHOCKING ENOUGH...
"...BUT EARLY AND UNCONFIRMED POLICE REPORTS SAY THAT FOSWELL WAS FOUND WITH HIS HEAD VIOLENTLY CRUSHED..."
...AND WEARING THE MASK OF THE MAN THE MEDIA HAS REFERRED TO AS SPIDER-MAN.
WAS THE BODY DUMPED INTO THE RIVER FROM ANOTHER LOCATION?
AND WHAT IS THE SIGNIFICANCE OF THE MASK?
THESE ARE THE QUESTIONS PLAGUING LAW ENFORCEMENT THIS EARLY MORNING.
WITH THE FEDERAL BUREAU OF INVESTIGATION REPORTING AN ENCOUNTER BETWEEN THIS PERSON KNOWN AS SPIDER-MAN AND THE LATE "MR. BIG" AS LATE AS LAST WEDNESDAY...
...ONE HAS TO WONDER WHAT THIS BIZARRE TURN OF EVENTS MEANS.
FICER, IS SPIDER-MAN SUSPECT IN THIS MURDER?
IF THE CORONER DOES INDEED RULE THIS A HOMICIDE IT WOULD GO WITHOUT SAYING THAT WHOEVER THIS SPIDER-MAN IS -- IS DEFINITELY ON THE SHORT LIST OF SUSPECTS -- YES.
SO, ARE YOU GOING TO...
MA'AM, AT THIS POINT IT IS JUST TOO EARLY TO SAY, EXCUSE ME.
YOU HEARD IT HERE, A DEAD BODY OF A KNOWN ORGANIZED CRIME FIGURE FOUND WEARING A SPIDER-MAN MASK.
A POLICE INVESTIGATION UNDERWAY. STAY TUNED FOR FURTHER DEVELOPMENTS.
NO, I WAS WRONG.
THEM TAKING MY MASK WASN'T THE WORST THING THAT COULD HAPPEN TO A SUPER HERO.
THIS! THIS IS THE WORST THING THAT CAN HAPPEN TO A SUPER-HERO.

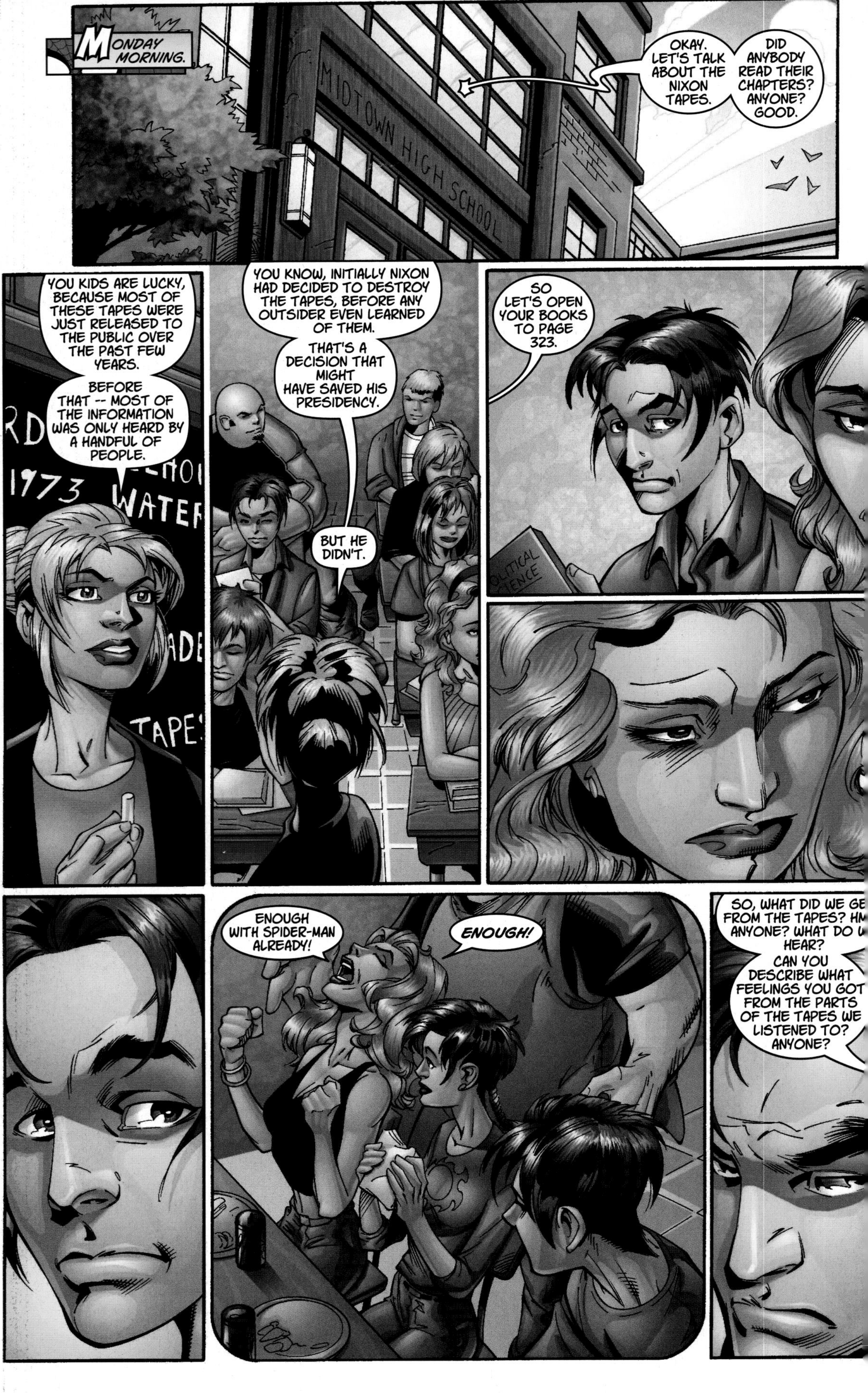
MONDAY MORNING.
MIDTOWN HIGH SCHOOL
OKAY. LET'S TALK ABOUT THE NIXON TAPES.
DID ANYBODY READ THEIR CHAPTERS? ANYONE? GOOD.
YOU KIDS ARE LUCKY, BECAUSE MOST OF THESE TAPES WERE JUST RELEASED TO THE PUBLIC OVER THE PAST FEW YEARS.
BEFORE THAT -- MOST OF THE INFORMATION WAS ONLY HEARD BY A HANDFUL OF PEOPLE.
1973
WATER
TAPES
YOU KNOW, INITIALLY NIXON HAD DECIDED TO DESTROY THE TAPES, BEFORE ANY OUTSIDER EVEN LEARNED OF THEM.
THAT'S A DECISION THAT MIGHT HAVE SAVED HIS PRESIDENCY.
BUT HE DIDN'T.
SO LET'S OPEN YOUR BOOKS TO PAGE 323.
ENOUGH WITH SPIDER-MAN ALREADY!
ENOUGH!
SO, WHAT DID WE GE FROM THE TAPES? HM ANYONE? WHAT DO W HEAR?
CAN YOU DESCRIBE WHAT FEELINGS YOU GOT FROM THE PARTS OF THE TAPES WE LISTENED TO? ANYONE?

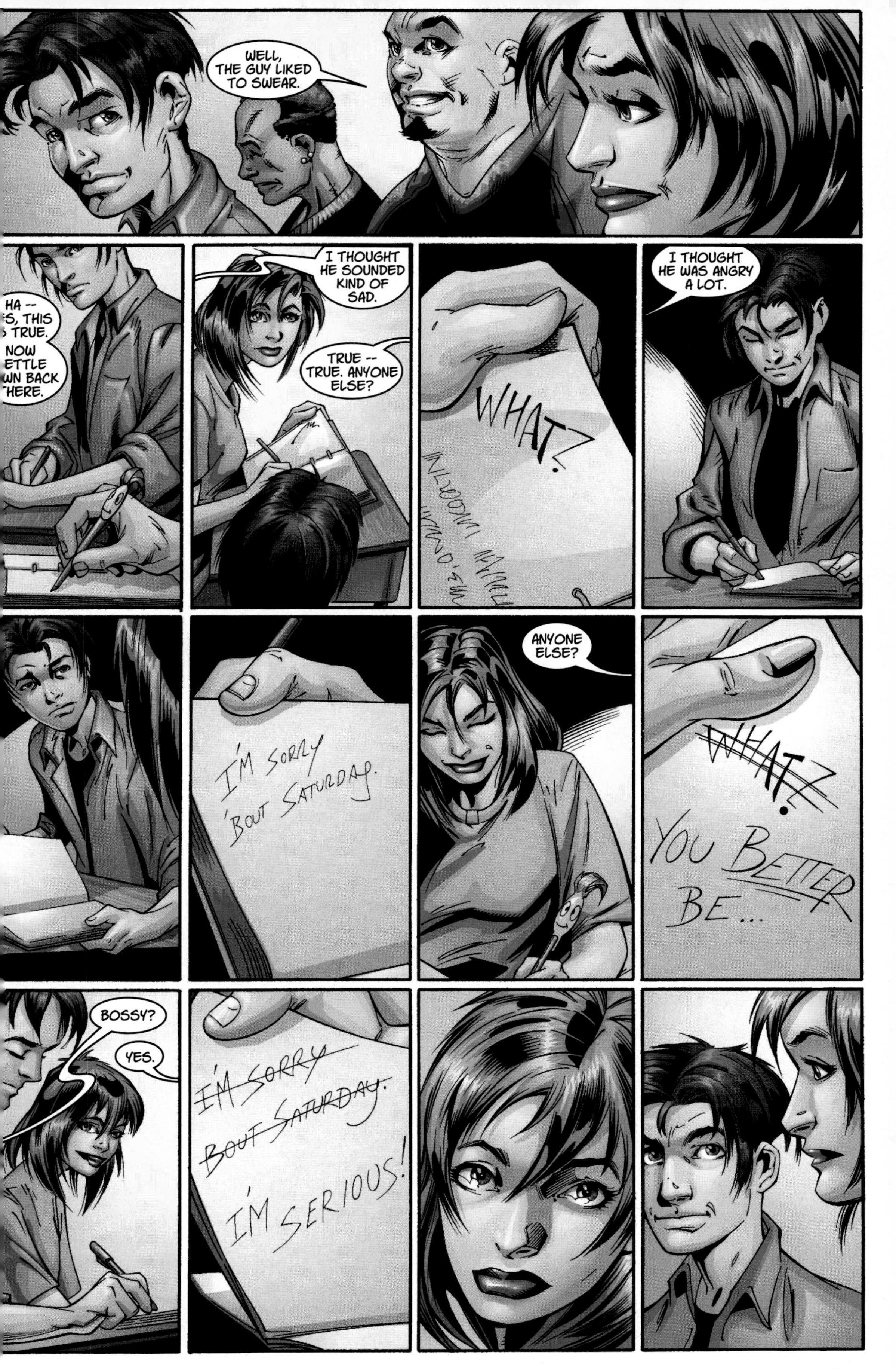
WELL, THE GUY LIKED TO SWEAR.
HA --
I THOUGHT HE SOUNDED KIND OF SAD.
TRUE -- TRUE. ANYONE ELSE?
WHAT?
I THOUGHT HE WAS ANGRY A LOT.
I'M SORRY 'BOUT SATURDAY.
ANYONE ELSE?
WHAT?
YOU BETTER BE...
BOSSY?
YES.
I'M SORRY 'BOUT SATURDAY.
I'M SERIOUS!

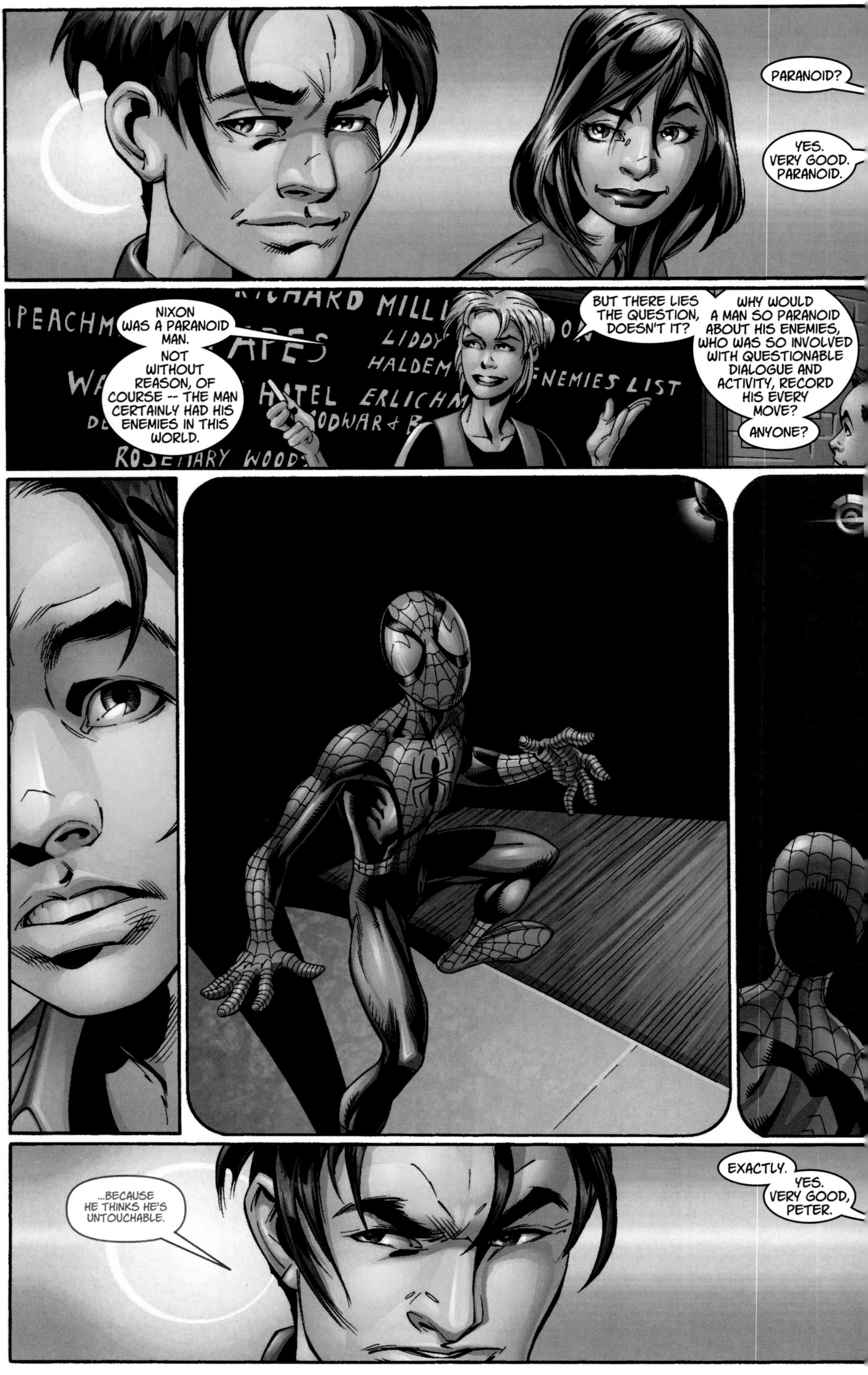
PARANOID?
YES. VERY GOOD. PARANOID.
RICHARD MILLI
IPEACHM
APES
LIDDY
HALDEM
WA
HOTEL
ERLICHM
ENEMIES LIST
ODWAR & B
ROSEMARY WOODS
NIXON WAS A PARANOID MAN.
NOT WITHOUT REASON, OF COURSE -- THE MAN CERTAINLY HAD HIS ENEMIES IN THIS WORLD.
BUT THERE LIES THE QUESTION, DOESN'T IT?
WHY WOULD A MAN SO PARANOID ABOUT HIS ENEMIES, WHO WAS SO INVOLVED WITH QUESTIONABLE DIALOGUE AND ACTIVITY, RECORD HIS EVERY MOVE?
ANYONE?
...BECAUSE HE THINKS HE'S UNTOUCHABLE.
EXACTLY.
YES. VERY GOOD, PETER.

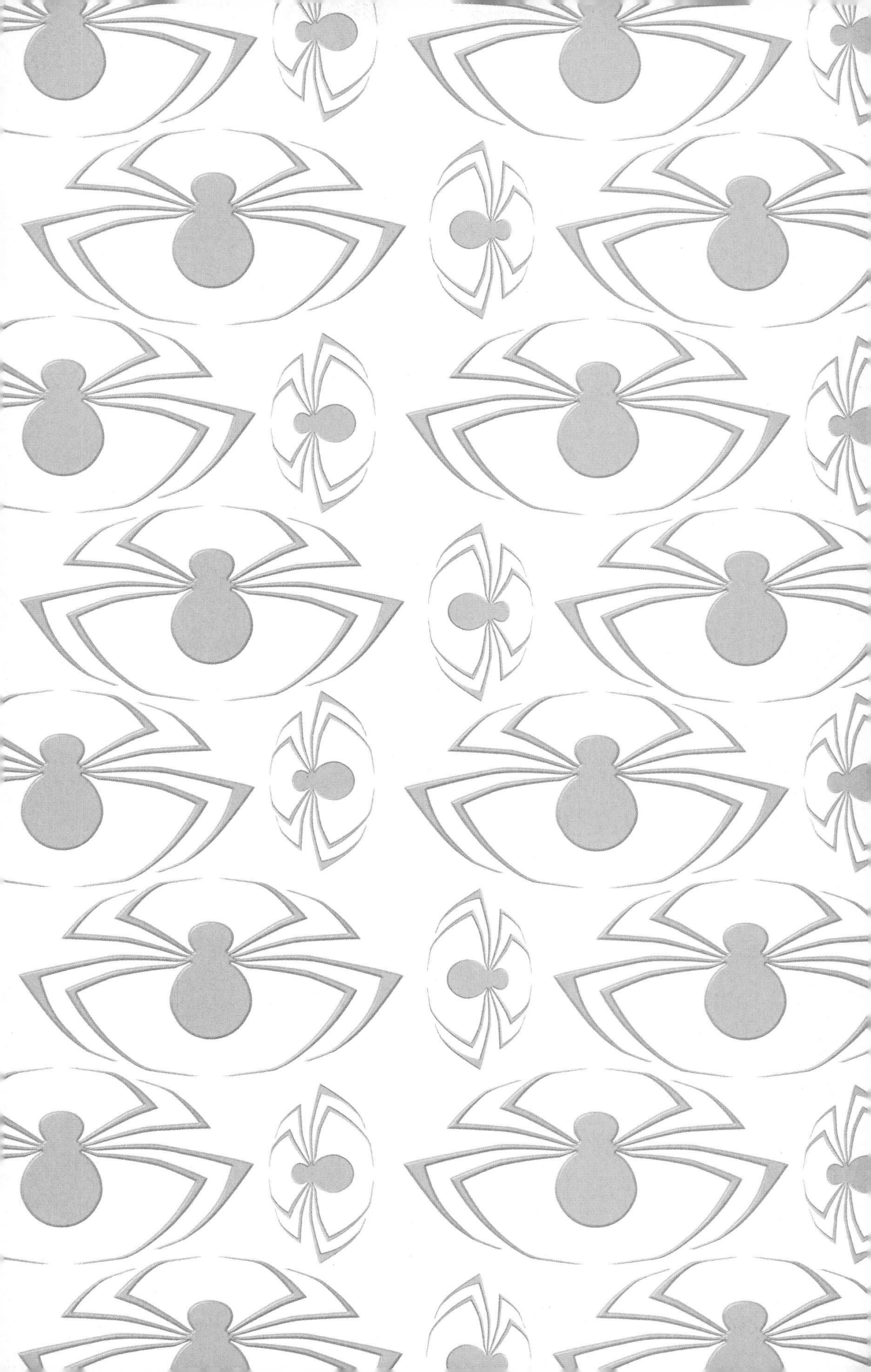

11

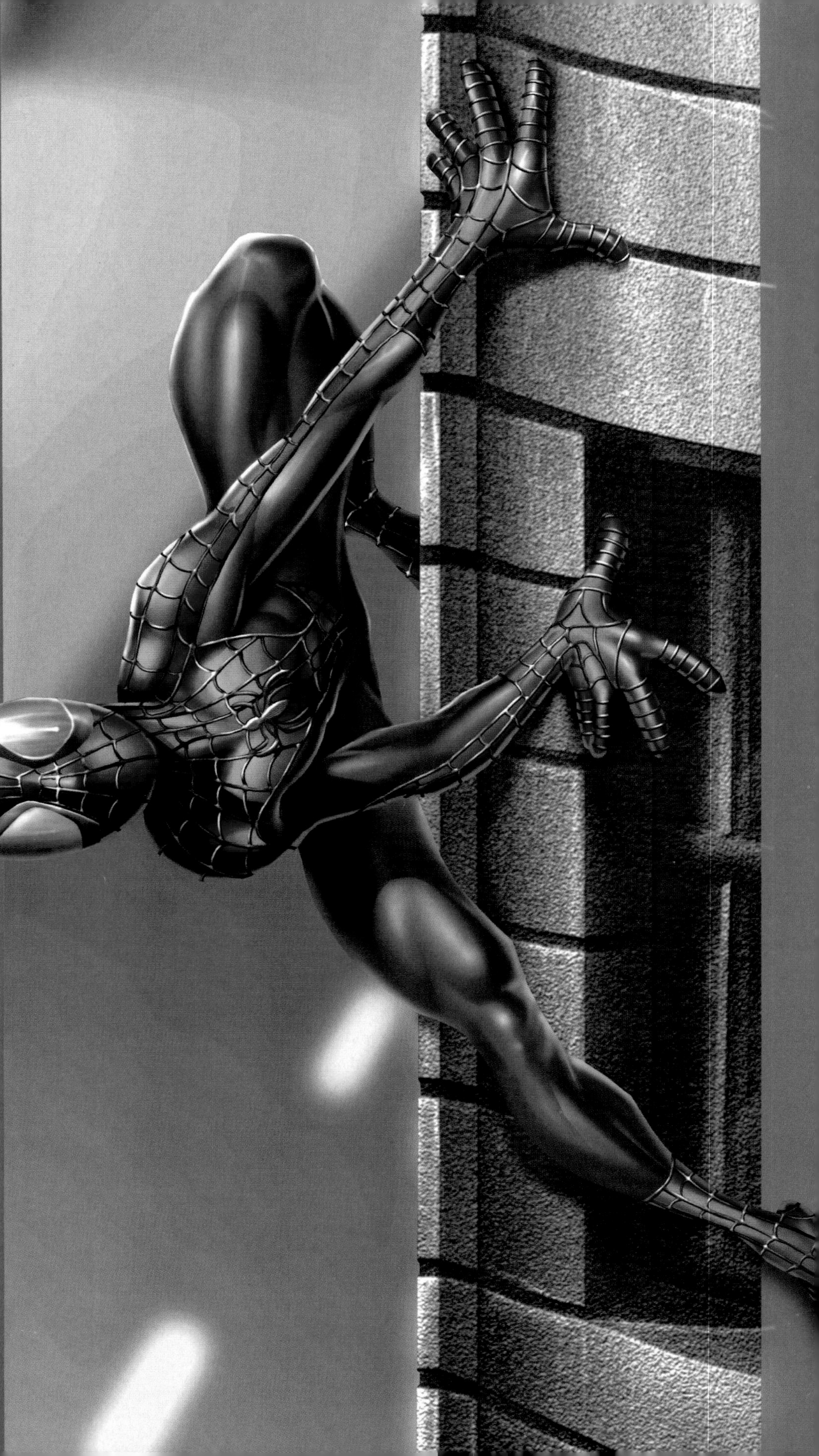

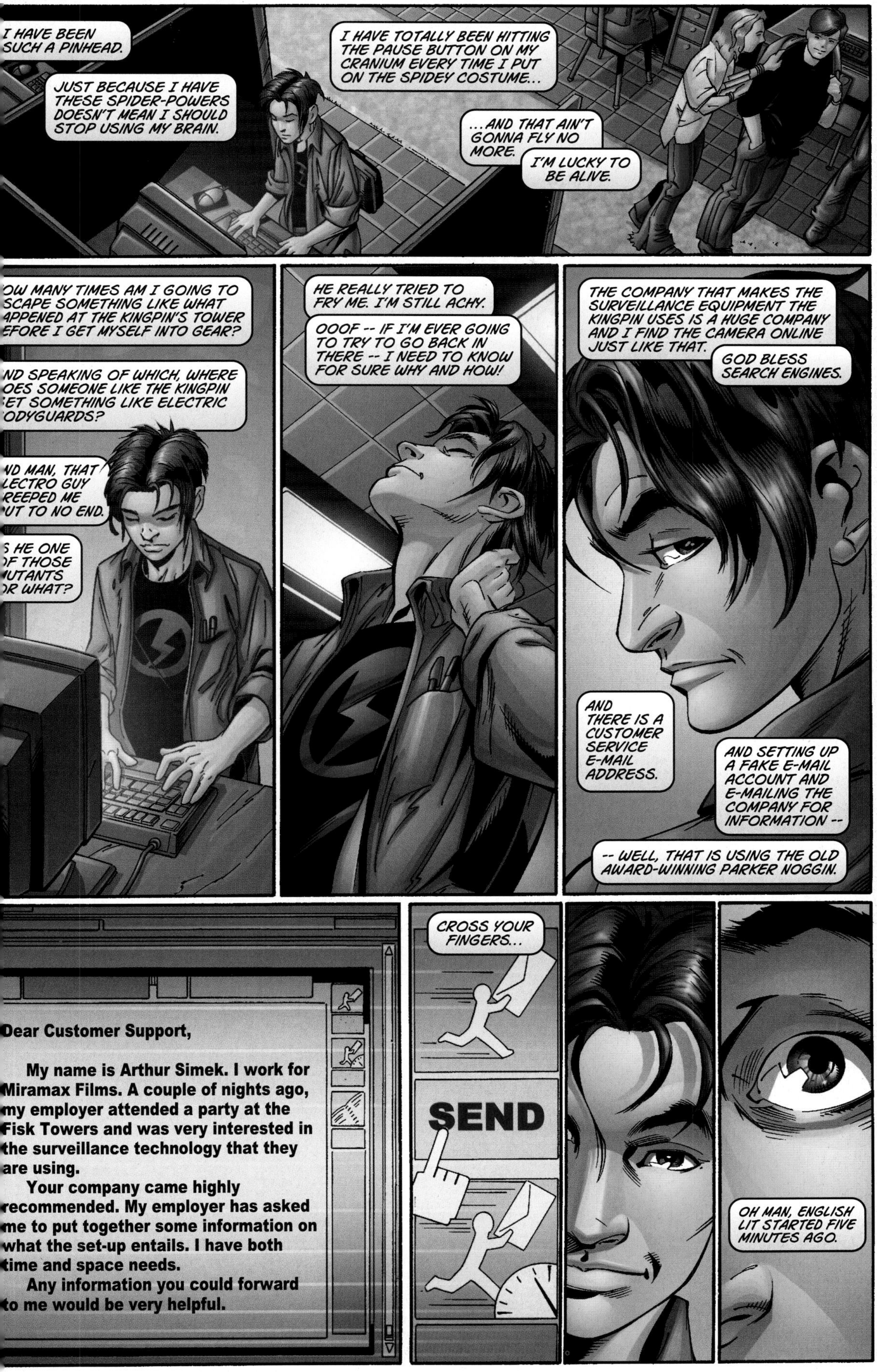
I HAVE BEEN SUCH A PINHEAD.
JUST BECAUSE I HAVE THESE SPIDER-POWERS DOESN'T MEAN I SHOULD STOP USING MY BRAIN.
I HAVE TOTALLY BEEN HITTING THE PAUSE BUTTON ON MY CRANIUM EVERY TIME I PUT ON THE SPIDEY COSTUME...
...AND THAT AIN'T GONNA FLY NO MORE.
I'M LUCKY TO BE ALIVE.
OW MANY TIMES AM I GOING TO SCAPE SOMETHING LIKE WHAT APPENED AT THE KINGPIN'S TOWER EFORE I GET MYSELF INTO GEAR?
ND SPEAKING OF WHICH, WHERE OES SOMEONE LIKE THE KINGPIN ET SOMETHING LIKE ELECTRIC ODYGUARDS?
ND MAN, THAT LECTRO GUY REEPED ME UT TO NO END.
S HE ONE F THOSE UTANTS R WHAT?
HE REALLY TRIED TO FRY ME. I'M STILL ACHY.
OOOF -- IF I'M EVER GOING TO TRY TO GO BACK IN THERE -- I NEED TO KNOW FOR SURE WHY AND HOW!
THE COMPANY THAT MAKES THE SURVEILLANCE EQUIPMENT THE KINGPIN USES IS A HUGE COMPANY AND I FIND THE CAMERA ONLINE JUST LIKE THAT.
GOD BLESS SEARCH ENGINES.
AND THERE IS A CUSTOMER SERVICE E-MAIL ADDRESS.
AND SETTING UP A FAKE E-MAIL ACCOUNT AND E-MAILING THE COMPANY FOR INFORMATION --
-- WELL, THAT IS USING THE OLD AWARD-WINNING PARKER NOGGIN.
Dear Customer Support,
My name is Arthur Simek. I work for Miramax Films. A couple of nights ago, my employer attended a party at the Fisk Towers and was very interested in the surveillance technology that they are using.
Your company came highly recommended. My employer has asked me to put together some information on what the set-up entails. I have both time and space needs.
Any information you could forward to me would be very helpful.
CROSS YOUR FINGERS...
SEND
OH MAN, ENGLISH LIT STARTED FIVE MINUTES AGO.

HI, PETER. MY NAME IS DOCTOR BRADLEY.

PLEASE -- PLEASE, SIT DOWN.

HERE?

ANYWHERE YOU LIKE.

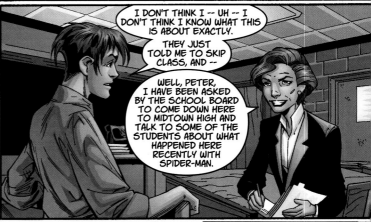

I DON'T THINK I -- UH -- I DON'T THINK I KNOW WHAT THIS IS ABOUT EXACTLY.

THEY JUST TOLD ME TO SKIP CLASS, AND --

WELL, PETER, I HAVE BEEN ASKED BY THE SCHOOL BOARD TO COME DOWN HERE TO MIDTOWN HIGH AND TALK TO SOME OF THE STUDENTS ABOUT WHAT HAPPENED HERE RECENTLY WITH SPIDER-MAN.

UH -- WHAT?

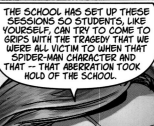

THE SCHOOL HAS SET UP THESE SESSIONS SO STUDENTS, LIKE YOURSELF, CAN TRY TO COME TO GRIPS WITH THE TRAGEDY THAT WE WERE ALL VICTIM TO WHEN THAT SPIDER-MAN CHARACTER AND THAT -- THAT ABERRATION TOOK HOLD OF THE SCHOOL.

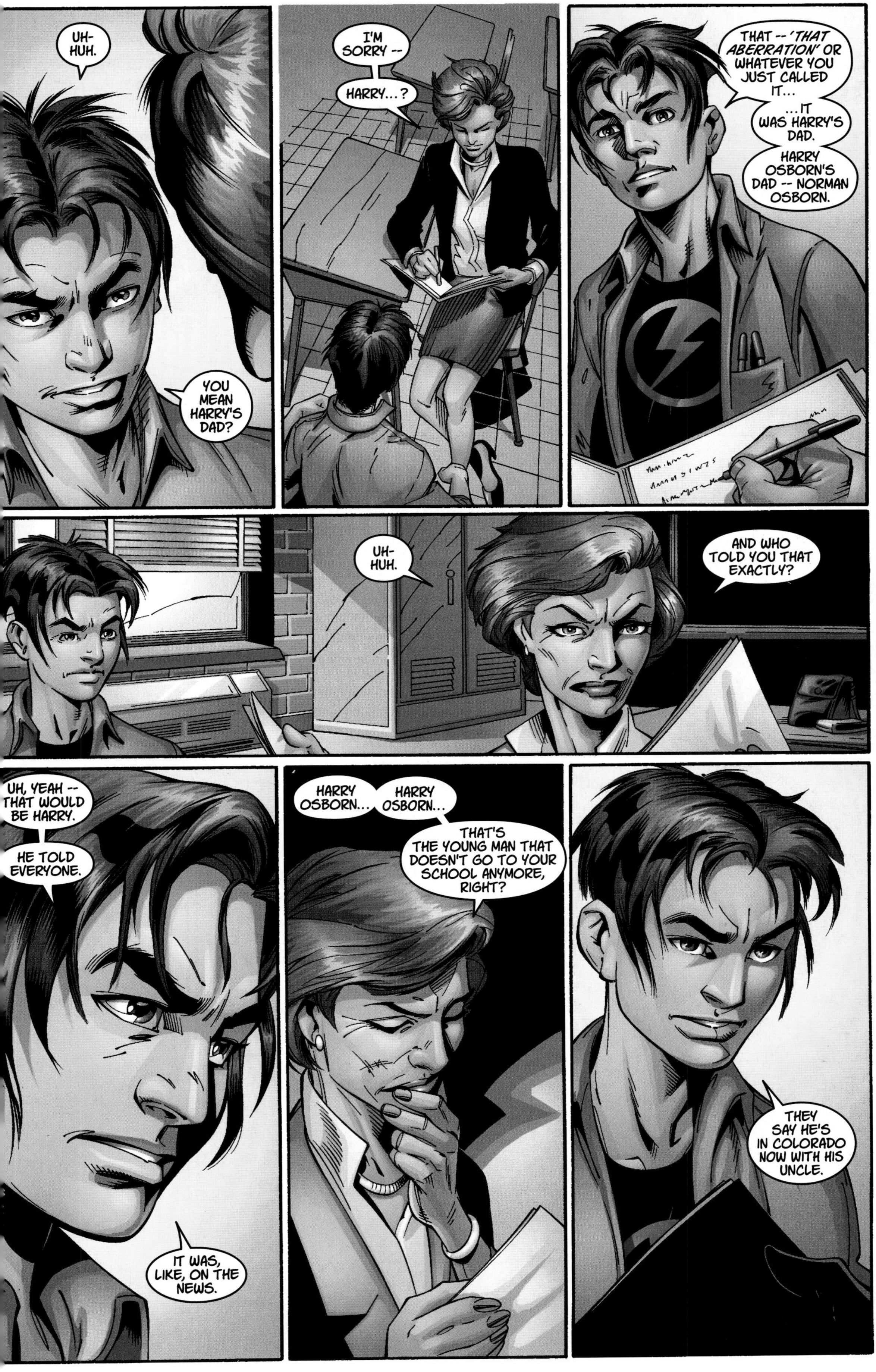

UH-HUH.
YOU MEAN HARRY'S DAD?
I'M SORRY --
HARRY...?
THAT -- '*THAT ABERRATION*' OR WHATEVER YOU JUST CALLED IT...
...IT WAS HARRY'S DAD.
HARRY OSBORN'S DAD -- NORMAN OSBORN.
UH-HUH.
AND WHO TOLD YOU THAT EXACTLY?
UH, YEAH -- THAT WOULD BE HARRY.
HE TOLD EVERYONE.
IT WAS, LIKE, ON THE NEWS.
HARRY OSBORN...
HARRY OSBORN...
THAT'S THE YOUNG MAN THAT DOESN'T GO TO YOUR SCHOOL ANYMORE, RIGHT?
THEY SAY HE'S IN COLORADO NOW WITH HIS UNCLE.

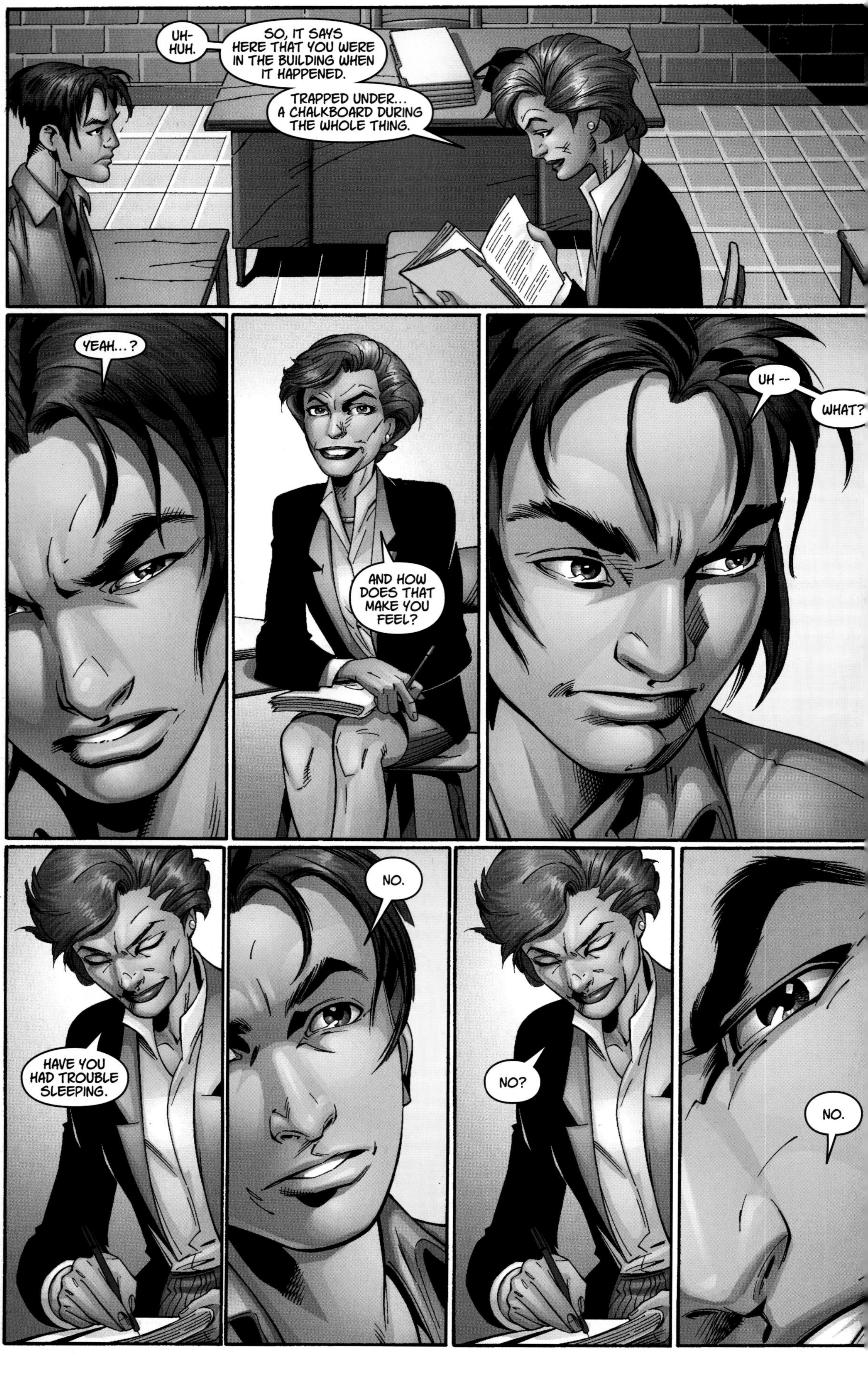

UH-HUH.
SO, IT SAYS HERE THAT YOU WERE IN THE BUILDING WHEN IT HAPPENED.
TRAPPED UNDER... A CHALKBOARD DURING THE WHOLE THING.
YEAH...?
AND HOW DOES THAT MAKE YOU FEEL?
UH --
WHAT?
HAVE YOU HAD TROUBLE SLEEPING.
NO.
NO?
NO.

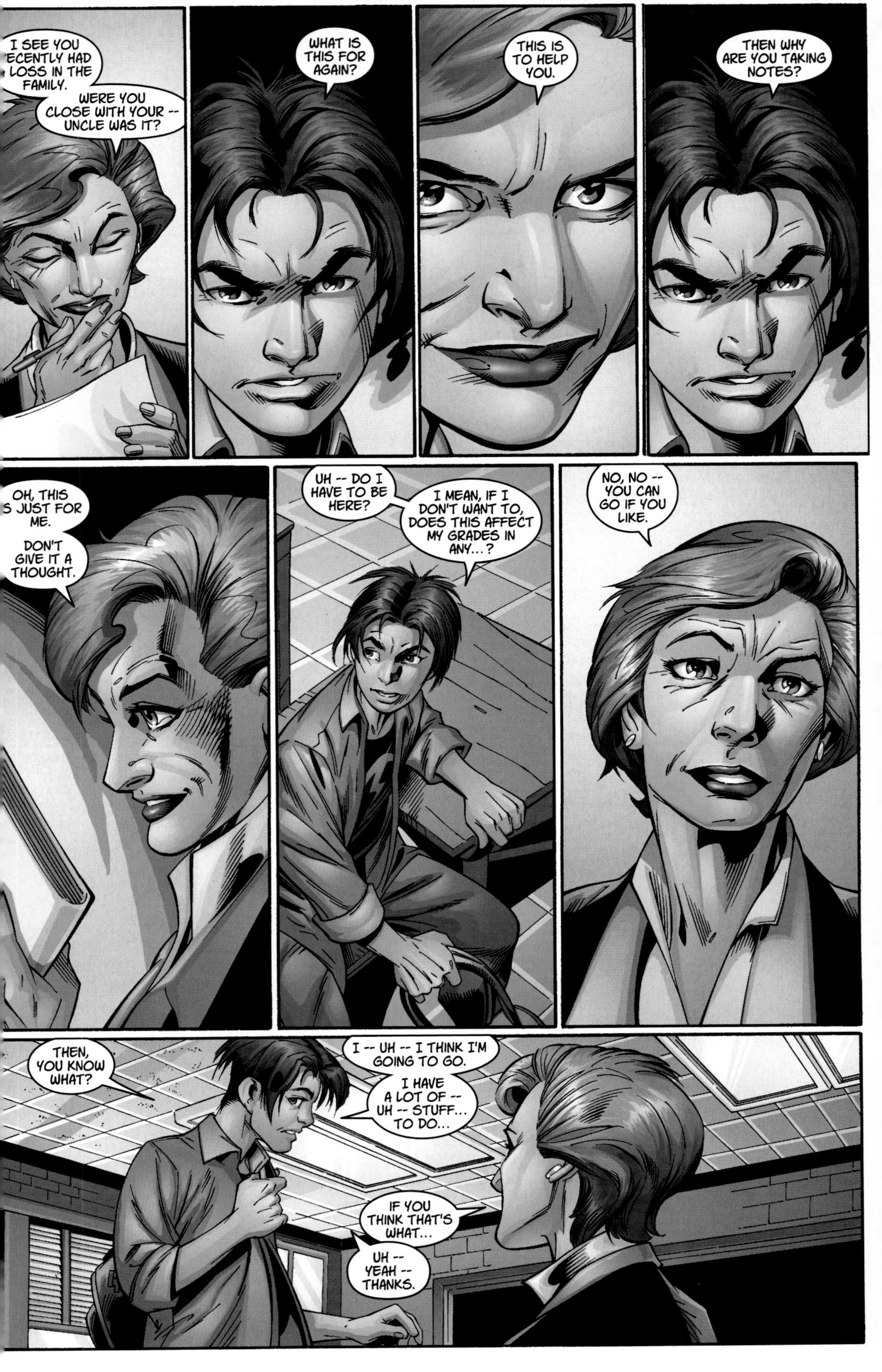
I SEE YOU
ECENTLY HAD
LOSS IN THE
FAMILY.
WERE YOU CLOSE WITH YOUR -- UNCLE WAS IT?
WHAT IS THIS FOR AGAIN?
THIS IS TO HELP YOU.
THEN WHY ARE YOU TAKING NOTES?
OH, THIS
S JUST FOR
ME.
DON'T GIVE IT A THOUGHT.
UH -- DO I HAVE TO BE HERE?
I MEAN, IF I DON'T WANT TO, DOES THIS AFFECT MY GRADES IN ANY...?
NO, NO -- YOU CAN GO IF YOU LIKE.
THEN, YOU KNOW WHAT?
I -- UH -- I THINK I'M GOING TO GO.
I HAVE A LOT OF -- UH -- STUFF... TO DO...
IF YOU THINK THAT'S WHAT...
UH -- YEAH -- THANKS.

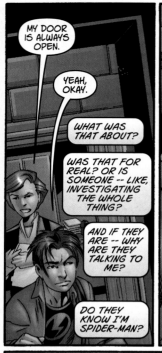

MY DOOR IS ALWAYS OPEN.

YEAH, OKAY.

WHAT WAS THAT ABOUT?

WAS THAT FOR REAL? OR IS SOMEONE -- LIKE, INVESTIGATING THE WHOLE THING?

AND IF THEY ARE -- WHY ARE THEY TALKING TO ME?

DO THEY KNOW I'M SPIDER-MAN?

LIKE I DON'T HAVE ENOUGH TO WORRY ABOUT WITH THE KINGPIN --

-- NOW I HAVE TO -- HEY...

OH HEY, LIZ...

HI, PETER.

THEY CALL YOU DOWN HERE TOO?

YEAH. WHAT'S THIS ABOUT ANYWAY?

I -- UH -- I DON'T KNOW. SOMEONE COVERING THEIR BUTT OR SOMETHING...

YOU OKAY?

I -- UH --

Y'KNOW? I DON'T REALL KNOW.

I DON'T KNOW.

KEEP OUT

WELL, YOU EVER, LIKE, WANT TO TALK ABOUT IT OR --

THAT'S NICE.

MAYBE, BUT --

BUT NOT TODAY IF THAT'S COOL.

OKAY.

YOU MUST BE LIZ ALLEN.

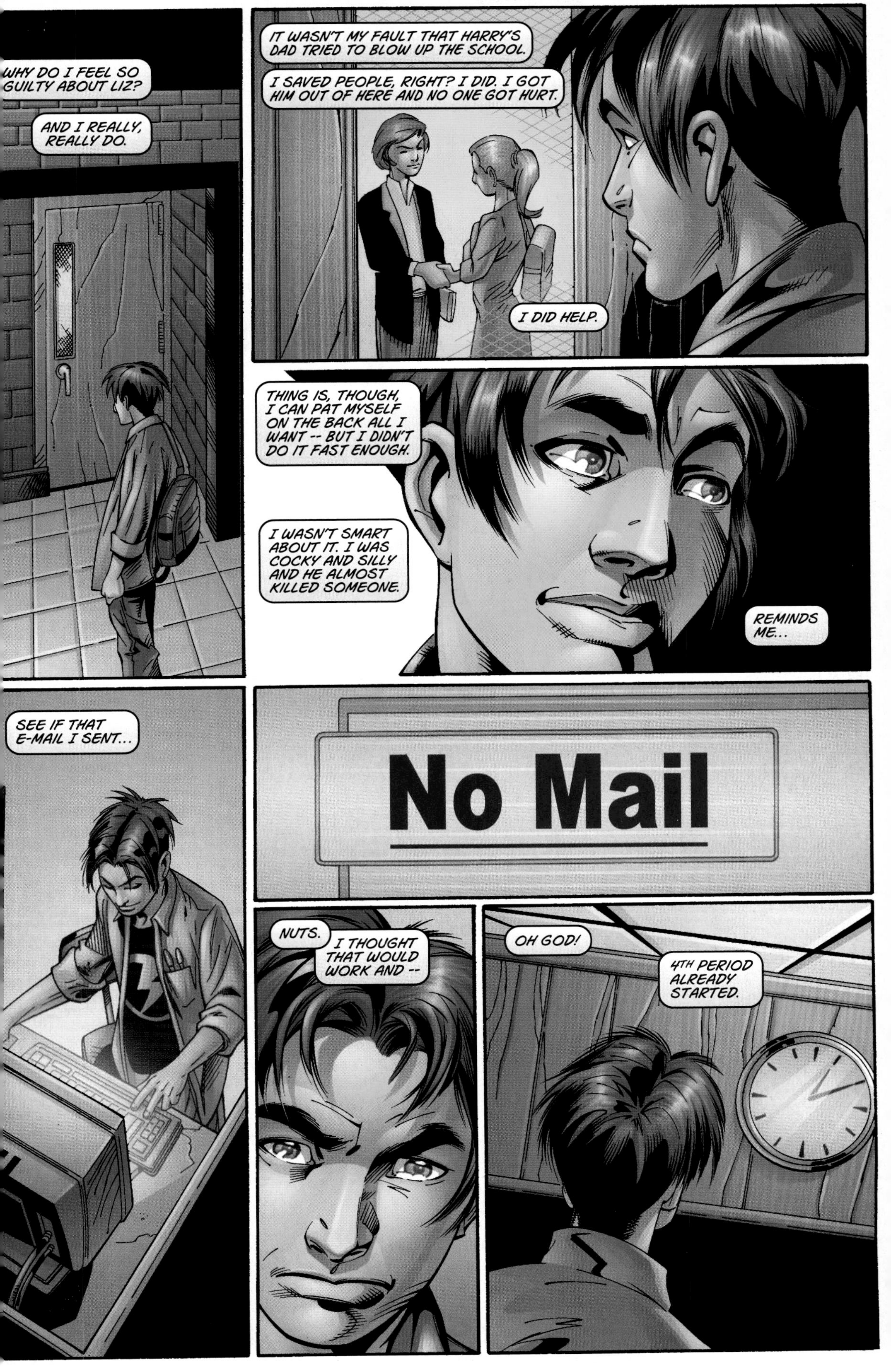
WHY DO I FEEL SO GUILTY ABOUT LIZ?
AND I REALLY, REALLY DO.
IT WASN'T MY FAULT THAT HARRY'S DAD TRIED TO BLOW UP THE SCHOOL.
I SAVED PEOPLE, RIGHT? I DID. I GOT HIM OUT OF HERE AND NO ONE GOT HURT.
I DID HELP.
THING IS, THOUGH, I CAN PAT MYSELF ON THE BACK ALL I WANT -- BUT I DIDN'T DO IT FAST ENOUGH.
I WASN'T SMART ABOUT IT. I WAS COCKY AND SILLY AND HE ALMOST KILLED SOMEONE.
REMINDS ME...
SEE IF THAT E-MAIL I SENT...
No Mail
NUTS.
I THOUGHT THAT WOULD WORK AND --
OH GOD!
4TH PERIOD ALREADY STARTED.

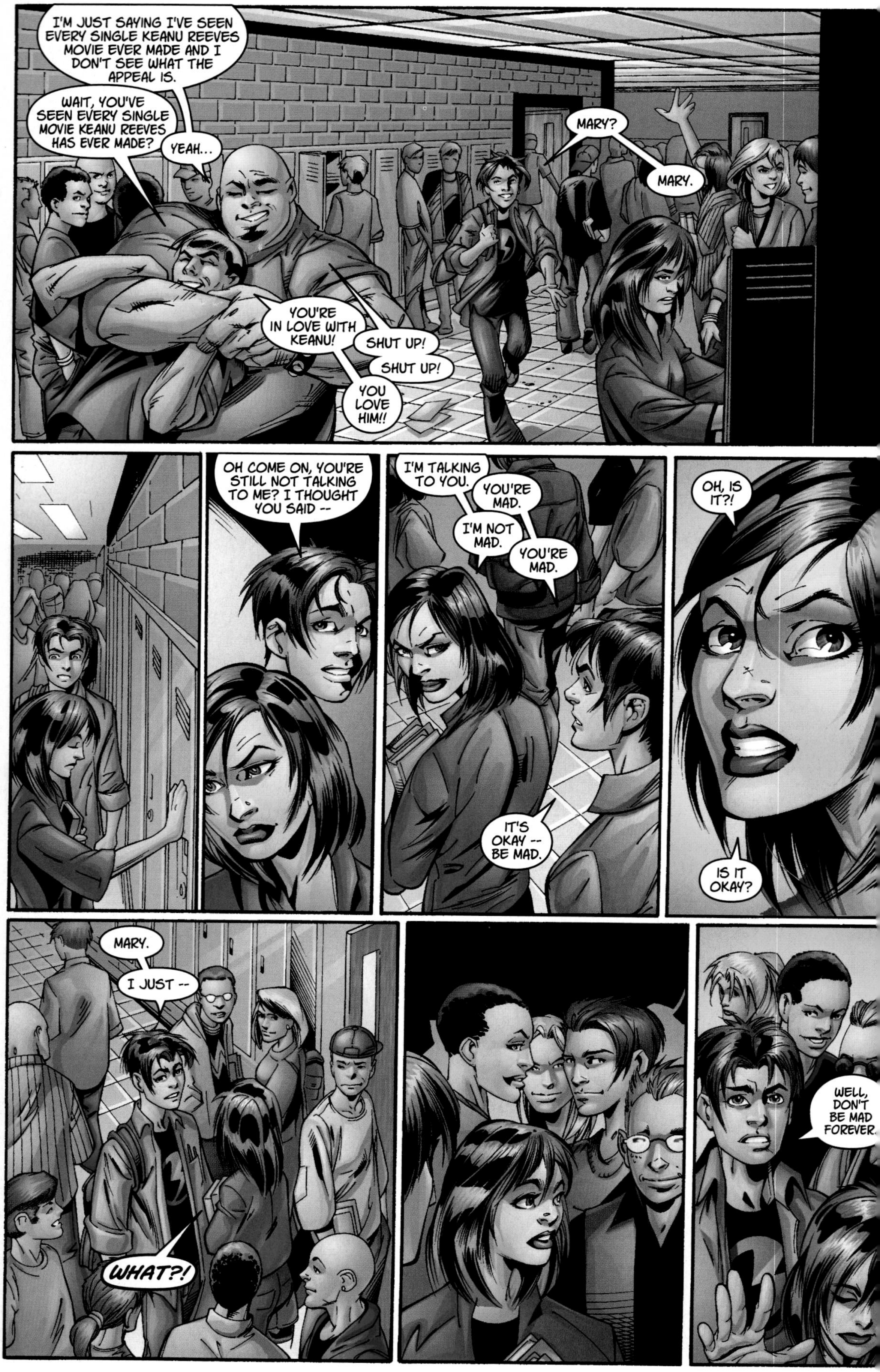
I'M JUST SAYING I'VE SEEN EVERY SINGLE KEANU REEVES MOVIE EVER MADE AND I DON'T SEE WHAT THE APPEAL IS.
WAIT, YOU'VE SEEN EVERY SINGLE MOVIE KEANU REEVES HAS EVER MADE?
YEAH...
YOU'RE IN LOVE WITH KEANU!
SHUT UP!
SHUT UP!
YOU LOVE HIM!!
MARY?
MARY.
OH COME ON, YOU'RE STILL NOT TALKING TO ME? I THOUGHT YOU SAID --
I'M TALKING TO YOU.
YOU'RE MAD.
I'M NOT MAD.
YOU'RE MAD.
IT'S OKAY -- BE MAD.
OH, IS IT?!
IS IT OKAY?
MARY.
I JUST --
WHAT?!
WELL, DON'T BE MAD FOREVER.

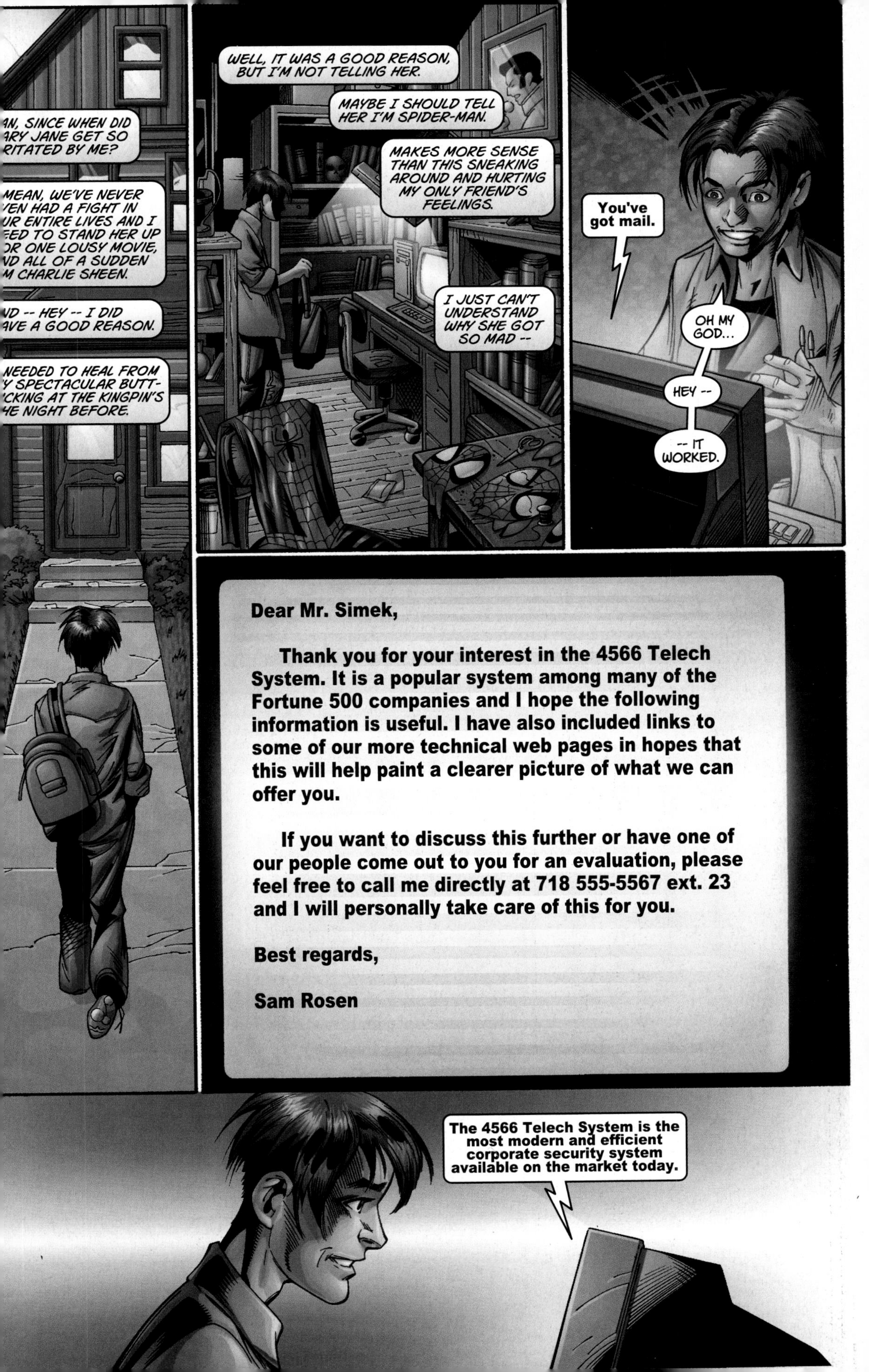

AN, SINCE WHEN DID
ARY JANE GET SO
RITATED BY ME?
MEAN, WE'VE NEVER
VEN HAD A FIGHT IN
UR ENTIRE LIVES AND I
EED TO STAND HER UP
OR ONE LOUSY MOVIE,
ND ALL OF A SUDDEN
M CHARLIE SHEEN.
ND -- HEY -- I DID
AVE A GOOD REASON.
NEEDED TO HEAL FROM
Y SPECTACULAR BUTT-
CKING AT THE KINGPIN'S
HE NIGHT BEFORE.
WELL, IT WAS A GOOD REASON, BUT I'M NOT TELLING HER.
MAYBE I SHOULD TELL HER I'M SPIDER-MAN.
MAKES MORE SENSE THAN THIS SNEAKING AROUND AND HURTING MY ONLY FRIEND'S FEELINGS.
I JUST CAN'T UNDERSTAND WHY SHE GOT SO MAD --
You've got mail.
OH MY GOD...
HEY --
-- IT WORKED.
Dear Mr. Simek,
Thank you for your interest in the 4566 Telech System. It is a popular system among many of the Fortune 500 companies and I hope the following information is useful. I have also included links to some of our more technical web pages in hopes that this will help paint a clearer picture of what we can offer you.
If you want to discuss this further or have one of our people come out to you for an evaluation, please feel free to call me directly at 718 555-5567 ext. 23 and I will personally take care of this for you.
Best regards,
Sam Rosen
The 4566 Telech System is the most modern and efficient corporate security system available on the market today.

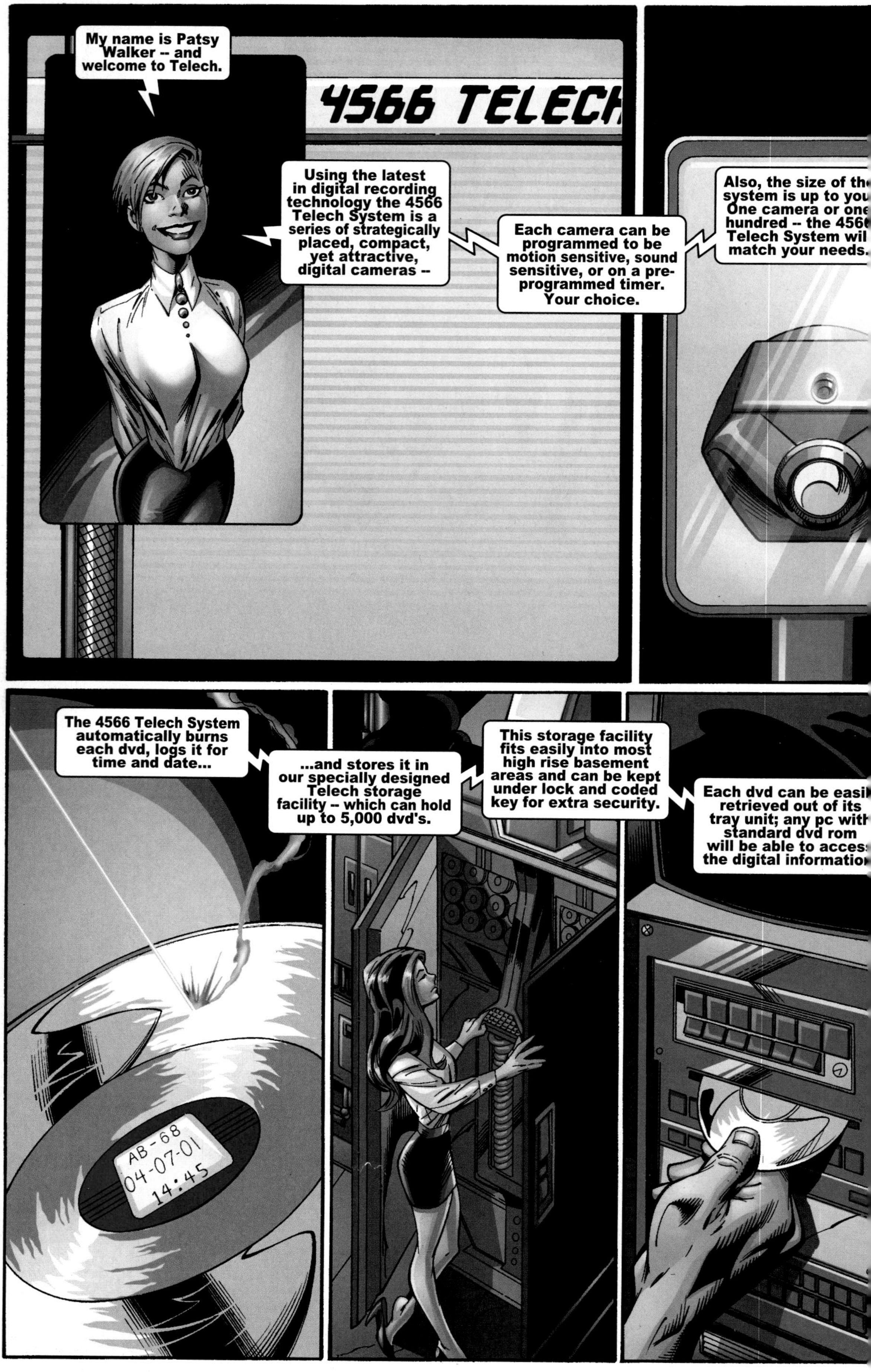

My name is Patsy Walker -- and welcome to Telech.
4566 TELECH
Using the latest in digital recording technology the 4566 Telech System is a series of strategically placed, compact, yet attractive, digital cameras --
Each camera can be programmed to be motion sensitive, sound sensitive, or on a pre-programmed timer. Your choice.
Also, the size of the system is up to you. One camera or one hundred -- the 4566 Telech System will match your needs.
The 4566 Telech System automatically burns each dvd, logs it for time and date...
AB-68 04-07-01 14:45
...and stores it in our specially designed Telech storage facility -- which can hold up to 5,000 dvd's.
This storage facility fits easily into most high rise basement areas and can be kept under lock and coded key for extra security.
Each dvd can be easily retrieved out of its tray unit; any pc with standard dvd rom will be able to access the digital information

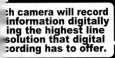
ch camera will record
information digitally
ing the highest line
solution that digital
cording has to offer.

Crisp, clear
picture and
sound.

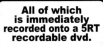
All of which
is immediately
recorded onto a 5RT
recordable dvd.

Each dvd can store
anywhere up to 12
hours of information.

he Telech System also
fers multi screen video
rveillance for use with
on site security staff.

Whether you have security
needs or just want to record
your board meetings for
accuracy or posterity...

4566 TELECH

...the 4566 Telech
System will meet
your needs.

Thank you for listening.
Hit reload to start the
presentation over.

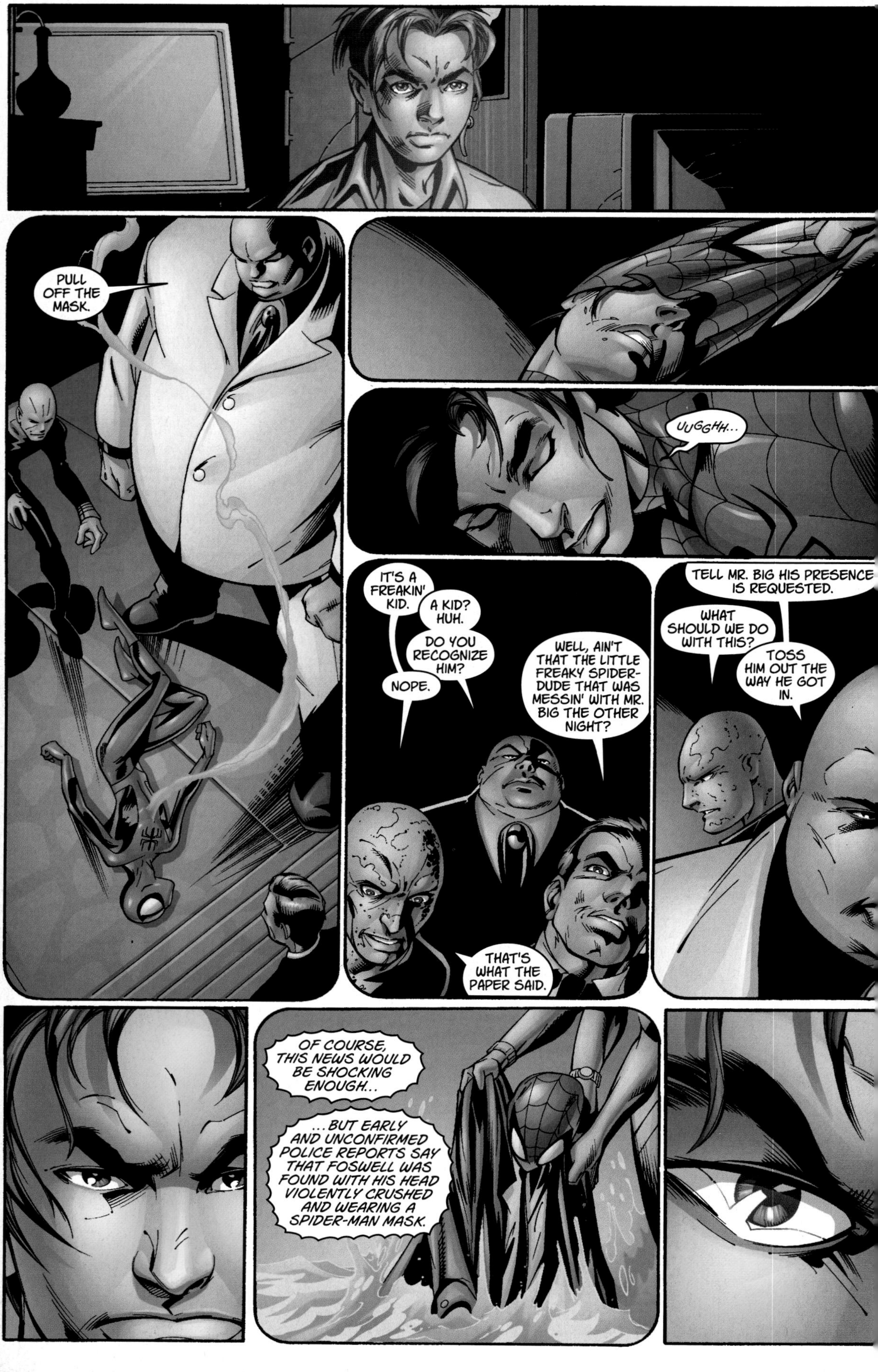
PULL OFF THE MASK.
UUGGHH...
IT'S A FREAKIN' KID.
A KID? HUH.
DO YOU RECOGNIZE HIM?
NOPE.
WELL, AIN'T THAT THE LITTLE FREAKY SPIDER-DUDE THAT WAS MESSIN' WITH MR. BIG THE OTHER NIGHT?
THAT'S WHAT THE PAPER SAID.
TELL MR. BIG HIS PRESENCE IS REQUESTED.
WHAT SHOULD WE DO WITH THIS?
TOSS HIM OUT THE WAY HE GOT IN.
OF COURSE, THIS NEWS WOULD BE SHOCKING ENOUGH...
...BUT EARLY AND UNCONFIRMED POLICE REPORTS SAY THAT FOSWELL WAS FOUND WITH HIS HEAD VIOLENTLY CRUSHED AND WEARING A SPIDER-MAN MASK.

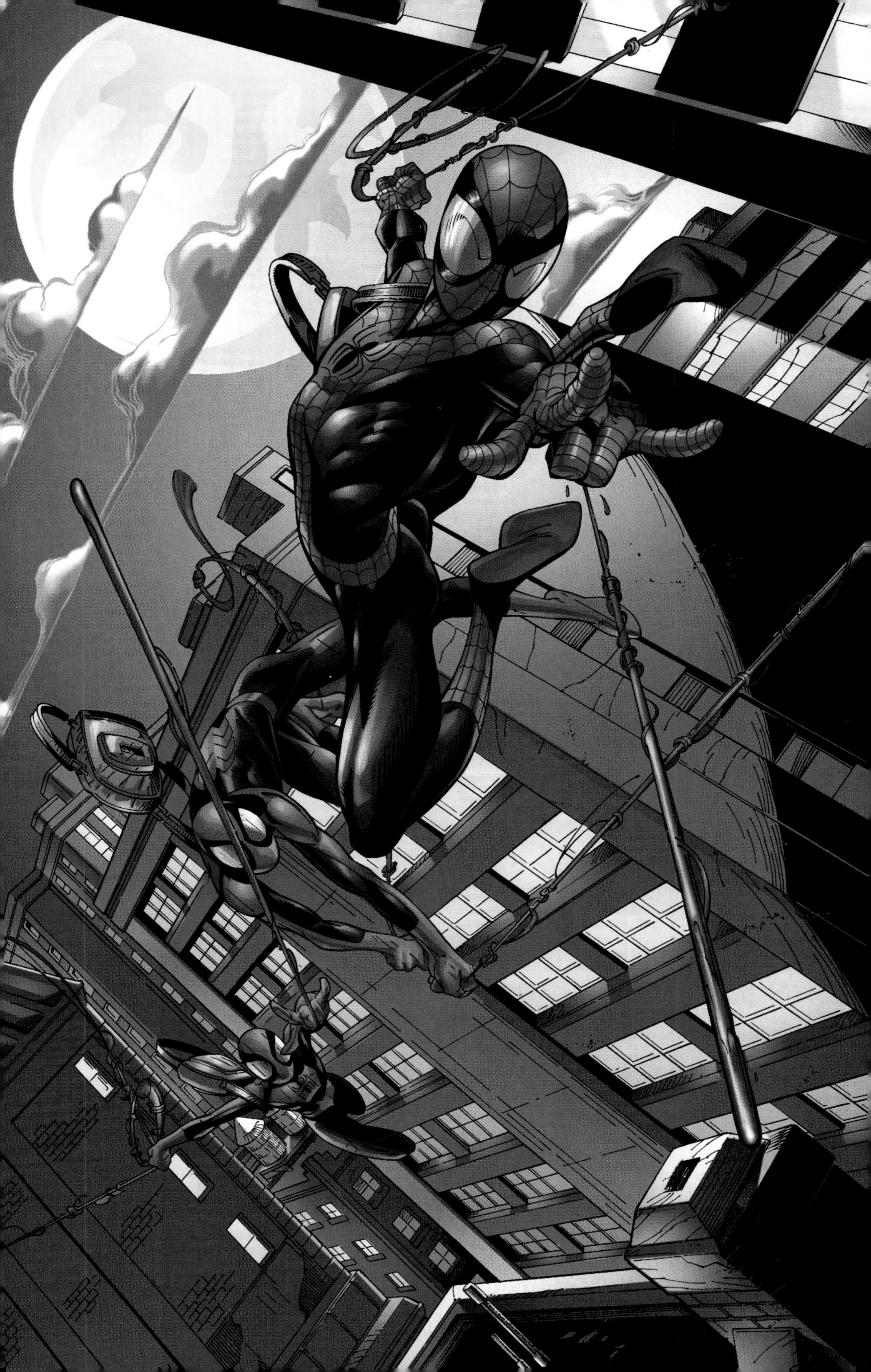

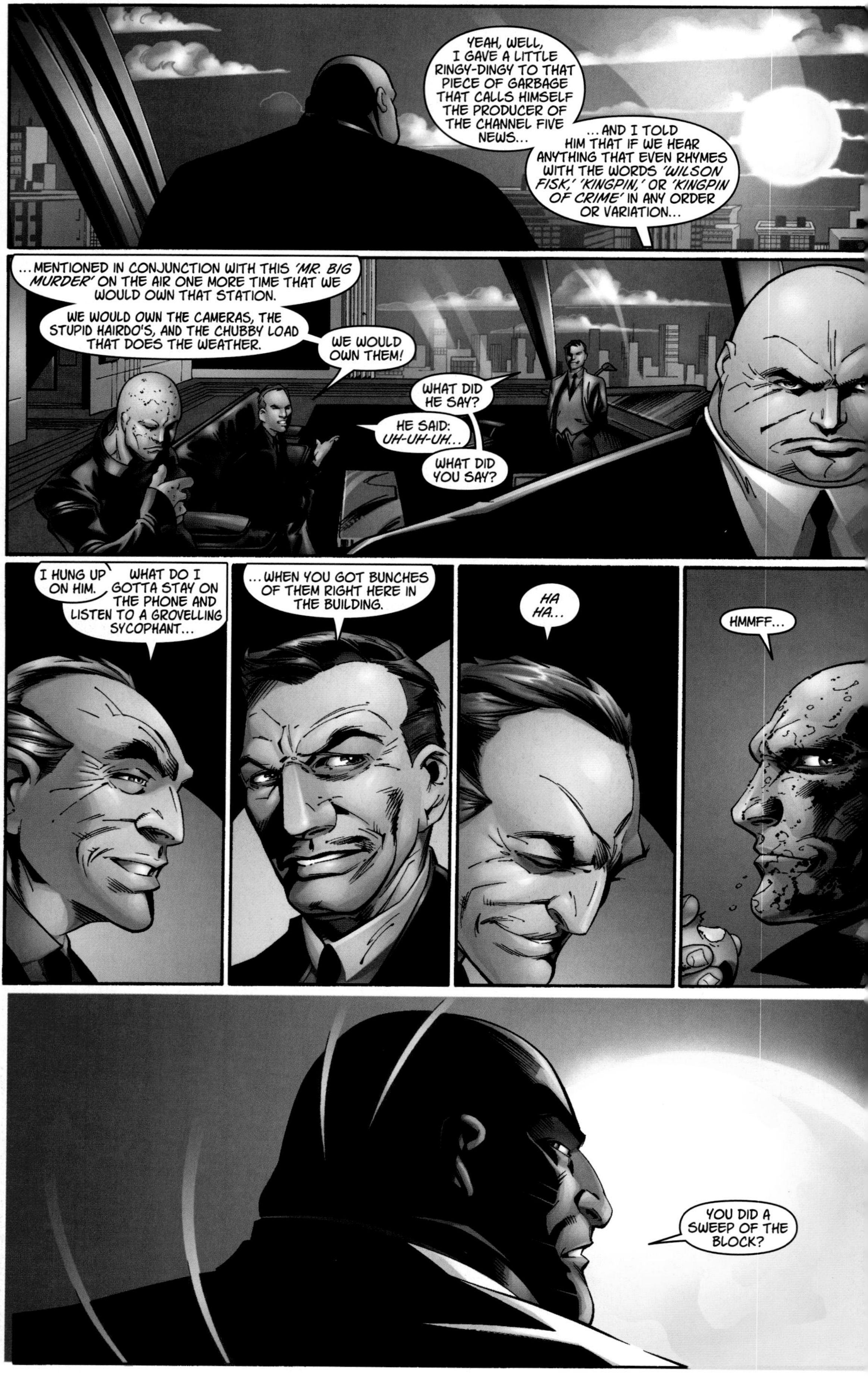
YEAH, WELL, I GAVE A LITTLE RINGY-DINGY TO THAT PIECE OF GARBAGE THAT CALLS HIMSELF THE PRODUCER OF THE CHANNEL FIVE NEWS...
...AND I TOLD HIM THAT IF WE HEAR ANYTHING THAT EVEN RHYMES WITH THE WORDS *'WILSON FISK,' 'KINGPIN,'* OR *'KINGPIN OF CRIME'* IN ANY ORDER OR VARIATION...
...MENTIONED IN CONJUNCTION WITH THIS *'MR. BIG MURDER'* ON THE AIR ONE MORE TIME THAT WE WOULD OWN THAT STATION.
WE WOULD OWN THE CAMERAS, THE STUPID HAIRDO'S, AND THE CHUBBY LOAD THAT DOES THE WEATHER.
WE WOULD OWN THEM!
WHAT DID HE SAY?
HE SAID: *UH-UH-UH...*
WHAT DID YOU SAY?
I HUNG UP ON HIM.
WHAT DO I GOTTA STAY ON THE PHONE AND LISTEN TO A GROVELLING SYCOPHANT...
...WHEN YOU GOT BUNCHES OF THEM RIGHT HERE IN THE BUILDING.
HA HA...
HMMFF...
YOU DID A SWEEP OF THE BLOCK?

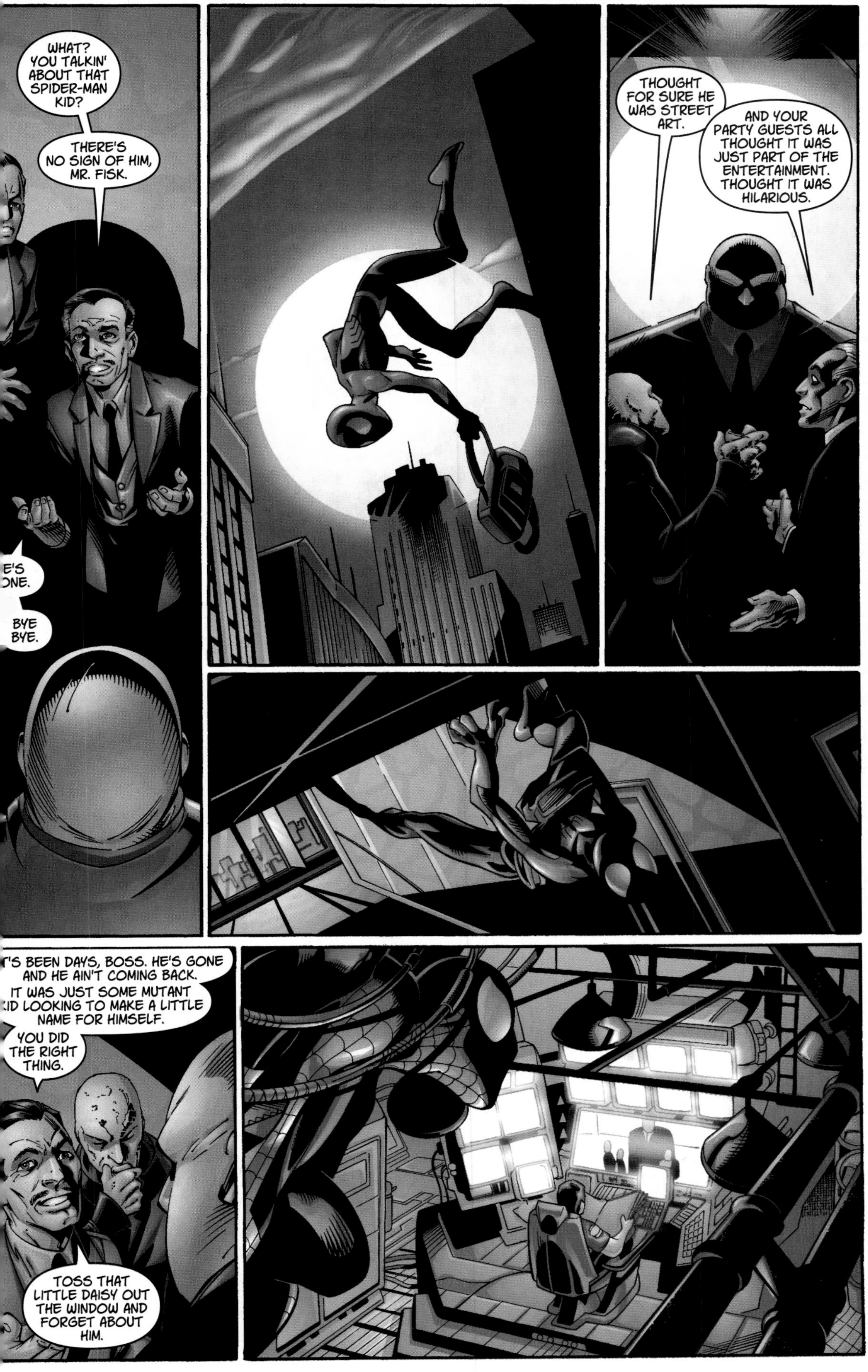
WHAT? YOU TALKIN' ABOUT THAT SPIDER-MAN KID?
THERE'S NO SIGN OF HIM, MR. FISK.
E'S ONE.
BYE BYE.
THOUGHT FOR SURE HE WAS STREET ART.
AND YOUR PARTY GUESTS ALL THOUGHT IT WAS JUST PART OF THE ENTERTAINMENT. THOUGHT IT WAS HILARIOUS.
'S BEEN DAYS, BOSS. HE'S GONE AND HE AIN'T COMING BACK. IT WAS JUST SOME MUTANT ID LOOKING TO MAKE A LITTLE NAME FOR HIMSELF.
YOU DID THE RIGHT THING.
TOSS THAT LITTLE DAISY OUT THE WINDOW AND FORGET ABOUT HIM.

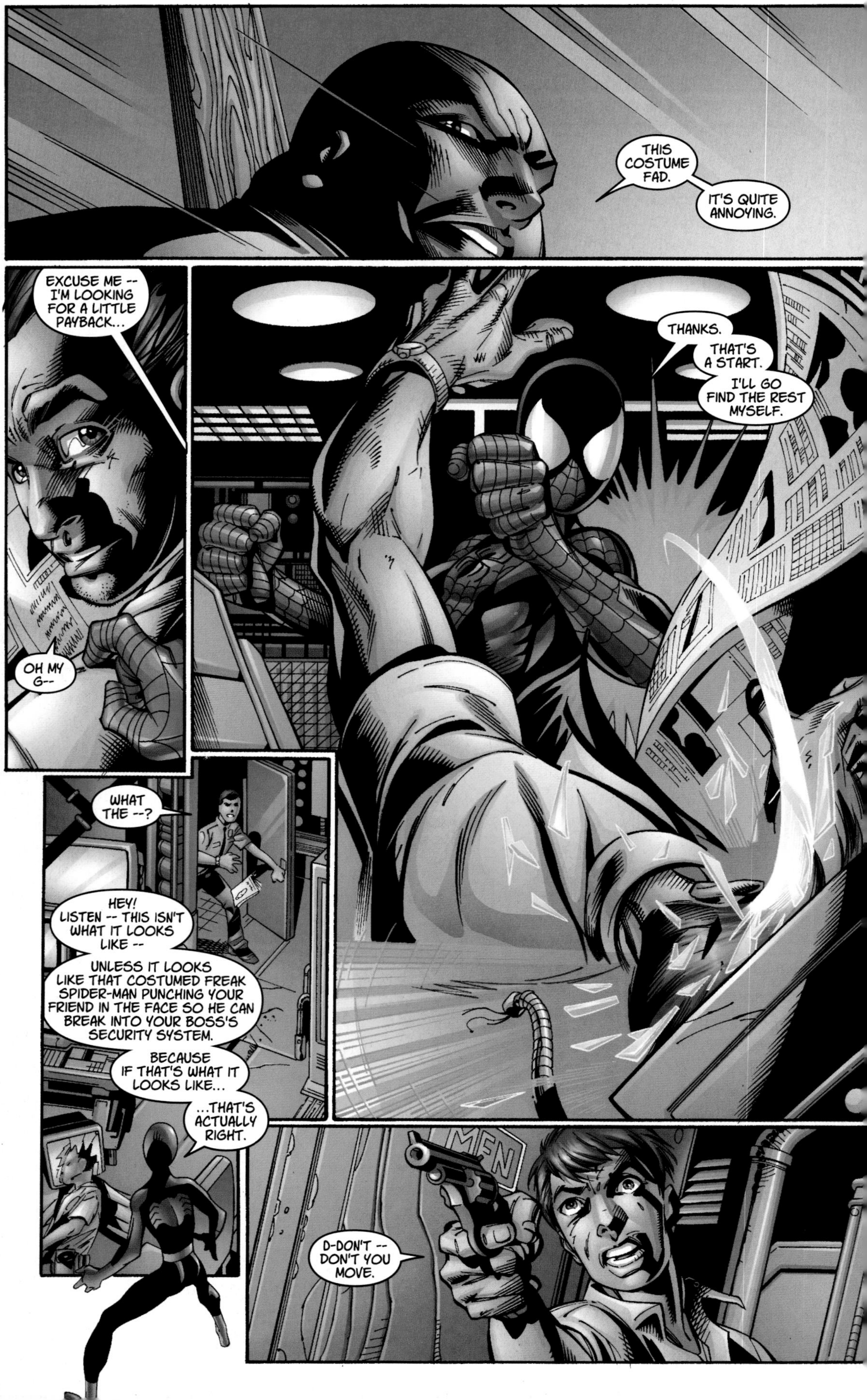
THIS COSTUME FAD.
IT'S QUITE ANNOYING.
EXCUSE ME -- I'M LOOKING FOR A LITTLE PAYBACK...
OH MY G--
THANKS.
THAT'S A START.
I'LL GO FIND THE REST MYSELF.
WHAT THE --?
HEY! LISTEN -- THIS ISN'T WHAT IT LOOKS LIKE --
UNLESS IT LOOKS LIKE THAT COSTUMED FREAK SPIDER-MAN PUNCHING YOUR FRIEND IN THE FACE SO HE CAN BREAK INTO YOUR BOSS'S SECURITY SYSTEM.
BECAUSE IF THAT'S WHAT IT LOOKS LIKE...
...THAT'S ACTUALLY RIGHT.
MEN
D-DON'T -- DON'T YOU MOVE.

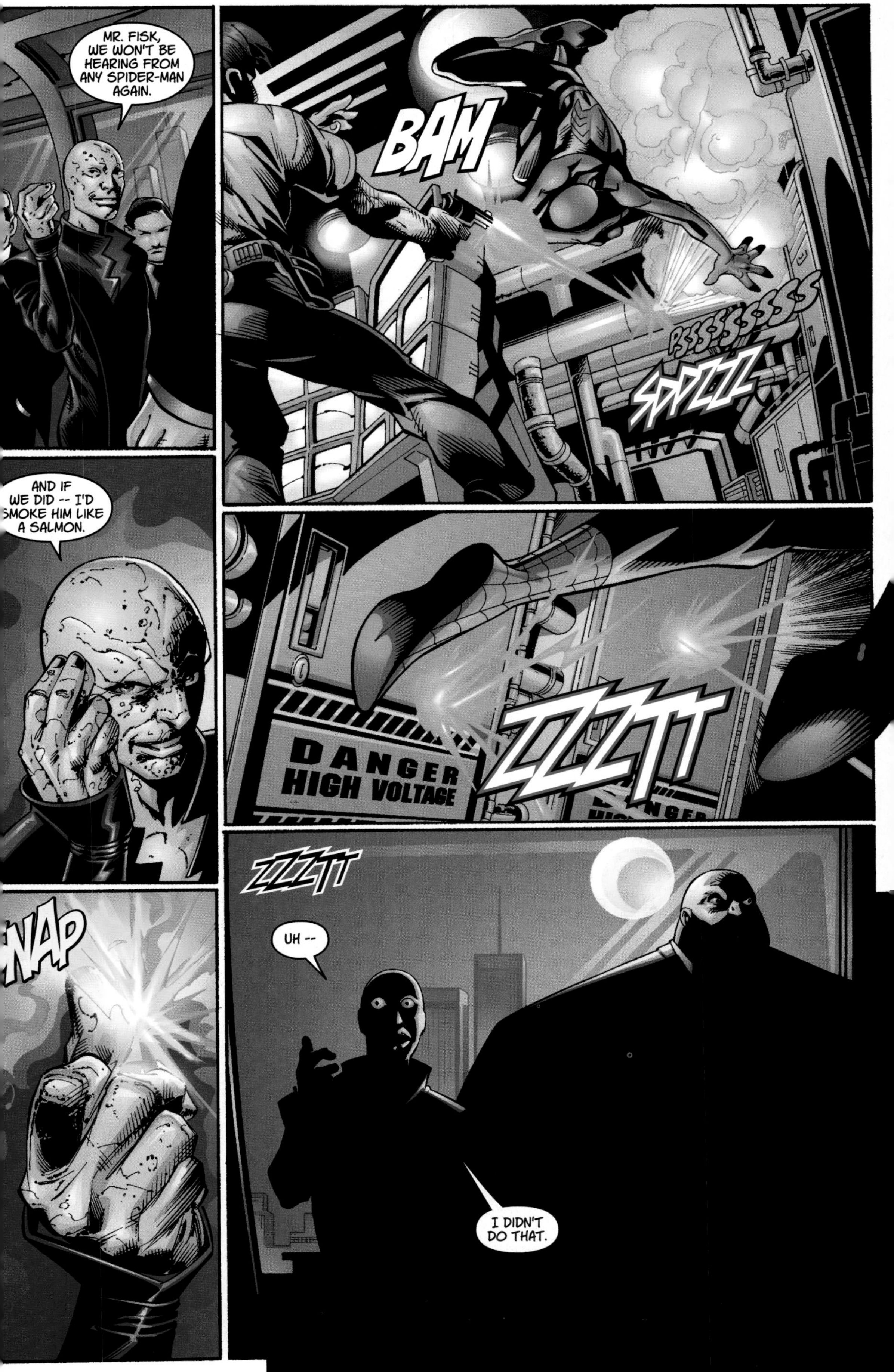
MR. FISK, WE WON'T BE HEARING FROM ANY SPIDER-MAN AGAIN.
BAM
PSSSSSSSSS
SPZZZ
AND IF WE DID -- I'D SMOKE HIM LIKE A SALMON.
DANGER HIGH VOLTAGE
ZZZTT
NAP
ZZZTT
UH --
I DIDN'T DO THAT.

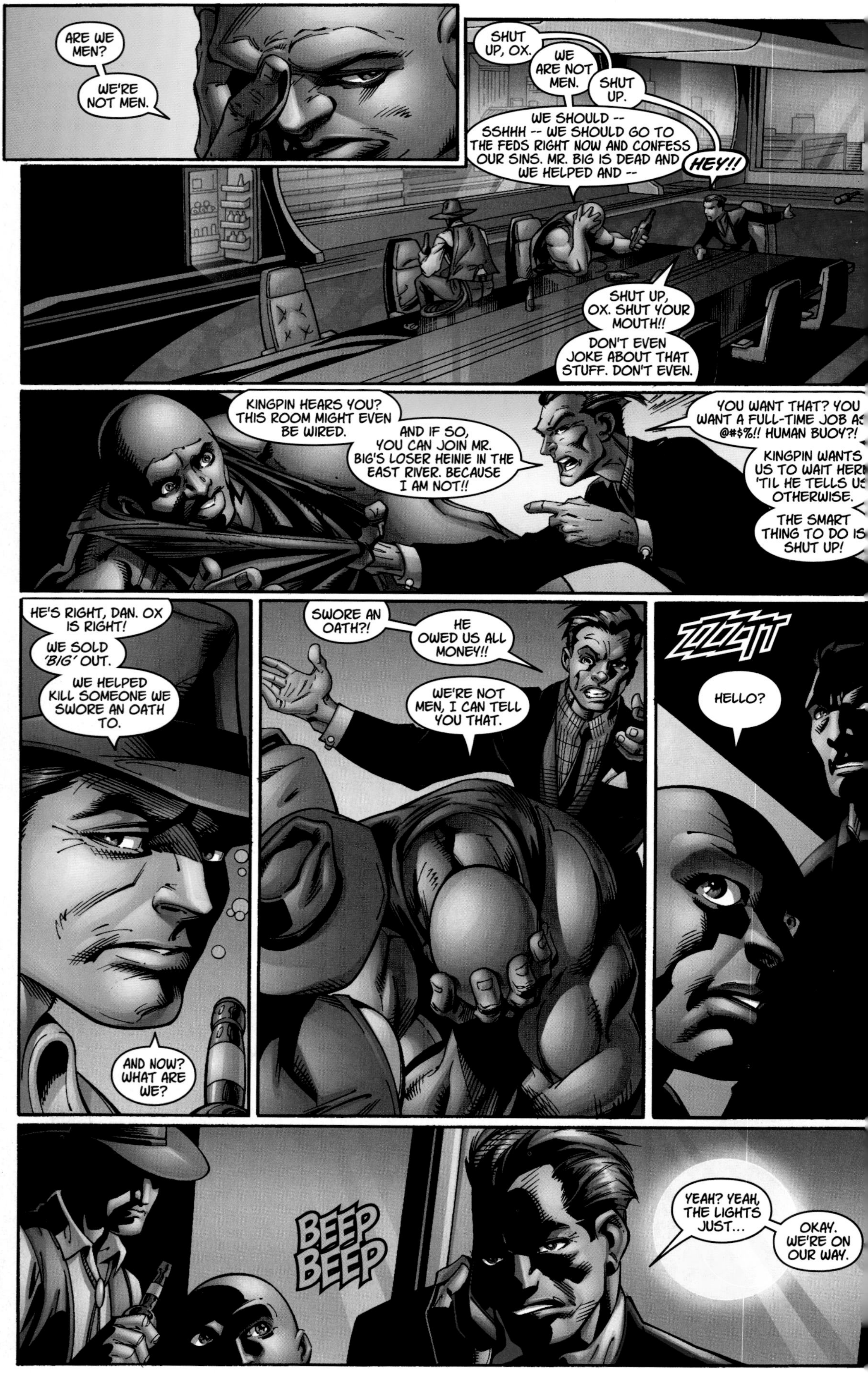

ARE WE MEN?
WE'RE NOT MEN.
SHUT UP, OX.
WE ARE NOT MEN.
SHUT UP.
WE SHOULD -- SSHHH -- WE SHOULD GO TO THE FEDS RIGHT NOW AND CONFESS OUR SINS. MR. BIG IS DEAD AND WE HELPED AND --
HEY!!
SHUT UP, OX. SHUT YOUR MOUTH!!
DON'T EVEN JOKE ABOUT THAT STUFF. DON'T EVEN.
KINGPIN HEARS YOU? THIS ROOM MIGHT EVEN BE WIRED.
AND IF SO, YOU CAN JOIN MR. BIG'S LOSER HEINIE IN THE EAST RIVER. BECAUSE I AM NOT!!
YOU WANT THAT? YOU WANT A FULL-TIME JOB AS @#$%!! HUMAN BUOY?!
KINGPIN WANTS US TO WAIT HERE 'TIL HE TELLS US OTHERWISE.
THE SMART THING TO DO IS SHUT UP!
HE'S RIGHT, DAN. OX IS RIGHT!
WE SOLD 'BIG' OUT.
WE HELPED KILL SOMEONE WE SWORE AN OATH TO.
AND NOW? WHAT ARE WE?
SWORE AN OATH?!
HE OWED US ALL MONEY!!
WE'RE NOT MEN, I CAN TELL YOU THAT.
ZZZZTT
HELLO?
BEEP BEEP
YEAH? YEAH, THE LIGHTS JUST...
OKAY. WE'RE ON OUR WAY.

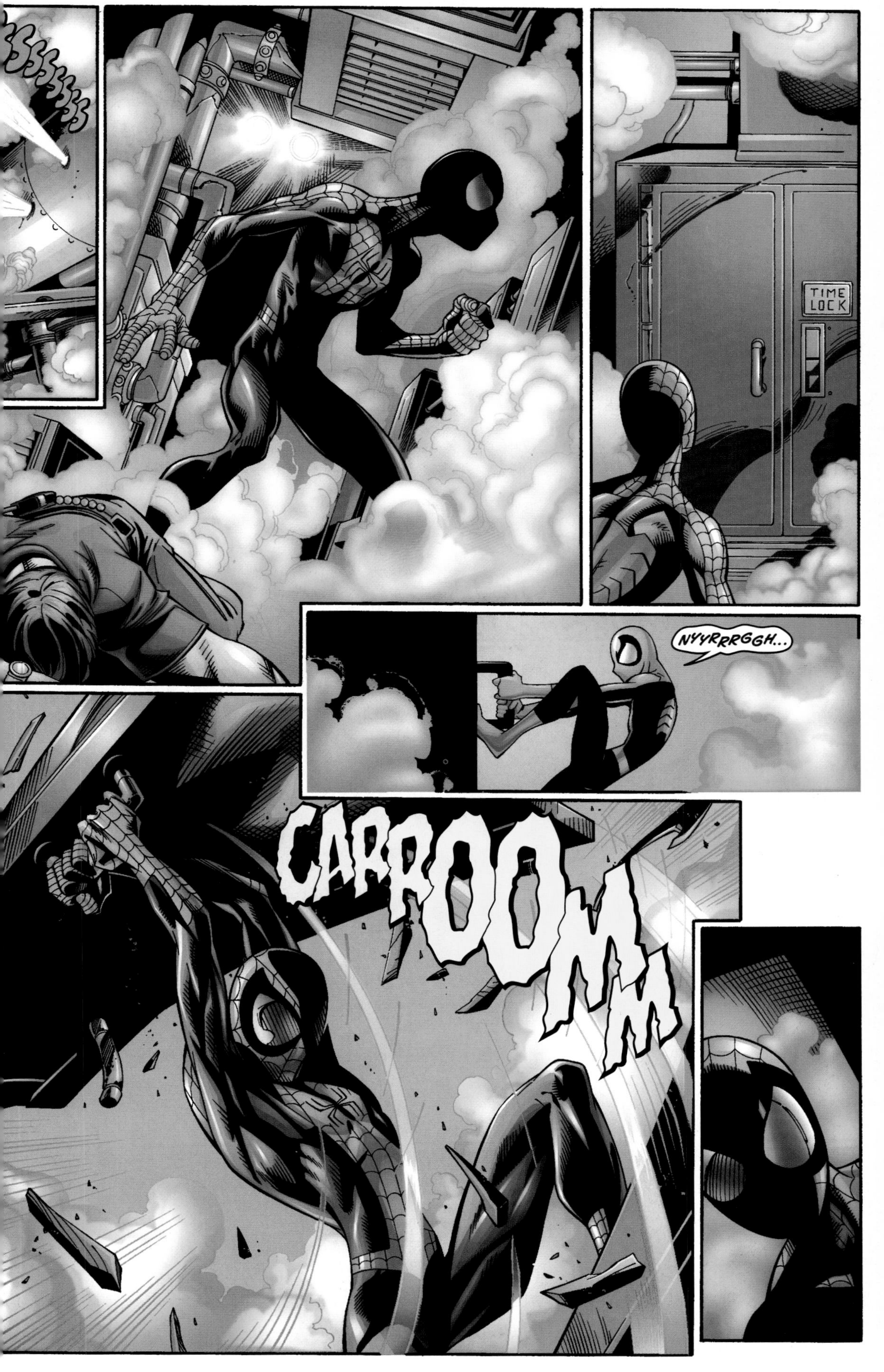
SSSSSSSSS
TIME LOCK
NYYRRRGGH...
CARROOMM

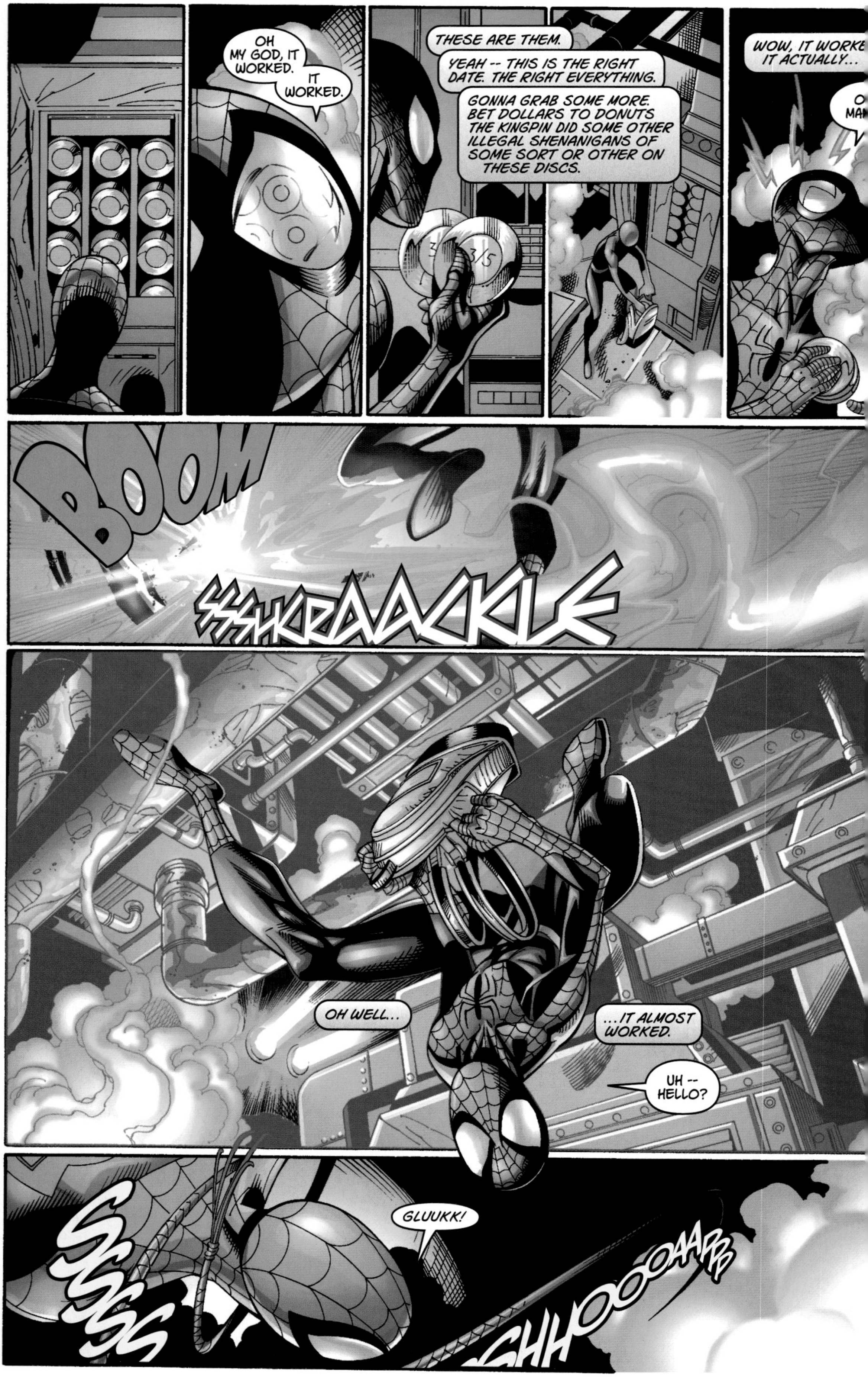
OH MY GOD, IT WORKED.
IT WORKED.
THESE ARE THEM.
YEAH -- THIS IS THE RIGHT DATE. THE RIGHT EVERYTHING.
GONNA GRAB SOME MORE. BET DOLLARS TO DONUTS THE KINGPIN DID SOME OTHER ILLEGAL SHENANIGANS OF SOME SORT OR OTHER ON THESE DISCS.
WOW, IT WORKE IT ACTUALLY...
BOOM
SSSHKRAACKLE
OH WELL...
...IT ALMOST WORKED.
UH -- HELLO?
GLUUKK!
SSSSG
GHHOOOOAARP

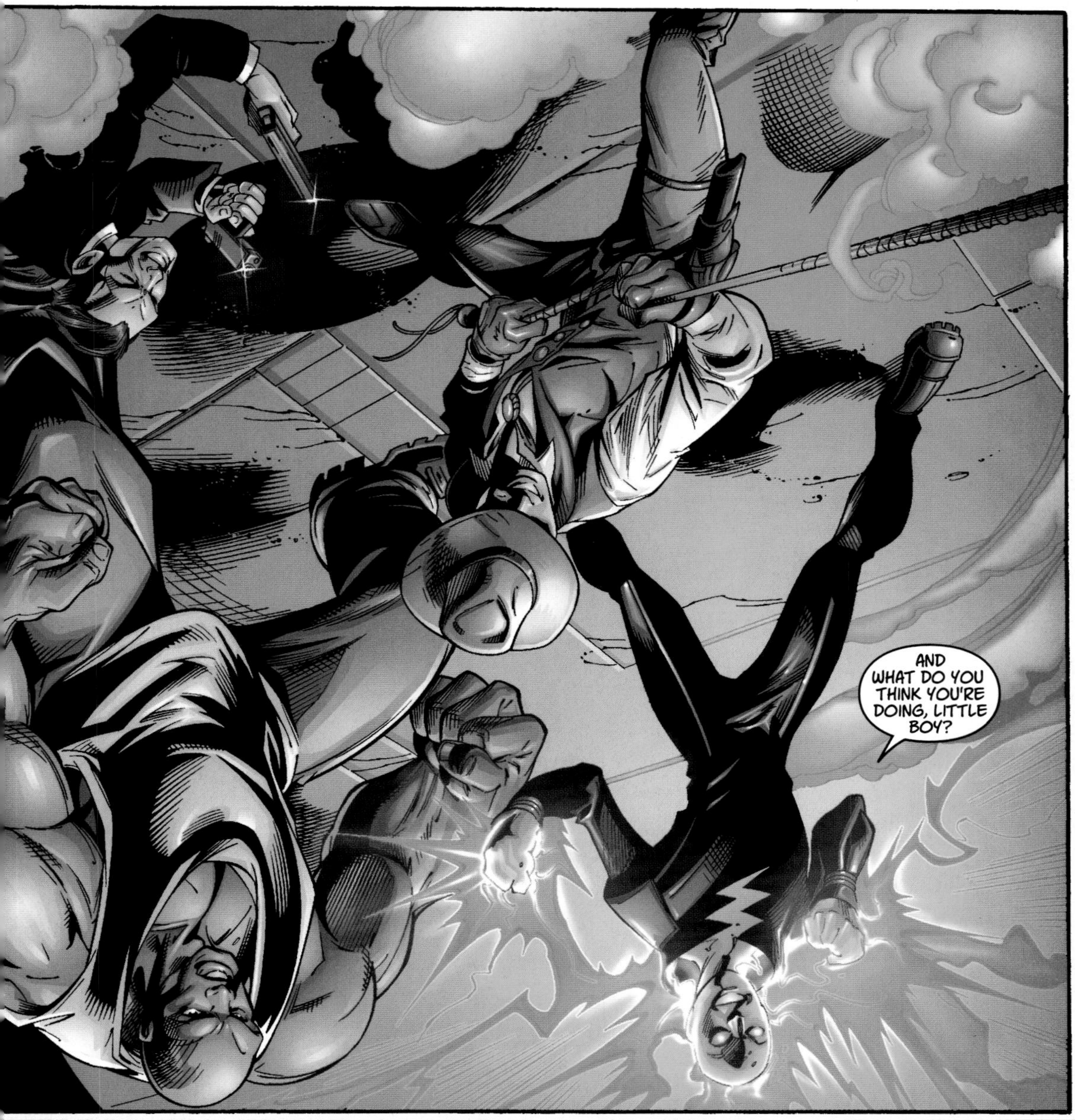
AND WHAT DO YOU THINK YOU'RE DOING, LITTLE BOY?
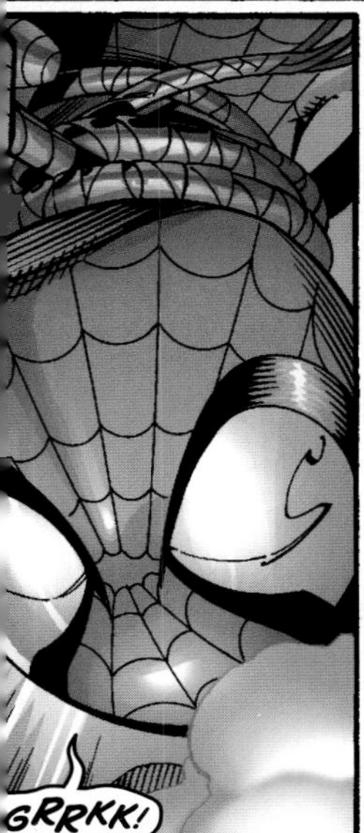
GRRKK!
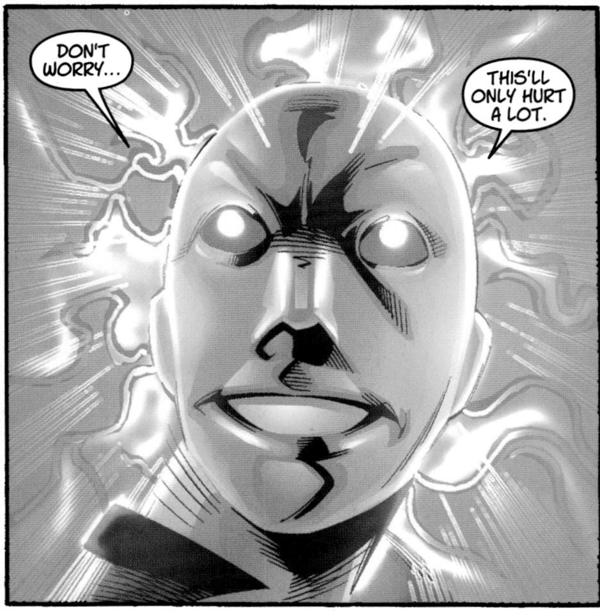
DON'T WORRY...
THIS'LL ONLY HURT A LOT.
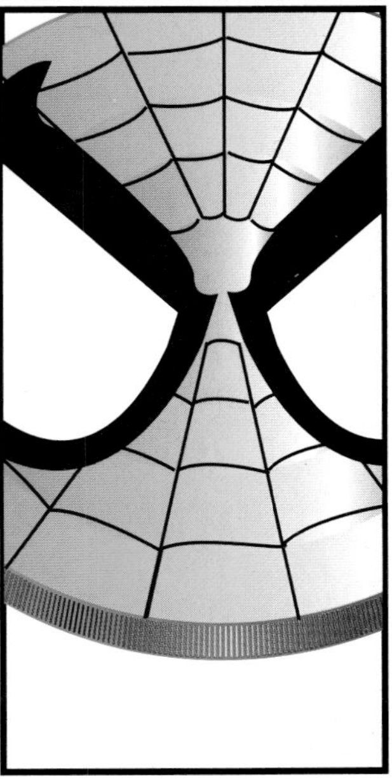

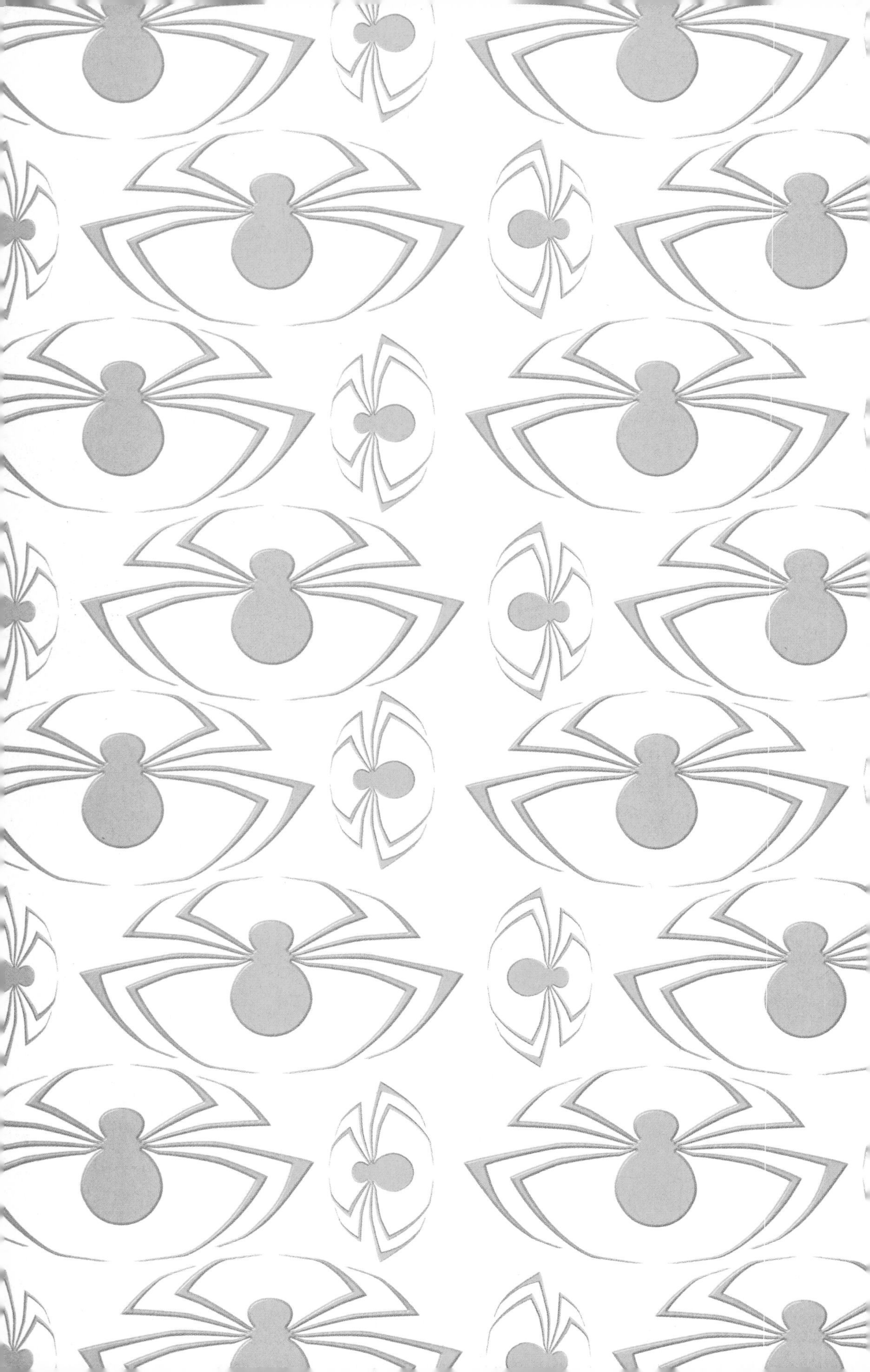

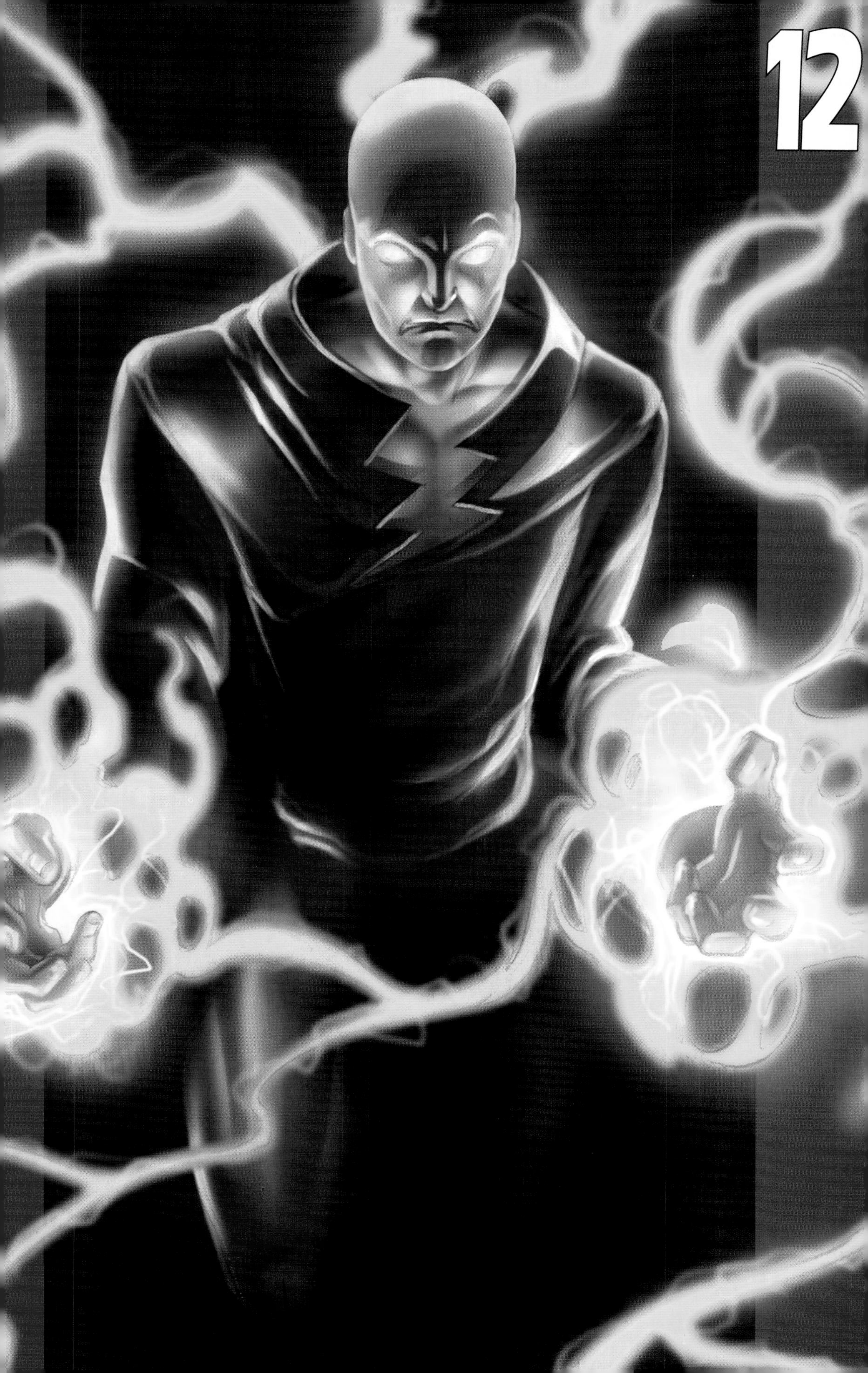
12

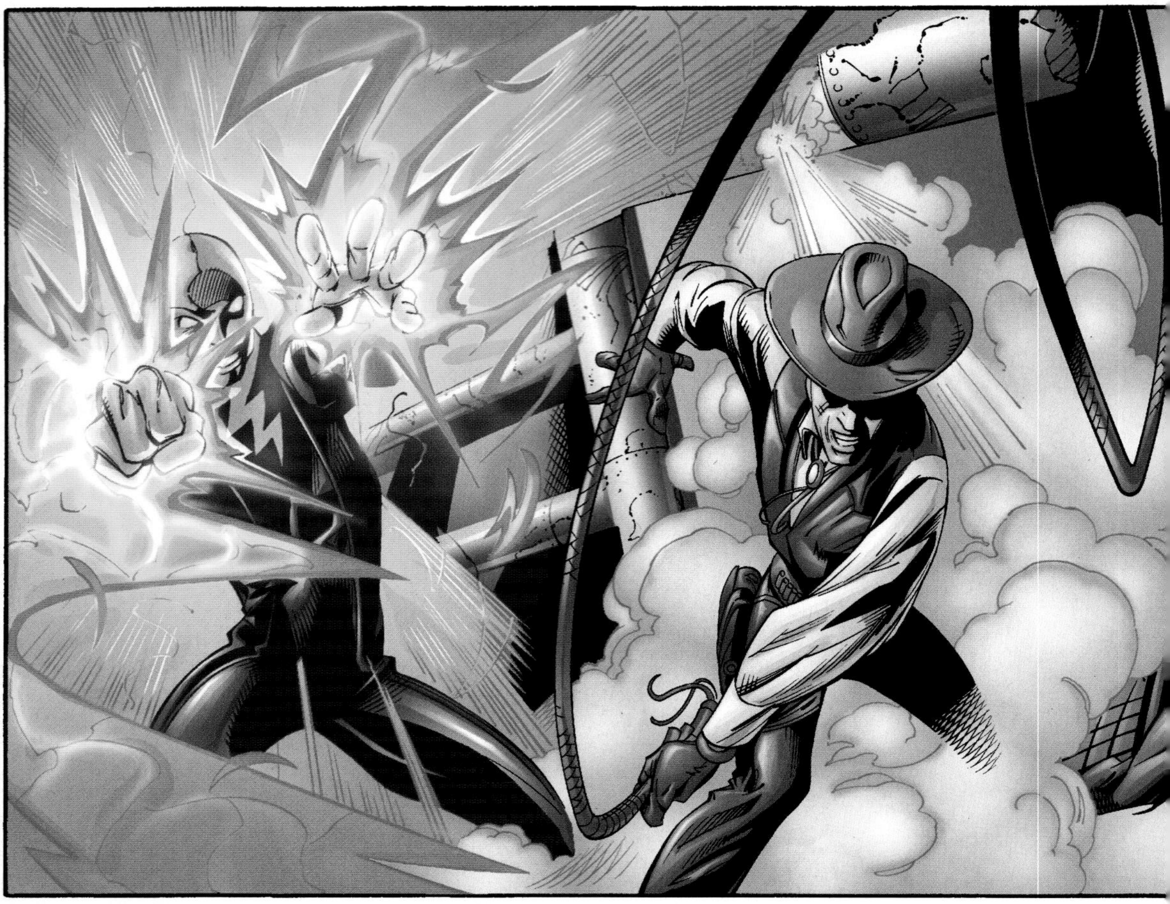

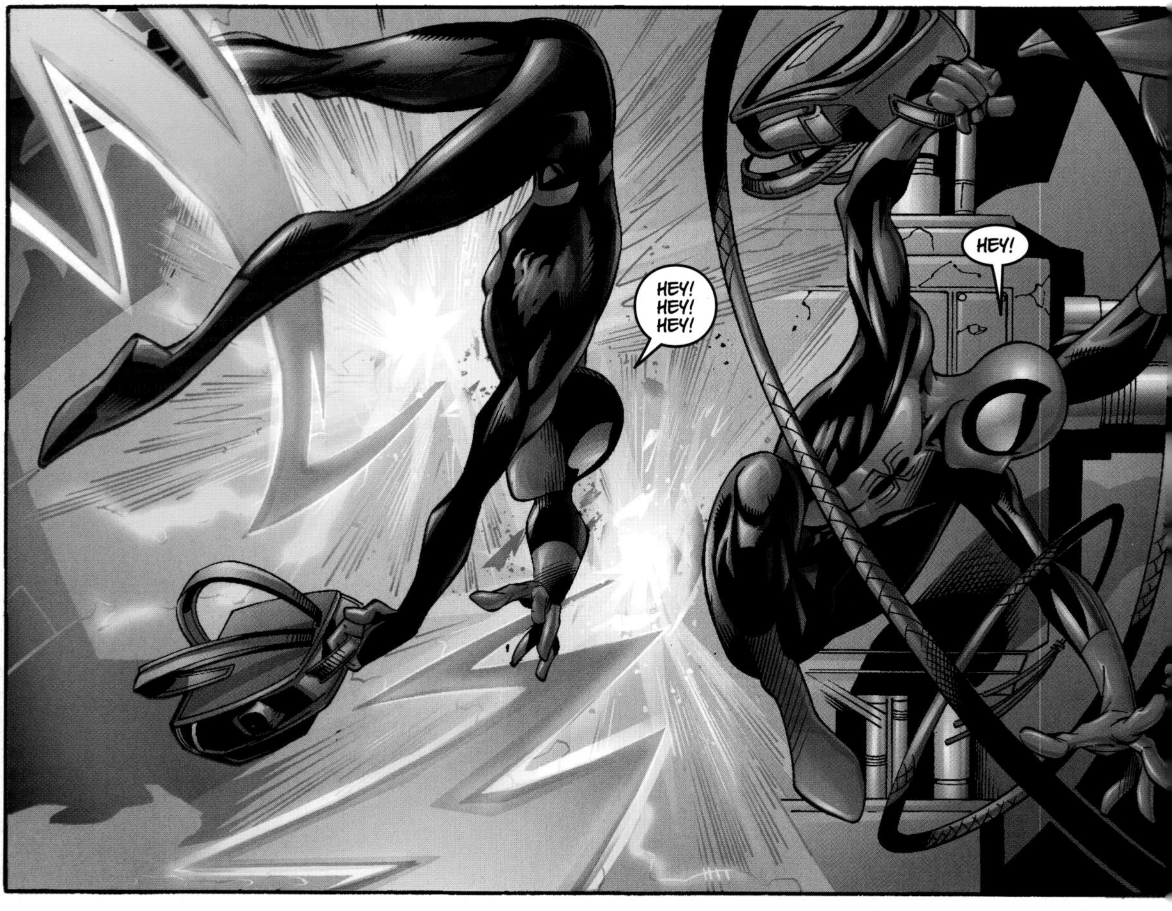
HEY! HEY! HEY!
HEY!

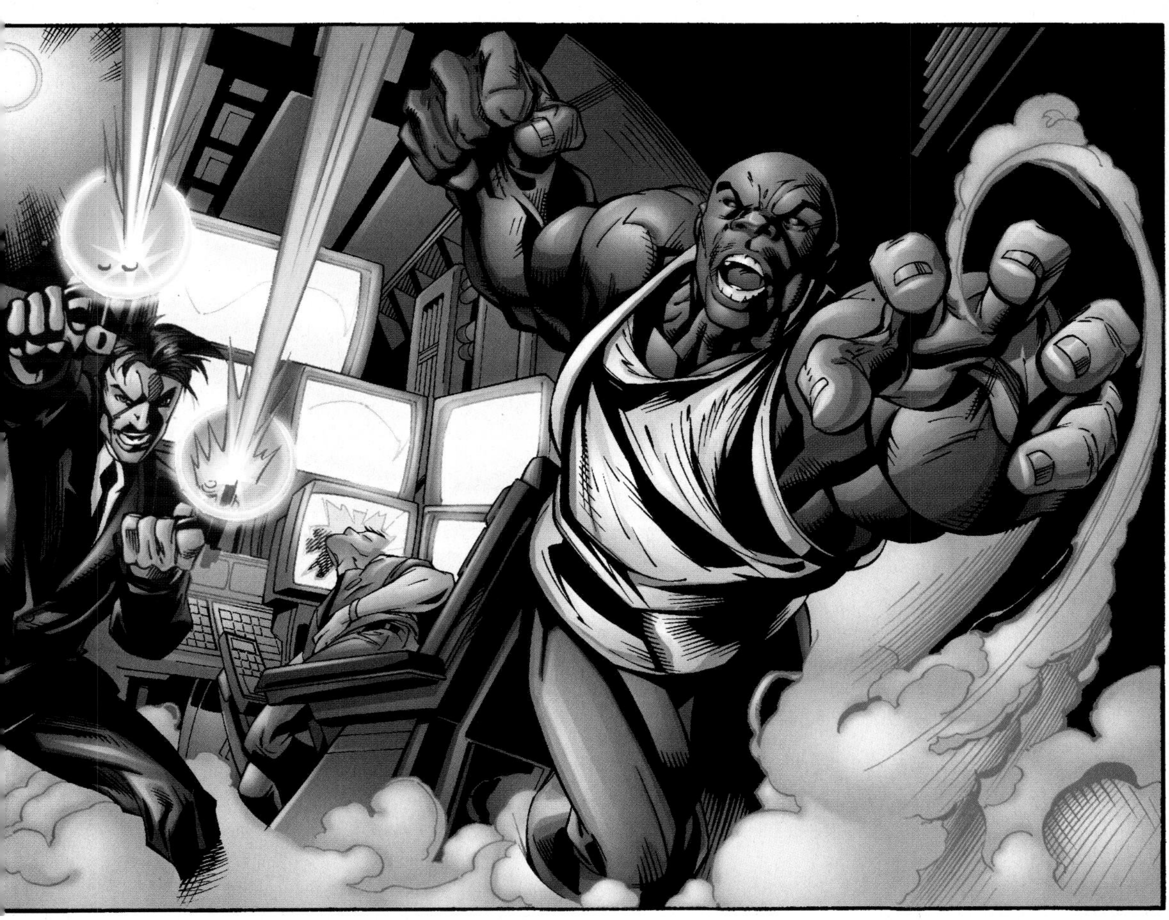

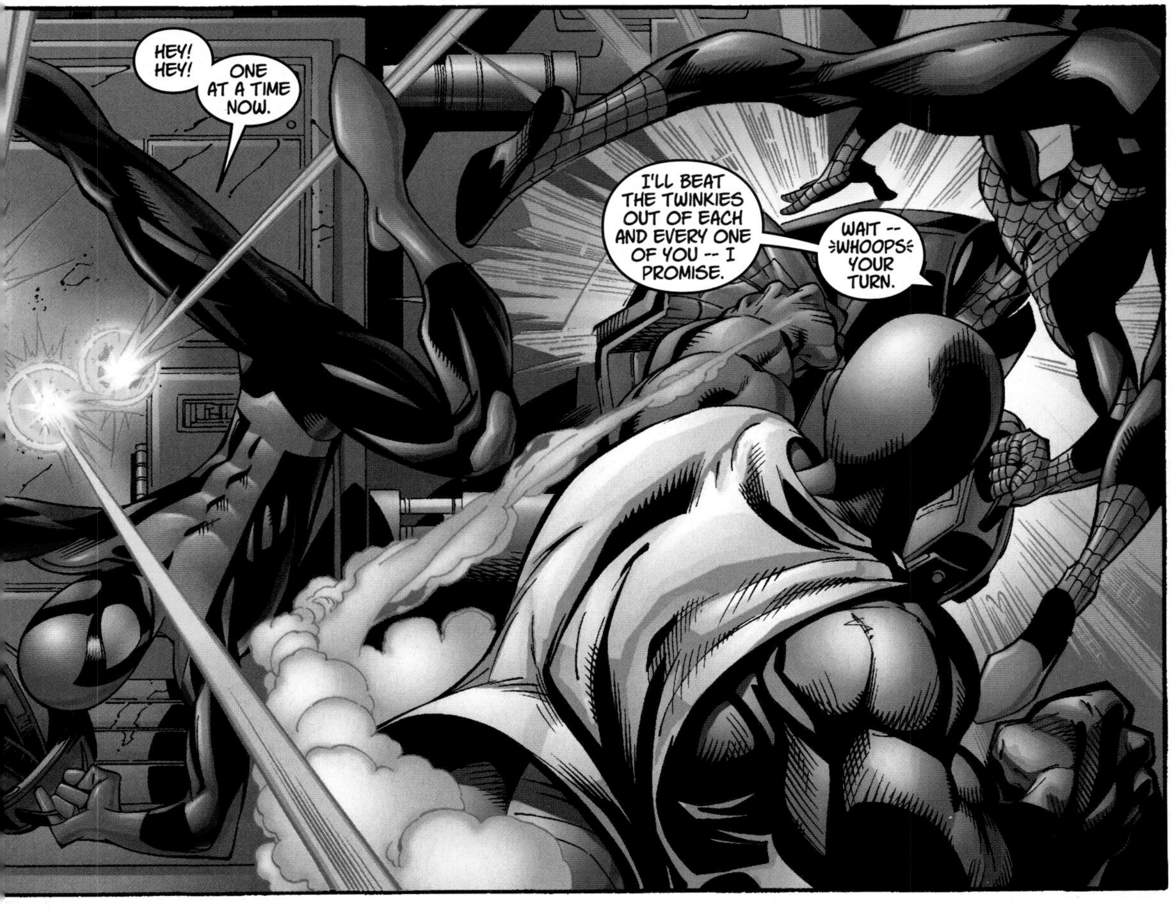

HEY! HEY!
ONE AT A TIME NOW.
I'LL BEAT THE TWINKIES OUT OF EACH AND EVERY ONE OF YOU -- I PROMISE.
WAIT -- WHOOPS YOUR TURN.

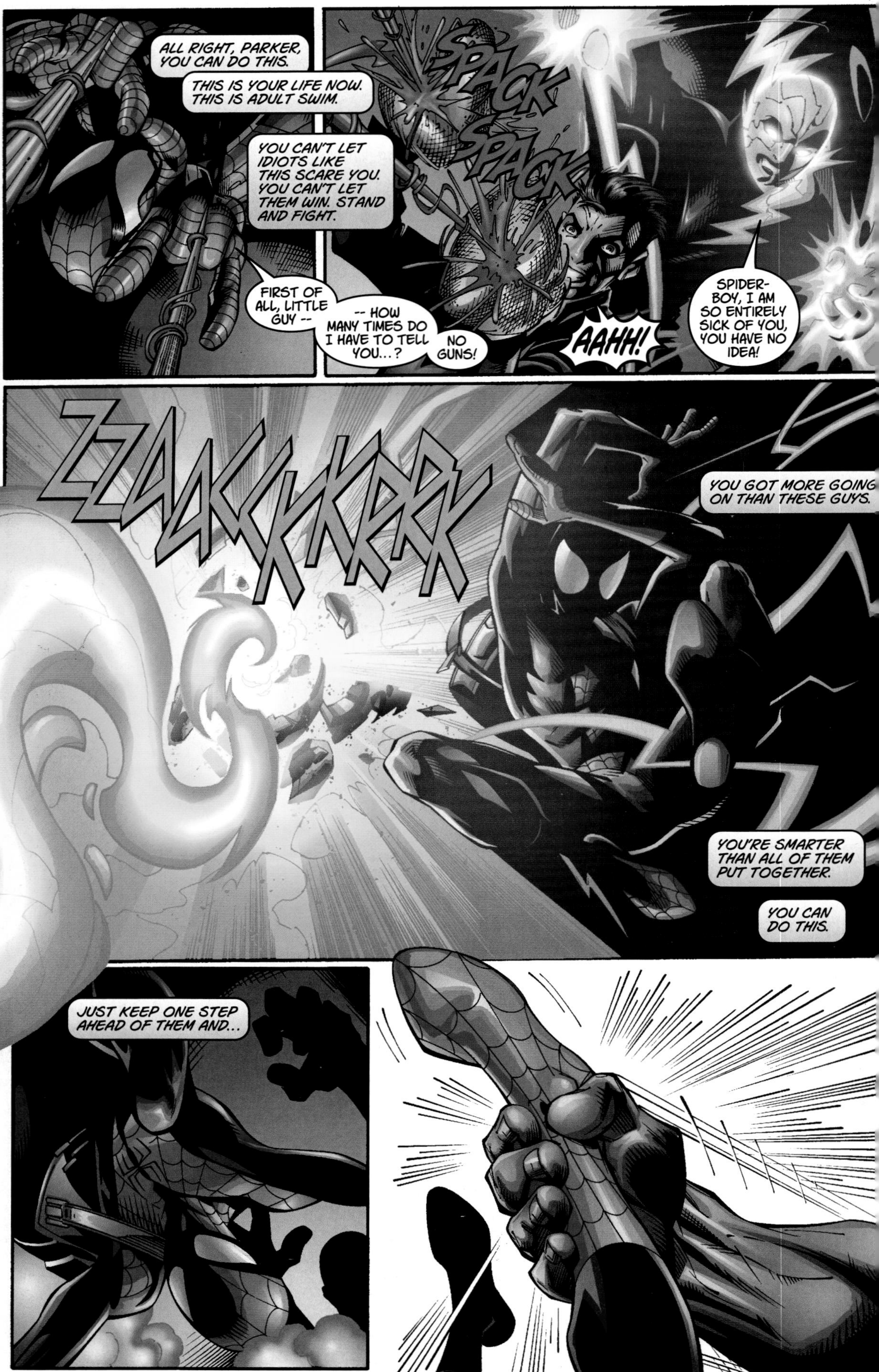
ALL RIGHT, PARKER, YOU CAN DO THIS.
THIS IS YOUR LIFE NOW. THIS IS ADULT SWIM.
YOU CAN'T LET IDIOTS LIKE THIS SCARE YOU. YOU CAN'T LET THEM WIN. STAND AND FIGHT.
FIRST OF ALL, LITTLE GUY --
-- HOW MANY TIMES DO I HAVE TO TELL YOU...?
NO GUNS!
SPACK SPACK
AAHH!
SPIDER-BOY, I AM SO ENTIRELY SICK OF YOU, YOU HAVE NO IDEA!
ZZAACKKRRK
YOU GOT MORE GOING ON THAN THESE GUYS.
YOU'RE SMARTER THAN ALL OF THEM PUT TOGETHER.
YOU CAN DO THIS.
JUST KEEP ONE STEP AHEAD OF THEM AND...

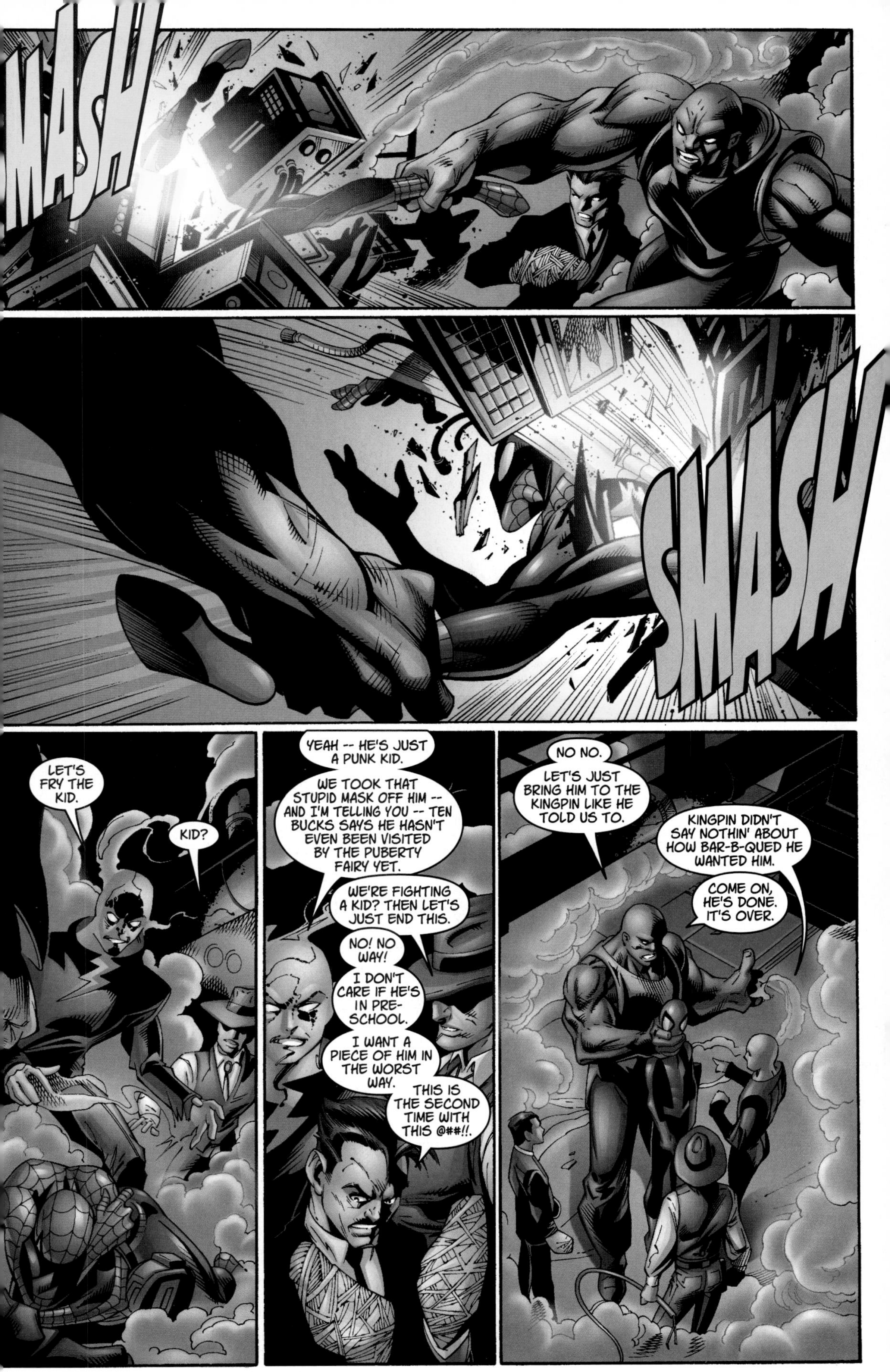
SMASH
SMASH
LET'S FRY THE KID.
KID?
YEAH -- HE'S JUST A PUNK KID.
WE TOOK THAT STUPID MASK OFF HIM -- AND I'M TELLING YOU -- TEN BUCKS SAYS HE HASN'T EVEN BEEN VISITED BY THE PUBERTY FAIRY YET.
WE'RE FIGHTING A KID? THEN LET'S JUST END THIS.
NO! NO WAY!
I DON'T CARE IF HE'S IN PRE-SCHOOL.
I WANT A PIECE OF HIM IN THE WORST WAY.
THIS IS THE SECOND TIME WITH THIS @##!!.
NO NO.
LET'S JUST BRING HIM TO THE KINGPIN LIKE HE TOLD US TO.
KINGPIN DIDN'T SAY NOTHIN' ABOUT HOW BAR-B-QUED HE WANTED HIM.
COME ON, HE'S DONE. IT'S OVER.

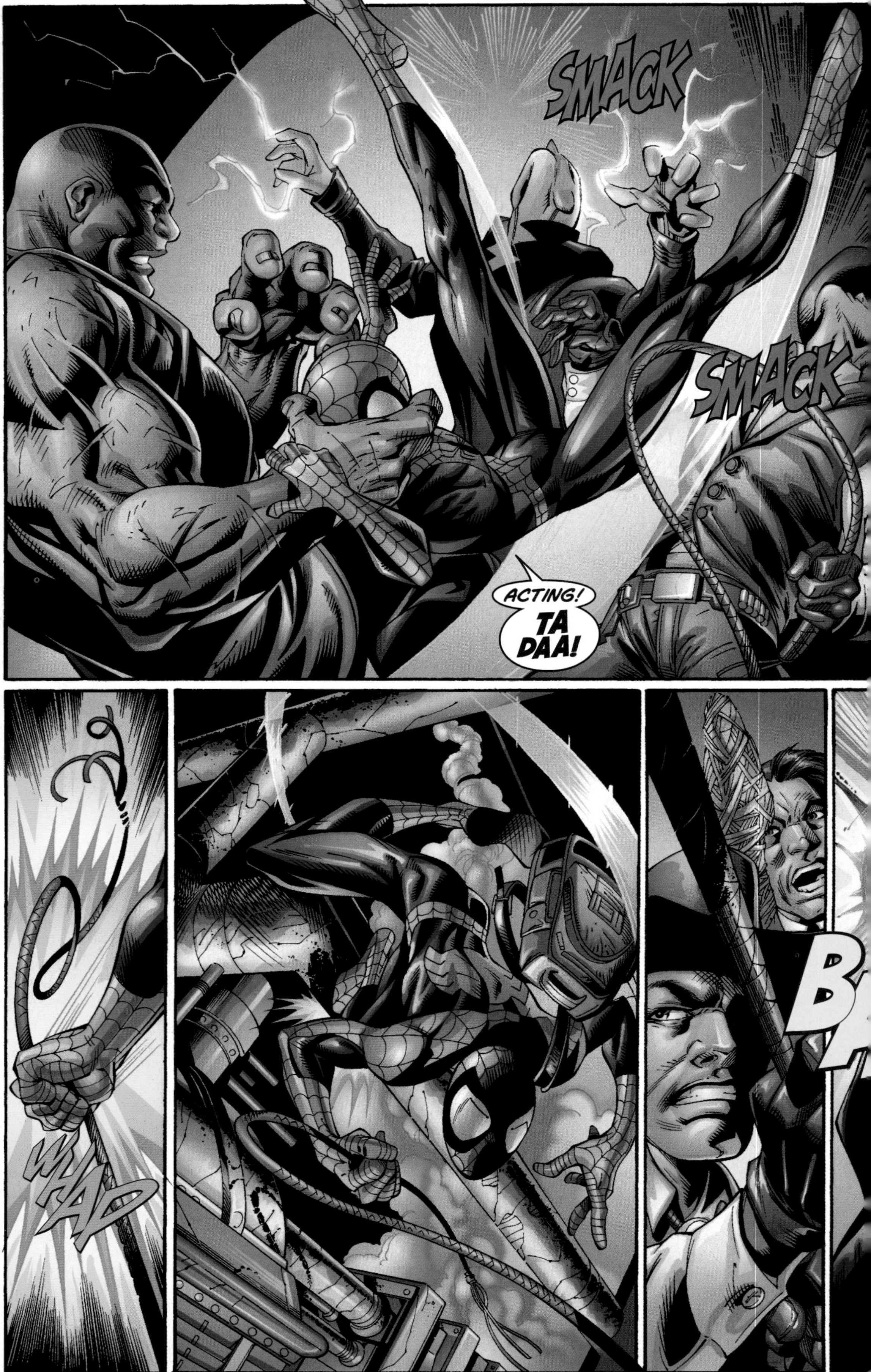
SMACK
SMACK
ACTING! TA DAA!
WHAP

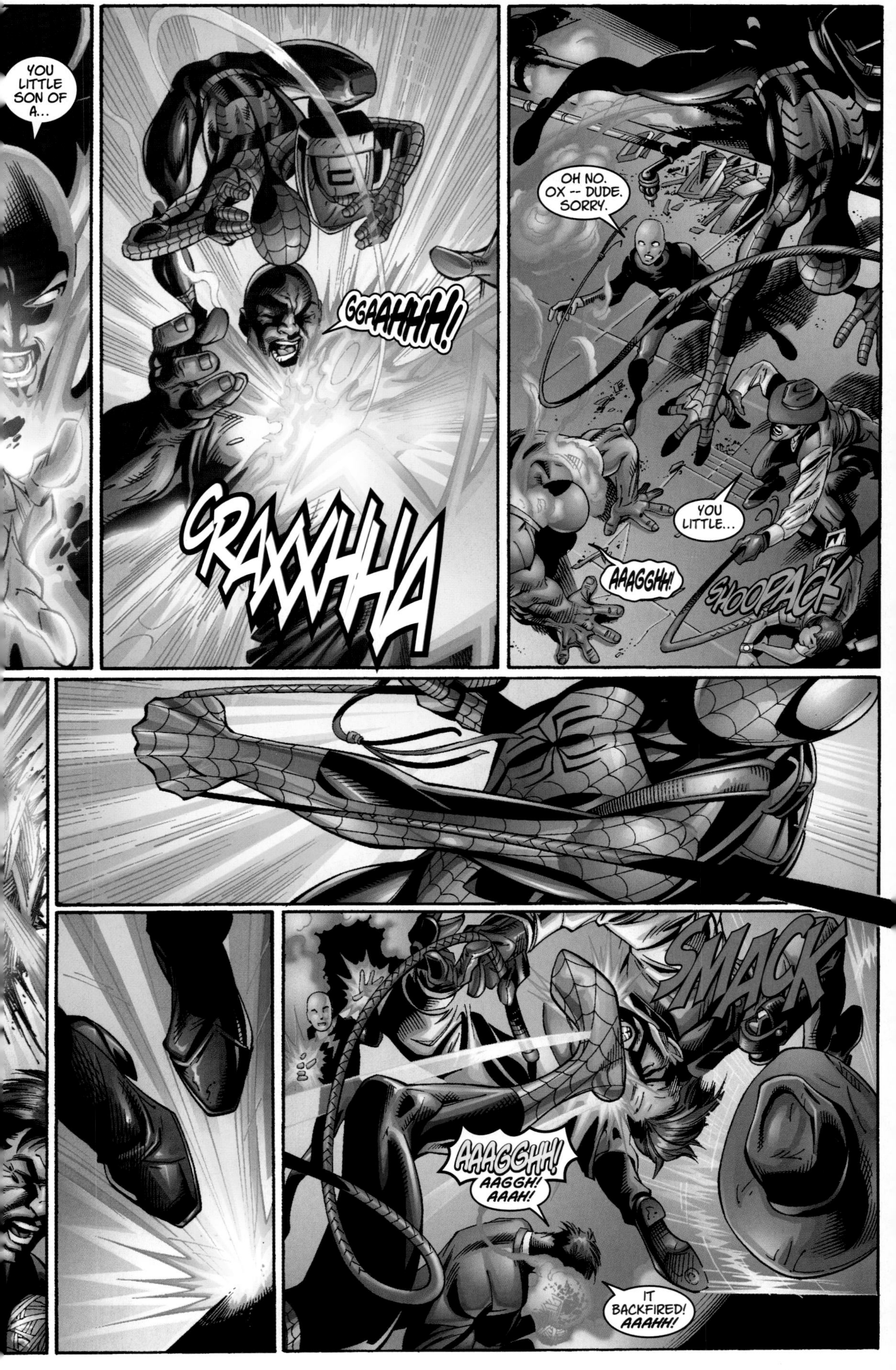

YOU LITTLE SON OF A...
GGAAHHH!
CRAXXHHA
OH NO. OX -- DUDE. SORRY.
YOU LITTLE...
AAAGGHH!
SHOOPACK
SMACK
AAAGGHH! AAGGH! AAAH!
IT BACKFIRED! AAAHH!

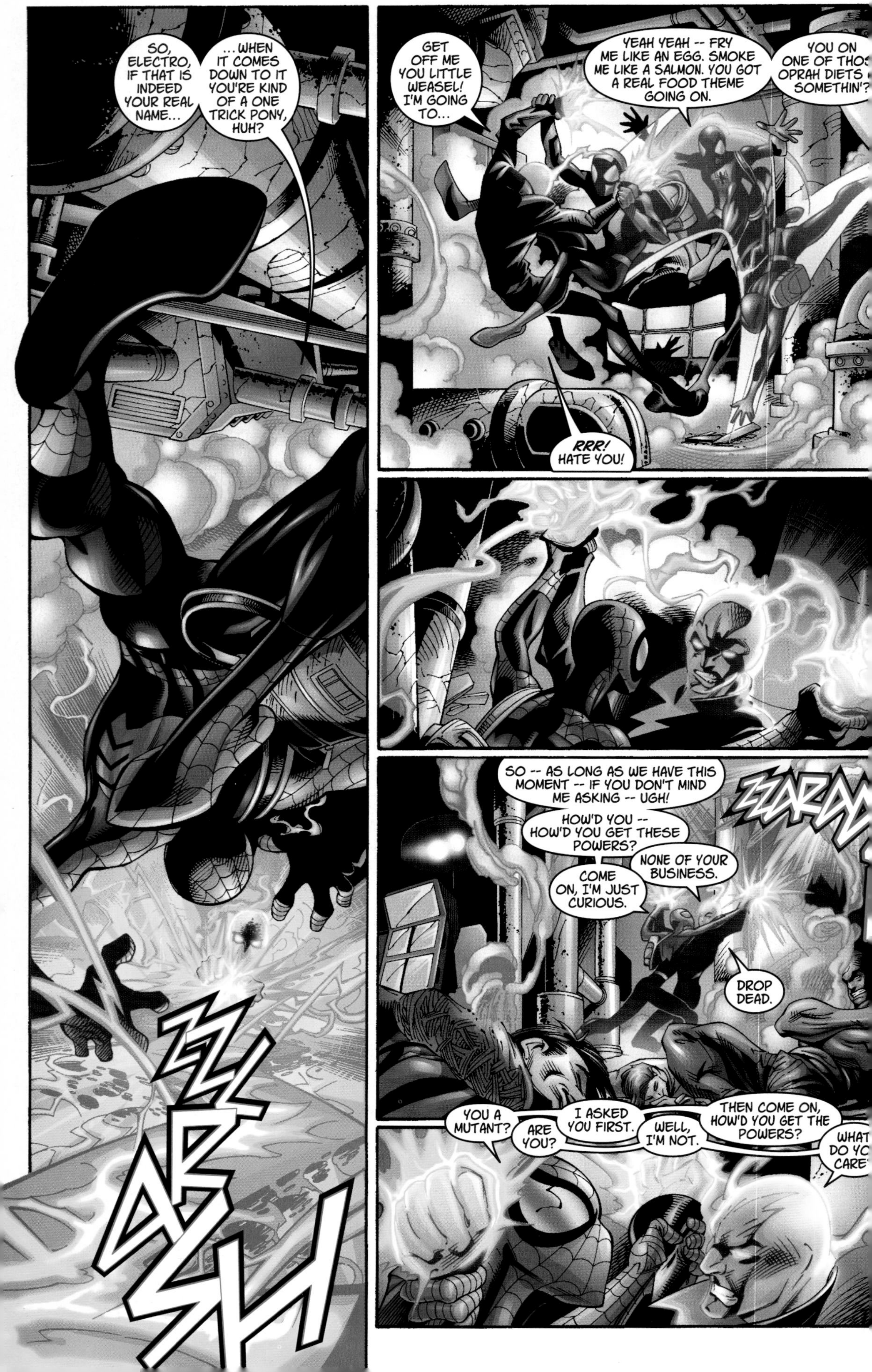
SO, ELECTRO, IF THAT IS INDEED YOUR REAL NAME...
...WHEN IT COMES DOWN TO IT YOU'RE KIND OF A ONE TRICK PONY, HUH?
ZZZAARASH
GET OFF ME YOU LITTLE WEASEL! I'M GOING TO...
YEAH YEAH -- FRY ME LIKE AN EGG. SMOKE ME LIKE A SALMON. YOU GOT A REAL FOOD THEME GOING ON.
YOU ON ONE OF THOS OPRAH DIETS SOMETHIN'?
RRR! HATE YOU!
SO -- AS LONG AS WE HAVE THIS MOMENT -- IF YOU DON'T MIND ME ASKING -- UGH!
HOW'D YOU -- HOW'D YOU GET THESE POWERS?
NONE OF YOUR BUSINESS.
COME ON, I'M JUST CURIOUS.
DROP DEAD.
YOU A MUTANT?
ARE YOU?
I ASKED YOU FIRST.
WELL, I'M NOT.
THEN COME ON, HOW'D YOU GET THE POWERS?

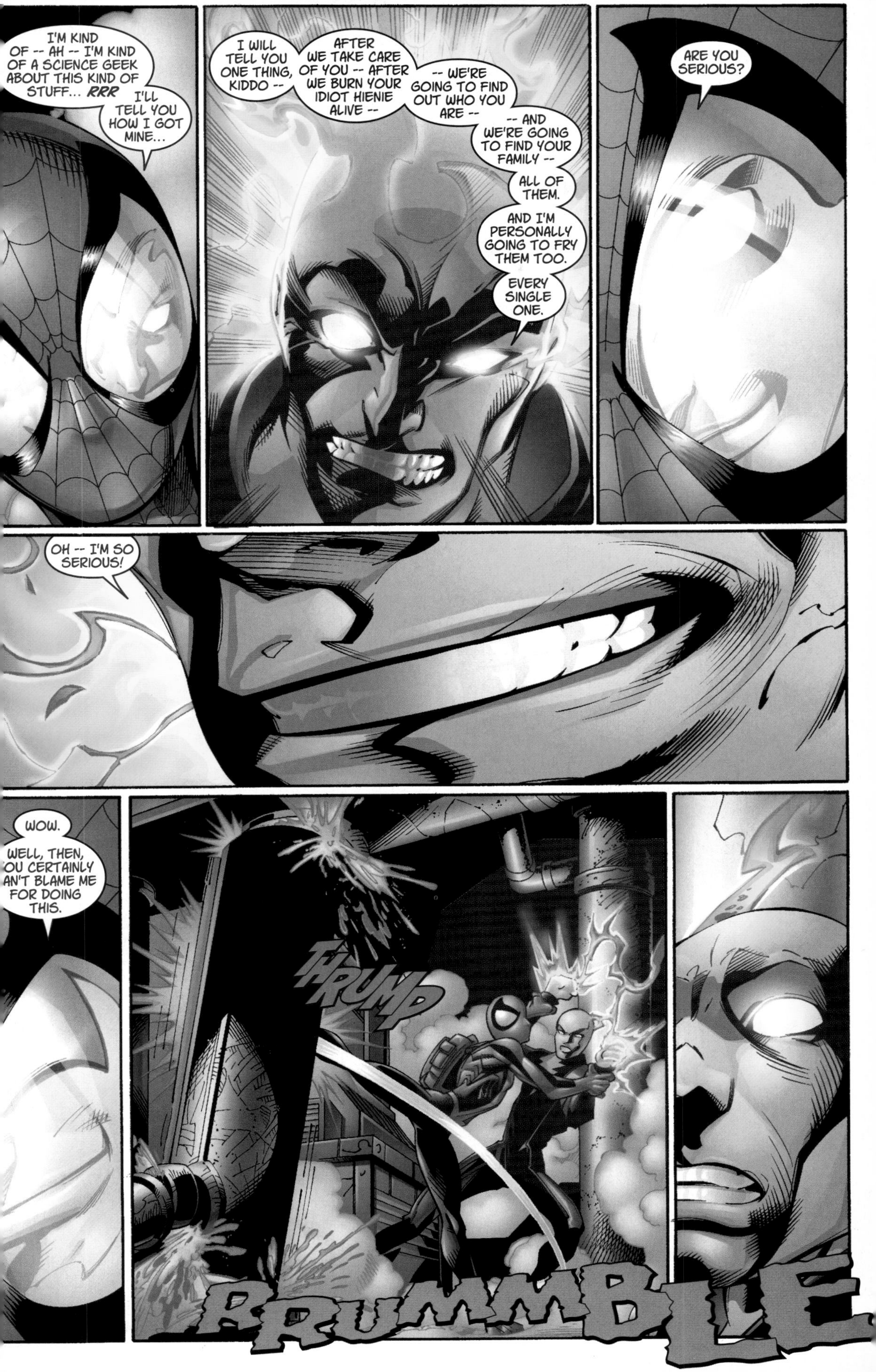

I'M KIND OF -- AH -- I'M KIND OF A SCIENCE GEEK ABOUT THIS KIND OF STUFF... RRR
I'LL TELL YOU HOW I GOT MINE...
I WILL TELL YOU ONE THING, KIDDO --
AFTER WE TAKE CARE OF YOU -- AFTER WE BURN YOUR IDIOT HIENIE ALIVE --
-- WE'RE GOING TO FIND OUT WHO YOU ARE --
-- AND WE'RE GOING TO FIND YOUR FAMILY --
ALL OF THEM.
AND I'M PERSONALLY GOING TO FRY THEM TOO.
EVERY SINGLE ONE.
ARE YOU SERIOUS?
OH -- I'M SO SERIOUS!
WOW.
WELL, THEN, OU CERTAINLY AN'T BLAME ME FOR DOING THIS.
THRUMP
RRUMMBLE

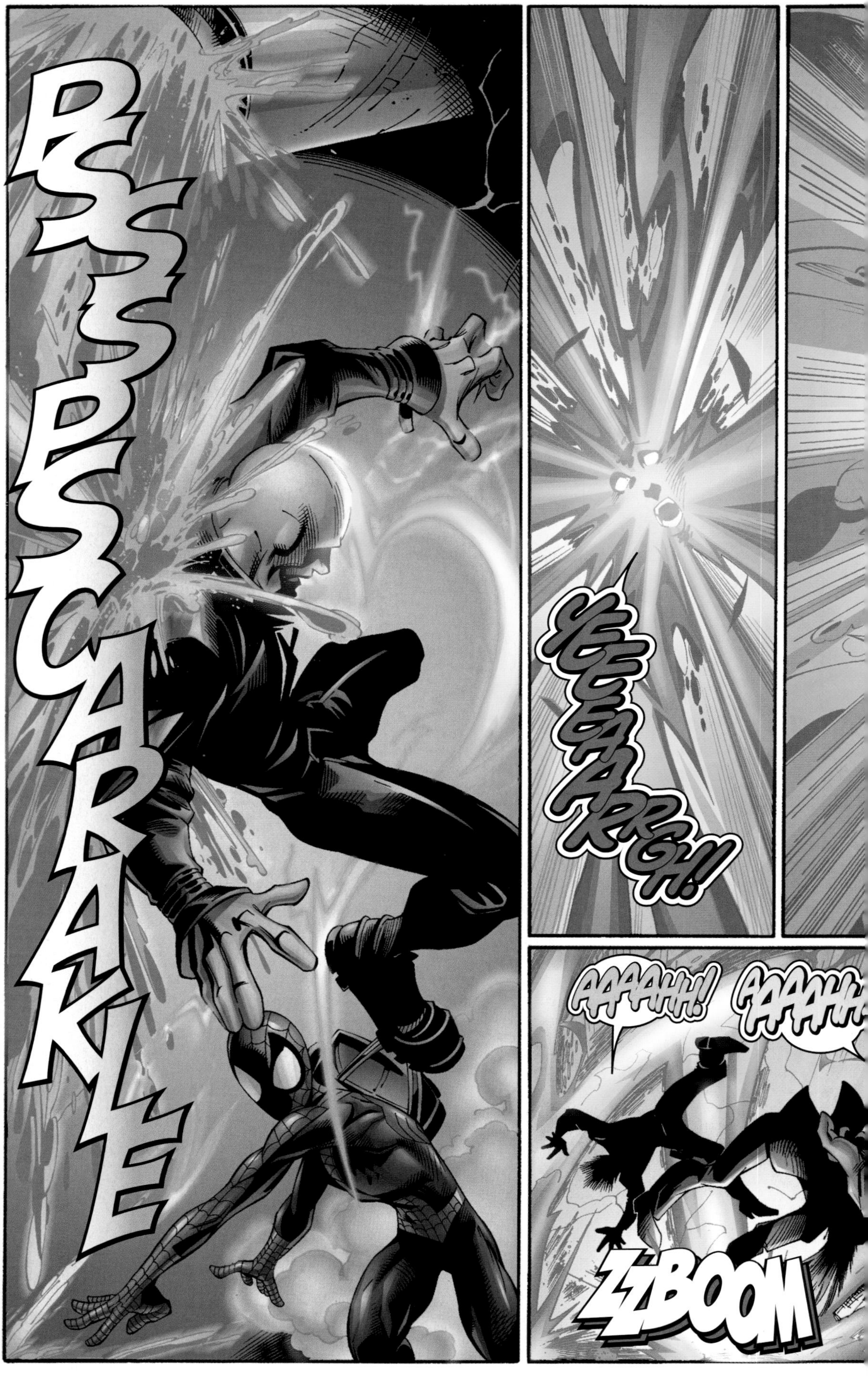
PSSPSCARAKLE
YEEAARRGH!
AAAAHH!
AAAAHH
ZZBOOM

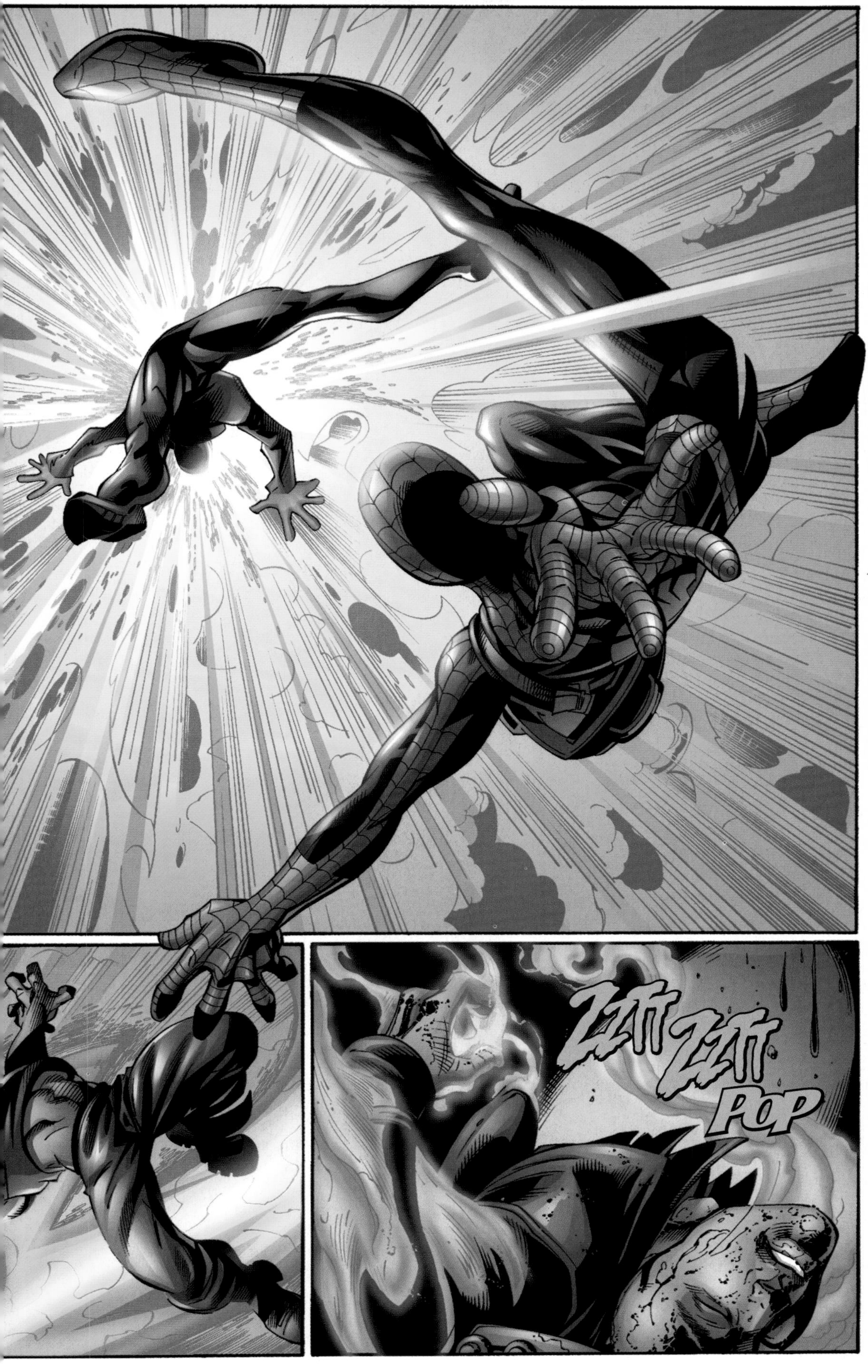
ZZZT ZZZT
POP

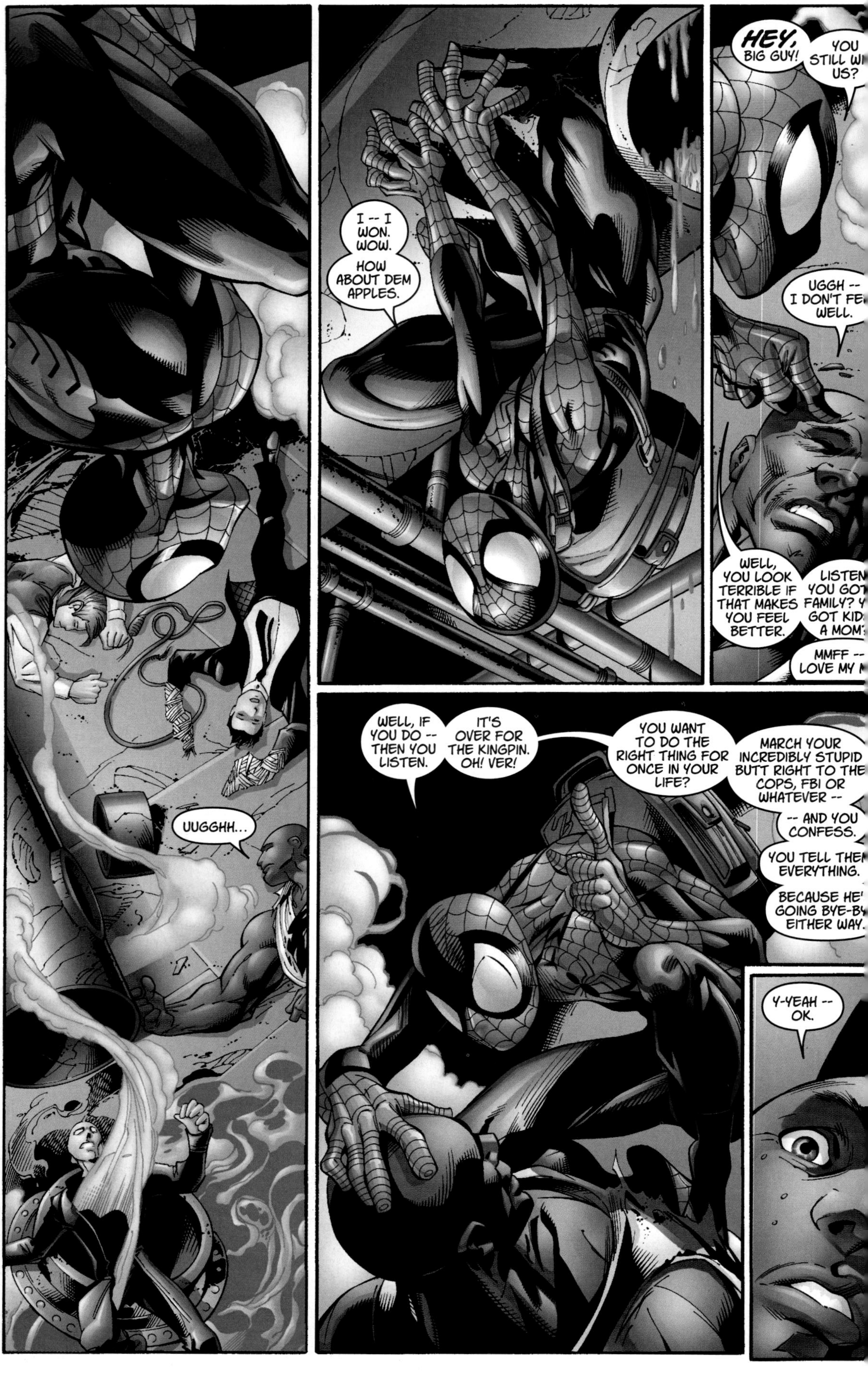
UUGGHH...
I -- I WON. WOW.
HOW ABOUT DEM APPLES.
HEY, BIG GUY!
YOU STILL WI US?
UGGH -- I DON'T FE WELL.
WELL, YOU LOOK TERRIBLE IF THAT MAKES YOU FEEL BETTER.
LISTEN YOU GOT FAMILY? Y GOT KID A MOM?
MMFF -- LOVE MY
WELL, IF YOU DO -- THEN YOU LISTEN.
IT'S OVER FOR THE KINGPIN. OH! VER!
YOU WANT TO DO THE RIGHT THING FOR ONCE IN YOUR LIFE?
MARCH YOUR INCREDIBLY STUPID BUTT RIGHT TO THE COPS, FBI OR WHATEVER --
-- AND YOU CONFESS.
YOU TELL THE EVERYTHING.
BECAUSE HE' GOING BYE-BY EITHER WAY.
Y-YEAH -- OK.

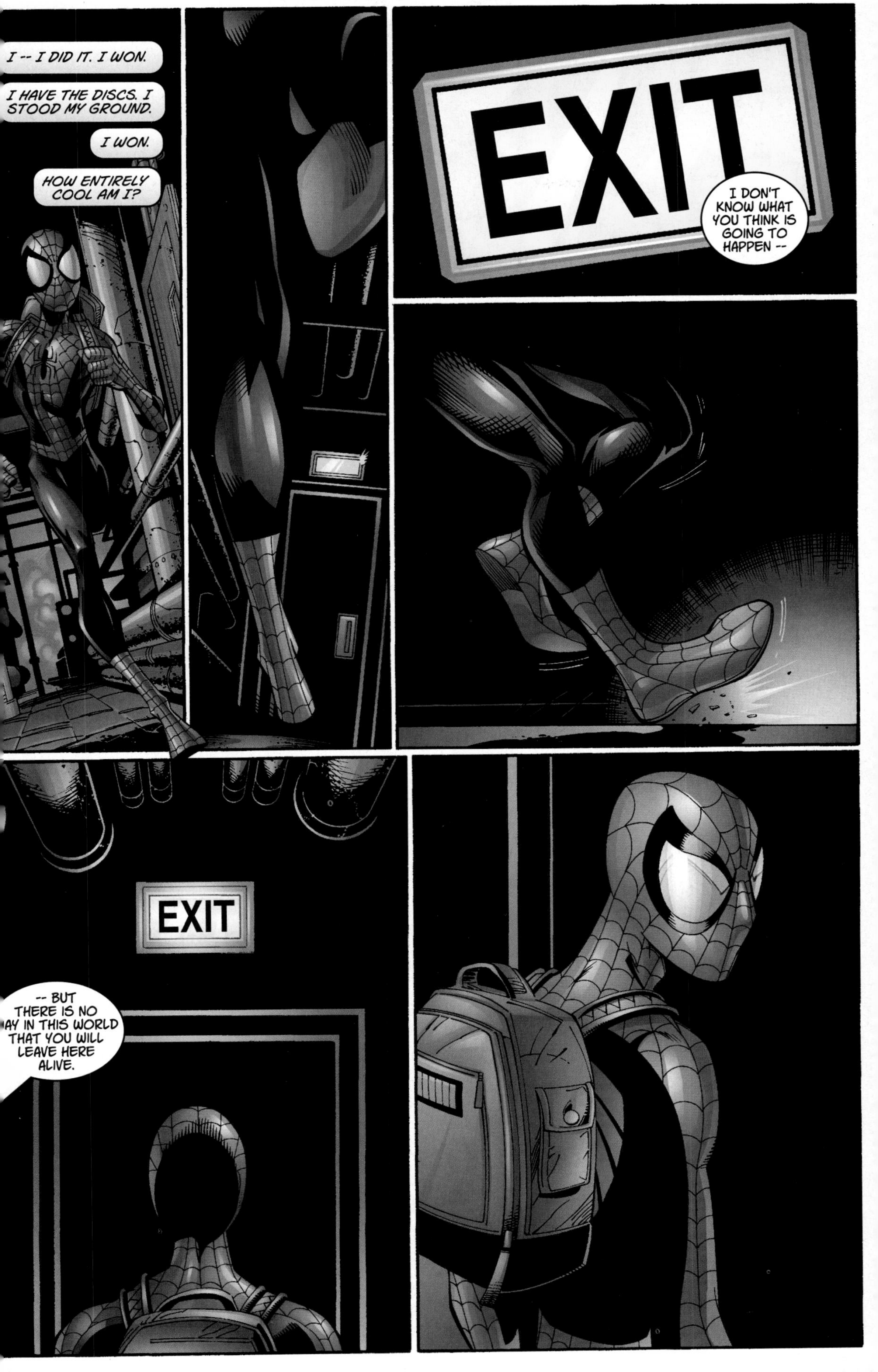
I -- I DID IT. I WON.
I HAVE THE DISCS. I STOOD MY GROUND.
I WON.
HOW ENTIRELY COOL AM I?
EXIT
I DON'T KNOW WHAT YOU THINK IS GOING TO HAPPEN --
EXIT
-- BUT THERE IS NO AY IN THIS WORLD THAT YOU WILL LEAVE HERE ALIVE.

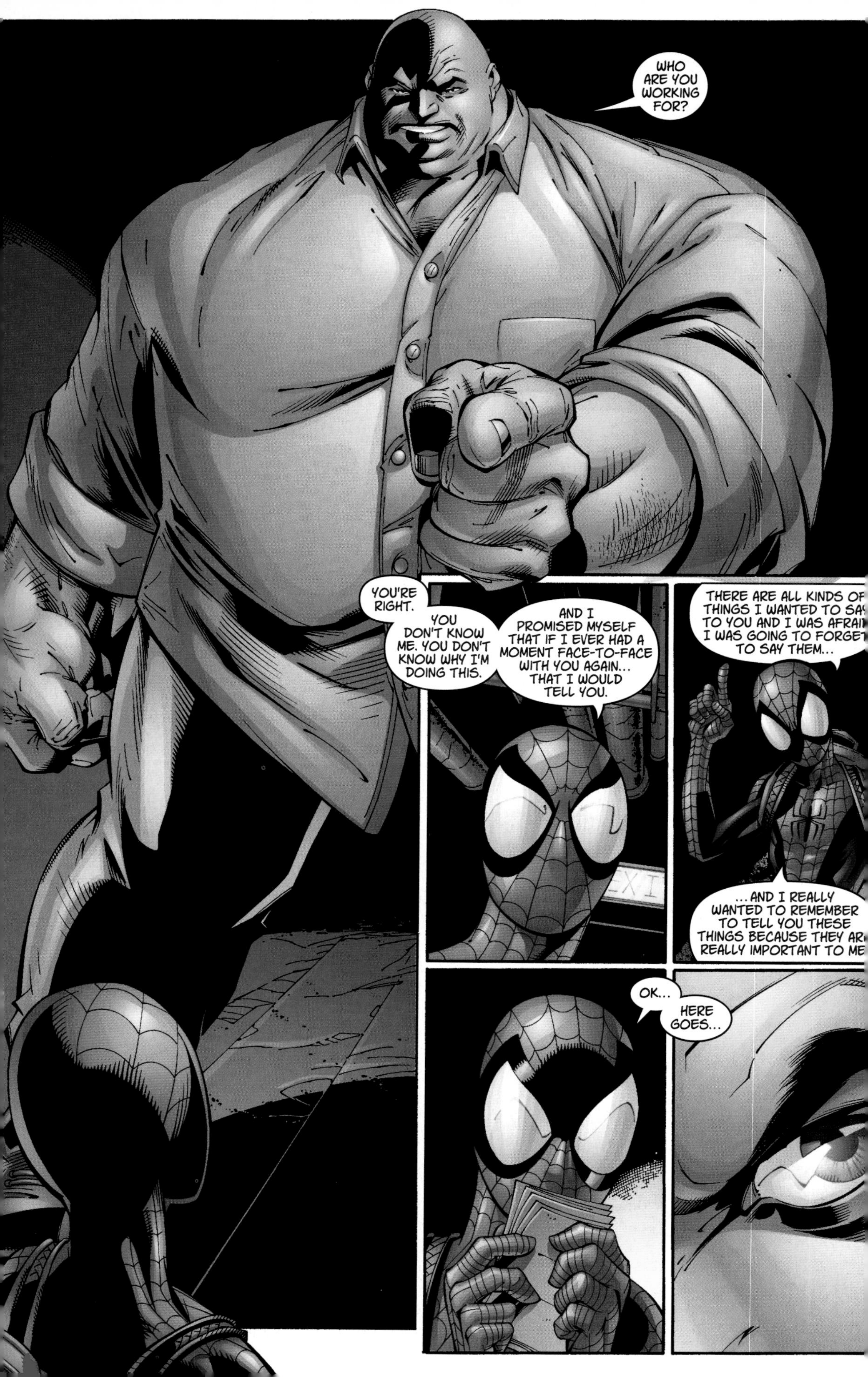

WHO ARE YOU WORKING FOR?
YOU'RE RIGHT.
YOU DON'T KNOW ME. YOU DON'T KNOW WHY I'M DOING THIS.
AND I PROMISED MYSELF THAT IF I EVER HAD A MOMENT FACE-TO-FACE WITH YOU AGAIN... THAT I WOULD TELL YOU.
THERE ARE ALL KINDS OF THINGS I WANTED TO SAY TO YOU AND I WAS AFRAID I WAS GOING TO FORGET TO SAY THEM...
...AND I REALLY WANTED TO REMEMBER TO TELL YOU THESE THINGS BECAUSE THEY ARE REALLY IMPORTANT TO ME.
OK...
HERE GOES...

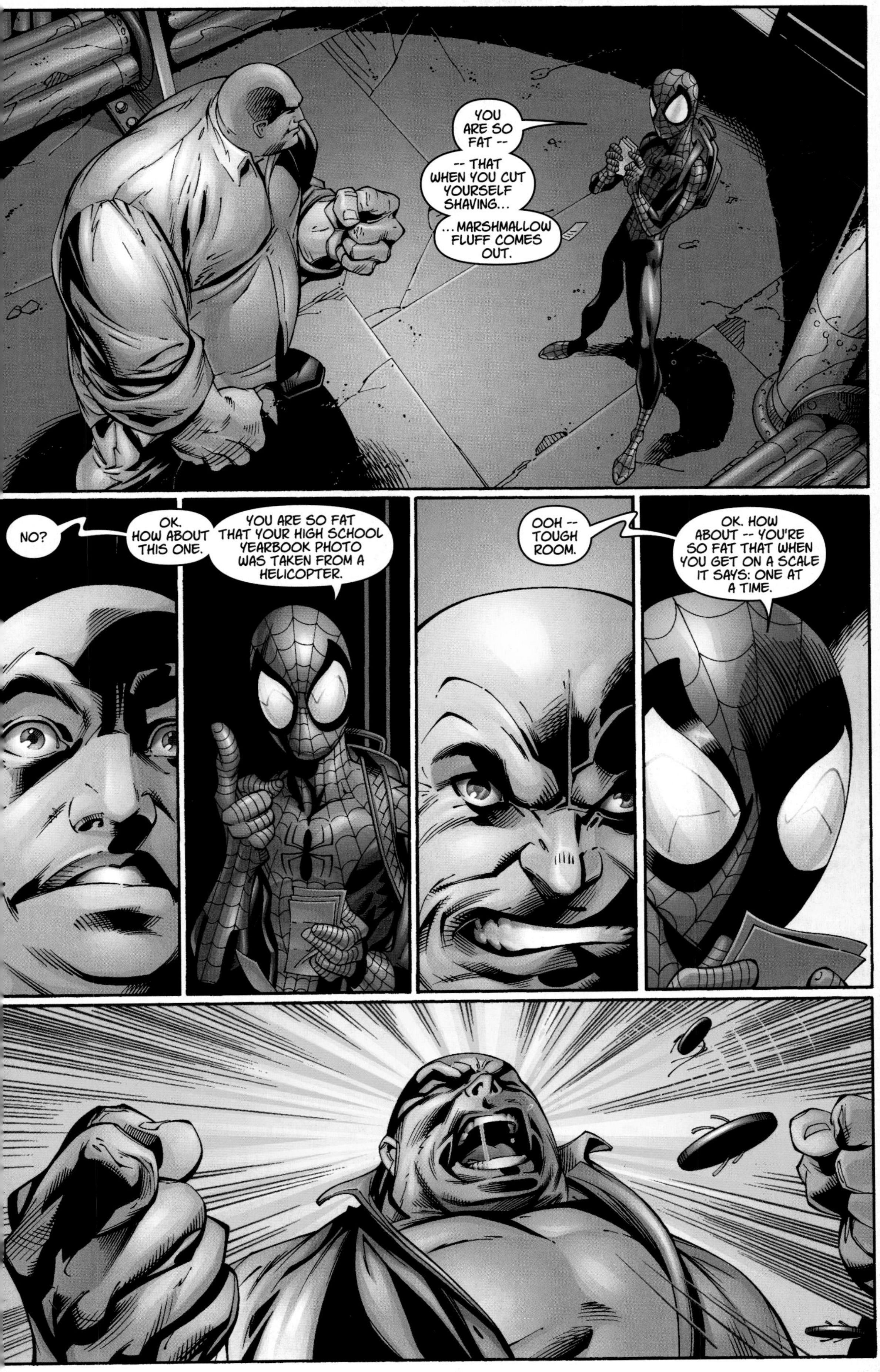
YOU ARE SO FAT --
-- THAT WHEN YOU CUT YOURSELF SHAVING...
...MARSHMALLOW FLUFF COMES OUT.
NO?
OK. HOW ABOUT THIS ONE.
YOU ARE SO FAT THAT YOUR HIGH SCHOOL YEARBOOK PHOTO WAS TAKEN FROM A HELICOPTER.
OOH -- TOUGH ROOM.
OK. HOW ABOUT -- YOU'RE SO FAT THAT WHEN YOU GET ON A SCALE IT SAYS: ONE AT A TIME.

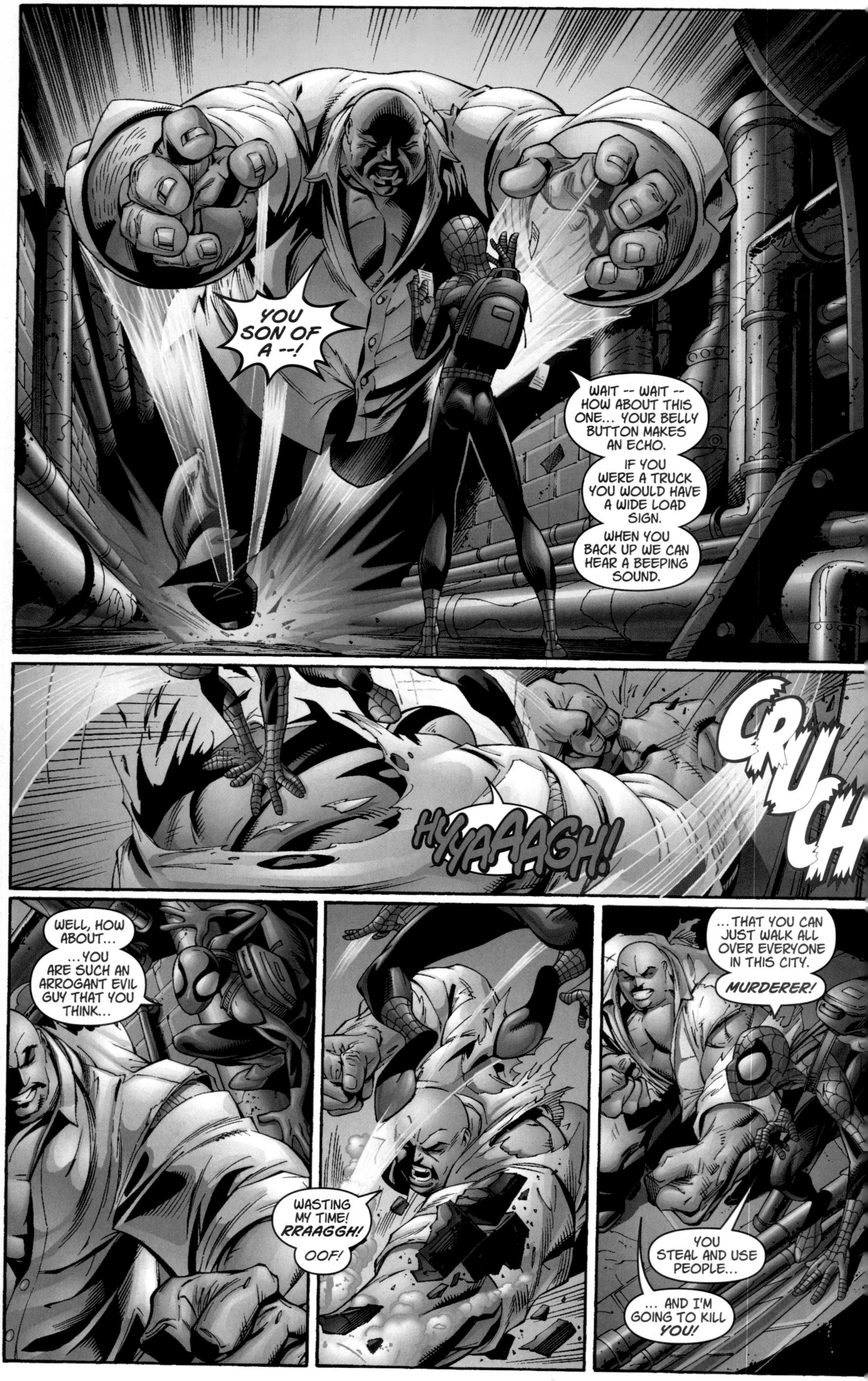

YOU SON OF A --!
WAIT -- WAIT -- HOW ABOUT THIS ONE... YOUR BELLY BUTTON MAKES AN ECHO.
IF YOU WERE A TRUCK YOU WOULD HAVE A WIDE LOAD SIGN.
WHEN YOU BACK UP WE CAN HEAR A BEEPING SOUND.
HYYAAAAGH!
CRUCH
WELL, HOW ABOUT...
...YOU ARE SUCH AN ARROGANT EVIL GUY THAT YOU THINK...
WASTING MY TIME! RRAAGGH!
OOF!
...THAT YOU CAN JUST WALK ALL OVER EVERYONE IN THIS CITY.
MURDERER!
YOU STEAL AND USE PEOPLE...
... AND I'M GOING TO KILL YOU!

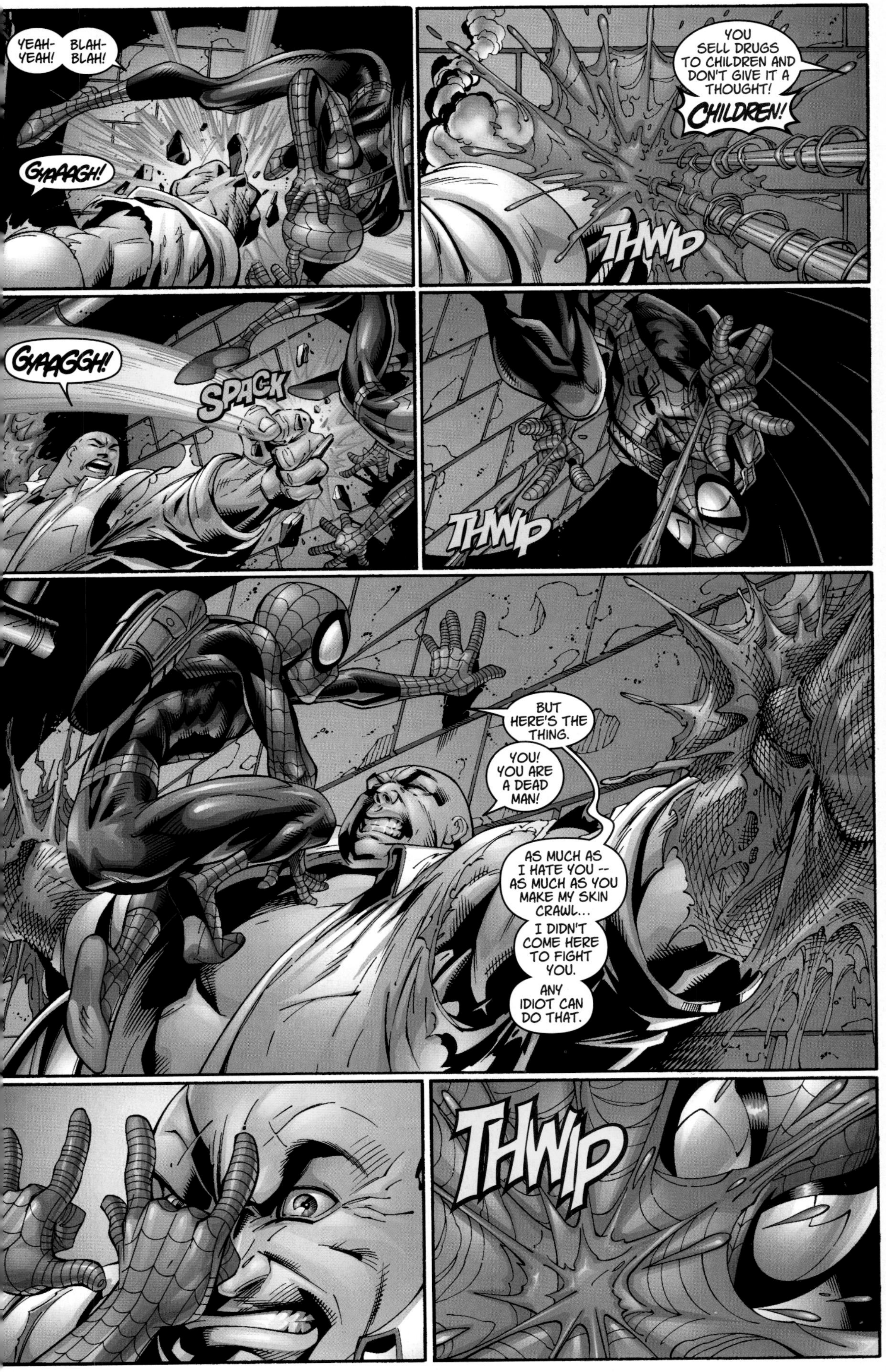
YEAH-YEAH!
BLAH-BLAH!
GYAAAGH!
YOU SELL DRUGS TO CHILDREN AND DON'T GIVE IT A THOUGHT!
CHILDREN!
THWIP
GYAAGGH!
SPACK
THWIP
BUT HERE'S THE THING.
YOU! YOU ARE A DEAD MAN!
AS MUCH AS I HATE YOU -- AS MUCH AS YOU MAKE MY SKIN CRAWL...
I DIDN'T COME HERE TO FIGHT YOU.
ANY IDIOT CAN DO THAT.
THWIP

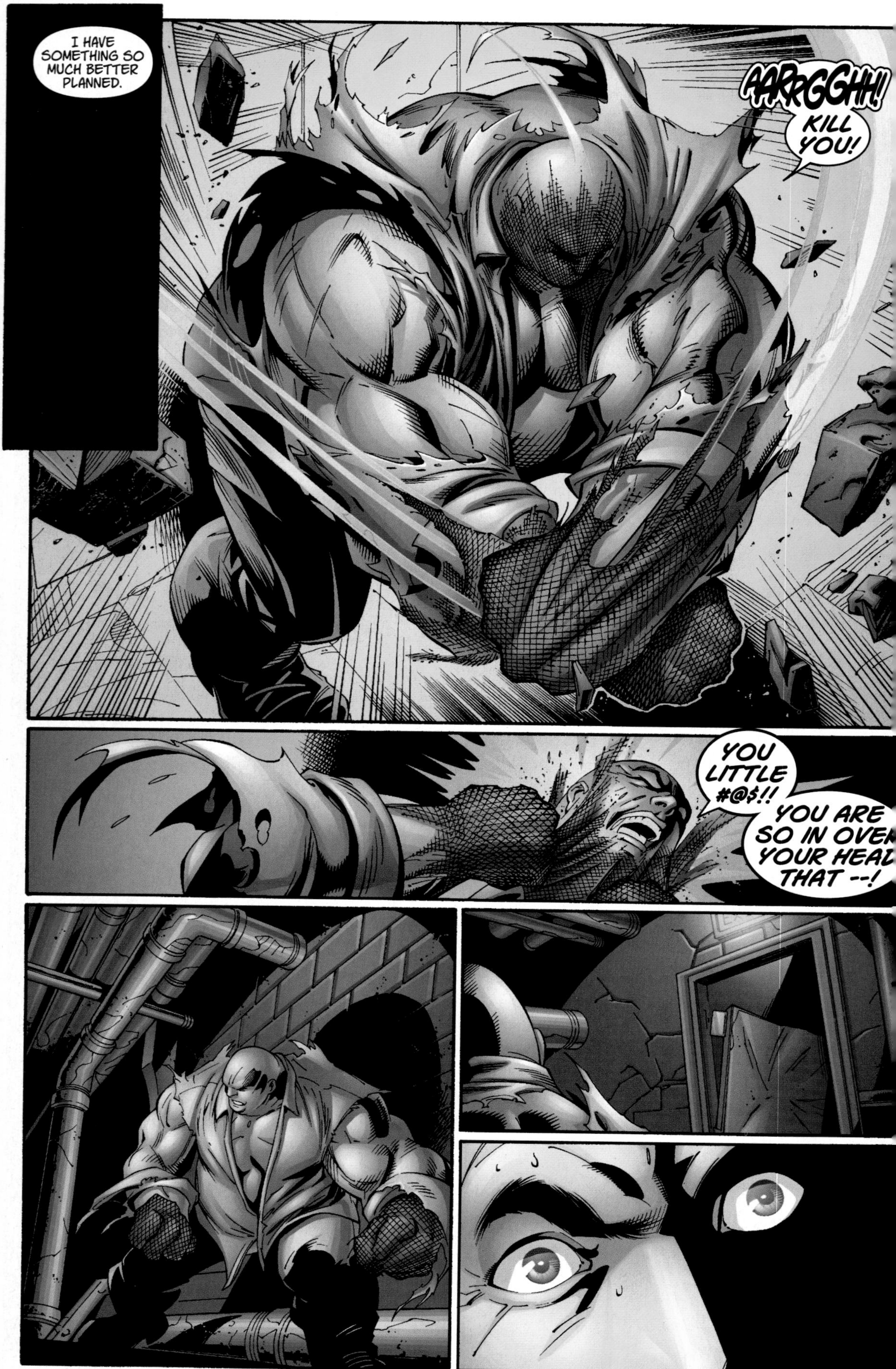
I HAVE SOMETHING SO MUCH BETTER PLANNED.
AARRGGHH!
KILL YOU!
YOU LITTLE #@$!!
YOU ARE SO IN OVER YOUR HEAD THAT --!

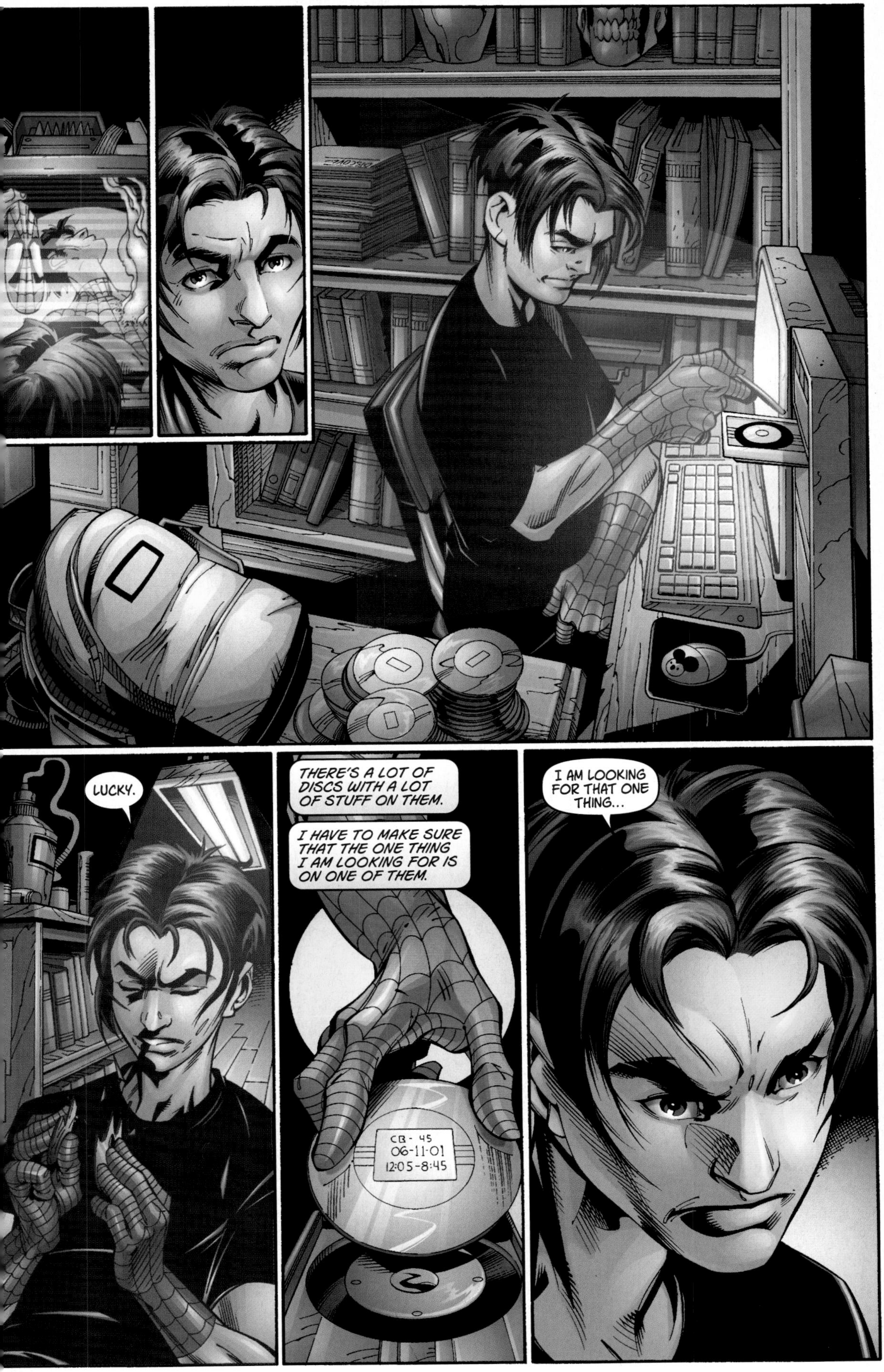

LUCKY.
THERE'S A LOT OF DISCS WITH A LOT OF STUFF ON THEM.
I HAVE TO MAKE SURE THAT THE ONE THING I AM LOOKING FOR IS ON ONE OF THEM.
CB - 45
06-11-01
12:05-8:45
I AM LOOKING FOR THAT ONE THING...

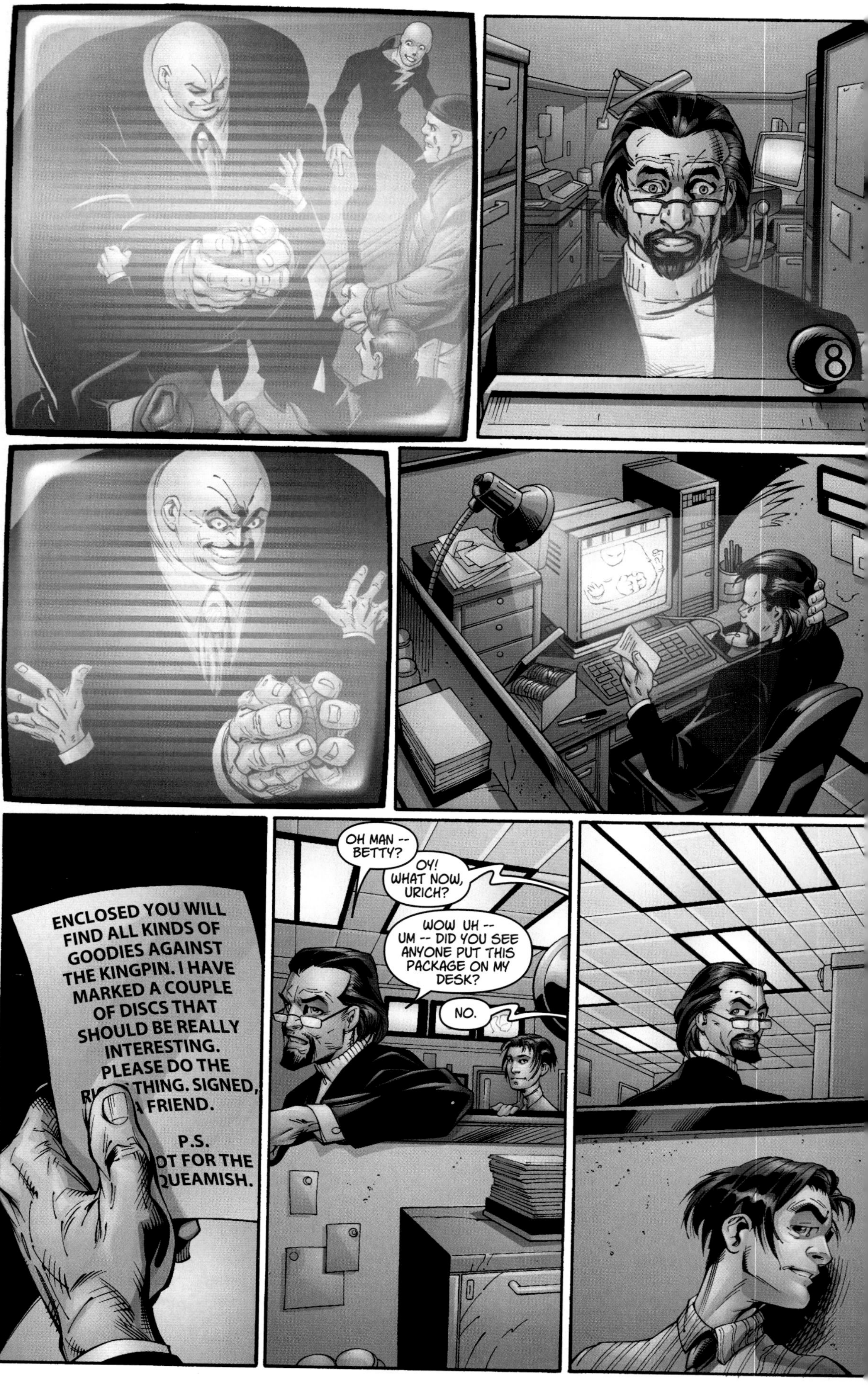

ENCLOSED YOU WILL FIND ALL KINDS OF GOODIES AGAINST THE KINGPIN. I HAVE MARKED A COUPLE OF DISCS THAT SHOULD BE REALLY INTERESTING. PLEASE DO THE RI THING. SIGNED, A FRIEND.
P.S. OT FOR THE QUEAMISH.
OH MAN -- BETTY?
OY! WHAT NOW, URICH?
WOW UH -- UM -- DID YOU SEE ANYONE PUT THIS PACKAGE ON MY DESK?
NO.

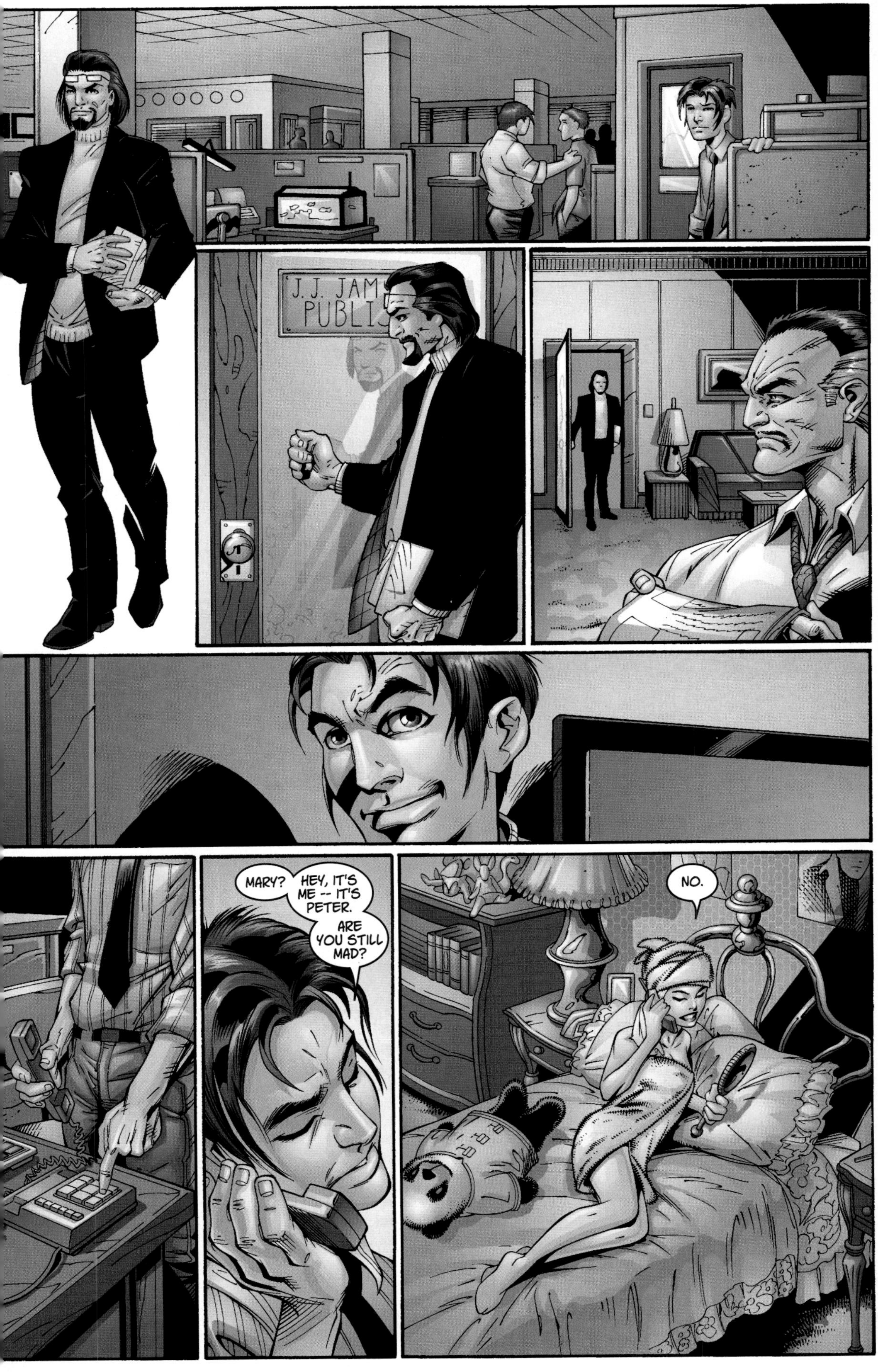
J. J. JAM
PUBLIS
MARY?
HEY, IT'S ME -- IT'S PETER.
ARE YOU STILL MAD?
NO.

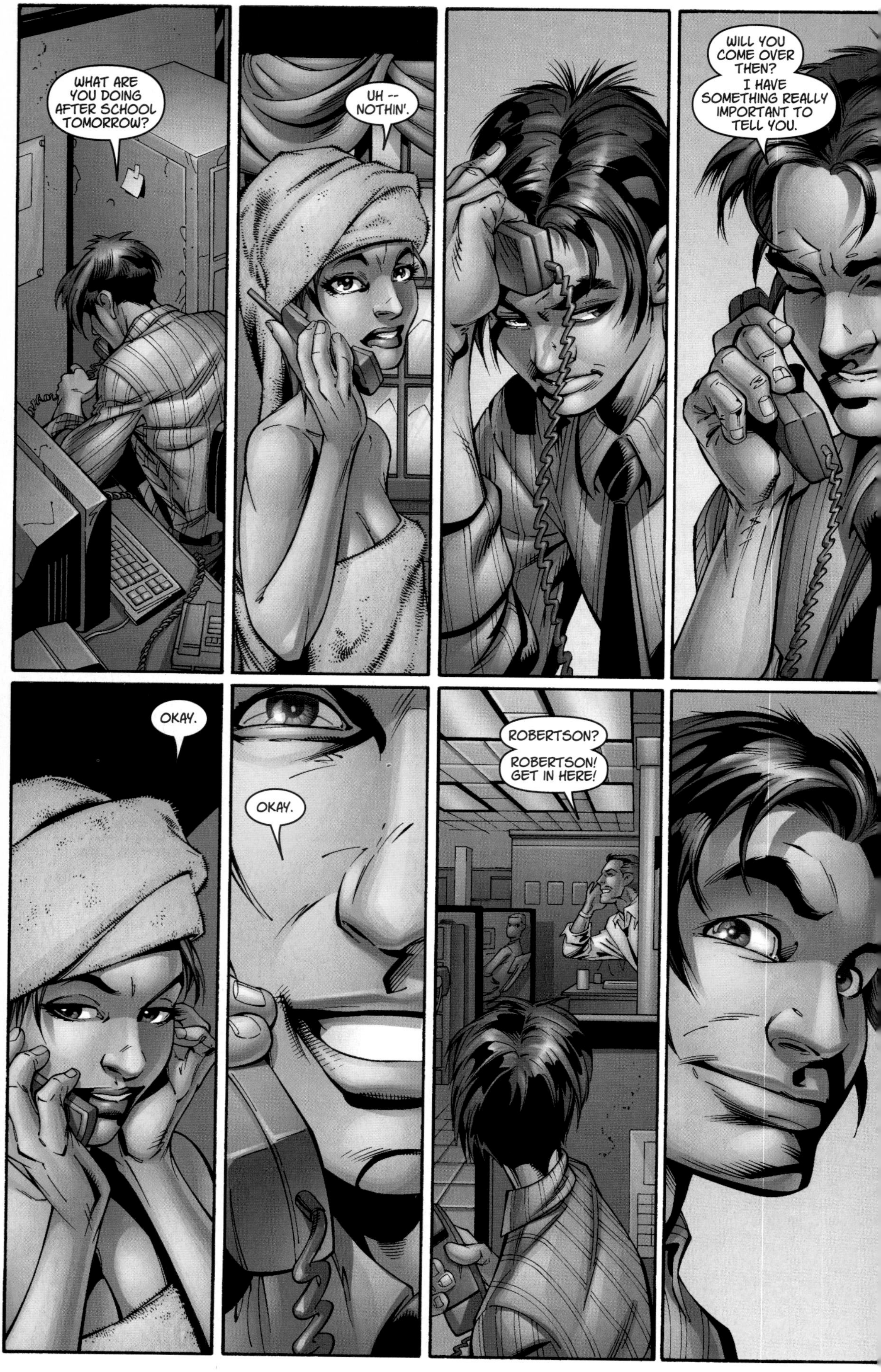
WHAT ARE YOU DOING AFTER SCHOOL TOMORROW?
UH -- NOTHIN'.
WILL YOU COME OVER THEN? I HAVE SOMETHING REALLY IMPORTANT TO TELL YOU.
OKAY.
OKAY.
ROBERTSON?
ROBERTSON! GET IN HERE!

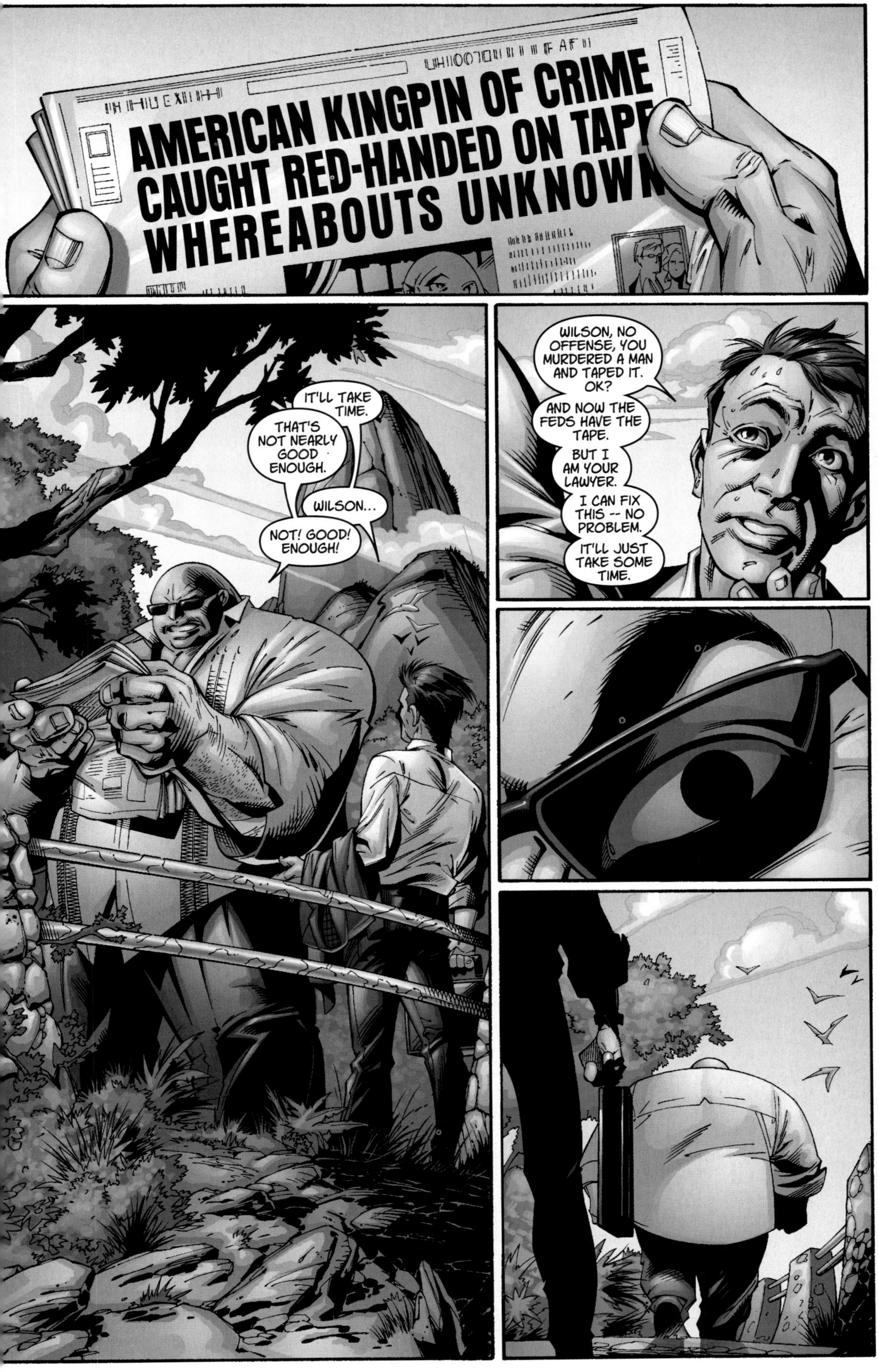
AMERICAN KINGPIN OF CRIME CAUGHT RED-HANDED ON TAPE WHEREABOUTS UNKNOWN
IT'LL TAKE TIME.
THAT'S NOT NEARLY GOOD ENOUGH.
WILSON...
NOT! GOOD! ENOUGH!
WILSON, NO OFFENSE, YOU MURDERED A MAN AND TAPED IT. OK?
AND NOW THE FEDS HAVE THE TAPE.
BUT I AM YOUR LAWYER.
I CAN FIX THIS -- NO PROBLEM.
IT'LL JUST TAKE SOME TIME.

13

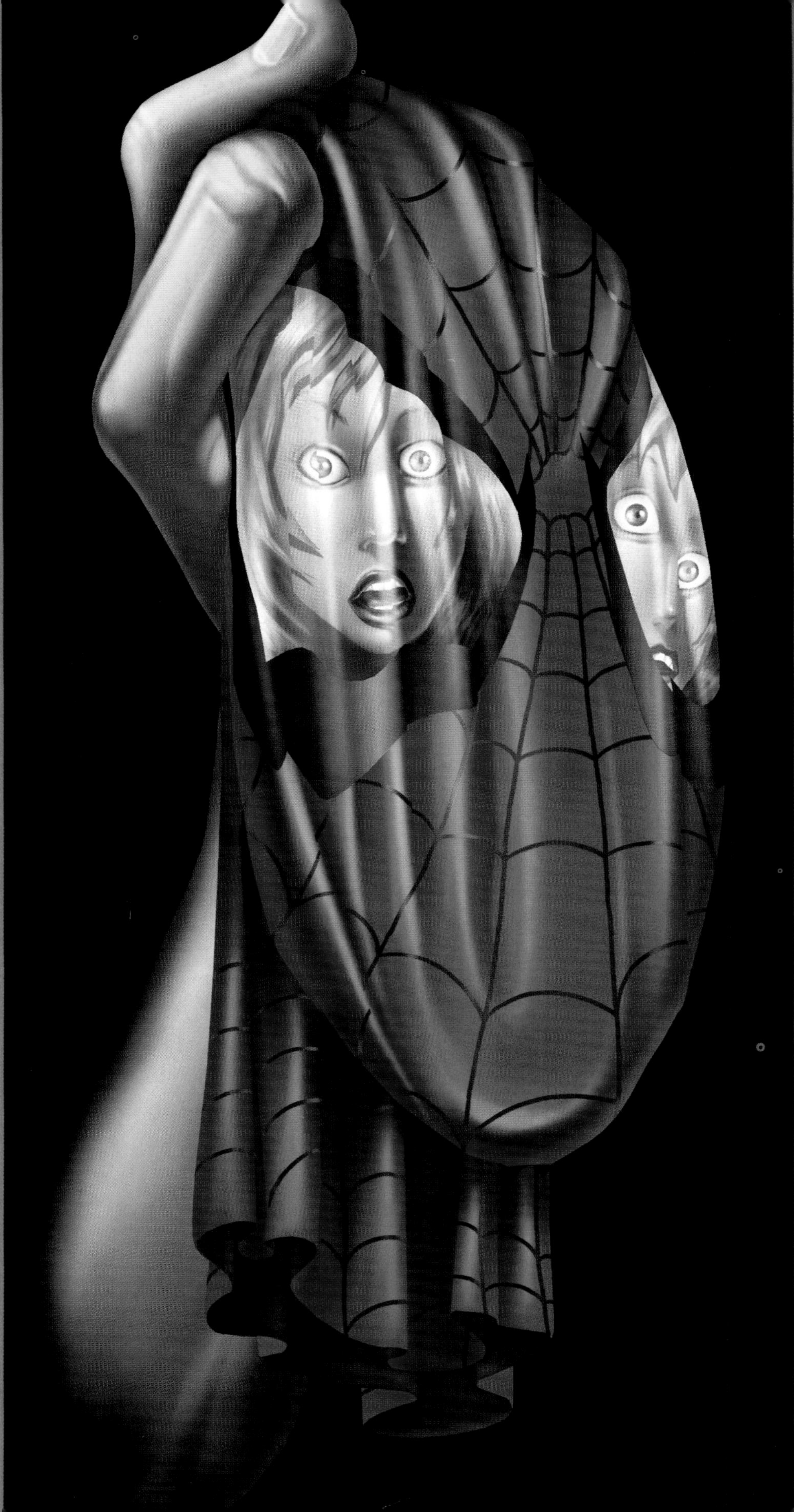

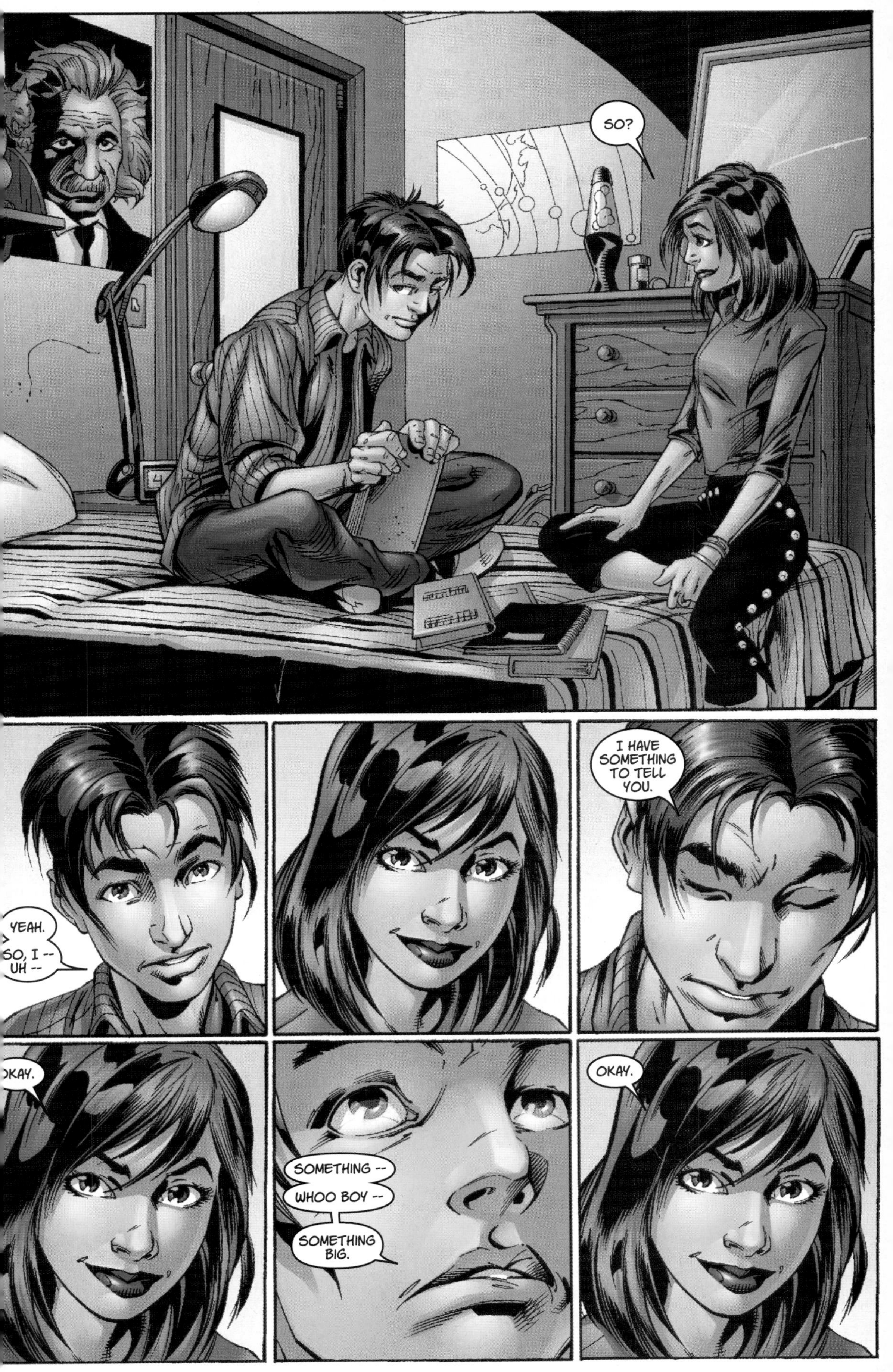
SO?
YEAH.
SO, I --
UH --
I HAVE SOMETHING TO TELL YOU.
OKAY.
SOMETHING --
WHOO BOY --
SOMETHING BIG.
OKAY.

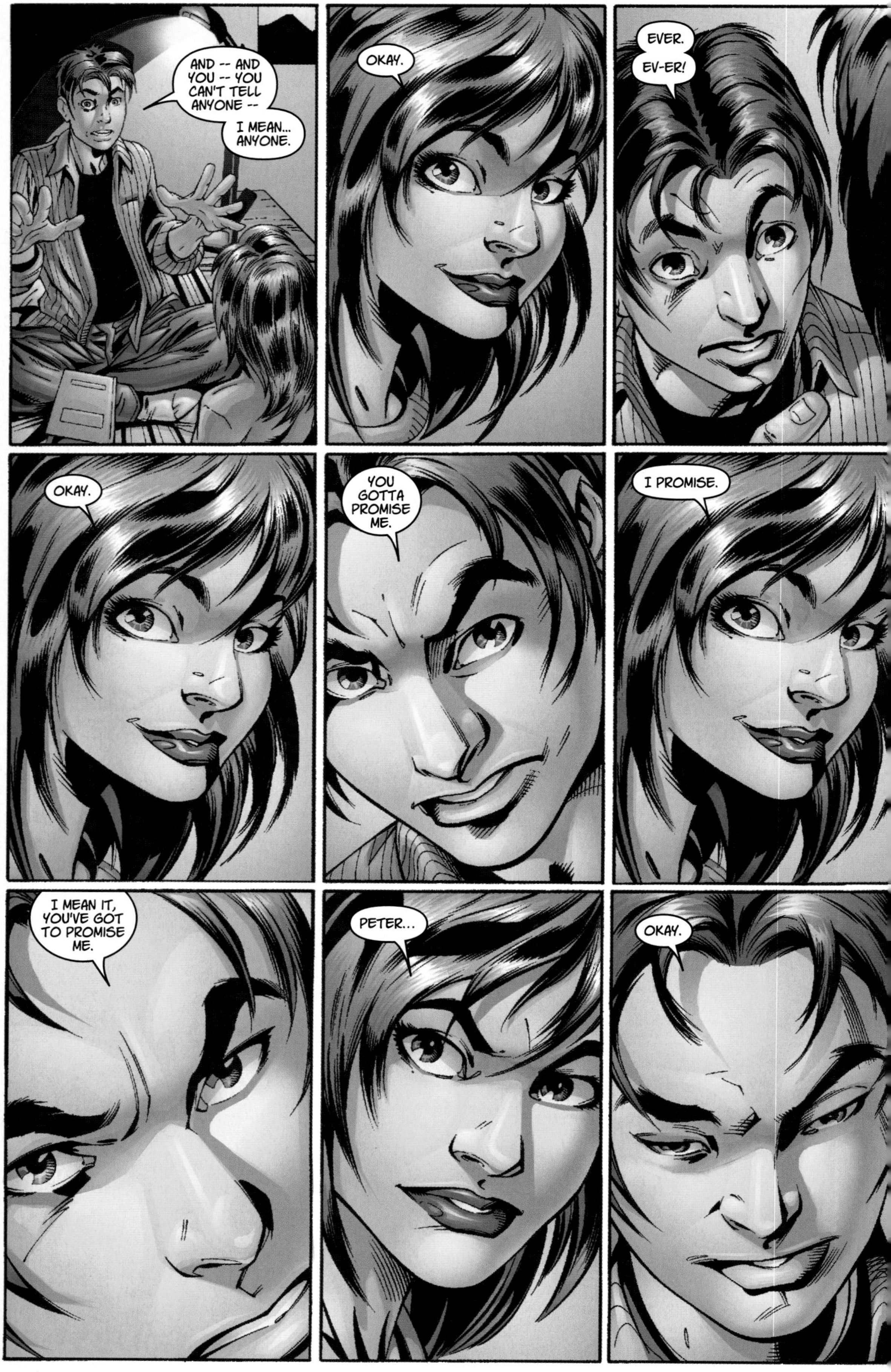
AND -- AND YOU -- YOU CAN'T TELL ANYONE --
I MEAN... ANYONE.
OKAY.
EVER.
EV-ER!
OKAY.
YOU GOTTA PROMISE ME.
I PROMISE.
I MEAN IT, YOU'VE GOT TO PROMISE ME.
PETER...
OKAY.

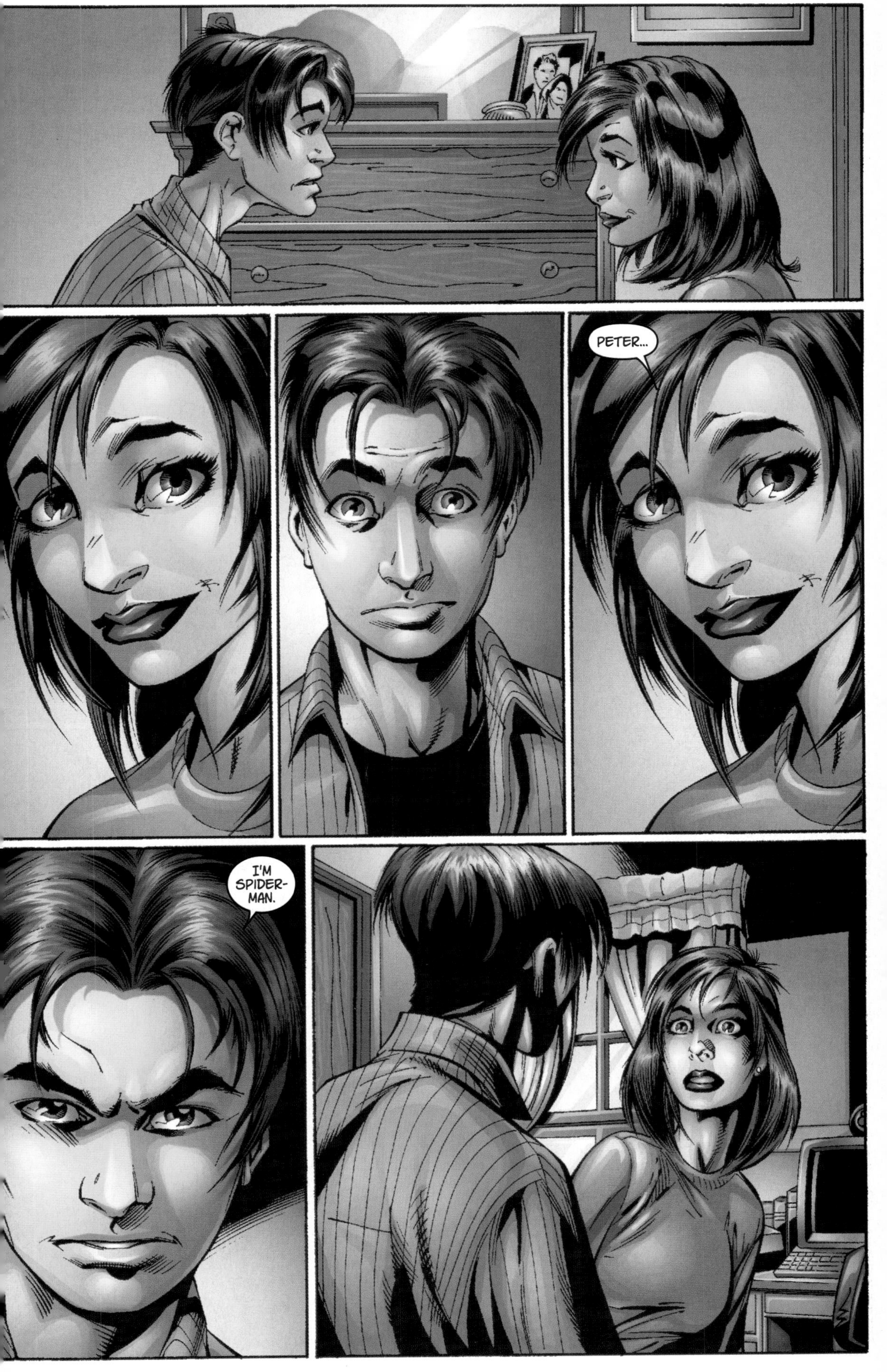
PETER...
I'M SPIDER-MAN.

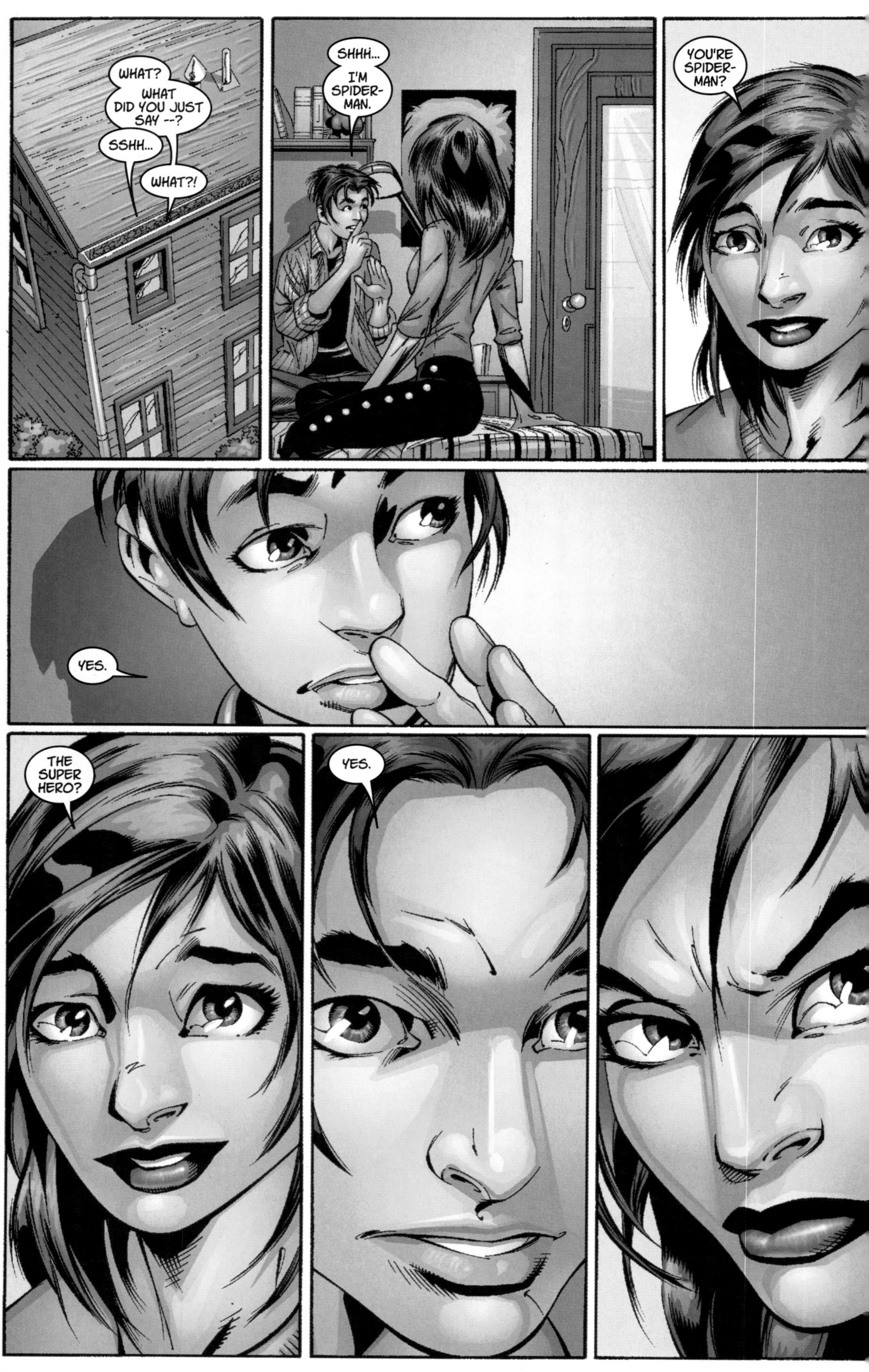
WHAT?
WHAT DID YOU JUST SAY --?
SSHH...
WHAT?!
SHHH... I'M SPIDER-MAN.
YOU'RE SPIDER-MAN?
YES.
THE SUPER HERO?
YES.

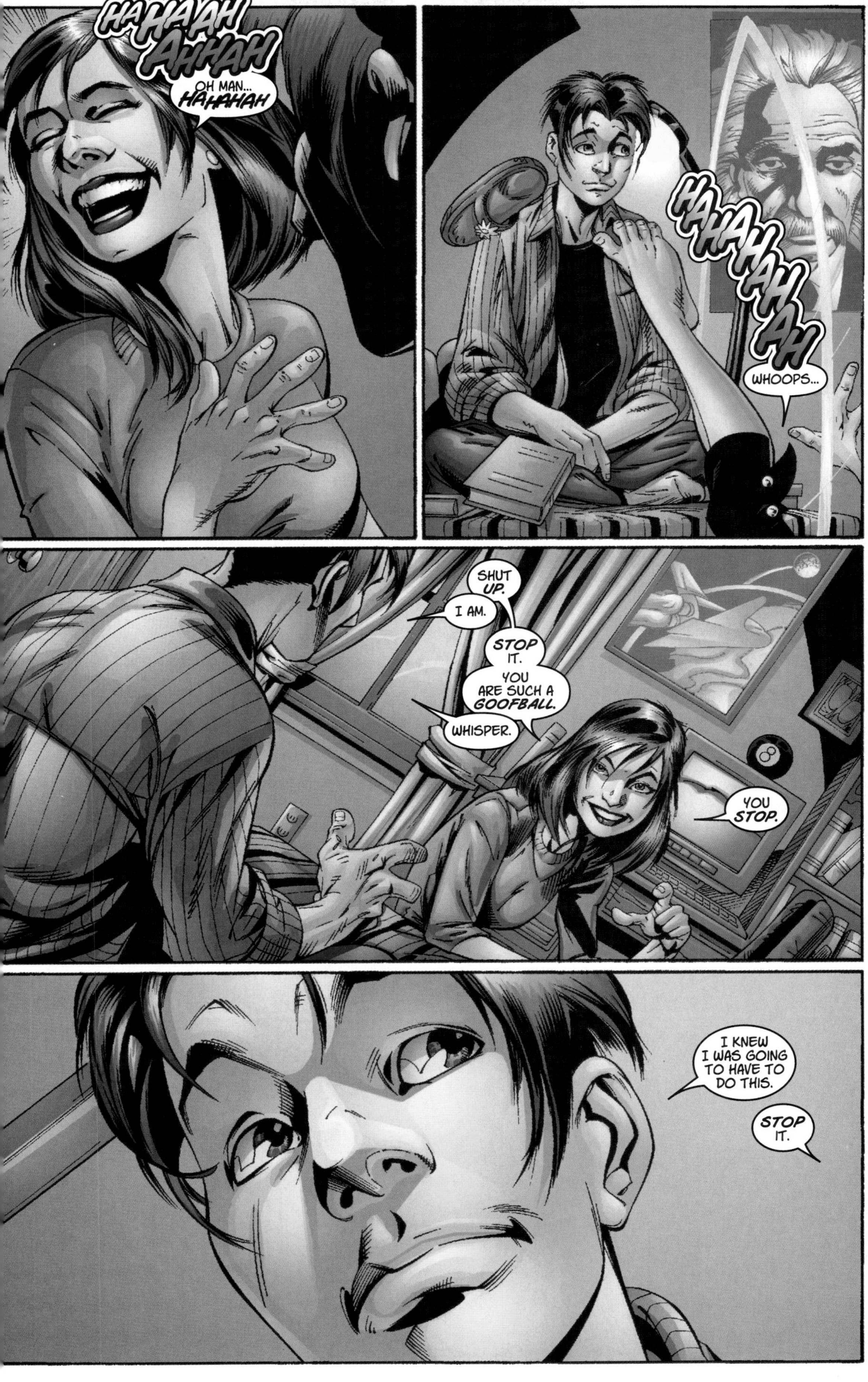
HAHAAH AHHAH
OH MAN... HAHAHAH
HAHAHAHAHAH
WHOOPS...
SHUT UP.
I AM.
STOP IT.
YOU ARE SUCH A GOOFBALL.
WHISPER.
YOU STOP.
I KNEW I WAS GOING TO HAVE TO DO THIS.
STOP IT.

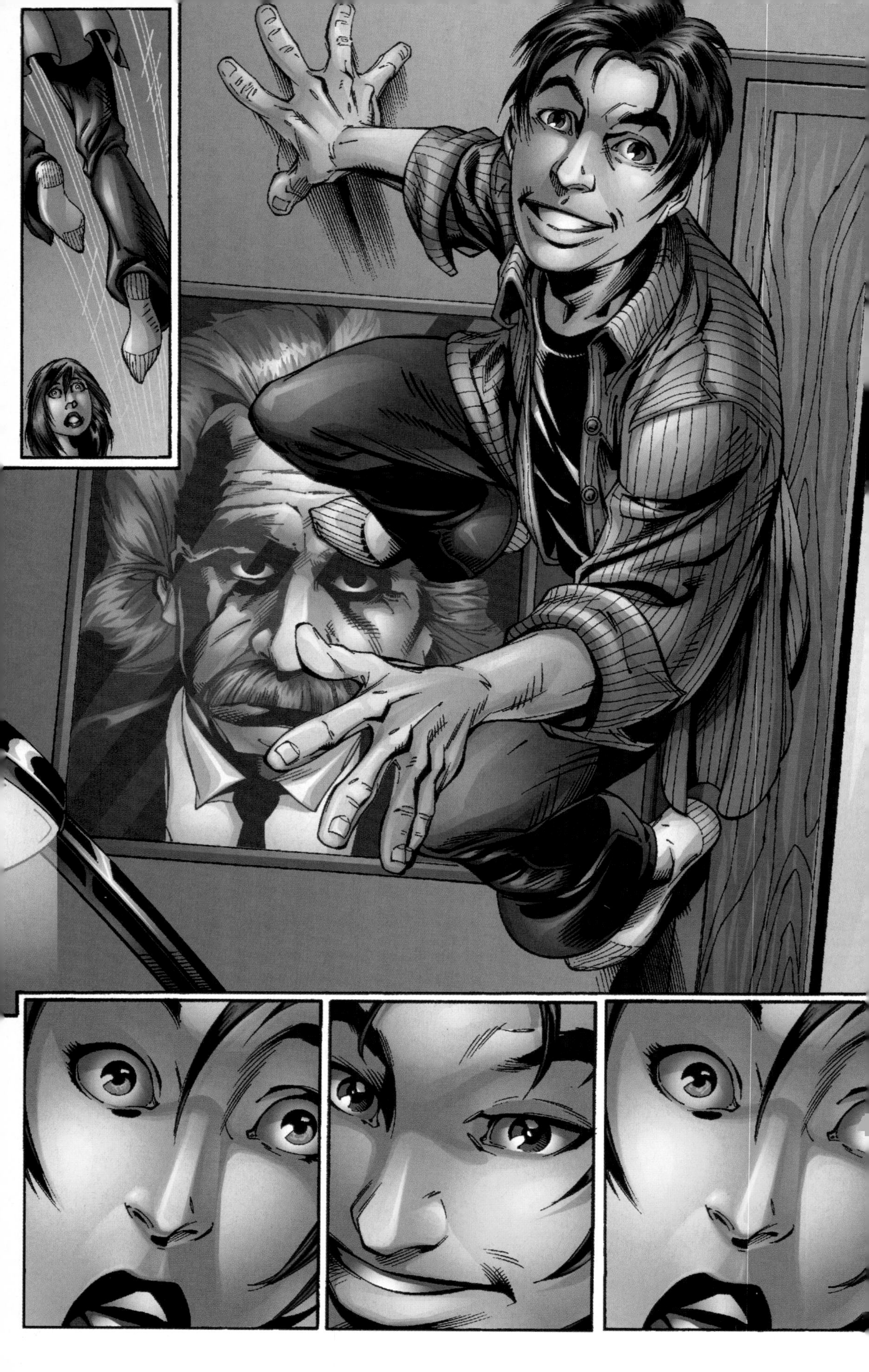

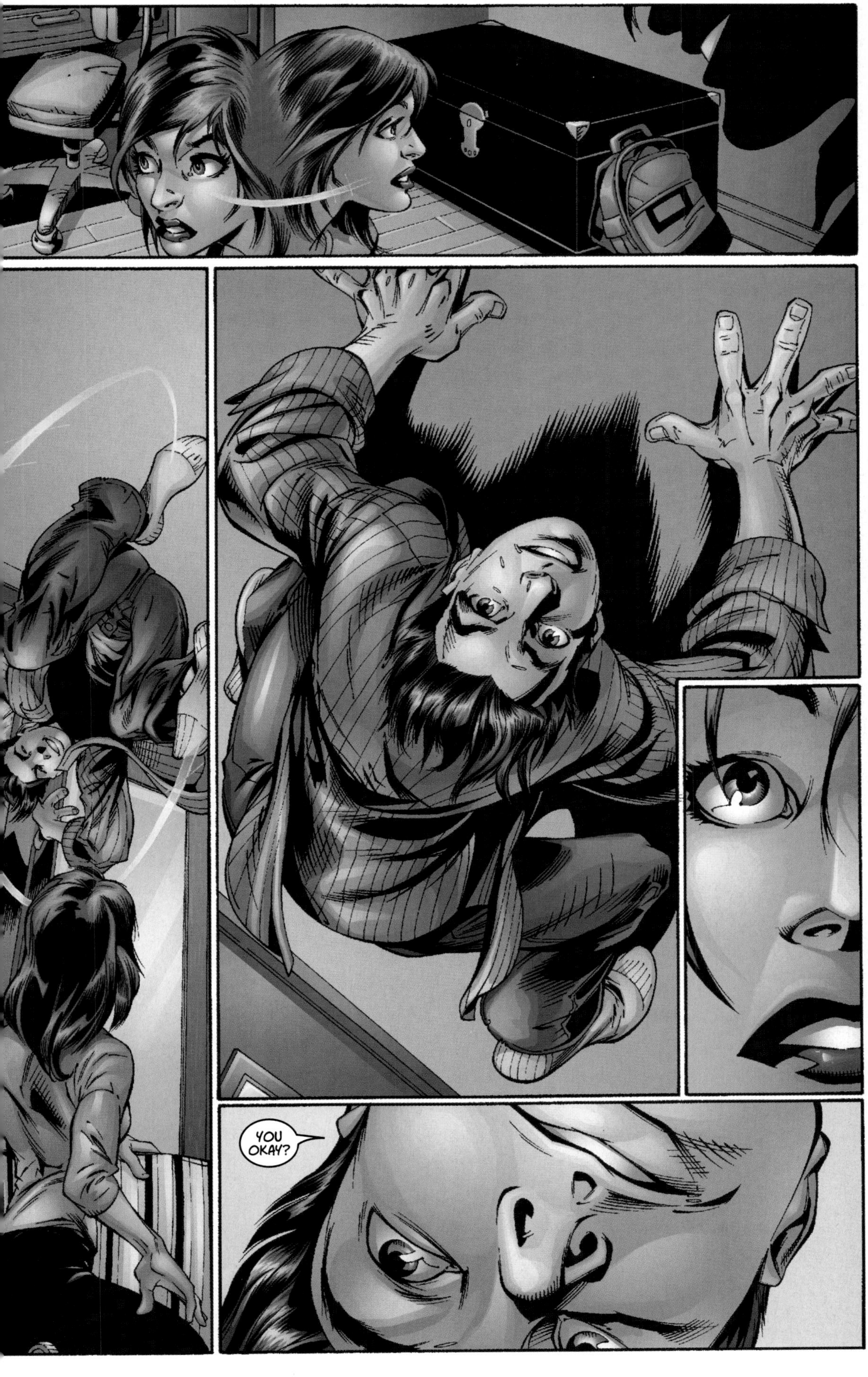
YOU OKAY?

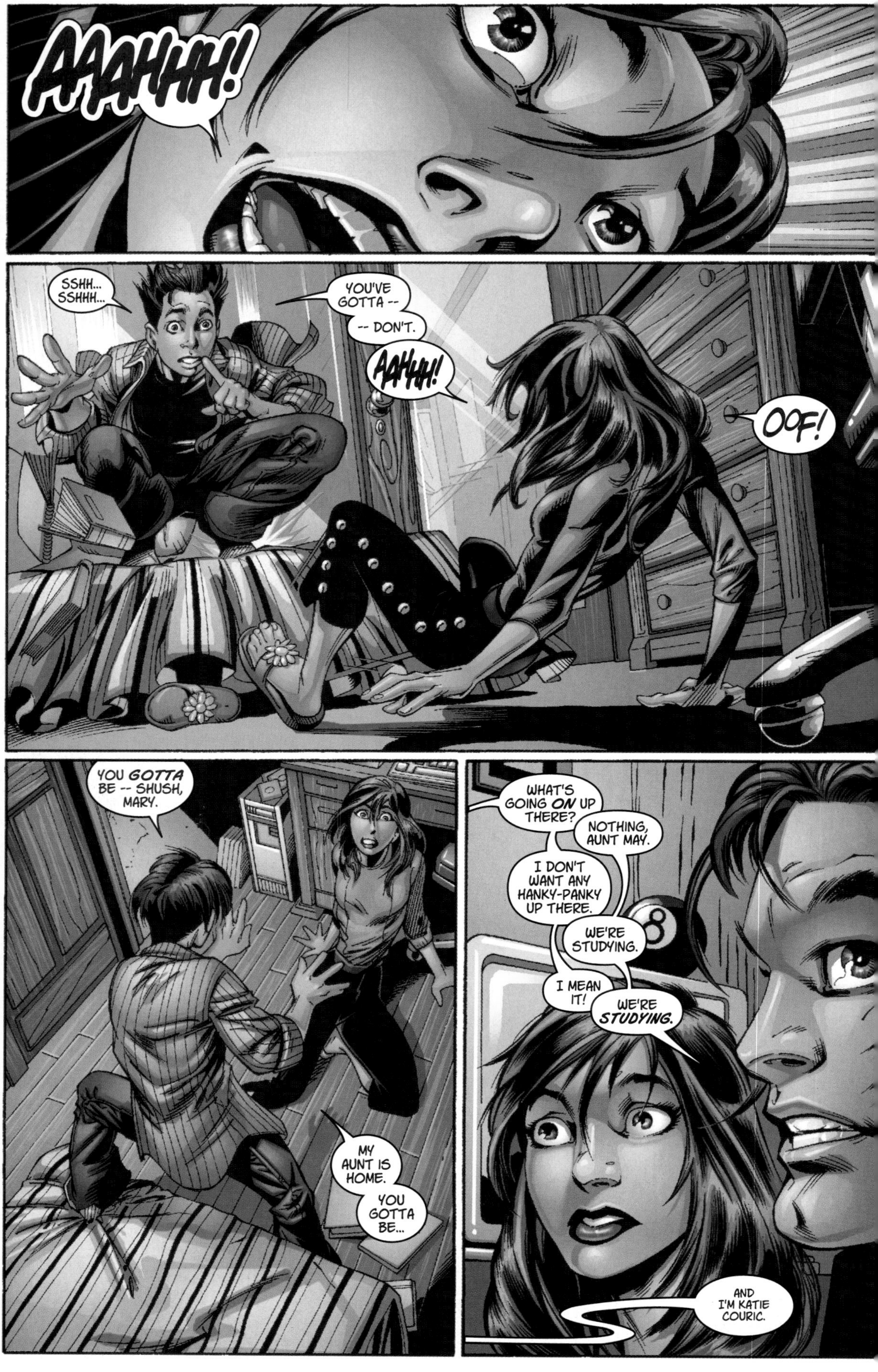
AAAHHH!
SSHH... SSHHH...
YOU'VE GOTTA --
-- DON'T.
AAHHH!
OOF!
YOU GOTTA BE -- SHUSH, MARY.
MY AUNT IS HOME.
YOU GOTTA BE...
WHAT'S GOING ON UP THERE?
NOTHING, AUNT MAY.
I DON'T WANT ANY HANKY-PANKY UP THERE.
WE'RE STUDYING.
I MEAN IT!
WE'RE STUDYING.
AND I'M KATIE COURIC.

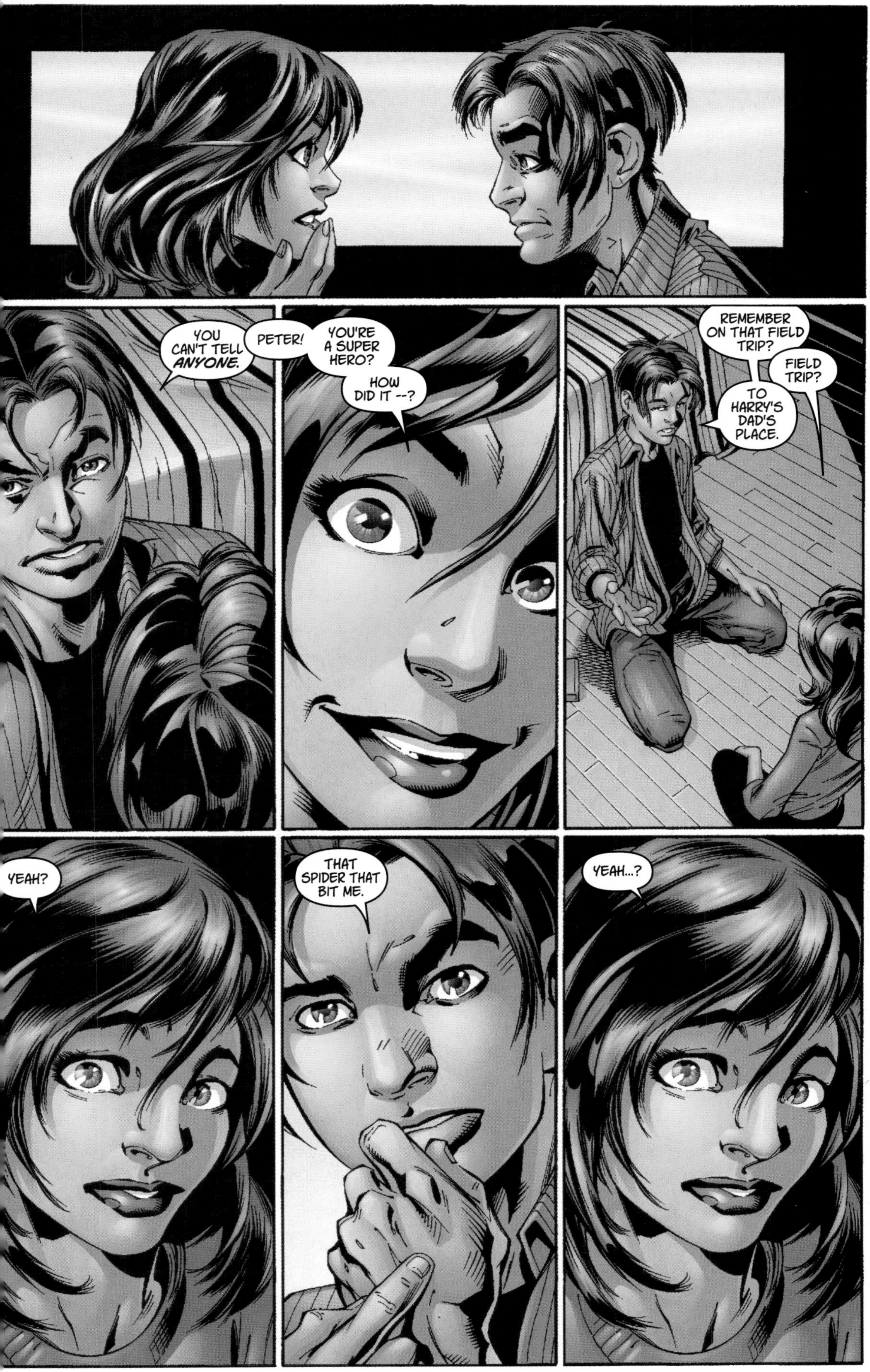
YOU CAN'T TELL *ANYONE.*
PETER!
YOU'RE A SUPER HERO?
HOW DID IT --?
REMEMBER ON THAT FIELD TRIP?
FIELD TRIP?
TO HARRY'S DAD'S PLACE.
YEAH?
THAT SPIDER THAT BIT ME.
YEAH...?

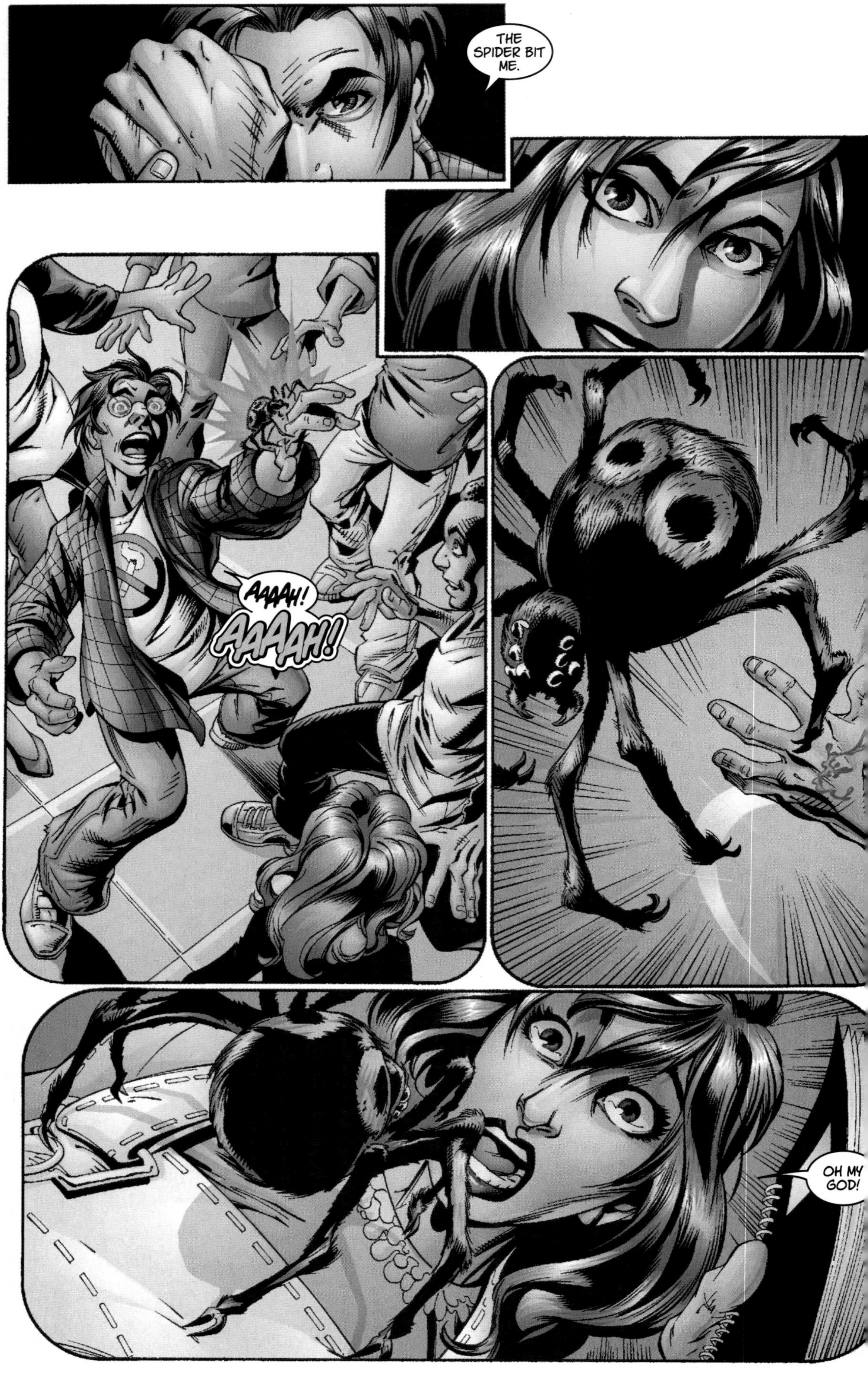
THE SPIDER BIT ME.
AAAAH!
AAAAH!
OH MY GOD!

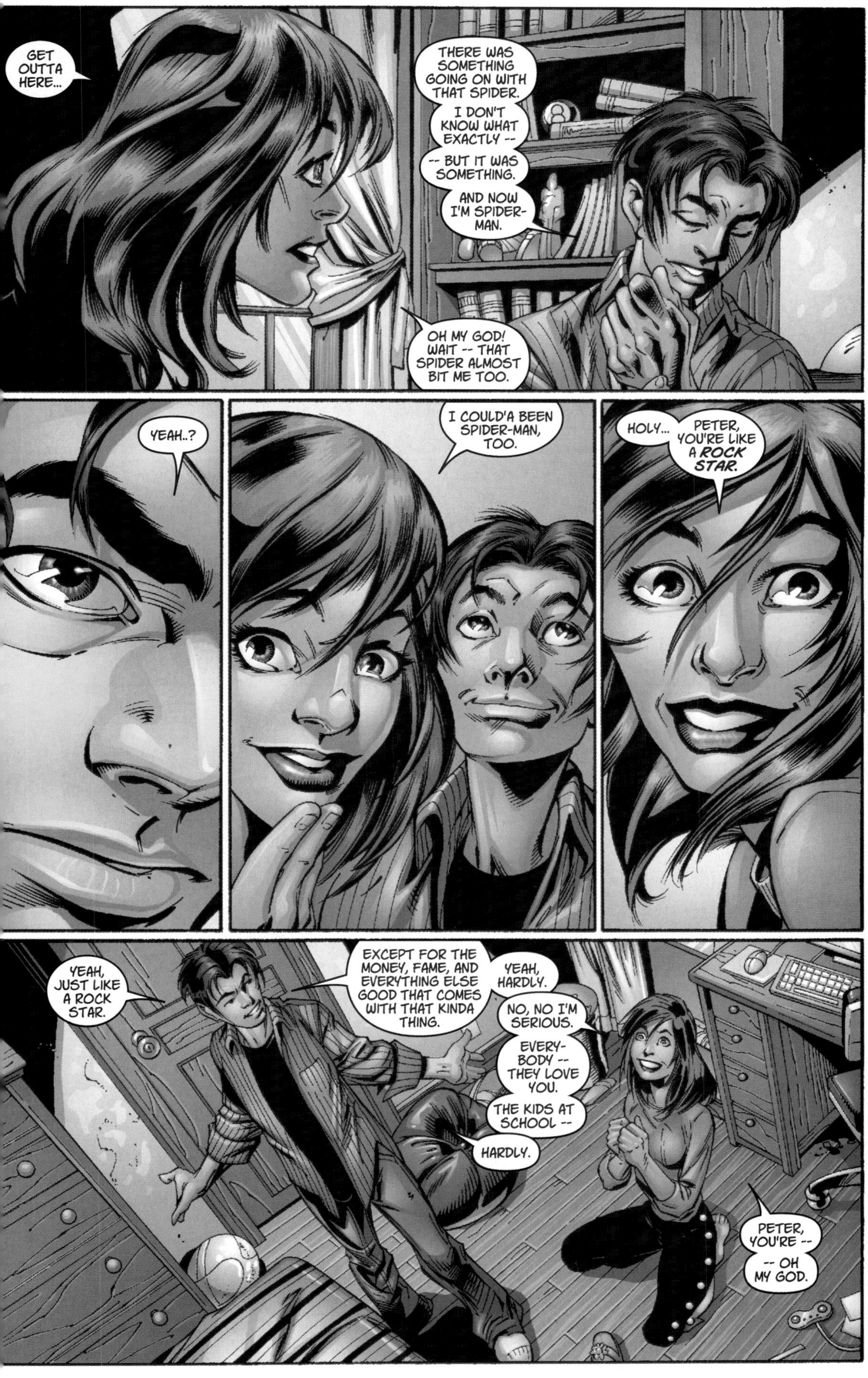
GET OUTTA HERE...
THERE WAS SOMETHING GOING ON WITH THAT SPIDER.
I DON'T KNOW WHAT EXACTLY --
-- BUT IT WAS SOMETHING.
AND NOW I'M SPIDER-MAN.
OH MY GOD! WAIT -- THAT SPIDER ALMOST BIT ME TOO.
YEAH..?
I COULD'A BEEN SPIDER-MAN, TOO.
HOLY...
PETER, YOU'RE LIKE A *ROCK STAR.*
YEAH, JUST LIKE A ROCK STAR.
EXCEPT FOR THE MONEY, FAME, AND EVERYTHING ELSE GOOD THAT COMES WITH THAT KINDA THING.
YEAH, HARDLY.
NO, NO I'M SERIOUS.
EVERY-BODY -- THEY LOVE YOU.
THE KIDS AT SCHOOL --
HARDLY.
PETER, YOU'RE --
-- OH MY GOD.

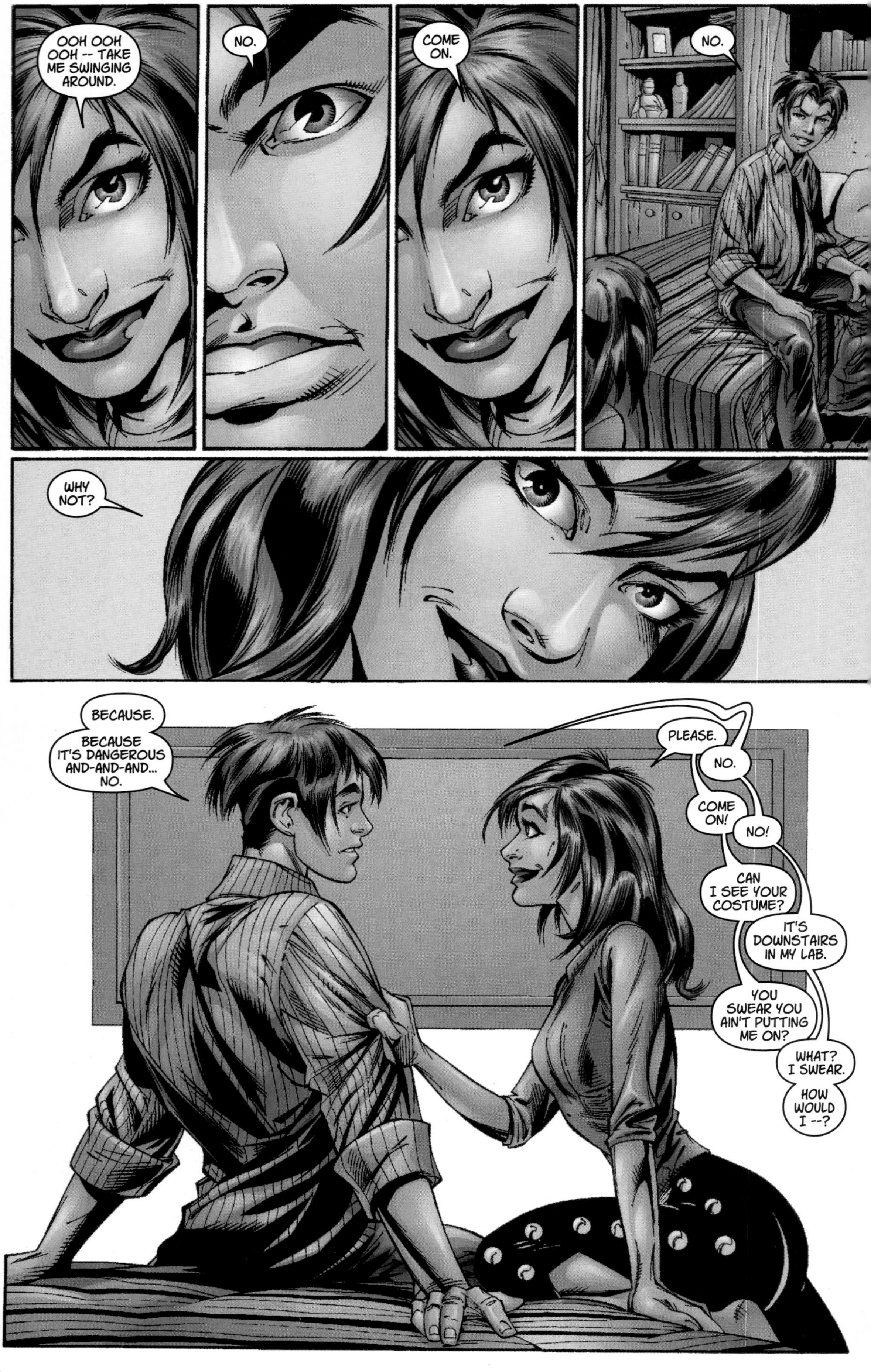
OOH OOH OOH -- TAKE ME SWINGING AROUND.
NO.
COME ON.
NO.
WHY NOT?
BECAUSE.
BECAUSE IT'S DANGEROUS AND-AND-AND... NO.
PLEASE.
NO.
COME ON!
NO!
CAN I SEE YOUR COSTUME?
IT'S DOWNSTAIRS IN MY LAB.
YOU SWEAR YOU AIN'T PUTTING ME ON?
WHAT? I SWEAR.
HOW WOULD I --?

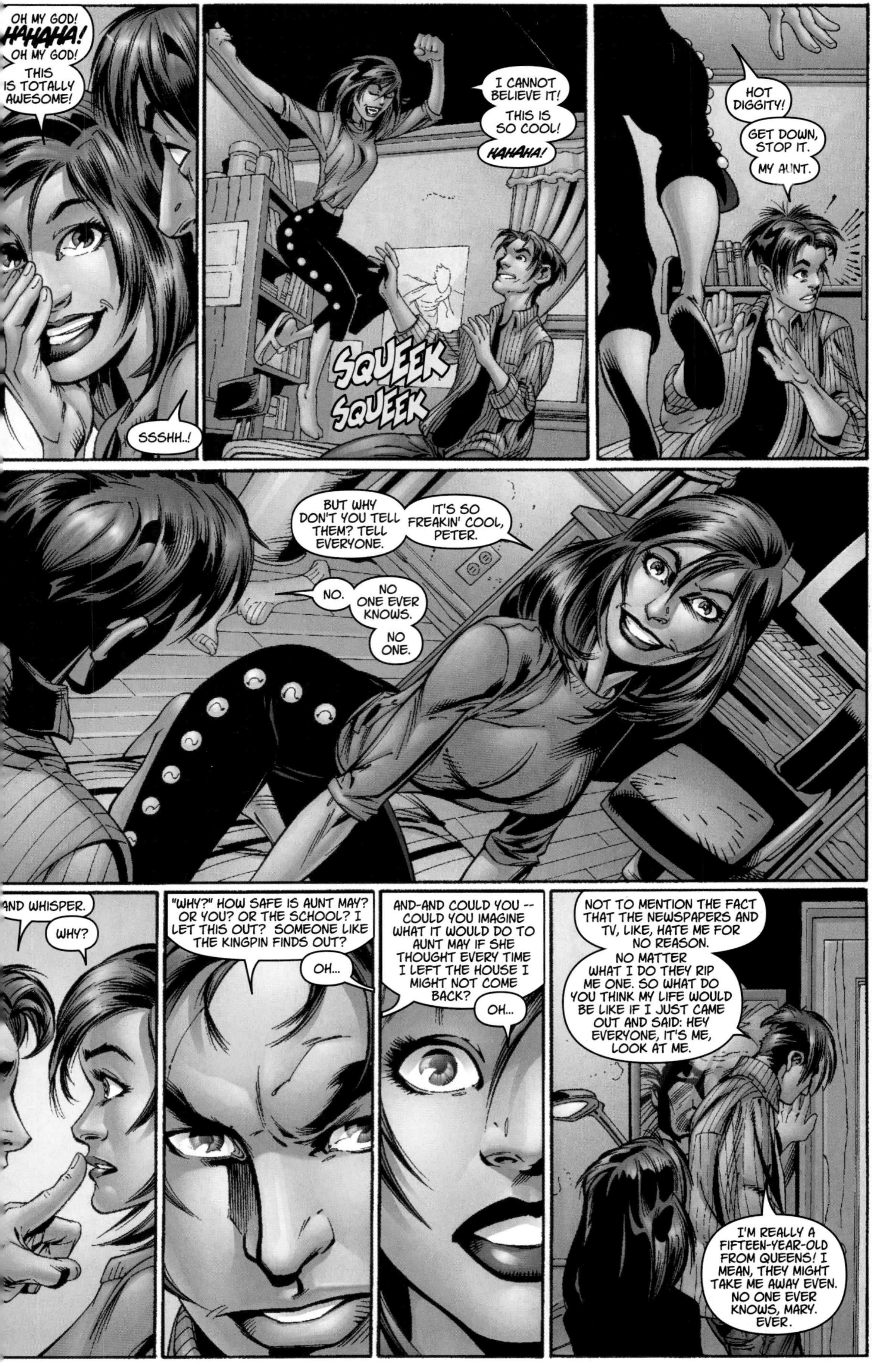
OH MY GOD! HAHAHA! OH MY GOD! THIS IS TOTALLY AWESOME!
SSSHH..!
I CANNOT BELIEVE IT!
THIS IS SO COOL!
HAHAHA!
SQUEEK SQUEEK
HOT DIGGITY!
GET DOWN, STOP IT.
MY AUNT.
BUT WHY DON'T YOU TELL THEM? TELL EVERYONE.
IT'S SO FREAKIN' COOL, PETER.
NO.
NO ONE EVER KNOWS.
NO ONE.
AND WHISPER.
WHY?
"WHY?" HOW SAFE IS AUNT MAY? OR YOU? OR THE SCHOOL? I LET THIS OUT? SOMEONE LIKE THE KINGPIN FINDS OUT?
OH...
AND-AND COULD YOU -- COULD YOU IMAGINE WHAT IT WOULD DO TO AUNT MAY IF SHE THOUGHT EVERY TIME I LEFT THE HOUSE I MIGHT NOT COME BACK?
OH...
NOT TO MENTION THE FACT THAT THE NEWSPAPERS AND TV, LIKE, HATE ME FOR NO REASON.
NO MATTER WHAT I DO THEY RIP ME ONE. SO WHAT DO YOU THINK MY LIFE WOULD BE LIKE IF I JUST CAME OUT AND SAID: HEY EVERYONE, IT'S ME, LOOK AT ME.
I'M REALLY A FIFTEEN-YEAR-OLD FROM QUEENS! I MEAN, THEY MIGHT TAKE ME AWAY EVEN. NO ONE EVER KNOWS, MARY. EVER.

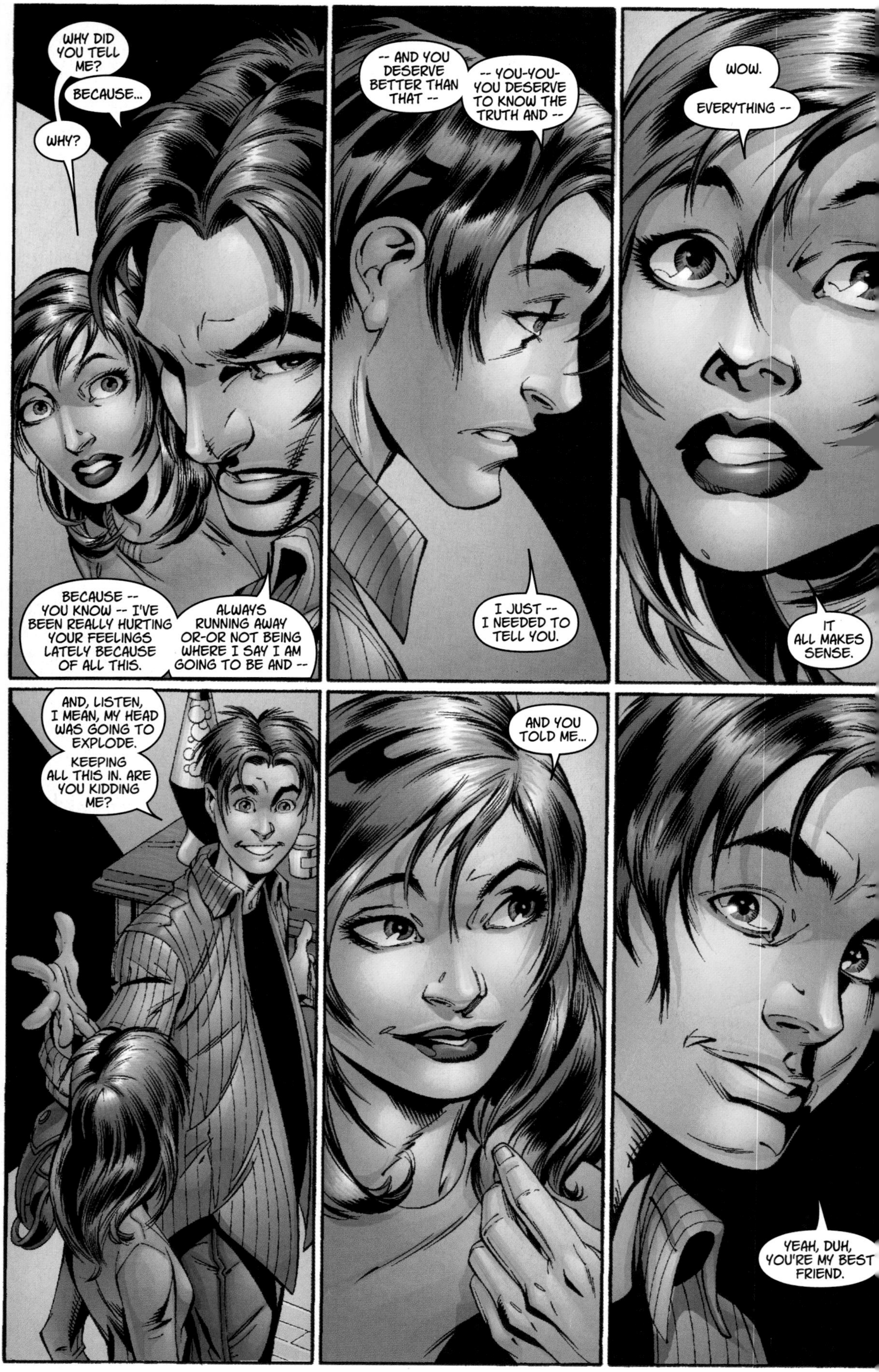
WHY DID YOU TELL ME?
BECAUSE...
WHY?
BECAUSE -- YOU KNOW -- I'VE BEEN REALLY HURTING YOUR FEELINGS LATELY BECAUSE OF ALL THIS.
ALWAYS RUNNING AWAY OR-OR NOT BEING WHERE I SAY I AM GOING TO BE AND --
-- AND YOU DESERVE BETTER THAN THAT --
-- YOU-YOU-YOU DESERVE TO KNOW THE TRUTH AND --
I JUST -- I NEEDED TO TELL YOU.
WOW.
EVERYTHING --
IT ALL MAKES SENSE.
AND, LISTEN, I MEAN, MY HEAD WAS GOING TO EXPLODE.
KEEPING ALL THIS IN. ARE YOU KIDDING ME?
AND YOU TOLD ME...
YEAH, DUH, YOU'RE MY BEST FRIEND.

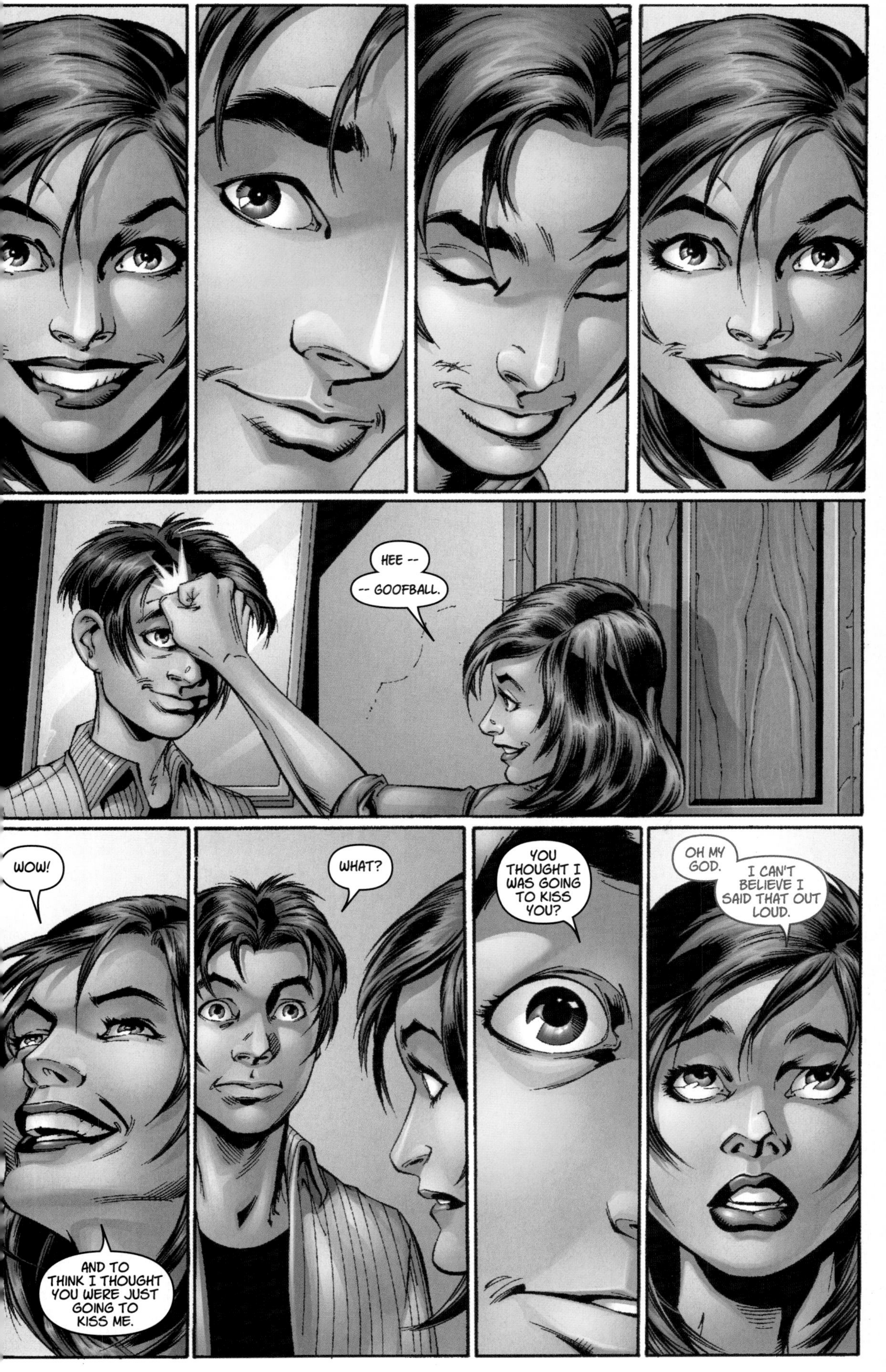
HEE --
-- GOOFBALL.
WOW!
AND TO THINK I THOUGHT YOU WERE JUST GOING TO KISS ME.
WHAT?
YOU THOUGHT I WAS GOING TO KISS YOU?
OH MY GOD.
I CAN'T BELIEVE I SAID THAT OUT LOUD.

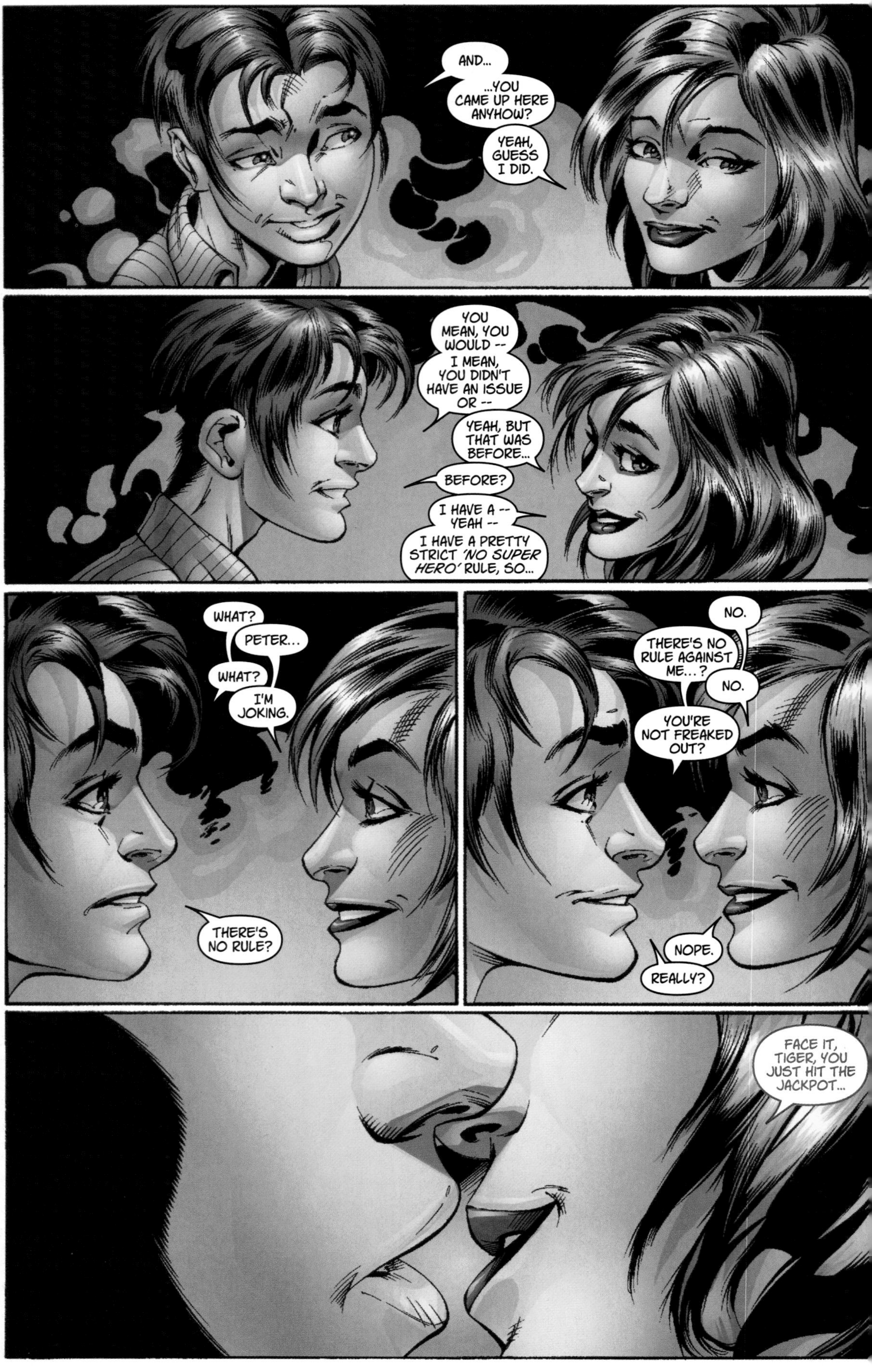

AND...
...YOU CAME UP HERE ANYHOW?
YEAH, GUESS I DID.
YOU MEAN, YOU WOULD -- I MEAN, YOU DIDN'T HAVE AN ISSUE OR --
YEAH, BUT THAT WAS BEFORE...
BEFORE?
I HAVE A -- YEAH -- I HAVE A PRETTY STRICT 'NO SUPER HERO' RULE, SO...
WHAT?
PETER...
WHAT?
I'M JOKING.
THERE'S NO RULE?
NO.
THERE'S NO RULE AGAINST ME...?
NO.
YOU'RE NOT FREAKED OUT?
NOPE.
REALLY?
FACE IT, TIGER, YOU JUST HIT THE JACKPOT...

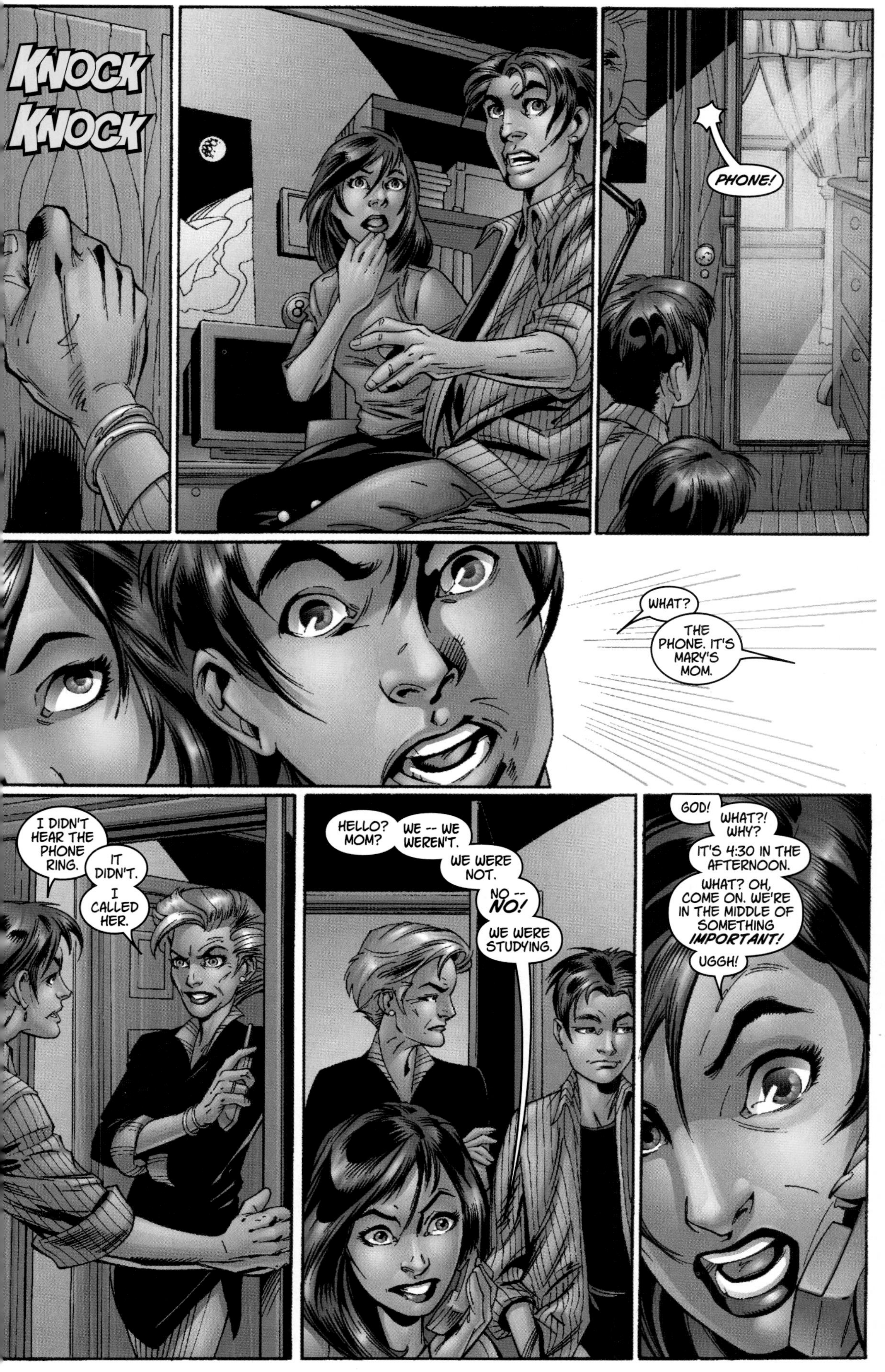
KNOCK
KNOCK
PHONE!
WHAT?
THE PHONE. IT'S MARY'S MOM.
I DIDN'T HEAR THE PHONE RING.
IT DIDN'T.
I CALLED HER.
HELLO? MOM?
WE -- WE WEREN'T.
WE WERE NOT.
NO -- NO!
WE WERE STUDYING.
GOD!
WHAT?! WHY?
IT'S 4:30 IN THE AFTERNOON.
WHAT? OH, COME ON. WE'RE IN THE MIDDLE OF SOMETHING IMPORTANT!
UGGH!

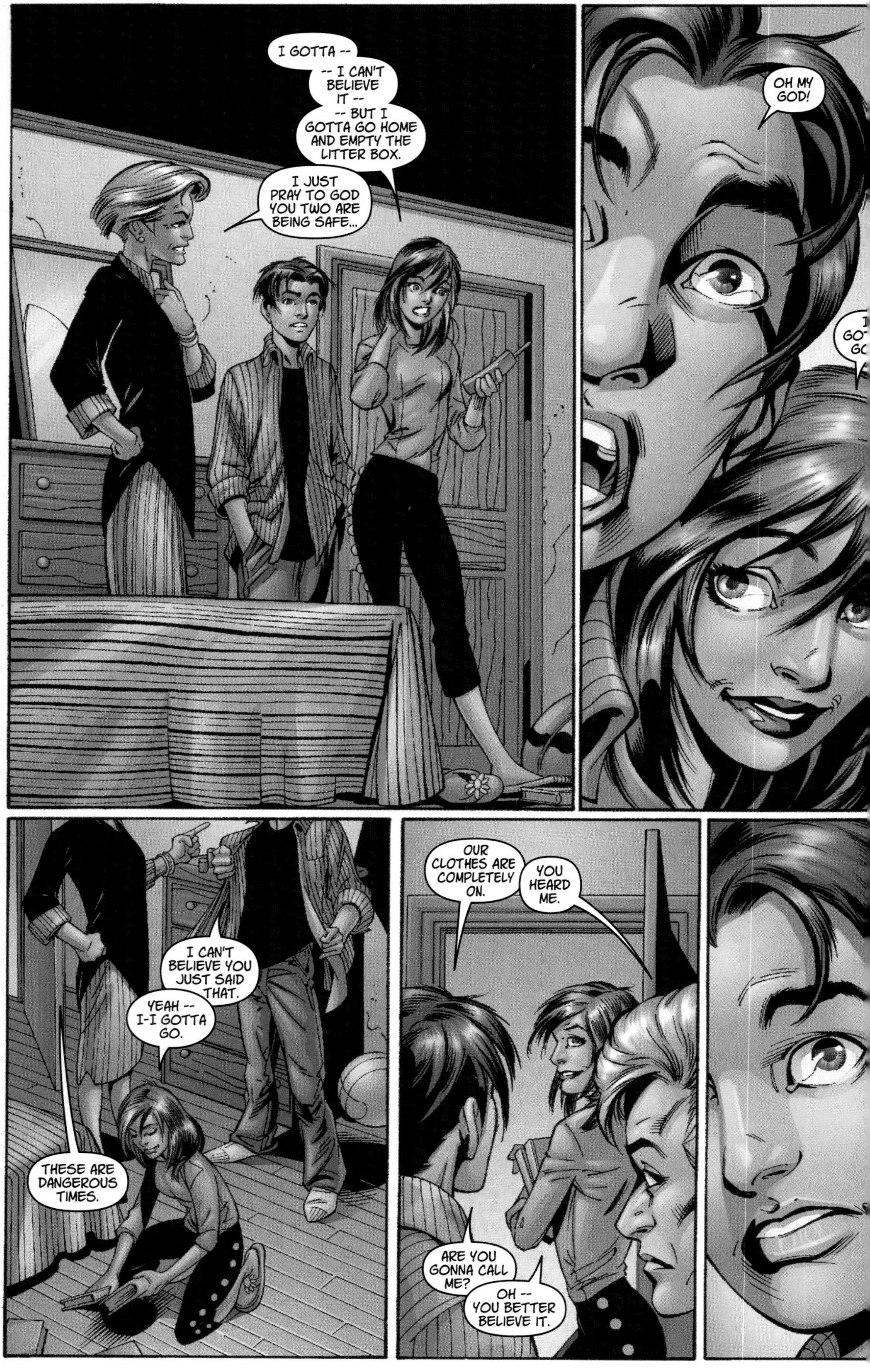
I GOTTA --
-- I CAN'T BELIEVE IT --
-- BUT I GOTTA GO HOME AND EMPTY THE LITTER BOX.
I JUST PRAY TO GOD YOU TWO ARE BEING SAFE...
OH MY GOD!
I CAN'T BELIEVE YOU JUST SAID THAT.
YEAH -- I-I GOTTA GO.
THESE ARE DANGEROUS TIMES.
OUR CLOTHES ARE COMPLETELY ON.
YOU HEARD ME.
ARE YOU GONNA CALL ME?
OH -- YOU BETTER BELIEVE IT.

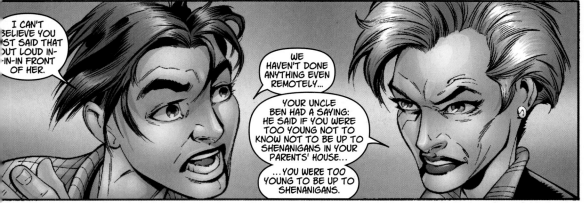

I CAN'T BELIEVE YOU JUST SAID THAT OUT LOUD IN--IN-IN FRONT OF HER.

WE HAVEN'T DONE ANYTHING EVEN REMOTELY...

YOUR UNCLE BEN HAD A SAYING: HE SAID IF YOU WERE TOO YOUNG NOT TO KNOW NOT TO BE UP TO SHENANIGANS IN YOUR PARENTS' HOUSE...

...YOU WERE TOO YOUNG TO BE UP TO SHENANIGANS.

WE -- WEREN'T -- DOING -- ANYTHING.

DO YOU KNOW ABOUT IT?

WHAT?

IT. DO YOU KNOW ABOUT --?

OH GOD! PLEASE STOP TALKING.

DO YOU?

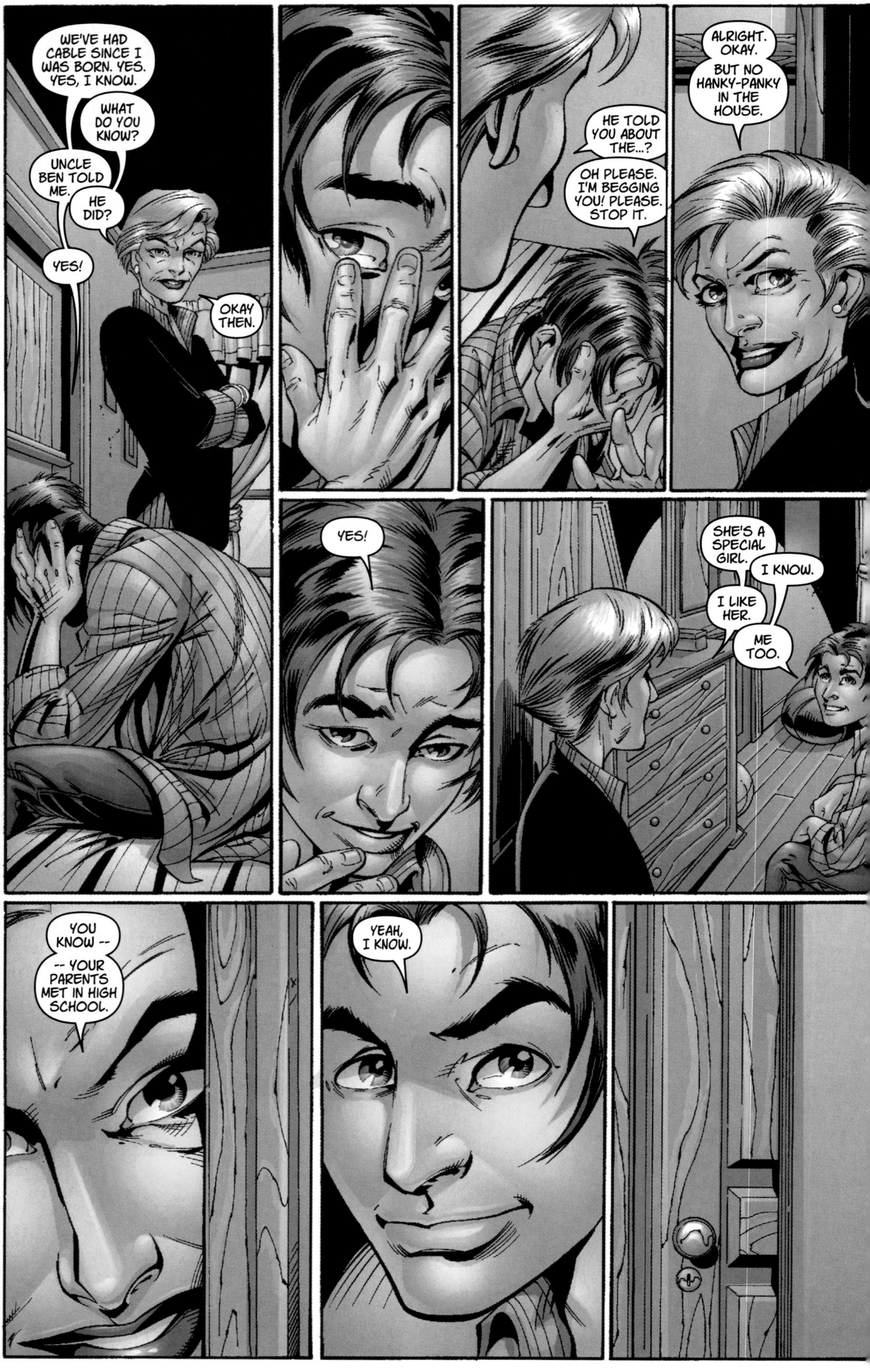
WE'VE HAD CABLE SINCE I WAS BORN. YES. YES, I KNOW.
WHAT DO YOU KNOW?
UNCLE BEN TOLD ME.
HE DID?
YES!
OKAY THEN.
HE TOLD YOU ABOUT THE...?
OH PLEASE. I'M BEGGING YOU! PLEASE. STOP IT.
ALRIGHT. OKAY.
BUT NO HANKY-PANKY IN THE HOUSE.
YES!
SHE'S A SPECIAL GIRL.
I KNOW.
I LIKE HER.
ME TOO.
YOU KNOW --
-- YOUR PARENTS MET IN HIGH SCHOOL.
YEAH, I KNOW.

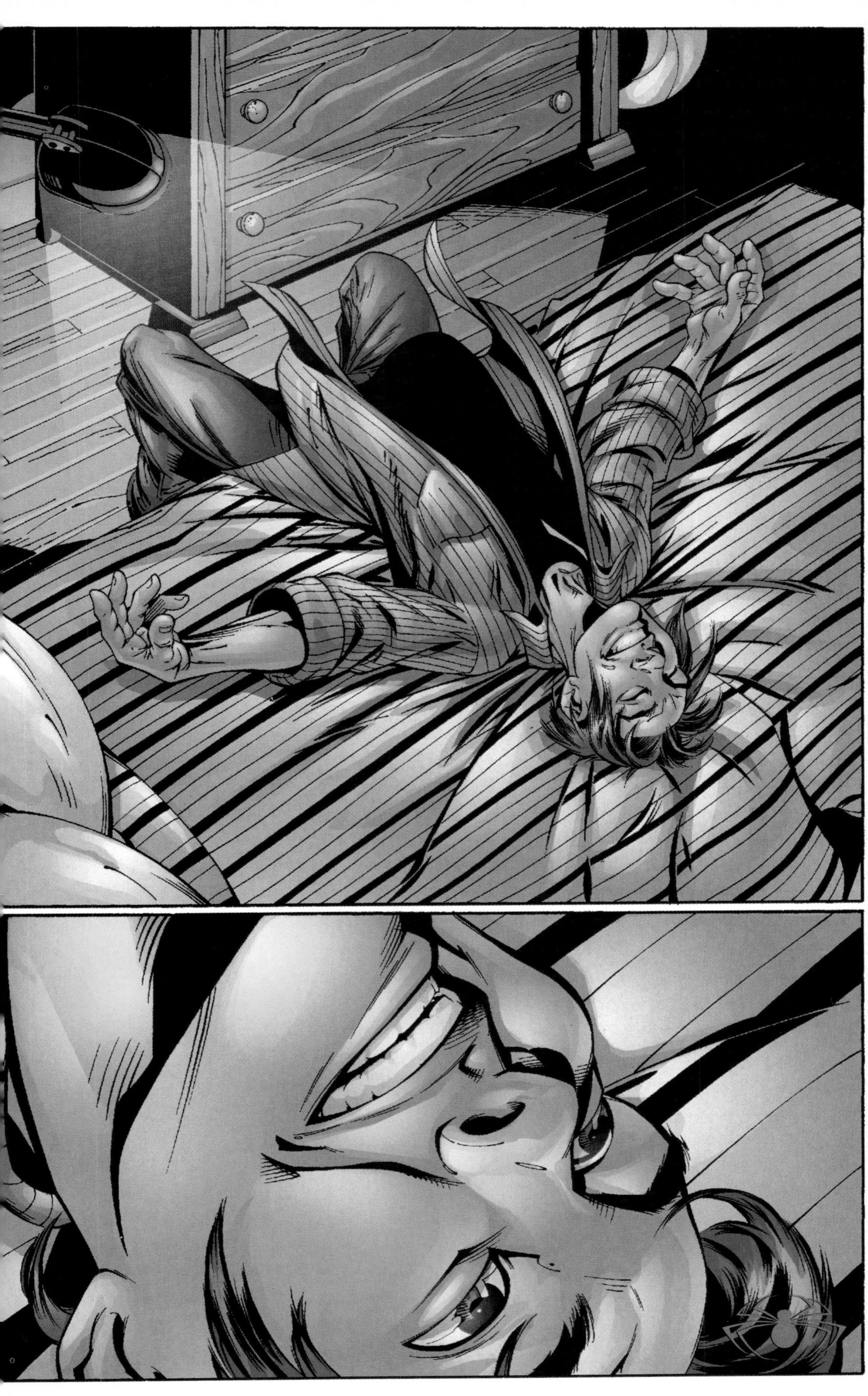

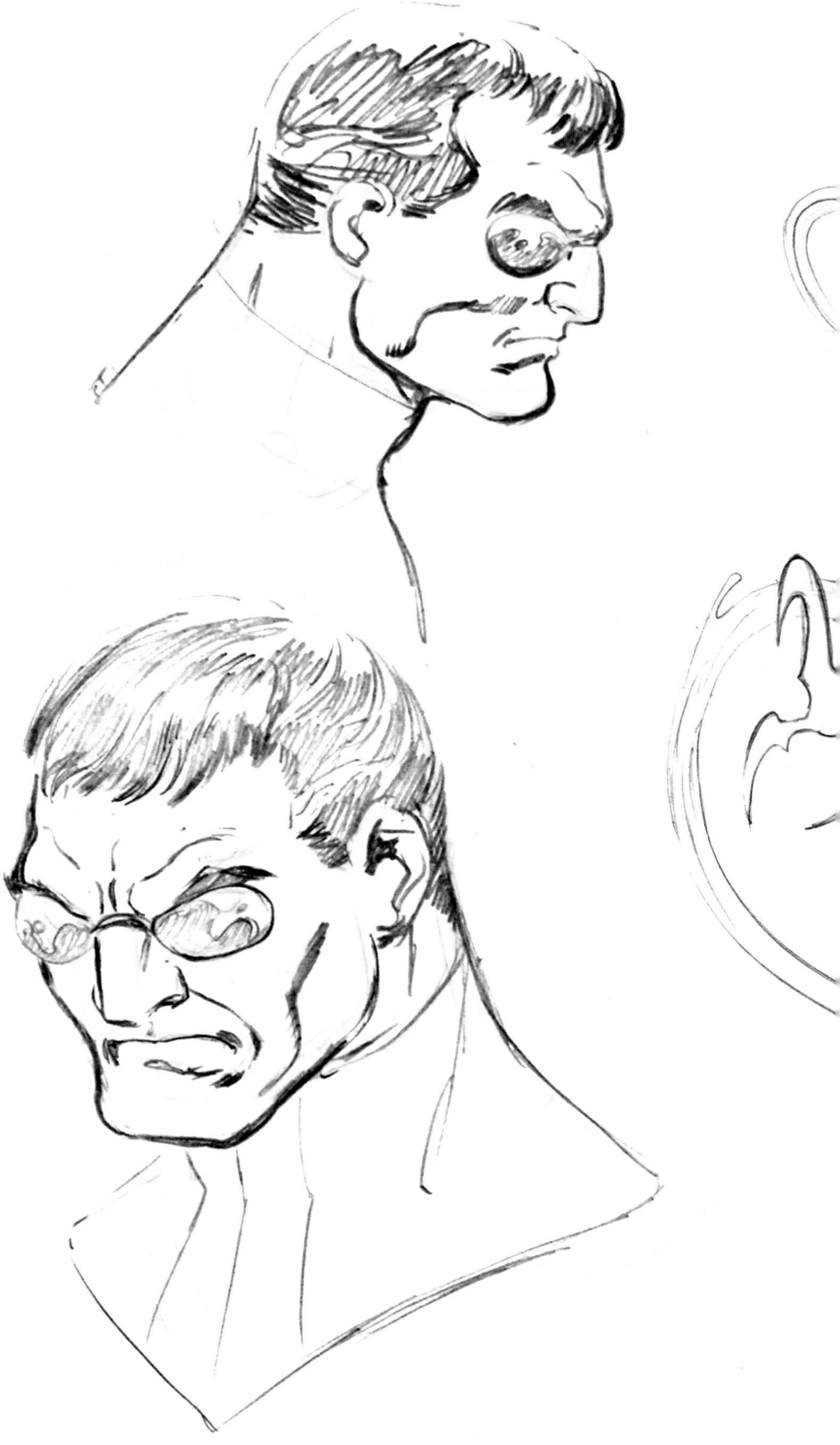

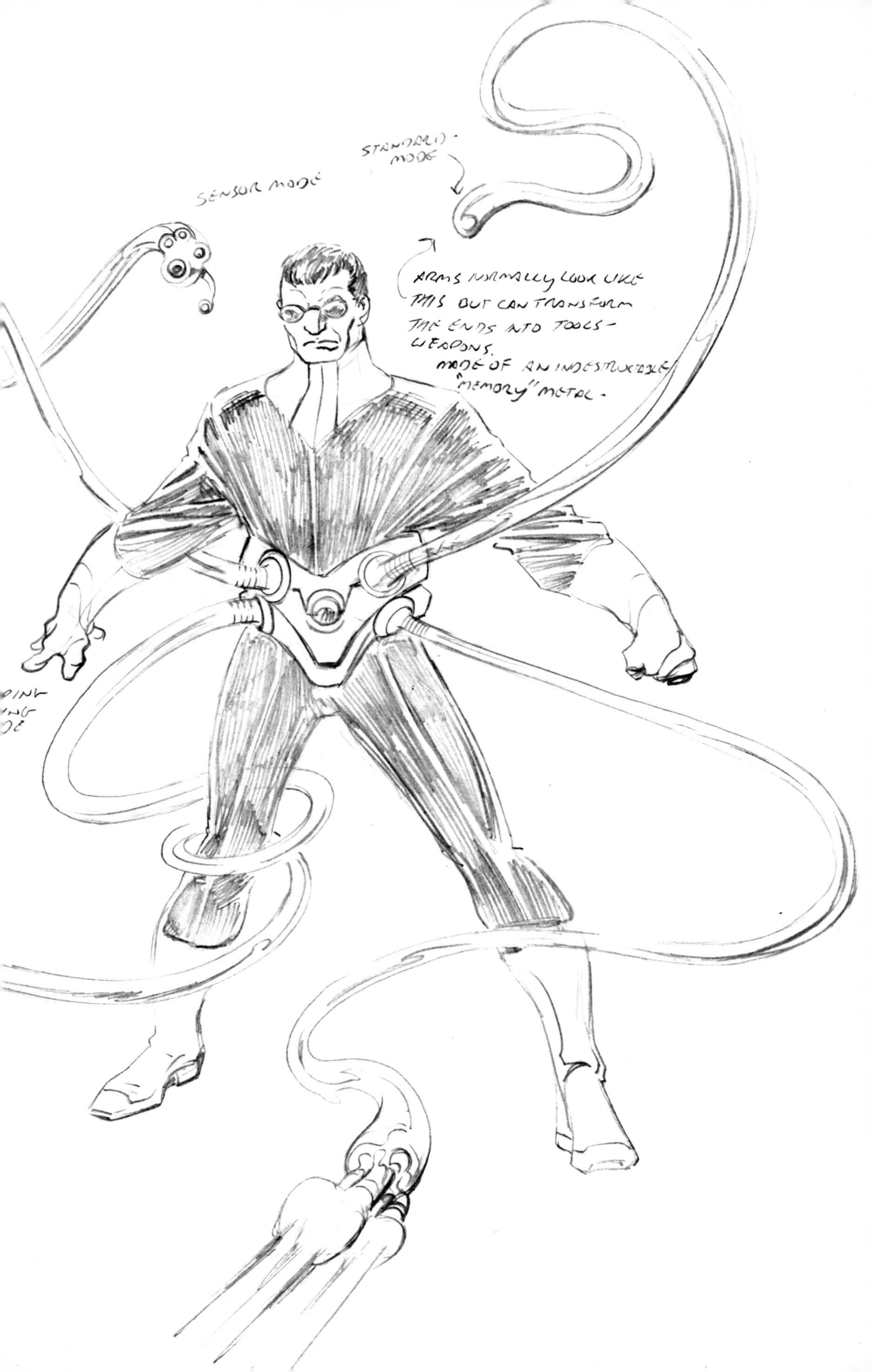
SENSOR MODE
STANDARD MODE
ARMS NORMALLY LOOK LIKE THIS BUT CAN TRANSFORM THE ENDS INTO TOOLS-WEAPONS.
MADE OF AN INDESTRUCTIBLE "MEMORY" METAL-

AUNT MAY

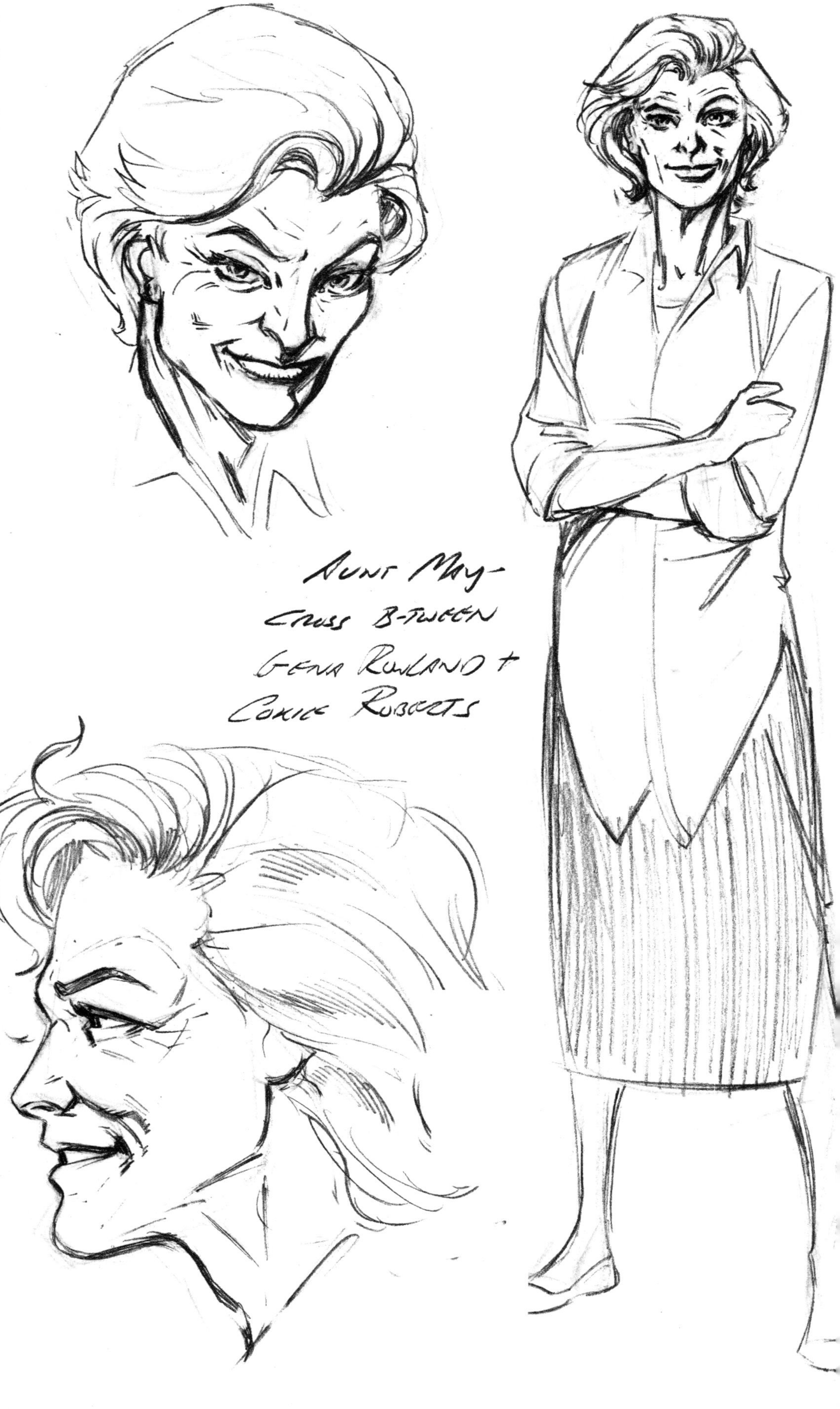
AUNT MAY-
CROSS B-TWEEN
GENA ROWLAND +
COKIE ROBERTS

GREEN GOBLIN

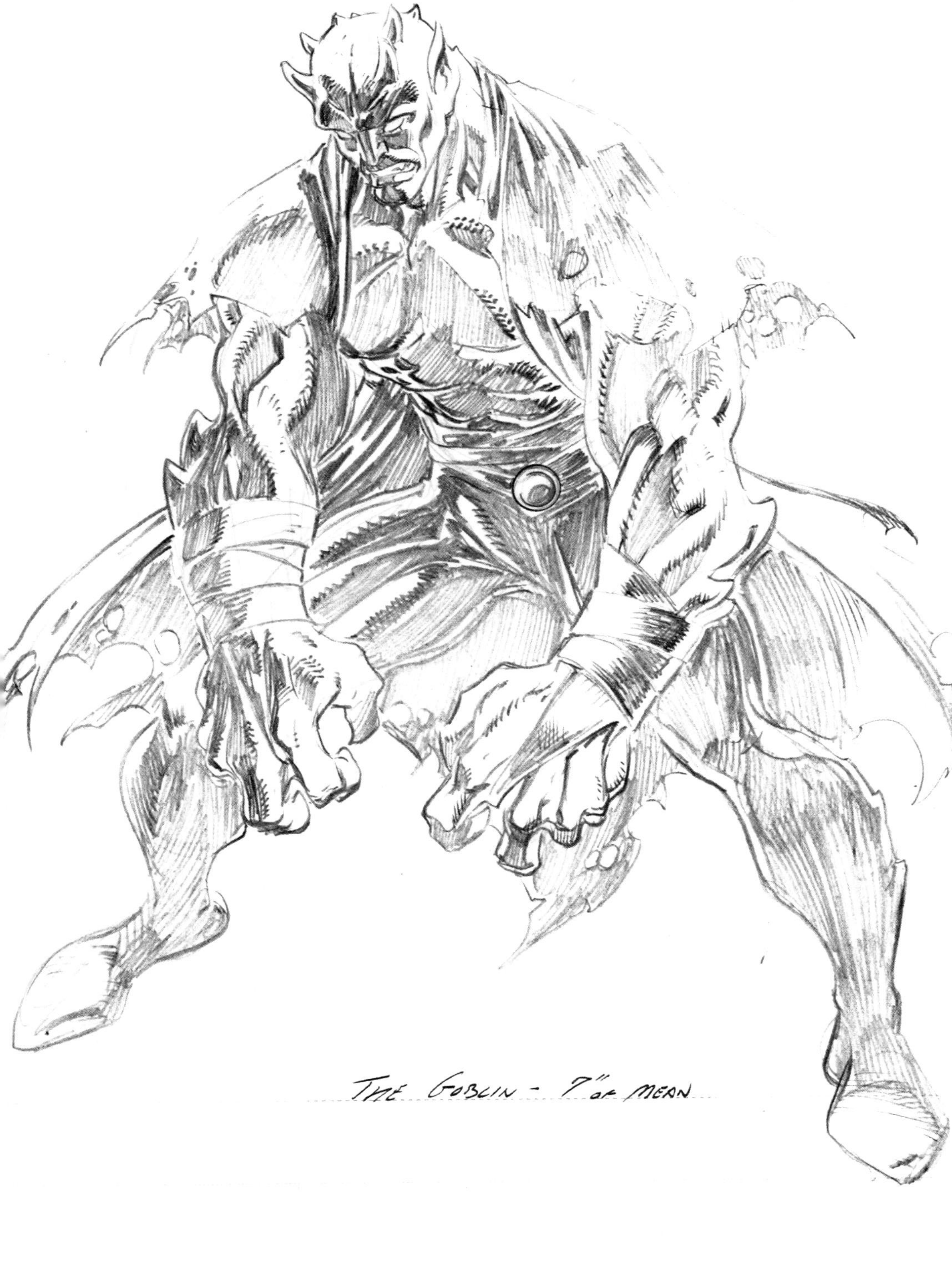
THE GOBLIN - 7" OF MEAN

ELECTRO

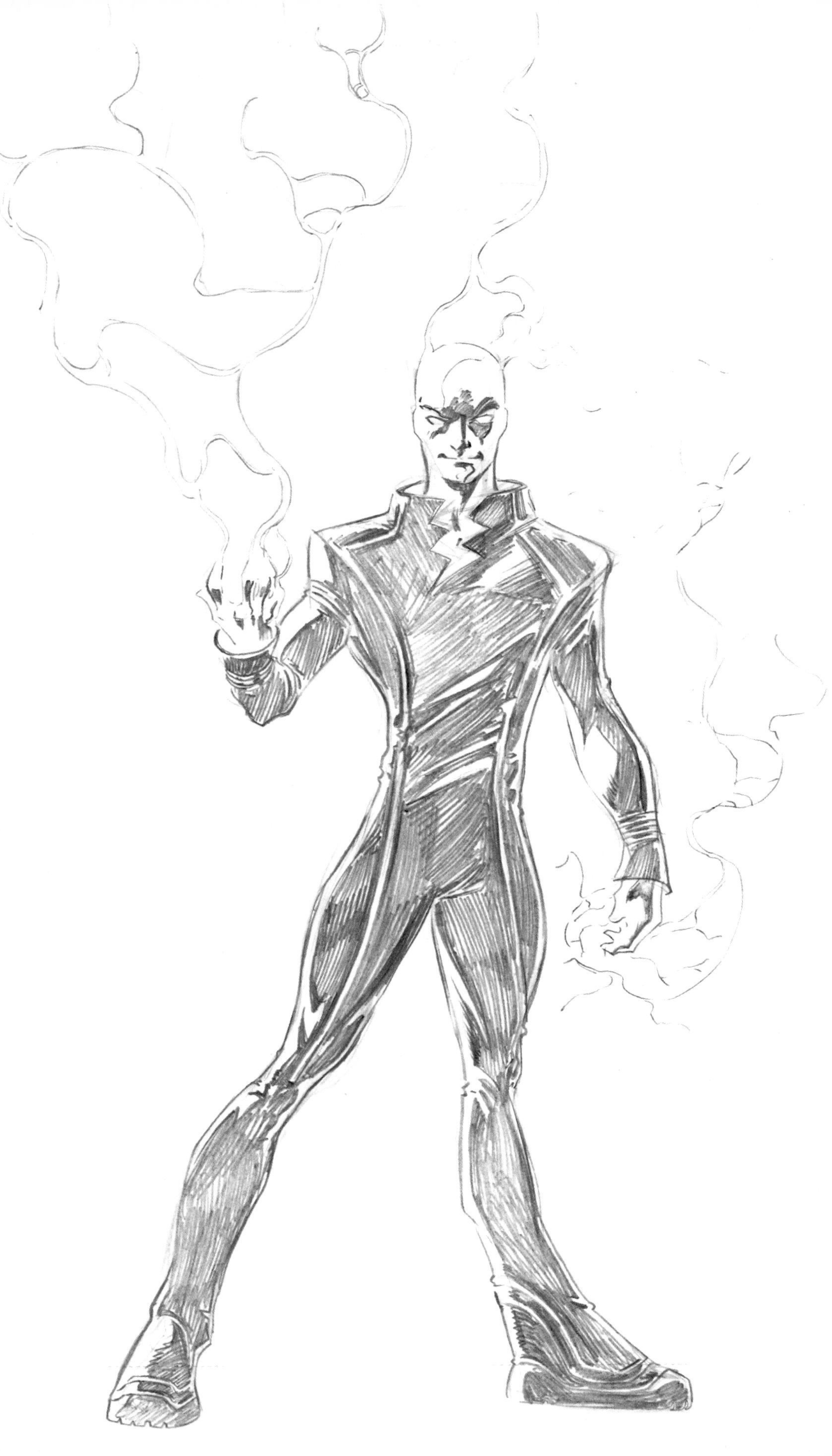

FANCY DAN

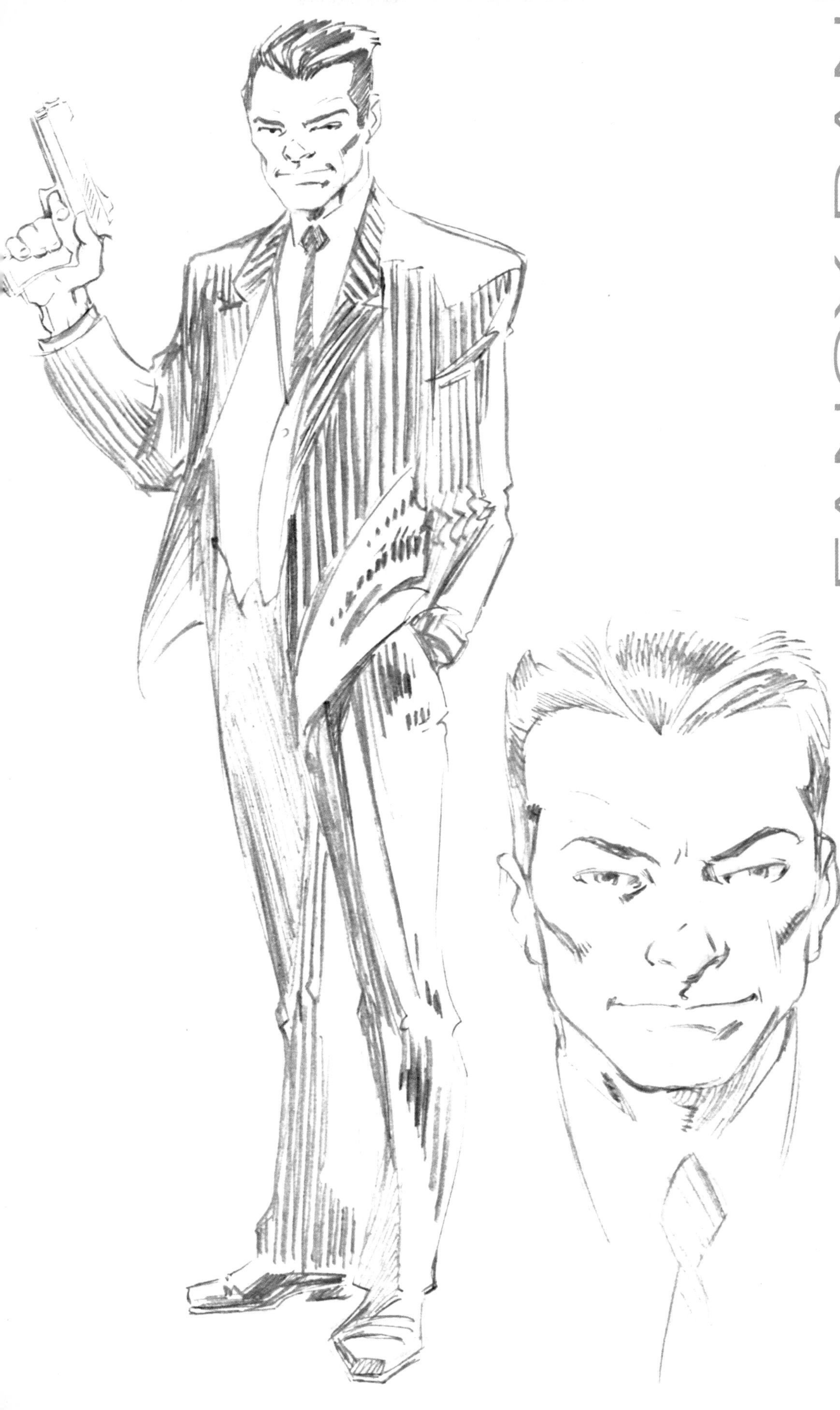

FLASH

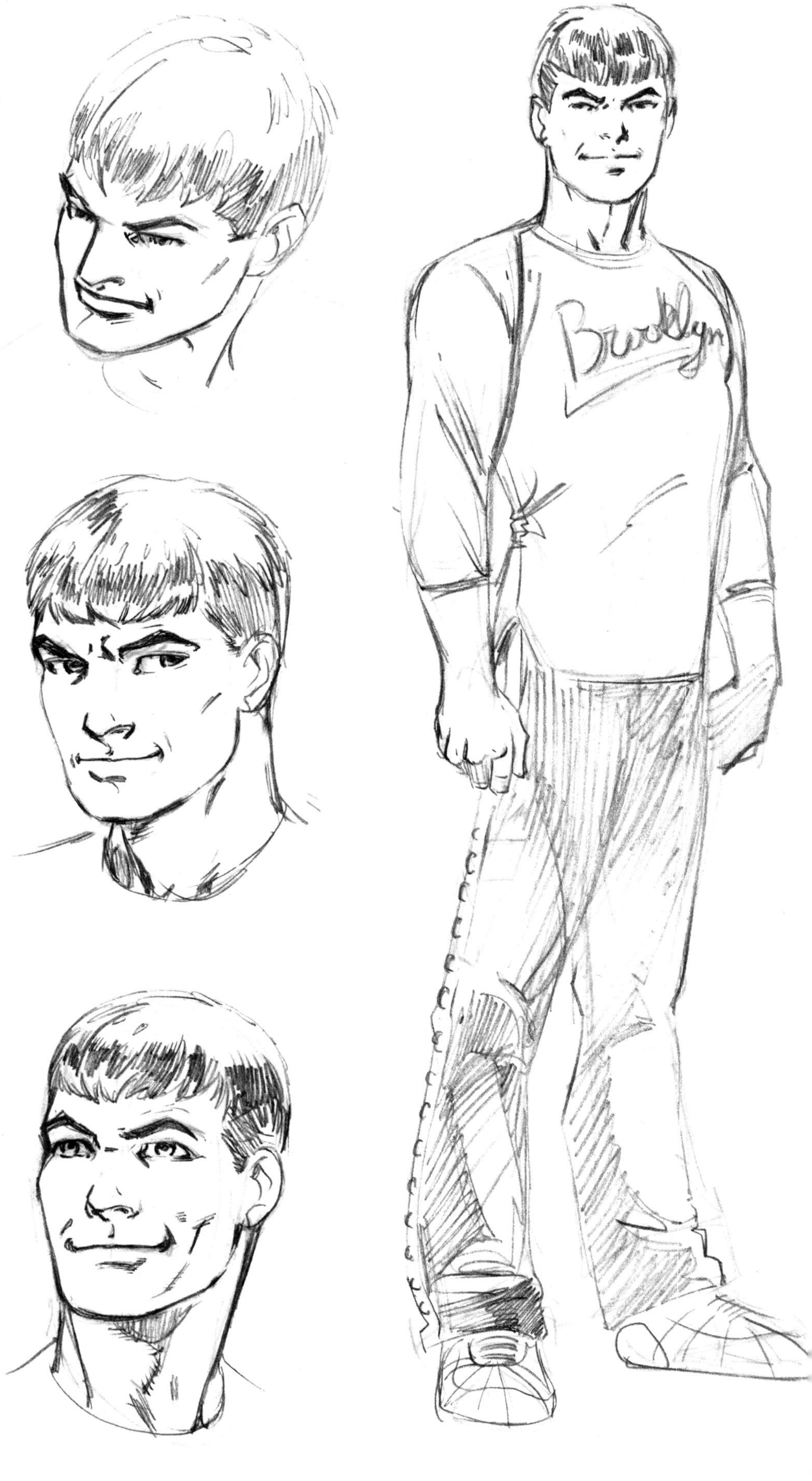
Brooklyn

HARRY OSBORN

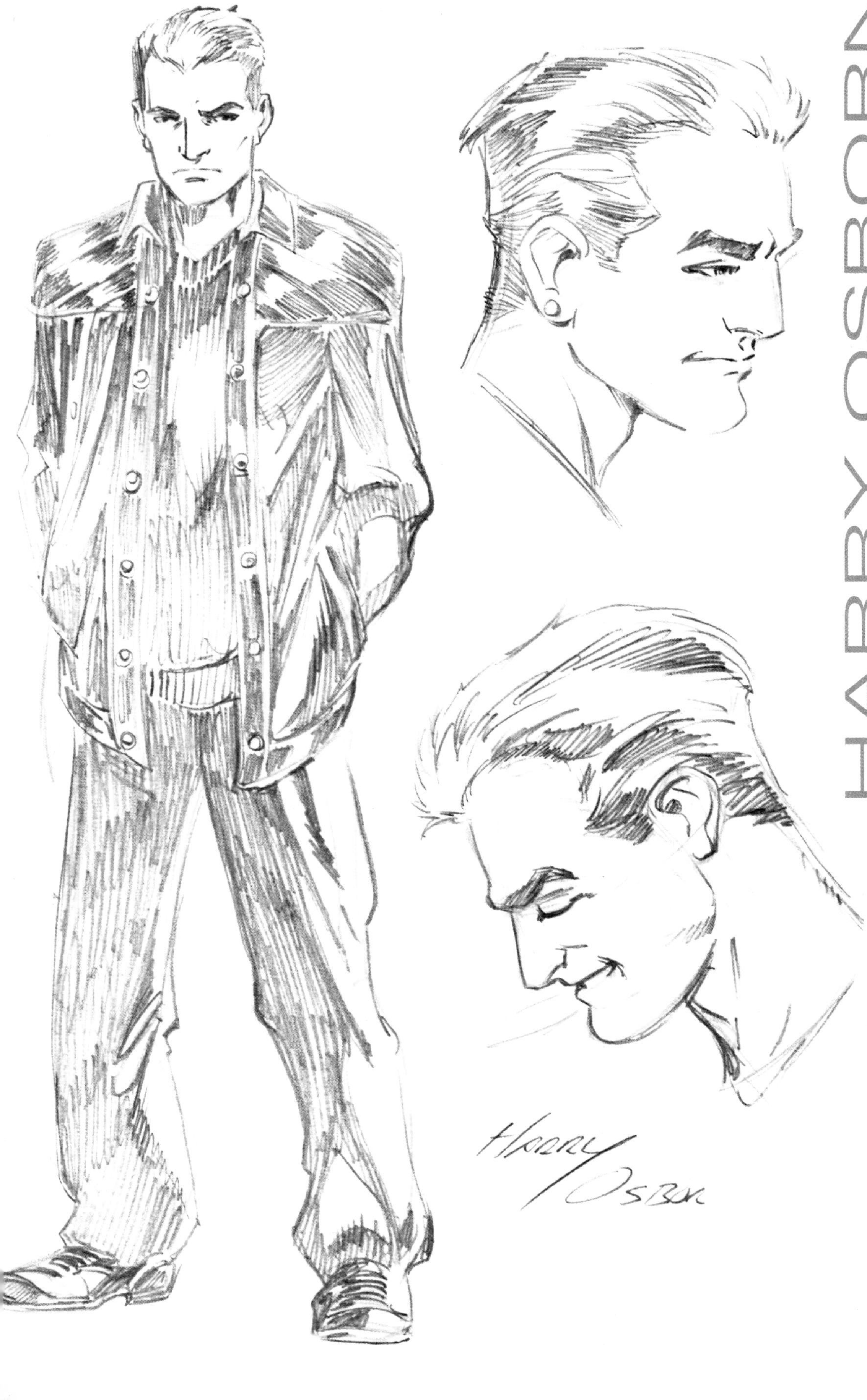
HARRY OSBORN

KINGPIN

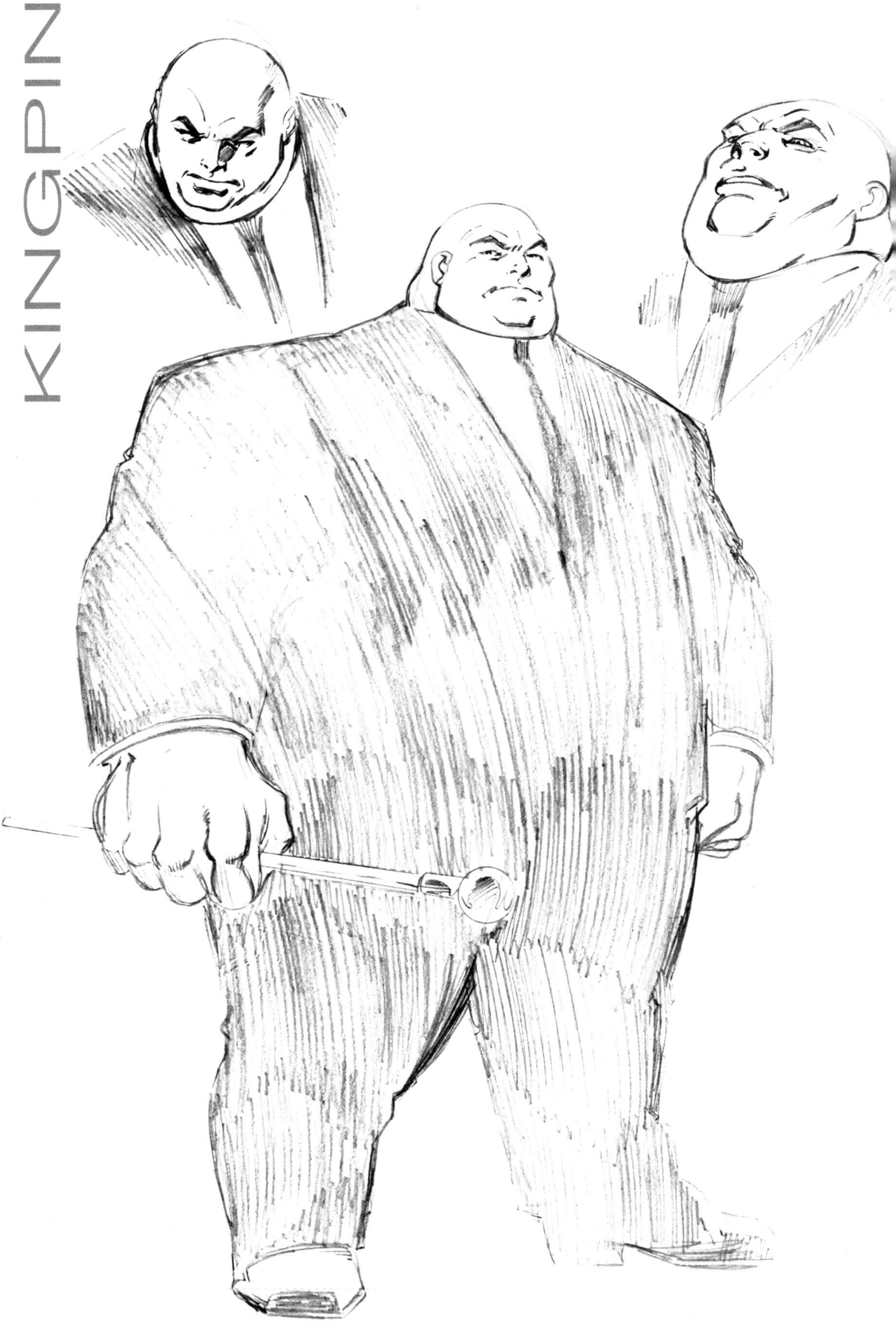

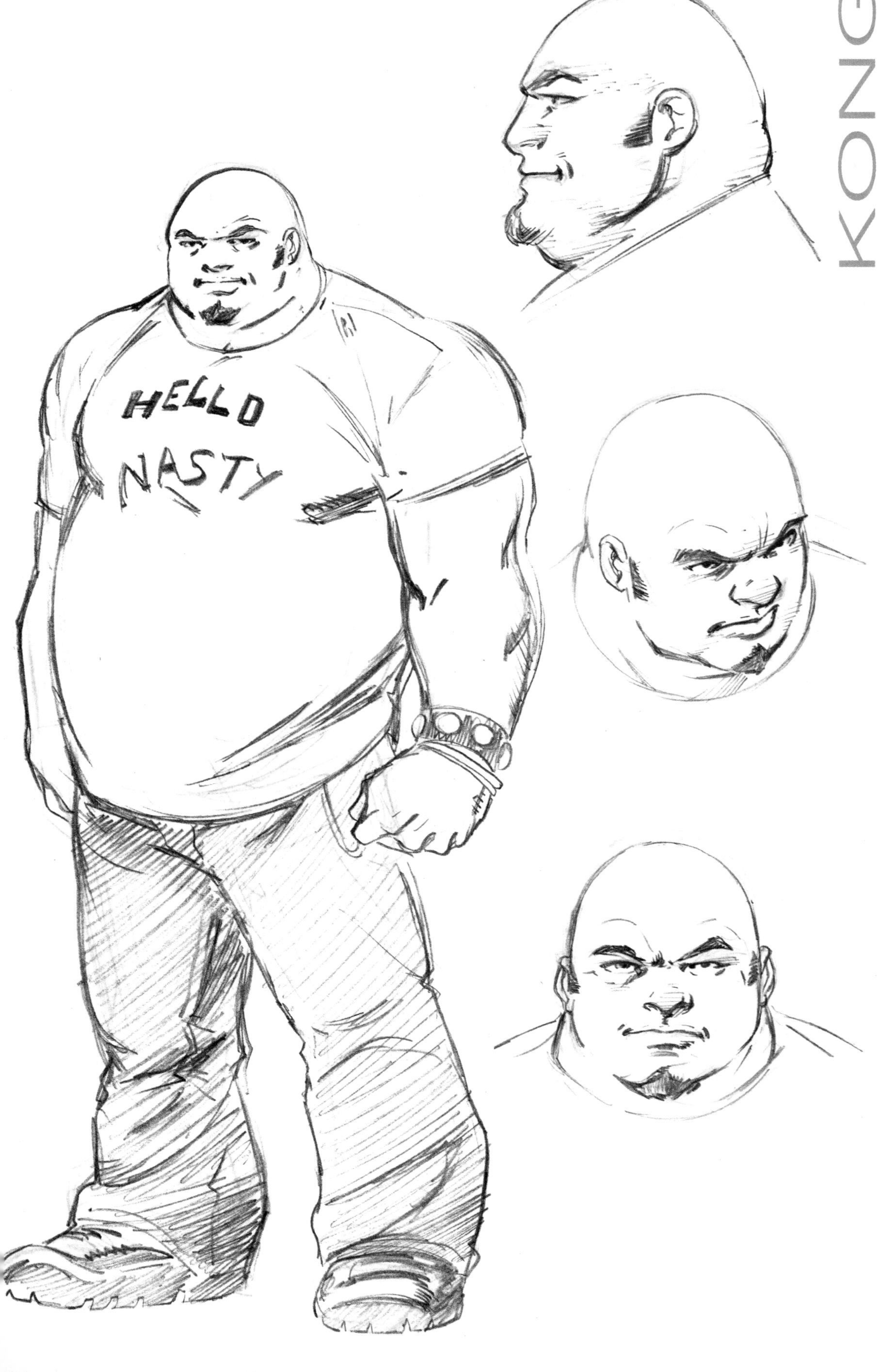
HELLO
NASTY
KONG

MARY JANE

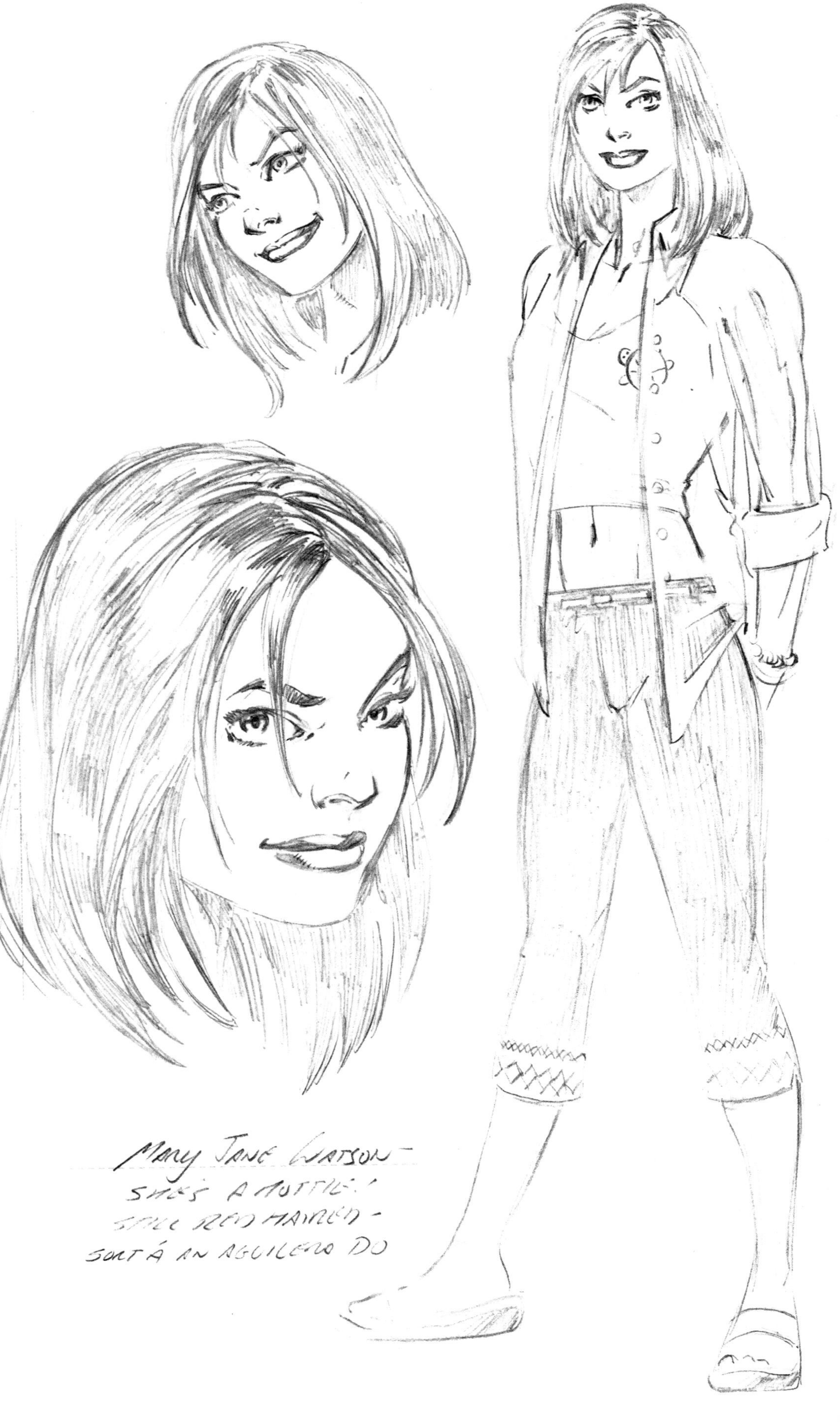
Mary Jane Watson -
She's a hottie!
Still red haired -
sort á an Aguilera do

MONTANA

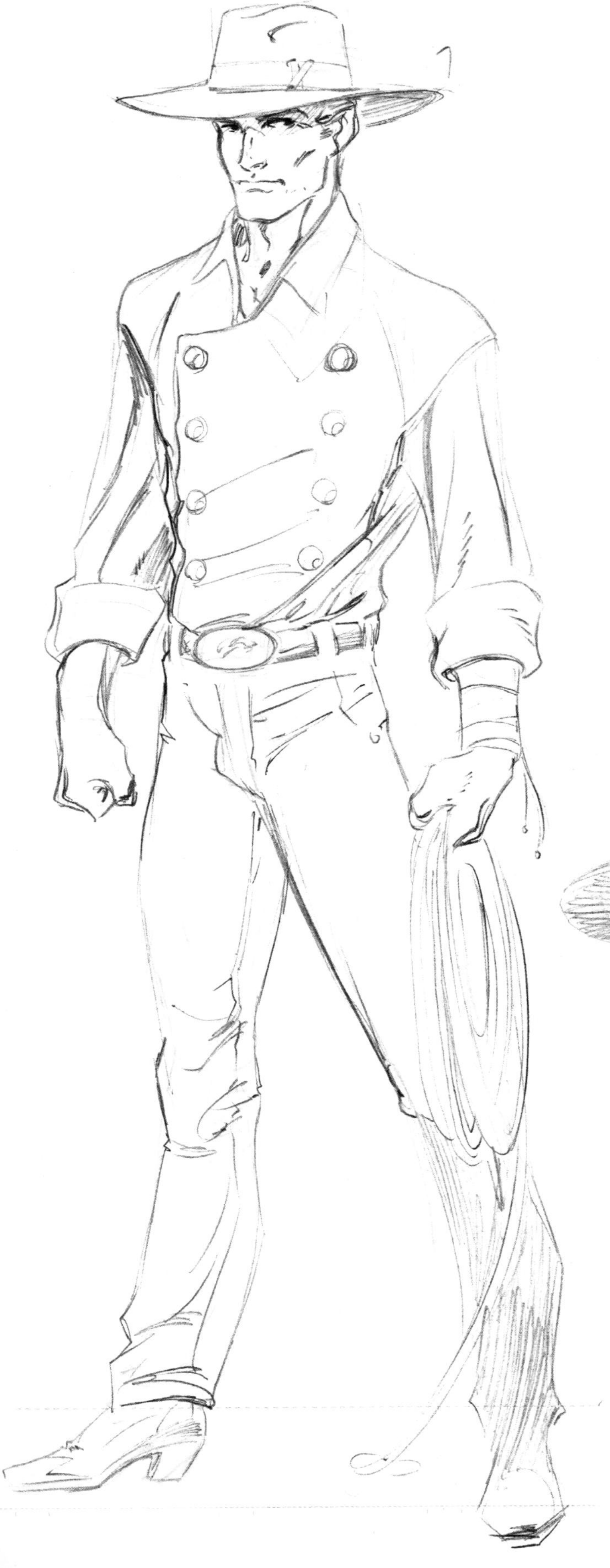

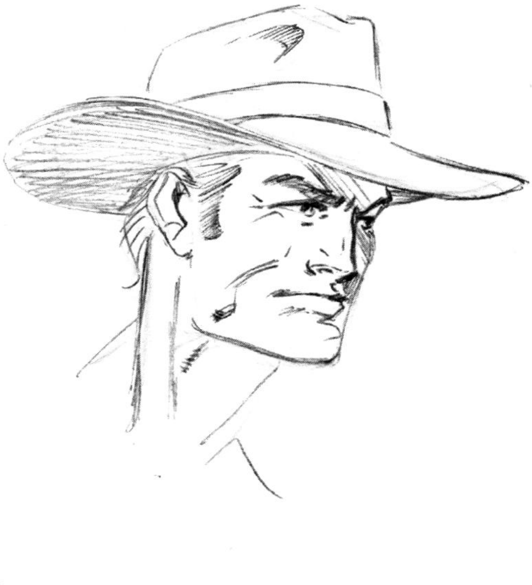

NORMAN OSBORN

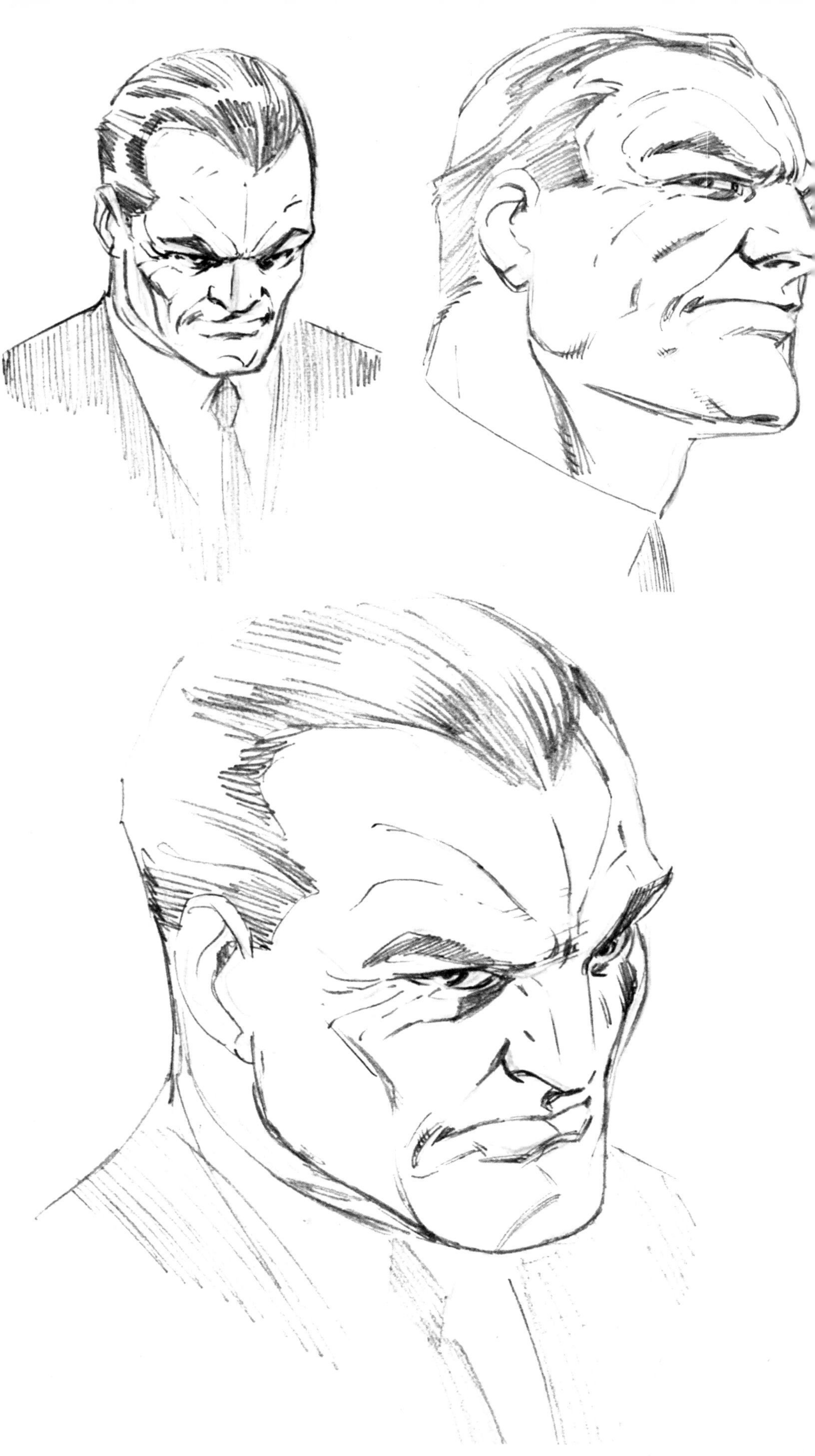

OX

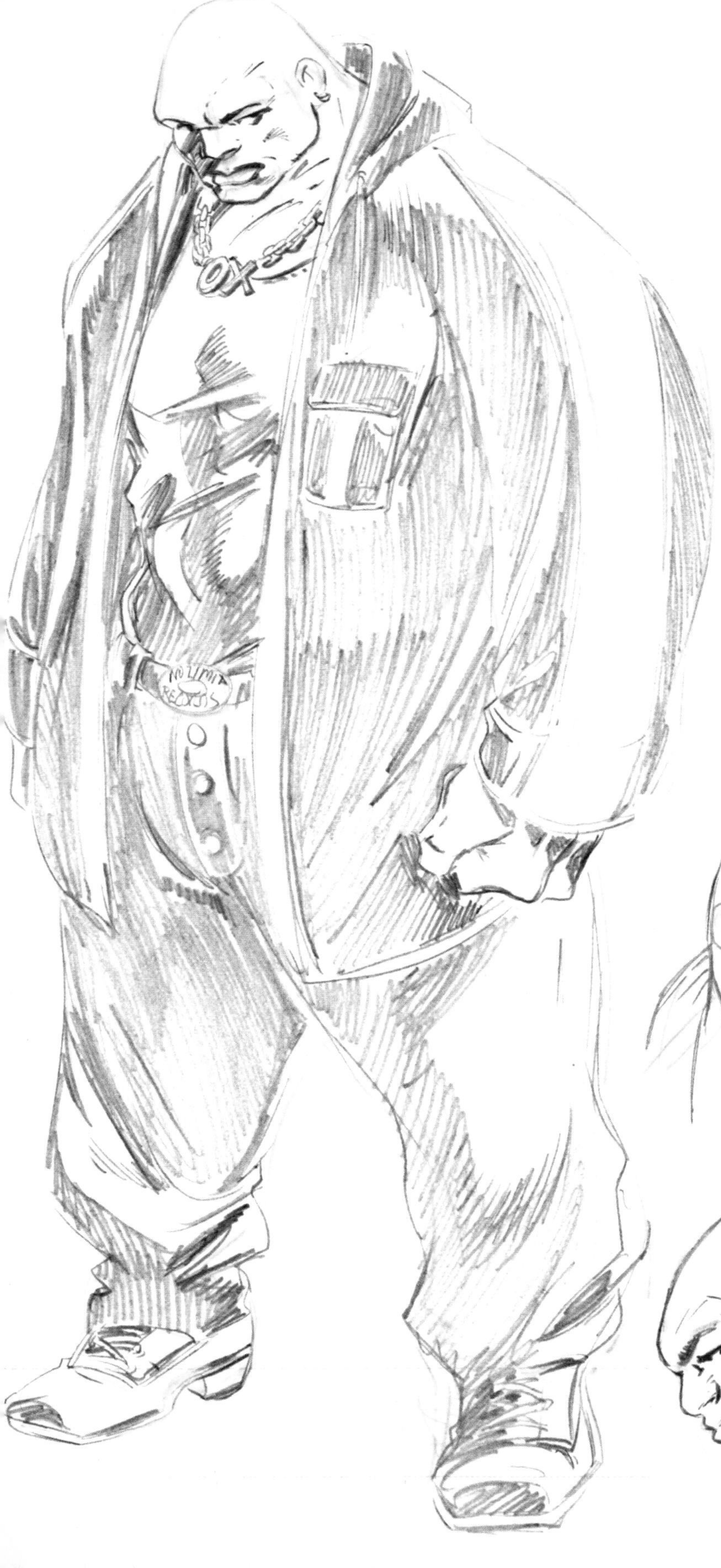
OX
NO LIMIT RECORDS

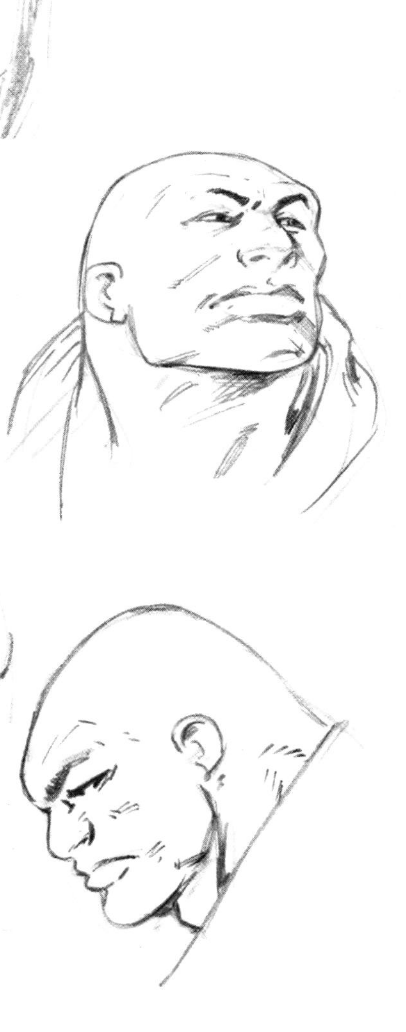

PETER PARKER

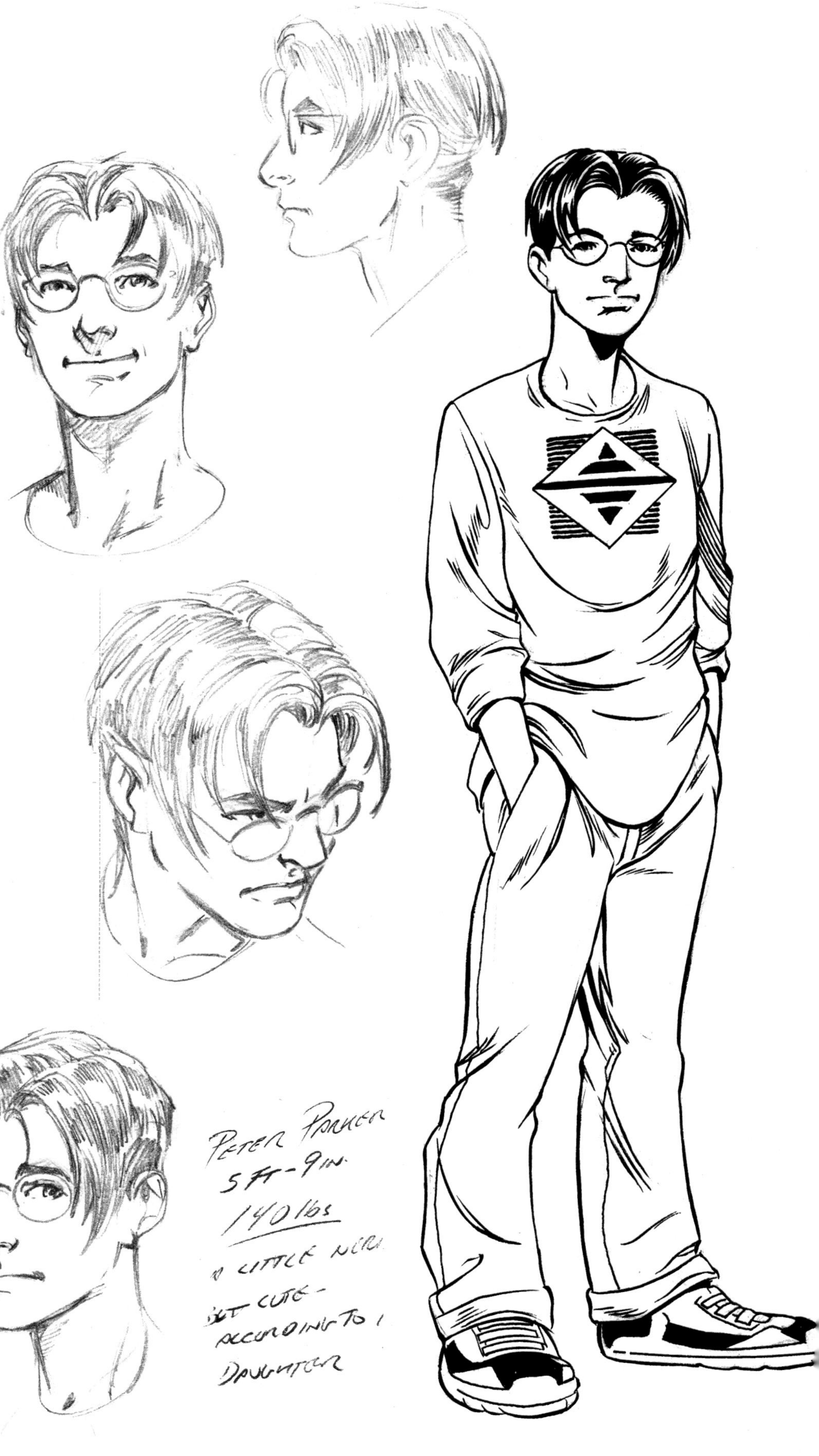
PETER PARKER
5 FT-9 IN.
140 lbs
A LITTLE NERI
BUT CUTE-
ACCORDING TO
DAUGHTER

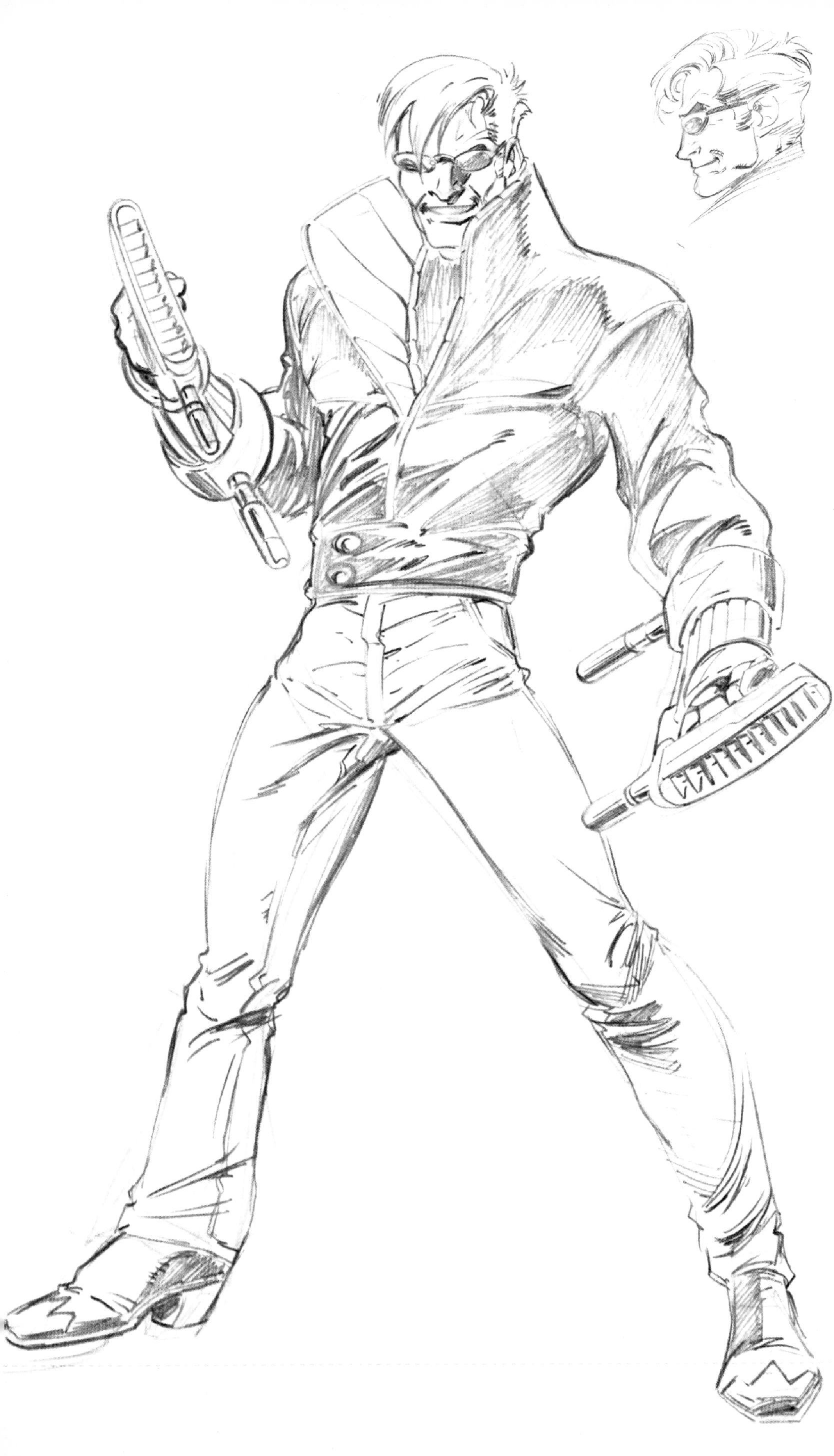

SHOCKER

SPIDER-MAN

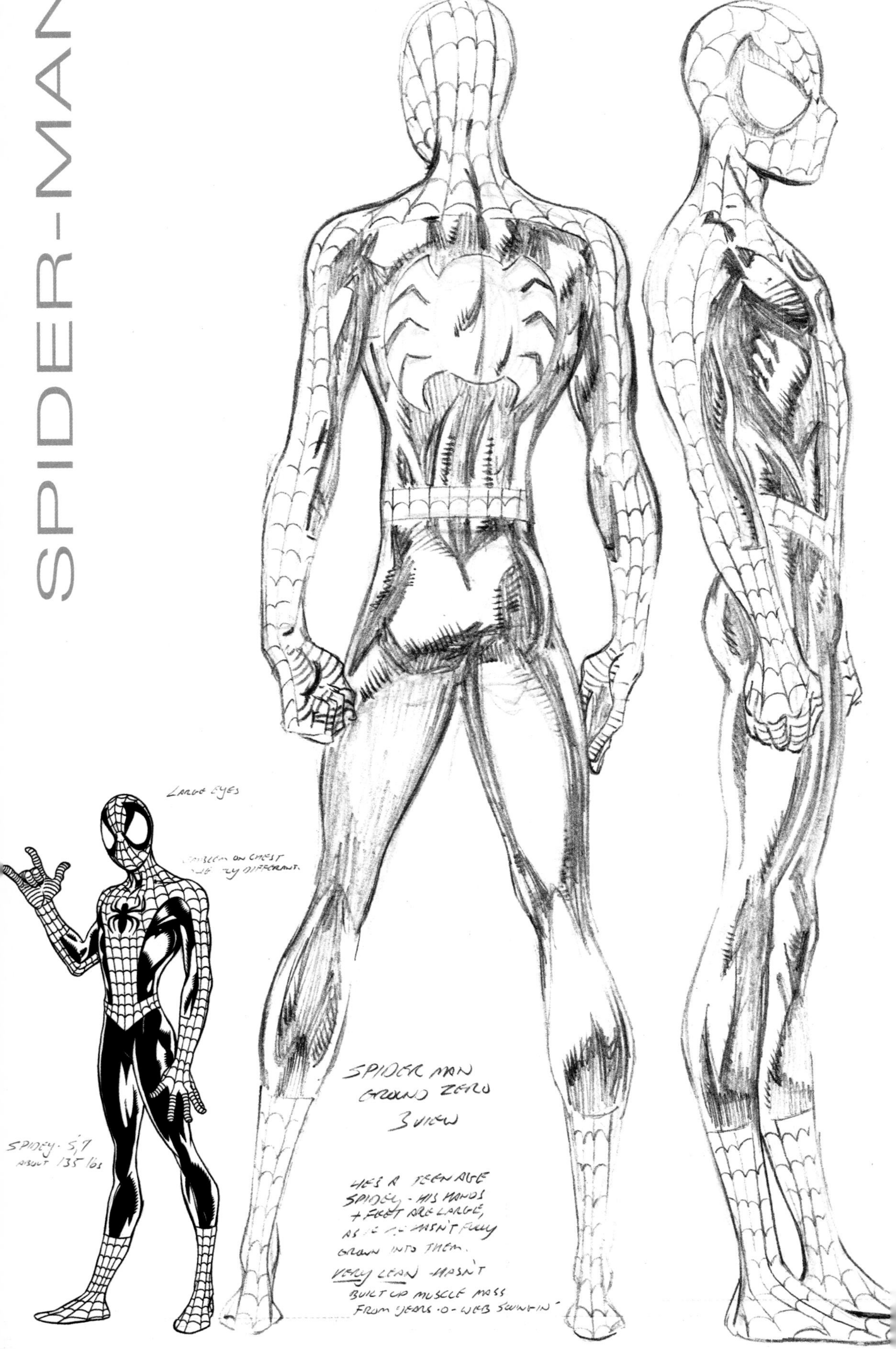
LARGE EYES
EMBLEM ON CHEST
DIFFERANT.
SPIDEY · 5'7
ABOUT 135 lbs
SPIDER MAN
GROUND ZERO
3 VIEW
HE'S A TEENAGE
SPIDEY - HIS HANDS
+ FEET ARE LARGE,
HASN'T FULLY
GROWN INTO THEM.
VERY LEAN - HASN'T
BUILT UP MUSCLE MASS
FROM YEARS · O - WEB SWINGIN'

UNCLE BEN

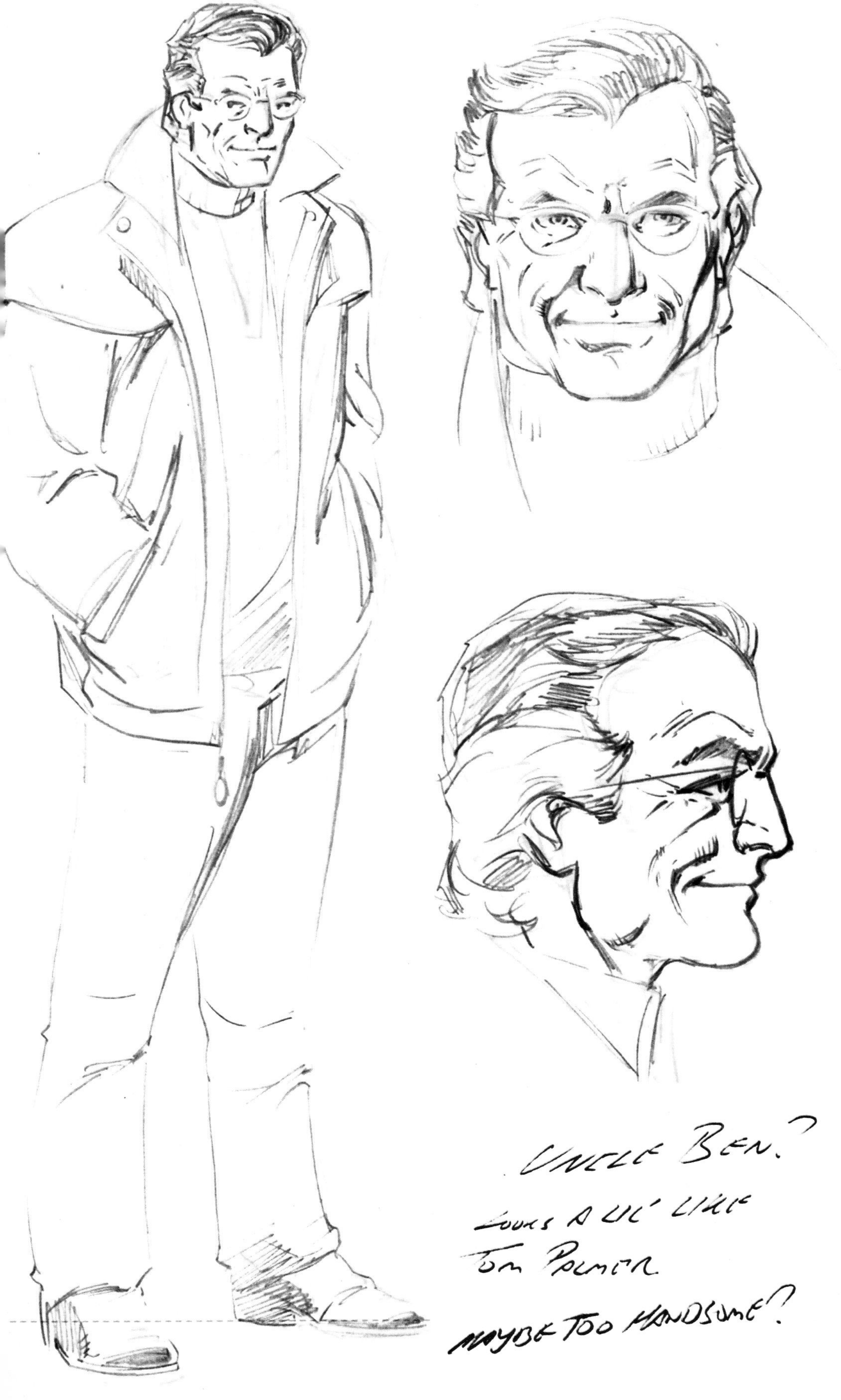

UNCLE BEN?
LOOKS A LIL' LIKE
TOM PALMER
MAYBE TOO HANDSOME?

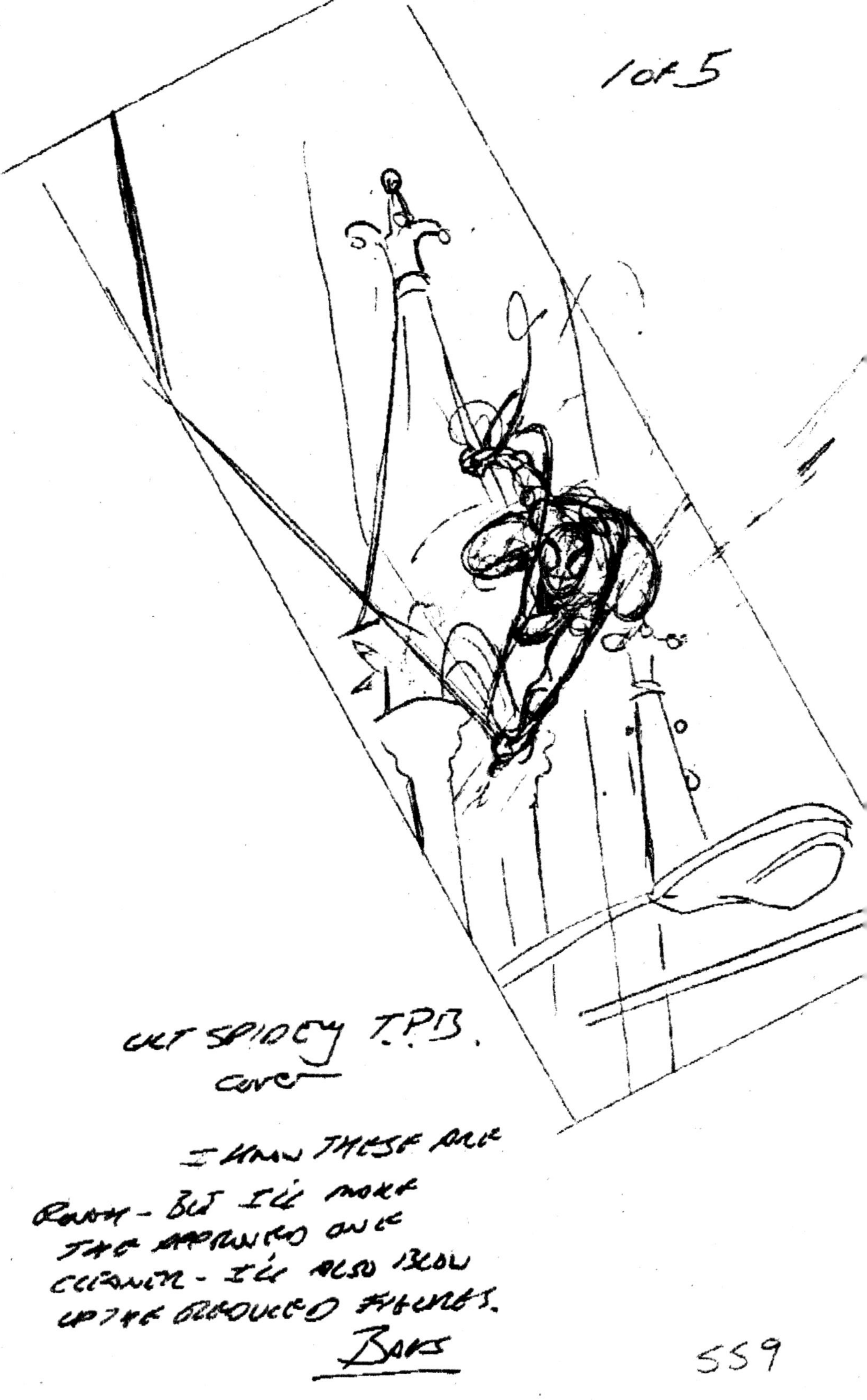
1 OF 5
ULT SPIDEY T.P.B.
COVER
I KNOW THESE ARE
ROUGH - BUT I'LL MAKE
THE DRAWINGS ONE
CLEANER - I'LL ALSO BLOW
UP THE REDUCED FIGURES.
BAGS
559

RAGS,
JOE Q
SEZ
THIS
ONE!

(A)

559

To Macchio!
Ext-213
Fm- Bagley-
2 to follow

Cover sketches
f. Ult. Spidey
#10

(B)

473

(C)

481

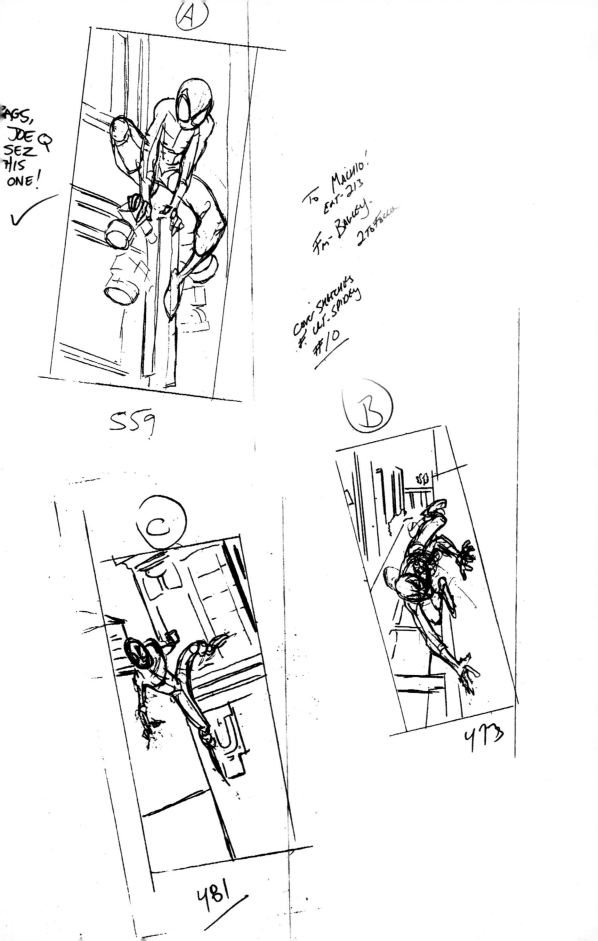

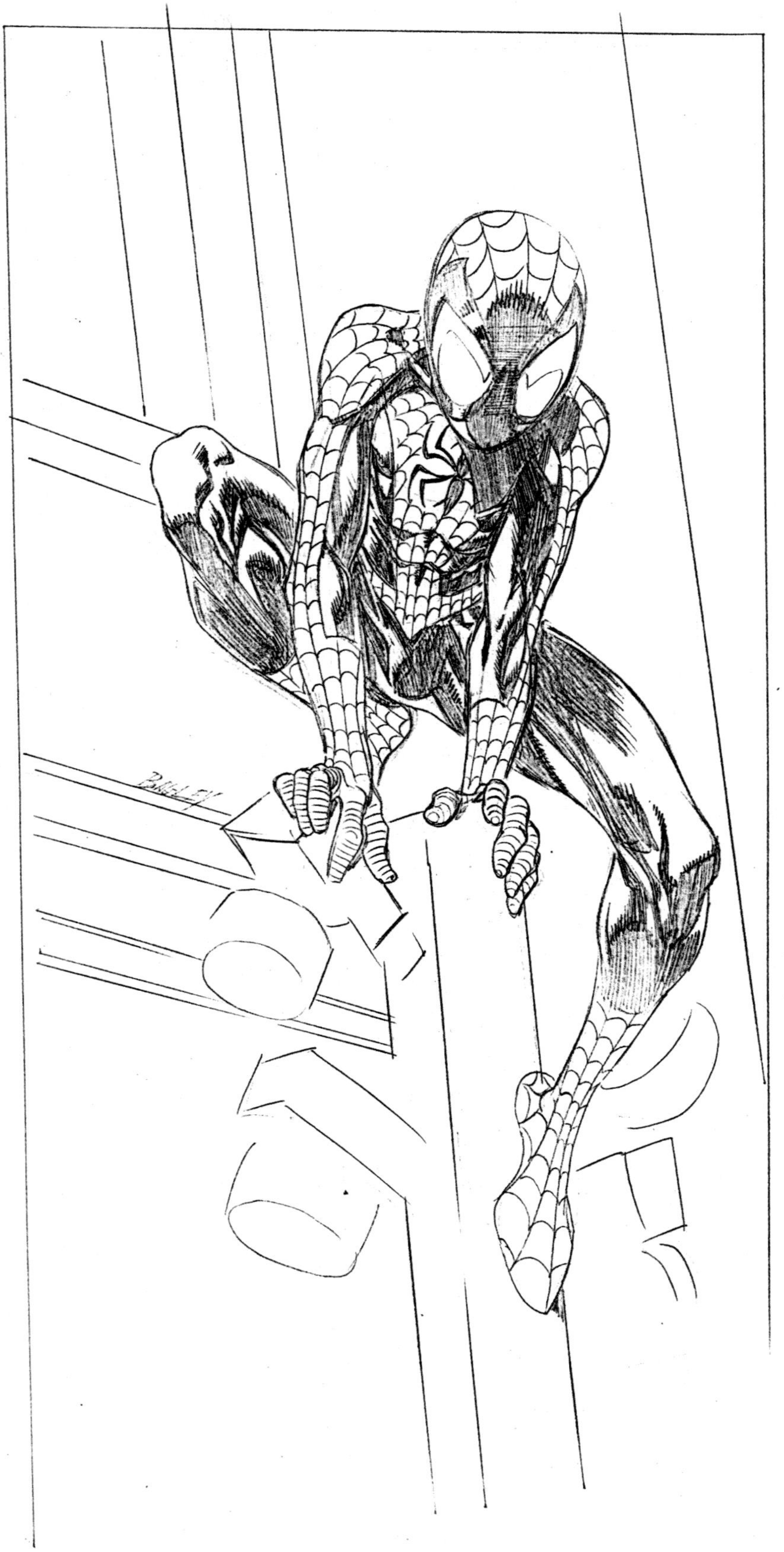
BAILEY

ULTIMATE SPIDER-MAN - #10 COVER

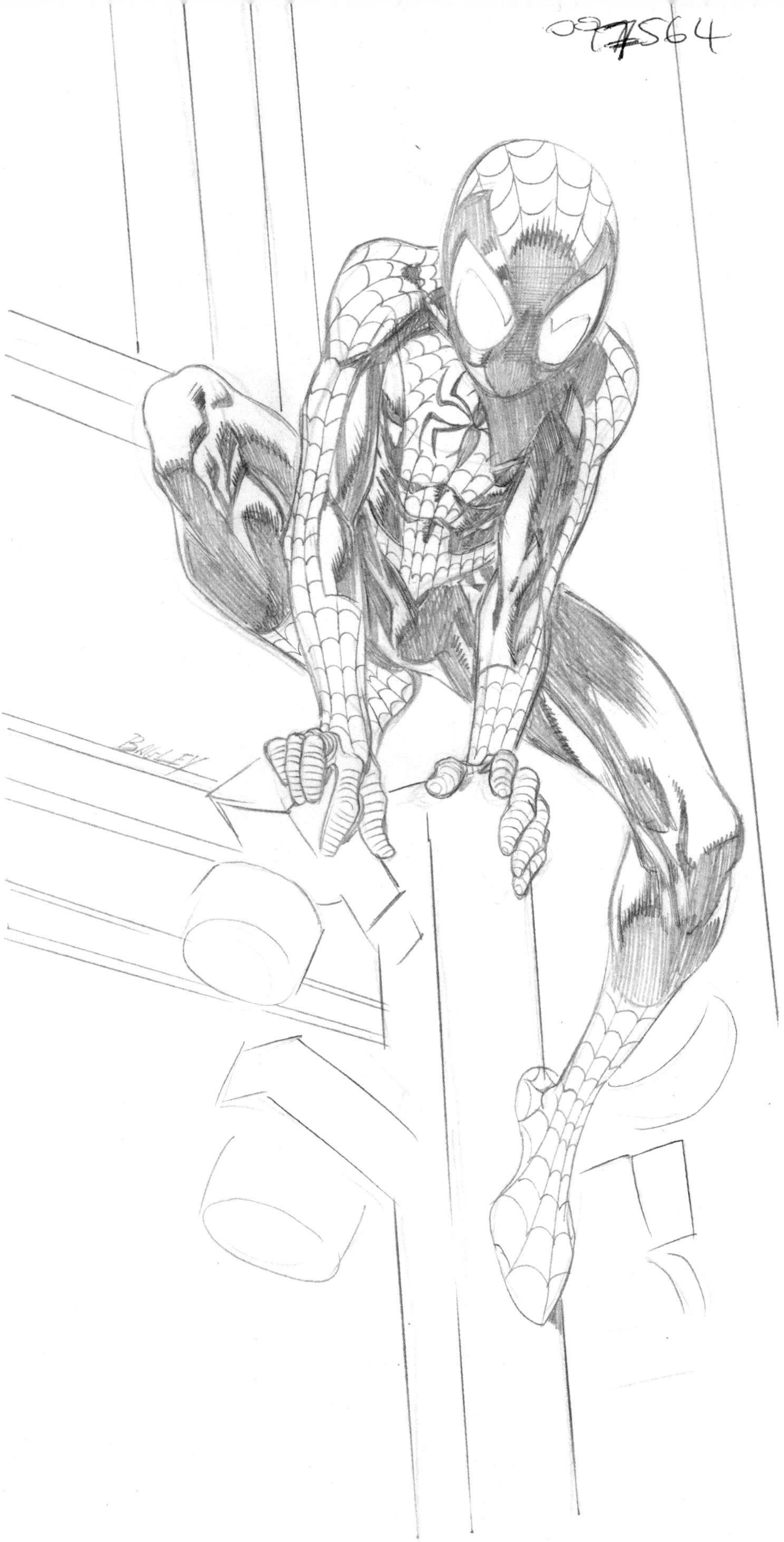
BAILEY

ISSUE 10 COVER PENCILS

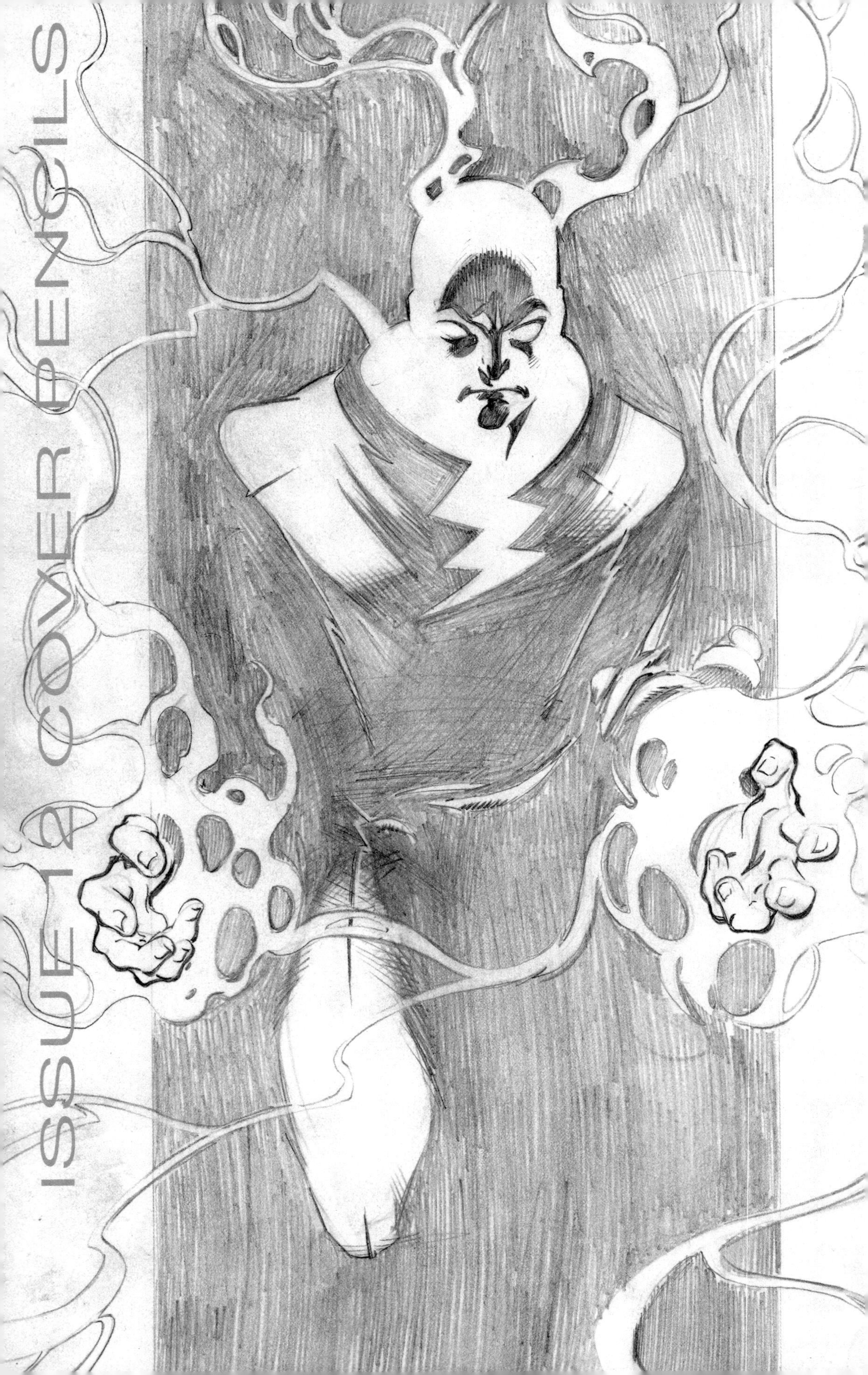
ISSUE 12 COVER PENCILS